"*Lazy, loves strong Drink, and is a Glutton*"

White Pennsylvania Runaways, 1720-1749

Compiled by
Joseph Lee Boyle

CLEARFIELD

Copyright © 2015 by
Joseph Lee Boyle

All Rights Reserved.

Reprinted for Clearfield Company by
Genealogical Publishing Company
Baltimore, Maryland
2015

ISBN 978-0-8063-5749-2

INTRODUCTION

One of the many neglected episodes of American history is that of the many thousands of white Europeans who did not come to the colonies as free men and women. Instead they came as indentured servants, political exiles, or transported convicts. White servitude was a major institution of the social and economic fabric of colonial British America. Bound whites preceded the use of black slaves in every colony. It is estimated that from 350,000 to 500,000 servants were imported through 1775. Though by the start of the eighteenth century the importation of black slaves increased dramatically in the Chesapeake and southern colonies, white bound labor remained significant until the American Revolution.

There were thousands of white people who wanted to leave their home countries, but were unable or unwilling to pay the cost of their passage, so as "free-willers" they became servants for a period of years to a colonial master who purchased them. Others were convicts or exiles. Some were not felons but shipped as "vagabonds." More than half the whites who came to the colonies south of New England were servants. Those who came voluntarily hoped for a better life. Most indentures were from four to seven years, though this varied over time.

Some were abducted to the colonies, as made famous in Robert Louis Stevenson's *Kidnapped*, but many are likely to have made the claim of being kidnapped to escape the terms of their indenture. Others may have runaway from home to leave families, debt, or other personal problems.

Of course, the numbers of both free and indentured immigrants depended on economics. Crop failures, wars, and economic disruptions in general added to the level of immigrants, in bondage or otherwise. There were more opportunities in the colonies for advancement after servitude than as a member of a traditional European society, though not as much as for free immigrants.

Not less than one-half, not more than two-thirds of all white immigrants to the colonies were convicts, redemptioners, or indentured servants. The convict and indentured servants were sold in America to citizens who bid the highest. The prices varied with men going for more than women, and those who claimed to be proficient in needed skills for more than the unskilled.

Underwriting of transportation was sometimes assumed by the planter, or more often by English merchants specializing in the sale of indentured servants. Recruiting agents called "crimps" hired drummers to recruit, sometimes making extravagant promises about the good life in the colonies. Illiterates were likely the most easily taken advantage of.

Though convicts were sent to the colonies before, the Transportation Act of 1718 opened the floodgates for exiled criminals, those convicted of minor crimes could be sent to the colonies for seven year terms. Capital crimes meant terms of fourteen years. After serving their time, they were eligible for royal mercy, and could return to England, but returning early was a capital offense. Convicts were attractive as they were relatively cheap, their sales prices were about one-third that of African slaves, and female felons sold for only two-thirds the price of males. From 1718 to 1775, some 50,000 convicts were banished to America from Britain. A "Contractor for the Transports" was paid to arrange transportation to the colonies, and upon arrival, the transported criminals were auctioned off in America for cash or goods such as tobacco.

Philadelphia was the major entrepôt for both free and indentured Europeans in the eighteenth century, as well as many convicts and slaves. As Philadelphia was one of the busiest ports in the American colonies, between 1720 and 1760, about twenty ships a year arrived from Ireland alone, most packed with servants for sale.

Early Pennsylvania was dominated by the Quakers and slaves were initially used for cheap labor. Though never done away with, cheaper white immigrant labor of various forms quickly expanded and surpassed slavery. In 1720 the estimated black population in Pennsylvania and Delaware was seven percent. By 1730 this had declined to three percent and remained about the same level through 1770.

There were numerous laws enacted in Pennsylvania during the colonial years to regulate the different classes of servants. There were also laws to protect servants from abuses and neglect by masters. For example in 1682 Pennsylvania forbade marriages between servants, and children were accounted to be bastards. Penalties were heavy, usually in the form of extra service. As late as 1768, a Chester County couple ran away, stayed thirteen days, and were brought back. The court judged each to serve thirty extra days for running away, five months for expenses, and one year for marrying.

In 1700 Pennsylvania passed "An Act for the better Regulation of Servants in this Province and Territories." One provision forbade selling a servant out of the province without his consent, and the consent of two justices in the area he lived. While there were provisions for apprehending fugitives, and fining those who hid them, for those "shall faithfully serve four years or more" would have a discharge and "be duly clothes with two complete suits of apparel, whereof one shall be new; one new axe, one grubbing-hoe, and one weeding-hoe at the charge of their master or mistress."

Some of those in bondage may have a better standard of living than they did in Europe. The master had paid for passage to the colonies, and had to provide for food, drink, clothing and shelter during the time of the indenture. A good master or mistress, as with bosses at any place and any time, could make the work far more pleasant.

With regard to convicts they were less well regarded than others in bondage. Benjamin Franklin noted convicts that "must be ruled with a Rod of Iron" and considered the British "emptying their jails into our settlements is an insult and contempt, the cruellest, that ever one people offered to another." While the colonists were incensed about receiving so many convicts, surviving court records do not show that they committed an inordinate number of crimes. Perhaps the lack of large towns, commercial activity, and general lack of opulence did not lend themselves to crimes the way the cities of England did, nor was there an existing criminal subculture.

After arrival in America, "soul drivers" sometimes drove coffles of convicts from town to town, selling them as they progressed into the interior of a colony. This was not without risks to the drivers. In 1774 a Baltimore merchant purchased a parcel of convicts, most of which he sold, except four men before he reached Frederick. One complained that he was too tired to go on, and they rested by a tree, the driver then insisted they go on, but they refused, threw him over a tree, dragged him into the woods, and cut his throat from ear to ear. All four were hanged for their crime.

Pennsylvania also enacted laws to regulate transported convicts. In 1722 a duty of £5 was placed on each convict, to be paid before landing in the province. The master was also required to provide "good and sufficient security" to the treasurer of £50 for the good behavior of each convict for a year.

Irish convicts were often disguised as indentured servants. Probably several thousand of the more than 25,000 Irish immigrants who came to Pennsylvania between the 1720s and the Revolution were convicts. There was also a duty on "Foreigners and Irish Servants" but while the Irish were unwanted, they were paradoxically irreplaceable "guest" laborers. Overall the Pennsylvania colony relied and thrived on cheap immigrant labor.

There were also "redemptioners," initially German, and then British. They promised to pay ship captains on their arrival in America. If they could not pay, or find a relative or countryman to do so, the captain was auction them off as indentured servants for a number of years, (usually two to seven) to defray the cost of their passage. For many this must have been a distress sale, as they could not return to Europe. Coming in family or large groups, they sold their own, or their children's labor for the cost of passage. The redemptioners were often called "free-willers." Rotterdam was the main port of embarkation for most German emigrants

Marianne Wokeck calculated that some 67,185 Germans arrived at Philadelphia from 1720 through 1760, at least half of whom were servants. The number of redemptioners is estimated to have been more than one-half, to two-thirds. An unknown number of families were broken up, as children and young people were in greater demand, while those more advanced in years found slower sale.

These potential immigrants had the opportunity to negotiate the cost before they embarked. The time involved varied, depending on the amount owed. Upon arrival the immigrant usually had up to fourteen days to negotiate a sale of his services. If he could not do so, the shipper recovered his costs by selling the indenture to the highest bidder, the immigrant having no choice what work he might have, or where he would go.

The Chesapeake colonies received the highest number of servants, followed by Pennsylvania. It received about one-tenth of all the men from the 1720s through the 1740s, and about one-fifth of the women in that period.

There was money to be made at multiple levels. The contractor who arranged the transportation profited, the ship owner and captain profited, and if the transport involved convicts, the county sheriff in England or Ireland had his palm out to facilitate the process. At one time Irish sheriffs received five pounds a head for convicts sentenced to transportation, but paid out only three pounds to the merchant transporters. Subject to supply and demand at the ports, agents would sometimes keep servants on shipboard or in houses until a sale at a good price could be arranged. Once in America, if the servant ran away, local officials were eager to earn rewards for their capture.

There were financial risks at all levels of the investment. Some individuals absconded before boarding the ship. While ship captains wanted to make as much as possible from transportation the servants, the less they paid for food, the more they made. Though high shipboard mortality was regrettable, some deaths always occurred after six to eight weeks at sea. While convict cargoes were generally chained, there were cases of uprisings with the ship's crew being overpowered.

Ship arrivals in the colonies tended to be seasonal, with the fall preferred, so that ships could take cured tobacco back to Europe, and new arrivals would have cooler weather to adjust to their new environment. The term "seasoning" was applied to newcomers, whose death rate varied, but was rarely less than ten percent, and as high as forty percent. Palatine fever, gaol fever, hospital fever, camp fever, and ship fever are all names applied to typhus, an acute febrile disease transmitted to man by body lice. The Palatine fever or ship fever was named for the disease German immigrants suffered during their passage to and arrival at Philadelphia. This was typhus, transmitted by body lice. Yellow fever, malaria, smallpox, and measles were also common eighteenth century killers.

Masters purchased their labor, not their bodies, but it was a risky investment. Death, injuries, chronic maladies, running away, or a shirking worker could mean loss of income. But cheap labor was more important than quality labor. Servants were required by law to work all day for six days a week. Masters could be fined for forcing their servants to work on Sunday

While the terms of indentures varied a great deal, the master was usually required to provide his servants with "sufficient meat, Drink, Apparell, Washing and Lodging." Of course what was "sufficient" from the master's view, was often not deemed such by the servant. White servants had the right to go appeal their treatment to the courts. But many likely were uniformed that their was a court system which might help them, others lived in remote areas with no immediate access to a court.

On the other hand, colonial courts could impose servitude on any citizen, usually for larceny or debt, if restitution could not be made, and fines and court costs paid. These individuals, as well as fugitive apprentices are included in this collection. Also included are escaped domestic criminals and even one renegade pirate captain.

Of course if servitude was to be a significant source of reliable labor, runaways could not be permitted to go free with impunity. As might be expected most runaways departed April through October, staying closer to home during winter weather. Non-English speakers might have runway less, whereas the Irish might have runaway more, due to the general anti-Irish feelings of the time. The not infrequent references to iron collars in these ads, show that running away was common. The collars were intended to make an example of the truants and to make identification easier. Servants were sometimes dangerous individuals. *The Pennsylvania Gazette*, December 11, 1755, has a report of the incarceration of seventeen year old Uriah Pearles, a runaway convict, for cutting James Peck's throat with an ax while Peck slept in bed with his wife.

Passes were required for those more than a certain distance away from home. Those who appeared to be suspicious characters, or could not give satisfactory accounts of themselves were committed to jail and held temporarily. Even if no master appeared to pay the costs of the man being held, he still might be remanded to servitude for failure to pay the costs of his own incarceration.

Unsuccessful flight also added to the time of servitude. This was done partly as punishment, and partly to compensate for the costs of capture, reward and return. On the other hand bad or abusive masters were sometimes punished by the judicial system with the shortening or cancelling of indentures.

For the ambitious servant, the term of servitude was a time of preparation. He was used to the climate and ways of the new land. He learned farming or another skill as practiced in the New World. He made contacts in the area he lived, and if an artisan, might have a list of customers when on his own. Abbott Emerson Smith estimated that one in ten would take up land and become prosperous, and that one in ten would become an artisan. The other eight died in servitude, returned to England, or became "poor whites."

The runaway ads presented here provide a first-hand view of history, as well as valuable demographic information with the age, sex, height, place of origin, clothing, occupation, speech, as well as physical imperfections, etc. They often display attitudes of the owners, and personality traits of the runaway, such as a common affection for alcohol. Some ads give extensive vignettes of individuals with their perceived idiosyncrasies. They provide a bonanza of information for the social historian. Those interested in tracking their ancestors will also find a goldmine of details.

It is impossible to know how many runaways there really were. Escapees of low value or close to the end of their terms may not have been advertised. Given that so many of the servants appear to be scapegraces, one wonders why their masters spent money to advertise for them, let alone pay a reward for their return. Those who were useful workers with lots of time remaining were likely to be the most sought after. Masters were likely to ignore those who left for a few days of dissipation, particularly planters during the agricultural slow season.

Some masters may have not wanted to pay the cost of the ads. Those masters whose servants absconded from more remote parts of the colony may not have bothered to advertise. A John Blowden was advertised eight times from 1729-1741, by three different masters, assumed to be the same man.

This compilation lists only white men and women. In the newspaper ads, wherein whites and blacks are listed together, I list the blacks are listed separately in the index. For black runaways, the reader is referred to Billy G. Smith and Richard Wojtowicz. *Blacks Who Stole Themselves: Advertisements for Runaways in the Pennsylvania Gazette, 1728-1790* (Philadelphia: University of Pennsylvania Press, 1989).

I have retained the original spelling, punctuation, and capitalization of the ads. Illegible words or letters are in brackets. Sometimes the ads in different papers are very similar and only the ad which occurs first in time is included, with references to the later ones. Minor differences in the advertisements are considered to be capitalization, spelling such as trousers/trowsers and 7/seven. If the ads are substantially different, each appears at the time it is first run. The majority are advertised in only one paper, many in two. Advertisements that are largely illegible are not included.

It will be noticed that far more men were runaways than women. In part this was due to the imbalance in the ratio of those who were indentured. Overall about nine-tenths of the registered indentured servants in the eighteenth century were men.

One wonders why James Claxton bothered to spend money advertising for 15 year old William Goodfellow, "an old offender, having ran away seven times since January last...." Or why Joseph Lynn of Philadelphia bothered to advertise in *The Boston Gazette* for Paul Raulisson, who had run away about three years earlier. Another charmer must have been David McQuatty. As "He is a small sized and thin visaged Man, pretty much Pock fretten, with a Roman Nose, and some small blue Spots on the right side of his Face & Nose, occasion'd by Gun-Powder. He is extremely affected with a trembling of the Nerves, so that he can scarcely hold any thing in his hand steadily" his usefulness to Ironmaster Samuel Nutt is speculative.

A unique ad is Thomas Clemson's poem for the "wretched Carcase" of Joseph Willard, who ran away in 1746. While Willard apparently ran away from Delaware, he was born in Bucks County, and made a servant in Lancaster. Along with others with Pennsylvania connections, who ran from other colonies, Willard is included here.

There are numerous variations in the spelling of names such as Edward Hambleton who ran way from Thomas Maybery in one ad, but appears as Edward Hamilton who ran away from Thomas Mayburry in another ad. Names can vary in the same ad such as Davis and Davies for one advertiser, and Kelly/Kelley in another.

In addition to creative spelling, the use of aliases was common. Good luck to the genealogist attempting to trace the line "*John Talifero*, alias *Luke Cell*, alias *John Dodso*n." Or "Elizabeth Barber, *alias* Rugstone, *alias* Burroughs."

Newspapers Consulted:

No newspapers with Pennsylvania runaways were found before 1720. It should be noted that none of these newspapers had a complete run for the period. Also, there were no newspapers published in Delaware or New Jersey for the entire period, colonies where ads for Pennsylvania runaways might have been numerous. In Maryland, where Pennsylvania runaways might also have been advertised, the first surviving newspaper was not published until 1728.

The American Weekly Mercury
Boston Evening-Post
The Boston Gazette
The Boston News-Letter
The Boston Post-Boy
The Maryland Gazette
The New-England Courant
The New-England Weekly Journal
The New-Hampshire Gazette
The New-London Summary
The Newport Mercury
The New-York Evening Post
The New-York Gazette, or Weekly Post-Boy
The New-York Weekly Journal
The Pennsylvania Gazette
The Pennsylvania Journal, or Weekly Advertiser
The Rhode-Island Gazette

For further reading:

Alderman, Clifford Lindsey. *Colonists for Sale: The Story of Indentured Servants in America* (MacMillan, 1975).

Blumenthal, Walter Hart. *Brides From Bridewell: Female Felons Sent to Colonial America* (1962, reprint, Westport, Conn.: Greenwood Press, 1973).

Coldham, Peter Wilson. *The Complete Book of Emigrants in Bondage, 1614-1775* (Baltimore: Genealogical Publishing Company, 1988).

Coldham, Peter Wilson. *Emigrants in Chains: A Social History of Forced Emigration to the Americas of Felons, Destitute Children, Political and Religious Non-Conformists, Vagabonds, Beggars and Other Undesirables, 1607-1776* (Baltimore: Genealogical Publishing Company, 1992).

Ekirch, A. Roger. *Bound for America: The Transportation of British Convicts to the Colonies, 1718-1775* (Oxford: Clarendon Press, 1987).

Galenson, David W. *White Servitude in Colonial America: An Economic Analysis* (Cambridge: Cambridge University Press, 1981).

Geiser, Karl F. *Redemptioners and Indentured Servants in the Colony and Commonwealth of Pennsylvania* (New Haven: Tuttle, Morehouse & Taylor, 1901).

Grubb, Farley. "German Immigration to Pennsylvania, 1709-1820," *Journal of Interdisciplinary History* 20, (1990), 417-36.

Grubb, Farley. "The Market for Indentured Immigrants: Evidence on the Efficiency of Forward-Labor Contracting in Philadelphia, 1745-1773," *The Journal of Economic History*, 45, (1985), 855-868.

Grubb, Farley. "Redemptioner Immigration to Pennsylvania: Evidence on Contract Choice and Profitability," *The Journal of Economic History*, 46, No. (1986), 407-418.

Grubb, Farley. "The Transatlantic Market for British Convict Labor," *The Journal of Economic History*, 60, (2000), 94-122.

Herrick, Cheesman A. *White Servitude in Pennsylvania: Indentured and Redemption Labor in Colony and Commonwealth* (Philadelphia: J. J. McVey, 1926).

Jordan, Don and Michael Walsh. *White Cargo: The Forgotten History of Britain's White Slaves in America* (Washington Square, N.Y.: New York University Press, 2007).

Lemon, James T. *The Best Poor Man's Country: A Geographical Study of Early Southeastern Pennsylvania* (Baltimore: Johns Hopkins Press, 1972).

Levy, Barry. "Levelers and Fugitives: Runaway Advertisements and the Contrasting Political Economies of Mid-Eighteenth-Century Massachusetts and Pennsylvania," *Pennsylvania History: A Journal of Mid-Atlantic Studies*, 78 (2011), 1-32.

McCoy, Michael Bradley. "Absconding Servants, Anxious Germans, And Angry Sailors: Working People And The Making Of The Philadelphia Election Riot Of 1742," *Pennsylvania History* 74, (2007), 427-451.

Meaders, Daniel. *Dead or Alive: Fugitive Slaves and White Indentured Servants Before 1830*. (New York: Garland Publishing, 1993).

Menard, Russell R. *Migrants, Servants and Slaves: Unfree Labor in Colonial British America* (Ashgate Varorium, 2001).

Menard, Russell R. "From Servants to Slaves: The Transformation of the Chesapeake Labor System," *Southern Studies*, 16 (1977), 355-388.

Salinger, Sharon V. "Labor, Markets, and Opportunity: Indentured Servitude in Early America," *Labor History*, 38, (19970, 311-38.

Salinger, Sharon V. "'Send No More Women'': Female Servants in Eighteenth-Century Philadelphia,' *The Pennsylvania Magazine of History and Biography*, 107, (1983), 29-48.

Salinger, Sharon V. *"To serve well and faithfully" Labor and Indentured Servants in Pennsylvania, 1682-1800* (New York: Cambridge University Press, 1987).

Smith, Abbot Emerson. *Colonists in Bondage: White Servitude and Convict Labor in America, 1607-1776* (1947; reprint; Gloucester, Mass.: Peter Smith, 1965).

Tomlins, Christopher L. *Reconsidering Indentured Servitude: European Migration and the Early American Labor Force, 1600-1775*. American Bar Foundation Working Paper #9920 American Bar Association, 1999.

Wokeck, Marianne. "The Flow and Composition of German Immigration to Philadelphia, 1727-1775," *The Pennsylvania Magazine of History and Biography*, 105 (1981), 249-278.

1720

RUN away from the Forge at *Monataunoy*, in the County of *Philadelphia*, a *Welshman*, midle siz'd about 21 Years of Age, of a clear Complexion, and fresh Cullour; Full Faced, with hollow Eyes and bottle Nose short brown hair a Little Curled; Full Shouldred, and when he Walks he stamps down his Feet,; his name is *Thomas Fare*, but has gone some time by the name of *Thomas Price*.
 Whoever can Secure the said Person and give notice thereof to *William Branson* in the Market place in *Philadelphia*, or to *William Coats* in the said City shall have *Forty Shillings* Reward and Reasonable Charges.
 The American Weekly Mercury, March 1, 1720; March 8, 1720; March 17, 1720.

This Day Run away from *John M'Comb*, Junier, an Indian Woman, about 17 Years of Age, Pitted in the face, of a middle Stature and Indifferent fatt, [*sic*] having on her a Drugat, Waistcoat and Kersey Petticoat, of a Light Collour. If any Person or Person, shall bring the said Girle to her said Master, shall be Rewarded for their Trouble to their Content.
 The American Weekly Mercury, March 24, 1720; March 31, 1720; April 14, 1720.

RUn away from *Philadelphia* in *October* last a Servant Man of Capt. *Joseph Mackintosh*; his Name is *William Minneman*, a Butcher by Trade He is a lean Man, pretty Tall, Long thin ill shaped Legs, something Pock-fretten, he is about 25 years of Age, & speaks broad *Scotch*. Whoever can take him up and bring him to *Andrew Bradford* in *Philadelphia*, or *William Bradford* in *New-York*, shall have Four Pounds Reward.
 The American Weekly Mercury, March 8, 1720; March 17, 1720; March 24, 1720.

RUN away the 17th of *March* last from *James Patterson* an Indian Trader, at *Pexton* on *Susquehanea* River, a Servant Lad named *John Maccahee* or *Makee* about Eighteen Years of Age, but of a small Stature and very much Marked in the Face with the small Pox and Freckles he hath been seen at one Indian Town called *Pehoquellamen* on *Delaware* River, There is also with him an Indian Man belonging to *Andrew Radford* at *Amboy Ferrey*, named *Toby*, of middle stature well set Aged about 23 Years he speakes good *English*, he goes like the Natives. Whoever shall take up said Servants and bring them to their said Masters or to *John Davis* in *Philadelphia* (next door

to the Printers) or give Notice thereof so that they may be had again shall have five Pounds as a Reward with Reasonable Charges, it is suposed they are gone towards *Albany* or *New-England*.
The American Weekly Mercury, April 21, 1720; April 28, 1720; May 5, 1728.

RUN away from his Master *Samuel Lewis*, of *Harford* in the County of *Chester*, a Servant Man Named *Thomas Roberts*, Aged about 20 Years of a Middle Stature thick brown Hair He has a Duroy Coat lined with Silk, and had a Leather Jacket when he went away but has changed in for another Coat, and leather Breeches. Whoever shall take up said servant and bring him to his Master or secure him so that he may be had again shall have Thirty shillings as a Reward besides Reasonable Charges paid them.
The American Weekly Mercury, May 26, 1720; June 2, 1720.

RUN away from *John Hyat* of *Philadelphia*, a Servant Man named *John Fenton* (but since his Departure Calls himself *John Steel*) He's about 22 Years of Age, of a Middle Stature, pretty well Set, of a Darkish complexion, his Haire cut close, had no Coat with him but a Striped Woolen Jacket, a pair of Britches, and a pair of Worsted Stockings of a Dirty gray Colour, a pair of Brass Buckels in a pair of Round Toe Shoes. He went from hence the 4th of this Instant *July*, he gave out he was destin'd for *New-York*, and *New-England*, per the way of *Delaware Falls*. Whosoever takes up said Runaway and Secures him so that his said Master may have him again, If taken within 20 Miles of this place *Ten Shillings*, but if further *Twenty Shillings* and Reasonable Charges.
The American Weekly Mercury, July 7, 1720; July 14, 1720; July 28, 1720.

RUN away the 10th of *June* last from his Master *Benjamin Denhall*, of *Concord* in the County of *Chester* in the Province of *Pennsilvania*, a Servant Man Named *Thomas Hardman*, about 40 Years of age, full Faced, thick Bodyed, Black Hair somewhat Curled, he had on an old Gray Kersey Vest, a New Black hat, an Ozenbrigs short apair Leather Breeches and Gray Stockings. Whosoever shall take up said Servant and give Notice to his said Master, or to the sheriff of *Philadelphia* shal have forty shillings as a Reward.
The American Weekly Mercury, August 11, 1720; August 25, 1720.

RUN away from *Israel Pembertons* Plantation in the County of *Bucks* in the Province of *Pennsilvania* the 20th of this Instant *September*, A Servant Man named *Thomas Jones* of Midle Stature well sett; aged about 21 Years, short dark hair not Long Enough to Cover his Eares, his face full of small pimples, and a dimple in one of his Cheeks, which appears pretty much when he smiles or Laughs: has taken with him in Cloths one Light Collered Sagathy Coat one Drugget Coat of a Brownish Collour, and a Vest of the same [both Coats without pocketts] a pretty good Carrelina Hatt, but not New: one ozinburg Jacket, and one pair of Leather one pair of Duroy and one pair of ozinbrigs britches; and two ozinbrigs shirts, one pair of yarn stockins, of dark Colour and Shoes almost New. whoever can take him up and Deliver to Samuel Bunting at the aforesaid Plantation or to Israel Pemberton in Philadelphia shall have forty Shillings as a Reward with reasonable Charges.

The American Weekly Mercury, September 22, 1720; September 29, 1720.

RUN away from *Edward Farmer* of *Whitemarsh* an English Servant Boy named *John Cowl*ey Aged about Seventeen Years, very short of Stature, fair hair, fresh Complexion, a course Dark collured Cloath Coat and Jackett the Coat has Large brass Buttons the Jackett lined with Yellow half thicks. Leather Britches and good Shoes and Stockings a black felt Hatt. Whoever shall take him up shall have 20*s*. as a Reward.

The American Weekly Mercury, October 6, 1720; October 13, 1720; October 20, 1720.

RUN away the 11th of this Instant *October*, from his Master *Peter Dicks* of *Upper Providence* in the County of *Chester*, a Servant Man named *Richard Skelton*, of a middle Stature, whitely favoured, aged about 18 Years, streight brown Hair, a black sharp Eye, an old Hat, a light colour'd Cloth Coat with cross Pockets, a brown Jacket, Linen Drawers, course Yarn Stockings and good Shoes. He rode away upon a dark brown Horse with a bald Face, four white Feet, a Wart on one of his Eyes; he has a Bridle and Saddle. Whoever shall take up the said Servant and bring him to his said Master, or secure him so that his said Master may have him again, shall have three Pounds as a Reward, with reasonable Charges.

The American Weekly Mercury, October 13, 1720.

RUN away from his Master *John Williams* Taylor, a Servant Lad named *John Peecock* aged about 17 Years, a thick well set Lad, short black courled hair, has a light coloured Loose and a Dark Coloured close bodied Coats lined

with read, a pair of Tickin and Leather Breeches, he has lost a joynt of one of his Fingers of his right Hand. Whoever shall take up said Servant and bring him to his Master or secure him and give notice shall have Twenty shillings as a Reward.
The American Weekly Mercury, October 27, 1720.

RUN away from *Frankford*, the 12th of this Month, *Hugh Willcox*, aged 30 Years, about 5 Foot 7 Inches high, had on then a Gray Coat and Jacket, with horn Buttons; took with him also a Gray Drugget Coat, lined and trimmed with black, and is supposed to have Stolen and carried with him a black Horse, with a Star in his Forehead, the off hind foot white, and a Cross on the off Shoulder. There are with him a Woman, called *Grace Mac-ward*, and a little Girle about 2 Months old the Woman passes for his Wife, she has the *Irish Brogue* on her Tongue, of middle Stature and Black Complexion. Whoever secures him, and gives Notice to the Printer or *Joseph Hawley* of *Frankford*, shall have Forty Shillings Reward.
The American Weekly Mercury, November 24, 1720; December 1, 1720; December 13, 1720.

RUN away from Shadrach Walley of New-Town in Bucks County, a Servant Man named Samuel Huff, an indifferent lusty young Man about Eighteen Years of Age, wore short brown Hair, but is supposed to have cut it off: He has with him two Suits of Cloths, the one a light coloured Kersey, and the other something darker. Whosoever takes up the said Servant, secures him, and gives Notice to his said Master, shall have Forty Shillings as a Reward.
The American Weekly Mercury, From Tuesday December 27, to Tuesday January 3, 1721; From Tuesday January 3, to Tuesday January 10, 1721.

1721

RUN away from his Master Samuel Kerk of the City of Philadelphia, Absalom Ayres, a Servant Lad about 18 Years of Age, he has a Face pox-broken, and pretends to be a Penman, wears a loose great Coat, Cinnamon coloured Drugget Jacket, Leather Breeches, and a worsted striped Cap. Whoever takes up the said Servant, or secures him and gives Notice to his said Master, shall have 30 *s*. Reward.
The American Weekly Mercury, From Tuesday January 31, to Tuesday February 7, 1721; From Tuesday February 7, to Tuesday February 14, 1721; From Tuesday February 14, to Tuesday February 21, 1721.

RUN away from his Master Robert Wills of the City of Philadelphia, Innholder, a Servant Man named Richard Weyman: he is tall and slim, aged about 22 Years, wears a Wig, a dark Duroy Coat, new Buckskin Briches. Whoever shall take up the said Servant, and give Notice to his said Master, shall have 40 s. Reward.

The American Weekly Mercury, From Tuesday February 7, to Tuesday February 14, 1721; From Tuesday February 14, to Tuesday February 21, 1721.

RUN away from Edward Brooks of Philadelphia, Butcher, an Irish Servant Man, named Miles Mac-ward, aged about 20 Years, middle Stature, dark Hair, has on a dark Serge Coat, grey Kersey Britches, light cinnamon-coloured Stockings and a new Felt Hat. Whoever secures him shall have 20 s. Reward and Charges.

The American Weekly Mercury, From Thursday March 23, to Thursday March 30, 1721. See *The American Weekly Mercury*, From Thursday March 23, to Thursday March 30, 1721, and *The American Weekly Mercury*, From Thursday June 1, to Thursday June 8, 1721.

RUN away from James Logan's Plantation near German Town the 28th Instant, an Irish Servant Lad, named Patrick Boyd, aged about 17 or 18 Years, with streight dark Hair, a freckled Face and a smooth Tongue, cloathed with a double-Breasted Pee-Jacket, a brownish Kersey Coat, a Pair of Leather Briches, and a good Felt Hat; but he had other Cloaths with him. Also a fine short Fowling Piece of a Carbine Length, or less. He went in company with one Miles Mac-Ward. Whoever takes and secures him shall be well rewarded for their Trouble.

The American Weekly Mercury, From Thursday March 23, to Thursday March 30, 1721; From Thursday March 30, to Thursday April 6, 1721. See above. See *The American Weekly Mercury*, From Thursday March 23, to Thursday March 30, 1721, for Macward, and *The American Weekly Mercury*, From Thursday June 1, to Thursday June 8, 1721, for both men.

RUN away from his Master William Noble of Warminster in the County of Bucks the 28th Instant, a Servant Man named Francis Mac-nemar, he is an Irishman, about 24 Years of Age, light brown curled Hair, a brown coloured Coat, striped Jacket, a Pair of Briches, one Leather, the other Woolen.

Whoever shall take up the said Servant, secure him and give Notice to Joseph Noble in Philadelphia, shall be well rewarded for their Pains.
The American Weekly Mercury, From Thursday March 23, to Thursday March 30, 1721; From Thursday March 30, to Thursday April 6, 1721.

RUN away from Thomas Jones of Philadelphia, the 28th Instant, a Servant Man named Nicholas Howell, about 25 Years of Age, tall of Stature, sandy Hair, light coloured Jacket, New Leather Briches, and new worsted Stockings. Whoever secures him shall have [10] *s*. Reward and Charges.
The American Weekly Mercury, From Thursday March 23, to Thursday March 30, 1721; From Thursday March 30, to Thursday April 6, 1721.

RUN away from Mr. Abel Pearson of Derby in the County of Chester, in the Province of Pennsylvania, a Servant Man, named John Renolds, aged about Twenty two Years, of short Stature, dark Complexion, short black Hair, wearing a brown Pee-Jacket, and a striped Flannel Jacket and Leather Breeches (being a Sailor.) Any Person that brings the said Servant to his said Master, or secures him so that his said Master may have him again, shall have 40 *s*. and reasonable Charges, paid by the said *Abel Pearson.*
The American Weekly Mercury, From Thursday March 23, to Thursday March 30, 1721; From Thursday March 30, to Thursday April 6, 1721.

Philadelphia, April 13.
RUN away from John Wleldon, March the 15th, 1721, a Servant Man named James Swaim, a Shoomaker, of a middle stature and swarthy Complexion, black bushy Hair, wears a brown coloured Coat and Leather Breeches, Whoever takes and secures him, so that his said Master may have him, shall have Fifty shillings Reward, paid by his said Master
John Wleldon.
The American Weekly Mercury, From Thursday April 6, to Thursday April 13, 1721; From Thursday April 13, to Thursday April 20, 1721; From Thursday April 27, to Thursday May 4, 1721; From Thursday June 8, to Thursday June 15, 1721. The third and fourth ads do not have the date and location at the top. The owner's last name is spelled Wheldon in all but the first ad. See *The American Weekly Mercury*, From Thursday May 10, to Thursday May 17, 1722.

RUN away from Philip Tayler of Chester County, a Servant Man named William Varnill, aged about 22 Years, fresh coloured, pretty tall, black Hat,

brown Hair, brownish coloured Sagathy Coat and Vest, New Leather Breeches, old Shoes and Stockings. He took with him a young Grey Horse, branded with *I. T.* on the near Side. Any Person that can take the said Man and Horse, or secure them so that his Master may have them again, shall have Thirty Shillings as a Reward, and reasonable Charges,
                 paid by me   Philip Taylor.
The American Weekly Mercury, From Thursday April 20, to Thursday April 27, 1721; From Thursday May 18, to May 25, 1721.

RUN away from William Chancellor *in Philadelphia, a Servant Man named,* Thomas Leicester, *aged about Twenty One Years, plump and fresh coloured, with short brown Hair, hanging down his Head as he goes: Having on a dark grey double-breasted Pee-Jacket lined, a speckled Shirt, and long Canvas Breeches, with another thin Pair under them: He looks very much like a Sailor. Whoever takes him up and brings him to his said Master shall be well rewarded.*
The American Weekly Mercury, From Thursday June 8, to Thursday June 15, 1721; From Thursday June 15, to Thursday June 22, 1721.

RUN away a second Time from *J. Logan's Plantation near German-Town, on the 4th Instant, an Irish Servant Lad named* Patrick Boyd, *aged about* 18 *Years, as may be judged by his Stature, with streight dark Hair, a freckled Face and Leather Breeches. He went off with two other of his Countrymen, herein also mentioned; viz* Miles Macward *and* Thomas Shaughnesay, *as it is supposed, in a small Boat stolen from Philadelphia. Whoever takes and secures him, so that his Master may recover him, shall be well rewarded for their Trouble.*
RUN away the 4th of this Instant June, from Edward Brooks *of Philadelphia, Butcher, an Irish Servant Man named* Miles Macward, *aged about Twenty Years, of a Middle Stature, dark Hair, a Felt Hat, has on a dark Serge Coat made fashionable, a Cinnamon coloured Jacket and grey Kersey Breeches, tied with Purple Leather at the Knees, Cinnamon coloured Yarn Stockings and good Shooes, being in Company with* Thomas Shauney *and* Patrick Boyd. *Whoever secures the said* Miles, *and brings his to his said Master, shall have Twenty Shillings Reward.*
RUN away the 4th of this Instant June, from Thomas Marle *of Bristol Township in the County of Philadelphia, a Servant Man from Ireland, named* Thomas Shaughnesay, *aged about Twenty Years, pretty tall Stature, but slender; a small Face and smiling, short brown curled Hair, a low Voice with a little of the Brogue. He had on a light brown Cloth Coat with open Sleeves, and fashionable; a striped Jacket, white Drawers, grey Stockings, good*

strong Shoos, and a Felt Hat. *Whoever secures him, and brings him to his said Master shall have Fifty Shillings Reward.*
The American Weekly Mercury, From Thursday June 1, to Thursday June 8, 1721. See The American Weekly Mercury, From Thursday March 23, to Thursday March 30, 1721, for Macward, and The American Weekly Mercury, From Thursday March 23, to Thursday March 30, 1721, for Boyd and Macward.

Philadelphia, June 7, 1721.

R*UN away from* Thomas Rutter *at the Iron-Works in the County of Philadelphia, a Servant Man named* William Newberry, *aged about Twenty Years: He is a West-country-Man, and talks like one; of a brown Complexion, his Hair cut off, wearing a brown Cap under his Hat. He is remarkable, having lost his Fore-Finger of his Left Hand. He has on very ordinary Habit and Leather Breeches. Whoever secures him, and gives Notice to his said Maser, or to* John Rutter *in Philladelphia, Smith, shall have Two Pistoles as a Reward.*
The American Weekly Mercury, From Thursday June 1, to Thursday June 8, 1721; From Thursday June 8, to Thursday June 15, 1721.

R*UN away from* John Orton *of the City of Philadelphia, Gun-Smith, a Servant Man named* Thomas Jones, *of a middle Stature, well-set, aged about 22 Years, short thick darkish Hair, His Face full of small Pimples, and a Dimple on one of his Cheeks, which appears pretty much when he laughs. He has on a grey Kersey Jacket with a short Cuff to the Sleeves, and has flat Pewter Buttons, a white Shirt mark'd* I. O. *on the Breast, a Pair of Leather Breeches, and Ozenbrig Trowsers. Whoever shall take up the said Servant, and bring him to his said Master, or secures him and gives Notice thereof, so that he may be had again, shall have Thirty Shillings as a Reward, with reasonable Charges.*
The American Weekly Mercury, From Thursday June 15, to Thursday June 22, 1721; From Thursday June 22, to Thursday June 29, 1721; From Thursday June 29, to Thursday July 6, 1721; From Thursday July 6, to Thursday July 13, 1721.

R*UN away from* Henry Rothwel *of the City of* Philadelphia *Cordwainer, two Servant Men, The one Named* Richard Allen, *a Slender young fellow with streight brown hair, he has a New Suite of Cinnamon coloured Cloaths lined with Sallune.*

The other a short thick fellow, with a dark coloured Coat lined with blue, dark coloured thick streight hair, Named Richard Middleton, they are both Shoe-Makers by Trade. Whoever shall take up said Servants and bring them to their said Master, or secure them and give Notice thereof so that he may have them again shall have three Pounds for each as a Reward with all reasonable Charges paid by   Henry Rothwell.

The American Weekly Mercury, From Thursday July 6, to Thursday July 13, 1721; From Thursday July 13, to Thursday July 20, 1721; From Thursday July 20, to Thursday July 20, 1721.

Philadelphia, July 13, 1721.
RUN away from Tobias Leech of Philadelphia County, a Servant Man named William Williams, about Thirty Years old, strong and well set, short black Hair, having on a Kersey Wastcoat, Linnen Breeches, and Woolen black and white Stockings. Whoever takes up the said Servant, secures him and gives Notice, so that his Master may have him again, shall have Forty Shillings Reward, besides reasonable Charges.   Tobias Leech.

The American Weekly Mercury, From Thursday July 6, to Thursday July 13, 1721; From Thursday July 13, to Thursday July 20, 1721.

RUN away from Evan Powel of the City of Philadelphia, about the 20th of June last, a Servant Man named John Williams: He is a Scotchman, of a Middle Stature, and very swarthy. He has a Scar on the Upper Part of his Forehead, very black Hair, is a Tinker by Trade, and has his Tools with him. Whoever shall take up the said Servant, secure him and give Notice to his said Master, or to Andrew Bradford in Philadelphia, shall have Forty Shillings Reward, besides reasonable Charges,
       paid by   Evan Powel.

The American Weekly Mercury, From Thursday August 3, to Thursday August 10, 1721.

Philadelphia, Novem. 20. 1721.
RUN away the 17th of this Instant, from Joseph Jones near Philadelphia, a Servant Man named John Palmer, but sometimes calls himself Plumly, aged about [9] Years, of a middle Stature, thick and well set, of a fresh ruddy Countenance, round faced and full, black bushy Hair and very hairy on his Breast. He took with him a homespun Coat of a Cinnamon Colour, lined with light-coloured Stuff, a Wastecoat almost the same Colour; a blew and white Striped Linsey-woolsey Jacket, another light-coloured Coat; also a very good Leather Jacket, with cross Pockets, lined with white Flannel or Half Thick, and Pewter Buttons, a Pair of very good Leather Britches with Brass

Buttons. He has 3 Shirts, one Cotton and Linnen, the other two homespun Cloth; a pretty good Hat, a S[ ]h Cloth Neckcloth fringed at both Ends, and one plain One; also a Pair of grey worsted Stockings, and 2 Pair of black and white Yarn Stockings and a Pair of Shoos almost new. He took with him a little black Mare, having a white Star in her Forehead, the off hind Foot a little white, a long bob Tail, a little round skirted, Old Saddle and a snaffle Bridle. Whoever takes him up, and secures him, that his Master may have him again, shall have Three Pounds Reward, paid them by me
Joseph Jones.
The American Weekly Mercury, From Thursday November 16, to Thursday November 23, 1721. See The American Weekly Mercury, From Tuesday February 13, to Tuesday February 20, 1722

1722

BROKE out of the Common Goal of Philadelphia, the 15th of this Instant February, 1721, [sic] the following persons:

John Palmer, alias Plumly, alias Paine, Servant to Joseph Jones, run away and was lately taken up at New-York, He is fully described in the American Mercury, Novem. 23, 1721. he has a Cinnamon coloured Coat on, a middle sized fresh coloured Man. His Master will give a Pistole Reward to any who shall secure him, besides what is here offered.

Daniel Oughtopay, a Dutchman, aged about 24 Years, Servant to Dr. Johnston in Amboy. He is a thin spare Man, grey Drugget Wastcoat and Breeches and light-coloured Coat on.

Ebenezer Mallary, a New-England Man, aged about 24 Years, is a middle sized thin Man, having on a Snuff colour'd Coat, and ordinary Ticking Wastcoat and Breeches He has dark brown strait Hair.

Matthew Dulany, an Irish Man, down-look'd swarthy Complexion, and had on an Olive-coloured Cloth Coat and Wastcoat with Cloth Buttons.

John Flemming, an Irish Lad, aged about 18, belonging to Mr. Miranda, Merchant in this City. He has no Coat, a grey Drugget Wastcoat and a narrow-brim'd Hat on.

John Corbet, a Shropshire Man, a Runaway Servant from Alexander Faulkner of Maryland, broke out on the 12th Instant. He has got a double-breasted Sailors Jacket on lined with red Bays, pretends to be a Sailor, and once taught School at Joseph Collings's in the Jerseys.

Whoever takes up and secures all, or any One of these Felons, shall have a Pistole Reward for each of them and reasonable Charges, paid them by John Wilson, Goaler.

The American Weekly Mercury, From Tuesday February 13, to Tuesday February 20, 1722; From Tuesday February 20, to Tuesday February 27, 1722; From Tuesday February 27, to Thursday March 1, 1722. See

The American Weekly Mercury, From Thursday November 16, to Thursday November 23, 1721, for Palmer.

Philadelphia, March 21, 1722.

RUN away the 10th Instant from Daniel Martin, living at Abraham Pride's in this City, a Servant Man named John Lee (*commonly known by the Name of Giff*), *of a middle Stature, fair Complexion, brown Hair. He has a black Hat new dress'd, and a Camblet Coat with two Rows of Buttons on the Breast, and one below, and three Jackets, one dark Drugget with red Lining, another striped Holland lined with checker'd Linnen, and the 3d of Ozenbrigs, and Leather Breeches with Buttons covered with Leather, grey woolen Stockings, and good round-toed Shoes. Any Body securing the said Person shall have 40s. Reward, paid them by* Daniel Martin.

The American Weekly Mercury, From Thursday March 25, to Thursday March 22, 1722; From Thursday March 22, to Thursday March 29, 1722; From Thursday April 12, to Thursday April 19, 1722.

Bristol, April 23, 1722.

RUN away from Thomas Wathell a Servant Man named Thomas Over, *aged about 21 Years, of a middle Stature, fresh Colour and light brown Hair. He is marked with Gun-Powder in the fleshy Part of one of his Arms, with the Jerusalem Arms, and the two first Letters of his Name. He has a New felt Hat, a light coloured Pea-Jacket and Leather Breeches, one Ozenbrig Shirt, grey woolen Stockings, and good round toed Shoos. Any Person who shall take up and secure the said Servant, and give Notice to his said Master, shall have Forty Shillings Reward, besides reasonable Charges, paid by me,*
Thomas Wathell.

The American Weekly Mercury, From Thursday April 19, to Thursday April 26, 1722; From Thursday April 26, to Thursday May 3, 1722; From Thursday May 3, to Thursday May 10, 1722.

Philadelphia, March 15, 1722.

RUN away from John Wheldon of this City, a Servant Man named James Swain, alias Smith, a Shoomaker, *of a middle Stature, swarthy Complexion, black bushy Hair, if it be not cut off, a big Nose with grey full Eyes, marked with the Small Pox in his Face. The said Servant hath done basely by his said Master, and left him at a Time when he could not help himself. He was some Time since at Mr. Bounds House, Never-sink, in Middle town, as I was informed. Whoever takes up the said Servant, and secures him, shall be paid Five Pounds by his said Master.*

The American Weekly Mercury, From Thursday May 10, to Thursday May 17, 1722; From Thursday May 17, to Thursday May 24, 1722; From Thursday May 24, to Thursday May 31, 1722; From Thursday June 28th, to Thursday July 5th, 1722; From Thursday July 12, to Thursday July 19, 1722; From Thursday July 19, to Thursday July 26, 1722. Only the first ad has the locaton and date at the top. See *The American Weekly Mercury*, From Thursday April 6, to Thursday April 13, 1721.

June 12. 1722.

RUN away from Robert Tunbroll in Philadelphia, one *Richard Harris*, a Carpenter, about 30 Years old, of a middle Stature, brown Complexion, having on a grey Drugget Coat, stript Breeches and speckled Shirt. He goes lamish or wobling. He has short Hair or a dark Wig. Whoever takes him up and secures him, so that his said Master may have him again, shall have a Pistole Reward.

The American Weekly Mercury, From Thursday June 7, to Thursday June 14, 1722; From Thursday June 14, to Thursday June 21, 1722; From Thursday July 12, to Thursday July 19, 1722; From Thursday August 20, to Thursday August 27, 1722.

June 12, 1722.

RUN away from John Sutton of Frankford, two Servant Men; one named *John Earle*, of a middle Stature, about Twenty Years of Age, wearing a Sailors Jacket, Leather Breeches, no Stockings, and a Pair of new Shoos, his Hair lately cut off, with a wollen Cap under his Hat. The other named *Peter Roads*, a Taylor by Trade, very swarthy Complexion and hath been lately sick; about the Age of Twenty One Years, having on a light coloured Coat and Breeches, and no Stockings. Whoever can secure the said Servants, so that their said Master may have them again, shall have a Pistole Reward for each of them.   By me, *John Sutton.*

The American Weekly Mercury, From Thursday June 7, to Thursday June 14, 1722; From Thursday June 14, to Thursday June 21, 1722.

RUN away from William Hunt of Bucks County, a Servant Man named Benjamin Hillyard, a Blacksmith, aged about 25 Years. Pretty lusty and tall, with a grey Broadcloth Coat, and a brown Home-spun Drugget Coat, an Ozenbrig Jacket, Leather Breeches, with Glass Buttons, black Stockings with round-toed Shoes, wearing a Wig or Cap, having no Hair on. And the said Hillyard hath stolen or taken with him a lusty well-set Negro-Man, belonging to Samuel Beaks, Called Quam, aged about 22 Years, having on a brown short Kersey Coat with Horn Buttons, a fine red-striped Vest and Breeches,

grey Stockings, Castor Hat and Garlicks Shirt, having his Right Hand burnt, between his Fore-Finger and Thum when a Child. Whoever can take up the said Servant Man and Negro, and secure them so that their Masters may have them, and gives notice to their said Masters, shall have Three Pounds current Money paid them, by
Delaware-Falls, William Hunt, and
June 17, 1722. Samuel Beaks.

The American Weekly Mercury, From Thursday June 14, to Thursday June 21, 1722; From Thursday June 28th, to Thursday July 5th, 1722; From Thursday July 12, to Thursday July 19, 1722. The American Weekly Mercury, From Thursday May 30, to Thursday June 6, 1723, for Quam. See The American Weekly Mercury, From Thursday August 8, to Thursday August 15, 1723, for Hillyard.

Philad. June 18, 1722.
RUN away from Zechariah Hutchins, Butcher, a Servant Man nam'd *Michael Hamlin*, an Irish Man, aged 24 Years, of a Small Stature, and has on a Cinnamon colour'd Coat and Vest, and long Ozenbrig Breeches and grey Stockings. He has black Hair and grey Eyes. Twenty Shillings Reward for taking of him, and reasonable Charges, By me, *Zechariah Hutchins.*

The American Weekly Mercury, From Thursday June 21, to Thursday June 28, 1722; From Thursday June 28, to Thursday July 5, 1722; From Thursday July 12, to Thursday July 19, 1722.

RUN away on the Twenty Seventh day of June last from James Armirage, Smith near the Welch-Tract an Apprentice Boy, between 14 and 15 Years of Age, Named Nathan Gumly having streight fair Hair, full fat faced of a fresh Complexion thick well-sett, having on when he went away a brownish gray Drugett Coat and Wastcoat, the Coat lined with white Flannen and the Wescote with striped Buckskin Breches with one button at each knee Yarn Stockings one thread of Black and the other of White, a felt Hat. Whoever takes up the said Boy and Secures him and gives notice thereof to his said Master so that he may have him again shall be well Rewarded for their pains.

The American Weekly Mercury, From Thursday July 5, to Thursday July 12, 1722; From Thursday July 12, to Thursday July 19, 1722; From Thursday July 19, to Thursday July 26, 1722.

RUN away from William Webb of Kennet Township in Chester County, On the 8th. Instant, a Servant Man named John Willson, Aged about 25 Years of a middle Stature, Swarthy Complexion, Short Hair, he has on a frize pea

Jacket lin'd with Red, a striped woolen Jacket, a Cotten and Linnen pair of Drawers a pair of White Stockings, and a felt Hat. Whoever takes him up and Secures him so that his said Master may have him again shall have Forty Shillings as a Reward and Reasonable Charges.

The American Weekly Mercury, From Thursday July 5, to Thursday July 12, 1722.

Septem. 14, 1722.

RUN away the 2d of this Instant September, from Ambrose Barecrost of Solebury near Buckingham-Meeting-House in Bucks-County, Pennsylvania, *Thomas Rolfe*, He is a short-set middle-ag'd Man with short sad coloured Hair, and took with him a Fustian Frock, a Snuff coloured Cloth Coat, two grey Kersey Wastecoats, one Pair of Buck-skin Breeches and a Pair of linnen Drawers, and several Pair of Stockings, all much wore; likewise one old speckled Shirt and 3 white Ones. He has a small Scar upon his Lower Lip, and a large Scar upon his upper Lip.

Whomsoever can secure him, and give Notice thereof to Ambrose Barcrost abovesaid, shall have Forty Shillings Reward and reasonable Charges, paid by   *Ambrose Barcrost.*

The American Weekly Mercury, From Thursday September 13, to Thursday September 20, 1722; From Thursday October 4, to Thursday October 11, 1722; From Thursday October 11, to Thursday October 18, 1722.

RUN away the 30th of September, 1722, from Philip Taylor, David Danis, Richard Bavenson and Thomas Marshall of Chester-County in the Province of Pennsylvania, 4 Servant Men; One named William Varnill, aged about 23 Years, pretty tall, fresh coloured, black Hat, brown Hair, brownish Coat and Vest, lined with Shalloon, new Linnen Drawers and old Shoes and Stockings. Another Man named William Beaumont, aged 24 Years, of a middle Stature, black bushy Hair, thin Visage, Pimples on his Cheeks, new Felt Hat, dark brown home-spun Coat, Old Leather Breeches, grey Yarn Stockings and New Shoes. Another Man named John Chapman, old Felt Hat, short black Hair, striped Jacket, Linnen Drawers, Ozenbrig Shirt, 2 Pair of Stockings, one old the other new, and a New Pair of Shoes. Another Man, low of Stature, named Edward Cooke, reddish Hair and Beard, new felt Hat, striped Jacket an Breeches, new Yarn Stockings, Shoos going back at the Heels.

Any Person or Persons that can take up and secure the said Servants, or any other them, so that their said Masters may have them again, shall have 30 s. per Head Reward, and reasonable Charges, paid them by their respective Masters.

The American Weekly Mercury, From Thursday September 27, to Thursday October 4, 1722; From Thursday October 4, to Thursday October 11, 1722; From Thursday October 18, to Thursday October 25, 1722.

RUN away the 16th Instant from *John Copson* of *Philadelphia*, a Servant Man named *Joseph Ceddles*, a Carpenter by Trade, speaks West-Country. He is a lusty tall Man, aged about 30 Years, wears a striped Cap, or a light bob Wig. Had on a light coloured Fustian Frock and Jacket, Ozenbrig Trowsers, and blackish Stockings. Whoever secures him, so that his Master may have him again, shall have a Pistole Reward.

The American Weekly Mercury, From Thursday October 18, to Thursday October 25, 1722.

RUN away from Daniel Durborow of Philadelphia, a Servant Man named Thomas Bingly, of a middle stature, thin Visage, has taken with him two Coats of a brown colour, one Duroy, and the other narrow Cloath, a Drugget Wastcoat, a striped Holland Wastcoat and Briches, two pair of long Linnen Breches, and a pair of Leather Britches a pair of new Shoes stitched about the quarters. Whoever can take up the said Servant or secure him so that his Master may have him again shall have a Pistole Reward,
        by Daniel Durborow.

The American Weekly Mercury, From Thursday October 25, to Thursday November 1, 1722; From Thursday November 1, to Thursday November 8, 1722.

RUN away from William Hunt at the Falls-Ferry in Bucks-County, a servant Man named David Rives, aged about Twenty Years, fair Hair, fresh Countenance, wears an old Felt Hat, or woolen Cap, a speckled shirt, a dark coloured Sailors Jacket lined with blue, course Kersey black and white Yarn Stockings, round toed shoes, speaks West Country, by Occupation a Farmer. Whoever takes up the said servant, and brings or seads [*sic*] him to his said Master, shall have a Pistole Reward, with reasonable Charges,
        paid by me   *William Hunt.*

The American Weekly Mercury, From Tuesday December 11, to Tuesday December 18, 1722; From Tuesday December 18, to Wednesday December 26, 1722; From Wednesday December 26, to Tuesday January 1, 1722; From Tuesday January 1, to Tuesday January 8, 1722; From Tuesday January 8, to Tuesday January 15, 1722. [*sic*]

RUN away from his Master, William Hays of Philadelphia, Shipwright, *Andrew Kees* an Irish Man, short stature, dark brown Hair somewhat curling, aged about 25 Years by Appearance, and round Visage. Whoever shall discover and take him, so as his Master may have him again, shall receive Thirty Shillings and reasonable Charges, paid by me
                        William Hayes.

The American Weekly Mercury, From Tuesday December 11, to Tuesday December 18, 1722; From Tuesday January 1, to Tuesday January 8, 1722; From Tuesday January 8, to Tuesday January 15, 1722. [*sic*]

1723

MADE an Escape last Night out of the Common Goal of Chester, one *William Pricket*, of a large Stature, well limbed, brown Complection, short black curled Hair, and is maim'd of his left Hand by the firing of a Gun, has on a narrow brimm'd Hat, and has on a short Fashionable Close bodied brown Coat a brown fashionable Cloth Pair of Breeches, square To'd Shoes, and dark grey Stockins. Whoever takes up and secures the said William Pricket, that he may be forth-coming, shall have Five Pounds Reward paid them by *Chester*, March 27, 1723.   John Taylor, Sheriff.

The American Weekly Mercury, From Thursday March 21, to Thursday March 28, 1723; From Thursday March 28, to Thursday April 4, 1723; From Thursday April 11, to Thursday April 18, 1723.

RUN away from *Joseph Townshend* and *Thomas Hayward* of Chester Pennsylvania, the 13th of this Instant *May* Two Servant Men, the one named *Edmund Jones*, a Shropshire Man, aged about 26 Years, a Tall slender Man, long Vissage, brown Hair, having on a new felt Hat, a thickset Fustion Coat, a blew Jacket and Leather Breeches, gray Yarn Stockings, Round to'd Shoes, two Osenbrigs Shirts, a Sailors Jacket of brown Cloth lined with red, by Trade a Weaver.   The other named *Thomas Coombes* a Somersetshire Man by Trade a Weaver, aged about 22 Years, a thick set short Fellow round Vissage, and a flat Nose, a Scare [*sic*] on his right Cheek occasioned by falling into the Fire, brown Hair, he has a light coloured Cloth Coat lined with Shalloon, Brass Buttons, and cross Pockets, an old Hat, and Osenbrigs westcoat and Breeches, grey Yarn Stockings and round to'd Shoes, also a sad Coloured Sailors Jacket lined with red, Breeches of same 2 Shirts of homespun Linnen he is also a Woolcomer by Trade. Whoever shall take up and secure the said Servants so that their said Masters may have them again shall have a Pistole Reward for each of them and Reasonable Charges paid by us

Joseph Townshend and *Thomas Hayward.*
The American Weekly Mercury, From Thursday May 9, to Thursday May 16, 1723; From Thursday May 23, to Thursday May 30, 1723; From Thursday May 30, to Thursday June 6, 1723; From Thursday June 13, to Thursday June 20, 1723; From Thursday June 27, to Thursday July 4, 1723.

RUN away from George Sheed, Perriwig Maker in Philadelphia, a Servant Man named James Robinson, of a middle Stature, fresh Complexion; he had on a Kersey Jacket, with Brass Buttons, an Ozenbrig Jacket and Breeches a speckled Shirt, dark colour'd Stockings and round toed Shoes, a light Wig and old Hat. He is very pert in Speech. Whoever takes him up, secures him, or brings him to his said Master, shall have Twenty Shillings Reward and reasonable Charges.
The American Weekly Mercury, From Thursday May 16, to Thursday May 23, 1723.

RUN away the 26th of this Instant *May,* from William Cooke of Concord in Chester=County; A Servant Man named Richard Shelton, aged about 23 Years, of Middle Stature, thin Fac'd, pale Complexion, short brown Hair, having on a felt Hat, a brown Coat, a light brown Jacket and gray Kersey Breeches with peices on the knees, gray Yarn Stockings and round to'd Shoes prety good with Steel Buckles in them. Whoever takes up the said Servant and gives Notices thereof to his Master that he may be had again shall have a Pistole Reward and Reasonable Charges, paid by me
William Cooke.
The American Weekly Mercury, From Thursday May 23, to Thursday May 30, 1723; From Thursday May 30, to Thursday June 6, 1723; From Thursday June 13, to Thursday June 20, 1723; From Thursday June 27, to Thursday July 4, 1723.

RUn away the 2d of this Instant June, from Robert Harris and William Hunt, at the Falls in Bucks County in Pennsylvania, Two Servant Men, the one named John Bealey, he is a tall Man, swarthy Complexion, dark short Hair, wears a black and white Kersey Coat, homespun Shirt and Drawers, yearn Stockings and Pumps. The other named David Reeves a short well set fellow fresh Complexion light hair, wears a Blue Gray Druget Coat, strip'd Jacket, home spun shirt and Drawers, yearn stockings & round to'd shooes, he is a Husbandman. Run away at the same time from Samuell Bonham of Trent Town in west Jersey, a servant man named Charles Brown a middle siz'd man fresh Complexion, light Brown hair, wears an old Snuff coloured Jacket, Leather Breeches with Brass buttons bluish stockings, new round to'd shooes, by trade a Baker, they have taken with them a Negro man named Quam belonging to Samuell Beaks of the Falls in Bucks County, he is a Lusty well sett fellow wears a black and white Kirsey Coat, Osinbrigs Jacket and drawers, home spun shirt and round to'd shooes; they are all about the age of Nineteen or Twenty (they are supposed to have taken Guns with them) Whosoever secures the said Servants or either of them so that their said Masters may have them again shall have a Pistole reward for each and reasonable Charges paid by their said *Masters.*

The American Weekly Mercury, From Thursday May 30, to Thursday June 6, 1723; From Thursday June 6, to Thursday June 13, 1723. See *The American Weekly Mercury,* From Thursday June 14, to Thursday June 21, 1722, for Quam.

RUN away the 13th of this Instant June, from Richard Hughs of Caln at the Head of Brandy-Wine, a Servant Man named William Eme, he is prety tall and slender, with short black Hair, having on an old Hat the Crown of one sort and the brim of another, an old white Shirt being torn below the Bosom, a Sailors Jacket of a dark Colour, a pair of Leather Breeches with Puffs at the knees without strings or Buttons; with a pair of Stockings without feet. Whoesever [sic] takes up said servant and gives notice thereof to his said Master or Mr. Rees Jones at the whitehorse in the Markett street Philadelphia, so that he may be had again, shall have Thirty shillings reward and reasonable Charges paid by me.   Richard Hughs.

The American Weekly Mercury, From Thursday June 13, to Thursday June 20, 1723; From Thursday June 27, to Thursday July 4, 1723.

DESERTED the 21st of this Instant June, from the Ship Richard and Mary at Philadelphia, One William Meredith, by Trade a Joyner, of about 21 years of Age, about five foot high short curl'd hair Eyes deep in his Head a lowring Countenance, he has a mill'd Cap on his head without a Hatt, Pee jacket and no Stockings, he was said to take the New-York road, he carried with him two joyners planes. Whoever brings him again to the said ship or to Samuel Dicker at Philadelphia, shall have Twenty Shillings as a reward besides all Reasonable Charges.

The American Weekly Mercury, From Thursday June 20, to Thursday June 27, 1723; From Thursday June 27, to Thursday July 4, 1723; From Thursday July 18, to Thursday July 24, 1723.

RUN away the 30th of June, from Thomas Moor of Calne in Chester-County, Yeoman, a Servant Man named James Sullevand, he is an Irish Man, aged about 25 Years, he is of a Middle Stature, well set, of a brown Complexion, brown bushey hair, a sandy Beard, he wears an Oszenbriggs Shirt, a blew duffuls Jacket with large Brass Buttons to it, a pair of Elk-Skin Breeches, a pair of blackish Stockings, a pair of Round to'd Shoes and a good felt Hat, he took a Gun with him. Whosoever takes up and secures the same Servant and gives Notice to his said Master so that he may be had again, shall have *Forty Shillings* Reward, and Reasonable Charges.

The American Weekly Mercury, From Thursday July 4, to Thursday July 11, 1723; From Thursday July 18, to Thursday July 24, 1723.

RUN away the 15th of this Instant July, from Nathan Watson of the Burrough of Bristol in the County of Bucks, two Servant Men, the one named John Amyet, aged about 22 Years, he is a West-Country Man, of middle Stature and goes stooping, he is a Sickly look'd Fellow, short brown Hair, and an old Felt Hat, he hath on a Saylors Jacket, light grey Yearn Stockings and round to'd Shoes. The other named John Cliff, aged about 19 or 20 Years, a thickset strong Fellow of a swarthey Complexion, sower look'd, when he went away he had on only his Shirt and Breeches, an old Felt Hat, and a Pair of round to'd Shoes. Whoever takes up the said Servants or either of them shall have a Pistole reward for each besides reasonable Charges.

The American Weekly Mercury, From Thursday July 11, to Thursday July 18, 1723; From Thursday July 18, to Thursday July 24, 1723.

RUN away from Robert Alexander, of Philadelphia, Merchant, Three Indentured Servants, being Palentines and some of those who were Imported about Five Months ago in Maryland, the first named *Peter Kures*, a middle aged Man, Tall of Stature and Swarthy Complexion, the second named *John Ierich Garlach*, aged about 30 Years, of a middle Stature, and brown Complexion, the third named *William Smith*, a middle aged Man, tall of Stature and Slender, or a brownish Complexion, he pretends to be a Miner. It is supposed they are about New-York.

Whoever takes up the said Servants and secures them, and gives Notice thereof to Mr. George M'Call Merchant, in Philadelphia, shall have Forty Shillings as a Reward for each, and Reasonable Charges.

The American Weekly Mercury, From Thursday July 18, to Thursday July 24, 1723; From Thursday September 19, to Thursday September 26, 1723.

RUN away from Major Richard Aldeburgh, on the 14th of this Month, a Servant Man named Benjamin Hilliard, by trade a black Smith, aged about 25 Years, of a brown Complexion, of tall stature and short brown hair, he has on a Double=Brested Jackett. Whosoever brings the said Man, to the above mentioned Major Alderburgh in the Arch Street in Philadelphia, shall have Two Pistoles as a Reward with all Reasonable Charges.

The American Weekly Mercury, From Thursday August 8, to Thursday August 15, 1723; From Thursday August 15, to Thursday August 22, 1723. See *The American Weekly Mercury*, From Thursday June 14, to Thursday June 21, 1722.

RUN away the 24th of August from The Honourable Sir *William Keith*, Bart. a Servant Man named *Richard Chamberlain*, by Trade a Taylor, of a middle Sature [sic] thin Visage, he weares sometimes a black Coat, sometimes a dark Coloured one, grey Stockins, and an old Hat. Whosoever takes up and secures the said Servant so that his said Master may have him again shall have Three Pounds as a Reward besides Reasonable Charges.

The American Weekly Mercury, From Thursday September 12, to Thursday, September 19, 1723; From Thursday September 19, to Thursday, September 26, 1723; From Thursday October 3, to Thursday October 10, 1723. See *The American Weekly Mercury*, From Tuesday December 31, to Tuesday January 7, 1723.

DEserted, the 7 of this Instant September, from the Brigantine Caesar, Robert Abbott Commander, one Henry Harmson, a German, but speaks indifferent good English, of a Middle Stature, pale Complexion, about 23 Years of age, he had on a brown bob Wigg, a light coloured Drab Coat, a Cinnamon coloured one underneath, and a Pair of Breeches of the same Colour, made French fashion, he is by Trade a Watch=Maker. Whoever takes up the said Henry Harmson and secures him, and gives Notice thereof to *Thomas Sobers* Merchant in Philadelphia, shall have Forty Shillings as a Reward besides reasonable Charges.

The American Weekly Mercury, From Thursday September 19, to Thursday, September 26, 1723; From Thursday October 3, to Thursday October 10, 1723.

RUN away on Wednesday the 16th of this Instant, from the Ship Gambol, Joseph Ruddock Commander, one /Forlong/Peter Furlong, a short wellset Man, black short Hair, swarthy Complexion, and a down look. Whoever takes up the said Peter Forlong and brings him to the said Ship, shall have Twenty Shillings as a Reward and Reasonable Charges.

The American Weekly Mercury, From Thursday October 17, to Thursday October 24, 1723; From Thursday October 24, to Thursday October 31, 1723 From Thursday October 31, to Thursday November 7, 1723.

RUN away on Fryday Morning the 29th of last Month from the Ship Joseph now at Philadelphia, John Bennet Master, Neal Tomson a Highlandman, of a middle Stature with sandy coulered Hair, he speaks Broken English, wearing a Light Brown Coat, with a Yellow Cloth Jacket and a Greyish coulered pair of searge Denim Breeches. Whosoever shall take up the said Man or secure him, or send word to the said Master or to Mr. John Francklin Marchant in Philadelphia, shall be very well Rewarded, besides all Reasonable Charges.

The American Weekly Mercury, From Thursday November 28, to Thursday December 5, 1723; *The American Weekly Mercury*, From Thursday December 5, to Tuesday December 10, 1723.

RUN away from his Excellency Sir *William Keith Bart* Governour, about the middle of September last, a servant man named *Richard Chamberlin*, by Trade a Taylor, of a middle stature, Thin Vissage, Wares sometim's his own black Hair, and other time's a Wigg, with a dark couler Cloth Coare, and other time's Black. Whosoever can Secure the said servant Man, so that his said Master may have him again, shall receive Five Pounds Reward and Reasonable Charges.

The American Weekly Mercury, From Tuesday December 31, 1723, to Tuesday January 7, 1724; From Tuesday January 7, to Tuesday January 14, 1724; From Tuesday January 21, to Tuesday January 28, 1724; From Tuesday February 18, to Tuesday February 25, 1724. See *The American Weekly Mercury*, From September 19, to Thursday, September 26, 1723.

1724

RUN away the 19th of this Instant January, from William Baldwin, at Namans Creek Mill, a Servant Man named William Potter, aged about 25 Years, of a middle Stature, he has on a very good Suit of brown Drugget Cloaths trim'd with black, a pair of good round to'd Shoes, and a felt Hat, he has brown Hair, he pretends to be a Black-Smith, he has with him a round Ey'd Ax which he says he made himself. Whoever takes up the said Servant

and secures him so that his said Master may have him again shall have *Forty Shillings* as a Reward and Reasonable Charges.
The American Weekly Mercury, From Tuesday January 14, to January 21, 1724; From Tuesday January 21, to January 28, 1724.

RUN away the 4th of December last, from Edward Weston of Philadelphia, a Servant Man named John Bradley, a Shropshire Man, about 25 Years of Age, of a middle Stature with short Brown Hair, if not cut off, brown Complexion, a low Voice but very Talkative, having on an old felt Hat, a plain Fustian Frock, an old black Jacket, an Ozenbrigs Shirt, brown Kersey Breeches, dark coloured Stockings, and a good pair of round to'd Shoes, having one of his little Fingers crumpled by Fire, he pretends to know somewhat of the Glass Trade, and has likewise given out that he is a Bricklayer. Whoever takes up and secures the said Servant, or brings him to his said Master shall have 40 s. as a Reward and Reasonable Charges,
The American Weekly Mercury, From Tuesday January 14, to January 21, 1724; From Tuesday January 21, to January 28, 1724; From Tuesday January 28, to Tuesday February 4, 1724.

THese are to give Notice, That there was stolen out of the Printing-House in *Philadelphia*, 5 or 6 sheets of the 10 *s*. and 5 *s*. Bills, of the New Impretsion *Paper Money*, some of which were Sign'd and uttered by one *John Jones*, who was apprehended on Thursday last and brought before the Mayor of this City, and Confessed the Fact, some Bills being found about him unsigned, and as the Officer was carrying him to Goal he made his Escape from him, leaving his Coat behind him. He is a Tall Slender Lad, of a pale Complexion, about Eighteen Years of Age, he wares a light bobb Wigg, but it is uncertain what other Cloaths he has on. Whosoever takes up the said *John Jones* and brings him to *Philadelphia* Goal, shall have *Fifteen Pounds* as a Reward and all Reasonable Charges, paid by   *Andrew Bradford.*
The American Weekly Mercury, From Tuesday January 28, to Tuesday February 4, 1724; From Tuesday February 4, to Tuesday February 11, 1724.

RUN away 2d day of April, from George Bostock of Chester County, a Servant Man named Valentine Vaughen, aged about 26 years, of a midle stature, Fresh Coloured thin Visage and brown Curled Hair, having on an old Hat, brown Home-spun Jacket and home-spun Shirt, pretty fine home-spun Cotten and Linnen Drawers course Stockings new Shoes. Whoever takes up the said Servant and secures him so that his said Master may have him again shall have Thirty Shillings as a Reward Paid by me, George Bostock.

The American Weekly Mercury, From Thursday April 23, to Thursday April 30, 1724; From Thursday May 7, to Thursday May 14, 1724; From Thursday May 21, to Thursday May 28, 1724.

RUN away the 26th of April *from* Thomas Paschall *of the Township of* Blockley, *near* Philadelphia, *and* John Marshall *of* Derby *two servant men, the one named* James Owen *of a middle Stature, well Set, and of a paleish Complection, straight brown Hair, and pretty well Cloathed, having a Fashionable Coat on, a dark Coloured Westcoat with Brass Buttons, Leather Breeches, Ozenbrigs Shirt, brown Stockings, old Shoes, and a Felt Hat.*

The other a Slender man, named Roger Lea, *of a middle Stature, a pale thin Complection, he has a blemish on one Eye, his hair Cut, and sometimes wears a Wigg, well Clothed having a Dark Coloured fashionable Coat with many Mettal Buttons on it, he took a Great Coat with him and two Shirts, several Neckcloaths. Whosoever aprehends and Secures the said servants so that their Masters may have them again, shall have four Pounds Reward, paid by their said Masters.*

The American Weekly Mercury, From Thursday April 23, to Thursday April 30, 1724; From Thursday May 7, to Thursday May 14, 1724. See *The American Weekly Mercury*, From Thursday June 18, to Thursday June 25, 1724, for Owen.

Run *away the 3d of this Instant* May, *from* John Wood *of* Philadelphia Mariner, *a Servant Man named* Jonathan Swindall, *he is of a middle Stature, aged about* 21 *Years, of a whitish Complexion, he has on a white Jacket lined with red, and small Brass Buttons, brownish coloured Stockings, a large pair of Canvas Trowsers, a good pair of round to'd Shoes, and an old Carolina Hat. Any Person that takes up the said Servant and Secures him so that his said Master may have him again, shall have* Twenty Shillings *as a Reward, and Reasonable Charges.*

The American Weekly Mercury, From Thursday May 7, to Thursday May 14, 1724; From Thursday May 21, to Thursday May 28, 1724.

RUN away, the 19th of this Instant May, from George Sheed, *Perriwigg Maker in Philadelphia, a Servant Man named* John Baptist Pollatto, *a French Man born, speaks but little English, by Trade a Barber, he is of a middle Stature, well set, a full Face and something Freckled, he had on a light Wigg, a gray Kersey Jacket lined with blue, a white Shirt, a light pair of Drugget*

Breeches, black roleup Stockings, square To'd Shoes, a red Leather Apron on, or about him when he went away Whoever takes up the said Servant and secures him so that his said Master may have him again, shall have Forty Shillings as a Reward and Reasonable Charges.

ALso Run away the same day, from George Cutts *of Philadelphia,* Tallow Chandler a servant man named *James Carr* an Irishman, but speaks as good French as a French man, prety Tall, black hair and down look, he had on a Dark Coulered silk Drugget Coat lined with Yellow silk, striped Flannel Jacket, Ozinbriggs pair of Breeches, new yarn Stockins, square to'd Shoes when he went away. He is supposed to be in Company with the above described Servant of Mr. *Sheed's*. Whoever takes up the said Servant and secures him so that his said Master may have him again, shall have *Forty Shillings* as a Reward and Reasonable Charges.

The American Weekly Mercury, From Thursday May 14, to Thursday May 21, 1724; From Thursday May 21, to Thursday May 28, 1724. In *The American Weekly Mercury*, From Thursday July 30, to Thursday August 5, 1724, the identical ad appears but begins "*RUN away, the 19th of last May....*" At the end of the ad is appended:

"N. B. *The above two Servants were taken up and Committed to Goal on Statin Island, but have since Broke Goal and made their Escape. These are therefore to desire all Persons to apprehend the aforesaid Servants, shall have the Reward as above mentioned.*"

RUN away the 22d *of this Instant* June, *from* Thomas Paschall *of the Township of* Blockley *near* Philadelphia, *a servant Man named* James Owen, *he is of a middle Stature, palish Complection, with Dark brown Hair, cut off Short, He had on a felt Hat, a brownish Coulered Coat pretty Fashionably made, a Dark Coulered Wastcoat, with Brass Buttons on it, linnen Breeches, Dark coulered Stockings, Shoepacks on his Feet, a pair of old Shoes with him, and a white Shirt.*

If any Person apprehends the said Servant and brings him to me shall have Four Pounds Reward paid by me   Thomas Paschall.

The American Weekly Mercury, From Thursday June 18, to Thursday June 25, 1724. See *The American Weekly Mercury*, From Thursday April 23, to Thursday April 30, 1724.

RUN away from David Marpole, *of* Abington *Township in the County of* Philadelphia, *the* 14th *of this Instant* June, *a Servant Man named* John Thomas, *a Short Thick well set fellow, black Curled Hair; about 23 Years of Age, he has on a course gray Kersey Jacket with brass Buttons, a Hat without a lining, Lether Breeches, and gray Worsted Stockings. Whosoever shall take*

up the said Servant and secure him, or bring him to his said Master, or the Sheriff of Philadelphia, shall have 30 Shilings as a Reward and Reasonable Charges.
The American Weekly Mercury, From Thursday June 18, to Thursday June 25, 1724.

RUN away the 5 of this Instant June, from John Cratho of the County of Philadelphia, a Welsh Servant Man Named Robert Ellis, aged about 23 Years, middle Stature pale Faced dark straite Hair; All the Cloaths he has on is Ozenbrigs Shirt and Breeches, He made his Escape from the Constable about Ancakers and calls himself John Dexter. Whoever shall take up and secures him so that his said Master may have him again shall have Five Pounds Reward and all reasonable Charges [   ]   Office   of Pensilvania, Ss.
The American Weekly Mercury, From Thursday June 25, to Thursday July 2, 1724.

WHereas Richard Brustall, a Short thick sett man, having a Bluber Lip with a rume or matter continually running from his Mouth, had very bad Teeth, drest in a short Pea Jacket and no Hair. Robert Clark, of a midle Stature having black Hair somewhat waiving, Aged between 40 and 50 Years, goes in a short Pea Jacket. Benjamen Herring, a little Man with white Eyebrows, sort Curled Hair of a Light sandy Couler, aged about 20 Years, being all Covenanted Servants to John Annis Commander of the Ship called the London Hope (now Lying at Jonathan Dickinsons Wharfe) have absented themselves and Run a way from the said John Annis's service, and whereas the said John Annis is Accountable at his Return to England for his said Servants, these are therefore to Desire all Persons, as well as Masters of Ships and other Vesels, not to Imploy or Entertain the aforesaid Persons, or either of them, but to Apprehend, take up, and secure the said Persons, or either of them, and as a Reward for so doing, the said John Annis doth hereby promise to Pay, for each Person secured, the Sum of 20 Shillings, and Reasonable Charges.   John Annis.
The American Weekly Mercury, From Thursday July 2, to Thursday July 9, 1724; From Thursday July 23, to Thursday July 30, 1724; From Thursday July 30, to Thursday August 5, 1724.

RUN away the 26th of August, from John Cassell upon Schuylkil a servant Man named Francis Turner, by Trade a Carpenter, and Sawyer, he's Aged about 21 Years, of a swarthy Complexion, short brown Hair, being Bald on the Crown, he having on a Pea Jacket, and Kersey Breeches, with a large

Check in his Shirt. *Whoever takes up the said Servant, and Secures him, and give Notice thereof to* John Cassell *aforesaid, or to* Arnold Cassell *in* Philadelphia, *shall have* 20 *Shillings as a Reward, and reasonable Charges, paid by either of them.*

The American Weekly Mercury, From Thursday August 20, to Thursday August 27, 1724.

RUN *away on Wednesday the 4th of this Inst.* November *from Sir* William Keith *Bart, Governour of* Pennsylvania, *a Servant Man, named* Henry Bell, *Aged about* 48 *Years, of a ruddy Complexion, and stoops as he walks: He was employed as a Carter, and had on when he went away, a prety good felt Hat, a brown Coat, a striped Woolen Jacket, and a pair of Boots; carrying with him a Bagg, wherein were a pair of Shoes and some other things.*

Whoever takes up and secures the said Servant so that he be returned to his said Master, shall have Three Pounds *as a Reward.*

The American Weekly Mercury, From Thursday November 12, to Thursday November 19, 1724; From Thursday November 19, to Thursday November 26, 1724; From Thursday December 3, to Thursday December 10, 1724.

RUN away from *John Moore* of *Philadelphia*, Esq; on the 25th of this Instant, a servant Man named *William Coats*, aged about 23 Years, of a fresh and fair Complexion, his Hair cut off, he carried with him two good suits of Apparel the one a Kersey and the other a black and white Drugget, a Drugget Wastcoat lined with dark Bays, a new black Hat, and good Shirts, &c. He was inticed away by one *Samuel Chaplen* a pretended Docter and piece of a Carpenter, who is gone with him. There is also a Woman gone with them who kept a Dram shop in Chestnut-street near the Coffee House back Gate, she claims them both for her Husbands. Whoever takes up and secures the said *William Coats* in the next Goal, so that his Master may have him again shall be very well Rewarded, and all Reasonable Charges allowed.

The American Weekly Mercury, From Tuesday December 22, to December 29, 1724; From Tuesday December 29, to Tuesday January 5, 1724-5; From Tuesday January 26, to Tuesday February 2, 1725. In the second and third ads, the first spelling to the runaway's name is "Courts".

RUN *away the 28th of this Instant* December, *from* Lawrence Reynolds *of* Philadelphia, *Currier, an Irish Man, named* Hugh Masterson, *speaks much upon the Irish Toan or Accent, about five Feet nine Inches high, wears a bob Wig tied behind with a string or thread, thick Eyebrows, pretty large Nosed,* a dark brown Coat on, and square Too'd Shoes. He hath stolen and taken with him, a Silver handled Sword broad shouldred Blade and a silver Chase to it, but 'tis supposed he has broke the Blade. He has also taken one pair of Shoes, a new Muslin Neckcloath, one Shirt and divers other things. Whoever secures the said Person, and gives Notice thereof to the said Lawrence Reynolds, shall have 40 Shillings and Reasonable Charges.

The American Weekly Mercury, From Tuesday December 22, to December 29, 1724.

1725

RUN away the 28th of *December* last from *Ralph Pile* of *Concord*, a Servant Man named *Elisha Perey*, aged about 18 or 19 Years, of a middle stature, smooth Complexion, he has on a new Country grey Drugget Coat lined with Woosted Druget, a dark blue Broadcloth Westcoat, and a Cotton and Linnen Westcoat, Buckskin Breeches with Puffs in them, and a fine Hat. He has also taken with him 6 or 7 Yards of Woosted Druget, the Chain being Blue and the Filling Orange collour. Whoever takes up the said Servant and brings him to his said Master, or secures him in the next Goal so that his Master may have him again shall have *Twenty Shillings* Reward and Reasonable Charges.

The American Weekly Mercury, From Tuesday December 29, to Tuesday January 5, 1724-5; From Tuesday January 5, to Tuesday January 12, 1725; From Tuesday January 12, to Tuesday January 19, 1725.

RUN away the 22d of this Instant, from *James Morris* Sawyer, in *Philadelphia*, an Irish Servant Man named *John Hayes*, of a middle size, aged about 22 years; pretty round favour'd with brown Hair, having on a dark coloured Irish Cloath Coat, 2 Jackets, one blue the other striped, and 2 Shirts, one Home-spun the other Ozenbrigs, a pair of white Blanketing Breeches, dark coloured Yarn Stockings pretty good Shoes, and a good felt Hat. Whosoever secures the said Servant so that his said Master may have him again, shall have Forty Shillings as a Reward and reasonable Charges.

The American Weekly Mercury, From Thursday March 18, to Thursday March 25, 1725; From Thursday March 25, to Thursday April 1, 1725; From Thursday April 1, to Thursday April 8, 1725.

RUN away the 25th of this Instant, from *Edward Thompson* of Edgmont, in Chester County, in Pennsylvania, a Servant Man named *Timothy Higgins*, aged about 22 Years; with short dark coloured Hair, fresh full Fac'd, of a middle Stature, speaks good English; he had on a large brim'd Hat, set up in three Corners, dark coloured Coat and Vest, Leather Breeches, with Brass Buttons mixt coloured Stockings, old Shoes, and 2 course Shirts [sic] Whoever takes up the said Servant and brings him to the Owner, shall have 30 s. Reward, besides reasonable Charges.

The American Weekly Mercury, From Thursday April 22, to Thursday April 29, 1725; From Thursday April 29, to Thursday May 6, 1725; From Thursday May 20, to Thursday May 27, 1725.

RUN away from his Master George Riscarrick, *at Cambray Brook, on the 24th of May, a Servant Man, named* Thomas Schowthrip, *of a middle Stature, thick set, and hath short Sandy coloured Hair, a light coloured fashionable made oat* [sic] *and Westcoat, an old pair of Leather Breeches with Brass Buttons, good Shoes, and Yarn Stockings. Whosoever takes up the said Servant and secures him, (or Brings him to his said Master,) so that he may be had again, shall have* Three Pounds *as a Reward, besides reasonable Charges.*

The American Weekly Mercury, From Thursday May 20, to Thursday May 27, 1725; From Thursday June 3, to Thursday June 10, 1725; From Thursday June 24, to Thursday July 1, 1725.

RUN away the 22d of this Instant *June*, from *John Naylor*, of the County of *Bucks*, a middle siz'd Servant Man, named *John Westron*, he has a Cut in his Lower Lip, and a Issue in one of his Legs just by his Knee; he wears his own Hair, Aged about 45, he came over in the Ship call'd the *Stanhope*, he was born in *Morchet* in *Devonshire*, in *England*; having on a *Felt-Hat*, and a *Woollen Cap*, a *Dark grey Coat*, with open Cuffs, and a striped Flannen Jacket, his Breeches and Stockings being of a Dark gray Colour, having on a Pair of Shoes pretty well worn.

N. B. Whoever takes up the said Servant, and secures him, so that his said Master may have him again, shall have 20 Shillings as a Reward, and reasonable Charges.

The American Weekly Mercury, From Thursday June 17, to Thursday June 24, 1725; From Thursday July 1, to Thursday July 8, 1725; From Thursday July 15, to Thursday July 22, 1725.

RUN *away the 20th Instant* June, *from* William Chancellor *of* Philadelphia, *a Servant Lad, named* James Prouse, *Aged about* 16 *Years, of a fair Complection, white Hair cut short, his Hands coloured with Tar, he is a Salt-Maker by Trade, having on a corded Druget Coat, Linen Jacket and*

Breeches, and Speckled Shirt. *Whoever shall take up the said Servant, or secure him so that his Master may have him again, shall have* 40 *Shillings Reward and reasonable Charges.*

The American Weekly Mercury, From Thursday June 17, to Thursday June 24, 1725.

RUN away from their Masters William Bissell *of the City of* Philadelphia, *Blacksmith, and* John Coats *of the same place, Brickmaker, Two* Carolina Indians, *a Man and a Woman, the Man's name is* Peter, *of a short Stature, and* 26 *Years of Age, he has a striped homespun Ticken Jacket and Breeches, also a Kersey Jacket, two Shirts one fine the other Ozenbrigs, two pair of Shoes, and a Felt Hat. The Woman's name is* Maria, *of a middle Stature, well set, about* 40 *Years of Age, she hath with her four striped Peticotes and several Jackets and other Cloaths, a new pair of Shoes, she has also a Blanket with her. They both speak good English.*

Whoever shall take up the said Indians, or either of them, and secures them, and gives Notice to their said Masters so that they may have them again, shall have 40 *Shillings for each as a Reward, besides all reasonable Charges.*

The American Weekly Mercury, From Thursday July 8, to Thursday July 15, 1725; From Thursday July 15, to Thursday July 22, 1725; From Thursday July 22, to Thursday July 29, 1725; From Thursday August 19, to Thursday August 26, 1725.

RUN away the 22d *of* July *last, from Sir* William Keith's *Plantation of* Horsham, *in the County of* Philadelphia, *a Servant Man named William Layworthy, by occupation a Farmer, of* Devonshire *in* Old England; *aged about* 40 *Years, a long Visage, his own black Hair, with a stoop in his Walk, and speaks the West Country accent; he carried with him of Cloaths a light blue Coat, with little Sleeves and long Pockets, a frize Jacket, with Gold thread Buttons and an old Linsey Woolsey Jacket, a pair of Buck Skin Breeches, a new pair of Home mad* [sic] *Trowsers, and a good felt Hat. Whosoever stops and secures the said* William Layworthy, *so as he may be returned to his Master Sir* William Keith, *shall have Three Pounds Reward and reasonable Charges, to be Paid in* Philadelphia,

by me Patrick Baird.

The American Weekly Mercury, From Thursday July 22, to Thursday July 29, 1725.

RUN away the 18th of this Instant, from *George Cartar* of the County of *Chester*, and Township of *Bradford*, near the Forks of *Brandewine*, a Servant Man named *John Double*, of a middle Stature, aged about 24 Years, he has short Hair, the end of his Nose flatish; he is in a Saylors habit, his Jacket with Red and White strips, he has a pair of grey Stockings, and round Toe'd Shoes, with Brass Buckles. Whoever takes up and secures the said Servant, to his said Master afore-mentioned, shall have 40 *Shillings* as a Reward.

The American Weekly Mercury, From Thursday August 19, to Thursday August 26, 1725; From Thursday August 26, to Thursday September 2, 1725.

RUN away the 18th of this Inst. *September*, from *Lawrence Rynolds* of the City of *Philadelphia*, a Servant Man named *George Rogers*, Aged about 30 Years, by Trade a Nailer, he is of a middle Stature, thin Vissage, short Hair, and a lump on his Throat, and also one on his Hand, like a Wen, about as big as a small Apple; he hath on a Check Shirt, and old gray Coat trim'd with black and a Pair of old Leather Breeches, Course Stockings, and new Round Toe'd Shoes, an old Hat. Whoever takes up the said Servant, and secures him so as his Master may have him again, shall have *Forty Shillings* Reward,

paid by me, *Lawrence Rynolds*.

The American Weekly Mercury, From Thursday September 16, to Thursday September 23, 1725; From Thursday September 23, to Thursday September 30, 1725; From Thursday October 7, to Thursday October 14, 1725. The second and third ads spell the advertiser's name as Reynolds.

MADE his Escape out of the Prison-Yard last Night, in *Phila.* on *William Billet*, of a middle Stature, fresh Colour, about 24 Years of Age, he looks very slie with his Eyes, having gray Jacket Breeches and Stockings, his Head is Shaven all over only a small Lock on the top of his Head and has a Scar over his left Eye, he is a Cooper by Trade, it is supposed he has also a Blew shag Coat, and some other Cloaths. Whosoever shall take up said *William Billet*, and bring him to *Owen Robert*, Esq; High-Sheriff, or secure him so as he may be had again shall have Five Pounds as a Reward and Reasonable Charges.

The American Weekly Mercury, From Thursday September 23, to Thursday September 30, 1725; From Thursday September 30, to Thursday October 7, 1725; From Thursday October 7, to Thursday October 14, 1725.

RUN away the 1st of this Instant *November*, from *Samuel Smith* of *Burlington*, a Servant Lad Named *Philip Dawfitt*, he is a Thick wellsett Lad of a Black Complexion, had on a Kersey Pea-Jacket a Blue Jacket, on under all Mealey, or else an Ozenbrigs Jacket, he had both with him an Ozenbrigs pair of Breeches of else Course Kersey, a Speckled Shirt, an Old Beaver Hat, Dark colour'd Stockings a new Pair of Round toed Shoes. Also from *Ennion Williams*, of *Bristol* in *Bucks* County, a Servant Lad, Named *Daniel Reynes*, he is a thick well set Lad, of a Black Complexion pretty much Pockfretten Short dark Hair, had on a new Felt Hat, a new Kersey Coat and Breeches of a Brownish colour, the Coat has on Horn Buttons, the Breeches Mettle buttons, a Specked Shirt, black Stockings, and a new Pair of Shoes, they are each of them about 18 Years of Age and took with them a Coverlie and a Hammock. Whoever shall take up the said Servants, shall have Thirty Shillings Reward for each besides Reasonable Charges paid by the said
Samuel Smith, and *Ennion Williams*.

The American Weekly Mercury, From Thursday October 28, to Thursday November 4, 1725; From Thursday November 4, to Thursday November 11, 1725.

Broke out of the Common-Goal of Chester, Oct. 28, 1725, between the Hours of Twelve and Four; Two Prisoners, one named William Bennet *(an Irishman,) of large Stature and well Set, with Short thick Brown hair, has on a Brown Cloath Coat, Ozenbrig Shirt, dirty Leather Breeches, brown Yarn Stockins, Old round Toe'd Shoes, and has no Hat unless he has got one since broke Prison. The other named* John Bull, *(an* English-man,*) thick and of short Stature, with short Brown Hair, has on a felt Hat, Copper Coloured Jacket, Ozenbrig Shirt, Leather Breeches, Cotten Stockings and old round Toe'd Shoes. Any Person that will take up the said* William Bennet *and* John Bull, *(they are Two Notorious Rogues) and secure them in the next Goal, so as they may be had or bring them to the Common Goal at* Chester, *aforesaid, shall have as a Reward* Four Pounds *or for each of them so Taken* Forty Shillings, *Paid them by,* William Weldon.

The American Weekly Mercury, From Thursday October 28, to Thursday November 4, 1725; From Thursday November 4, to Thursday November 11, 1725.

STOLE out of Joshua Lawrence's *Pasture near* Philadelphia, *the* 11*th of* August *last, (by one* William Powel, *otherwise calls himself* William Rogers, *being a Well Set Fellow, given much to talk, blind in one Eye with a White of Felm over the same; a little Pock fretten in the Face, Speaks broken English, short dark Hair sometimes wears a Wigg, he calls himself a Welsh Man,) a*

small bright Dun Pacing Horse, mentioned in the former New Papers. If any can secure the said Fellow so that he may be brought to Justice, shall be well Rewarded.
   The American Weekly Mercury, From Thursday November 4, to Thursday November 11, 1725.

RUN away from his Master *Henry Enocks* of the County of *Bucks*, *Black Smith*, a Servant Lad, named *James Smart*, of Middle Stature round Visage Brown curl'd Hair, about 17 Years of Age, having on a Strip'd Jacket a Leather pair of Breeches, new Hat, and several other Cloaths, he has Stolen or taken away his Indenture from his said Master, Whoever shall take up said Servant and bring him to his said Master, or give Notice thereof, so that his Master may have him again, shall have *Twenty Shillings* and reasonable Charges,   by *Henry Enocks*.
   The American Weekly Mercury, From Thursday November 25, to Thursday December 2, 1725; From Thursday December 2, to Thursday December 9, 1725; From Tuesday January 18, to Tuesday January 25, 1726. See The American Weekly Mercury, From Thursday May 26, to Thursday June 2, 1726.

1726

Philadelphia, Feb. 9th 1725-6.
THen Run away from *Zachariah Hutchins*, a Servant Man named *Thomas Thompson*, of a middle Stature, with Black short Hair, and black Eyes, of a thin Visage, with a Sinamon colour'd Coat, trim'd with Black, and burnt on the Flap before, and a white Coat under, with a black West [sic] and Leather Breeches with Brass Buttons, and new Shoes, an Ozebrig Shirt white Sleeves. Whoever secures the said Servant to his said Master, shall have 40 *Shillings* Reward and reasonable Charges, by me   *Zach. Hutchins.*
   The American Weekly Mercury, From Thursday February 8, to Thursday February 15, 1726.

RUN away the 6th of the first Month 1726. from his Master Jeremiah Effreth, a Servant Lad named Thomas Davis aged about Nineteen Years he has brown Hair, is of a dark Complexion and well set, has on a Dark coloured kersey Coat Felt Hat and Home spun Shirt, new Ozenbrigs Breeches Gray yarn Stockins and new shoes. Whoever secures the said Servant so that his Master may have him again shall have twenty Shillings Reward and Reasonable Charges, paid by me,   Jeremiah Effreth.

The American Weekly Mercury, From Tuesday March 1, to Tuesday March 8, 1726. See *The American Weekly Mercury*, From Thursday July 31, to Thursday August 7, 1729.

RUN away on the 6th of this Instant March, from John Hutton of Philadelphia, a Servant Man named Tho. Tidman, Aged 22 Years, of a middle stature, pale Face; short brown Hair, one of his Hips is higher than the other, he had on a Felt Hat, a course shirt new Neck't, a Broad Cloath Sinnamon colour'd Coat turn'd, a pair of course Linnen Breeches, grey Yearn Stockings, and a pair of old shoes new cover'd. Whoever takes up the said runaway and secures him so that he may be had again, shall have 40 s. Reward, and Charges.
The American Weekly Mercury, From Tuesday March 1, to Tuesday March 8, 1726.

RUN away *March* 3d 1726. From the Ship *John Gally John Ball* Master, two Men named: *Joseph Newell*, and *James Ensworth*, the former is a Man of a middle Stature, and of a brown Complection full favored, gray Eyes short brown Hair, his Cheeks spotted with little black specks like Gun-Powder. *James Ensworth*, is a tall spare young Man full favored with short Hair, sometimes he wears a Wigg with a short brown Jacket. Whosoever can secure the said Runaways, so as they may be had again shall have Five Pounds Reward with Reasonable Charges,
  John Ball. *Philadelphia, March* 13. 1726.
The American Weekly Mercury, From Thursday March 17, to Thursday March 24, 1726; From Thursday March 24, to Thursday March 31, 1726; From Thursday March 31, to Thursday April 7, 1726. The second and third ads do not have the date at the bottom.

RUN a way from their Masters two Men Servants, one from *Robert Shephard*, of the County of *Philadelphia*, Carter, named *Joseph Knight*, he is about 28 Years of Age of a Short Stature, black bushy Hair, and Rudy Complection, having on a gray homespun Jacket, Ozenbrig Shirt and Trousers, Wooden Heel'd Shoes, stitch d on the Quarters, he had on a narrow brim'd Hat.

 The other from *John Hutton* of the City of *Philadelphia*, Cordwainer, named Thomas Ridinan Aged Twenty Three Years; He has on a Felt Hat, short curl'd brown Hair, a Cinamon coloured Coat course Shirt a striped Ticken Jacket and old Leather Breeches with gray Yarn Stockings and old Shoes covered, one of his Hips is higher than the other. Whoever takes

either of the said Servants and secure them, shall have *Forty Shillings* Reward besides Reasonable Charges.
The American Weekly Mercury, From Thursday April 21, to Thursday April 28, 1726. See *The American Weekly Mercury*, From Thursday April 28, to Thursday May 5, 1726, for Knight.

RUN away from his Master *Robert Shephard*, of the County of *Philadelphia*, Carter, a Servant Man named *Joseph Knight*, he is about 28 Years of Age, of a Short Stature, black bushy Hair, and is of a Rudy Complection, having on a gray homespun Jacket, Ozenbrig Shirt and Trousers, Wooden Heel'd Shoes, stitch'd on the Quarters, he had on a narrow brimm'd Felt Hat.
The American Weekly Mercury, From Thursday April 28, to Thursday May 5, 1726. See *The American Weekly Mercury*, From Thursday April 21, to Thursday April 28, 1726.

RUN *away on the* 8*th of this Instant* May, *from* Edmond Farrel *Tanner, of* Philadelphia, *two Servant Men, one is named* Peter Clare, *Aged about* 24 *Years, of a middle Stature, a Tanner by Trade, his Face thin and Freckl'd, he has streight brown Hair, an old Felt Hat, a brown Cloath Coat and a Fustin Jacket. The other named* John Hynes, *of a middle Stature, Aged about* 20 *Years, a Skynner by Trade, he has very short Hair, a black Fustin Frock with Mother of Pearl Buttons, and a white Flannen Jacket.*
Run *away in Company with the above two Servants, from* Lawrence Reynolds *Currier, a Servant Man named* John Willson, *Aged about* 20 *Years, by Trade a Butcher, of a small Stature, with short brown Hair, he has an old Pea Jacket, a striped Flannel Jacket under it, and an old Felt Hat. They are all Irish Men, and was lately brought into* New-Castle, *by Mr.* Patterson *Merchant, from* Dublin. *Whoever takes up the said Servants or either of them, so that they may be had again, shall* have 40 Shillings *as a Reward for Each, with reasonable Charges.*
The American Weekly Mercury, From Thursday May 5, to Thursday May 12, 1726. See *The American Weekly Mercury*, From Thursday June 16, to Thursday June 23, 1726.

DESERTED *from the Ship* Betty, Samuel Manthorpe *Master at* Philadelphia, *the following Persons.* May *the* 3*d.* Edward Willson *a slender Man, Aged about* 20 *Years; with his own curled dark brown Hair, of a fresh Complection.* Robert Collet *middle Stature Man, with his own dark brown Hair, very much Pock fretten, and Aged about* 20 *Years.* May *the* 10*th.* James Twhaits *a Boy about* 15 *Years of Age; with his own light coloured slanck*

[sic] *Hair, of a Pale Complection, small and slender in Stature; they have all Sailors Habit. Whoever takes up and secures them so that they may be had again, shall have* 40 Shillings *as a Reward for each, and reasonable Charges.*

The American Weekly Mercury, From Thursday May 5, to Thursday May 12, 1726;

TWO Sailors Deserted from the Ship Betty, Timothy Williamson, *on Monday the* 16th *at 6 in the Evening, both Scotch Men, the one named* John Hall *a short black Man, his own black short Hair, wearing a light coloured Pea Jacket, a Pair of large Silver Buckles on his Shoes, The other named* Archiba Hall, *his own brown Hair, a thin Complection, and pitted with the small Pox, he has on a dark Pea Jacket; both Aged about* 28 *Years. Whoever takes up and secures them so that they may be had again, shall have* 40 Shillings *as a Reward for Each, and reasonable Charges.*

The American Weekly Mercury, From Thursday May 12, to Thursday May 19, 1726; The American Weekly Mercury, From Thursday May 5, to Thursday May 12, 1726.

RUN away from their Masters two Servant Lads, *viz.* one on the 19th of *May*, from *Joseph Suckly* of *Philadelphia*, Merchant, named *Richard Tickum*, born in *Malbrough* in *Wiltshire*, about 18 or 20 Years of Age, by Trade a Baker; he has dark coloured short Hair, a Pea Jacket, an Ozenbrig Shirt, Jacket and Breeches, a dark gray pair of Stockings, a pair of Wooden Heel'd Shoes, and a fine Hat much Torn in the Brim.

The other Run away at the same Time, from *Benjamin Rhodes*, Bricklayer; he is about 17 or 18 Years of Age, named *Evan Edwards*, a Saddletree maker by Trade, pretty Tall and full Fac'd, with short black Hair, he had on an old Felt Hat, a brown Drugget Coat, no Jacket, a pair of other Leather Breeches, and a pair of light grey Worstead Stockings. Whoever takes up the said Run aways or either of them, so that they may be had again, shall have *Forty Shillings* as a Reward for Each, and reasonable Charges.

The American Weekly Mercury, From Thursday May 19, to Thursday May 26, 1726.

RUN away from *Henry Enoch* of *Bensalem Township* on *Bucks County*, the 29th of this Instant *May* 1716. [sic] A Prentice Lad, named *James Smart*, Aged about Eighteen or Nineteen Years, of a Middle Stature, with brown Hair very good, He had on a Cinnamon coloured Coat with Brass Buttons of two sorts, a homespun Jacket and Breeches striped, the Collar of the Jacket unbound, black Stockings good Shoes, an Ozenbrig Shirt, a good Felt Hat. Whoever takes the said Apprentice and brings him to his said Master, shall have *Twenty Shilling* Reward and Reasonable Charges.

The American Weekly Mercury, From Thursday May 26, to Thursday June 2, 1726; From Thursday June 2, to Thursday June 9, 1726; From Thursday June 9, to Thursday June 16, 1726. See *The American Weekly Mercury*, From Thursday November 25, to Thursday December 2, 1725.

RUN away from *John Crosby* of *Ridley* in the County of *Chester*, in the Province of *Pennsylvania*, a Servant Man of a well proportioned Body, of a middle Stature, Thin white Vissage, short black Hair, being about the Age of 28 or 30 Years, an Englishman by Birth, being Cloathed, with a new Caster Hat, a lightish Coloured Drugget Coat lined with light Shalloon, a Wastcoat and Breeches of German Town blue and white striped Linnen, an Ozenbrigs Shirt, a Pair of old Gray worsted stockings footed with Gray woolin Yarn, he is Indented by the Name of *John Jackson* having lost 2 Joints of his Fore finger off his Right Hand. The Horse he had is taken at *Amboy* Ferry. Whoever takes up the said Servant and brings him to his said Master or to *Andrew Bradford* in *Philadelphia*, or to *William Bradford* in *New-York*, so that his Master may have him again shall have *Five Pounds* Reward and reasonable Charges.

The American Weekly Mercury, From Thursday May 26, to Thursday June 2, 1726; From Thursday June 2, to Thursday June 9, 1726; From Thursday June 9, to Thursday June 16, 1726.

RUN away on the *8th of this Instant* May, *from* Edmond Farrel *Tanner, of* Philadelphia, *two Servant Men, one is named* Peter Clare, *Aged about* 24 *Years, of a middle Stature, a Tanner by Trade, his Face thin and Freckl'd, his Hair being cut off, an old Felt Hat, a brown Cloath Coat and a Fustain Jacket. The other named* John Hynes, *of a middle Stature, Aged about* 20 *Years, a Skinner by Trade, he has very short Hair, a white Flannen Jacket. Whoever takes up the said Servants or either of them and secures them, shall if taken within Ten Miles of this City have* 20 *shillings, but if further* 40 *shillings, as a Reward for each and reasonable Charges.*

The American Weekly Mercury, From Thursday June 16, to Thursday June 23, 1726. See *The American Weekly Mercury*, From Thursday May 5, to Thursday May 12, 1726.

RUN away June 22. from the *Township* of Richland in Bucks *County, an Irish Man, named* William Bannet, of large Stature, palish Complexion light colour'd Hair, having on a homespun Wastcoat and Trousers, dark colour'd Coat, old Leather Breeches, gray Yarn Stockings, a Pair of Pumps and Shoes, and old Felt Hat, he formerly belonged to Mr. *Hunter*, in *Chester* County Tanner, and having Committed several Villanies was committed to Chester Gaol, from whence he broke loose some time ago, and he has also taken with him a Dark colour'd pacing Mare, having a Star in her Forehead, and branded with **B** as also a Gun about Five Foot long. Whoever takes up the said runaway, and secures him in the next common Goal shall have Seven Pounds Ten Shillings as a Reward paid them by *William Moore* of the Great Swamps, in the County of Bucks aforesaid.

N. B. It is supposed he has a Counterfeit pass with him.

The *American Weekly Mercury* From Thursday June 23, to Thursday June 30, 1726.

RUN away the 11th of this Instant August, from *John Sewers* of *Philadelphia*, a Servant Man named *Thomas Tomlinson*, he's a *East-India* Indian, about Two or Three and Twenty Years of Age, of a middle Stature, no Hair, he had on a Blue and White striped Jacket and Breeches, a light coloured Coat, good Shoes and Stockings, a new Hat; he talks very good English. Whoever takes the said Servant, and brings him to his said Master *John Sewers* shall have 3 Pounds Rewarded.

The *American Weekly Mercury*, From Thursday August 11, to Thursday August 18, 1726; From Thursday August 18, to Thursday August 25, 1726.

RUN *away the 2d of this Instant from* Thomas Ashton, *of the City of* Philadelphia *Ship-wright, a Servant Man, named* James Riley, *about 25 Years of Age, of a middle Stature, fresh Colour'd and Pock-fretten; he has no Hair on his Head, but wears a white Cap; he took with him a Cinnamon coloured Duroy Coat, and a pair of new Shoes. Whoever secures the said Servant to his said Master shall have* Twenty Shillings *Reward and reasonable Charges.*

The *American Weekly Mercury*, From Thursday August 11, to Thursday August 18, 1726; From Thursday September 8, to Thursday September 15, 1726.

RUN *away the* 13*th of this Instant* August, *from* Frederick Engle *of* Chester County, *a Servant Man, named* William Cooper, *of a short stature, short* curl'd Hair, he is much Pock-fretten, he has on a dark coloured Fashionable Coat and Jacket, with Plush Breeches, green Yarn Stockings and Wooden heel' shoes; he is a Shoemaker by Trade, & has took with him a Bay Mare with a Blaze down her Face.

Whoever takes up said servant and brings him to Owen Owen Esq; High sheriff of Philadelphia, or to his Master in Chester, shall have Five Pounds Reward and reasonable Charges.

The American Weekly Mercury, From Thursday August 11, to Thursday August 18, 1726.

RUN away on the 3d of this Instant *September*, from *John Sherburn* Joyner, of the City of *Philadelphia*, a servant and an Apprentice; the Man named *John Spring*, of a middle Stature, Aged about 25 or 26 Years, a Joyner by Trade, he had on an old Beaver Hat, and an old Wigg, one fine shirt and one Home-spun shirt, a Cinamon colour'd Coat, grey West-coat and Breeches, a Chocolate colour pair of stockings, with good new shoes, and a pair of Trousers: The Apprentice named *John Evans*, of a middle stature, with short red curl'd Hair; he had with him a Felt Hat, a fine shirt and a course one, with a brown Coat, grey Wast-coat and Breeches, a pair of grey Yarn stockings and new shoes. Whoever takes up said servant and Apprentice, and brings them to *John Sherburn* Joyner, shall *Five Pounds* Reward for Each, and reasonable Charges.

RUN away the 3d ult. from *William Hays*, of *Philadelphia*, Ship-wright, a servant Man named *Philip*— he is a Tall thin Man, with a hooked Nose, long Face, sandy Complexion, about 23 or 24 Years of Age; he has on a good dark colour'd Wigg, a short snuff colour'd Jacket, white shirt, old Hat, and a good silk Handkerchief, he is a strong well proportioned Man. Whoever shall take up and secure the said servant, so that his Master may have him again, shall have *Five Pounds* Reward and reasonable Charges, paid by me
William Hays.

RUN away at the same Time, from *James Wood*, Boat builder, a servant Man named *John Bromley*, of a middle stature, pale Complexion, a large Nose, no Hair, having on a striped Jacket and Breeches, with a pair, of Trowsers, ordinary Hat and shoes, a great Coat of a snuff colour. Whoever takes up the said servant and brings him to his said Master, shall have *Five Pounds* Reward and reasonable Charges.

☞ *The above mentioned Three Servant Men and Apprentice are all supposed to be gone together towards* New-England.

The American Weekly Mercury, From Thursday September 8, to Thursday September 15, 1726; From Thursday October 6, to Thursday October 13, 1726.

RUN away from the Ship *Constantine*, *Edward Foy* Commander; Three Sailors, One named *William Fortune*, Aged about 24 Years, about 5 Foot 4 Inches high, with his own Hair; he is of a dark Complexion, well Proportioned and well Cloathed. The other named *Philip Gammon*, Aged about 24 Years, about 5 Foot 3 Inches high, with his own Hair; he is of a dark Complexion, something squarer Set than the other: These above Two Sailors are Comrades and supposed to be together.

The other named *John Jennings*, a Servant to Captain *Edward Foy*, Aged about 45 Years, well Set, about 5 Foot 8 Inches high, his hair is cutoff, and had on when he went away a Pea-Jacket and Swanskin Wastecoat. Whosoever takes up the abovesaid Sailors, or either of them, and brings them to the said Commander, shall be very well Rewarded: These are likewise to forwarn all Persons from Entertaining any of the above Sailors, as they will Answer the Contrary at their Peril.

The American Weekly Mercury, From Thursday October 13, to Thursday October 20, 1726; From Thursday November 17, to Thursday November 24, 1726.

RUN away the 31st of *October* last, from *John Brackenbury*, of the City of *Philadelphia*, Sadler, a Prentice Lad named *Alexander Mac-Colester*, he is of a short Stature, a pale Complexion, with little Bumps in his Face, his Hair cut off, he wears a white Cap under his Hat, a Great Coat made of Homespun, it's Burnt a little in one of the Flaps, a Black Coat and Vest, a Pair of white Fustain Breeches trim'd with Black, two pair of Wooden heel'd Shoes, one pair new and the other pair lately mended, when he walks his Toes turns in. Whoever takes up said Prentice and secures him, so that his said Master may have him again, shall have *Forty-Shillings* Reward and Reasonable Charges, paid by me,   *John Brackenbury*.

The American Weekly Mercury, From Thursday October 27, to Thursday November 3, 1726; From Thursday November 3, to Thursday November 10, 1726; From Thursday November 17, to Thursday November 24, 1726. See *The American Weekly Mercury*, From Thursday August 10, to Thursday August 17, 1727.

RUN away from John Worral *and* Henry Grubb, *in* Edgment *in* Chester County, *Two servant Men, the 6th of this Instant* November, *One of them an English Man, Age about 22 Years, with a fair complexion and short Hair, he had on a Felt Hat, Lincey Jacket, and Linnen Drawers, a Home-spun shirt, and good Worsted Stockings, and indifferent good shoes; his Name is* Henry Renton, *by Trade a Butcher: The other is a Swead, named* Henry Turcy, *Aged* about 29 Years, of a short stature, with a small bump on his Nose, and swarthy complexion, he stuters in his speech, and wears a large Felt Hat, a silk Handkerchief about his Neck, a wide Coat of a brown colour, and a Jacket much of the same colour, One fine shirt, and Two Ozenbrigs shirts, a pair of Leather Breeches, white Yearn stockings and old shoes: It is supposed that a Boy about sixteen Years of Age, with curl'd Hair; is with them. Any Person or Persons, that shall take up said Run-aways so that their said Masters may have them again, shall have 40 s. as a Reward for Each and reasonable Charges.

The American Weekly Mercury, From Thursday November 3, to Thursday November 10, 1726; From Thursday November 17, to Thursday November 24, 1726.

RUN away from *Charles Read*, the 19th of *November* last, an *Irish* Servant Man, belonging to the *Iron-Works*, named *James Crouders*, of a middle Stature, about 22 Years of Age, long dark brown Hair curling on his Shoulders, of a pale Sickly Complexion and sore Leggs, he wore away with him, an Old Felt Hat a Dark Colour'd Kersey Pea-Jacket, with a striped Flannel under Vest, a new Ozenbrig Shirt, an Old pair of dark Colour'd Drugget Breeches, a new pair of Yarn Stockings, and a New Pair of Shoes. Whoever takes him up and brings him to the said *Charles Read* or to *Robert Ellis* of *Philadelphia*, shall be well Rewarded. And all Persons are forbid to Entertain him at their Peril.

The American Weekly Mercury, From Thursday November 24, to Thursday December 1, 1726; From Thursday December 1, to Tuesday December 13, 1726; From Tuesday January 10, to Tuesday January 17, 1727.

RUN away from the Ship *Apphia, George Smith*, Commander, one —— *Hendricks* a Passenger, in said Ship, he is about 60 Years of Age, short White Hair he wears generally a Blew Coat, when he looks any Person in the Face, he commonly shuts one of his Eyes. Whosoever shall apprehend said Runaway, and bring him to said Commander, or to *Andrew Bradford* in *Philadelphia*, shall have *Fifty Shillings* Reward and all reasonable Charges.

The American Weekly Mercury, From Thursday December 1, to Tuesday December 13, 1726; From Tuesday December 13, to Tuesday December 20, 1726; From Tuesday December 20, to Tuesday December 27, 1726; From Tuesday January 10, to Tuesday January 17, 1727.

1727

RUN away from the Ship *Shadwell* on Saturday last, one *Henry Pearson* a Saylor; he is a tall swarthy Man, aged about 35 Years, having on a brown Pea Jacket, wearing a Cap, and sometimes a Wigg. Whoever brings the said *Henry Pearson* to *John Jones* Master of said Ship, shall have 30 *Shillings* as a Reward and reasonable Charges.
The American Weekly Mercury, From Tuesday February 21, to Tuesday February 28, 1727.

RUN away on Sunday the fifth of *March*, from *Richard Barry* and *Nathaniel Grubb* of *Willistown* in *Chester* County, two Servant men, one named *John Mac Nayle*, Aged about 20 Years, of a middle Stature, short black Hair, he has on a good felt Hat, a gray Kearsey Jacket, an old pair of Leather Breeches, with Linnen Leggins upon his Stockings: The other named *Arthur Mulholland*, younger than the first, of a brown Complection, with long Hair of a brown Colour, having on a dark Cinnamon colour'd Suit of Cloaths. Whoever takes up the said Servants, so that their said Masters may have them again, shall have Five Pounds Reward and reasonable Charges
               paid, by me   *Richard Barry.*
The American Weekly Mercury, From Tuesday February 28, to Tuesday March 7, 1727; From Thursday April 6, to Thursday April 13, 1727.

RUN away on the 20th of this Instant *March*, from *Martha Rawle* (Widdow of *Francis Rawle* deceas'd) near *Philadelphia*, a Servant Man named Charles *Mugglew[ay]* an *Irish* Man, of a middle Stature, having round Shoulders, a thin sharp Face; carry'd away with him, one Shirt of Irish Linnen, and another Ozenbrig, one pair of gray Stockings, one pair of gray Duroy Breeches, and another pair Home-spun, one light Cinnamon colour Duroy Wastcoat, and another of black and white Home-spun, a Cinnamon colour Cloath Coat, and one Felt Hat. Whoever shall take him up and bring him to William Rawle in Philadelphia, or secure him so that the Owner may have him again shall have Forty Shillings Reward.
The American Weekly Mercury, From Thursday March 30, to Thursday April 6, 1727.

RUN away on the 9th Instant April, *from* Thomas Pryer, *of the City of* Philadelphia, Baker, *a Servant Man, named* Nicholas Park, *he is of a middle stature, he has on a Kearsy Coat, a short Wigg, long Breeches, a striped*

Flannen Jacket; he is a staring Fellow with a hooked Nose, and is very Fluent in Speech, as Lattin *and* French.

RUN *away on the 9th Instant* April, *from* John Bryant, *Baker, a Servant Man, named* Samuel Bond, *a likely young Fellow, of a middle stature, with his own Hair very bushy and long, had on a good Broad-cloth Coat, a good Felt Hat, Ozenbriggs Wastcoat and Breeches, with good Shoes and Stockings; he had with him also a strip'd Flannel Wastcoat, a pair of Leather Breeches, a pair of Trowsers, and a brown Holland Wastcoat.*

RUN *away at the same Time from* Charles West, *Ship-Carpenter, a Servan* [sic] *Man named* John Elford, *a likely Fellow, with a remarkable Scar on his left Arm or Hand; he has on a new Duroy Coat, strip'd Holland Wastcoat and Breeches, with new Shoes and Stockings. They are about 22 Years of Age each, and suppos'd to be gone together. Whoever secures the above said Runaways so that their said Masters may have them again, shall have* Forty Shillings *Reward for each, and reasonable Charges paid by their said Masters.*

N. B. *It is supposed the above Four Servants are all together, they stole a small Boat, with was found about Nine Miles up the River towards* Burlington.

The American Weekly Mercury, From Thursday April 6, to Thursday April 13, 1727.

RUN *away in* December *last a Servant Woman named* Elizabeth Cyphers *alias* Willson, *about 23 Years of Age, a middle Stature full Bodied Woman, round Shoulders, Pockfretten; she had on a dark coloured Shalloon Gown. Whoever shall bring her to* Samuel Holt *of* Philadelphia, *shall have* Forty Shillings *Reward and reasonable Charges paid them by me* Samuel Holt. *There is something now come from* Bristol *for her, from her Mother.*

The American Weekly Mercury, From Thursday April 27, to Thursday May 4th, 1727.

RUN away the 20th of this Instant *May*, from *William Bantoff* Baker, of the City of *Philadelphia*, two Servant Men. The one named *John Thompson*, aged about Twenty Years, a large well-set Fellow much Pock-fretten, having his Hair cut off, and wearing an Ozenbrigs Vest and Breeches, as also a Duroy Jacket a good Hat and Cinamon colour'd Stockings. The other named *Andrew Hillton*, a short bow Legged Fellow with fine Cloth Vest and Breeches, short dark colour'd Hair, having on a felt Hat Shoes and Stockings. Whoever will take up or secure the said Servants so that their Master may have them again, shall have Five Pounds as a Reward, and all Reasonable Charges, paid by *William Bantoff*.

The American Weekly Mercury, From Thursday May 18, to Thursday May 25, 1727; From Thursday June 1, to Thursday June 8, 1727; From Thursday June 15, to Thursday June 22, 1727; From Thursday June 29, to Thursday July 6, 1727. See *The American Weekly Mercury*, From Thursday June 29, to Thursday July 6, 1727, for Thompson. This ad, and the other by Bantoff for Thompson, were both in the paper for From Thursday June 29, to Thursday July 6, 1727.

RUN away from his Master *Stephen Jackson* near *Scuilkill-Ferry*, a Servant Lad about 17 Years old, named *John Humphry*, having short white Hair, he took with him two Dark Wiggs, two Vests one of Cloth a Cinnamon colour, the other a gray Drugget home made but without Sleeves, a pair of Leather Breeches, a pair of new strong Shoes, a pair of Old black Worsted Stockings an old light colour riding Coat with a Cape. Whosoever takes up and secures the said Servant so that his Master may have him again, shall be payed *Thirty Shillings* if found within Twenty Miles, and Twenty Shillings more for every Twenty Mile further from *Philadelphia*, which shall be paid by me
     Stephen Jackson.
The American Weekly Mercury, From Thursday May 25, to Thursday June 1, 1727; From Thursday June 1, to Thursday June 8, 1727. See *The American Weekly Mercury*, From Thursday July 6, to Thursday July 13, 1727.

RUN away the 9th of this instant *June*, from the Widdow *Sheppard* of *Philadelphia*, a Servant Man, named *John Blanchet*, about 24 Years of Age, Pockfretten and Freckled, red Hair, very thick Legs; wears a short Wigg of a light Colour, an old fine Cloth Vest, a pair of Ozenbrig Trowsers and shirt, a Felt Hatt, speaks broad West-Country. Whoever takes up said Servant and secures him so that he may be had again, shall have *Five Pounds* as a Reward and reasonable Charges, by   *Aemy Sheppard.*
The American Weekly Mercury, From Thursday June 8, to Thursday June 15, 1727; From Thursday June 15, to Thursday June 22, 1727; From Thursday June 22, to Thursday June 29, 1727; From Thursday June 29, to Thursday July 6, 1727.

RUN away the 9th Instant *June*, from *George Bowels* of *Philadelphia*, Blacksmith, a Servant Man named *Thomas Seamore*, of a small stature, thin Visage, pale Complection, dark brown short Hair, he has lost two of his upper Fore=teeth, having on a light Coloured Keasey Coat, Ozenbrig Jacket and

Breeches, a pair of Trowsers, grey Worsted stocking, round Toed shoes, and a Felt Hat, supposed to have taken a Brace of Pistols with him. Whoever takes up the said servant and secures him so that he may be had again, shall have Five Pounds as a Reward and reasonable Charges, by me
                    George Bowels.
N. B. *The aforesaid two Run-aways are supposed to be gone together towards* New-York.
    The American Weekly Mercury, From Thursday June 8, to Thursday June 15, 1727; From Thursday June 15, to Thursday June 22, 1727; From Thursday June 22, to Thursday June 29, 1727.

RUN away on the 12th of this Instant *June*, from *Joseph Jackson* of *London-Grove*, in *Chester* County, a Servant Man named *Richard Prat*, Aged about 18 Years, of a small Stature, Sandy Coloured short Hair and Curled, with a grey Linsey Coat, and a good Felt Hat. Whoever takes up the said Servant, or secures him so that his Master may have him again, shall have Twenty five Shillings as a Reward and all reasonable Charges, paid by me
                    Joseph Jackson.
    The American Weekly Mercury, From Thursday June 8, to Thursday June 15, 1727; From Thursday June 22, to Thursday June 29, 1727.

RUN away the 23d of *June* last, from *William Bantoff* Baker, of the City of *Philadelphia*, a Servant Man named *John Thompson*, (but now goes by the Name of *John Collins*,) about Twenty Years of Age, a large well set Fellow much Pockfretten, and there is a Scare a-cross [*sic*] his Chin, he wear'd a Pea-Jacket, a new Pair of Ozenbrig Breeches and Wooden heel'd Shoes, he carried a small Book of *John Collin's* with him, so that his Master may have him again, shall have Three Pounds as a Reward and reasonable Charges, paid by *William Bantoff.*
N. B *He was Advertised in the* Weekly Mercury, *in the 25th of* May *last, but has been taken since, and is run away again.*
    The American Weekly Mercury, From Thursday June 29, to Thursday July 6, 1727. See *The American Weekly Mercury*, From Thursday May 18, to Thursday May 25, 1727, for Thompson. This ad, and the other by Bantoff for Thompson, were both in the paper dated From Thursday June 29, to Thursday July 6, 1727.

RUN away the 9th of July 1727. *from his Master* Stephen Jackson *on Schuylkill, a lusty Servant Lad, named* John Humphrey *about* 18 *years old, very Short white hair a felt Hat, an Ozenbrig Shirt and Breeches, a Pair of large Square To'd Shoes, large Brass Buckles, old black Worsted Stockings, a gray homespun vest without Sleeves, 'tis supposed he took with him a small black Mare branded on her near Buttock with W thus and on the near Shoulder branded with the Letter ↔ thus Cross her Buttock, and one white Foot behind. Whoever takes up and secures said Servant so that his Master may have him again, shall be paid Twenty Five Shillings if took 20 Miles from Philadelphia, and one Shilling more for every Mile about Twenty Miles, paid by* Stephen Jackson.

The American Weekly Mercury, From Thursday July 6, to Thursday July 13, 1727; From Thursday July 13, to Thursday July 20, 1727; From Thursday August 3, to Thursday August 10, 1727. See *The American Weekly Mercury*, From Thursday May 25, to Thursday June 1, 1727.

RUN away of the 14th Instant from *George Farinton* of the City of *Philadelphia*, a Servant Man, named *William Davis*, of a short Stature, but very thick, Aged about 28 Years; with a Claret mark on his left Cheek, no Hair, wears a short bob Wigg of a Flaxen Colour, a light Broad-cloth Coat with a small Cuff, a new Felt Hat, good Shoes & Stockings, an a small bundle of Cloaths with him.

Whoever takes up and secures the said Servant, and brings him to his said Master, shall have *Three Pounds* as a Reward and reasonable Charges.

The American Weekly Mercury, From Thursday August 10, to Thursday August 17, 1727.

RUN away two Servant Men, one from *Ruth Hoskins* of *Chester*, named *Gregory Cock*, a lusty well Set Man, a thick courl'd Head of Hair, of a swarthy Complection, has lost some of his fore Teeth, and much shows the rest: he has several Suits of lining Jackets and Breeches Ozenbrigs, a Snuff colour'd Pea-Jacket, a Felt Hat, and a pair of new Shoes. The other from *Edward Smout* of the same Place, named *David Gibbens*, of a small Stature, without Hair, excepting some behind, which is not long: he is of a fair rudy Complection, long Visage, peeked Chin with a Scar about an Inch long across it, may have with him a black Wigg; took with him a dark brown Broad-Cloth Coat full Fashion, and breeches of the same, his Wast-Coat without Lining of Homespun, and sow'd with Yellow, a good Beaver Hat, Shoes, stitch'd round the Quarters, Silver Buckles; has in his Pocket a Silver Needle-Case, with two Letters SS on the Top, a pair of Worstead Roll-up Stockings of a mixt Colour Cinamon and white.

Whoever takes up the said Servant and brings them as aforesaid, shall have *Two Pounds* for Each with reasonable Charges, by us
Ruth Hoskins, Edward Smout.

The American Weekly Mercury, From Thursday August 10, to Thursday August 17, 1727; From Thursday August 17, to Thursday August 24, 1727. See *The American Weekly Mercury*, From Thursday August 31, to Thursday September 7, 1727, for Gibbens.

RUN away on the 14th of this Instant, from *John Knowles* of *Philadelphia*, a Servant Man named *Hugh Brown*, about 35 Years of Age, a short well Set *Irish* Man having a Brogue on his Tongue, he has short Hair, and wears a Callico Cap, a broad Chequer Shirt, a dark Colour'd Kersey Pea-Jacket lin'd up with Blue; he has in his Bundle a Great Coat, and another broad Chequer Shirt. Whoever takes up and secures said Servant so that his said Master may have him again, shall have 30 Shillings as a Reward and reasonable Charges, Likewise Run away at the same Time from *John Brackenbury* of the City of *Philadelphia* Sadler, an Apprentice Lad, Named *Allexander Mac-Collister*, aged about Twenty Years, he has Bumps in his Face, he had on when he went away, an old Shirt, an old worsted Cap, Short Stature and short Hair; an old Felt Hat, and old Leather Breeches, a pair of Yearn stockings, and wood-heel'd Shoes, torn a-Cross both Toes. Whoever takes up said Apprentice and secures him, so that his Master may have him again, shall have for the first 30 *Shillings*. And for the last *Twenty shillings*, and all reasonable Charges paid by us,   John Knowles, and *John Brackenbury*.

The American Weekly Mercury, From Thursday August 10, to Thursday August 17, 1727; From Thursday August 17, to Thursday August 24, 1727; From Thursday August 24, to Thursday August 31, 1727. See *The American Weekly Mercury*, From Thursday October 27, to Thursday November 3, 1726, for MacCollister.

RUN away from *George House* of *Philadelphia*, Shoemaker, the 29th of 6 Mo. 1727, an Apprentice Lad named *Thomas Crosset*, about Twenty Years of Age, middle Stature, freckled Face, with short black curled Hair, having on a dark Kersey Jacket, Ozenbrigs Shirt, Leather Breeches, light coloured Worsted Stockings, large Wooden Heel'd Shoes, and a Beaver Hat. Whoever secures said Apprentice so that his Master may have him again, shall have *Three Pounds* Reward, and reasonable Charges,
by me   *George House*.

The American Weekly Mercury, From Thursday August 24, to Thursday August 31, 1727; From Thursday August 31, to Thursday September 7, 1727.

RUN away from *Edward Smout* of *Chester* a Servant Man named *David Gibbens*, of a small Stature without Hair excepting some behind, which is not long: he is of a fair rudy Complection, long Visage, peeked Chin with a Scar about an Inch long a-crose it, may have with him a black Wigg; took with him a dark brown Broad-Cloth Coat full Fashion, and Breeches of the same, his Wast-Coat without Lining of Homespun, and sow'd with Yellow, a good Beaver Hat, Shoes stitch'd round the Quarters, Silver Buckles; had in his Pocket a Silver Needle-Case, with two Letters AA on the Top, a pair of Worstead Roll-up Stockings of a mixt Colour Cinamon and white.

Whoever takes up the said Servant and brings him as aforesaid, shall have *Two Pounds* Reward and reasonable Charges,

    by me *Edward Smout.*

The American Weekly Mercury, From Thursday August 31, to Thursday September 7, 1727. See *The American Weekly Mercury*, From Thursday August 10, to Thursday August 17, 1727.

RUN away the 24th of this Instant *September* from *William Hudson*, a Servant Lad named *Clament Charadon*, about 18 Years of Age, he is tall and slim, with short brown Hair, somewhat Curl'd, has on an old felt Hat, Ozenbrig Shirt, striped Flannel Jacket, and Breeches, Light brown Worsted Stockings, a Lock with a round Iron Heater on his Legg Except Cut off, a good pair of Shoes. Whoever takes up the said Servant and brings him to his said Master shall have *Forty Shillings* Reward,

    paid by *William Hudson* Jun.

The American Weekly Mercury, From Thursday September 21, to Thursday September 28, 1727; From Thursday September 28, to Thursday October 5, 1727.

RUN away the 21st of *Sepember*, from *Benjamen Fairman*, living near *Philadelphia*, a servant Man named *John Johnson*, of a middle stature, black Complection, black short Hair, having on a new Felt Hat, Ozenbrigs shirt & Breeches, an old light colour'd Pea-Jacket, white Yearn stockinks. Whoever takes up the said servant and secures him, so as his Master may have him again, shall have *Thirty shillings* as a Reward, and reasonable Charges, paid by *Benjamin Fairman.*

The American Weekly Mercury, From Thursday September 28, to Thursday October 5, 1727; From Thursday October 5, to Thursday October 12, 1727.

RUN away October 10, *from* Robert Miller *in* Caln, *a Servant Man named* John Sitch, *about 24 Years of age, of a small Stature, swarthy Complection,*

brown Hair; when he went off, he took with him a new Felt Hat, and another old one, an old Jacket, grey Kearsey Coat, Linnen Drawers, and an old pair of Trowsers, brown Yarn Stockings, and a new pair of Shoes; he also took with him a Hemp Halter, *Whoever secures the said Servant, so that his said Master may have him, shall have* 20 Shillings *Reward,*
     by me Robert Miller.

The American Weekly Mercury, From Thursday October 12, to Thursday October 19, 1727; From Thursday October 19, to Thursday October 26, 1727; From Thursday November 2, to Thursday November 9, 1727.

RUN away the 3*d of the* 8*th Month, called* October, 1727, *from* Samuel Jones *of* Cadbury *in the County of* Chester, *a Welch Servant Man, named* William Williams, 21 *Years of age, of a middle stature, round shoulder'd, thin Visage, brown Coloured Hair; having on a striped Jacket, a green Plush Cap, or Felt Hat, grey Yarn Stockings, round Toe'd Shoes: Whosoever shall take up the said Runaway and secure him shall have* Forty shillings *Reward, or bring him home, shall have the Sum of Four Pounds paid them*
     by me Samuel Jones.

The American Weekly Mercury, From Thursday October 12, to Thursday October 19, 1727; From Thursday October 19, to Thursday October 26, 1727; From Thursday November 2, to Thursday November 9, 1727.

RUN away the 9*th of this Instant from* Alexander Frame *of the City of* Philadelphia, *Taylor, a Servant Lad named* John Man, *Aged about Eighteen Years, (a Taylor by Trade) Short Stature he had on when he went away a Grey Sagathea Coat, and a Fustain Frock under the Coat, Ozenbrig Breeches, a Course white shirt, Yearn Stockings, old Shoes, old Hat and a short Dart Wigg, pale Complection. Whoever secures the said Servant, so that his Master may have him again, shall have* Thirty shillings *Reward and Reasonable Charges,* paid by *Alexander Frame.*

The American Weekly Mercury, From Thursday October 19, to Thursday October 26, 1727; From Thursday October 26, to Thursday November 2, 1727; From Thursday November 2, to Thursday November 9, 1727.

RUN away the 26*th of this Instant from* James Steward *Taylor, of the City of* Philadelphia, *a Servant Man named* John Jones, *aged about* 20 *Years of a middle stature and slender Fair Complection, large Eyes somewhat soreish,*

Lame and Crumpled on his left Foot, has on a large broad brim'd Hat with a hole worn out near the Edge a light Colour'd Duroy Coat and Jacket with new Fashion cut Sleeves, also a Linnen striped Jacket and breeches with brown Holland Trousers, Two white Holland shirts, two pair of stockings, one Cotton and one Worsted, old shoes Light coloured Wigg, or Cap, pretends to make Leather Breeches and Gloves, but was willing to serve the said steward [sic] to Learn the Taylors Trade. Whoever Brings him to his said Master shall have Forty Shillings Reward and Reasonable Charges.
N. B. *He pretends to be a Relation to Judge* Lloyd.

> *The American Weekly Mercury*, From Thursday October 19, to Thursday October 26, 1727; From Thursday October 26, to Thursday November 2, 1727; From Thursday November 2, to Thursday November 9, 1727. See *The American Weekly Mercury*, From Tuesday December 12, to Tuesday December 19, 1727.

RUN away from *Anthony Wilkinson* of *Philadelphia* Carver, *November* 1st, a Servant Man, named *Richard Peckford* a Stone Cutter by Trade, he is a tall raw Bone Fellow, little round Shoulder'd, he stoops with him Neck; had on a Felt Hat edged round the Brim, a light blue thick Woollin Cap, a light white Kearsey Coat full trimm'd, a dark pair of Yearn Stockings, a pair of Leather Breeches with Brass Buttons. Whoever takes up and secures the said Servant, and gives Notice thereof to his said Master, shall have *Forty Shillings* as a Reward and all other reasonable Charges,
    paid by me *Anthony Wilkinson.*

> *The American Weekly Mercury*, From Thursday November 2, to Thursday November 9, 1727; From Thursday November 9, to Thursday November 16, 1727.

RUN away on Tuesday the 21*st of* November, *from* George King, *Mastmaker, of the City of* Philadelphia, *a Servant Man named* Thomas Watkins, *aged about* 40 *Years, of a middle Stature, long Visage, having a large Tooth in his upper Jaw, he had on an old Felt Hat and Worsted Cap, an old Great Blue Coat, and a Pea-Jacket lined with Red, Orenbrig Breeches, old Stockings and Shoes. Whoever takes up and secures said Servant to his said Master, so that he may be had again, shall have* 20 *Shillings as a Reward and reasonable Charges, paid by me* George King.
☞*If he returns to his said Master he shall be kindly Receiv'd.*

> *The American Weekly Mercury*, From Thursday November 23, to Thursday November 30, 1727; From Thursday November 30, to Thursday December 7, 1727; From Thursday December 7, to Tuesday December 12, 1727. Last line not in the last advertisement.

RUN away on the 3d of this Instant *December*, from *James Steward*, Taylor of the City of *Philadelphia*, a Servant Man, named *John Jones*, aged about 20 Years, of a middle Stature and slender, fair Complection, large Eyes somewhat soreish, lame and crumpled on his left Foot, he has a fine Beaver Hat, a dark brown Natural Wigg, a light colour'd Duroy Coat and Jacket, with new Fashion cut Sleeves; also a Linnen striped Jacket and Breeches, with two Holland Shirts, a pair of striped Holland Trousers, brown Worsted Stockings and new Shoes. Whoever takes up the said Servant and secures him so that his said Master may have his again, shall have Three Pounds as a Reward and all reasonable Charges:

☞ *He pretends to make Leather Breeches and Gloves, but was willing to serve the said Steward to learn the Taylors Trade; this is the third Time of his runing away from said Steward.*

The American Weekly Mercury, From Tuesday December 12, to Tuesday December 19, 1727; From Tuesday December 19, to Tuesday December 26, 1727; From Tuesday December 26, 1727, to Tuesday January 2, 1728. See *The American Weekly Mercury*, From Thursday October 19, to Thursday October 26, 1727.

1728

WHereas *Conrad Kann* and his Wife *Marina*, two Palantines, (the former a Tall black grain'd Man, with his own long black Hair, commonly wears a Blue Coat with Brass Buttons; the latter a middle siz'd Young Woman, of around Face, brown Complection) who arrived here the 30th of *October* last from *London*, in the Ship John Galley, have now absented themselves for seven Weeks, with intent to screen themselves from paying their Passage: If any one will bring the said Man and Woman, (or the Man alone) or give Notice so as they may be had, shall have 30 *Shillings* reward, and reasonable Charges; paid by *John Ball*,

Master of the aforesaid Ship, in *Philadelphia*.

The American Weekly Mercury, From Tuesday January 9, to Tuesday January 16, 1728; From Tuesday January 16, to Tuesday January 23, 1728; From Tuesday January 23, to Tuesday January 30, 1728; From Tuesday February 13, to Tuesday February 19, 1728. [*sic*]

Philadelphia, March 29, 1728.

RUN away from the *Iron-Works* on the *French-Creek*, in the County of *Chester*, a Servant Man named *Rich. Snaggs*, of a very short Stature, about 26 Years of Age, of a Sworthy Complection, and has a Scar over one of his Eyes, and goes a little lame with his Feet, his Hair is cut off, and he sometimes wears a little short light Colour'd Wigg: He has on a grey Kersey Jacket, and

Breeches, with small Pewter Buttons. Whoever secures said Servant, so that his Masters may have him again, shall have *Forty Shillings* Reward, and Reasonable Charges, paid by us,   *William Branson, Samuel Nutt.*
    The American Weekly Mercury, From Thursday April 4, to Thursday April 11, 1728. See *The American Weekly Mercury*, From Tuesday April 17, to Thursday April 24, 1729.

JOHN Rogers late of the City of *Philadelphia* Potter, having absconded some Time in *December* last, and took with him a likey [sic] young Negroe Lad about 18 Years of Age, named *Limos*, he is of a yellowish Complection, and a Malagascow Negroe, he had on an Ozenbrig Shirt and Frock, a Frize Jacket and Breeches without lining with Brass Buttons. These are to forwarn all Persons from Buying the above said Negroe, he belonging to *Solomon Goard* of *Philadelphia*. And whoever will take up said Negroe and secure him and give Notice thereof to *Andrew Bradford* in *Philadelphia*, or *William Parks* in *Maryland*, shall have *Three Pounds* and Reasonable Charges.
    The American Weekly Mercury, From Thursday May 2, to Thursday May 9, 1728; From Thursday June 6, to Thursday June 13, 1728; From Thursday June 27, to Thursday July 4, 1728.

RUN away from John Hyatt, *of* Philadelphia, *on the* 19*th Instant a servant man named John Hill, by Trade a Brasider of middling Stature Black curled Hair, Thin Vissage little Pockfretten had on a Cherry derry Jacket and Breeche,* (or dark Duroy) *a new shirt of scotch Linning, Grey mild stockings Wooden heeld shooes and large Beaver Hat much worn. It is supposed he is in Company with two sailors which have absconded from the Grain Brigantine, lately arrived from Madera. The one of which is a Yorkshire man of small stature Pockfretten, stradles wide in his gate hath on a Brown cloth coat and Jacket his Name* Thomas Wittaher, *aged about 30. The other an Irishman,* James Letcher *slender in Body, aged about 21 Years with Black Lank Hair, White cloth Pea Peacket* [sic] *and Breeches, and sloucht Hat Whoever secures said* Hill *and gives Notice to this Master so that he may be had again shall have Fifty shillings Reward and Reasonable Charges,*
           paid by   John Hyatt.
    The American Weekly Mercury, From Thursday May 16, to Thursday May 23, 1728.

RUN away from *William Bareford* of the City of *Philadelphia*, a Servant Man, named *Thomas Wilson*, a short well set Fellow, by Trade a Butcher, he has short sandy Hair, a plain light grey Cloth Coat, striped Jacket and

Breeches, he is a talkive [sic] Fellow. Whosoever shall take up said Servant, and brings him to his said Master, shall have Forty Shillings Reward and reasonable Charges, paid by   William Bareford.
The American Weekly Mercury, From Thursday May 30, to Thursday June 6, 1728; From Thursday June 6, to Thursday June 13, 1728; From Thursday June 13, to Thursday June 20, 1728.

RUN away the 4th of this Instant *June*, from *Thomas Wilcox*, a Servant Man, named *Thomas Ryon*, an *Irish*-Man, of a short Stature, well set, short black Hair, somewhat curl'd (or he may have on a dark colour'd Wigg, which he had in his Pocket) of a fresh Complection, he has on a Linsey-woolsey Coat with large Pewter Buttons, a brown Jacket, a Ozenbrig Shirt and Breeches, a good Raccoon-Hat, grey Yarn Stockings, and a Pair of new single Sole Shoes. Whoever secures the said Servant or brings him to the Work-House in *Philadelphia*, or to his Master in *Concord, Chester*-County, shall have *Forty Shillings* as a Reward, and reasonable Charges,
    paid by   *Thomas Wilcox*.
The American Weekly Mercury, From Thursday May 30, to Thursday June 6, 1728; From Thursday June 6, to Thursday June 13, 1728; From Thursday June 13, to Thursday June 20, 1728.

RUN away the 10th of this Instant *June*, from *Andrew Bradford*, of the City of *Philadelphia*, a Servant Man named *Nicholas Classon* a Printer by Trade, and a sprightly young Fellow, about 21 Years of Age, fresh Complection, much Pockfretten, and has on a grey Drugget Coat lin'd and trim'd with Black, a white Demity Jacket, also a white Fustain Coat with mettle Buttons, and faced in the Neck with red Velvit, a Pair of Leather Breeches, and a Pair of striped Linnen homespun Breeches, he wears a short bob Wegg, he has several other Cloaths with him, and good Shoes and Stockings, (He formerly served with *William Parks* Printer in *Annapolis*). Whoever takes up said Servant and brings him to his said Master, or to *William Bradford* in *New-York*, or to *William Parks* in *Annapolis*, shall have *Three Pounds* Reward, and reasonable Charges, paid by me *Andrew Bradford*.
The American Weekly Mercury, From Thursday June 6, to Thursday June 13, 1728; From Thursday June 13, to Thursday June 20, 1728; From Thursday June 27, to Thursday July 4, 1728.

RUN away from the Ship Waring, a Servant Man, named *Backer Irish* Extract, a well set Fellow, about 25 Years of Age, with short Hair, having on a Sailor Jacket and Breeches; he is supposed to be gone to *New York*.

Whoever takes him up, and brings him to *John Hopkins*, shall have 20 Shillings as a Reward and all reasonable Charges.

The American Weekly Mercury, From Thursday June 27, to Thursday July 4, 1728; From Thursday July 4, to Thursday July 11, 1728; From Thursday July 18, to Thursday July 25, 1728.

RUN away from *Anthony Willkerson*, a Servant Man, named *Richard Pickford*, a tall Man, short brown curl'd Hair, by Trade a Stone-cutter, he has a dark Coat with flat white Mettle Buttons, he stoops much in his Neck, he is about 23 Years of Age: As also run away from *Thomas Boude*, in Company, a Servant Man, named *Patrick Kenedy*, a very short Fellow, pitted with the Small-Pox, aged about 22 Years, no Hair, but wore a Wigg or Cap, he has a dark Coat with red Cuffs, and lin'd with red, a Pair of Tickin Breeches, a good Felt Hat. Whoever takes up and secures the said Servant, so that their Masters may have them again, shall have *Thirty Shillings* Reward for each and Reasonable Charges paid by us,

Anthony Wilkerson and *Thomas Boude*.

American Weekly Mercury, From Thursday June 27, to Thursday July 4, 1728; From Thursday July 4, to Thursday July 11, 1728.

RUN away on the 27th of May last, from *Richard Loudon* in the Town of *Chester*, a Servant Man, named *William Smith* a Shoe maker by Trade, he is of a middle stature, with black Hair, pretty fresh Complection, aged about 23 or 24 Years, having on darkish coloured Cloaths trim'd with Black, Linnen Drawers, gray Yarn Stockings, pretty good Shoes, with small Brass Buckles in them; he is an *Irish-man* born, and supposed to be gone to *New-York.* Whoever takes up the said Servant and secures him so that his said Master may have him again, shall have *Forty shillings* as a Reward and reasonable Charges.

The American Weekly Mercury, From Thursday June 27, to Thursday July 4, 1728. See *American Weekly Mercury*, From Thursday July 4, to Thursday July 11, 1728, and *The American Weekly Mercury*, From Thursday July 18, to Thursday July 25, 1728.

RUN away on the 27th of May last, from *Duncan Dummond* in the Town of *Chester*, a Servant Man, named *William Smith* a Shoe maker by Trade, but served his Time at *Dublin*, to a Clog-maker, he is of a middle stature, with black Hair, pretty fresh Complection, aged about 23 or 24 Years, having on darkish coloured Cloaths trim'd with Black, Linnen Drawers, gray Yarn Stockings, pretty good Shoes, with small Brass Buckles in them: he is an

Irish-man born, and suppos'd to be gone to *New-York*. Whoever takes up the said Servant and secures him so that his said Master may have him again, shall have *Three Pounds* as a Reward and reasonable Charges.

American Weekly Mercury, From Thursday July 4, to Thursday July 11, 1728. See *The American Weekly Mercury*, From Thursday June 27, to Thursday July 4, 1728, and *The American Weekly Mercury*, From Thursday July 18, to Thursday July 25, 1728.

RUN away the 16th of this Instant from *John Pasmore* of *Kennet* in *Chester* County, a Servant Man named *Roger Burn*, an *Irishman* aged about 27 Years, of a low Stature, something Freckl'd, his Hair is cut off, he had a dark bob Wigg a dark Cloath Coat with Eight brass Buttons, an Ozenbrig Shirt, Course Linnen Breeches, and a pair of grey Stockings and Felt Hat. Whoever shall take up said Servant and bring him to his said Master, or to the Work house in *Philadelphia*, shall have *Forty Shillings* as a Reward, and Reasonable Charges.

The American Weekly Mercury, From Thursday July 18, to Thursday July 25, 1728; From Thursday July 25, to Thursday August 1, 1728.

RUN away on the 27th of May last from *Richard Lawden* Shoe-maker, in *Chester*, a Servant Man, named *William Smith*, who served his Time at *Dublin*, in *Ireland*, to a Clog and Patten-maker, properly belonging to one *Duncan Dummond* Mercht. in the County of *New-Castle*; of a middle stature, with black Hair, pretty fresh Complection, aged about 23 or 24 Years, having on darkish coloured Cloaths trimm'd with Black, Linnen Drawers, gray Yarn Stockings, pretty good Shoes, with small Brass Buckles in them; he is an *Irish-man* born, and supposed to be gone to *New-York*. Whoever takes up the said Servant and secures him so that his said Master may have him again, shall have Three Pounds as a Reward and reasonable Charges.

The American Weekly Mercury, From Thursday July 18, to Thursday July 25, 1728. See *The American Weekly Mercury*, From Thursday June 27, to Thursday July 4, 1728, and *American Weekly Mercury*, From Thursday July 4, to Thursday July 11, 1728.

RUN away the 15th Day of this Instant *July* from *Charles Crosly* of middle Town in *Chester* County, a Servant Man named *Roger Carey*, aged betwixt Thirty and Forty years, of a middle Stature, black Complexion, dark colour'd Streight Hair, and a dark coloured Coat, and a Cinnamon coloured vest and striped Tickin Breeches, black Worsted Stockings and good Shoes, and a good Felt Hat, and a fine Shirt, and a Course homespun Shirt, he is by Trade a Weaver and Coomber. Whoever takes up the said Servant and secures him, again, shall have *Twenty Shillings* reward and reasonable Charges paid by me   Charls Crosleys.

The American Weekly Mercury, From Thursday August 1, to Thursday August 8, 1728.

RUN away the 6th of *July* last, from *Samuel Worthington*, of the Manner of *Moorland*, in the County of *Philadelphia*, two Servant Men; one named *James Purnel*, a short Man with black Hair, aged about 30 Years: He had on a brown Drugget Jacket, Linnen Drawers, Caster Hat, two Pair of Stockings, and a Pair of Silver Buckles at his Shoes: He is Burst (or broken Belly'd) for which Cause he wears a Leather Apron: He hath with him four Cancelled Bonds, which he sheweth, to make People believe he is a Free man, (for which Bonds, and other Money paid he became bound.) The other is a lusty young Man, named *Richard Bowen*, with brown Hair, a large Felt Hat, a good brown Kersey Jacket, lin'd with Shalloon, a Pair of Leather Breeches, and Linnen Drawers, two Pair of Shoes, and other Cloaths. Whoever secures the said Servant, so as their Master may have them again, shall have *Five Pounds* Reward and all reasonable Charges, paid by   *Samuel Worthington.*

The American Weekly Mercury, From Thursday August 8, to Thursday August 15, 1728; From Thursday August 15, to Thursday August 22, 1728; From Thursday August 22, to Thursday August 29, 1728. See *The Pennsylvania Gazette*, From April 23, to April 30, 1730.

RUN away the 18*th of this Instant* August, *from* Samuel Bowls *of* Philadelphia *Black smith, a Servant Man named* Launcelot H*erne, aged about* 24 *Years, of a tall Stature, and light Hair, a Naylor by Trade, he carried away with him, a new Felt Hat, a light Serge Jacket, Ozenbrig and Buckskin Breeches, Holland Shirt and white Stockings. Whoever takes up said Servant and brings him to his said Master shall have Five Pounds as a Reward and Reasonable Charges, Samuel Bowls.*
Philadelphia *August* 18. 1728.

RUN *away at the same Time from* John Sherburn, *of* Philadelphia *Joyner, a Servant Man named* Neal M'Coy *a Scotchman, a Joyner by Trade, aged about* 24 *Years, thin Vissage, of a pale Complection, short brown curl'd Hair a Snuff colour'd Coat Jacket and Stockings, and Leather Breeches, a good Felt Hat, one Checkt and one White shirt, and Ozenbrig Trousers. Whoever takes up the said servant and brings him to his said Master shall have* Five Pounds *as a Reward and all Reasonable Charges paid by*
John Sherburn.   Philadelphia, *August* 18 1728

The American Weekly Mercury, From Thursday August 15, to Thursday August 22, 1728; From Thursday August 22, to Thursday August 29, 1728.

Philadelphia, August 28. 1728.
RUN away the 15th Instant *August* from *John Rutter*, at the Iron works, at *Manatawney*, a Servant Man named *Timothy Brandriff*, a Weaver by Trade, born at *Cape May*, aged Twenty Three Years of a middle Stature, sandy Complection, bushy Hair, small Visage and freckled in the Face, he stoops in the Shoulders, he has two or three Suites of Cloaths, also went away with him one *Richard Hether*, a Freeman a Blacksmith by Trade, he formerly lived in *West-Jersey* Whosoever shall take up the said Servant and bring him to the said *John Rutter* in *Philadelphia* or secures him; so that he may have him again, shall have *Four Pounds* Reward, and Reasonable Charges,
paid by me,   *John Rutter.*

The American Weekly Mercury, From Thursday August 22, to Thursday August 29, 1728; From Thursday August 29, to Thursday September 5, 1728.

RUN away the 8th of this Instant *September*, from *Joseph Taylor*, jun. of *Kennet* Township in *Chester* County, a Servant Man, named *Joseph Hodges*, aged about 19 Years, a tall slender Man, long Visage, Pockfretten, with short light colour'd Hair, a Felt Hat, a grey colour'd Kearsy Coat and Jacket with Brass Buttons, a pair of Ozenbrig Breeches and Trousers, a Pair of Worsted Ash colour'd Stockings, and old Shoes; he had also with him when he went away one Ozenbrig Shirt and a fine one. Whoever takes up the said Servant and brings him to his said Master, shall have *Fifty Shillings* Reward and reasonable Charges, paid by me,   *Joseph Taylor.*

The American Weekly Mercury, From Thursday September 5, to Thursday September 12, 1728; From Thursday September 12, to Thursday September 19, 1728; From Thursday September 26, to Thursday October 3, 1728.

RUN away the 1st of this Inst. *September* from *Henry Pugh*, of *Merrion* in the County of *Philadelphia*, a Servant Man named *Peter Mack Collick* an *Irishman*, of a middle Size, about Twenty Years of Age, he had on a bob Wigg and sometimes wears a Cap, a dark Cloath Coat and Wastcoat lined, a pair of Leather Breeches, he took with him a white Horse, and an old Russet Saddle Branded with the letters B. H. Whoever shall take up the said Servant and bring him to his said Master, or to the WorkHouse, or give Notice thereof, so that he may be had again, shall have *Twenty Shillings* Reward and Reasonable Charges.

The American Weekly Mercury, From Thursday September 5, to Thursday September 12, 1728; From Thursday September 12, to Thursday September 19, 1728; From Thursday September 26, to Thursday October 3, 1728.

Run away from John Wheldon *Cord-wainer of* Philadelphia, *a servant Man named* Edward White, *a shoe-maker, middle Stature, thin Vissage, a fair spoken Man, but pretends to be a Bath Man, and some Times a Doctor; having on a Felt Hat, a light Wigg, a Pea-Jacket lined with Blue, Homespun Breeches, a white Shirt, grey Stockings, round Toe'd shoes, supposing to have the other Cloaths which he ran away with before, a fashionable grey colou'd Drugget Coat, a stript Flannel Jacket, Leather Breeches, Ozenbrigs Trousers, Purple colour'd stockings. Whoever takes up the said Servant and secures or brings him to his said Master, shall have 30 s. Reward and reasonable Charges.*

The American Weekly Mercury, From Thursday September 26, to Thursday October 3, 1728; From Thursday October 3, to Thursday October 10, 1728; From Thursday October 17, to Thursday October 24, 1728; From Thursday October 24, to Thursday October 31, 1728.

THIS Day Run away from *John Bayley* Cordwainer, Two servant Men Shoemakers, and both *Irish*, the one Named *George Newman*, short and well set, had on a Light colour'd Cloth Coat, strip'd Holland Jacket and Breeches, has also a Pair of Buckskin-Breeches, good Wood heel shoes, Yarn Rockins, [sic] short Brown Hair, and smooth Face about Thirty years old; the other Named *Michael Brazil*, short and Dark Complexion'd, has on a Dark Colour'd Frize Coat and Waste-coat; a pair of New Buckskin Breeches, a Black Wigg, good shoes and Yarn stockings, and Thirty years old. Whoever takes up the said Servants, so that their Masters may have them again, shall have Five Pounds reward, or Fifty shillings for each, and reasonable Charges
        paid by me.   *John Bayley.*

The American Weekly Mercury, From Thursday November 13, to Thursday, November 21, 1728. [*sic*]

RUN away the 16th. of *November*, from the Ship *Borden*, *William Harbert* Commander, a Servant Man, Named *Edward Conron*, (an *Irish* Man, but denies his Country,) of a middle Size, about Twenty one years of age, pretends to be a Barber Surgeon, pretty Fat, his Face mark'd with the small

Pox; supposed to have on when he went away, a Suit of Black Cloth Cloathes, with an old Red thread bare Duffell Coat, a Light short Horse hair Wigg, and Black Stockings, hath pretty much of the *Irish* Accent in his Speech: Whoever takes up the said Servant, and brings him to the said Ship, or to *Edward Horne* in *Philadelphia*, shall have Forty Shillings Reward, and reasonable Charges paid, *Edward Horne.*

The American Weekly Mercury, From Thursday November 28, to Thursday, December 5, 1728; From Thursday December 5, to Tuesday December 18, 1728.

Philadelphia, *December the* 11th. 1728.
RUN away on the First day of *Nov.* from *Andrew Cornish*, of *Conestogoe* in *Chester* County, a Servant Woman, named *Mary Rawlinson*, who since has changed her name to *Sarah Wood*; she has on a brown Gown and Petty-coat, with one under Petty-coat of Gray Kersey joyn'd at the Top with Blue: Who ever takes up the said Servant Woman, and brings her to her said Master, shall have Forty Shillings Reward and all reasonable Charges paid by, *Andrew Cornish.*

The American Weekly Mercury, From Thursday December 5, to Tuesday December 18, 1728; From Thursday December 18, to Thursday December 24, 1728.

1729

RUn away from *Daniel Prichard*, in the County of *Bucks*, a Servant Woman, named *Elizabeth Skit*, of a short stature, thick and fat, light Hair'd, with a broad red Face, had on a strip'd Linsey-Woolsey Petticoat and Wastecoat, a Gown with broad red Stripes, blue Stockings, and Leather-heel'd Shoes. Whoever secures the said Servant, so that her Master may have her again, shall have Forty Shillings Reward and reasonable Charges.

The Pennsylvania Gazette, January 2, 1729; January 7, 1729; January 21, 1729.

RUN away from *Richard Whitten*, of *Dublin*, in the County of *Philadelphia*, a Servant Man, named *James Cundun*, an *Irishman*, a short well set Fellow, aged about 22 Years; has curl'd black Hair; Brownish Complexion, inclining to Fat; with a Dent upon the upper Part of one of his Cheeks; wears an old Beaver-Hat; two Wollen Jackets, the uppermost being a dark Sheep's Grey, a Pair of Linnen Breeches, with short Trousers over them, a Pair of course Woollen Stockings, and ordinary Shoes.

Whoever secures the said Runaway, so as his Master may have him again, shall have Twenty Shillings Reward, and reasonable Charges

paid by me,   *Richard Whitten.*
The Pennsylvania Gazette, January 29, 1729; February 4, 1729; February 11, 1729.

Philadelphia, *January t*he 3d 1728-9
RUN away from *William Farmer Yerbury*; a Servant Man nam'd *Thady Ternan* an *Irishman*, sometimes by the name of *Timothy*, a Taylor by Trade, about six Foot high, aged about 36 Years, he wears sometimes a Light, and sometimes a Dark colour'd Wigg, with a Black Complexion, wears a good Felt Hat, with a good Brown Cloath-Coat and Jacket and Brown Cloth Briches and Stockins.

Whoever secure the said Run-away, so as his Master may have him again, shall have *Three Pounds* Reward, and reasonable Charges
paid by me,   *William Farmer Yerbury.*
The American Weekly Mercury, From Tuesday, February 4, to Tuesday, February 11, 1729; From Tuesday, February 11, to Tuesday, February 18, 1729; From Tuesday, February 18, to Tuesday, February 25, 1729.

WHEREAS Joseph Sturgus *of the City of* Philadelphia, *in the Province of* Pennsilvania, *Saddletree-maker by an Order was of Court in this City was adjudged to serve* Caleb Ransted *of the same place Turner, a certain Term of Years not yet expired, Notwithstanding the said Servant has Absented himself from his said Masters Service, for the space of Eight Months in Nine Months Time, and is now Absent, he is of a middle Stature, thin Visage Squint ey'd ill look'd he is supposed to have on Yarn Stockins, Buckskin Breeches, Elkskin Jacket, Cinnamon colour'd Broadcloth Coat, Felt Hat. These are therefore to Inform all Persons that is they can take up the said Servant and bring him again shall have* Twenty Shillings *as a Reward and Reasonable Charges*
Caleb Ransted.
The American Weekly Mercury, From Tuesday, February 18, to Tuesday, February 25, 1729; From Tuesday [*sic*] March 27, to Thursday, April 3, 1729.

RUN away from *Christopher Smith* Merchant, a Servant Maid, named Mary Wilson, a *Londoner*, she is a Mantua-maker by Trade. She has on a brown Gown fac'd with Black, a red Petticoat of pale Complexion, high Forehead; Whoever brings the said Servant to *Samuel Ferguson*, in Walnut-street, shall have Twenty Shillings reward paid by the said *Samuel Ferguson.*
The Pennsylvania Gazette, March 27, 1729; April 3, 1729; April 10, 1729.

RUN away the 19th of this Instant, from the Ship Mary, Robert Deglish Commander, an Apprentice to the said Vessel, named Patrick Lamenon, an Irish-man, a Cooper by Trade, aged about thirty Years, he's a thin Fac'd Fellow, of a middle Stature, with long lank brown Hair, a light Colour'd Jacket with Canvas Patches on the Shoulders, Canvas Trowsers, a large Hat, light grey Stockings. Whoever takes up the Servant, and brings him to Robert Deglish, or John Morrison, at Henry Dexter's in Philadelphia, shall have Twenty Shillings reward, and Reasonable Charges paid, by John Morrison.
  The Pennsylvania Gazette, March 27, 1729; April 3, 1729; April 10, 1729.

RUN away the 5th of this Instant *April*, from *Zachariah Hutchins*, Butcher of the City of *Philadelphia*: a Servant Man, named *Thomas Chit*, a short well set Fellow, of a fresh Complexion, about 35 Years of Age, having his Hair cut off, or a Light Wig, having on an old Hat, with Brim sow'd on to the Crown, a Cinnamon colour'd Coat, with bright Metal Buttons upon Wood, a Light Sagathie Jacket, a Pair of Buckskin Breeches something Gresey, a New Garlick Shirt, a Butcher by Trade: Any Person that can take up the said Servant, and secure him, so that his Master may have him again, shall have *Three Pounds* as a Reward, besides all reasonable Charges,
          paid by me.   *Zachariah Hutchins.*
  The American Weekly Mercury, From Tuesday April 3, to Thursday April 10, 1729; From Tuesday April 10, to Thursday April 17, 1729; From Tuesday April 17, to Thursday April 24, 1729.

RUN away the 10th of this Instant *April*, from *John Hutchinson*, at the *Falls* of *Delaware*; a Servant Man, named *Thomas Richards*, a Taylor by Trade, born at *London*, of very low stature, well set, a Wart on his Right Cheek, short black Hair, cuts with his Left Hand, and Sows with his Right; he had with him when he went away Two Coats, one of dark coloured of homespun Serge, and Jacket of the same, the other Coat Brown Linsey much worn, Buckskin Breeches, a pair of Yarn Stockings, a pair of Shoes one pair Wooden heel stitchd about the Quarters, with large Silver Buckles, the other pair Leather-heel'd with large Steel Buckles, two Hats one a Castor, the other a Felt. Whoever secures the said Servant s that his Master may have him again shall have *Three Pounds* as a Reward, and reasonable Charges
          paid by me,   *John Hutchinson.*
  The American Weekly Mercury, From Tuesday April 10, to Thursday April 17, 1729; From Tuesday April 17, to Thursday April 24, 1729; From Tuesday April 24, to Thursday May 1, 1729. Newspapers dated

as shown. See *The American Weekly Mercury*, From Thursday, November 25, to Thursday, December 2, 1731.

RUN away the 7th of this Instant *April*, from *Wm. Iddings* of *Nantmeal*, a Servant Man named *Richard Snags*, of low Stature, about 30 Years of Age, Swarthy Complexion, a Scar over one of his Eyes, he had a Striped Jacket, Blew and White Cotten and Linnen, Greyish Coloured great Coat, with Blackish Woollen Stockings, and old Leather Breeches. Whoever takes up the said Servant and brings him to *Hugh Roberts* at the *Indian King* in *Philadelphia*, or to *Wm. Iddings* of *Nantmeal* shall have *Thirty Shillings* as a Reward and reasonable Charges paid by me,   *Wm. Iddings*.

The American Weekly Mercury, From Tuesday April 17, to Thursday April 24, 1729; From Thursday May 15, to Thursday May 22, 1729. See *The American Weekly Mercury*, From Thursday April 4, to Thursday April 11, 1728.

RUN away from *John Bentley* of *Burmingham*, and *Richard Clayton* of *Concord*, both of the same County, two Servant Men, the one named *John Gray*, an Englishman, of a short Stature, dark Complexion, short curl'd Hair, a Mole upon his right Cheek: He had on when he went away, a good Felt Hat, a blue Jacket with a Cinnamon-colour'd Jacket under it, grey stockings, good Shoes. The other named *Richard Middleton*, an Englishman, of a short Stature, a pale Complexion, strait Hair, a good Felt Hat, a light colour'd Coat, Leather Breeches, yellow Stockings, good Shoes. Whoever secures the said Servants, in the next Goal, and gives Notice to their Masters, so that they may have 'em again, shall have Fifty Shillings Reward, and reasonable Charges paid by us,   *John Bentley, Richard Clayton.*

The Pennsylvania Gazette, May 1, 1729; May 8, 1729; May 15, 1729; June 5, 1729.

RUN away from the Ship *Salisbury*, the 9th of this instant *May*; Two Servant Men, one named *Richard Mabbot*, of a Light Brown Complexion, middle Stature, having on a Seaman's Kersey upper Jacket, a Ship Swanskin one under it; his Hair lately cut off.

George Rigby, of sandy Complexion, some sign of the Small-Pox in his Face, of a middle Stature; having on when he went away, a Drugget Coat with small Buttons, a strip'd Jacket, wearing a Light Wig. Any Person that shall bring them to *Thomas Sharp*, or *Samuel Bromage*, shall have *Three Pounds* Reward for Each of them, with reasonable Charges.

The American Weekly Mercury, From Thursday May 8, to Thursday May 15, 1729; From Thursday May 15, to Thursday May 22, 1729.

RUN away the 19th Instant May, *from* Benjamin Armitage, *of* Bristol-Township *and County of* Philadelphia, *a Servant Man named* George Palmore, *an Englishman, aged 33 Years, of a middle Stature, well-set, a little pock-fretten, his Hair off, wearing a Felt Hat, strip'd yellow and white Silk Handkerchief, speckled Shirt, pied Jacket, brown colour'd Breeches of the same, under which a strip'd blue and white Flannel Jacket, grey worsted Stockings, new Shoes. Whoever secures the said Runaway, so as he may be had again, shall have Forty Shillings Reward, and reasonable Charges paid by me,* Benjamin Armitage.

The Pennsylvania Gazette, May 22, 1729; May 29, 1729; June 5, 1729; June 12, 1729.

RUN away the 18th Instant, from *Samuel Richardson*, of *Bristol* Township, a Servant Man named *John Mackmaman*, an Irishman, a short brisk Fellow, talks much, wearing black curl'd Hair, aged about 30, pock-fretten, brownish broad Cloth Coat and Jacket lin'd with Camlet, with curl'd Brass Buttons with Wooden Moulds, an Ozenbrig or Homespun Shirt, new long Ozenbrig Trouzers, strip'd Ticken Breeches, Worsted Stockings, purple colour'd, good Shoes. Whoever secures the said Servant, or gives Notice to *Hugh Roberts* of *Philadelphia*, so as his Master may have him again, shall have Three Pounds Reward, and reasonable Charges paid,
            by me   Samuel Richardson.

The Pennsylvania Gazette, May 29, 1729; June 5, 1729.

R*Un away from* James Chalmers *out of* Philadelphia, *the* 10*th of this instant June; a Servant Man, named* Alex. Sloane, *a well set little Fellow, Black Wigg, swarthy Complexion, New Coat of a dark Brown colour, White-wastecoat, Brown Breeches and Stockins.*

Also from Samuel Worthington *the same Day, out of the same Place.*

One William Setgriffon, *his servant, a pretty Tall and Lusty Fellow about Twenty Years of Age, a Brownish Coat much worn, very large Breeches, Brown Worsted Stockings: He took from his Master Five Pair of silver sleeve Buttons.*

The American Weekly Mercury, From Thursday May 29, to Thursday June 5, 1729; From Thursday June 5, to Thursday June 12, 1729; From Thursday June 19, to Thursday June 26, 1729; From Thursday June 26, to Thursday July 3, 1729.

Philadelphia, *June the* 17th 1729.

RUN away the 15th of this Instant *June*, from *Thomas Stackhouse* in *Bucsks* [*sic*] County; a Servant Man named *Thomas Roberts*, a middle siz'd well set broad Shoulder'd Fellow, short stubbed Sandy Hair, a Red Complexion, and Gray Eyes, an *Englishman*, he has on a Drugget Jack, [*sic*] Light Russet colour, with flat Pewter Buttons, also an Ozenbrig patch'd Shirt, and a Course Pair of Linnen Draws, and a Pair of Gray Stocking Legings, and a Pair of Old Squar'd Toe'd Shoes, and an Old Caster Hat. Whoever secures the said Servant, and gives notice to his Master, shall have *Forty Shillings* as a Reward.

The American Weekly Mercury, From Thursday June 12, to Thursday June 19, 1729.

RUN away on the 9th. of this Instant *June*, Two Servant Men belonging to *Thomas Arrold* of the Township of *Bradford*, in the County of *Chester*, and is named *John Burk*, he is about 18 Years of age, of a Middle Stature, Fresh Colour'd, with short Black Hair; he had on when he went away a Felt Hat, Black Coat, a white Jacket, Leather Breeches, and Brown Yarn Stockins.

The other belonging to *Thomas Thernbury*, of the Township aforesaid, in Named *James Cownden*, he is about Twenty five Years of Age, Tall of stature, thin Fac'd, long hock'd [*sic*] Nose'd, with straight Light colour'd Hair; he had on when he went away, a Felt Hat, a Gray Double-Brested Pea-Jacket with Brass Buttons, a New Pair of Linnen Drawers, Black Stokins, and Pair of Shoes newly Tap'd.

Whoever secures either of the above-mention'd Servant Men, shall have Three Pounds Reward; Paid by Us.

The American Weekly Mercury, From Thursday June 12, to Thursday June 19, 1729; From Thursday June 19, to Thursday June 26, 1729.

RUN away from *George Shad*, Peruke-maker, in *Front-street Philadelphia*, the 30th of *June*; a Servant Man named *John Granger*, a short fellow hard Favoured, long Vissage, a Scar under his Chin like the Evil, he waddles in his Gate; and had on a Felt-Hat, light Wig, an Ozenbrig Jacket and Breeches, White Garlick Shirt, round Toe'd Shoes and no Stockins on when he went away: Whoever takes up the said Runaway, and bring him to his said Master, or secures him so that his Master may have him again, shall have *Forty Shillings* reward, and all reasonable Charges for ten Miles from *Philadelphia*.

The American Weekly Mercury, From Thursday June 26, to Thursday July 3, 1729; From Thursday July 3, to Thursday July 10, 1729.

RUN away on the 15th of *June* past, from *Arthur Wells* of this City; a Servant Man named *John Blowden*, aged about 22 Years, by Trade a Shoemaker; he is of a middle Stature, full Faced, of a fair Complection, and Effeminate Voice, with short Brown Bushy Hair: He has on a Striped Homespun Jacket, and Breeches of the same, without Pockets. and Patched on the Knees, Garlick Shirt half worne an old Beaver Hat, with sides Flopping down, Brown Worsted Stockings, and Wooden Heel'd Shoes cover'd over the Toes.

N. B. He has been seen Lurking near this Town this Fortnight past, and last Sunday Night, having procured a Duroy Coat, he went further, he has also since changed his Breeches for others of a narrower *S*tripe, and has got a New pair of *S*hoes which being too little for him he was forced to cut them in the *S*ides; he often pretends to be worth a great deal of Money, by which he has imposed on several.

Whoever shall secure the said Servant, so that his Master may have him again, shall have *Forty Shillings* Reward, and reasonable Charges,
             paid by   *Arthur Wells.*

The American Weekly Mercury, From Thursday July 3, to Thursday July 10, 1729; From Thursday July 17, to Thursday July 24, 1729; From Thursday July 24, to Thursday July 31, 1729. See *The Pennsylvania Gazette*, From March 4, to March 11, 1731; *The American Weekly Mercury*, From Tuesday March 13, to Tuesday March 20, 1733; *The Pennsylvania Gazette*, From March 8, to March 15, 1733; *The American Weekly Mercury*, From Thursday October 4, to Thursday October 11, 1733; *The Pennsylvania Gazette*, From September 28, to October 11, 1733; *The Pennsylvania Gazette*, From November 13, to November 20, 1735, and *The Pennsylvania Gazette*, January 29, 1741.

RUN away the 16th of this Instant July; from his Master, *William Ruttenhousen* of *German Town*, Paper-Maker; a Servant Man named *Edward Guest*, about Twenty two Years of Age, a Middle sized fellow, his Hair cut off, and has two Letters of his Name markt with Blew on his Wrist, he Stutters in his Speech, having on two Jackets, one a Stript, the other Plain, Strip'd Linnen Breeches, Old Shoes and Stockings: Whoever shall take up the said Servant, and bring him to his Master, or to the Workhouse, and give Notice to *Andrew Bradford*, shall have *Thirty Shillings* Reward, and reasonable Charges.

The American Weekly Mercury, From Thursday July 10, to Thursday July 24, 1729; From Thursday July 17, to Thursday July 24, 1729.

RUN away from *Jeremiah Elfreth*; a Servant Man named *Thomas Davis*, he is about 21 Years of age, he took with him a Light colour'd Cloth Vest, and dark Cloth Breeches, a White Shirt, and a Ozenbrig Shirt and Breeches, an Old fine Hat, and Gray Worsted Stockins, he is of a short Stature, black Hair and Complection, he hath a Hole or Scar in his Forehead. Whoever shall take up the said Servant, and bring him to *Jeremiah Elfreth* of *Philadelphia*, or *John Elfreth* of *Bristol*, or *James Sykes* at *New Castle*, shall have *Thirty Shillings* as a Reward, Paid by me,   Jeremiah Elfreth.

The American Weekly Mercury, From Thursday July 31, to Thursday August 7, 1729; From Thursday August 7, to Thursday August 14, 1729. See *The American Weekly Mercury*, From Tuesday March 1, to Tuesday March 8, 1726.

R*UN away from Daniel Palmer, of the Township of* Makefield, *in the County of* Bucks, *and Province of* Pennsylvania, *a Servant Man, named* Cesar Hyde, *aged* 28 *Years, short Stature, and Pock-freten, dark coloured Hair; he had on when he went away, a Felt Hat, and a yellow coloured Coat with Brass Buttons, a striped Jacket, a white Pair of Breeches, a light coloured Pair of Worsted Stockings, and round Toed Shoes. Whoever secures said Runaway, so that his Master may have him again, shall have Thirty Shillings Reward, and Reasonable Charges paid by* Daniel Palmer.

The Pennsylvania Gazette, September 11, 1729; September 18, 1729

B*Roke out of the Goal of* Philadelphia, *the* 30*th of* August *last, Two Men, one named* Joseph Prowse, *about Twenty Years of Age, tall and slender, of a fair Complexion, white Hair lately cut off, brown stuff Jacket, Gray stockings, and an Old Beaver-Hat. The other named* James Mitchel, *a short Down=look'd Fellow, Freckled in the Face, black Hair lately cut off, with a large fresh scar on the Left side of his Head, pretends to be a sailor.*

Whoever takes up the said Persons, or either of them, shall have Forty shillings Reward for each, and reasonable Charges
    Paid by   CHARLES READ, Sher.

The American Weekly Mercury, From Thursday September 28, to Thursday October 5, 1729. [sic]

RUN away on the 10th of *September* past, from *William Dewees* of Germantown Township, in *Philadelphia* County, a Servant Man named *Melchizedeck Arnold*, of a middle Stature, and reddish curled Hair: he had on when he went away, a good Felt Hat, a dark Cinnamon-colour'd Coat, black Drugget Jacket, mouse-colour'd drugget Breeches, grey Stockings, and new Shoes.

Whoever secures the *said Runaway, to that his Master may have him again, shall have Twenty* Shillings Reward, and reasonable Charges
            paid, by me   *William Dewees.*
The Pennsylvania Gazette, From September 25, to October 2, 1729; From October 2, to October 9, 1729; From October 9, to October 16, 1729.

RUN away on the 25th of September past, from *Rice Prichard* of Whiteland in Chester County, a Servant Man named *John Cresswel,* of a middle Stature and ruddy Countenance, his Hair inclining to Red. He had on when he went away, a little white short Whig, an old Hat, Drugget Wastcoat, the Body lined with Linnen; coarse Linnen Breeches, grey woollen Stockings, and round toe'd Shoes.
    Whoever shall secure the said Servant so that his Master may have him again, shall have *Three Pounds* Reward, and reasonable Charges paid by *Rice Prichard.*
    The Pennsylvania Gazette, From September 25, to October 2, 1729.

RUN away the 8th of *September* last, from *Samuel Eastbourn,* of *Soldbury,* in the County of *Bucks;* an Apprentice, Named, *James Morgan,* of a Middle stature, well set, a thick short fellow, having on, when he went away, a New Felt Hat, Linnen Trousers, good Shoes, New Stockings, a Linnen Jacket, a Gray Coat, an Ozenbrig Shirt, having spotted with Gun=Powder very much. Whosoever bring, or secure him, so that his Master may have him again, shall have *Forty Shillings* as a Reward, and all reasonable Charges
           paid by me,   *Samuel Eastbourn.*
    The American Weekly Mercury, From Thursday October 2, to Thursday October 9, 1729; From Thursday October 9, to Thursday October 16, 1729.

RAN away from *David Davies* of *Goshe*n, in the County of *Cheste*r, on the 6th of this Instant, a Servant Man, named *George Curren,* aged about Twenty-one. He is an *Irishman,* of a middle Stature, pale Complexion, pretty much Pockfretten, short black Hair, some times wears a light-coloured strait Wigg; at other times a knit Cap; he has a good Felt Hat, a dark brown Frize Coat, and an old Sheep-russet Wastcoat, old dark coloured Breeches, with a great deal of Pitch on them, and a good strip'd Pair under them; also a strip'd Shirt, dark brown Stockings, and old Shoes. Whosoever will secure the said Runaway, and give Information to his Master, so that he may have him again, shall have *Twenty Sh*illings Reward, and all reasonable Charges, paid by me *David Davies.*

The Pennsylvania Gazette, From November 6, to November 10, 1729; From November 10, to November 13, 1729; From November 13, to November 17, 1729; From November 20, to November 24, 1729.

BRoke out of *Newtown* Goal the 6th of *October* last, the following Persons, viz. *Thomas Lamb,* of a Middle stature, Black Complexion; had on when he went away, a Light colour'd Broad Cloath Coat without Pocket Holes, or Flaps, Burnt in several Places on one of the Fore Skirts, had with him two Wigs, one Black, and Ty'd behind, the other a White short Wig, and he has a great Scar over his Right Ear: At the same Time broke out of the said Goal, one *Edward Garland,* who pretends himself Mate of a Ship, also a Ship Carpenter, nigh six Foot high, Pale Vizage, and a little Pock broken; is supposed to have on a good fine Hat, and Light colour'd Wig, Ty'd with a black Ribbon behind, or else a Double Worsted Cap, a good White Shirt, a Double Breasted Cinamon colour'd Broad Cloath Coat Trim'd with the same, a Gray Broad Cloath Vest, and Black Breeches, Light Gray Worsted Stockings, good Wood Heel'd Shoes, and Brass Buckles: Escaped at the same time, one *George Tesdall,* a Labourer, of a Middle Size, Pale Vizige, very much Pock-Broken; and had a Stuttering, or Impediment in his Speech, also Brown Hair, supposed to have on an Old Blew Gray Broad Cloath Coat, an Old Light Gray Kersey Vest, an Ozenbrigs Shirt, and Trousers, Leather Breeches, Gray Yarn Stockings, and old Leather-Heel'd Shoes, but no Buckles.

Whoever takes up the said Men, and brings them to *John Millnors* of *Newtown,* or secures them, so as they may be had again, shall have Fifty Shillings for Each, as a Reward, and reasonable Charges, paid by
Timothy Smith, Sheriff.

The American Weekly Mercury, From Thursday November 13, to Thursday November 20, 1729; From Thursday November 20, to Thursday November 27, 1729.

RUN away the 24th of this Instant *November,* from *John Bell,* Carpenter of *Chester* County, a Servant Lad, named *John Edwards,* aged about Seventeen Years, a Welch Lad, of a Middle Stature, blackish Hair, a Yellow Cloath and a Linnen Jacket, Leather Breeches, Ozenbrick Shirt, and a Felt Hat. Whosoever shall take up said Lad, and secure him, so that his Master may have him again, shall have Forty Shillings Reward and reasonable Charges, paid by *John Bell.*

The American Weekly Mercury, From Thursday November 20, to Thursday November 27, 1729; From Thursday November 27, to Thursday December 4, 1729; From Thursday December 4, to Tuesday December 9, 1729.

RUN away from *Edward Brooks* of *Philadelphia*, Butcher, the Second Day of the Fair, a lusty Servant Maid, aged about 25 Years, named *Anne Dod*, of a likely fresh Countenance, dark Brown Hair, mark'd near the Bent of one Arm with *A. D.* 1705. having on a Plat Bonnet, Lin'd with Flesh colour'd Silk, and a Strip'd Blew and White Linnen Gown, and a Greenish Peticoat. Any one that can bring her, to her said Master, or give Intelligence, so that he may have her again, shall have Thirty Shillings reward, and reasonable Charges.

The American Weekly Mercury, From Thursday November 27, to Thursday December 4, 1729; From Thursday December 4, to Tuesday December 9, 1729.

RUN away from *Evan Thomas*, of *Willis Town*, in the County of *Chester*, on the 22d Day of this Instant *November*, a Servant Man, named *William Vippin*, a Irish Man, a Weaver by Trade; he has with him a Gray Drugget Coat, a pair of Gray Drugget, and a pair of Calamanca Breeches, two White Flannel wast=Coats, two fine Shirts, several pair of Stockings, a Light Gray Peruke, new Shoes and Buckles, and Twenty Shillings in Money; he is of a Middle Stature, and pretty fresh Complexion. If any Person or Persons will Secure the said Run=away, so that he may be had again, shall have Forty Shillings reward, and reasonable Charges, paid by me,
    Evan Thomas.

The American Weekly Mercury, From Thursday November 27, to Thursday December 4, 1729; From Thursday December 4, to Tuesday December 9, 1729.

RUN away on the 13th Instant, from *Moses Hewes* of this City, a Servant Woman named *Jane Mackelanen*, aged about 23 Years, of a middle Stature, round Visage, fresh Complexion, dark Hair; having on two Suits of Apparel, the one a blue Stuff Jacket and Petticoat, the other a brown shalloon Gown, and light coloured Petticoat, Oznaburgh Shift, blue Stockings and old Shoes. Whoever shall take up the said Servant and bring her to her Master, or secure or so that he may have her again, shall have *Twenty Shillings* Reward, and all reasonable Charges paid by, me *Moses Hewes.*

The Pennsylvania Gazette, From December 16, to December 23, 1729; From December 23, to December 30, 1729; From January 6, to January 13, 1730.

RUN away about the last Day of *November* past, from *John Naglee* of *Germantown* in this County, Butcher, a Dutch Servant Man, named *Johannes Fetterly*, who speaks very little English, and has formerly been a Trooper in the Emperor's Service, aged about 34 Years, of middle Stature, swarthy Complexion, grry Hair if not cut off, with a Scar over the Knuckle of the Fore-finger of his Right Hand; he had on a new Felt Hat, an old turn'd grey Coat with black Buttons, blue Wastecoat, coarse Linen Shirt, old Leather Breeches, black or grey Stockings, and old Shoes new soal'd. Whoever secures the said Servant so that his Master may have him again, shall have *Three Pounds* Reward, and reasonable Charges paid, by *John Naglee*.

The Pennsylvania Gazette, From December 16, to December 23, 1729; From December 23, to December 30, 1729; From January 6, to January 13, 1730.

RUN away on the 5th Instant, from *Nicholas Scull* of this City, Innholder, a Servant Man named *Lawrence Herne*, aged about 22 Years; he is low of Stature, of a black Complexion, with black curl'd Hair and has on a grey Coat either of Serge or Duroy, with black Cuffs; a Wastecoat of the same, but more worn than the Coat; an old Hat, a good Shirt, Leather Breeches, grey worsted Stockings, and good Shoes. Whoever secures the said Servant so that his Master may have him again, shall have *Forty Shillings* Reward, and reasonable Charges paid, by   *Nicholas Scull*.

The Pennsylvania Gazette, From December 16, to December 23, 1729; From December 23, to December 30, 1729; From December 30, 1729, to January 6,1730; From January 20, to January 27, 1730.

1730

RUN away from the *John Galley*, of *Dublin*, Capt. *Richard Murphy*, a Servant Man named *William Gilliam*, a black-Smith by Trade, he is short and well-set, he was but indifferently Cloathed when he went away, having but part of a Shirt to his Back, and yellow coloured Jacket with Pewter Buttons, his Hair very short, wearing an old Wig over it. He is supposed to be gone towards *Philadelphia*. Whoever takes up said Servant, and secures him, so that the said Murphy may have him again, or give Notice to *Richard Ashfield* in *New-York*, or to *Andrew Bradford* in *PhilGelphis*, [sic] shall have Forty Shillings Reward, besides all reasonable Charges, paid by Richard Ashfield.

The American Weekly Mercury, From Tuesday December 30, to Tuesday, January 6, 1729 [*sic*]; From Tuesday, January 6, to Wednesday, January 14, 1729 [*sic*]; From Tuesday, January 14, to Wednesday, January 20, 1729 [*sic*]. Actual year is 1730.

RUN away the 5th of this Instant *January*, from *Jonathan Cooper* of *Wrights* Town, in the County of *Bucks*, in the Province of *Pennsylvania*; a Servant Man, named *Thomas Murry*, an *Irish* Man, he is thin Fac'd, hath had the Small-Pox, Light Brown Hair a little Curl'd behind, with a Dark colour'd Irish Ratten or Frise Coat unlin'd, with Cross Pockets, an Old Brown Kearsey Coat torn at the Sleeves and Sides, a Double Breasted Pea-Jacket with Pewter Buttons, Two Pair of Leather Breeches, one Pair good, without buttons at the Knees, only Strings and Puffs, the othe [*sic*] pair Old with some Brass and some Pewter Buttons, Two Pair of Stockings, one pair good White Yarn of Sheeps Black to above the *M*iddle of the Leg, Three Shirts, one of Homespun Linnen, the other Two finer, one very much worn, a Pair of good *S*hoes, and a Pair of *S*patterdashes with Brass Buttons, a good Felt. He hath taken with him from his said Master, a little Bay *M*are, with a Scar like a Heart, with a Switch Tail and Branded on the near Buttock and Shoulder this, *I. S. C.* and a good Old Round Scirted Saddle a little torn before; he hath a Bag with him to put his Things in.

Whosoever takes up the said Servant, and secures him, so that he may be had again, and give Notice to *Jonathan Cooper* at *Wrights* Town, or to *Christopher Toppin* at *Lewis Town*, shall have Three Pounds Reward, an reasonable Charges, paid by me,

Jonathan Cooper, or *Christopher Toppin*.

The American Weekly Mercury, From Tuesday, January 6, to Wednesday, January 14, 1729 [*sic*]; From Tuesday, January 14, to Wednesday, January 20, 1729 [*sic*]; From Tuesday January 20, to Tuesday January 29, 1729 [*sic*]. Actual year is 1730.

RUN *away from the Iron-Works at* French Creek, *in* Chester-*County, on Saturday the* 21st *Instant* February; *Two Servant Men.*

The one named Joseph Bartam, *of a Tall stooping stature, much Pitted with the small-Pox, short dark brown Hair, about* 30 *Years of Age: he had on when he went away a Castor Hat, a brown double Breasted Pea Jacket, with Mohair Buttons of the same Colour, and Breeches of the same, with an Ozenbrig shirt, he is a Taylor by trade.*

The other named Nathaniel Ford, *of a Middle stature swarthy Complection, black Hair he has Two broad Teeth before, about* 25 *Years of*

Age; he had on when he went away an old Castor Hat, dark coloured Sarge Coat, lined with Bleu, he is a Carpenter by Trade; and has taken his Tools with him, and it is supposed he has taken a Gun. Whoever shall take up said Servants, or either of them, and bring them to Samuel Nut at the Iron-Works at French Creek or to William Branson in Philadelphia, or secure them, and give Notice; shall have Forty Shillings Reward for Each, and Reasonable Charges.

The American Weekly Mercury, From Thursday February 19, to Tuesday February 24, 1730; From Tuesday March 3, to Thursday March 5, 1730; From Tuesday March 5, to Thursday March 12, 1730; From Tuesday March 12, to Thursday March 19, 1730. [sic]

RUN away on Sunday Night last, from *John Clark* of *Bucks* County; an *Irish* Servant Woman, named *Anstis Downing*, alias *Agnes Mac Daniel*, aged about 22 Years, she speaks clear English, is of middle Stature, swarthy Complexion, black Hair and black Eyes, and something round-shoulder'd. She has on a Gown Yellow and Green striped, a Petticoat of Yellow and Red striped, and an old brown Gown and Petticoat, and new Leather-heel'd Shoes. She has stolen her Indentures, and went away with one *George Welsby*, who lately married her, of which they have a Certificate with them. He is a short Fellow, with a down roguish Look, pale Complexion, grey little Eyes, and thin brown Hair, if cut off he wears a Cap. He has with him a light-colour'd close made Cloath Coat, and Breeches of the same; an old dark-colour'd Coat with red Lining, a dark-colour'd Great Coat, Leather Breeches with Berry Buttons cap'd with Silver, two Felt Hats one old the other new, a speckled Shirt and other Shirts. He has a *Maryland* Pass with him, sign'd *Charles Markland*; and they have taken a long Pine Canoo with an Iron Chain. Whoever secures the said Servants shall have Twenty Shillings Reward for each, and reasonable Charges paid, by
John Clark. March 11, 1729-30

The Pennsylvania Gazette, From March 5, 1730, to March 13, From March 13, to March 19, 1730; From March 19, to March 26, 1730.

RUN away from *John Parker*, Joiner, at *William Bile's*, in *Bucks* County, a Servant Man named *Robert Naylor*, aged about 20 Years, of low Stature, fresh Complexion, brown lank Hair, wears an old Felt Hat, a brown Pea-Jacket with brass Buttons, Indian-dress'd Leather Breeches, old pair of dark brown worsted Stockens, a new pair of Shoes. Whoever secures the said Servant, so as his Master may have him again, shall have 40 s, Reward, and reasonable Charges paid by   John Parker.

The Pennsylvania Gazette, From March 5, 1730, to March 13, 1730; From March 13, to March 19, 1730; From March 19, to March 26, 1730; From March 26, to April 2, 1730; From April 9, to April 16, 1730. See *The Pennsylvania Gazette*, From August 13, to 20, 1730.

R*UN away the Third of this Instant* April, *from his Master* Thomas Robinson, *of the Township of* Solesbury, *in the County of* Bucks; *a Servant Man named* Henry Rice, *he has Black Hair, a Swarthy Complexion, Long Stature, a Weaver by Trade; he had on, when he went away, a Whitish Coloured Coat, with Mettle Buttons, a Homespun Shirt, Buckskin Breeches, with Mettle Buttons. Whoever shall take up said Servant, and secure him, or bring him to his Master, or give Notice, shall have Thirty Shillings as a Reward, and reasonable Charges, paid by* Thomas Robinson.

The American Weekly Mercury, From Thursday April 9, to Thursday April 16, 1730; From Thursday April 16, to Thursday April 23, 1730.

RUN away on the 14th Instant, from *Stephen Hollingsworth* of *Philadelphia*, Cordwainer, a Servant Man named *John Talifero*, alias *Luke Cell*, alias *John Dodso*n. He is short and thick, full-fac'd, pale and freckled; has on a short black Wig, an old Hat, a blue Camlet Coat with white Metal Buttons, a reddish Camlet Jacket, grey Stockings and old Shoes. He is a great Rambler, a noted Rogue, and pretty well known as such in all the neighbouring Colonies. Whoever secures him so that he may be had again, shall have *Thirty Shillings* Reward; and reasonable Charges paid, by
                    Stephen Hollingsworth.

The Pennsylvania Gazette, From April 9, to April 16, 1730; From April 16, April 23, 1730; From April 23, to April 30, 1730.

RUN away on the 19th Instant from *Abraham Wood* of *Bucks* County, a *French* Servant Man named *Isaac Barone*, aged about 25 Years; a little well-built Man, black Hair, swarthy Complexion, round Visage. Has on a light coloured Kersey Coat made fashionable, a blue and white striped Jacket, a Felt Hat, fine Shirt and an Oznaburgh Shirt, and Trowsers.

    Run away at the same Time from *Nicholas Parker* of the same County, an *Irish* Servant Man, named *Henry Brewer*, about 50 Years of Age, middle Stature, short black Hair, but sometimes wears a white Wig or a worsted Cap, has a teering Look with his Eyes. He wears a brownish colour'd broad Cloth Coat and Vest trim'd with the same Colour, Oznaburgh Breeches, fine and coarse Shirts, brownish Yarn Stockings, old Shoes and a good Felt Hat. *Note*, They are supposed to be gone together, and to have false Passes with them.

Whoever secures the said Servants, so that their Masters may have them again, shall have *Three Pounds* Reward for each, and reasonable Charges paid, by *Abraham Wo*od, and *Nicholas Parker.*

The Pennsylvania Gazette, From April 16, April 23, 1730; From April 23, to April 30, 1730; From April 30, to May 7, 1730.

RUN away on the 19th Inst. from *John Baldwin* of *Kennet* in *Chester* County, a Servant Man named *George Smith*, of a middle Stature, thin Visage, wide Mouth, blackish Hair, aged 21 Years: he took with him two Suits of *French* Drugget, one white the other Snuff colour'd, with Silver Clasps on one of the Garments; also a blue shagg'd Great Coat or Cloak, a Silver hilted Sword, a brown bay Horse branded with E on the near Shoulder, and a Star in the Forehead. Whoever secures the said Servant and Effects so that his said Master may have them again, shall have *Five Pounds* Reward, and reasonable Charges paid, by John Baldwin.

The Pennsylvania Gazette, From April 23, to April 30, 1730; From April 30, to May 7, 1730. See *The Pennsylvania Gazette*, From May 7, to May 14, 1730.

RUN away on the 19th Instant from *Isaac Walker* of *Tredyffryn* in *Chester* County, an *Irish* Servant Man, named *Joseph Cummins*, about 22 Years of Age, of middle Stature, well sett, freckled Face, sandy Hair but short; he wears a white linnen Cap, a good Felt Hat, a copper colour'd Drugget Coat with light colour'd Linings, a Linsey-wolsey Jacket, and good Leather Breeches with Brass Buttons, Oznaburgh Shirt, reddish Handkerchief, light brown worsted Stockings, a new Pair of Shoes with brass Buckles. *Note*, The Back of his Hand is lately much bruised, and he wears a Cloth about it. Whoever secures the said Servant so that his said Master may have him again, shall have *Thirty Shillings* Reward, and reasonable Charges paid, by *Isaac Walker.*

The Pennsylvania Gazette, From April 16, April 23, 1730; From April 23, to April 30, 1730; From April 30, to May 7, 1730.; From May 7, to May 14, 1730.

RUN away the 19th of this Instant from *John Wallace* in *Derby*, a Servant Man named *Samuel Hughs*, of a low Stature, goes stooping, and sharp Shins, one more sharp than the other; he looks to be 30 Years of Age, but says he is but 25. He served some Time in *Frankford*; He hath got a large felt Hat, short black Hair, striped Handkerchief, a darkish-coloured homepsun cloth Coat and Jacket, a pair of Trowsers, bluish Stockings and new Shoes; He is one

that hath a great deal of Assurance, and is a *West Country-man*. Whoever secures the said Servant so that his Master may have him again, shall have *Twenty Shillings* Reward and reasonable Charges
paid, by   John Wallace.
The Pennsylvania Gazette, From April 23, to April 30, 1730; From April 30, to May 7, 1730; From May 7, to May 14, 1730.

RUN away the 3d of this Instant *May*, from his Master *Joseph Lyn*, Shipwright, an *Irish* Servant Lad, named *Arthur Flening*, about Seventeen Years of Age; he had on a Brown Broad Cloath Coat and Vest, and also a Blew Jacket, a good White Shirt, and long Breeches, good Yarn Stockings, he is of a Dull Complexion, and is well grown of his Age. Whosoever can take up said Servant or secure him, so that his Master may have him again, shall have Forty Shillings as a Reward, and reasonable Charges.
The American Weekly Mercury, From Thursday April 30, to Thursday May 7, 1730.

RUN away on the 25th of this Instant from *Samuel Worthington* of the Manor of *Moreland* in this County, two Servant Men, viz *Richard Bowen*, aged 22 Years, well set, has short dirty brown Hair; a grey Kersey Coat and Jacket, woollen and worsted Stockings, and good Shoes. *James Purnel*, aged 30 Years, of low Stature, black Complexion, without Hair; he is bursten, and commonly wears an Apron to conceal it; also his little Finger, by reason of a Cut among the Sinews, stands streight, and will not bend with the rest; his Cloaths are much the same with those of *Bowe*n described above. They have taken with them two Guns, a pair of Boots, a Castor Hat, and a copper-coloured Sagathee Jacket.

RUN away at the same Time from *Henry Comeley* of the same Place, a Servant Man named *Abel Philips*, aged 24 Years, lusty and well-sett, short black Hair, broad Face, large Nose, and small hollow Eyes; he has a coarse grey Kersey Coat and Wastcoat, Leather Breeches, a Light-coloured Great Coat, good Stockings and Shoes.

RUN away also at the same Time from *Thomas Dussell* of the same Place, an *Irish* Servant Man named *Peter Kelley*, of middle Stature and well-sett, black Hair, swarthy Complexion, much pockfretten; he has a home made brown cloth Coat, a grey drugget Jacket, and a thick Buckskin Jacket, leather Breeches, a blue great Coat with pewter Buttons, grey Stockings and good Shoes. He speaks good *French*. It is thought all four are gone together.

Whoever secures the said Servants in some Goal, and gives Notice to their Masters, shall have *Fifty Shillings* Reward for each, and reasonable Charges paid, by *S. Worthington, Henry Comeley, Thomas Duffell [Dussell]*

The Pennsylvania Gazette, From April 23, to April 30, 1730; From April 30, to May 7, 1730; From May 7, to May 14, 1730. See *The American Weekly Mercury*, From Thursday August 22, to Thursday August 29, 1728, for Bowen and Purnel.

RUN away from *White* and *Taylor*; a Servant Man named *John Hedford*, of a middle Stature and Pale Complexion, had on when he went away, an Old Beaver Hat; a Cap; one light grey Cloath Coat, and Strip'd Swanskin Jacket; a Check'd Shirt, a Redish Coarse Pair of Woollen Stockings, and a good Pair of Shoes. Whoever secures said Servant, so that he may be had again, shall have Forty Shillings Reward, and all reasonable Charges,
   paid by *White* and *Taylor*.
The American Weekly Mercury, From Thursday May 7, to ThursdayMay 14, 1730; From Thursday May 21, to Thursday May 28, 1730; From Thursday July 2, to Thursday July 9, 1730; From Thursday July 9, to Thursday July 16, 1730. See *The Pennsylvania Gazette*, From May 7, to May 14, 1730.

RUN away on the 5th Instant from *Evan Morgan* of this City, a Servant Man named *John Frost*, by Trade a Taylor and Staymaker, aged about 30 Years, small of Stature, hath a very short Neck, and a thick fat chin which almost rests upon his Breast. He wears a light-coloured Duroy Coat, strip'd Cherryderry Jacket and Breeches, light grey worsted Stockings, two good white Shirts, a brown Wig, an old Castor Hat, and good Shoes; but may have other Cloaths unknown; and also an old Indenture which has been cancelled. Whoever secures the said Servant, so that he may be had again, shall have *Four Pounds* Reward and reasonable Charges
   paid, by *Evan Mor*gan.
The Pennsylvania Gazette, From April 30, to May 7, 1730.

RUN away from *White & Taylor* a Servant Man named *John Hedford*, of a middle Stature and pale Complexion. Had on when he went away, an old Beaver Hat; a Cap; one light grey Cloth, and one strip'd Swanskin Jacket; a check'd Shirt; a reddish coarse Pair of Stockings, and good Shoes. Whoever secures the said Servant so that he may be had again, shall have *Forty Shillings* Reward, and reasonable Charges paid, by *White & Taylor*.
 The Pennsylvania Gazette, From May 7, to May 14, 1730; From May 14, to May 21, 1730. See *The American Weekly Mercury*, From Thursday May 7, to Thursday May 14, 1730.

RUN away on the 6th of *April* past, From *Jeremiah Clement* of *Chester*, Hatter, a Servant Man named *Lawrence Murphey*, of middle Stature, well sett, short black Hair, fair Complexion; He had with him but ordinary working Cloaths, to wit, a brown broad-cloath Coat made like a Sailor's Jacket, a dark coloured Coat with small Cuffs; an ordinary Shirt with a blue Patch near the Collar, a Felt Hat, grey Kersey Breeches, yarn Stockings, and old Shoes; but may have procured better Cloaths since. He was born in *Ireland*, and can speak *Irish*, but commonly talks good *English*, having lived several Years in *England*. He is a very good Workman at the weaving Business, especially Woollen Weaving; he also can work at the Hatters Trade; also writes a good Hand and has been a Schoolmaster. Whoever shall secure the said Servant so that he may be had again, and give Notice thereof to his abovesaid Master, or at the *New Printing Office* in *Philadelphia*, shall have Eight Pounds Reward, and reasonable Charges

paid, by   *Jeremiah Clement.*

The Pennsylvania Gazette, From May 7, to May 14, 1730; From May 14, to May 21, 1730; From May 217, to May 28, 1730.

RUN away on the 25th of this Instant from *Samuel Worthington* of the Manor of *Moreland* in this County, two Servant Men, *viz. Richard Bowen*, aged 22 Years, well set, and no Hair; also his little Finger, by reason of a Cut among the Sinews, stands streight, and will not bend with the rest; he has a brown Coat, Kersey Jacket, woollen and worsted Stockings, and good Shoes. *James Purnel*, aged 30 Years, of low Stature, black Complexion, without Hair; he is bursten, and commonly wears an Apron to conceal it; has on a light-colour'd Cloth Coat, and a grey Duroy Jacket.

RUN away at the same Time from *Henry Comeley* of the same Place, a Servant Man named *Abel Philips*, aged 24 Years, lusty and well-sett, black Hair lately cut off, broad Face, small Beard, large Nose, and small hollow Eyes; he has a brown Kersey Coat, strip'd blue and white Ticken Jacket, good Stockings and Shoes.

Run away on April 19, from *John Baldwin* of *Kennet* Township in *Chester* County, a Servant Man named *George Smith*, of a middle Stature, thin Visage, wide Mouth, blackish Hair, aged 21 Years. He has with him a Suit of Snuff-coloured French Drugget with long Skirts.

N. B. *The above four Servants, having been advertis'd in this Gazette, were apprehended and put into* Amboy *Jail, but made a second Escape at the* Raritons, *as they were bringing home.*

Whoever secures the said Servants in *Trentown* Goal, or brings them home to their said Masters, shall have *Fifty Shillings* Reward for each, and reasonable Charges paid, by

S. Worthington, Henry Comeley, John Baldwin.
The Pennsylvania Gazette, From May 7, to May 14, 1730. See *The Pennsylvania Gazette*, From April 23, to April 30, 1730, for all but Smith. See *The American Weekly Mercury*, From Thursday August 22, to Thursday August 29, 1728, for Bowen and Purnel. See *The Pennsylvania Gazette*, From April 23, to April 30', 1730, for Smith.

RUN away from *Joseph England* of *Nottingham*, in *Chester* County in *Pennsylvania*, upon the First of this Instant *June*; a Servant Man, named *Alexander Mac Connel*, an *Irish* Man indifferent Tall, a Lusty well set Man, very Swarthy, thick Lips, his Hair cut off, and having on an Old Pisburn'd Wig, a good Felt Hat, and a Strip'd Lincy Jacket, a Pair of Leather Breeches, or Ozenbrig Trousers, and Light Grey Stockings, and a Pair of New Shoes, too short for him to wear. Whoever shall take up the abovesaid Servant, or secure him, or send him to the Work=house in *Philadelphia*, and give Notice to his Master, or *Andrew Bradford*, shall have Five Pounds Reward,
   paid by me,   *Joseph England.*
The American Weekly Mercury, From Thursday May 28, to Thursday June 4, 1730; From Thursday June 4, to Thursday June 11, 1730; From Thursday June 11, to Thursday June 18, 1730.

         Philadelphia, June 8, 1730.
RUN away from *William Smith* of *Philadelphia*, Shoemaker; a Servant Man, named *John Norris*, aged about 24 Years, of Middle Stature, smooth Fac'd, (his Hair cut off) and sharp Shin'd, he had on when he went away, a dark colour'd Coat with cut Sleeves, Strip'd Homespun Jacket and Breeches, and a pair of Leather Breeches and Trouzers, with two White Shirts; supposed to be in Company with one *James Curry*, an Apprentice to Mr. *Paris* of *Philadelphia*, Brass Founder; he is about 19 Years of Age, Tall and Slender, with Ash colour Cloathes; Whoever secures the said Servant, so that his said Master may have him again, shall have Five Pounds Reward, and reasonable Charges, paid by me,   *William Smith.*
The American Weekly Mercury, From Thursday June 4, to ThursdayJune 11, 1730; From Thursday June 11, to Thursday June 18, 1730; From Thursday June 18, to Thursday June 25, 1730; From Thursday June 25, to Thursday July 2, 1730; From Thursday July 9, to Thursday July 16, 1730. See *The Pennsylvania Gazette*, From June 4, to June 11, 1730.

RUN away from the Ship *Salisbury, Daniel Williams*, Master, Four Sailors, viz, Joseph Lob, Carpenter of the said Ship, a full fac'd well-set Man, with either a red or a black Pair of Breeches, and a Cap under his Hat. *Emanuel Roche*t, a short spare Man, with his own Hair, and a long Coat. *Thomas Crab*, a Lad, with sandy Hair, and a blue Jacket: The other a Scotchman. Run away also from the same Vessel, an indented Servant, named *George Sc*ot, of middle Stature, sly Look, and sandy Eyebrows. Whoever secures the said Men shall have *Twenty Shill*ings Reward for each of the Sailors, and *Three Pounds* for the Servant, reasonable Charges, paid by   *Simon Edgell.*

> *The Pennsylvania Gazette*, From May 28, to June 4, 1730; From June 4, to June 11, 1730; From June 11, to June 18, 1730.

RUN away on the 20th of *May* past, from Matthew Hughes of *Buckingham* in the County of *Bucks*, a Servant Lad named *John Ford*, about 17 Years of Age, pretty well set but short, red complection and freckled, with rusty sandy Hair; he has very flat Feet, and goes with his Knees close together and his Feet a little out: He is a West-country Lad and came from *Crookhorne*: Had on a new Felt Hat, a brown Drugget Coat lin'd with light Shalloon, oznaburgh Shirt and Trowsers, and old shoes with Nails in them. Whoever secures the said Servant, so that he may be had again, shall have *Forty Shillings* Reward, and reasonable charges paid by   *Matthew Hughes.*

> *The Pennsylvania Gazette*, From May 28, to June 4, 1730; From June 4, to June 11, 1730; From June 11, to June 18, 1730.

RUN away the 23d Instant, from *Hannah Pritchett* of *Philadelphia*; an *Irish* Servant Man, named *Robert Griffin*, a Taylor by Trade, he is of a Middle Stature, Black Complexion, he hath a large Mouth, hollow'd Ey'd, and a Shambling way in his walking, when he talks to them he looks them starking in the Face, he hath short Black Hair, having lately wore a Wig; had on when he went away a Blue and White Linnen Jacket, and Brown Cloath Cloathes, with Red Facings to them, a Pair of Grey Worsted Stockings too large for him, a Pair of Shoes almost New, a White Shirt: He absented himself from his said Mistress the 16th of *April* last, and returned again the 20th Instant and said he was at Work while away, and one *Martins* near *Shamony=Ferry*: Whoever secures the said Servant, and brings him to the Work-house in *Philadelphia*, or to *John Jenkinson*, at the Widow *Walkers*, in *Frontstreet*, shall have Twenty Shillings Reward, and reasonable Charges,
     paid by,   *John Jenkinson.*

> *The American Weekly Mercury*, From Thursday June 18, to Thursday June 25, 1730; From Thursday June 25, to Thursday July 2, 1730; From Thursday July 2, to Thursday July 9, 1730; From Thursday July

9, to Thursday July 16, 1730; From Thursday July 16, to Thursday July 23, 1730.

RUN away from *William Smith* of *Philadelphia*, Shoemaker, a Servant Man, named *John Norris*, aged about 24 Years, of middle Stature, smooth Fac'd, with sharp shins, his Hair cut off; He had on a dark colour'd Coat with cut Sleeves, a strip'd homespun Jacket and Breeches, and a pair of Leather Breeches, and Trowsers, with two white Shirts; supposed to be in Company with one *James Curry*, an Apprentice to Mrs. *Paris* of *Philadelphia*, Brass Founder; he is about 19 Years of Age, tall and slender, with ash-colour Clothes. Whoever secures the said Servant, so that his said Master may have him again, shall have *Five Pounds* Reward, and reasonable Charges, paid by me, *William Smith*. June 8.
N. B. He has taken with him several Working Tools belonging to the Shoemakers Trade.

The Pennsylvania Gazette, From June 4, to June 11, 1730; From June 11, to June 18, 1730; From June 18, to June 23, 1730; From June 25, to July 2, 1730; From July 2, to July 9, 1730; to June 23, 1730; From July 9, to July 16, 1730. See *The American Weekly Mercury*, From Thursday June 4, to Thursday June 11, 1730.

RUN away on *Sunday* Night the 15th Instant, from *James Brendly* of this City, a Servant Man named *John Tyler*, by Trade a Hatter, aged about 22 Years, middle Stature, pale Complexion, dark short Hair shav'd about 4 Months since, grey Eyes and an impudent Look; hath a brown Pea Jacket scarce long enough for him, a half-worn white Shirt, one Pair of Leather Breeches and two Pair of ozenbrig Breeches, a strip'd flannel Wastcoat, and an ozenbrig Jacket over it, black worsted Stockings, half worn wooden-heel'd Shoes and a Felt Hat.

RUN away at the same time from *Charles Blake*, at the Sign of the *Brigantine* in this City, a Servant Man named *Thomas Tamerlane*, an *East Indian*, by Trade a Rigger, about 23 Years of Age, small of Stature, with round Shoulders, no Hair, speaks and writes good English: Had on a speckled Shirt, strip'd blue and white flannel Jacket, Tarry Trowsers, good Shoes, and a Felt Hat. 'Tis supposed they are gone together.

Whoever secures the above said Servants, so that they may be had again, and gives Notice to their said Masters, shall have *Forty Shillings* Reward for each, and reasonable charges paid, by
James Brendly, and *Charles Blake*.

The Pennsylvania Gazette, From June 11, to June 18, 1730; From June 18, to June 23, 1730; From June 25, to July 2, 1730. See *The American*

Weekly Mercury, From Thursday, October 8, to Thursday October 15, 1730, for Tamerlane.

RUN away on *Sunday, June* 21, from *John Dexter*, of *Philadelphia*, Sadler, a Servant Man named *William Brown*, aged about 20 Years, a tall slim Fellow, pretty much pock-mark'd, his Hair cut off; he had on a light colour'd Coat, with ozenbrigs Jacket and Breeches, and two Shirts. Whoever secures the said Servants, so that his Master may have him again, shall have *Thirty Shillings* Reward, and reasonable Charges paid, by *John Dexter*.
    The Pennsylvania Gazette, From June 18, to June 23, 1730; From June 25, to July 2, 1730; From July 2, to July 9, 1730.

RUN away the 12th of this Instant *July*, from *Richard Sunley*, near *Wrights=Town*, in *Bucks* County, in the Province of *Pennsylvania*, a Servant Man named *James MacGinnis* an *Irish* Man, aged 21 Years, a thick short well=set Fellow, full Fac d, fresh Colour'd, something Pockbroken, and has dark brown curl'd Hair, had on when he went away, a Snuff colour'd Broad Cloth Jacket with Brass Buttons, Buckskin Breeches with Brass Buttons, a new Ozenbrigs Shirt, a Holland Shirt, two Pair of Stockings, the one Gray, the other White, single soled Shoes narrow Toe'd, a good fine Hat. He took also when he went away from his said Master, a fine Beaver Hat, three Muslin Neckcloths, whipt at the End, a Cotton Handcherchief not made, a Coat and Wastecoat of Sagathy of White and Redish colour, which was cut out, but not made up, about six Yards and a half of the same in two Pieces, also a strip'd Jacket cut out, but not made up, about six Yards of Duroy, of Blewish colour, four Yards of Shalloon, of a Whitish colour, three Pair of Buckskin Breeches, cut out, but not made up, a Homespun Light colour'd Drugget Coat cut out, and part of a Brown Duroy, with large Quantities of other Things. Whosoever secures the said Runaway, and gives Notice to his said Master, or to a*Abraham Chapman* in *Wrights Town* in *Bucks* County, or to *Andrew Bradford* in *Philadelphia*, shall have Five Pounds Reward, and reasonable Charges, paid by me,   *Robert Sunley.*
    The American Weekly Mercury, From Thursday, July 9, to Thursday July 16, 1730; From Thursday, July 16, to Thursday July 23, 1730; From Thursday, July 23, to Thursday July 30, 1730.

RUN away the 19th Instant *July*, from her Master *Charles Sandiford* (lately from *Barbados*) a Covenanted Servant Woman, named *Jane Braiser*, she is of a Middle Stature, Pockfretten and Freckled, she has a striped Callaminco Gown of a Red and White stripe, a Yellow Quilted Petticoat; she has taken the followings [*sic*] Goods, viz. a White Fustian Gown, the Sleeves turn'd up with an Indian Chints, a Blue Camblet Riding-Hood, also a Gallon China Bowl, and many other valuable Goods (if any Person will give any Intelligence of any of the above Goods, shall be very well Rewarded.) Whosoever shall take up the said Servant, and bring her to the Work-house, or give Notice to her Master, shall have Five Pounds Reward, and Reasonable Charges.

The American Weekly Mercury, From Thursday, July 16, to Thursday July 23, 1730; From Thursday, July 23, to Thursday July 30, 1730.

RUN away the 22d of this Instant *July*, from *Jonathan Fisher* of *Philadelphia*, Glover, a Servant Man named *Thomas Forrest*, he is a middle sized Man, has a Squinting Look, is about Thirty Years of age, a Skinner by Trade; had on when he went away, a Light coloured plain made Duroy Coat without Pockets, Strip'd Jacket and Breeches, good round Toe'd Shoes almost new, Light Grey Worsted Stockings, a New Hat, wears a Wig or Cap, has with him two White Shirts, and a Speckled one, supposed to be in Company with one *William Varnall*, who is run-away from his Creditors. Whosoever takes up said run-away, and brings him to his Master, or secures him, so that his Master may have him again, shall have Five Pounds Reward, and Reasonable Charges,   by *Jonathan Fisher.*

The American Weekly Mercury, From Thursday, July 23, to Thursday July 30, 1730; From Thursday, July 30, to Thursday August 6, 1730; From Thursday, August 6, to Thursday August 13, 1730; From Thursday, August 13, to Thursday August 20, 1730. See *The Pennsylvania Gazette*, From July 23, to July 30, 1730.

RUN away the 22d Instant *Jonathan Fisher* of *Philadelphia*, Glover, a Servant Man named *Thomas Forrest*; he is a middle siz'd Man of a squinting Look, about 30 Years of Age, a Skinner by Trade: He had on when he went away a light-coloured Duroy Coat, plain without Pockets, strip'd Jacket and Breeches, a new Philadelphia made Hat, wears a Wigg or Cap, good round toe'd Shoes and fine gray worsted Stockings, two white Shirts and one speckled. Is in Company with one *William Varnell*, who is run away from his Creditors. Whoever shall secure the said Runaway, so as his Master may have him again, shall have *Five Pounds* Reward and reasonable Charges,
     by   *Jonathan Fishe*r.

The Pennsylvania Gazette, From July 23, to July 30, 1730; From July 30, to August 6, 1730; From August 6, to August 13, 1730. See *The American Weekly Mercury*, From Thursday, July 23, to Thursday July 30, 1730.

RUN away last Night from *Joshua Cowpland* of *Cheste*r, a Servant Man named *Michael Eades*, aged 24 Years, a Shoemaker by Trade; very small Stature, brown short Hair, thin Beard, fair Complexion. He had on when he went away, a striped woollen Jacket without Sleeves, Ozenburgh Shirt and Breeches, grey yarn Stockings, new round toed Shoes, and felt Hat.

    Whoever secures the said Servant, so as his Master may have him again, shall have *Forty Shillings* Reward and reasonable Charges paid, by *Philadelphia, August 8.*   *Joshua Cowpland.*

    The Pennsylvania Gazette, From August 6, to August 13, 1730.

R*UN away from his Master,* Nicholas Roach, *of* Philadelphia, *Hatter on the* 11*th of* July, 1730, *a Servant Man, named* Thomas Harris, *he is a square built Fellow, down Look'd, Stoops and Rowls as he walks, of a Pale Complexion, and has Black Hair and Beard. He had on when he went away, a New Dowlas Shirt, Blue and White striped Cotten and Linnen Jacket and Breeches, Black Stockings, and round Toe'd Shoes, a good Raccoon Hat, he is a Hatter by Trade. Whoever secures this Fellow, so as to bring him to his Master, shall have Thirty Shillings Reward, and all reasonable Charges*
        paid by me,   Nicholas Roach.

    The American Weekly Mercury, From Thursday, August 13, to Thursday August 20, 1730; From Thursday, August 20, to Thursday August 27, 1730; From Thursday, August 27, to Thursday September 3, 1730.

RUN away on the 16th Instant at Night, from John Parker, Joiner, of *Bristo*l in *Bucks* County, a Servant Man named *Robert Naylor*, aged about 20 Years; he is short and thick sett, lank brown Hair, and a fresh Complexion; he is Left handed, and has two great Scars on his Right Hand, just below his Thumb: He had on when he went away a new Felt Hat; 2 Shirts, 2 Jackets, 1 pair of Breeches, and 1 pair of Trowsers all of ozenbrigs, new grey yarn Stockings with white Tops, and new Shoes. It is supposed he is gone with his Father of the same Name. Whoever secures the said Servant, so that his Master may have him again, shall have *Forty Shillings* Reward and reasonable Charges
        paid, by   *John Parker*.

    The Pennsylvania Gazette, From August 13, to 20, 1730; From August 20, to 27, 1730. See *The Pennsylvania Gazette*, From March 5, 1730, to March 13, 1730.

Run away from *William Anderson* of *Whitemarsh*, near Justice *Farmer's*, a Servant Man named *Owen O Donolly*, an Irishman, aged about 26 Years, broad well-set Man, bow-legged, a great Boaster and Lyar, and full of Talk; when he walks, his Head leans to one side; black Hair but wears a white Wig: has a brown cloth Coat, a light-colour'd cloth Jacket, Shirt and Breeches of ozenbrigs, a pair of white Stockings, and a pair of blue grey. He professes to be a Brickmaker and a Mason. Whoever secures the said Servant, and gives Notice so that his Master may have him again, shall have *Fifty Shillings* Reward, and reasonable Charges paid, by *William Anderson.*

The Pennsylvania Gazette, From August 27, September 3, 1730; From September 3, to September 10, 1730; From September 10, to September 17, 1730.

RUN away from *John Lloyd* of *Philadelphia,* a Servant Man named *Joseph Dalloway,* middle sized, well-set, dark Hair a little curl'd, about 35 Years of Age, a Blacksmith by Trade. He had on a Kersey Coat with Breeches of the same, a strip'd Ticken Jacket, grey Yarn Stockings, Garlix Shirt, and a coarse Shirt, 1 Fine Hat, and the other a Felt, Leather heel'd Shoes. It is supposed he is gone towards *Minnysinks* or *Sopu*s in *York* Government. Whoever secures the said Runaway, so that his Master may have him again, shall have *Thirty Shillings* Reward, and reasonable Charges paid,
by *John Lloyd.* Sept. 8, 1730.
The Pennsylvania Gazette, From September 3, September 10, 1730; From September 10, to September 17, 1730; From September 17, to September 24 1730.

RUN away on the 14th of this Instant, from the several Persons following, being Residents in *Philadelphi*a: the several Servants herein after named and described, viz. FROM *Nicholas Rogers* one named *Nicholas Mac Donnell*, an Irishman, by Trade a Baker, of middle Stature, well sett, aged Twenty three Years or thereabouts, bald on the Top of his Head occasion'd by a Scald: *Apparel*, a light-colour'd old Drugget Coat, Jacket and Breeches of broad striped Linen, a light-colour'd Wig, or a Cap FROM *Thomas Lindley,* one named *John Roe,* aged about 24 Years, by Trade a Smith, a lusty well-set Fellow, pale Complexion, high Nose, and heavy ey'd: *Appare*l, a dark colour'd drugget Coat, plain without Pockets, and full short; new ozenbrigs Jacket and Breeches, a new Carolina Hat, and a Wig or Cap; he took with him a Gun. FROM *Thomas Hart,* one named *Thomas Grigg,* by Trade a Mason, aged 17 or 18 Years, his Eyes are red and watery, and he has no Hair: *Apparel*, a brown Coat new fashion'd with brass Buttons, a homespun striped Jacket and Breeches, white yarn Stockings. FROM *Esther Lowdon,* one named *Mark Woods,* aged about 24 Years, a pretended Bricklayer, of short Stature, round-shoulder'd, the little Finger of his left Hand crooked, and has no Hair. *Apparel*, a dark colour'd fashionable Coat, a homespun small striped Jacket and Breeches, and homespun Shirt. FROM *John Hart*, one named *Garrett White*, aged about 22 Years, a short thick well-set Fellow, short Black Hair, and is hollow ey'd: *Apparel*, a light South-sea green Broad Cloth Coat, felt Hat, white plush Breeches, dark worsted Stockings, and good Shoes. Whoever shall secure the said Servants, or any of them, for each shall receive *Forty Shillings* Reward, and reasonable Charges paid by us

        Nicholas Rogers, Thomas Lindley, Thomas Hart, Esther Lowdon, John Hart.

The Pennsylvania Gazette, From September 10, to September 17, 1730. See *The Pennsylvania Gazette, The Pennsylvania Gazette*, From April 27, to May 4, 1732, for Roe.

        Philadelphia, *Sept.* 27, 1730.
THIS Day Run away from the Ship *John Frigate,* Thomas Smith, *Master, a Servant Lad named* John Gibbs, *(alias* Griffitts*) aged about* 19 *Years, Short Stature, round Fac'd and fresh Colour'd, had on a Tarry Ozenbriggs Frock and Trousers, a Blew Jacket, Grey Yarn Stockings, thin Double Soled Shoes, and an old Hat very Narrow in the Brim: Whoever can take up the said Runaway, and bring him to the Ship by the* 1*st of* November *next, shall have Forty Shillings Reward and reasonable Charges,*
        paid by   Thomas Sober.

The American Weekly Mercury, From Thursday, September 24, to Thursday October 1, 1730; From Thursday, October 8, to Thursday October 15, 1730; From Thursday, October 22, to Thursday October 29, 1730.

RUN away on the 5th of this Instant from the several Persons following, being Residents in *Philadelphia*, the several Servants herein named and described, viz. FROM *Duncan Mackenzie*, one named *John Wicks*, a little Fellow with a black Wig, his Face lately much scratches, bow-legged; has on an orange-coloured Coat, and ozenburgh Trowsers. FROM *Joseph Flower*, Joiner, one *Joseph Woore*, a little Man, no Hair and wears a Cap, stammers much, has a Pea Jacket with red Lining, and Trowsers. FROM *Armstrong Smith*, Shipwright, one Servant Man, having on the right Side of his Mouth a remarkable Bit of Flesh as big as a Plumb. FROM *John Jones*, one named *Robert Willis*, low Stature, pale Complexion, black Hair, a Mole on one side of his Face, by Trade a Shoemaker; has on a light-coloured drugget Jacket, speckled Shirt, and new ozenburgh Trowsers. FROM *Jonathan Fisher*, Glover, a Servant Boy named *James Fitzgerald*, 18 Years of Age, no Hair, wears a Cap or a light Wig, fair Complexion; had on dark-coloured broad cloth Coat with white metal Buttons and long Pockets, a strip'd ticken Jacket and Breeches. Whoever secures the said Servants, shall have *Twenty Shillings* for each, and reasonable Charges paid by their Masters above named.

The Pennsylvania Gazette, From October 1, to October 8, 1730. See *The Pennsylvania Gazette*, From September 9, 1731, to September 23, 1731, for Fitzgerald.

RUN away from *Charles Blakey*, at the Sign on the Brigantine in Water=Street, an East Indian Man, named *Thomas Tamerlin*, has on a Pea-Jacket, a Leather Pair of Breeches, and on Ozenbriggs Pair of Trowsers over them, a good Raccoon Hat; he is of small Stature, round Shouldered, speaks and writes good English. Whoever secures the said Runaway so that his Master may have him again shall have Thirty Shillings Reward, and reasonable charges paid by   *Charles Blakey.*

The American Weekly Mercury, From Thursday, October 8, to Thursday October 15, 1730; From Thursday, October 15, to Thursday October 22, 1730; From Thursday, October 22, to Thursday October 29, 1730. See *The Pennsylvania Gazette*, From June 11, to June 18, 1730.

RUN away on the 1st of this Instant from *Samuel Bunting* of *Bucks* County near *Joseph Kirkbride's*, a Servant Man named *John Taft*, of a middle Stature, short red Hair, about 35 Years of Age, a wry Neck, freckled Face, and a Weaver by Trade: he took with him two Suits of Cloaths, one a dark brown serge, Buttons of the same, and a strip'd Holland Jacket: The other a Homespun brown cloth Coat with large brass Buttons, Leather Breeches, grey Stockings, good Shoes, and an old Hat. Whoever secures the said Servant and brings him to his abovesaid Master, or to *Israel Pemberton* in *Philadelphi*a, shall have *Forty Shillings* Reward and reasonable Charges.

The Pennsylvania Gazette, From October 1, to October 8, 1730; From October 8, to October 15, 1730; From October 22, to October 29, 1730; From October 29, to November 5, 1730; From November 5, to November 12, 1730. Last ad shows he ran away "on the 1st of October last."

RUN away the 29th of *October* last, from *John Warren* of *Wicako*, within a mile of this City, a Servant Man named *Henry Carter*, aged about 23 Years, indifferent tall and slender, of a Swarthy Complexion, dark brown Hair, he had a brown great Coat, a whitish pea=Jacket turn'd, with dark lining, also a brown Duroy Jacket, new Ozenbrigs Breeches and Trowsers, a fine Holland

Shirt and a Muslin Stock, Coarse White Yarn Stockings, new Wooden heel'd Shoes stitch'd round the Quarters and a Midling good Beaver Hat. He has taken with him several Pieces of Garterings, several Pair of New Gloves and Silk Handkerchiefs and some fine Thread, and a small gilded Trunk of about 2*s*. 6*d*. price, as also some Ballads, he formerly belonged to Mr. *John Budd.* Whoever takes up the said Servant and secures him, and gives Notice to his said Master, shall have *Forty Shillings* Reward, and all reasonable Charges, paid by me   *John Warren.*

The American Weekly Mercury, From Thursday, November 5, to Thursday November 12, 1730; From Thursday, November 12, to Thursday November 19, 1730; From Thursday, November 19, to Thursday November 26, 1730.

RUN away the 21st of this Instant *October*, from *Joseph Foster* of *Bibery* Township, in the County of *Philadelphia*, a Servant Man named *Michael Donahe*, about 19 Years of Age, of a Middle Stature, fresh Complexion, straight Black Hair, he has lost one of upper fore Teeth; he had on a new Felt Hat, a light colour'd Cloth Coat and Jacket, the Jacket having Pewter Buttons on it, Strip'd Homespun Ticking Breeches, Black and White Woollen Stockings, or Grey Worsted Stockings, New Shoes Double Sol'd, with Brass Buckles. Whoever secures the above mentioned Servant, and gives Notice to his said Master, shall have Forty Shillings Reward, and all reasonable Charges, paid by me,   *Joseph Foster.*

The American Weekly Mercury, From Thursday, November 5, to Thursday November 12, 1730; From Thursday, November 12, to Thursday November 19, 1730; From Thursday, November 19, to Thursday November 26, 1730.

RUN away on the 6th Instant at Night from *John Orr*, near *Skuylkill, Philadelphia*, a Servant Man named *James Mitchel*, of middle Stature, brown curling Hair, smooth faced, with one black Eye by Boxing lately, about 28 Years of Age, a Cooper by Trade. Has with him a brown Kersey Coat and Jacket, short made in the Waste; a blue grey Broadcloth Coat, plain made, with long Pockets and a black Velvet Cape; an old Great Coat of black Kersey; fine Linen Shirts; black Broadcloth Breeches, and brown Kersey Breeches; knit Mittens, mixt with red, blue and white; a Felt Hat, light grey Stockings and good Shoes; He has been a Traveller, and can talk *Dutch, Spanish* and *Irish*. He took with him a small brown Mare, having a Slit in the near Ear, branded T L with a flower-de-luce between, a fine Pacer, shod before, with an old Saddle and a new curb Bridle. Whoever secures the said

Servant and Mare, so that they may be had again, shall have *Four Pounds* Reward for each, and reasonable Charges paid by *John Orr*.

The Pennsylvania Gazette, From November 5, to November 12, 1730; From November 12, to November 19, 1730; From November 19, to November 26, 1730. See *The Pennsylvania Gazette*, From May 13, to May 20, 1731.

RUN away from *George Parker*, Butcher, near *Philadelphia*, about the 4th of the 9th Month, a Servant Man named *Andrew Hilton*, aged about 30 Years, a short Man with black Hair, and a Scar under his Chin, much like the King's Evil, with crooked Legs, a Pair of strong Shoes, brown Worsted Stockings, a Pair of Leather Breeches and Trowsers, an Ozenbrigs Shirt, a Linnen Jacket, a dark colour'd Kersey Coat and Felt Hat; there is supposed to be with him, a little Woman with back [sic] Hair, named *Ann Pearce*, an English Woman, with a black Gown and Petticoat. Whoever secures the said Servant, so that his Master may have him again, shall have *Thirty Shillings* Reward, and reasonable Charges, paid by me   *George Parker*.

The American Weekly Mercury, From Thursday, December 3, to Tuesday, December 8, 1730; From Tuesday, December 8, to Tuesday, December 15, 1730; From Tuesday, December 15, to Tuesday, December 22, 1730.

1731

RUN away the 31*st* of *December* last, from John Hood of the City of *Philadelphia*, Shoemaker, an Irish Servant Man named *John Downing*, about 23 Years of Age, of middle Stature, long thin Visage, dark brown Hair. Has on an old Felt Hat, an old brown Jacket, a black one under it, and a blue one under both; good Buckskin Breeches, blue-grey Worsted Stockings, a pair of good round-toed Shoes. Whoever secures the said Runaway so as his Master may have him again, shall have Fifty Shillings Reward, and reasonable Charges paid,   by *John Hood*.

N. B. If the said Servant will Return he shall pay no Charges his Master has been at.

The American Weekly Mercury, From Tuesday, January 5, to Tuesday, January 12, 1730; From Tuesday, January 12, to Tuesday, January 19, 1730 [*sic*]; From Tuesday, January 19, to Tuesday, January 26, 1731.

RUN away on the 30th of January past, from *John Wallace* of *Chester*, Smith, a Servant Man names *Joseph Horsley*, about Twenty five Years of Age, a well-set Fellow, very full fac'd. He had on when he went away, a dark coloured Cloth Coat, full trimm'd; an ozenbrigs Jacket and Breeches; three Pair of Stockings, black. brown, and grey. He took along with him seven Yards of brown Holland. Whoever secures the said Servant, and brings him to *Chester* Prison, shall have Four Pounds Reward, and all reasonable Charges paid, by me   *John Wallace.*

The Pennsylvania Gazette, From January 26, to February 2, 1731; From February 2, to February 9, 1731; From February 9, to February 16, 1731; From February 16, to February 23, 1731.

RUN from *Nathan Dix* and *James Portell* of *Octorar*a in the Township of *Nottingham, Chester* County, Two Servant Men aged about 20 Years, named *Cornelius Kelly* and *Edward Greagin*, both native *Iri*sh; the one being a pretty tall slim Fellow, with strait black Hair; a linsey Jacket and a linen one under it, leather Breeches, a large brim'd felt Hat, Stockings mixt with blue and black, and a Tow Shirt. The other having two Thumbs upon each Hand is remarkable enough. Whoever apprehends and secures the said Servants, so that their Masters may have them again, shall have *Five Pounds* Reward and reasonable Charges paid, by
     Nathan Dix, James Portell. Philadelphia, Jan. 25, 1730,1.

The Pennsylvania Gazette, From February 2, to February 9, 1731; From February 9, to February 16, 1731; From February 16, to February 23, 1731.

RUN away, the 4th of this Month, from his Master *James Wilson* of the Northern Liberties of *Philadelphia*, a Servant Man named *Henry Prichard*, of a middle Stature, dark brown Hair, aged about 22 Years, he had on a brown homespun Coat, a light colour'd Vest with Brass Buttons, and a brown Broad-Cloath Vest with Brass Buttons, a pair of Cloath Breeches, a Felt Hat and yarn Stockings. Whoever brings said Servant to his Master, or secures him on the Work-House in *Philadelphia*, so that he may have him again, shall have *Thirty Shillings* Reward if taken within 20 Miles of home, and *Fifty* if farther, and all Reasonable Charges.

The American Weekly Mercury, From Tuesday, February 16, to Wednesday February 24, 1731; From Wednesday, February 24, to Tuesday March 2, 1731; From Tuesday, March 2, to Thursday March 9, 1731. [*sic*]

RUN away from the Snow *Dolphin*, two Servant Men, the one named *Francis Darby*, an *Irish* Man aged about 22 Years, with light colour Coat with white Mettle Buttons, and wears a Wig.

The other named *William Hughes* an *English* Man, of a middle Stature, short black curl'd Hair, aged about 24 Years with a dark Grey Coat: Whoever secures the said Servants, shall have *Thirty* Shillings Reward.
The American Weekly Mercury, From Wednesday, February 24, to Tuesday March 2, 1731. See *The American Weekly Mercury*, From Thursday May 20, to Thursday May 27, 1731, for Darby.

RUN away on *Wednesday* Morning last, from *Arthur Wells* of this City, a Servant Man named *John Blowden* (but will probably alter his Name as he travels) by Trade a Shoemaker; he is of middle Stature, full fac'd, of fair Complexion, and low womanish Voice, brown bushy Hair, a great Lyar and extravagant Boaster, He has on a dark brown Drugget Coat, with a Patch on the Sleeve, a close Cuff, and a Piece cut out among the Plaits at the side; a Jacket of the same, having a Piece cut out of the skirt behind, and the Edges of the Hole sew'd to the Lining; old Leather Breeches, Garlix Shirt, old Hat, grey Yarn Stockings, good Shoes. He has with him some scarps of Silk of various sorts, and Paint of several Colours, being somewhat ingenious at making artificial or counterfeit Flowers and Posies. N. B. *He was once before gone 6 Months, the greatest Part of which Time he spent in lurking about from one Part of the Country to another: When he unaccountably imposed upon the Country People in several Places, and persuaded them to conceal him Time after Time, and accommodate him with their best Victuals, Drink and Lodging, by strange invented Stories, that he as a rich Man's Son in Philadelphia, and obliged to abscond for a little Time while his Father made up some Difference or Trouble he was engaged in; sometimes he said he was a Doctor or Surgeon, &c. and by such Pretences not only abused the Credulity and Good Nature of honest and well-meaning People, but most commonly found an Opportunity of Pilfering something wherever he was kindly entertained.* Whoever shall apprehend and secure the said Servant, so that his Master may have him again, shall have *Forty Shillings* Reward, and reasonable Charges paid,
     by Arthur Wells. *Philadelphia, March* 5, 1730-1.
The Pennsylvania Gazette, From March 4, to March 11, 1731. See *The American Weekly Mercury*, From Thursday July 3, to Thursday July 10, 1729; *The American Weekly Mercury*, From Tuesday March 13, to Tuesday March 20, 1733; *The Pennsylvania Gazette*, From March 8, to March 15, 1733; *The American Weekly Mercury*, From Thursday October 4, to Thursday October 11, 1733; *The Pennsylvania Gazette*, From September 28, to October 11, 1733; *The Pennsylvania Gazette*, From November 13, to November 20, 1735, and *The Pennsylvania Gazette*, January 29, 1741.

RUN away about the 15th of March, 1730-31, from *John Bayly* of the City of *Philadelphia*, Cordwainer, a Servant Man named *William Lester*, a tall fellow pale Fac'd and Pockfretten; his Cloathing was an oldish Grey Cloth Coat and Waste-coat, Leather Breeches, he had likewise a new brownish Duroy Coat, strip'd Holland Waste-coat and Breeches, a black Wooll Wig, and a good brownish hair Wig, a fine new Hat and an old one, a pair of new Calf-skin Shoes and good Worsted Stockings besides others. It is supposed he has taken a Woman with him whom he used to call his Wife. Whosoever takes up said Servant or secures him, so that his Master may have him again, shall have *Fifty Shillings* Reward and reasonable Charges,
     paid by John Bayly.
 The American Weekly Mercury, From Thursday, April 1, to Thursday, April 8, 1731; From Thursday, April 15, to Thursday, April 22, 1731; From Thursday, April 29, to Thursday, May 6, 1731.

RUN away from *William Biddle*, of *Philadelphia*, a Servant Man named *Charles Callehan*, aged about twenty Years; low Stature but well-sett, short light brown Hair, he hath lost two of his upper Teeth; and had on an old Great Coat with brass Buttons, oznaburgh Shirt, and old Drugget Breeches: Took with him a new pair of Shoes. Whoever secures the said Servant, so that his Master may have him again, shall have *Twenty Shillings* Reward, and reasonable Charges paid,
    by *William Biddle. Philadelphia, M*arch 30, 1731
 The Pennsylvania Gazette, From March 25, to April 1, 1731.

RUN away from John Owen, Sheriff of *Chester*, an *Indian* Man who went by the Name of *Ham*, but his right Name is *Jacob Tomson*; he is a broad set Man, full faced, with long black Hair. He hath an old brown Coat, a pair of old Trowsers, old white Stockings, old Shoes, and an old Beaver Hat; he speaks pretty good English, being New-England born; Whoever secures the said Man so that the Sheriff aforesaid may have him again, shall have *Thirty Shillings* Reward, and reasonable Charges paid by *John Owen.*
 The Pennsylvania Gazette, From April 22, to April 29, 1731; From April 29, to May 6, 1731; From May 13, to May 20, 1731.

RUN away on Monday last, from *John Comely* of the Mannor *Moreland*, a Servant Man, named *William Green*, aged about 20, of middle Stature, pale Complection, long Visage, large Nose, and dirty light brown Hair. Had a new ash-colour Kersey Jacket, a Coat of near the same Colour with Horn Buttons, Leather Breeches, blue-grey and other Stockings, homespun Shirts and old

Shoes. Whoever secure the said Servant so that his Master may have him again, shall have 25 s. Reward, and reasonable Charges
        paid, by   *John Comely.*
The Pennsylvania Gazette, From May 6, to May 13, 1731; From May 13, to May 20, 1731; From May 20, to May 27, 1730; From May 27, to June 3, 1731.

RUN away on the 16th of May from *John Orr*, near *Skuylkill*, Philadelphia, a Servant Man named *James Mitchel*, of middle stature, brown hair, smooth faced, about 28 Years of Age; his right Arm marked with 2 Fishes, the Letters I.M. and the Date of the Year, in blue; by Trade a Cooper; has been a Traveller, and can talk *Dut*ch, *Spanish* and *Irish*. Has with him a brown Ratteen Jacket, ozenbrigs Shirt and Breeches, black Stockins, and 3 pair of Stockins beside of three different colours; brown Breeches patch'd on the Knees. Whoever secures the said Servant so that his Master may have him again, shall have *Five Pou*nds Reward, and reasonable Charges
        paid by   *John Orr.*
The Pennsylvania Gazette, From May 13, to May 20, 1731; From May 27, to June 3, 1731.

                      Philadelphia, *May* 24. 1731.
RUN away, Yesterday Morning, from *Thomas Davis* of *Bucks* County, a Servant Man named *Francis Darby*, aged about 22 Years, a short thick fat well-set Man, thick Legs, full Fac'd, having on a light colour'd double breasted Coat with white Mettle Buttons, a Seamans Jacket blue Worsted Stockings, shock Hair, and sometime he wears a Cap; he has a Bundle of other Cloaths with him; he was seen in *Philadelphia* Yesterday at 12 a-Clock. Whoever secures the said Servant so that his Master may have him again, shall receive *Forty Shillings* Reward, and Reasonable Charges.
    N. B. He once Run away from Capt. *Hore*, and went by the Name of *John Moore.*
The American Weekly Mercury, From Thursday May 20, to Thursday May 27, 1731; Thursday June 3, to Thursday June 10, 1731; Thursday June 10, to Thursday June 17, 1731. See *The American Weekly Mercury,* From Wednesday, February 24, to Tuesday March 2, 1731.

RUN away from *David Potts*, at *Socken* above the Great Swamp, a Servant Boy named *John Williams*, about seventeen Years of Age, of swarthy Complexion, has black Hair, and two Molds on his Forehead. Had on a brown linsey-wolsey Jacket, Leather Breeches, a pair of Shoepacks, and Stockings footed with White. He is suppos'd to have with him a big Bay Horse, with a switch Tail, and a Star in the Forehead, a half-crop and a half penny in one Ear, and banded on the near Shoulder IP with a Dagger over it. He went away on the 17th Instant. Whoever secures him, and gives Notice to *George Shoemaker*, Innkeeper in *Philadelphia*, so that his Master may have him again, shall have *Forty Shillings* Reward, and reasonable Charges paid, by *David Potts*.

The Pennsylvania Gazette, From May 20, to May 27, 1731; From May 27, to June 3, 1731; From June 3, to June 10, 1731.

RUN away, the 18th of *May* last from his Master *Thomas Tatnall* of *Chester* County near *Darby*, a Servant Man named *Thomas French*, about 22 Years of Age, of a low Stature, brown Complexion and no Hair, had on a good Felt Hat, a brown Jacket lined with Red, an old pair of Linnen Breeches, a new pair of Shoes. Whosoever shall take up said *S*ervant, and bring him to his Master, or to the Workhouse in *Philadelphia*, or secure him so that he may be had again, shall have *Fifty Shillings* Reward and Reasonable Charges.

The American Weekly Mercury, From Thursday May 27, to Thursday June 3, 1731; Thursday June 10, to Thursday June 17, 1731; Thursday June 24, to Thursday July 1, 1731. See *The American Weekly Mercury*, From Thursday May 4, to Thursday May 11, 1732.

Philadelphia, June 10, 1731.
RUN away, early this Morning, form [sic] the Sloop *Maryland*, of *Boston*, *Edward Sunderland* Master, a Servant Man named *Robert Hancock*, aged about 20 Years, of a middle Stature, swarthy Complexion, pretty thick set, black Hair, has taken with him a dark colour'd Duroy Coat, Jacket and Breeches striped red green and white, the Breeches having red silk Puffs; he has also a Sute of light coloured Summer-Cloaths, several pair of Stockins, and several other Things. Whoever takes up the said Servant and brings him to his Master, or to Mr. *Peter Baynton* in *Philadelphia*, shall have *Thirty Shillings* as a reward beside all reasonable Charges.

The American Weekly Mercury, Thursday June 3, to Thursday June 10, 1731; Thursday June 10, to Thursday June 17, 1731.

RUN away the 11th of this Month, from *William Nichols* of *Calan*, Turner in *Chester* County, a Servant Man named *Henry Damsel*, of a low Stature and well-set, short black Hair, red Complexion, talks thick, he has one Crooked Leg, and had on a Lincy Jacket with Pewter Buttons, a Homespun Shirt and coarse Drawers, Brown Thread Stockings, a good pair of Shoes. Whosoever shall take up the said Servant, and bring him to his said Master, or to the

Work-house in *Philadelphia*, shall have Forty Shillings Reward, and Reasonable Charges.

N. B. *There was one Giles — went away with him.*

The American Weekly Mercury, Thursday June 10, to Thursday June 17, 1731; Thursday June 24, to Thursday July 1, 1731; Thursday July 1, to Thursday July 8, 1731. See *The Pennsylvania Gazette*, From July 1, to July 8, 1731.

RUN away on the 13th of this Instant, from *Richard Stanley*, of *Philadelphia*, Potter, an *Irish* Servant Man named *Jendey Forlindey*, a Weaver by Trade; speaks good *English*, about 30 Years of Age, short curled Hair, thin Visage, sharp Nose and pale Complexion; had with him a grey Duroy Coat pretty much worn, a brown Drugget Jacket, ozenbrigs Shirt and a fine Shirt, and two pair of Shoes. Has with him a large black Horse, about 14 Hands high, with a small Star, a switch Tail, branded M on the near Shoulder and Buttocks, and a Fistula on his Shoulder. Whoever secures the said Servant and Horse, so that they may be had again, shall have *Three Pounds* Reward and reasonable Charges paid,

by *Richard Stanley.* Philadelphia, June 16, 1731.

The Pennsylvania Gazette, From June 10, to June 17, 1731; From June 17, to June 24, 1731; From June 24, to July 1, 1731; From July 1, to July 8, 1731.

RUN away from *Joseph Richards*, of *Philadelphia*, a Servant Woman named *Sarah M'Nahme*, about 20 Years of Age, brown Complexion, and pretty much Pockbroken, having on when she went away, a striped Blue and White Linnen Gown, a Lincy-wolsey Petticoat, a White Apron and Muslin Handkerchief. Whosoever brings her to her Master *Joseph Richards*, shall be well Rewarded for their Pains, they that detain her, be it at their Peril.

The American Weekly Mercury, From Thursday, June 17, to Thursday, June 24, 1731.

RUN away the 28th of the 4 Month, 1731. from *David Davis* of *Goshen* in the County of *Chester*, an *Irish* Servant Man named *George Curren*, of a middle Stature, pretty slender, pale Complexion, Pock-freckel'd and dark Hair; he had on a pretty good Felt Hat, a new Course Shirt, a dark Grey Course Kersey Coat, a good pair of Leather Breeches with Pewter Buttons, a midling good pair of round Toed Shoes, and Grey Yarn Stockings.

Whosoever will take up and secure the said Servant, and bring him to *David Davies* [sic] aforesaid, shall have *Twenty Shillings* as a Reward, and all reasonable Charges, paid by   *David Davies.*
The American Weekly Mercury, From Thursday July 1, to Thursday, July 8, 1731; From Thursday July 8, to Thursday, July 15, 1731; From Thursday July 15, to Thursday, July 22, 1731.

RUN away from *Evan Mor*gan of this City, Shopkeeper, a Servant Woman named *Mary Davi*s, a short thin slender Body, fresh Complexion; had on a new Gown of yard wide Bristol Stuff of Red and Green; and the Neck and Sleeves turn'd up with Green a yellow pair of Bodice, and other good Apparel. Whoever brings home the said Servant shall be
                    rewarded by   *Evan Morgan.*
The Pennsylvania Gazette, From June 24, to July 1, 1731.

RUN away together on Sunday the fourth of *July*, from *Caln* in *Chester* County, the 3 following Servant Men, *viz*. From *Thomas G*reen, one named *John Par*ker, about 20 Years of Age, short and well set, brown Hair; has on an old Coat, a new Felt Hat, a new Shirt, with Trowsers, and Drawers under them. FROM *Moses White*, junior, one named *Giles Greenwich*, short and thick, with a down Look, brown Hair, has on new Trowsers, old Shoes, lightish Kersey Coat with great white-metal Buttons. FROM *William Nichol*s, one named *Henry Damsel*, short and well set, talks thick, has on an old Hat, a Linsey Jacket, and a dirty Shirt. Whoever secures the said Servants, so that they may be had again, shall have *Three Pounds Ten Shillings* Reward, and reasonable Charges paid, by
         Thomas Green, Moses White, William Nichols.
The Pennsylvania Gazette, From July 1, to July 8, 1731; From July 15, to July 22, 1731; From July 22, to July 29, 1731. See *The American Weekly Mercury*, Thursday June 10, to Thursday June 17, 1731, for Damsel and Giles.

RUN away the 25th of *June* last, from the Ship *John Galley, John Ball* Commander, Two Sailors, the one named *George Bordman*, the other *John Gilling*, they are both of Middle Stature, they are in Sailors Habit, and have several other Cloaths. Whoever shall take up said Sailors, and bring them to the said Ship, shall have *Forty Shillings* reward,
         paid by   Capt. *John Ball.*
The American Weekly Mercury, From Thursday July 22, to Thursday, July 29, 1731.

RUN away on the 28th of *July* past, from the Widow *Wragg* of *Philadelphia*, a Servant Man named *John Harding*, (but sometimes changes his Name) by Trade a Butcher, aged about 30 Years, of small Stature, black Complexion, and short black Hair. Had on when he went away, ozenbrigs Breeches, Cotton and Linen Shirt, an old Felt Hat, a leather Belt about him, and an Apron. Whoever secures the said Servant so that his Mistress may have him again, shall have *Twenty Shillings* Reward, and all reasonable Charges
               paid, by   *Mary Wragg.*
The Pennsylvania Gazette, From July 25, to August 5, 1731.

RUN away on Sunday last from *Jonathan Park*, of *Bradford* Township in *Chester* County, an *Irish* Servant Man named *James Condon*, aged about 25 Years, short black curl'd bushy Hair, shaved pretty high on his Forehead, dark down Look, middle Stature, is a Weaver by Trade. Had on when he went a way a striped ticken Jacket, fine Shirt, new Felt Hat, old white Linnen Breeches, and linnen Leggins, old Shoes. He took with him a small bay Horse about 3 Years old, branded IL (in one Letter with a ω over it) on the near Shoulder I think, and a Star in the Forehead. Whoever secures the said Man and Horse, so that they may be had again, shall have *Forty Shillings* Reward, and reasonable Charges paid,
               by *Jonathan Park. August 10. 1731.*
The Pennsylvania Gazette, From August 5, to August 12, 1731; From August 12, to August 19, 1731; From August 19, to August 26, 1731.

BROKE out of *Philadelphia* Goal on the 18th Instant, in the Night, one *Cornelius Thompson*, (in Company with 5 others who are since taken) aged about 40 Years, tall and slender, has a large Scar upon his left Cheek; had with him a brown Kersey Coat, Dimitty Vest and Breeches, grey worsted Stockings, one square-toe'd Shoes, an old light-coloured Wig, Holland Shirt, ruffled at the Breast.

Whoever apprehends and secures the said Person, shall have Forty Shillings Reward, and reasonable Charges paid,
               by   *Charles Read*, Sher.
The Pennsylvania Gazette, From August 19, to August 26, 1731; September 2, to September 9, 1731.

Bucks, Ss.   *August* 29, 1731.
LAST night Broke out of *Newtown* Goal, two Prisoners, the one named *Obediah Owen*, a *New-England Man*, about 25 Years old, committed for Horse Stealing; he is a tall well-sett Man, of a swarthy Complexion, short

brown Hair; had on when he went away a dark colour'd Coat, a fine Shirt, Check Trowsers, black Worsted Stockings and round Too'd Shoes with wooden Heels. He was taken at *Perth-Amboy* for the said Felony about 10 Weeks ago

The other an *Irish* Man, named *George Beman*, aged about 24 Years, a Felon, of middle Stature, swarthy Complexion but looks Fair having lain in Goal about 5 Months; he had on a redish Camblet Coat, Cloth Breeches of a yellowish colour with black Puffs, an old Osnabrigs Shirt, grey Yarn Stockings and round Too'd Leather Heel'd Shoes

Whoever secures then and brings them to *Newtown* Goal, shall have Four Pounds Reward for each, Paid by   *Timothy Smith*, Sheriff

IT is supposed the above Felons have taken with them a Negro Man named *Jo*, belonging to *Henry Nelson*, aged about 20 Years, he had on a Linsey-Woolsey Coat of a grey colour, a Leather Jacket lined with white Linsey-woolsey, a pair of Leather Breeches with blue Glass Buttons, a good Hat, two new Shirts made of fine homespun Linnen, a pair of Thread Stockings and good round Too'd Shoes He took with him three of his Masters Horses and three Saddles and Bridles, viz one a grey Flea bitten Horse, branded I on his Near Shoulder, Shod before, about 14 Hands high and Paces well: A white Horse about 14 Hands high, branded (I think) on the near Shoulder H and on the Near Thigh N, a Swallow Fork in the Far Ear and a Half Penny under it: The other a Dunnish Bay Horse about 14 Hands high, branded and Ear mark't as aforesaid. A new black Breasted Saddle made of a Hogs-Skin; a good square Skirted black Saddle, and an old Saddle. Also two Guns with some Powder and *S*hot.

Whoever secures the said Negro and Horses, *&c* and brings them to their Owner near *Newtown*, shall have *Eight Pounds* Reward,
    Paid by   *Henry Nelson.*

The American Weekly Mercury, From Thursday August 26, to Thursday, September 2, 1731; From Thursday September 23, to Thursday, September 30, 1731.

RUN away the 5th of this Instant *September*, from *William Burge* of *Philadelphi*a, a Servant Man named *Peter Reed*, an *Irishman*, by Trade a Sadler, aged about 29 Years, well-set, of Middle Stature, much Pockfretten, small Eyes, sharp Nose, his Head shaved, and has on a brown Wig or Cap, a new Cloath Drugget Coat, dark Olive colour, full Trim'd, with Staines on it, a Cloth Jacket of a redish Drab colour, Leather Breeches with flat Brass Buttons, a pair of light Grey coarse Worsted Stockings, a Caster-Hat above half worn, round Toed Shoes, an old fine Cloth-Riding Coat light colour. If any Person secures the said Servant, so that the said *Burge* may have him again, shall have *Forty Shill*ings Reward, and reasonable Charges, paid by William Burge.

RUN away the 4th of this Instant *September*, from *George Sheed*, Peruke-Maker in *Front-Street*, *Philadelphia*, a Servant Man named *Stephen Roe*, a Barber and Peruke-Maker, a well-set Fellow, of Middle Stature, fresh Complexion, very much Pockfretten in the Face, he walks quick, he is an *Irishman* born, he was a Runaway 23 Weeks from his former Master, and taken at *New-Town* in *Maryland*, he is about 20 Years of age; he had on a dark brown Cloath Coat well wore, with a large Stain on the Back, a Yellow Linnen Jacket, striped Ticking Breeches, an Osnabrigs Jacket and Breeches, two Garlick Shirts, one old Holland one, sharp Toed Pumps, he has several pair of Stockings, he wears a light Wig or Cap, his Hat Cock'd close to the Crown. Whosoever takes up the said Servant, and brings him to his said Master, or secure him, so that his Master may have him again, shall have *Three Pounds* Reward and reasonable Charge,

paid by George Sheed.

RUN away on Sunday the 5th of this Instant *September*, a Servant Man belonging to *James Lewis* of *Philadelphia*, named *Patrick Tearney*, he is a short well-set Man, aged about 22 Years, had on when he went away, a blue Broad Cloath Coat, a yellow Canvas Waste-Coat and Breeches, Thread Stockings, a pair of good Summer Shoes, a dark brown Wigg and a Felt Hat; he is a Taylor by Trade, an *Irishman*, Writes very well, a very smooth Tongue'd Fellow, suppos'd to have a Counterfeit Pass. Whoever takes up the said Servant and secures him, so that his said Master may have him again, shall have *Forty Shillings* as a Reward, and all reasonable Charges,

paid by Thomas Biles.

N. B. *It is thought that the above three Servants are gone together.*

The American Weekly Mercury, From Thursday September 2, to Thursday, September 9, 1731; From Thursday September 9, to Thursday, September 16, 1731.

RUN away last Night from *Patrick Carrigan*, a servant man named *Hugh Wear*, aged about 22 years, long visage, fresh-colour'd, tender eyes, short dark brown hair lately cut. Had on a black broadcloth jacket and breeches, a strip'd cheery-derry jacket, a fine shirt and a coarse shirt, a broad brimm'd felt hat with holes made thro' it by small shot, yarn stockings, strong shoes with shoe-strings. He was lately a servant to Mr. *James Mackay* in *Philadelphia*, and is by trade a spinner and worker in linnen. Whoever

secures the said servant so that his master may have him again, shall have *Thirty Shillings* Reward, and reasonable Charges
paid by *Patrick Carrigan. Septembe*r 6. 1731.
The Pennsylvania Gazette, From September 2, to September 9, 1731; From September 9, to September 23, 1731; From September 23, to September 30, 1731.

RUN away last Night the two following Servants, *viz.* FROM *Isaac Corin* at the Center, one named *James Fitzgerald*, about 19 Years of Age, has a long thin Visage and a sharp Look, short Hair, clean Limb'd; is a leather-dresser breeches-maker and glover by trade: had on a new felt hat, a thin silk cap, a light colour'd kersey great coat, a strait brownish coat with long pockets and brass buttons to the waste and up the sides; another coat of dark brown with white metal buttons, ozenbrigs wastecoat, kersey breeches, grey woollen stockins, and black worsted stockins, and a pair of shoes. FROM *Caleb Ranstead* an Irish servant named *Daniel Brian*, about 18 years of age, short but well set, short hair, a cast in one eye, and one of his legs crooked near the ancle having been broke; has on a cloth drugget coat almost new [ ] cinnamon colour, with broad flat pewter buttons, an ozenbrigs jacket, a white shirt of homespun linnen, leather breeches, yarn stockings, old shoes, old hat; and has taken an old pair of black cloth breeches, and an old grey cloth jacket without sleeves. Whoever secures the said servants shall have *Thirty Shillings* Reward for each, and reasonable charges paid,
by *Isaac Corin, Caleb Ramstead. September* 20. 1731.
The Pennsylvania Gazette, From September 9, 1731, to September 23, 1731; From September 23, to September 30, 1731. See *The Pennsylvania Gazette*, From October 1, to October 8, 1730, for Fitzgerald.

RUN away from his Master *Samuel Johnson* of the City of *Philadelphia*, Painter, a Servant Man named *Francis Stading*, a Dutchman, of a smooth Complexion and middling Stature, speaks good English, wears a dark colour'd bod [sic] Wigg, a New Hat, a light colour'd Fustian Frock, Searsucker Jacket and Breeches, lightish Stockings, a pair of old Shoes and a pair of Trousers much coloured with Paints. He is a bold impudent Fellow both in Look and Behaviour. Whoever takes up and secures the said Servant so that his Master may have him again, shall have Forty Shillings Reward and Reasonable Charges, paid by   Samuel Johnson.
The American Weekly Mercury, From Thursday September 23, to Thursday, September 30, 1731; From Thursday September 30, to

Thursday, October 7, 1731; From Thursday October 7, to Thursday, October 14, 1731.

LAST night broke out of *Chester* Goal, the three following Persons, *viz.*

Peter Moorhouse, an Englishman, of middle stature, dark complexion, short black Hair, wears a cap, has a dark colour'd coat, and a light colour'd fustian coat with metal buttons tip'd with mother of pearl, leather breeches, old shoes and stockins.

William Mack, an Irishman, a tall thin look'd fellow, has lately had the small pox and is very much pitted; has on a dark homespun coat, striped breeches, old shoes and stockins.

William Cain, an Irishman, of middle stature, well set, is of a brown complexion, hath black hair; has a lightish colour'd coat full trimm'd, linnen jacket and breeches, thread stockings, and good shoes.

Whoever apprehends the said persons, and brings them to *Chester* Goal, shall have *Thirty Shillings* reward for each, and reasonable charges paid, by
        September 25.   John Owen, Sher.

The Pennsylvania Gazette, From September 23, to September 30, 1731; From September 30, to October 7, 1731; From October 7, to October 14, 1731.

RUN away the 19th of this Instant, from *Richard Thomas* of *Whiteland* Township in *Chester* County, a certain *Thomas Maguire*, an *Irish* Man, aged about 20 Years, of Middling Stature, longish Visage, and pretty much Pockfretten, large grey Eyes, and ratting [*sic*] Speech, had on a New light colour'd Camblet Coat with whitish Trimming, a striped Wast-Coat, Leather Breeches flourished at the Button Holes, light colour Stockings, good Shoes, a Caster Hat and a Muslin Cap with a black Ribbond behind. He has also several fine Shirts, a grey Broad Cloth Coat with Scollop Sleves, and several Jackets both Linnen and Cotton. He writes a pretty good hand, and understands some Latin, he was seen in *Philadelphia* on the 21st Instant. Whoever takes up and secures the said *Thomas Maguire* in *Philadelphia* or *Chester* Goal, or brings him to the said *Richard Thomas*, shall have *Five Pounds* as a Reward and all reasonable Charges,
        paid by   *Richard Thomas.*

The American Weekly Mercury, From Thursday October 21, to Thursday, October 28, 1731; From Thursday November 4, to Thursday, November 11, 1731.

RUN away on *Sunday* Night last, the two following Servant Men, *viz*. FROM *Thomas Hart*, Bricklayer, one named *James Biddle*, by trade a Chimney-sweeper, of middle stature, much pockfretten, short brown Hair and wears a cap; had on a lightish-colour'd duroy coat, and breeches of the same, garlick shirt, a fine hat, strip'd cotton jacket, thin low-heel'd shoes. FROM *William Davies*, one named *John Edwards*, by trade a Bookbinder, of middle stature, his hair cut off, has a large scar on his left cheek, and is a little pockfretten; had on an old castor hat, silk cap, lightish colour'd plain coat with brass buttons, dark jacket, leather breeches, and also a linnen jacket and breeches, dark worsted stockins, and low-heel'd shoes seam'd round the quarters. 'Tis supposed they have a red great coat with them. Whoever *secures the said servants so that they may be had again*, shall have *Twenty* Shillings Reward for each, and reasonable charges paid,

by *Thomas Hart*, and *William Davies*. *Octob*. 12.

The Pennsylvania Gazette, From October 7, to October 14, 1731.

RUN away on the 19th of this Instant *October*, from *Isaac Norris* of *Fairhill*, a Servant Man named *John Wood*, a slender active Man, about 22 Years of Age, his Hair Cut off, thinish but lively Visage: born as he says at *Birmingham* in *Great Britain*, came a Servant from *Bristol* in 1730. He is a Carpenter and Sawyer, and has been a Sailor, and about two Weeks ago Cut his Leg with an Ax, above and on one side his Instep; is well Cloathed, and has taken away much others, viz. a good Leather Jecket and Breeches with Brass Buttons, a Fine but worn Sagathee Coat without Cuffs, several, perhaps Four or Six white and Spekle Shirts, a good Broad Cloth Coat with no Cuff, a Riding Coat; a new lightish brown Drugget Jacket lin'd with Shalloon, strip'd Holland Jacket and Breeches, a Pair of Duroy Breeches the Puffs white Silk; a new fine Hat, a Light brown Wigg & a Cap, & as is supposed several other things. Also a black Trotting Gelding about Seven Years old, Mark'd E on the near Shoulder, and a Notch in the far Ear, no white about him save a snip on his upper Lip, a good whole Skirt Saddle, Bridle and spitt boots. Whoever shall take up the said Servant and Horse, and bring them to me, or secure them that I may have them again, shall have *Forty Shillings* Reward, besides reasonable Charges, paid by *Isaac Norris*.

The American Weekly Mercury, From Thursday October 21, to Thursday, October 28, 1731; From Thursday November 4, to Thursday, November 11, 1731; From Thursday November 11, to Thursday, November 18, 1731. See *The Pennsylvania Gazette*, From October 21, to October 28, 1731.

RUN away on the 19th Instant, from *Isaac Norris* of *Fairhill*, a Servant Man named *John Wood*, a slender active Man, about Twenty-two Years of Age, his Hair cut off, a thin but lively Visage: born as he says at *Birmingham* in *Great Britain*, came a Servant from *Bristol* in 1730, is a Carpenter and Sawyer, and has been a Sailor, and had about two Weeks ago cut his Leg with an Ax above and on one Side of his Instep; is well cloath'd, and has taken away much other, *viz.* A good Leather Jacket and Breeches with brass Buttons; a fine, but worn Sagathee Coat; several, perhaps 4 or 6 white and speckled Shirts; a Broadcloth Coat with no Cuff, a riding Coat; a new lightish brown Drugget Jacket and Breeches; a pair of Duroy Breeches, the Pufts white Silk; a new fine Hat, a light brown Wig, a Cap, and is suppos'd several other Things. Also a black trotting Gelding, about seven Years old, mark'd E on the near Shoulder, and a Notch in the far Ear, no White about him save a snip in the upper Lip, a good whole Skirt Saddle, Bridle, and Spit-Boots. Whoever shall take up the said Servant and Horse, and bring him to me, or secure him so that I may have them again, shall have *Forty Shillings* Reward, besides reasonable Charges paid, by *Isaac Norris.*

    The Pennsylvania Gazette, From October 21, to October 28, 1731; From October 28, November 4, 1731; From November 4, to November 11, 1731. See *The American Weekly Mercury,* From Thursday October 21, to Thursday, October 28, 1731.

ESCAPED from the Sheriff of *Lancaster* a Man named *John Brown*, alias *Robinson*, of middle Stature, very broad Shoulders, well set, forward and bold in Talking, and has a rogueish Look: Had on an old light colour'd Coat, brown Cloth Breeches very old, old Shoes, old Yarn Stockins, and an old Hat. Whoever secures him shall have *Forty Shillings* Reward, and reasonable Charges paid, by   *John Galbreth*, Sher.

    The Pennsylvania Gazette, From November 4, to November 11, 1731; November 11, to November 18, 1731.

RUN away, the 17th of this Instant *November*, from *Edward Clayton* of *Bradford* Township in *Chester* County, a Servant Man named *William Kehind*, aged about 18 Years, a lusty Man and much Pockfretten, he had on when he went away a grey Pea-Jacket, a striped Shirt, Leather Breeches, new Worsted Stockings of a deep Cinnamon Colour, good Shoes and an old Castor Hat edged with the same; he is a Saylor. He also took with him a black-grey Horse and a new Bridle, but no Saddle. Whosoever takes up and secures the said Servant and Horse, or either of them, so that they may be had again, shall have *Two Pounds* Reward and all reasonable Charges, paid by *Edward Clayton.*

    The American Weekly Mercury, From Thursday, November 18, to Thursday, November 25, 1731.

RUN away from *John Hutchison* of *Bucks* County, a Servant Man named *Thomas Richardson*, by Trade a Taylor, aged about 24 Years, a short well-set Fellow, full Faced and of a pale Complexion, had on a striped Cap bound with blue Ferritin and tied with the same, a brown Cloth Searge Coat and a black Broad-Cloth Coat or Jacket, also three other Jackets whereof one is Searsucker, no Sleves to any of them, a pair of black Breeches and Stockings and low heel'st Shoes. He also took with him a black pacing Mare with a long Tail, branded on the near Shoulder and Buttock **I. H.** and **E. G.** Whosoever will take up the said Servant and Secures him so that his Master may have him again shall have *Fifty Shillings* as a Reward and reasonable Charges.

The American Weekly Mercury, From Thursday, November 25, to Thursday, December 2, 1731; From Thursday, December 2, to Thursday, December 9, 1731; From Thursday, December 6, to Tuesday, December 14, 1731. See *The American Weekly Mercury*, From Tuesday April 10, to Thursday April 17, 1729 [*sic*].

RUN away on the 16th Instant, from *William Pywell* of this City, Tanner, a Servant Man named *Patrick Connor*, a Currier by Trade, about 27 Years of Age, middle stature, much pock-fretten, a large Scar under his right Eye, and has an ill Look: Had on a light colour'd duroy Coat, blue and white striped Wastecoat and Breeches, fine worsted stockins. Whoever apprehends the said Servant, shall have *Three Pou*nds Reward; or if he is in *New-*York or *Maryland*, Five Pound, with reasonable Charges, paid by *William Pywell*.

The Pennsylvania Gazette, From November 18, to November 27, 1731; December 2, 1731

RUN away on the 28th past, the two following Servant Men, viz. From John Fruin, *Baker, one named* Peter Humphries; *about 26 years of age, middle stature, well set, spreading knees, and goes tenderly on his feet, thick lips, and has a tooth out before towards the left side. Had on a castor hat, a lightish natural wig, striped homespun jacket, leather breechies, white frock, black stockins, good shoes, and took with him 2 speckled shirts, 3 white shirts, and 5 pair of stockins, and was seen with a small bundle at his back. From* William Biddle, *one named* Charles Calahan, *aged about 22 years, a short well set fellow, sandy complexion, has lost one or two of his upper fore teeth, short curl'd hair, and has on a grey kersey great coat, white broad-cloth close bodied coat, corded dimmitty jacket, black breeches, and white stockins. 'Tis suppos'd there are more gone with them, and that they have counterfeit passes. Whoever shall apprehend and secure the said servants,*

so that their masters may have them again, shall have Forty Shillings *Reward for each, and reasonable charges paid, by* John Fruin, William Biddle
The Pennsylvania Gazette, From November 27, to December 2, 1731; From December 2, to December 14, 1731; From December 14, to December 28, 1731.

1732

RUN away from *Jonathan Tatnal* near this City, an *Irish* Servant Man named *John Reddy*, is pretty tall, of black complexion, wears his Hair, stoops a little in the Shoulder, has a sly Look, and a smooth Tongue without much of the Brogue, wears his Hat over his Eyes, and pretends to be a *Quaker*; works at Husbandry, and has been among the *Indians*. Took with him a grey Duroy Suit, Stockins of the same Colour, a coarse Shirt, a blue Jacket, a lightish colour's Kersey Jacket, and a homespun greyish Coat, all plain made. Whosoever secures the said Servants so that his Master may have him again, shall have *Forty Sh*illings Reward, and reasonable Charges,
      paid by   *Jonathan Tatnal*, or *John Croker*.
The Pennsylvania Gazette, From December 28, 1731, to January 4, 1732; From January 4, to January 11, 1732; From January 11, to January 18, 1732.

RUN away *January* the 14th, from *Robert Shewell*, Cooper, at Judge *Langhorne's* Mill in *Middletown*, near *Bristol* in *Bucks* County, an Apprentice Fellow named *Abraham Wells*, aged about 18, of middle stature, well set, full faced, with a fair complexion, fresh colour, and light brown hair. Had on a good homespun drugget coat, lined with thin stuff, brass buttons a row of them down each sleeve, and long pockets; a vest of the same but not lined; ozenbrigs shirt, leather breeches, fine grey yarn stockins, good shoes, a red silk handkerchief, and a good felt Hat. He also took with him a pair of striped drawers, two pair of men's shoes, new, one pair of womens shoes, a little gun, and a new sheepskin apron of tann'd leather. Whoever secures the said Apprentice, so that he may be had again, shall have Forty Shillings Reward and reasonable charges paid by *Robert Shewell*.
The Pennsylvania Gazette, From January 18, to January 25, 1732; From January 25, to February 1, 1732; From February 1, to February 8, 1732.

Philadelphia, Feb. 1.
RUN *away about six Weeks since from* Andrews *and* Postlethwaite, *a Servant Man named* William Miller, *of middle Stature, about 45 Years of Age, wearing his own Hair, curl'd, bushy, and of a sandy colour; having with him*

Age, wearing his own Hair, curl'd, bushy, and of a sandy colour; having with him a great Coat, and a tight-bodied Coat, both of greyish Kersey; yarn Stockings and Felt Hat. He formerly kept the Upper (commonly called Roach's) Ferry. Whoever secures the said Servant, so that he may be had again, shall have Forty Shillings Reward, and reasonable Charges paid, by Andrews and Postlethwaite.

The Pennsylvania Gazette, From January 25, to February 1, 1732; From February 1, to February 8, 1732; From February 8, to February 15, 1732.

RUN away the 23d of this Instant from on board the Ship *Mary*, lying at Mr. *Clymer's* Wharff (near *Market-Street* End) *James Benn* Master, a Servant Man named *Corlius Pearson*, by Trade a Hatter, aged about 30 Years, he is a lusty Man, above six Foot high, of a very Swarthy Complexion, and short Hair; he had on a dark Frize Coat and Jacket, a pair of striped Ticking Breeches, a pair of grey Stockings and bad Shoes. Whoever takes up the said Servant, and bring him to the said *James Benn*, or Capt. *Anthony Peele* in *Philadelphia*, shall have Thirty Shillings as a Reward and all reasonable Charges, paid by   *James Benn* or *Anthony Peele*.

The American Weekly Mercury, From Tuesday, February 22, to Tuesday, February 29, 1732; From Tuesday, March 7, to Thursday, March 16, 1732; From Thursday, March 23, to Thursday, March 30, 1732.

RAN away on the 20th of September last, from James Yates, jun *of* Newtown in Bucks-County, a Servant Man named Charles O-Neal, but is supposed to have changed his Name, and call himself Thomas Davis: He is of short size, fresh Complexion, down-looked, thick Lips, and a short Nose, had on when he went away, an old great Coat, white Jacket, Leather Breeches, grey Stockings, round-toed Shoes. Whoever takes up the said Servant, and secures him so that his Master may have him again, shall have Three Pounds *Reward, and reasonable Charges paid, by*   James Yates, jun.

The Pennsylvania Gazette, From February 22, to February 29, 1732; From February 29, to March 7, 1732; From March 16, to March 23, 1732.

RUN away on the first Instant, from Thomas Mills, of Middletown in Chester County, a Servant Man named John Homer, by Trade a Shoemaker, of short

Stature, pale Complexion, one of his Feet hath been half cut off, and three Toes off the other: He had on a light double-breasted Coat with light colour'd buttons, and he rode on a small dark bay Horse. Whoever secures the said Servant, so that his Master may have him again, shall have Twenty Shillings Reward, and reasonable Charges paid, by Thomas Mills.

The Pennsylvania Gazette, From February 29, to March 7, 1732; From March 7, to March 16, 1732.

ON Thursday the Ninth of this Instant *March*, Escaped from the Jail of the City of *Philadelphia*, John M' Ferson, being the Captain of a Crew condemn'd for Piracy, at a Court of Vice-Admiralty held at the City Aforesaid. He is a short well set Man, brown Complexion, a fresh Colour much Pockfretten, he had on when he went away, a black Wigg, a dark colour'd double breasted Coat, a Searsucker Jacket and Breeches, a white Holland Shirt, a good Pair of Shoes and Stockings. All Persons are forbid to entertain him at their Peril, and whoever secures him, so that he may be return'd to the said Goal, will receive from the Honourable *Patrick Gordon* Esq; Governor of *Pennsylvania*, &c. the Sum of *Twenty Pounds*, and be paid the further Sum of *Ten Pounds* by   *Charles Read*, Sheriff.

The American Weekly Mercury, From Tuesday, March 7, to Thursday March 16, 1732; From Thursday, March 16, to Thursday March 23, 1732; From Thursday, March 30, to Thursday April 6, 1732. See *The Pennsylvania Gazette*, From March 16, to March 23, 1732; From March 23, to March 30, 1732.

ON Thursday the 9th of this Instant March, Escaped from the Goal of the City of Philadelphia, John M'Farson, being the Captain of a Crew condemn'd for Piracy, at a Court of Admiralty held at the City aforesaid. He is a short well set Man, brown Complexion and fresh coloured much pock-fretten: He had on when he went away, a black Wig, a dark-colour'd double breasted Coat, a Seersucker Jacket and Breeches, a white Holland Shirt, and good Shoes and Stockings. All Persons are forbid to entertain him, at their Peril: And whosoever secures him so that he may be return'd to the said Goal, will receive from the Honourable PATRICK GORDON Esq; Governor of Pennsylvania, &c. the Sum of Twenty Pounds, and be paid the further Sum of Ten Pounds by   C. READ, Sher.

The Pennsylvania Gazette, From March 16, to March 23, 1732; From March 23, to March 30, 1732. See *The American Weekly Mercury*, From Tuesday, March 7, to Thursday March 16, 1732

RUN away from Jacob Wright of the Great Valley in Chester County, on the 3d Instant, a Servant Man named Patrick Burgan, aged about 23 years, of middle stature, with short black Hair, a whitish colour'd cloth Coat, a striped linsey Jacket, leather Breeches with brass buttons, black stockings, coarse shoes, with several other sorts of Apparel. Whoever secures the said Servants, so that his Master may have him again, shall have Forty Shillings Reward, and reasonable Charges paid by   Jacob Wright.

The Pennsylvania Gazette, From March 30, to April 6, 1732; From April 6, to April 13, 1732. See *The American Weekly Mercury*, From Thursday June 8, to Thursday June 15, 1732, and *The Pennsylvania Gazette*, From June 8, to June 15, 1732.

RUN away the 20th instant, from John Riley *near Chester, a Servant Man named* Henry Edwards, *a West-countryman, by Trade a Wool-Comber, tall and slim, with good dark brown Hair, and writes a pretty good hand. He had on a new snuff-colour'd homespun Coat and Jacket with brass Buttons, Leather Breeches, an old Shirt, woollen Stockins near the colour of his clothes, old Shoes and a Felt Hat. He had near Three Pounds in his Pocket, and was seen the same Night at 9 o'clock, at Mr.* Dunning's *the* George Inn, *in this City. Whoever secures the said Servant, and gives Notice to his Master, or to* Abraham Prat *of* Philadelphia, *shall have* Forty Shillings *Reward, and reasonable Charges paid* by   John Riley.

The Pennsylvania Gazette, From April 20, to April 27, 1732; From April 27, to May 4, 1732; From May 4, to May 11, 1732; From May 11, to May 18, 1732; From May 18, to May 25, 1732.

RUN away the 29th of April last from Thomas Lindley *of* Philadelphia *Smith, a Servant Man named* John Roe, *aged about 25 Years, a lusty well set man, of a pale complexion, full nose and large heavy eyes. Had on a fine Hat, brown natural Wigg, plain brown drugget Coat, light colour'd Kersey Wastecoat, dark cloth Breeches, grey worsted Stockings and old Shoes (went in Company with a woman of short stature, brown Complexion, long nose, and has a large scar on one of her Arms) Whoever secures the said Servant so that his Master may have him again, shall have* Twenty Shillings *Reward, and reasonable Charges paid by*   Thomas Lindley.

The Pennsylvania Gazette, From April 27, to May 4, 1732; From May 4, to May 11, 1732; From May 11, to May 18, 1732; From June 1, to June 8, 1732. See *The Pennsylvania Gazette*, From September 10, to September 17, 1730.

RUN away from Richard Wright, *April 17, a Servant Man named* William Cole, *aged about 24 Years, a little short Man, with a smooth Face, fresh-colour'd, and has short black Hair. Had on an old Beaver Hat, and a grey Kersey Coat with brass Buttons, a light colour'd cloth Great Coat with a Cape, and one Corner of the Coat torn off, leather Breeches, ozenbrigs Shirt, grey yarn Stockings, strong Shoes, and has a small Lock on one of his Legs. Whoever secures the said Servant, so that his Master may have him again, shall have* Forty Shillings *Reward, and reasonable Charges*
   paid by R. Wright.
 The Pennsylvania Gazette, From May 4, to May 11, 1732; From May 11, to May 18, 1732; From May 18, to May 25, 1732.

RUN *away the 9th of this Instant* May, *from* Thomas Tatnall *of* Chester County, *a Servant Man named* Thomas French *a short Fellow, he had on an old Hat and a mixt coloured Linsey-Woolsey Coat, a pair of Linnen Breeches, a pair of old Stockings cut off about his Shoes, and good Shoes, he is an* Englishman *and a good Scholar, he has been a Sailor. Whoever takes up the said Servant and secures him in the Work-house in* Chester, *or brings him to his said Master, shall have* Twenty Shillings *Reward and reasonable Charges, paid by me,* Thomas Tatnall.
 The American Weekly Mercury, From Thursday May 4, to Thursday May 11, 1732. See *The American Weekly Mercury*, From Thursday May 27, to Thursday June 3, 1731.

RUN *away the 1st of this Instant* May *from* John Rigley, *a Servant Man named* Nicodemus Carpenter; *had on when he went away, a white Homespun Jacket, an old black pair of Breeches patch'd, when he went away he had neither Cap or Hat, his Hair cut off, with only a Neck-Lock left behind, he is of a fair Complexion, aged about 20 Years, Tall and Slender. Whoever secures the said Servant, so that his said Master may have him again, shall have* Thirty Shillings *as a Reward and reasonable Charges,*
   paid by me, John Rigley.
 The American Weekly Mercury, From Thursday May 4, to Thursday May 11, 1732.

RUN *away from* Peter Cuff, *a Servant Man named* John M'kinzey, *about* 30 *Years of Age, speaks broad Scotch, is well-set, of a middle Stature, full round Face and Brown Complexion with short black Hair, he had on when he went away a new Drab colour'd Fustian Coat, with white-mettal Buttons, and lined with Shaloon, and Breeches of the same, an Ozenbrigs, Wastcoat and Shirt,* yarn Stockings and a new Felt Hat. Whoever brings him back or secures him and gives Intelligence to his said Master in Philadelphia, shall have Forty Shillings Reward, and reasonable Charges allowed.

N. B. He has been a Soldier in Flanders, and can speak a little Dutch and French.

The American Weekly Mercury, From Thursday May 25, to Thursday June 1, 1732; From Thursday June 15, to Thursday June 22, 1732; From Thursday June 22, to Thursday June 29, 1732. See The Pennsylvania Gazette, From May 25, to June 1, 1732.

RUN away from Peter Cuff, a Servant Man named ,John Mackenzy, about 30 Years of Age, speaks broad Scotch, is well sett. of middle Stature, full round Face and Brown Complexion, with short black Hair: Had on when he went away, a new drab colour'd Fustian Coat, with white metal Buttons, and lin'd with Shalloon; Breeches of the same; ozenbrigs, Wastecoat and Shirt, yarn Stockings, and a new felt Hat. Whoever brings him back, or secures him and gives Intelligence to his said Master in Philadelphia, shall have Forty Shillings Reward, and reasonable Charges allowed. N. B. He has been a Soldier in Flanders, and can speak a little Dutch and French.

The Pennsylvania Gazette, From May 25, to June 1, 1732; June 8, 1732. See The American Weekly Mercury, From Thursday May 25, to Thursday June 1, 1732; From June 1, to June 8, 1732; From June 8, to June 15, 1732.

RUN away, the 11th of this Instant June, from Jacob Wright and Richard Anderson of Whiteland Township in Chester County, two Servant Men the one named Patrick Burgain, an Irish Man, about 20 Years of Age, of a middle Stature, black Hair, dark Eyes, and fresh Colour'd; he took with him a brown colour'd Coat made plain with large Brass Buttons, a new homespun Tammey Jacket of a Cinnamon Colour, Leather Breeches with Brass Buttons, homespun Shirts, Stockings several sorts, old Shoes and a Felt Hat. The other named John Flood, an Irish Man, aged about 20 Years, of short Stature and short black Hair, but commonly wears a Cap, dark Eyes and dull Complexion with a down Look, he is very hard of hearing; he took with him a brown Jacket, Leather Breeches, two pair of Trowsers, Ozenbrigs Shirts, yarn Stockings, strong Shoes and a Felt Hat; by Trade a Weaver. 'Tis supposed they have changed their Names.

Whoever takes up and secures the said Servants so that their Masters may have them again, shall have Forty Shillings as a Reward, for each, and reasonable Charges, paid by us

Jacob Wright, Richard Anderson.

The American Weekly Mercury, From Thursday June 8, to Thursday June 15, 1732; From Thursday June 22, to Thursday June 29, 1732; From Thursday June 29, to Thursday July 8, 1732. See *The Pennsylvania Gazette*, From March 30, to April 6, 1732, and *The Pennsylvania Gazette*, From June 8, to June 15, 1732.

RUN away on the 15th *of April last, from* Michael M'Guire, *of* Birmingham *in* Chester *County, a Servant Man named* John Higgins, *of middle Stature, down looked, pale Complexion, by Trade a Worsted Comber. Had on an ozenbrigs Jacket with brass Buttons, a pair of Leather Breeches, supposed to have with him a linsey wolsey Coat, brown worsted Stockins, and middling good Shoes. Whoever takes up the said Servant, so that his Master may have him again, shall have* Three Pounds *Reward, and reasonable Charges paid by* Michael M'Guire. *June* 3. 1732.

The Pennsylvania Gazette, June 1, to June 8, 1732; From June 8, to June 15, 1732; From June 15, to June 19, 1732.

RUN away on Sunday the fourth Instant, from Jacob Scuten of Blockley Township in Philadelphia County, near Roche's Ferry, a Servant Man named John Jones, aged about 22 Years, of middle Stature, round shoulder'd, round visag'd, smooth Countenance with no Beard, full Eyes, and short dark curl'd Hair. Had on a light-colour'd homspun drugget Coat, plain made; striped blue and white homespun Jacket and Breeches, grey worsted Stockings, Calfskin Shoes stitch'd round the Quarters, an old Garlick Shirt, and a Felt Hat about half worn. Whoever secures the said Servant, so that his Master may have him again, shall have* Forty Shillings *Reward, and reasonable Charges paid.*

The Pennsylvania Gazette, From June 8, to June 15, 1732; From June 15, to June 19, 1732.

RUN away on the 11th Instant, from Jacob Wright and Richard Anderson of Whiteland Township in Chester County, two Servant Men; one named Patrick Burgain, an Irishman, about 20 Years of Age, middle Stature, black Hair, dark Eyes, fresh coloured; took with him a brown plain Coat, with large brass Buttons, a new homespun tammey Jacket of a cinnamon colour, Leather Breeches with brass Buttons, homespun Shirts, several Sorts of Stockings, old Shoes, and old Felt Hat. The other named John Flud, an Irishman, about 20 Years of Age, short siz'd, very thick of Hearing, short black Hair and commonly wears a Cap, has dark Eyes, is of dull Complexion, and down Look; He took away with him, a brown Jacket, Leather Breeches,* two pair of *Trowzers, ozenbrigs Shirts, yarn Stockings, strong Shoes, Felt Hat: He is by Trade a Weaver. Whoever secures the said Servants, so that their Masters may have them again, shall have* Forty Shillings *Reward for each, and reasonable Charges paid, by* Jacob Wright, Richard Anderson.

The Pennsylvania Gazette, From June 8, to June 15, 1732; From June 15, to June 19, 1732; From June 26, to July 3, 1732. See *The Pennsylvania Gazette*, From March 30, to April 6, 1732, and *The American Weekly Mercury*, From Thursday June 8, to Thursday June 15, 1732.

RUN away the 5th of May last, from Obediah Eldridge *of this City, Cordwainer, a Servant Man named* Thomas Landsdown, *aged about 26 Years, he is a* Bristol *Man, by Trade a Shoemaker, had on when he went away a Felt Hat, a Drugget Coat of a deep ash Colour, without Cuffs, Ozenbrigs Shirt, and Linnen Breeches, Yarn, Stockings and round To'd Shoes. He is of a Middle Stature, large Eyes and full large Teeth, some lost before, he is very round Shoulder'd. Whoever takes up the said Servant and secures him, so that his Master may have him again, shall have Forty Shillings Reward and all reasonable Charges, paid by me* Obediah Eldridge.
N. B. *These are therefore to forewarn all Persons to Entertain the said Servant, at their Peril.*

The American Weekly Mercury, From Thursday June 29, to Thursday July 6, 1732; From Thursday July 6, to Thursday July 13, 1732; From Thursday July 13, to Thursday July 20, 1732. The third ad shows he ran away "*the 16th of May last*".

RUN away July the 2d. from Edmund Farrel, *Skinner and Tanner in* Philadelphia, *a Servant Man named* Alexander Nealson, *aged about 24 Years, of middle Stature, smooth fac'd, short curl'd brown Hair: Had on when he went away, an olive-colour'd cloth Coat with small Cuffs, a white dimmity Jacket, Buckskin Breeches with brass Buttons, black Stockings, and good Shoes, and went in Company with a Servant Man belonging to* William Hudson *jun. Whoever secures the said Servant, so that his Master may have him again, shall have* Forty *Shillings Reward, and reasonable Charges paid,* by Edmund Farrel.

The Pennsylvania Gazette, From June 26, to July 3, 1732; July 10, 1732.

RUN away Yesterday from *Joseph Hayes* of *Haverford* in Chester County, a Servant Man named *Joseph Sandimont*, about 19 or 20 Years of Age, of middle Stature, curl'd black Hair, is much pockfretten, and pretends to be a Glover by Trade. Had on a new pair of Trowsers, a new homespun Shirt, a striped linnen Jacket, and an old Felt Hat. Whoever secures the said Servant, so that his Master may have him again, shall have *Forty Shillings* Reward, and reasonable Charges paid, by   Joseph Hayes. July 11.
  The Pennsylvania Gazette, From July 3, to July 10, 1732; From July 10, to July 17, 1732.

RUN away the 23d of this Instant July, from William Dickie *of East* Sudbury, *in* Chester *County, a Servant Man named* John Scandelan, *by Trade a Cooper, of middle Stature, well-set, short black Hair. Had on when he went away, a black Homespun Cloath Coat, lined with black Shalloon, Linnen Drawers, brown Yarn Stockings, high Heel'd Shoes. Supposed to be in Company with one* Thomas Russel. *Any Person that brings said Servant to his Master, or secures him, so that his said Master may have him again, shall have Three Pounds Reward, paid by me,*   William Dickie.
  The American Weekly Mercury, From Thursday, July 20, to Thursday, July 27, 1732; From Thursday, August 17, to Thursday, August 24, 1732; From Thursday, August 24, to Thursday, August 31, 1732.

RUN away on the 9th Instant, from Joseph Jackson *of* Bristol, *a Servant Man of middle Stature, dark Complexion, has a sly roguish Look, pretends to be one of the People called Quakers, and once attempted to preach amongst them but was repulsed. Had on a lead colour'd duroy Wastecoat, ozenbrigs Shirt and Trowsers, old Shoes and old Beaver Hat. Whoever secures him shall have* Twenty Shillings *Reward, and reasonable Charges paid by* Joseph Jackson.
  The Pennsylvania Gazette, From July 17, to July 24, 1732; From July 24, to July 31, 1732; From July 31, to August 7, 1732.

R*UN away from their Master & Mistress of* Concord *in* Chester *County, the 31st of* July *past, Two Servant Men, the one from* Henry Pierce, Esq: *named* James Boyd (*an* Irishman) *about 18 Years of Age, a short thick Fellow, round Visage, and black Hair, he had on when he went away, a dark brown Coat without Cuffs, a Pair of Leather Breeches, and an old Pair of Trowsers.*
  The other from Jane Newlin, *named* John Forrester, *of a middle Stature, pale Complexion, long brown Hair and large Teeth, about 20 Years of Age,*

he had on a light grey Coat, and a Pair of Linnen Breeches, Ash coloured Worstod Stockings, and good Shoes.

Whoever shall take up said Servants, or either of them, so that their Master and Mistress may have them again, or give Notice thereof, shall have Thirty Shillings *for each, as a Reward, and reasonable Charges,*
          paid by   Henry Pierce & Jane Newlin.

The American Weekly Mercury, From Thursday, July 27, to Thursday, August 3, 1732; From Thursday, August 17, to Thursday, August 24, 1732; From Thursday August 31, to Thursday September 7, 1732.

RUN away the 24th of *July* last, from *Joseph Harrison* of *Philadelphia*, Carpenter, an Apprentice Boy named *Thomas Rush*, about 18 Years of Age, small and short Stature, has a down Look, brown Hair a little Curl'd. Whoever takes up the said Apprentice and secures him, so that his Master may have him again, shall have 40 Shillings as a Reward and all reasonable Charge,
          paid by   *Joseph Harrison.*
N. B. All Persons are forewarned not to Entertain the said Apprentice, as they will answer the same at their Peril.

The American Weekly Mercury, From Thursday, August 17, to Thursday, August 24, 1732; From Thursday August 31, to Thursday September 7, 1732; From Thursday, September 7, to Thursday, September 14, 1732; From Thursday, October 5, to Thursday, October 12, 1732; From Thursday, October 12, to Thursday, October 19, 1732; From Thursday, October 26, to Thursday, November 2, 1732.

August 27. 1723. [*sic*]
RUN *away from* Peter Hatton *of* Concord *in the County of* Chester, *a Servant Man named* James Ryon *an Irishman, aged about* 24 *Years, he had on when he went away, a homespun Shirt and a light colour'd Linsey Jacket with Brass Buttons on it, and Linnen Draws and Leggings; He also took a Pair of brown Woollen Stockings and good Shoes he is of a Middle Stature and fair Complexion, he wears short black curled Hair. Whoever takes up the aforesaid Servant and secures him, so that his Master may have him again, shall have Thirty Shillings as a Reward and all Reasonable Charges,*
          paid by me,   Peter Hatton.

The American Weekly Mercury, From Thursday, August 24, to Thursday, August 31, 1732; From Thursday August 31, to Thursday September 7, 1732; From Thursday September 7, to Thursday September 14, 1732.

RUN away, the 20th of this Instant, from Obadiah Bonsal *of* Darby, *in* Chester County, *a* Servant Man *named* Thomas Pollock, *he is a* North Britain, *about* 22 Years of age, short of Stature and pretty brown Complexion, his Hair cut off; he had on when he went away a Cloath colour'd homespun Coat lined with Linsey Woollsey, Leather Breeches with Brass Buttons and work'd round the Holes at the Knees, sky or blueish Colour'd Worsted Stockings, had with him a fine Shirt and a course one, he pretends to be a Shoemaker.

Whoever takes up the said Servant and brings him to his said Master, or secures him so that he may be had again, shall have* Forty Shillings *as a Reward and reasonable Charges, paid by me*   Obadiah Bonsal.
N. B. *He has a false Pass with him.*

> *The American Weekly Mercury*, From Thursday, August 24, to Thursday, August 31, 1732; From Thursday August 31, to Thursday September 7, 1732; From Thursday September 7, to Thursday September 14, 1732.

RUN away Aug. 30. from Philip Yarnal, *in* Edgmont, Chester County, *an* Irish Servant Lad *named* Joseph Richardson, *about* 18 Years of Age, of short Stature, well set, short brown Hair somewhat curled. Had on a black & white cloth Coat, a new Felt Hat, homespun Shirt, coarse linen Drawers, brown woollen Stockins, and a good pair of strong shoes. Whoever secures him so that his Master may have him again, shall have* Thirty Shillings *Reward, and reasonable Charges paid, by me*   Philip Yarnal, jun.

> *The Pennsylvania Gazette*, From August 28, to September 7, 1732; From September 7, to September 12, 1732; From September 12, to September 18, 1732; September 18, to September 26, 1732.

RUN away Aug. 28. from Daniel Walker, *of Chester County, an Irish Servant Man named* Dennis Neal, *aged about* 19, *he is tall and well set, fair Complexion, short light brown Hair somewhat curled, broad Face with a flat Irish Nose, the third Finger of his left Hand is mortified near the fore Joint, a Scar on the bottom of the same Finger and in the Palm of his Hand. Had on a light colour'd Kersey Wastecoat and Breeches trimm'd with black, a halfworn Felt Hat, homespun Shirt, black and blue yarn Stockings, and round toed Shoes. Whoever secures the said Servant, so that his Master may have him again, shall have* Forty Shillings *Reward and reasonable Charges paid by*   Daniel Walker.

> *The Pennsylvania Gazette*, From August 28, to September 7, 1732; From September 7, to September 12, 1732; From September 12, to September 18, 1732; September 18, to September 26, 1732.

RUN away from *John Leacock* at *Pool*-Forge in *Philadelphia*-County, the 17th of this Instant *September*, a Servant Man named *Thomas Forde*, of middle age and low Stature, very talkative, born at *New-Castle* in *England* and speaks broad English, had on a Felt Hat and long striped Linnen Cap, a new Ozenbrigs Jacket, Ozenbrigs Shirt and Trowsers, and pretty good double soal'd Shoes. He pretends to be a Copper-Miner.—He went in Company with a Servant Man of *Thomas Mayberey's*, named *Edward Hambleton*, an Irishman, a very forward Fellow; Young and Tall and speaks good English, very apt to shew his Teeth, had on when he went away a Drugget Coat and Jacket of a brown Collour, a pair of Leather Breeches and suppos'd to take a pair of Ozenbrigs Trowsers with him, a pair of whitish blue Stockins, a fine Shirt torn about the Neck, and but indifferent Shoes. Whoever takes up the said Servants, or either of them, and brings them to their said Masters, or secures them in *Philadelphia* Goal, shall have *Forty Shillings* as Reward for each, and all reasonable Charges, paid by their respective Masters,

    John Leacock. Thomas Mayberey.

The American Weekly Mercury, From Thursday September 14, to Thursday September 21, 1732. See, *The American Weekly Mercury*, From June 30, to July 7, 1737, *The American Weekly Mercury*, From July 14, to July 21, 1737, and *The American Weekly Mercury*, From Thursday August 4, to Thursday August 11, 1737, for Hambleton/Hamilton.

RUN away from Ralph Sandiford, *a Servant Man named* John King, *sometimes he writes his Name* John Landman King, *he is marked* I K *on one of his Thumbs with Gunpowder; he is a Weaver by Trade, short in Stature, but fat and well set, and when he moves his Mouth he has a Dimple in his Cheek, he has short curled black Hair, and had on an ozenbrigs Shirt Vest and Breeches, and a brown Coat. He is a* Devonshire *Man, and has taken with him a grey Mare marked with a halfpenny cut on the left Ear, also a Silver Spoon marked* C. H. *Whoever secures the said Servant, so that he may be had again, shall have Forty Shillings Reward and reasonable Charges paid, by* Ralph Sandiford.

The Pennsylvania Gazette, September 18, to September 26, 1732; September 26, to October 5, 1732; From October 9, to October 19, 1732.

RUN away the 2d of this Instant October, from *John Clows* of *Makefield* in the County of *Bucks*, and Province of *Pennsylvania*, a Servant Man named *Jonathan French*, aged about 25 Years, of small Stature, down Look, droping

Nose, Pockmark'd Had on when he went away, a black and white Worsted Drugett Coat, Linnen Wastecoat, fine Shirt, a double Worsted Cap, new Felt Hat, strip'd Holland Breeches, Purple coloured Yarn Stockings and good Shoes Whoever brings the said Servant to his Master, or secures him, so that his Master may have him again, shall have *Five Pounds* as a Reward, and reasonable Charges, paid by   John Clows.

The Pennsylvania Gazette, September 28, to October 5, 1732; October 12 to October 19, 1732; October 26, to November 2, 1732.

RUN away on Octob. 2. *from* John Parry, *of Tredyffryn in Chester County, a Servant Man named* Humphrey Reynolds, *aged about 22 Years, an Englishman, short and well set, strait blackish Hair, fair Complexion, down Looks, and shews his Teeth much when he speaks, and waddles as he walks. He had on when he went away, an old Leather Jacket lined with blue, with Brass Buttons, an old striped Jacket, an old Felt Hat, a new homespun Shirt, Leather Breeches with brass Buttons, yarn Stockins and old Shoes. Whoever secures the said Servant, so that his Master may have him again, shall have* Forty Shillings *Reward, and reasonable Charges paid, by* John Parry.

The Pennsylvania Gazette, From October 9, to October 19, 1732; From October 19, to October 26, 1732; From October 26, to November 2, 1732.

RUN away from *Joseph Reyner* of *Chester*-County, Cordwainer, a Servant Man named *William M'Guire*, an Irishman, about 24 Years of age, short of Stature and round Vissag'd, by Trade a Shoemaker, he had on a lightish Coat, his other Apparel uncertain. Whoever takes him up and secures him so that his Master may have him again shall have *Twenty Shillings* as a Reward and reasonable Charges, paid by   Joseph Reyner.

The American Weekly Mercury, From Thursday, October 19, to Thursday, October 26, 1732; From Thursday, October 26, to Thursday, November 2, 1732; From Thursday, November 9, to Thursday, November 16, 1732; From Thursday, November 16, to Thursday, November 23, 1732. See *The Pennsylvania Gazette*, From October 19, to October 26, 1732.

RUN away, the 3d of *October*, from his Master, *Peter Lycon* of *Horsham*, Black-Smith, a Servant Man named *John Murrey*, an Irishman, about 24 years of age, of middle Stature and well-set, gray Eyes, short black Hair and swarthy Complexion, had on a blue and white striped Linnen Jacket and Breeches, a homspun [*sic*] Shirt, old Stockings and Shoes and a Felt Hat. It is supposed he has chang'd his Apparel, and he has a false Pass. Whosoever takes up the said Servant and brings him to his Master, or to the Work-House in *Philadelphia*, and gives Notice thereof so that he may be had again, shall have *Forty Shillings* as a *R*eward and all reasonable Charges.

> *The American Weekly Mercury,* From Thursday, October 19, to Thursday, October 26, 1732; From Thursday November 9, to Thursday November 16, 1732; From Thursday, November 9, to Thursday, November 16, 1732.

RUN away from Joseph Reyner *of* Chester, *a Servant Man named* William Mc. Guire, *an Irishman, a Shoemaker by Trade, of a short Stature, and is round visaged. Has on a lightish colour'd Coat. Whoever secures him so that he may be had again, shall have Twenty Shillings Reward and Reasonable Charges paid, by* Joseph Reyner.

> *The Pennsylvania Gazette,* From October 19, to October 26, 1732; From October 26, to November 2, 1732; From November 2, to November 9, 1732; From November 9, to November 16, 1732. See *The American Weekly Mercury,* From Thursday, October 19, to Thursday, October 26, 1732.

LAST night made their Escape out of the Goal of Philadelphia, *one* Peter Harpe, *a Palantine, aged about* 40 *Years. He is a short well set Fellow, with black Eyes, and thin Visage pretty much pockfretten; had on a grey homespun Coat with brass Buttons, Trowsers, grey Stockings, & new Shoes. Also one* Francis M'Ginnis, *of small Stature, thin Visage, with an effeminate Voice, and Legs somewhat crooked; he pretends to understand Clerkship: Had on a Camlet Riding-Coat, old leather Breeches, grey worsted Stockings, and took with him several Wigs. Whoever secures the said Prisoners so that they may be had again, shall have* Five Pound *Reward for* Peter Harpe, *and Forty Shillings for* Francis M'Ginnis, *paid by*
    Novem. 15. 1732.   S. ROBINSON, *Sher.*

> *The Pennsylvania Gazette,* From November 9, to November 16, 1732; From November 16, to November 23, 1732; From November 23, to November 30, 1732.

RUN away on the 25th *of December past, from* Stephen Armit, *of* Philadelphia, *Joiner, a Servant Man named* Thomas Holt, *aged about* 21 *Years, a likely well set Fellow, an Irishman, with a good Head of Hair. Had on a grey cloth Coat full trim'd, a light-colour'd broadcloth Coat under it, with long Pockets; striped holland Jacket, Leather Breeches, and a good*

Beaver Hat. Whoever secures the said Servant so that he may be had again, shall have Twenty Shillings Reward, and reasonable Charges paid by   Stephen Armit.

The Pennsylvania Gazette, From January 4, to January 11, 1733; From January 18, to January 25, 1733; From January 25, to February 1, 1733.

RUN *away on Jan 14. from* Samuel Hurfoot, *near Frankfort, an Irish Servant Man named* Valentine Clarke, *about* 19 *Years of Age, of middle size, fresh Complexion. Took with him a light colour'd Camlet Coat, a brown Coat, a dark grey Duroy Jacket, Leather Breeches, yarn Stockins, strong Shoes, and three Shirts, one of them fine. Also a dark brown Mare, and an old Saddle. Also he hath stolen away Six Pounds in Money. Whoever secures him so that he may be had again, shall have* Forty Shillings *Reward, and reasonable Charges paid, by*   Samuel Hurfoot.

The Pennsylvania Gazette, From January 11, to January 18, 1733; From January 18, to January 25, 1733.

RUN away from his Master *Charles Hargrave*, an Apprentice Lad named Samuel Stretch, a lusty Rawbone Fellow about 18 Years of Age, he has taken sundry sorts of Cloathes with him. Whosoever shall take up said Apprentice and bring him to his Master, shall have *Forty Shillings* Reward and reasonable Charges.

The American Weekly Mercury, From Thursday January 30, to Tuesday February 6, 1733; From Tuesday February 6, to Tuesday February 12, 1733.

RUN *away on* Jan. 24. *from* Samuel Worthington, *of the Manor of Moreland, an Irish Servant Man, named* Malachi Garvi, *about* 34 *Years of Age, of good Stature, red Beard, light brown Hair, his Face swelled and somewhat broke out by reason of his late Sickness, in which I took him in almost naked, paid his Expences, Doctor, &c. for which he became my Servant. He is well known in most of these Provinces, having travel'd about some Years. He had on a blueish grey strait body'd Coat, a coarse Kersey Jacket, reddish brown Stockins, old Shoes, & Leather Breeches. Whoever secures him so that he may be had again, shall have* Three Pounds *Reward, and reasonable Charges paid, by*   Samuel Worthington.

The Pennsylvania Gazette, From January 25, to February 1, 1733; From February 1, to February 8, 1733; From February 8, to February 15, 1733; From February 15, to February 22, 1733; February 22, to February 28, 1733.

RUN away the 11th of this Instant *March*, from *William Smith*, of Philadelphia, Cordwainer, a Servant Man named *John Blowden*, aged about 25 Years, smooth Face, he had on when he went away, an old Beaver Hat, a brown Wigg, with a large black Patch on his right Cheek; an old Kearsey Great-Coat, too short for him, a dark Kearsey Coat with Brass Buttons, a Red and White strip'd Holland Jacket and Breeches, white Stockins and round toe'd Shoes, he was formerly a Servant to *Arthur Wells* of this City, and ran away from his several Times, he has a smooth Tongue, and sometimes passes for a Gentleman, sometimes for a Merchant, and sometimes a Doctor; he generally harbours within a few Miles of this City for some Time, and has imposed on several People with a pretence that he has quarl'd with the Watch, and keeps out of the Way til his Friends have made it up for him.

Whoever takes up the said Servant so that his Master may have him again, shall have *Five Pounds* Reward, and reasonable Charges paid, by me, *William Smith.*

The American Weekly Mercury, From Tuesday March 13, to Tuesday March 20, 1733; From Tuesday March 20, to Tuesday March 27, 1733. See *The American Weekly Mercury*, From Thursday July 3, to Thursday July 10, 1729; *The Pennsylvania Gazette*, March 18, 1731; *The Pennsylvania Gazette*, From March 4, to March 11, 1730; *The American Weekly Mercury*, From Thursday October 4, to Thursday October 11, 1733; *The Pennsylvania Gazette*, From September 28, to October 11, 1733; *The Pennsylvania Gazette*, From November 13, to November 20, 1735, and *The Pennsylvania Gazette*, January 29, 1741.

RUN away from William Smith, *of* Philadelphia, March 11, *a Servant Man named* John Blowden, *aged about 25 Years, smooth faced. He had on an old Beaver Hat, a brown Wig, a large black Patch on his right Cheek, an old Kearsey Great Coat too short for him, a dark Kersey Coat with brass Buttons, a striped red and white holland Jacket and Breeches, white Stockings, round toed Shoes, He was formerly a Servant to* Arthur Wells *of this City, and ran away from him several times. He has a smooth Tongue, and sometimes passes for a Gentleman, sometimes for a Merchant, and sometimes for a Doctor; he generally harbours within a few Miles of this City, for some Time, and has imposed on several People with a Pretense that he has quarrel'd with the Watch and keeps out of the Way til his Friends have made it up for him. Whoever secures him so that he may be had again, shall have* Five Pounds Reward, *and reasonable Charges paid,* by William Smith.

The Pennsylvania Gazette, From March 8, to March 15, 1733; From March 15, to March 22, 1733. See *The American Weekly Mercury*, From Thursday July 3, to Thursday July 10, 1729; *The Pennsylvania Gazette*, From March 4, to March 11, 1731; *The American Weekly*

Mercury, From Tuesday March 13, to Tuesday March 20, 1733; *The American Weekly Mercury*, From Thursday October 4, to Thursday October 11, 1733; *The Pennsylvania Gazette*, From September 28, to October 11, 1733; *The Pennsylvania Gazette*, From November 13, to November 20, 1735, and *The Pennsylvania Gazette*, January 29, 1741.

RUN away Mar. 14. from Edmund Farrel, *Tanner, a Servant Man named* Alexander Nelson, *an Irishman, aged about* 24 *Years, of middle Stature. He has a black Wig, a lead colour Camlet Coat, a black Drugget Jacket, Buckskin Breeches, fine Hat, grey worsted Stockings, new Shoes; gas also taken with him a Quantity of Paper Money, and some Silver, and also the old Indentures of one* James Mac Daniel, *now free, and the Pass of the said* Mac Daniel *out of Maryland, and probably may use his Name. Whoever secures the said Servant so that he may be had again, shall have* Three *Pounds Reward, and reasonable Charges paid, by* Edmund Farrel.

The Pennsylvania Gazette, From March 8, to March 15, 1733; From March 15, to March 22, 1733; From March 22, to March 29, 1733.

RUN away March 25. *from the Ship* Swift, *a Servant Man named* Robert Low, *aged about* 24 *Years, of middle Stature and sandy Complexion, wearing his own short Hair. Whoever secures said Servant so that he may be had again, shall have* Three Pounds *Reward, and reasonable Charges paid,*
by David Russan, *Master of said Ship.*

The Pennsylvania Gazette, From March 22, to March 29, 1733; From March 29, to April 5, 1733; From April 5, to April 12, 1733; From April 19, to April 26, 1733.

L*AST Night absented himself from his Master's House,* (Peter Cuff *Brewer in* Philadelphia) *a Servant Man named* Thomas Probert *a Welshman, but speaks good English, he is a lusty thick set Fellow of middle stature with short Hair, had on a coarse Felt Hat,* 2 *blue check Shirts, dark colour'd Kersey Coat lin'd with blue Linsey, torn Breeches of the same Kersey, brass Buttons, has with him several Pair of Yarn and Worsted Stockings. Whoever takes up said Servant, and brings him to his said Master, shall have* Three Pounds *Reward and reasonable Charges paid by* Peter Cuff.

N. B. He has taken Paper-Money, it cannot be said how much at present. April 2.

The Pennsylvania Gazette, From March 29, to April 5, 1733; From April 5, to April 12, 1733; From April 19, to April 26, 1733.

RUN away from *William Parker*, of *Philadelphia*, a Servant Man belonging to *Thomas Bacley*, of *Falls* Township in *Bucks* County; named *John Kees*, very much Pockfretten, a fresh Colour and longish Chin, brownish Complexion, his Hair cut off, pretty free in Speech & Writes pretty well, had on a Copper Colour'd Coat with Brass Buttons, no Jacket, a pair of blue roaded Stockings, a Check Shirt, and a pretty good Felt Hat Whoever takes up the said Servant and brings him to *William Parker* in *Water Street*, shall have *Twenty Shillings* Reward, and reasonable Charges,
                  paid by   *William Parker.*

The American Weekly Mercury, From Thursday, April 19, to Thursday, April 26, 1733; From Thursday, April 26, to Thursday, May 3, 1733; From Thursday May 10, to Thursday May 17, 1733.

RUN away on Sunday Night last from Thomas Shoemaker, *an English Servant Man named* John White, *about* 30 *Years of Age, middle sized, well set, short strait brown Hair. Had on a fine Hat somewhat worn, a darkish Kersey Jacket, a light-coloured Kersey wide Coat, Leather Breeches, woollen Stockings of blue and white mixed, good Shoes. Whoever secures the said Servants so that he may be had again, shall have Three Pounds Reward, and reasonable Charges paid, by* Thomas Shoemaker.   April 24.

The Pennsylvania Gazette, From April 19, to April 26, 1733.

RUN away, the sixth of this Instant, from *Joseph Richardson* of *Perckomey*, in the Township of *New-Providence*, in the County of *Philadelphia*, a Servant Man named *William Brown*, alias *William Dorrell*, aged 21 Years, of middle Stature, hollow Ey'd, large Nose, a down Look and very round Shoulder'd, his Hair lately cut off; he had on when he went away, a new Felt Hat, a close body'd Coat and a great-Coat of a lightish Colour with Brass Buttons, a pair of round-toe'd Boots and a pair of Pumps with peaked Toes. He took with him a large black Gelding branded with **WB**, Paces well, sho'd all round, and took a Man's Saddle and Bridle, likewise a small Trunk having in it some Womens Apparel, *viz.* some Handkerchiefs, Capes and a black Padesway Hood, and six Shillings in Money, Whoever takes up the said Servant and Horse, and brings them to *Joseph Richardson* aforesaid, or to *George Emlen* in *Philadelphia*, or Secures them so as they may be had again, shall have *Eight Pounds* as a Reward, and reasonable Charges,
                paid by me   *Jos. Richardson.*

The American Weekly Mercury, From Thursday May 10, to Thursday May 17, 1733; From Thursday May 24, to Thursday May 31, 1733. See *The Pennsylvania Gazette*, From May 10, to May 17, 1733.

RUN away the 6th of this Instant May, from Joseph Richardson of Perkiomy, in the Township of New-Providence, in the County of Philadelphia, a Servant Man named William Brown, alias William Dorrell, aged 21 Years, he is of a middle Stature, hollow Ey'd, large Nose, down Look and very round Shoulder'd, his Hair lately cut off; he had on when he went away, a new Felt Hat, a close body'd Coat and a great Coat of a Lightish colour and brass Buttons, a pair of round Toe'd Boots, and a Pair of Pumps with Peaked Toes; he took with him, a large black Gelding branded with **W.B.** Paces well, shod all round, and took a Mans Saddle and Bridle; likewise a small Trunk, having in it some Womens Apparel, viz. Some Handkerchiefs, Caps, and a black Padesway Hood, and Six Shillings in Money. Whoever takes up said Servants and Horse, and brings them to Joseph Richardson aforesaid, or to George Emlen in Philadelphia, or secures them so as they may be had again, shall have Eight Pounds as a Reward and reasonable Charges paid by me.
            Joseph Richardson. May 9. 1733.
    The Pennsylvania Gazette, From May 10, to May 17, 1733; From May 17, to May 24, 1733. See *The American Weekly Mercury*, From Thursday May 10, to Thursday May 17, 1733.

LAST Night broke out of the Goal of this City, Joseph Watt, who was convicted of counterfeiting Bill of Credit of this Province, and had his Sentence executed by standing in the Pillory, and his Ears cropt. He is about Forty Years of Age, with long strait brown Hair, and has a Scar in his Throat where he attempted to cut it. Whoever takes him, or can give Intelligence of him, are desired to advertise the Sheriff thereof, that he may be brought to Prison again.   June 14.
    The Pennsylvania Gazette, From June 7, to June 14, 1733; From June 28, to July 5, 1733.

RUN away the 25th of *June* last, from *Richard Clymer* of *Philadelphia*, two Servant Men, the one an elderly Man aged about 40 Years or upwards, he had short Hair and a long Nose, he had on when he went away, a Linnen Jacket and Trowsers, he speaks pretty much West-Country, his Name is *Aaron Thomas*. The other an *Irish* Lad, with short white Hair, about 19 Years of age, speaks very good *English*, he is small of Stature, (they are both of one heigth) he had on a Linnen Jacket and long Trousers, his Name is *Michael Glandon*. Whoever takes up the said Servants, and secures them so that their Master may have them again, shall have *Five Pounds* as a Reward for each, and reasonable Charpaid, [sic] by me,
            Richard Clymer.

The American Weekly Mercury, From Thursday July 5, to Thursday July 12, 1733; From Thursday July 12, to Thursday July 19, 1733; From Thursday July 19, to Thursday July 26, 1733; From Thursday July 26, to Thursday August 2, 1733.

RUn away, the 7th of this Instant *August*, from *Mathew Dwalt* [sic] of the City of *Philadelphia*, Cordwainer, a Servant Man named *Robert Winter*, aged about 24 Years, a tall well-set fresh-collour'd Fellow, had on a light colour'd Kersey Pea-Jacket lined with red, gray Kersey Breeches, Yarn Stockings, good Shoes with but one Buckle in them, and a speckled Shirt, he has no Hair but a white Cap. Whoever takes up the said Servant and brings him to his Master, or secures him so that he may be had again, shall have *Four Pounds* as a Reward and all reasonable Charges,
   paid by *Matthew Dwalt.*
The American Weekly Mercury, From Thursday, August 9, to Thursday, August 16, 1733; From Thursday, August 16, to Thursday, August 23, 1733.

RUn away, the 28th of *May* last, from *John Powell*, of *Providence* Township, in *Chester*-County, a Dutch Servant Man named *Nicholas Bogert*, a lusty well-set Fellow with dark long Hair, he has lost several of his fore Teeth out of the upper Jaw, he had on or with him when he went away a homespun Coat lined, and a blue Coat lined with red, a wastcoat without Sleves and mended under the Arms with light colour'd Cloth, a Felt Hat, three pair Breeches one Cloth and two Leather, white Stockings, old Shoes, three Shirts; he has a large straight Foot.

Whoever secures the said Servant so that he may be had again, shall have *Forty Shillings* Reward and reasonable Charges,
   paid by *John Powell.*
The American Weekly Mercury, From Thursday, August 16, to Thursday, August 23, 1733; From Thursday, August 23, to Thursday, August 30, 1733; *The American Weekly Mercury*, From Thursday, August 6, to Thursday, September 13, 1733. [sic]

RUN away, the 19 of *August* last, from *Thomas Crispin* and *Hance Lican*, two Servant Men, the one named *Joseph Trull*, of a middle Stature, thin Visag'd, strait brown Hair, a Bump on the right side of his under Lip, he is a down looking Fellow; he had on an old gray Coat, homespun striped Jacket and Breeches, gray yarn Stockings, and a new Felt Hat. The other named *James Norton*, a short Fellow of brownish Complexion and thin Visage, dark

curl'd Hair, had on when he went away, an Ozenbrigs Jacket, homespun Linnen Shirt and Breeches, old Shoes and Stockings, the Shoes ty'd with strings and a new Felt Hat. Whoever takes up the said Servants and secures them so that they may be had again, shall have *Three Pounds* for each as a Reward, and all reasonable Charges,
                paid by   *Thomas Crispin & Hance Lican.*
The American Weekly Mercury, From Thursday, August 30, to Thursday, September 6, 1733; *The American Weekly Mercury,* From Thursday, August 6, to Thursday, September 13, 1733 [*sic*]; From Thursday September 13, to Thursday, September 20, 1733.

THis is to give Notice, That on the 26 of *August* last, there went away from *Nathaniel Pooles,* Shipwright, in *Philadelphia,* a certain Gentleman named *David Hopkins,* of a pale Complexion, supposed to be troubled in his Mind, his Apparel when he went away was a whitish Broad Cloath Coat, white Westcoat and Breeches, blue and white striped Cap and a large pair of Silver Buckles in his Shoes Whoever can give any Intelligence of the said Person to *Reece Jones* at the White Horse in *Market Street,* or to *Robert Davis* at the Queens Head in *Water Street,* shall have *Twenty Shilling* Reward and reasonable Charges, paid by
                Reece Jones or *Robert Davis.*
The American Weekly Mercury, From Thursday, August 6, to Thursday, September 13, 1733 [*sic*]; From Thursday, September 13, to Thursday September 20, 1733.

RUN away *Aug.* 19 from their Masters, three Servants, the one from *Abel Preston,* Baker, a Man of about 22 Years of Age named *William Hasey,* short of Stature, black Hair but cut off and wears a Wigg, he had on an Oznaburgs Shirt, Jacket and Trousers, a pair of yellowish Stockings and good Shoes.
    Two belonging to *Jacob Medcalf* Esq; of *Cooper's Ferry,* in *New-Jersey,* the one named *William Dorrington,* about 30 Years of age, of middle Stature and lightish Hair, had on a Felt Hat, an ash coloured Coat, Oznaburgs Trousers, and a striped homespun Flannel Jacket. The other named *Benjamin Greenstreet,* a short thick Fellow, fresh colour'd, about 24 Years of age, bushy sandy colour'd Hair, a whitish colour'd Kersey Jacket, a pair of Oznaburg Breeches with two Silver Buttons, an Oznaburg Shirt, a Felt Hat cut round the Brim, and half worn Shoes. There is another servant with them belonging to some one about 6 Miles from *Philadelphia.*
    Whoever takes up the said Servants or either of them and secures them so that [their] Masters may have them again, shall have *Forty Shillings* as a Reward for each and all reasonable Charges, paid by

Abel Preston & Jacob Medcalf.
The American Weekly Mercury, From Thursday, August 16, to Thursday, August 23, 1733.

RUn away, the 18th of this Instant *September*, from *Samuel Garrat*, jun. near *Goshen*, a Servant Man named *John Shanay*, an *Irish* Man of about 20 Years of Age, short of Stature and brown curl'd Hair, of pailish [sic] Complexion, had on when he went away a double Breasted blue Broad-Cloath Coat, a black Jacket, two pair of Linnen Drawers, light colour'd Worsted Stockings, and Neets Leather Shoes. He is mark'd on his Right Hand with J S. and reads and writes well. Whoever secures the said Servant so that he may be had again, and gives Notice to *Thomas Oldman* in *Philadelphia*, or *Samuel Garrat* at *Darby*, shall have *Forty Shillings* Reward and reasonable Charges, paid by *Samuel Garrat*, jun.
The American Weekly Mercury, From Thursday, September 13th, to Thursday September 20th, 1733; From Thursday, September 20th, to Thursday September 27th, 1733; From Thursday, September 27th, to Thursday October 4th, 1733.

RUN away from *William Smith* of *Philadelphia*, Cordwainer, a Servant Man named *John Blowden*, of middle Stature and pale Face, he had on when he went away an old dark colour'd Kearsey Coat with Brass Buttons, Oznaburgs Jacket, Shirt and Trousers, old Shoes and Stockings, no Hat unless he has got one since. He formerly belonged to *Arthur Wells* of this City deceas'd, and has often run away from him. He generally harbours about the Town, with an excuse that he has been Fighting and keeps out of the way till his Friends makes it up for him, generally staying two or three Days at one House, till he finds an opportunity to get farther. He sometimes passes for a Doctor, sometimes a Gentleman, or else a Merchant. Whoever takes him up and secures him so that his Master may have him again, shall have *Three Pounds* as a Reward and all reasonable Charges,
paid by me   *William Smith.*
The American Weekly Mercury, From Thursday October 4, to Thursday October 11, 1733. See *The American Weekly Mercury*, From Thursday July 3, to Thursday July 10, 1729; *The Pennsylvania Gazette*, From March 4, to March 11, 1731; *The American Weekly Mercury*, From Tuesday March 13, to Tuesday March 20, 1733; *The Pennsylvania Gazette*, From March 8, to March 15, 1733; *The American Weekly Mercury*, From Thursday October 4, to Thursday October 11, 1733; *The Pennsylvania Gazette*, October 18, 1733; *The Pennsylvania

Gazette, From November 13, to November 20, 1735, and *The Pennsylvania Gazette,* January 29, 1741.

RUN away from *William Smith* of *Philadelphi*a, Cordwainer, a Servant Man named *John Blowden,* of middle Stature and pale Face, he had on when he went away an old dark coloured Kersey Coat with Brass Buttons, Ozenbrigs Jacket, Shirt and Trowsers, old Shoes and Stockings, no Hat unless he got one since. He formerly belonged to *Arthur Wel*ls of this City deceas'd, and has often run away from him. He generally harbours near Town, with an excuse that he has been Fighting and keeps out of the way till his Friends make it up for him, generally staying 2 or 3 Days at one House till he finds an Opportunity to get farther. He sometimes passes for a Doctor, sometimes a Gentleman, or else a Merchant. Whoever takes him up and secures him so that his Master may have him again, shall have *Three Pounds* as a Reward and all reasonable Charges, paid by me   *William Smith.*

The Pennsylvania Gazette, From September 28, to October 11, 1733; October 18, 1733. See *The American Weekly Mercury,* From Thursday July 3, to Thursday July 10, 1729; *The Pennsylvania Gazette,* From March 4, to March 11, 1731; *The American Weekly Mercury,* From Tuesday March 13, to Tuesday March 20, 1733; *The Pennsylvania Gazette,* From March 8, to March 15, 1733; *The American Weekly Mercury,* From Thursday October 4, to Thursday October 11, 1733; *The Pennsylvania Gazette,* From November 13, to November 20, 1735, and *The Pennsylvania Gazette,* January 29, 1741.

R*UN away October the 21st, from the Ship* Diligence, *Samuel Wood, Master, Two Sailors, One of them is taken, and is now in the Work-House. The other is a black Complexion Man, wearing his own Hair, with a down Look, named Michael Griffis, having with him a red Rug Coat, a brown Pea-Jacket, and a blue and white striped Wast coat and Breeches. Whosoever shall take up the said Man, so that he may be had again, shall be paid all reasonable Charges by me*   Samuel Wood.

The Pennsylvania Gazette, From October 18, to October 25, 1733; November 1, 1733.

RUN away the 22d of *September* last, from his Master *James Queen* of the Township of *Nottingham* in *Chester* County, a Servant Man named *William Bell,* aged about 23 Years, he is a skinner and Glover by Trade, he had on when he went away a blue Cloath Jacket lined with Green, an old gray Coat with Brass Buttons, a pair of Leather Breeches, a pair of Country Shoes with

Strings in them, a course Shirt and brown worsted Stockings. He is of a middle Stature and hath brown Hair. Whoever takes up the said Servant and secures him so that his Master may have again, shall have *Three Pounds* as a Reward and all reasonable Charges, paid by   *James Queen.*

The American Weekly Mercury, From Thursday, November 1, to Thursday November 8, 1733; From Thursday, November 8, to Thursday, November 15, 1733; From Thursday, November 29, to Thursday, December 6, 1733.

RUN away from on board the Bristol Hope, *Arthur Tough*, Master, a Servant Man belonging to *George Fleming*, named *John Hopkins*, he is pockfretten, and hath an Impediment in his Speech, short white Hair, short thick Neck, and is a chunky fellow, by Trade a Cook. He had on when he went away, a half-wore frize Coat, a sort of silk Wastecoat much torn, lightish blew Breeches, blew worsted Stockings and new round to'd Shoes.

Whoever secures the said Servant, and delivers him to the Workhouse-keeper shall have *Forty Shillings*, Reward, and reasonable Charges paid,
by *Tho. Campbel*, in Sec. Street.

The Pennsylvania Gazette, From October 25, to November 1, 1733; From November 1, to November 8, 1733; From November 16, to November 22, 1733; November 22, to November 29, 1733.

RUN away on Sunday Morning last the two following Servant Men, viz. From Joseph Gray *at the Middle Ferry on* Skuylkill, *a Dutch Servant Man speaks a little English and French, named Andreas Baseener, about 25 Years of Age, long strait Hair of a Pissburnt colour, tall, swarthy Complexion; Had on a Broadcloth Coat and Breeches somewhat worn, Felt Hat, wears a Stock with a large Brass Clasp, Ozenbrigs Shirt, Grey Yarn Stockings, strong Shoes.*

From Christian Grassholt *a Dutch Servant Man, by Trade a Taylor, talks little or no English, named* Hans Wulf Eisman, *no Hair, about 22 Years old, wears a white Cap under his Felt Hate, [sic] white Hatband, an old Olive green Duroy Coat, one Sleeve a little torn, a black Cloth Wastecoat and Breeches, white Yarn Stockings, and dark Stockings, square toe'd Shoes with large Brass Buckles, coarse Linen Shirt. Whoever secures the said Servants so as they may be had again, shall have* Forty Shillings *Reward for the first and* Twenty Shillings *for the other, and reasonable Charges paid by*
Jos. Gray & Ch. Grassholt. Novem. 13.

The Pennsylvania Gazette, From November 8, to November 16, 1733; From November 16, to November 22, 1733; From November 29, to December 6, 1733; From December 6, to December 13, 1733.

RUN away the 27th of *August* last, from *James Anderson* Minister of the Gospel in *Donigal*, in the County of *Lancaster* in *Pensilvania*, a Servant Man named *Hugh Wier*, aged about 30 Years of a middle Stature and fresh Complexion, sandy Beard, and short dark brown Hair, he went off very bear [sic] in Cloathing, and is supposed to have got himself dress'd in *Indian* Habit, (He having been used among *Indians*, when he run away from other Masters before) He is by Trade a Flax-dresser, Spinster and Woolcomber, and it is supposed he can Weave, He also does most sort of Women Work, such as washing of Cloaths or Dishes, milking of Cows, and other Kitchen Work, and usually Changes his Name, Whoever takes up said Servant and secures him either in this or any of the neighbouring Provinces and let his Master know of it, by Post or other-ways, so as his said Master may have him again, shall have *Three Pounds* as a Reward, and all reasonable Charges paid by me, James Anderson.

The American Weekly Mercury, From Thursday, November 29, to Thursday, December 6, 1733; From Thursday, December 14, to Friday, December 21, 1733; From Saturday, December 22, to Saturday, December 29, 1733.

RUN from the Ship *Vigor*, *Wm. Harris* Master, lately arrived from *Bristol*, 3 Servant (*viz.*) *George Haynes*, a lusty jolly Man, with large and full Eyes, a Cooper by Trade, and aged about 28 Years, the second named *Samuel Wood*, a middle siz'd Man, has a Boil or Sore on the left side of his Chin, as he walks his Knees turns much in, and his Feet out, he has been formerly in *Virginia*. The Third named *John Williams*, a small thin Man, fair Complexion, he wears his own Hair, when he speaks 'tis but slow, they have all Servants Pea-Jackets on, (and Samuel Wood a Tarpaulin Jacket) and all gone in Company together. Whoever takes up or secures the said Servant so that they may be had again, shall have Forty Shillings as a reward for each and all reasonable Charges paid by   Willing and Shippen.

The American Weekly Mercury, From Thursday, November 29, to Thursday, December 6, 1733; From Thursday, December 6, to Friday, December 14, 1733; From Thursday, December 14, [sic] to Friday, December 21, 1733. See *The Pennsylvania Gazette*, November 29, to December 6, 1733.

RUN away from the Ship Vigor, William Harris, *Master, lately arrived from* Bristol, *three Servant Men, viz.* George Haynes, *a lusty jolly Man, with large and full Eyes, by Trade a Cooper and about* 28 *Years of Age.* Samuel Wood, *a middle siz'd Man, a Boil or Sore on the left Side of his Chin; as he walks his Knees turn much in and his Feet out; he has been formerly in* Virginia.

The other John Williams, *a small thin Man, fair Complexion, his own Hair, when he speaks 'tis but slow: They have all Servants Pea-Jackets on (and* Samuel Wood, *a tarpaulin Jacket) and all gone in Company. Whoever takes up, or secures the said Servants so that they may be had again, shall have Forty Shillings Reward for each, and all reasonable Charges paid by*
Willing & Shippen. *December* 3. 1733.

The Pennsylvania Gazette, From November 29, to December 6, 1733; From December 6, to December 13, 1733; From December 13, to December 20, 1733. See *The American Weekly Mercury,* From Thursday, November 29, to Thursday, December 6, 1733.

Philadelphia, Decemb. 28, 1733.
RUN away, last Night, a Servant Man named *Samuel Cammock*, a squat Fellow with a down look, has the *Irish* Brogue pretty strong, has on a Sailors *Pee* Jacket of light colour'd Cloth. He has taken away with him a Bay Mare pretty low but well set, she has no Gates but a ntural [sic] Pace, with a black Maine a switch Tail and a small speck in her Forehead, markt on the near Buttock with **K**. Whoever brings the said Servant and Mare to the Post-Master of Philadelphia, shall have Five Pounds Reward.

The American Weekly Mercury, From Thursday, December 22, to Thursday December 29, 1733.

RUN away, the 23*d* of this Instant *December*, from *John Hyatt* of *Philadelphia*, a Servant Man named *James Rigley*, he's of midling Stature, fresh Complexion and black curled Hair, by Trade a Brass-Founder. He had on a Cinnamon colour'd old Camblet Coat rent a little on the Back, under that a Linnen Coat Searsuccor Jacket and Breeches and a pair of old Trowsers, had with him three shirts, one of Holland and two of course Linnen. He's in Company with a Man in a light colour'd Cloth Coat, old Trowsers and a large Hat, his name is *George Rochell*, a Carpenter by Trade. Whoever secures the said Servant and gives Notice thereof to his Master so that he may have him again, shall have *Forty Shillings* reward and reasonable Charges,
paid by   *John Hyatt.*

The American Weekly Mercury, From Thursday, December 22, to Thursday December 29, 1733; From Tuesday, January 1, to Tuesday January 8, 1734; From Tuesday, January 8, to Tuesday January 15, 1734; From Tuesday, January 15, to Tuesday January 22, 1734. See *The American Weekly Mercury,* From Tuesday February 4, to Tuesday February 11, 1735.

RUN away, the 26th of this Instant *December*, from *Robert Hannum* of *Birmingham* in *Chester* County, near *Brandy-Wine*, a Servant Man named *Richard Field*, aged about 24 Years, of middle Stature, thin Visag'd and squints inward with both Eyes, with short light colour'd Hair, had on a new Felt Hat, a Cinnamon coloured Coat much worn and faded, with large Brass Buttons; a Jacket of natural black Wollen with Brass Buttons, a pair of Orange colour'd Wollen Breeches with side Pockets and a Patch on one Knee, black Wollen Stockings, and half worn double Sole'd Shoes a Sole of one being cut off. Whoever takes up and secures the said Servant so that his Master may have him again, shall have *Thirty Shillings* Reward and all reasonable Charges paid by   *Robert Hannum*.

The American Weekly Mercury, From Thursday, December 22, to Thursday December 29, 1733; From Tuesday, January 1, to Tuesday January 8, 1734; From Tuesday, January 8, to Tuesday January 15, 1734.

1734

RUN away, the 26th of *December* last from *Obediah Eldridge* of *Philadelphia*, a Servant Man named *William Richman*, by Trade a Shoemaker, about 22 Years of age, a slender thin Vissag'd Fellow, stoops forward as he walks, has light colour'd Hair, one of his Hands is mark'd with Gun-powder the two first Letters of his Name, WR, with the date of the Year, 1729. He had on when he went away a Felt Hat, a dark Olive colour'd Camblet Coat, a Cloth Jacket, a white Shirt, Leather Breeches, Worsted Stockings and peaked-toed Shoes. He is a *Wiltshire* Man and speaks West-Country. Whoever takes him up and brings him to his Master, or secures him so that he may have him again, shall have *Three Pounds* Reward and all reasonable Charges, paid by   *Obediah Eldridge*.

The American Weekly Mercury, From Saturday, December 29, to Tuesday January 1, 1734; From Tuesday, January 1, to Tuesday January 8, 1734; From Tuesday, January 8, to Tuesday January 15, 1734; From Tuesday, January 15, to Tuesday January 22, 1734; From Tuesday, January 22, to Tuesday January 29, 1734.

RUN away on the 23d Instant from Ralph Lees, *Taylor, an Irish Servant Lad named* William Dryskyl, *by Trade a Taylor, about 17 Years of Age, has a large Dent on his right Cheek, took with him an old gray Kersey Jacket, light colour'd cloth Breeches pretty much worn, and white dimity Breeches, two Pair of Stockins, one white, the other cinnamon colour; and a Felt Hat.*

have Thirty Shillings *Reward, and reasonable Charges paid,*
        by Ralph Lees. Philadelphia, January 24. 1733, 4.
The Pennsylvania Gazette, From January 16, to January 23, 1734; January 30, 1734.

RUN away from *Henry Smith's* Plantation above *Tulpahocke*n, the 12th of last Month, a Servant Man named *Thomas Bently*, aged 18 Years, fresh colour'd, something Freckled, had on a brown Kersey Coat, blue Cloth Cap, Indian Shoes and Stockings and a Garlix Shirt. He took with him the following Goods belonging to his Master, Twelve Yards of Strowds, three Indian Blankets, Twelve Pounds of Powder, Twenty Bars of Lead, Two Dozen clasp Knive, [*sic*] one short Gun, a roan Horse marked **ID** on his near Shoulder or Buttock, (or both) with a narrow White Slip on his forehead; the said Servant went in Company with *William Mack*, a hired Man to the said *Henry Smith*, pretending to go *Indian* Trading.
Whoever takes up the said *Bently* and brings him to Philadelphia, to *Edward Shippen*, shall have *Three Pounds* and reasonable Charges,
        paid by   *Edward Shippen.*
The American Weekly Mercury, From Tuesday February 26, to Tuesday March 5, 1734; From Thursday March 21, to Thursday March 28, 1734. See *The Pennsylvania Gazette*, March 6, 1734.

RUN away from *Henry Smith's* Plantation above *Tulpehocke*n, the 12th Inst. a Servant Man named *Tho. Bently*, aged eighteen years, fresh colour'd, something freckled, had on a brown Kersey, blue Coat cloth cap, Indian Shoes and Stockings, a Garlix Shirt; took with him the following Goods belonging to his Master; Twelve yards of Strowds, Three Indian Blankets, Twelve Pounds of Powder, Twenty Bars of Lead, Two dozen clasp Knives, one Shot Gun, a roan Horse marked *I. D.* on the near shoulder or buttock, or both, with a narrow white Slip on his forehead; the said Servant went in Company with *Wm. Mark*, a hired Man to the *Henry Smith*, pretending to go Indian Trading. Whoever takes up the said *Bently*, and brings him to Philadelphia, to *Edward Shippen*, shall have Three Pounds and reasonable Charges paid by,   *Edward Shippen.*
The Pennsylvania Gazette, From February 20, to February 27, 1734; From February 27, to March 6, 1734. See *The American Weekly Mercury*, From Tuesday February 26, to Tuesday March 5, 1734.

RUN away, the 4th of this Inst. *March*, from George Robison of *West-Nottingham* in *Chester* County, a Servant Man named *Thomas Johnson*, an

Englishman, of a middle size, very much Pock mark'd, and clean Shaved. Wore when he went away, a Flaxen fair Wigg or new Worsted Cap, two white Coats one lined with red, a black Coat trim'd with Mohair, a blue Jacket and a pair of scarlet shagg Breeches. He also took from his Master Gold and Plate to the Value of 20 or 30 Pounds, besides Cloaths and a good Mare with Furniture. Whoever takes up and secures the said Servant, and give Notice to his Master, so that he may have him again, shall have *Three Pounds* as a Reward, and reasonable Charges, paid by *George Robison.*

The American Weekly Mercury, From Tuesday March 12, to Thursday March 21, 1734; From Thursday, March 29, to Thursday, April 18, 1734; From Thursday, April 18, to Thursday, April 25, 1734.

*RUN away the 5th of this Instant Ma*rch, from James Boyd of Chester County, and Township of Sudsbury, a Servant Man named John Edwards, he is a small, short, thin Fellow, black Complexion, had on when he went away a brownish coloured Homepsun Coat, with a Linnen Cinnamon coloured Jacket, an old fine Shirt, old Cloth Breeches, old Worsted Stockings and new Shoes. He took with him a falling Ax, he has also a sore leg that was cut with an Ax. Any Person that can apprehend, or secure the said Servant, so that his Master may have him again, shall have *Twenty Shillings* Reward, and reasonable Charges, paid by me *James Boyd.*

The Pennsylvania Gazette, From March 13, to March 21, 1734; From March 21, to March 28, 1734; From March 28, to April 4, 1734; From April 4, to April 11, 1734; From April 11, to April 18, 1734; From April 18, to April 25, 1734.

RUN away, the 15th of this Instant *April*, from *Andrew Robinson*, a Servant Lad named *James Bell*, aged about 18 Years, a middle siz'd Fellow of a sandy Complexion, long Vissag'd, pretty much Pock-broken and grey Ey'd; he had on when he went away a half worn Beaver Hat, a white Holland Cap mark'd I. B. a fine white Shirt, a homespun black and white Drugget Coat and Vest lined with Lead colour'd Shalloon, good Leather Breeches with Brass Buttons, brown Stockings and good Shoes. Whoever takes up the said Servant, and secures him so that he may be had again, shall have *Five Pounds* as a Reward, and reasonable Charges, paid by *Andrew Robinson.*
N. B. He speaks good *High-Dutch.*

The American Weekly Mercury, From Thursday March 28, to Thursday April 18, 1734; From Thursday April 18, to Thursday April 25, 1734.

RUN away the 20th of this Instant April, from Daniel Davis of Chichester, (or Marcus-Hook) Sawyer, a servant man named Joseph Millwater, alias Grimes, of low stature, well set, aged near 40 Years, short brown Hair, a flat Nose, can saw, and has been us'd to spin. Had on a Felt Hat about half worn, a light coloured Tammey Jacket lin'd with a snuff colour'd Tammey, a pair of old leather Breeches, light coloured worsted stockings, sharp toed shoes with low heels, and a shirt made of Homepsun Linnen not wash'd. Whoever takes up the said Servant, and brings him to this said Master, or secures him so that he may be had again, shall have Three Pounds Reward, and all reasonable Charges paid, by   Daniel Davis.

The Pennsylvania Gazette, From April 18, to April 25, 1734; From April 25, to May 2, 1734.

RUN away, the 6th of this Inst. *May,* from *Thomas Potts* of *Colebrook*-Dale Iron-Works, in *Philadelphia* County, *Pennsylvania,* a Servant Man named *Evan Thomas,* a Welchman, aged about 22 Years, of short Stature, fresh Complexion, round Vissag'd, a chunky well-set Fellow: had on when he went away a brown Kersey Coat trimm'd with Mohair Buttons of the same colour, an old brown Kearsey Jacket with Brass Buttons, a homespun Shirt, a pair of Linnen Drawers, a pair of Yarn Stockings, a pair of old Shoes and a Felt Hat. Also a Negro Man named *Jo Cunfy,* about 20 Years of age, of tall Stature, had on an old Beaver Hat, a Tickin Cap, an Orange colour'd Cloth Coat with Brass Buttons, a striped Ticken Jacket & Breeches, an Ozenbrigs Shirt, a pair of gray Worsted Stockings and a pair of old Shoes; he's *Pennsylvania* born and speaks good *English.* They took with them two Horses, the one a Sorrel with a flxen [*sic*] Mane, branded with an undistinguishable Mark on the far Buttock; the other supposed to be a Bay Horse, a Pacer. Whoever takes up the said Servant and Negro, or either of them, and brings them or either of them to the said *Thomas Potts,* or secures them so that they may be had again, shall have *Fifty Shi*llings for each and all reasonable Charges,
            paid by   Thomas Potts.

The American Weekly Mercury, From Thursday, May 9, to Thursday May 16, 1734; From Thursday, May 30, to Thursday June 6, 1734; From Thursday, June 13, to Thursday June 20, 1734; From Thursday, June 20, to Thursday June 27, 1734.

RUN away, the 16th of this Instant *May,* from *James Allcorn* of *Marlborough* Township in *Chester* County, a Servant Man named *James Loonin,* aged about 25 Years, a Native of *Ireland,* he has two Letters drawn on one of his Hands with Gun Powder, he is of short Stature and well-set, short black Hair, hollow Eyes, and a ruddy Complexion, had on a Coat of black and white

natural Wool with Brass Buttons and no Lining, a gray Linsey Jacket, a pair of Leather Breeches with a single Brass Button at each Knee and a pair of old Trowsers over them, pretty good Shoes and Stockings, a white Lambskin Wigg and a pretty good Felt Hat. He has part of his Indenture with him, and is suppose to have a false Pass. Whoever takes up the said Servant and brings him to his Master, or secures him so that he may be had again, shall have Three Pounds Reward and all reasonable Charges,
                paid by me   James Allcorn.
The American Weekly Mercury, From Thursday, May 16, to Thursday May 23, 1734; From Thursday, May 23, to Thursday May 30, 1734; From Thursday, May 30, to Thursday June 6, 1734.

RUN away, the 26th of *May*, from *John Leacock*, at *Pool*-Forge, two Servant Lads, one named *Anthony Lee*, a tall Fellow, bandy Leg'd, he is talkative and can tell his Story very plausibly, born in *Lancashire* in *England,* had on when he went away a blue great Coat, Ozenbriggs Jacket and Trowsers, blue worsted Stockings, a good Felt Hat, a blue Shirt and good Shoes. The other a small Boy, about 14 or 15 Years old, named *James Esington*, he has a cast with his Eye, he Reads and writes pretty well, and was born in *London*, had on a blue great Coat, Ozenbrigs Jacket, Leather Breeches, and striped Cap. They went away in Company with a Servant of *Samuel Brown*, a full Faced chunkey Fellow of a red Complexion. Whoever takes up the said Servants and brings them to *John Leacock* in *Philadelphia*, or to Pool Forge, shall have Forty Shillings for each, and reasonable Charges
                paid, by   *John Leacock.*
The American Weekly Mercury, From Thursday, May 23, to Thursday May 30, 1734; From Thursday, May 30, to Thursday, June 6, 1734; From June 6, to June 13, 1734; From June 13, to June 20, 1734. See *The Pennsylvania Gazette*, June 6, 1734, and *The Pennsylvania Gazette*, From September 5, to September 12, 1734. Lea/Lee.

RUN away, the 4th of this Instant *June*, from *John Lock* of *Philadelphia*, a Servant Man named *William Colston*, a Yorkshire Man, about 30 Years of Age, round smooth Fac'd and long black Hair, he had on when he went away, a course [*sic*] *Russia* Linnen Frock and Trowsers, an Ozenbrigs Shirt, a pair of double Soal'd Shoes almost new and an old Felt Hat with a very narrow Brim. Whoever takes up the said Servant and brings him to his Master or secures him so that he may be had again, shall have *Three Pounds* Reward and all reasonable Charges, paid by   *John Lock.*
N. B. If he returns home to his Master speedily he shall be forgiven.

The American Weekly Mercury, From Thursday, May 30, to Thursday, June 6, 1734.

3d of the 4th Mo. 1734.
RUN away, last Night, from *John Salkeld* of Chester, a Servant Man named *William Green*, about 25 Years of age, an English man born, of middle Stature, somewhat stooping as he walks, lank brown Hair, thin Vissag'd, had on when he went away on old Duroy Coat plain made, two striped Tickin Jackets, one pair of striped Linnen Drawers, two pair of Trowsers with each a [lon]g Pocket on the right side, a pair of Worsted Stockings and a pair of Yarn Stockings footed with a pair of Calf-Skin Shoes, five Shirts two of old chequer'd Linnen two of fine homespun Linnen not well whiten'd and one of old Ozenbrigs. Whoever takes up said Servant so that his Master may have him again, shall have *Forty Shillings* Reward and reasonable Charges,
   paid by *John Salkeld.*
The American Weekly Mercury, From Thursday, May 30, to Thursday, June 6, 1734; From Thursday, June 27, to Thursday, July 4, 1734; From Thursday, July 4, to Thursday, July 11, 1734.

RUN away from John Leacock, from Pool Forge, the 26th of this Instant, Two Servants, one named Anthony Lea, a tall fellow, bandy legged, and talkative, can tell his Story very plausibly, born in Lancaster in England; had on when he went away a blue great Coat, Ozenbrigs Jacket and Trowsers, blue worsted Stockings, a good Felt Hat, a blue Shirt and good Shoes. The other a small Boy about 14 or 15 Years old, named James Esington, a cast with his Eye, and reads and writes pretty well, born in London; had on a blue great Coat, Ozenbrigs Jacket and Leather Breeches, and strip'd Cap. They went in Company with a Servant of Samuel Brown's, a full Faced chunky Fellow of a red Complexion. Whoever takes up the said Servants, and secures them in any County Goal, or brings them to John Leacock, or to Pool Forge, shall have Forty Shillings for each, and reasonable Charges
   paid, by John Leacock.
The Pennsylvania Gazette, From June 6, to June 13, 1734. See *The American Weekly Mercury*, From Thursday, May 30, to Thursday, June 6, 1734, and *The Pennsylvania Gazette*, From September 12, to September 19, 1734. Lea/Lee.

RUN away, the 16th of this Instant *June*, from *Robert Chalfin* of *Birmingham* in *Chester*-County, a Servant Man named *Edward Hemphill*, of middle Stature, thick set, swarthy Complexion and short black Hair, he has several blue Spots on one of his Hands, he had on a dark colour'd Cloath Coat with

Brass Buttons, a blue Jacket with Horn Buttons, Leather Breeches with Brass Buttons, course Linnen Leggings, good Shoes, a pretty good Felt Hat and a good course Shirt. Whoever takes up the said Servant and secures him so that his Master may have him again, shall have *Twenty Shillings* as a Reward and all reasonable Charges, paid by *Robert Chalfin*.

The American Weekly Mercury, From Thursday, June 13, to Thursday, June 20, 1734.

June 27. 1734.

RUN away, last Sunday Night from the Sloop *Union*, *Robert M'Cullock* Master, a Servant Man named *James Bennerman*, of low Stature and round Shoulder'd, has short brown Hair, and talks broad Scotch; he was cloath'd, when he went away, with an Ozenbrigs Frock and Trowsers, and a pair of Shoes ty'd with Rope-Yarns. Whoever secures him so that he may be had again, or brings him to Mr. *Andrew Bradford*, Post-Master, in *Philadelphia*, shall have *Thirty Shillings* Reward and reasonable Charges,
        paid by   *John Inglis.*

The American Weekly Mercury, From Thursday, June 20, to Thursday, June 27, 1734.

RUN away Yesterday Morning from Samuel Hale of this City Potter, a Servant Man named *Edward Pain*, about 26 Years of Age, of middle Stature, walks very upright with a lively Look; the Letters E.P. are marked below his Thumb, with blue, and the Effigies of Christ on the Cross in the same Colour on the Inside of his Arm, no Hair, but wears a Cap or a new light colour'd Wig, he is a Potter by Trade, and pretends to be a Sailor. He had on a new Castor Hat, a reddish colour'd Kersey Coat new made, Fly fashion, good Leather Breeches, two new fine Shirts, and new Shoes and Stockings. Whoever secures the said Servant so that his Master may have him again, shall have *Five Pounds* Reward, and reasonable Charges
        paid, by   *Samuel Hale. Philadel. June* 14, 1734.

The Pennsylvania Gazette, From June 13, to June 20, 1734; From June 20, to June 27, 1734; From June 27, to July 4, 1734; From July 4, 1734, to July 11, 1734; From July 11, to July 18, 1734; July 18, to July 25, 1734; From July 25, to August 1, 1734. See *The New-York Weekly Journal*, July 1, 1734.

RUN away the 18th Instant, from *Owen Owen* of this City, a Servant Lad named *James Roe*, about 18 Years of Age, born in *Dublin*, short Stature, well set, fresh Complexion; took with him two Coats, several Jackets, Drawers

and Shirts, and sundry other things besides; he is suppos'd to wear a whitish Fustian Coat with frosted Buttons, and strip'd Jacket and Breeches.
Whoever takes up and secures the said Servant, so that his Master may have him again, shall have *Forty Shillings* Reward, and reasonable Charges paid, *by Owen Owen.*

The Pennsylvania Gazette, From June 13, to June 20, 1734; June 27, 1734. See *The Pennsylvania Gazette*, From September 12, to September 19, 1734.

RUN away on *Friday* Night last from *Anthony Wilkinson* of this City, Carver, a Servant Man named *John Nicholson*, about 27 Years of Age, of middle Stature, short brown Hair, swarthy Complexion, thin jaw'd, and the End of his Nose very red. He had on a thick grey Kersey Pea Jacket lin'd with red Shaloon, a pair of new Trowsers, an old Castor Hat, no Stockings, and old Shoes which had been new soal'd: He pretends to be a Chair carver, and can speak a little *Indian*, having lived a Twelve month among those People.

Whoever secures the said Servant so that his Master may have him again, shall have *Three Pounds* Reward, and reasonable Charges paid, by Anthony Wilkinson. Philadel. June 17. 1734.

The Pennsylvania Gazette, From June 13, to June 20, 1734; From June 20, to June 27, 1734; From June 27, to July 4, 1734; From July 11, to July 18, 1734; From July 18, to July 25, 1734; From July 25, to August 1, 1734.

RUN away the 14th of *June*, from *Samuel Hale*, of the City of *Philadelphia*, Potter, a Servant Man, named *Edward Pain*, about 26 Years of Age, is of a middle Stature, walks very upright, with a lively Look. He is Marked on the out-side of His Hand (between his Thumb and Fore-finger) with the Letters E. P. in blue, and the Effigies of Christ on the Cross on the inside of his Arm, in the same Colour. His Hair is cut off, and he wears a Cap, and sometimes a light coloured Wig. He has a new Castor Hat, a New reddish colour'd Kersey Coat, made Fly-Fashion, good Leather Breeches, two New fine Shirts, and New Shoes and Stockings. He is a Potter by Trade, and pretends to be a Sailor.

Whoever takes up the said Servant Man, and secures him, so that his Master may have him again, shall have *Five Pounds* as a Reward, and all Reasonable Charges paid, by *Samuel Hale.*

When taken up, give Notice to his Master in *Philadelphia*, or to *William Bradford* or *John Peter Zenger*, in *New-York.*

The New-York Weekly Journal, July 1, 1734. See *The Pennsylvania Gazette*, From June 13, to June 20, 1734.

R*UN* away June 27, from George Aston *of the Township of* East-Caln *and County of* Chester, *and Province of* Pennsylvania, *the following Servants, viz.*

James Cavenaugh, *an Irishman, a middle siz'd Man, fresh coloured, the Skin grows over the corner of one of his Eyes next to his Nose.* Thomas Wiltshire, *an Englishman, of short Stature, thin Beard, and swarthy complexion; by Trade a Sadler, and has working Tools with him, and Buck skin cut for a Woman's Saddle.* Josiah Coasher, *an hired Man, tall, thin and spare, of a swarthy complexion, New England born. They have taken away with them five fine Shirts with four Buttons and four Button holes on the collar of each Shirt; and five muslin Stocks made to buckle; two striped Jackets and three pair of Breeches all lined; three pair of white thread Stockings, and a pair of very good worsted Stockings; two muslin Handkerchiefs, and a red silk One striped round the Edges; and a dark coloured Kersey Coat, with brass Buttons, and two felt Hats with a new ozenbrigs Wallet. Whoever apprehends and secures the said Servants so that they may be had again, shall have* Five Pounds *Reward, or Forty Shillings for either of them, with reasonable charges paid. Note, The two Servants* Thomas Wiltshire *and* James Cavenaugh *have some wearing Apparel of their own, but 'tis supposed they will wear some of the Above mentioned clothes, which they have feloniously taken, with sundry other valuable Goods too tedious to mention here.* George Aston.

The Pennsylvania Gazette, From June 27, to July 4, 1734; From July 4, to July 11, 1734; From July 11, to July 18, 1734; From July 18, to July 25, 1734; From July 25, to August 1, 1734. See *The American Weekly Mercury*, From Thursday July 25, to Thursday August 1, 1734.

Philadelphia, June 27. 1734.
RUN away from *George Aston* of the Township of *East Caln* and County of *Chester*, and Province of *Pennsylvania*, the following Servants, viz.

James Cavenaugh, an *Irishman*, a middle siz'd Man, fresh Coloured, the Skin grows over the Corner of one of his Eyes next to his Nose.

Thomas Wiltshire, an *Englishman*, of short Stature, thin Beard, and swarthy Complexion; by Trade a Saddler, and has Working Tools with him, and Buck-skin cut out for a Woman's Saddle.

Josiah Coasher, a hired Man, tall, thin and spare, of a sworthy Complection, *New-England* born.

They have taken away with them five fine Shirts with four Buttons and four Button-holes on the Collar of each Shirt; and five Muslin Stocks made to buckle; two striped Jackets and three pair of Breeches all lined; three pair of white thread Stockings, and a Pair of very good worsted Stockings; two Musling Handkerchiefs, and a red silk One striped round the Edges; and a dark colour'd Kersey Coat with Brass Buttons, and two Felt Hats, with a new large Ozenbrigs Wallet.

Whoever apprehends and secures the said Servants. so that they may be had again, shall have *Five Pounds* Reward, and reasonable Charges, or *Forty Shillings* for either of them, paid by me *George Aston*.

Note, That the two Servants *Thomas Wiltshire*, and *James Gavenaugh*, had some wearing Apparel of their own, but 'tis supposed they will wear some of the above-mentione'd Clothes, which they have feloniously taken, with some other valuable Goods to tedious to mention here.

The American Weekly Mercury, From Thursday July 25, to Thursday August 1, 1734; From Thursday August 15, to Thursday August 22, 1734. See *The Pennsylvania Gazette*, From June 27, to July 4, 1734.

RUN away from *Jacob Lightfoot* of *Chester*, a Man named b*William Davis*, a *Welchman*, speaks broken *English*, of sandy Complexion, he has his Hair, of middle Stature, he had a brown Coat, white Fustian Coat, an old Felt Hat, a pair of Leather Breeches, a pair of grey Stockings; he is very remarkable by his Teeth, which stand very much awry, some being longer than the rest, and also one Finger, broken formerly by a Cart; he is about 30 or 40 Years of Age, and pretends to be a great Miner. Whoever takes up the said Man and secures him so that he may be had again, or brings him to *Chester* Goal, shall have Five Pounds Reward, and reasonable Charges, paid by
Chester, Aug. 3. 1734.   *Jacob Lightfoot.*

The Pennsylvania Gazette, From August 1, to August 8, 1734; From August 8, to August 15, 1734; From August 22, to August 29, 1734.

*T*Aken up on Suspicion of being a Runaway, on the 23d of July past, and put into the Goal at *Burlington*, one **Robert Oldham** *(as he tells his Name) about 17 or 18 Years of Age; he says he served his Time with one* **Charles Gross** *near Justice* Gatchel's *in* Nottingham, *Chester County, and has been about 7 Years in the Country. He had with him a brown home-spun Coat with brass Buttons, a striped homespun Linnen Jacket, ozenbrigs Trowsers, black Yarn Stockings and strong Shoes. He is of low Stature, slender Body, brown Hair, and pale Complexion.*

The Pennsylvania Gazette, From August 1, to August 8, 1734; From August 22, to August 29, 1734.

RUN away from **Pool Forge** *on the 9th Inst. a Servant Man named* **Anthony Lea**, *tall and slender, being bandy-kneed his Knees meet as he walks, aged about 20 years, born in Lancashire, a lively look'd Fellow, talks a little West*

Country, and is very sawcey. Had on when he went away a dark-colour'd fine broadcloth second hand Coat fashionably made, two ozenbrig Shirts and some speckled ones, an old blue great Coat, a good felt hat, bluish worsted Stockings and pretty good Shoes. He went in Company with a young lusty Woman named Elizabeth, *of a dark swarthy Complexion, speaks good English and Dutch, she had on a brown dutch Jacket or two, a striped linen Gown, a linsey wolsey Petticoat fill'd in with black Wooll. Whoever secures the said Servant and brings him to* John Leacock *at* Pool Forge *or at* Philadelphia, *or puts him in any County Goal, and gives Notice so that he may be had again, shall have* Forty Shillings *Reward and reasonable Charges, paid by* John Leacock.

The Pennsylvania Gazette, From September 5, to September 12, 1734; September 19, 1734. See The American Weekly Mercury, From Thursday, May 30, to Thursday, June 6, 1734, and The Pennsylvania Gazette, June 6, 1734, for Lea/Lee.

RUN away from *Thomas Dunning*, at the George-Inn, in Second-Street, *the 15th Instant, a Servant Man, named* Richard Ashton, *well set, about 25 Years of Age, of a sandy Complexion (without Hair) had on, a pair of round Toe'd Shoes, the Soles of English bend Leather, an Ozenbrigs Coat with Brass Buttons, a pair of Buckskin Breeches. Whoever shall secure him in any Goal, shall have Five Pounds Reward, and reasonable Charges, paid by* Tho. Dunning.

N. B. He has with him Five Pistoles, a Half Moidore, and a considerable Sum of English Coin.

The Pennsylvania Gazette, From September 19, to September 25, 1734; From September 25, to October 3, 1734; From October 3, to October 10, 1734; From October 10, to October 17, 1734. See The American Weekly Mercury, From Thursday September 19, to Thursday September 26, 1734.

RUN *away Yesterday Afternoon, the two following Servant Lads, viz. From* Owen Owen, *one named* James Roe *(Dublin born) of short stature, well set, his Hair off. Took with him several Coats, Jackets, shirts and breeches, is supposed to wear a Fustian Coat with yellowish frosted Buttons, and striped Jacket and Drawers; has with him besides, an old brown Coat and Leather Breeches. From* Thomas Stapleford, *Joiner, a Lad named* Joseph Land, *about 18 Years old, of short stature, swarthy complexion, thick Lips, his Hair off, and has several Wiggs, with a light colour'd Great Coat, a light colour'd Camlet Coat, a Duroy Coat, a striped Linnen Jacket, Leather Breeches, and new Shoes.*

Whoever secures the said Servants, so that their Masters may have them again, shall have Forty Shillings Reward for each, and reasonable Charges, paid by Owen Owen, Tho. Stapleford. Phila. Sept. 17. 1734.

The Pennsylvania Gazette, From September 12, to September 19, 1734; September 25, 1734. See The Pennsylvania Gazette, From June 13, to June 20, 1734, for Roe.

RUN away, the 15th of this Inst. *Sept.* from *Thomas Dunning* at the *George-Inn* in *Second* street a Servant Man named *Richard Ashton*, about 25 Years of age, well set, of a sandy Complexion, without Hair, had on a pair of round Toe'd Shoes the Soals of English bend Leather, an Ozenbriggs Coat with Brass Buttons, and a pair of Buckskin Breeches. Whoever shall secure him in any Goal, shall have *Five Pounds* Reward, and all reasonable Charges,
paid by   *Thomas Dunning.*
N. B. He has with him five Pistoles, a half Moidore & a considerable Sum of English Silver Coin.

The American Weekly Mercury, From Thursday September 19, to Thursday September 26, 1734; From Thursday October 24, to Thursday October 31, 1734. See The Pennsylvania Gazette, From September 19, to September 25, 1734.

RUN away, the 6th of this Instant *September*, from *James Moyes* of *Philadelphia*, Rope-maker, a Servant Man named *William Garwood*, aged about 19 Years, tall of Stature, indifferent square in the Shoulders, short black Hair, black full Eyes, he has a Scar on his right Cheek from his Nose downwards, had on when he went away a dark brown Drab Coat bound with black Quality, he had besides a new Drugget Coat of a brown Cinnamon collour, a striped Holland Jacket and Breeches, black Stockings, good Shoes, a good Hat, a red spotted Handkerchief, a Garlix Shirt, he also took with him an Ozenbrigs Coat, two white and three Ozenbrigs Shirts, one new, and two striped Holland Jackets Whoever shall take him up so that he may be had again, shall have *Three Pound* as a Reward, paid by me   *James Moyes.*

The American Weekly Mercury, From Thursday September 12, to Thursday September 19, 1734; From Thursday September 19, to Thursday September 26, 1734; From Thursday September 26, to Thursday October 3, 1734; From Thursday October 10, to Thursday October 17, 1734.

R*UN away the First of this Instant at Night, from Capt.* Christopher Postgate, *a Servant Lad named* Thomas M'Callon, *about* 19 *Years of age, by Trade a*

Taylor, short Stature, his own brown Hair. Had on a dark Suit of Frize, a Felt Hat, dark Yarn Stockings. Whosoever takes up and secures the said Servant Lad, and gives Notice to his aforesaid Master, or Mr. Mackay, shall have Twenty Shillings *Reward, and Reasonable Cha*rges. C. Postgate.

The Pennsylvania Gazette, From September 25, to October 3, 1734; From October 3, to October 10, 1734; From October 17, to October 24, 1734; From October 24, to October 31, 1734.

RUN away, the 13th of this Inst. *Octob.* from *John Bringhurst* of *Philadelphia,* a Servant Man named *John Doyle*, an Irishman, aged about 22 Years, a short thick budge Fellow, of a fresh Complexion; had on a Suit of dark Irish Frize, close sleev'd Coat, old Hat, a light colour'd Wigg, Thread Stockings and new Shoes. He had also with him an old brown Camblet Coat, a pair of Leather Breeches and several good Shirts By Trade a Cooper. He pretends to be a Scholar, and writes a good hand. Whoever secures the said Runaway so that he be had again, shall be well rewarded by *John Bringhurst.*

The American Weekly Mercury, From Thursday October 17, to Thursday October 24, 1734; From Thursday October 24, to Thursday October 31, 1734; From Thursday October 31, to Thursday November 7, 1734; From Thursday November 7, to Thursday November 14, 1734.

RUN away from *Robert Buchanan,* Esq; High Sheriff of *Lancaster* County in the Province of *Pennsylvania,* one *Leonard Milburn,* a Carpenter and Joyner by Trade, aged about 38 or 40 Years , his Hair cut off, his Beard of a sandy colour, walks with his Knees bending in and his Ancle Joints bending out, had an a [sic] light coloured Fustian Coat with Mettle Buttons, and a brown coloured linsey-woolsey Jacket. Whoever secures the said *Milburn* in any Goal, and sends Word to *Andrew Bradford* in *Philadelphia,* or to the said Sheriff, so that he may be had again, shall have Forty Shillings as a Reward and all reasonable Charges, paid by *Robert Buchanan,* Sheriff.

The American Weekly Mercury, From Thursday October 17, to Thursday October 24, 1734; From Thursday October 24, to Thursday October 31, 1734.

Philadelphia, Octo. 14 1734.

RAN-away from *Joseph Lyn* Shipwright *of Philadelphia, about* 3 *years past, a servant man named* Paul Raulisson, *a sawyer by Trade, about* 33 *Years of Age, he wore his own strait black Hair, tall of Stature, white Looks. He had on when he went away, a good suit of black broad cloth full trim'd, good white shirt, good shoes and stockings, good Hatt; he is supposed to be in New England and it is thought that is Wife is with him, her Name is* Sarah,

she worn a Green Calliminco Gown, flour'd with white. Whoever takes up the said servant and secures him so that his Master may have him again, shall have Five Pounds *Boston Money Reward, and reasonable charges paid by,   Messrs.* John *and* Joseph Gooch, *in* Boston.
The Boston Gazette, From December 2, to December 9, 1734.

RUN away the 11*th Day of* November *past from* Rees Pritchard *of* Whiteland, Chester *County, an* Irish *Servant Man named* Lawrence Keron, *aged about* 22 *Years, well set Man, freckled Complexion and mark'd with the Small-Pox, sandy curl'd Hair; brownish Cloth Coat, Buttons of the same, and Breeches of the same Cloth; Cotton and Linnen Shirt, blue and white mixt Yarn Stockings, and another Pair of light colour'd Yarn Stockings, footed with dark colour'd Yarn a good deal above the Shoe; an old Felt Hat, with a Piece cut out of the Brim, and cock'd up so as to hide it, wooden heel'd Shoes, and a Pair of old Shoes that have been mended and cover'd. Whoever takes up and secures the above mentioned Servant, so that his Master may have him again, shall have* Forty Shillings *Reward, and reasonable Charges paid by* Rees Prichard. N. B. *It is supposed he is gone towards* Maryland.

The Pennsylvania Gazette, From December 5, to December 12, 1734; From December 12, to December 19, 1734; From December 19, to December 26, 1734; From December 26, 1734, to January 2, 1735; From January 2, to January 9, 1735; From January 9, to January 16, 1735; From January 16, to January 23, 1735; From January 28, to February 4, 1735; From February 18, to February 25, 1735; From February 25, to March 4, 1735; From March 11, to March 20, 1735.

RUN away, the 15th of this Instant *December*, from his Master *William Peters* of *Ash* Town near *Concord* in *Chester* County, a Servant Man named *John Gryer*, of short Stature, well set and long Visag'd; he has a Scar on the lower part of his Cheek occasioned by the Kings Evil; he had on a dark gray Jacket and Breeches, a Felt Hat, Cap or Wigg, a speckled Shirt and Yarn Stockings; he has also a red and white striped Jacket. Whoever takes up the said Servant and secures him so that his Master may have him again, shall have *Thirty Shillings* Reward and reasonable Charges,
           paid by   *William Peters.*
The American Weekly Mercury, From Tuesday December 17, to Tuesday December 24, 1734; From Tuesday December 24, to Tuesday December 31, 1734; From Tuesday December 31, to Tuesday January 7, 1734-35; From Tuesday January 14, to Tuesday January 21, 1735.

1735

RUN away, the 2d of this Inst. *January*, from *Samuel Richey* of *Northampton* Township in *Buck*-County, [sic] a Covenanted Servant named *John Cary*, by Trade a Weaver, of middle Stature and well set, fair of Complexion and pretty much Pock-fretten, had on an old Felt Hat, a black Wool Wigg, a brown homespun Coat and Westcoat, a pair of Leather Breeches and a pair of dark gray Duroy Breeches, a pair of brown purple Yarn Stockings and a pair of Thread Stockings, three homspun Shirts, two Muslin Stocks mark'd S. R. and a pair of half-worn Leather Heel'd Shoes. Whoever takes up the said Fellow and Secures him so that he may be had again, shall have *Three Pou*nds Reward and all reasonable Charges, paid by me *Samuel Richey*.

The American Weekly Mercury, From Tuesday December 31, 1734, to Tuesday January 7, 1735; From Tuesday January 7, to Tuesday January 14, 1735; From Tuesday January 14, to Tuesday January 21, 1735.

WHereas one *Nathaniel M' Br*ide of *Marlborough* Township in *Chester* County, hath stole divers Good from *Nathaniel Jenkins*, Store-keeper , at *New-Garden*, in the said County, (with whom he work'd) and hath left those parts since the 10th or 11th of this Instant, he had on when he went away a suit of bright gray Duroy Cloaths with close round Cuffs to the Coat, a good fine Hat, a thin pair of sad colour Worsted Stockings, a new pair of thick Shoes with round Toes, with Brass Buckles not fellows, he also took with him a sute of lightish colour'd Kersey almost new, and Kersey great Coat, a new pair of Boots with striped Straps, he is about 23 or 24 Years of age, of middle Stature, straitish black Hair, dark Complexion, of a sober down look, speaking drollingly, walks stooping as tho' he followed the Plow, he is of no Trade but pretends to have skill in Horses, he came from the North of *Ireland* and hath been in this Country about 5 Years.

Whoever shall take up the said *M'Bride* and bring him to *Philadelphia*, or secure him so that he may be brought to Justice, and give Notice to the Printer hereof, shall have *Five Pounds* Reward and reasonable Charges, paid by me   *Nathaniel Jenkins*.   *Philadelphia, Jan*, 24. 1734.

N. B. He hath a Pass drawn and sign'd by one *Simon Hadly* a Justice in *New-Castle* County, dated in last *July or August*.

The American Weekly Mercury, From Tuesday January 21, to Tuesday January 28, 1735; From Tuesday January 28, to Tuesday February 4, 1735; From Tuesday February 4, to Tuesday February 11, 1735

RUN away the 10*th* of this Instant *Feb.* from *Lawrence Rennalds* a Servant Man named *Valentine Clark*, about 23 Years of age, he is tall and slender, Raw-Bon'd and of a fresh Colour, a long Visage and down look. he had on a white homespun Jacket, a dark Olive colour'd Cloath Jacket, also a brown Jacket with Brass Buttons, a good Beaver Hat, a speckled Shirt, a new homespun Shirt and an Ozenbrigs Shirt, grey Worsted Stockings and a pair of good Buckskin Breeches with Brass Buttons.

Whoever takes up and secures the said Servant so that his Master may have him again, shall have *Three Pounds* as a Reward and reasonable Charges, paid by   *L. Rennalds.*

The American Weekly Mercury, From Tuesday February 4, to Tuesday February 11, 1735. See *The Pennsylvania Gazette*, From Thursday, July 8, to Thursday, July 15, 1736.

RUN away, the 4th of this Inst. *February*, from *John Hyatt* of *Philadelphia*, a Servant Man named *James Ridsley*, of middle size, about 25 Years of age, with short black curl'd Hair, fair Complexion and smooth Fac'd. Had on a good light colour'd fine Duroy Coat with several large greasy Spots on the Back, a lightish colour'd good Broad Cloath Jacket, a pair of black Leather Breeches, with Pewter Buttons cover'd with black Leather, an Ozenbrigs Shirt and good strong Shoes old Hoase. He is a Brass-Founder by Trade and speaks good English. Whoever secures the said Servant and give Notice thereof to his Master, so that he be had again, shall have *Forty Shillings* Reward and reasonable Charges.

RUN away, the 4th of this Instant *Feb.* from *Francis Richardson* of *Philadelphia*, Gold-smith, an Apprentice Lad named *Isaac Marceloe*, born in *London* but of French Extraction which may be discovered by his speech, of short Stature and thin Visage, limps in his gate as if he had been Lame. He was formerly Apprentice to *William Heurtin*, Gold-smith, in *New-York*. Had on when he went away, a grey Cloath Coat which had been his Masters and was turn'd for him, a brown Cloath Jacket with most of the Buttons off, a pair of Plush Breeches with Horn Buttons turn'd round and tip'd with Silver, a thick pair of mil'd grey Stockings and a pair of old Shoes worn thro', he has a light Wigg and a Cap with him. Whoever takes up and secures the said Lad so that his Master may have him again, shall have *Thirty Shillings* as a Reward and reasonable Charges, paid by me *Francis Richardson.*
N. B. 'Tis suppose the above Runaways are in Company.

The American Weekly Mercury, From Tuesday February 4, to Tuesday February 11, 1735; From Tuesday February 11, to Tuesday February 18, 1735; From Tuesday February 18, to Tuesday February 25, 1735; From Tuesday February 25, to Tuesday March 4, 1735; From Thursday March 20, to Thursday March 27, 1735. The last ad amends the final line to conclude with "and gone towards *Maryland* or *Virginia*." See *The American Weekly Mercury*, From Thursday, December 22, to Thursday December 29, 1733, for Ridsley/Rigley

RUN away, the 23d of this Inst. *Febr.* from their Masters *Samuel Parr* and *William Moode*, two Servant Men, the one named *Robert Reney*, about 21 Years of age, of short Stature, long sandy colour'd Hair, pail of Complexion, an *Irish*-man, had on when he went away a good suit of blue gray Cloath, Worsted Stockings of the same colour and a pair of yarn Stockings, a Beaver Hat half worn, 2 white Shirts and white mettle Buckles in his Shoes. The other named *Henry Yawes*, short of Stature, short black Hair and a blackish Complexion, a pouch Mouth and full Eyes with a wild look, aged about 21 years, he had on when he went away a brown Pea Jacket, an old Hat, a striped Flanell Jacket, 2 striped Shirts and several white ones, a pair of Breeches and Trowsers over them, gray yarn Stockings and 2 odd Buckles in his Shoes the one large Steel the other Bath Mettle.

Whoever takes up and secures the said Servants or either of them so that their Masters may have them again, if taken within 10 Miles of Philadelphia, shall have *Twenty Shillings* for each, if farther *Three Pounds*, as a Reward and all reasonable Charges.

N. B. One of them has a Pocket Compass, and they may have changed their Cloaths.

The American Weekly Mercury, From Tuesday February 18, to Tuesday February 25, 1735.

RUN *away the* 11*th Instant from* Evan Price *in* Robinson *Township in* Lancaster *County, a* New-England *Servant Lad, named* John Patridge, *tall and slim, about* 17 *Years of Age, short black Hair, Pockfretten; with a Pea-Jacket, mill'd Cap, old Hat, is something of a Sailor, and pretends to talk French. He took a Gun with him. Whoever secures him, so that he may be had again, shall have* Forty Shillings *Reward, and reasonable Charges paid by* Evan Price.

The Pennsylvania Gazette, From March 4, to March 11; 1735; From March 11, to March 20, 1735; From March 20, to March 27, 1735; From March 27, to April 3, 1735; From April 24, to May 1, 1735; From May 1, to May 8, 1735.

STOLEN *away last Night from* William Herbert, *a small Bay Horse, suspected to be taken by one* John Mitchel *who sold him but a few Hours before; He is a Man of middle Stature, wears a yellowish or brownish Coat,*

a flaxen Wig or a Cap, no Shoes but sharp-toed Boots, a large Scar under his Cheek in his Neck; He has a good Horse besides, which he rides on, and 'tis thought a young Welch Woman he has with him rides on the stolen Horse above-mentioned. Whoever secures the said Mitchel, *and the Horse, so that the Owner may have him again, shall have* Forty Shillings *Reward and reasonable Charges paid. And about a Week since, the said* Herbert *hired a sorrel Horse with a white Face, to a young Man, a Gingerbread Baker, to go to* Bristol, *and the Horse is not yet returned: Whoever brings the said Horse home again, shall have* Twenty Shillings *Reward, paid by*
Philad. March 20. 1734-5   William Herbert.

The Pennsylvania Gazette, From March 11, to March 20, 1735; From March 20, to March 27, 1735; From March 27, to April 3, 1735; From April 3, to April 10, 1735; From April 17, to April 24, 1735; From April 24, to May 1, 1735; From May 1, to May 8, 1735.

RUN away, the 25th of last *March*, from *William Wright* of *Conestoga* in *Lancaster* County in *Pennsylvania*, a Servant Man named *Anthony Garrad*, an Englishman, pretty tall of Stature but slender, much scarified with the Small-Pox, of redish Complexion and walks with his Toes inward, about 37 Years of age; he had on when he went away a Beaver Hat half wore, a yellow Cap or Wigg, a homespun brown Cloath Coat newly turned with Brass Buttons, a light gray Cloath Jacket much wore with Brass Buttons, a pair of Buckskin Breeches about half worn with Brass Buttons, a pair of homespun Yarn Stockings almost black and a pair of old Shoes. He hath stolen a considerable quantity of Silver and Gold Mill'd Money, Guineas, and Crown Pieces, and same [sic] other Gold, also a Watch with a Tortois-shell Case studded with Silver, the inside Case Silver, a Steel Key but no Chain. Whoever secures the said Man so that he may be brought to Justice, shall have Forty Shillings Reward and reasonable Charges,
             paid by me   William Wright.

The American Weekly Mercury, From Thursday April 3, to Thursday April 10, 1735.

RUN away, the 25th of this Inst. *May*, from *Edward Horne's* Plantation, in the Northern Liberties of *Philadelphia*, a Servant Man named *John Matthews*, of a sandy Complexion and down look, a strong well-set Fellow, about 23 Years of age, had a short light Wig, a good Felt Hat, a homespun gray Cloth Coat which hath been let out at both the sides, a blue pair of course Cloth Breeches, two pair of homespun Stockings one gray the other brown, a good pair of Shoes the grain outward and large Buckles, took with him a thick Leather Jacket with Brass Buttons and lined with blue; pretends he is a

Maltster and can comb Wool. Whoever secures the said Servant so that his Master may have him again, shall have *Forty Shillings* Reward and reasonable Charges paid by   *Edw. Horne.*
    The American Weekly Mercury, From Thursday May 22, to Thursday May 29, 1735.

RUN away the 16th *of this Instant from* Armstrong Smith, *Shipwright, a Servant Man named* David Steadman, *an Irishman, very tall, with dark or black Hair, about* 35 *Years of age; had on when he went away a new Ozenbrigs Shirt, old Trousers, a dirty old Duck Linnen Coat with mettal Buttons, and old grey yarn Stockings patcht with blue, an old Hat and old Shoes. Whoever takes up and secures the said Servants, shall have* Twenty Shillings *Reward and reasonable Charges, paid by*   Armstrong Smith.
    The Pennsylvania Gazette, From May 15, to May 22, 1735; From May 22, to May 29, 1735

RUN away on the 23d Instant from the Widow Ann Amos *at* Poqueston, *a welsh Servant Man named* Thomas Roberts, *he is marked on his right Hand with the Letters T. R. about* 22 *Years of Age, had short curl'd brown Hair, but perhaps has cut it off since he went away, is round visag'd, full-faced, and fresh colour'd, has wide Nostrils and small grey Eyes, is pretty tall and slim, speaks good English and Irish, is much addicted to Liquor, sings well, and sometimes alters his Voice like a Woman. He had on when he went away a blue grey broadcloth Coat, it has been turn'd and very few Plaits in the Sides; an old fine white Shirt, fine homespun Linnen Jacket which being too big for him is took up in the Sides and Back, coarse homespun Trowsers, brown woollen Stockings, round toed Shoes, brass Buckles and has took an Ax with him. 'Tis supposed he is gone towards* York. *Whoever takes up and secures the said Servant so that he may be had again, shall have* Forty Shillings *Reward and reasonable Charges paid by*   Ann Amos.
    The Pennsylvania Gazette, From June 26, to July 3, 1735; From July 3, to July 10, 1735; From July 10, to July 17, 1735; From July 17, to July 24, 1735. The third ad has " *June* 26, 1735." at the bottom.

RUN away, the 27th of *July,* from *Roger Ball* of *Darby* in *Chester* County, *Pennsylvania,* an Irish Servant Lad named *William Rowlands,* about 17 Years of age, small of Stature, thin Visag'd, full Ey'd & Pock-fretten, and black Hair lately cut off; had on a brown Jacket, grey Cloth Breeches, brown Stockings, new Shoes and pretty good Hat. Whoever takes up and secures the said

Servant so that his Master may have him again, shall have *Thirty Shillings* as a Reward, and reasonable Charges, paid by   *Roger Ball.*

The American Weekly Mercury, From Thursday July 24, to Thursday July 31, 1735; From Thursday July 31, to Thursday August 7, 1735; From Thursday August 7, to Thursday August 14, 1735.

RUN away, the 21st of *July,* from *John Hannum* of *Concord* in *Chester* County, a Servant Man named *Josiah Coger, New-England* born, a tall slender Fellow, of a swarthy Complexion and short brown Hair and red Beard, his Teeth pretty much gone before, he had on when he went away an old Beaver Hat the Brims cut narrow, a grey Jacket with carved Pewter Buttons, Tow-Cloath Trowsers and old Shoes. He has a Scar in one of his Legs by a Bullet received in the Indian War. Whoever takes up and secures the said Servant so that his Master may have him again, shall have *Three Pounds* as a Reward, paid by   *John Hannum.*

The American Weekly Mercury, From Thursday July 24, to Thursday July 31, 1735; From Thursday July 31, to Thursday August 7, 1735; From Thursday August 7, to Thursday August 14, 1735.

RUN away the 24th of *July*, 1735, a Servant Man named *David Brown*, came from *Scotland*, about 25 Years old, lusty and well set, had on a white flourished quilted Cap, a light coloured Cloath Coat, a white Fustian Wastcoat and a pair of Oznabrig Trousers, he is very apt to be in Liquor and then appears like a Mad Man and pretends Relation to the Duke of Argyl.

Whoever secures him and gives Notice to *Daniel Flexney* at *Philadelphia*, shall have reasonable Satisfaction for their Trouble.

The American Weekly Mercury, From Thursday July 31, to Thursday August 7, 1735.

R*UN away on the 4th Inst. from* Joseph Hargrave *at* Point Nopoint, *a servant Man named* William Ronane, *aged about 24 Years, of thin Visage, brown Complexion, middle Stature and slim. Had on when he went away, a striped worsted Cap, a brown Jacket with Metal Buttons, dark brown Kersey Breeches, light grey yarn Stockings, and good Shoes. 'Tis suppos'd he is gone towards Conestogoe. Whoever secures the said Servant so that he may he had again, shall have* Forty Shillings Reward, *and reasonable Charges paid, by*   Joseph Hargrave.

The Pennsylvania Gazette, From July 31, to August 7, 1735; From August 7, to August 14, 1735; From August 14, to August 21, 1735;

From August 28, to September 4, 1735; From September 4, to September 11, 1735; From September 11, to September 18, 1735.

R*UN away the 3d of this Inst. from* Joseph Burleigh, *at the Sign of the* Crown *in* New-Bristol, *a servant Man named* Robert Hambleton, *about* 21 *Years of Age, no Hair, pale Complection, walks heavy; had on when he went away, an old Pea Jacket lin'd with blue, and a speckled Shirt, ozenbrigs Trowsers, pretty good Shoes, took with him a drab coloured Pea Jacket, one check'd Shirt, and one ozenbrigs; was formerly a servant to* John Elfreth *Shipwright in* Philadelphia. *Whoever takes up the said Servant so that he may be had again, shall have* Three Pounds *Reward and reasonable Charges paid by* Joseph Burleigh.

The Pennsylvania Gazette, From July 31, to August 7, 1735; August 14, 1735.

RAN-away the 12th of this Instant *August,* from *Alexander Crukshank* of the City of *Philadelphia,* Shoe-maker, a Servant named *William Forest,* a short Fellow, sandy Complection, and short curl'd Hair; had on when he went away, a light colour'd Kersey Coat, striped Flanel Wastcoat, Leather Breeches, dark Stockings, old Shoes, a good Hat, and two Shirts, one white the other check'd. Any Person that secures the said Servant so that his Master may have him again, shall have *Forty Shillings* Reward and reasonable Charges, paid by   Alex. Crukshank.   August 21.

The American Weekly Mercury, From Thursday August 14, to Thursday August 21, 1735.

STOLEN from *James Claypoole,* a large roan Horse with a trimmed Mane, short switch Tail, branded with **I C** on the near Buttock, and shod all round: supposed to be taken by a Person that had a Pass granted him in this City by the Name of *John Hopkins,* a lusty Irish Man, and was seen the same Day going up *Wisahickan* Road, and is gone towards *Potowmock.* Whoever secures the said Man and Horse, shall have *Three Pounds* Reward, or *Forty Shillings* for the Horse only, and reasonable Charges
             paid by   James Claypoole.

The Pennsylvania Gazette, From August 21, to August 28, 1735.

RAN-away on the 29th of *August* last, from his Master *James Shields* of *West-Bradford* in *Chester-*County, a *Devonshire* Servant Man named *Samuel Hooper,* a woollen Weaver by Trade; he is about 23 Years of age, pretty small

Stature, and of a swarthy Complexion; he has a long sharp Nose, black Eyebrows, and black bushy Hair; when he speaks he cuts short his Words: He had on when he went away, a narrow brimm'd Felt Hat, an old snuff colour'd Drugget Coat full Trimm'd, striped Flanel Jacket, grey Kersey Breeches lin'd with Linen, coarse Linen Shirt without shoulder straps, grey yarn Stockings, and old Shoes. He took a Dun Horse with him neither Branded nor Earmark'd.

Whoever shall take up said Servant and secures him so that his said Master may have him again, shall have *Twenty Shillings* Reward, and all reasonable Charges, Paid by   *James Shields.*

The American Weekly Mercury, From Thursday August 28, to Thursday September 4, 1735; From Thursday September 4, to Thursday September 11, 1735; From Thursday September 11, to Thursday September 18, 1735; From Thursday September 18, to Thursday September 25, 1735.

RAN-away on the 22*d* of *August* last, from *Joseph Cumly* of the Mannor of *Mooreland* in the County of *Philadelphia*, an Irish Servant Man named *Martin Farrell*, a pretty lusty Man, of a sandy Complexion; he has large grey Eyes, no Hair but wears a Cap; he had on a light colour'd Kersey Coat without Cuffs, and has Pewter Buttons with a flap over the Button holes, a pair of Trowsers and Drawers, homespun Shirt, good Stockings and Shoes, and a Castor Hat.

Whoever takes up the said Servant and brings him to *Philadelphia* Goal, shall have *Six Pounds* Reward, and all reasonable Charges,
          paid by   *Joseph Cumly.*

The American Weekly Mercury, From Thursday September 18, to Thursday September 25, 1735; From Thursday September 25, to Thursday October 2, 1735; From Thursday October 2, to Thursday October 9, 1735.

STOLEN out of the Shop of Marcus Kuhl *in* Market-Street, *a Piece of Calimanco with narrow Striped of red, green and blue, and two broad stripes of yellow: It was stolen by* John Fulks *and his Wife* Elizabeth, *who have since left this Place: He is a thin visaged Man, with dark brown strait Hair, wears a grey drugget Jacket and on old patch'd black Coat; and when he is dress'd, a white Garlick Jacket and Breeches, white Cotton Stockings, pretty good Shoes, and speaks thro' his Nose a little.* Elizabeth Fulks, *is a lusty fat Woman much Pockfretten, of red Complexion, has with her, a Callico Gown with a large running Sprig, of a pale purple and red, it is cuff'd and robed with Linnen, an old Bengal Gown of a light Mouse colour, cuff'd and robed*

with small spotted Callico, and old striped Calimanco quilted Petticoat, a short brown camlet cloak, faced down with a dirty colour'd Silk, and a new Gown made of the stolen Calimanco above mention'd, cuff'd and robed with green Persian, and tied down before with a broad green Ribband. Note, *They stole a Parcel of Handkerchiefs and other things, besides the Calimanco above mentioned. Whoever secures the said Persons in any Goal of this Province so that they may be brought to Justice, shall have* Forty Shillings Reward *and reasonable Charges paid by* Marcus Kuhl.
The Pennsylvania Gazette, From September 19, to September 25, 1734; From October 17, to October 24, 1734.

RAN-away on the 1*st* of *May* last, from *Ann Roberts* of the Township of *Nantmeal* in *Chester* County, an Irish Servant Man named *John Obrian*, alias *John Right*, about 24 Years of Age, of middling Stature. He pretends to be a Butcher. Had on a Felt Hat, a Cinamon colour'd Coat, a striped Jacket, an Oznabrigs Shirt, a pair of Purple Breeches, dark yarn Stockings, and strong Shoes. He has dark Hair.
Whoever takes up said Servant and Returns him to his said Mistress, or to *John Roberts* in Market-street, *Philadelphia*, shall have *Forty Shillings* Reward, and reasonable Charges, paid by *Ann Roberts.*
The American Weekly Mercury, From Thursday November 20, to Thursday November 27, 1735; From Thursday December 4, to Thursday December 11, 1735.

RAN-away on *Nov.* 15. at Night, from *George House*, an Irish Servant Man named *John Hendry*, aged about 22 Years, of middle Stature, no Hair but wears a Wig or a Cap; by Trade a Shoe-maker. Had an a brown Drugget Coat with close or slash Sleeves, striped Linen Jacket, and Leather Breeches, a narrow brimm'd Hat, good Shoes and grey Stockings; and has taken some Tools with him belonging to his Trade.
Whoever secures the said Servant, so that he may be had again, shall have *Five Pounds* Reward, and reasonable Charges,
paid by *George House.*
The American Weekly Mercury, From Thursday November 20, to Thursday November 27, 1735; From Thursday November 27, to Thursday December 4, 1735; From Thursday December 4, to Thursday December 11, 1735; From Thursday December 11, to Thursday December 18, 1735. See *The Pennsylvania Gazette*, From November 13, to November 20, 1735.

RUN away from *William Perkins*, a Servant Man named *William Ains*worth, about 29 Years of Age, black Complexion, black lank Hair and black Eyes, middle siz'd and well set: Had on a dark brown Coat, full trimm'd, red striped woollen Jacket, and Leather Breeches, lead coloured woollen Stockings and good strong Shoes. Whoever secures the said Servant so that he may be had again, shall have *Twenty Shillings* Reward and reasonable Charges paid by *William Perkins*.

The Pennsylvania Gazette, From November 13, to November 20, 1735; From November 20, to November 27, 1735; From December 11, to December 18, 1735; From December 18, to December 24, 1735; From December 24, to December 30, 1735; From December 30, 1735, to January 6, 1736; From January 6, to January 15, 1736.

RUN away last Sunday Night from *George House*, an Irish Servant Man named *John Hendry*, aged about 22 years, of Middle Stature, no hair but wears a cap; by trade a Shoemaker. Had an a brown Drugget Coat with close Sleeves, and Leather Breeches, a narrow brimm'd Hat, good Shoes and Stockings; and has taken some Tools belonging to his Trade. Whoever secures the said Servant so that he may be had again, shall have *Five Pounds* Reward and reasonable Charges by *George House*.

The Pennsylvania Gazette, From November 13, to November 20, 1735; From November 20, to November 27, 1735; From November 27, to December 4, 1735. See *The American Weekly Mercury*, From Thursday November 20, to Thursday November 27, 1735; From December 4, to December 11, 1735; From December 11, to December 18, 1735; From December 18, to December 24, 1735.

RUN away the 9th Inst. from *James Norrel* of *Oley* in this County, an hired Servant Man named *John Blowden*, well set, of short Stature, black Hair, fair Complexion, and has a smooth Tongue. He has taken with him belonging to his Master, a black Horse branded with I N on the near Shoulder, a small Star like a Clover Leaf, and not dock'd, about 9 Years old: Like wife belonging to his Master, a homespun Kearsey great Coat clothcolour'd with large Brass Buttons on it, a new pair of brown Yarn Stockings, two new pairs of shoes, one of Mens, and the other Womens, a pewter Pocket Bottle that will hold a Pint, a pair of Silver Buttons, and some Money. He had also a homespun

Camlet inside Coat of Cinnamon-colour patch'd, and a black Caliminco Jacket and Breeches, a Pair of striped linnen trowsers, and a Pair of old Shoes picked-toed, white Linnen Stockings, white Linnen Cap, a Caroline Hat. He was formerly servant to *Arthur Wells* and afterwards, to *William Smith* both of this city, and often ran away from them both. He pretends to be a doctor, sometimes a Gentleman or a Merchant, and endeavours to cheat all he comes acquainted with. Whoever secures him in any Goal, so that his Master may have Justice from him, and secures the Horse so that he may be had again, shall have *Three Pounds* Reward and reasonable Charges

    paid by *James Norrel. Philad. Nov.* 20.

The Pennsylvania Gazette, From November 13, to November 20, 1735; From November 20, to November 27, 1735; From December 4, to December 11, 1735; From December 11, to December 18, 1735; From December 18, to December 24, 1735; From December 24, to December 30, 1735; From December 30, 1735, to January 6, 1736; From January 6, to January 15, 1736. See *The American Weekly Mercury*, From Thursday July 3, to Thursday July 10, 1729; *The Pennsylvania Gazette*, From March 4, to March 11, 1731; *The American Weekly Mercury*, From Tuesday March 13, to Tuesday March 20, 1733; *The Pennsylvania Gazette*, From March 8, to March 15, 1733; *The American Weekly Mercury*, From Thursday October 4, to Thursday October 11, 1733, *The Pennsylvania Gazette*, From September 28, to October 11, 1733, and *The Pennsylvania Gazette*, January 29, 1741.

RAN-away the 10*th* of *May* last, from *John Powel* of *Lancaster*, an Irish Servant Man named *James Kavanaugh*, about 25 Years of Age, of middling Stature, and redish Complexion; he has a Scar under one of his Eyes. His Apparel uncertain.

He was formerly a Servant to *Joseph Stone* of *Lancaster*.

Whoever takes up and secures the said Servant so that his Master may have him again, shall have *Forty Shillings* as a Reward, and reasonable Charges, paid by me *John Powel.*

The American Weekly Mercury, From Thursday December 11, to Thursday December 18, 1735; From Thursday December 18, to Tuesday December 23, 1735; From Tuesday December 23, to Tuesday December 30, 1735.

RUN away on the 12th Inst. from *James Mackey*, an *Irish* Servant Man named *William Crosbery*, alias *M'clauskey*, about 22 Years of Age, well set, and wears a pissburnt Wig, by Trade a Taylor: Had on a Coat, Jacket and Breeches of very ordinary coarse Kersey, and good Shoes and Stockings;

took with him an ozenbrigs Frock. Whoever secures the said Servant so that he may be had again, shall have *Twenty Shillings* Reward and reasonable Charges paid by   *James Mackey.*

The Pennsylvania Gazette, From December 11, to December 18, 1735; From December 18, to December 24, 1735; From December 24, to December 30, 1735; From December 30, 1735, to January 6, 1736; From January 6, to January 15, 1736; From January 15, to January 22, 1736.

1736

RAN-away (some time ago) from *Samuel Bethel* of the Town of *Lancaster,* an Irish Man called *John Hagget,* a Hatter by Trade, a short well set Fellow. He had on an old gray Coat, Leather Breeches, and white Stockings.

Whoever shall take up the said *John Hagget,* and bring him to *Lancaster-*Prison, shall have *Three Pounds* Reward, and all reasonable Charges paid by me   *Samuel Bethel.*

The American Weekly Mercury, From Tuesday January 13, to Tuesday January 20, 1736; From Tuesday January 20, to Tuesday January 27, 1736.

RAN-away on the 3d of *March,* Inst. from his Master *Richard Hughes,* Inn keeper at the Sign of the Three Tons in *Merion* in *Philadelphia* County, an Irish Servant Man, named *Edward Brown,* a Skinner and Glover by Trade, of a middle Stature, bottle-nos'd, and is about 44 Years of Age. He had on when he went away, a dark brown homespun Coat something too wide, a serge dove colour'd Wastcoat, and striped Flanel Jacket, two homespun Shirts, leather Breeches with brass Buttons, three pair of yarn Stockings, good old Shoes new tapp'd, with Bath-metal Buckles, a double worsted Cap, and half wore Felt Hat. Has short black Hair.

Whoever takes up the said Servant Man, and secures him so as his said Master may have him again, shall have *Thirty Shillings* Reward and reasonable Charges, paid by   *Richard Hughes.*

The American Weekly Mercury, From Tuesday March 2, to Tuesday March 9, 1736; From Tuesday March 9, to Tuesday March 16, 1736; From Tuesday March 16, to Tuesday March 23, 1736; From Tuesday March 23, to Tuesday April 1, 1736.

RUN away last Night from *Richard Baily* of this City, Weaver, a Servant Man named *Robert Perkinson,* aged about 30 Years, a likely Man, a smooth he went away a homepsun light grey Coat with Brass Buttons, and a light coloured fine Broad-cloth Coat, Cloth Breeches with Silver Buttons, and another Pair of blue, a new Pair of fashionable Calfskin Shoes, a Pair of Black and a Pair of blue grey Stockings, a Beaver Hat half worn.

Whoever takes up the said Servant and secures him, so that his Master may have him again, shall have *Forty Shillings* Reward and reasonable Charges paid by   Richard Baily. *Philad. March* 26. 1736,

The Pennsylvania Gazette, From April 1, to April 8, 1736; From April 22, to April 29, 1736; From April 29, to May 6, 1736; From May 6, to May 13, 1736.

RUN away on the 6th of May *from* Thomas Wynne, *of* Blockley *Township, a Servant Man named* Thomas Mc Coun, *born in* Dublin, *talks good English, aged about* 22 *Years, walks upright, short black Hair, old woollen Cap; his Hat cocked close, he says he is a Weaver by trade, and can draw Pictures of any kind very well. Had on a brown Broad cloth Coat trimmd with the same, an old Broad cloth Jacket with brass Buttons, a linnen one under it, Camblet Breeches, grey yarn Stockings, good Shoes: He took away with him a Gun and a brindle grey Spaniel Dog. Whoever secures the said Servant so that his Master may have him again, shall have* Forty Shillings *Reward and reasonable Charges paid by*   Thomas Wynne.

The Pennsylvania Gazette, From May 20, to May 27, 1736; From May 27, to June 3, 1736; From June 3, to June 10, 1736; From July 1, to July 8, 1736.

Pensilvania, *SS*.
A*Bsented from the Service of the Honourable the Proprietary on the* 18*th Instant. An Indented Servant Man, named* Tobias Shewen, *aged about* 23 *Years, of middle stature, brown Hair something curl'd, his Apparel was a good fine light-colour'd Kersey Coat, a brown mixt colour'd Drugget Jacket, a pair of Leather Breeches, gray worsted Stockings, a good Hat, good Linnen and Shoes. Whoever shall take up the said Servant, and bring him to the Subscriber, shall be well Rewarded for so doing.*
Philad. 22. 3 mo. 1736.   James Steel.
The Pennsylvania Gazette, From May 20, to May 27, 1736.

RUN away from Edmund Peers, *of* New-York, *a Servant Maid, named* Grissel Miller, *a Scotch Girl aged about* 20 *Years; had on when she went away, a black Crape Gown, and a quilted Petticoat, a Pair of blew Stockings white clocks, a new Pair of Shoes, she speaks broad Scotch, middle size, full*

breasted. *Whosoever takes her up and brings her to* Henry Hartley, *at the* Compass *and* Horse-Shoe, *in* Strawberry-Alley, Philadelphia, *shall have* Forty Shillings *Reward and reasonable Charges paid by* Henry Hartley.
    The Pennsylvania Gazette, From May 20, to May 27, 1736; From May 27, to June 3, 1736.

RUN away on *Sunday* last from *John Ingram*, Bricklayer, an English Servant Lad named *John Hall*, aged about 19 Years, of middle Stature, thin visage, much Pockfretten, no Hair. Had on an Ozenbrigs Jacket, a pair of Diaper Breeches lind with checkd Linnen, an Ozenbrigs Shirt, thread Stockings and old Shoes, a good Silk Handkerchief about his Neck, an old Beaver Hat. Whosoever takes up and secures the said Servant so that his Master may have him again, shall have *Twenty Shillings* Reward and reasonable Charges paid by   John Ingram.
    The Pennsylvania Gazette, From May 27, to June 3, 1736; From June 3, to June 10, 1736

STOLEN on Monday Night last, from *Hugh Flanagan* living near *Wall-kills* about 25 Miles from *Esopes*, but was stolen near *Prince-Town, Somerset* County, in *New-Jersey*, a large coal-black Stallion, no white about him, his Mane hanging on both Sides, has a large Scar on his Shoulder, where he had a Fistula, no brand, shod before, is a natural Pacer. He was stolen by one *John Brown*, a lust [sic] well-set Fellow, with curled black Hair, red Face and pockbroken; had on a striped Jacket and Breeches, a Pair of Trowsers, brown close-bodied Coat, and a dark red great Coat with a double Cape, tied behind him. Whoever secures the said Man and Horse, shall have *Forty Shillings* Reward for both, and *Twenty Shillings* for the Horse alone, and reasonable Charges paid by   Hugh Flanagan.   *Philad. June*, 3. 1736.
    N. B. *The said* John Brown *pick'd one* Thomas M'Gee's *Pocket of* Nine Pounds One Shilling *at the House of* Owen Owen *in* Market Street, Philadelphia.
    The Pennsylvania Gazette, From May 27, to June 3, 1736; From June 3, to June 10, 1736; From June 10, to June 17, 1736; From June 17, to June 24, 1736; From July 15, to July 22, 1736.

RAN-away from *Nicholas Fred* of *Birmingham*, in *Chester* County, on the 14th of this Instant, a Servant Lad named *Patrick Trener*, about 18 Years of Age, he is fresh colour'd, and has brown Hair. He had on a pretty good Hat, a good fine Shirt, old homespun Trowsers, and New Pumps.

Whoever takes up and secures the said Runaway so that his said Master may have him again, shall have *Forty Shillings* Reward and all necessary Charges paid by   *Nicholas Fred.*

The American Weekly Mercury, From Thursday June 10, to Thursday June 17, 1736; From Thursday June 17, to Thursday June 24, 1736; From Thursday June 24, to Thursday July 1, 1736.

RAN-away about the 10th of *June*, from on Board the Ship Mary & Hannah, *Henry Savage* Master, two Men viz. *John Hamilton* and *Peter Gambarto*. *Hamilton* is a *Scotchman* and talks as such, he is about five Foot high, and pitted with the Small-Pox, dress'd as a Sailor newly come on Shore. *Gambarto* is about the same Size, and had a brown Jacket on.

Whoever takes up the said *Hamilton* and *Gambarto*, or either of them, and brings him or them to the said *Henry Savage* on board his Ship at *Arch-Street* Wharfe, or to Mr. *John Reynolds*, Merchant, in *Water-Street*, shall have *Twenty Shillings* Reward of each and reasonable Charges,
 paid by   *Henry Savage.*

The American Weekly Mercury, From Thursday June 17, to Thursday June 24, 1736; From Thursday June 24, to Thursday July 1, 1736; From Thursday July 1, to Thursday July 8, 1736.

RAN-away from *Christian Stone* of the County of *Lancaster*, a Servant Man named *Thomas MacKnapp*, of a middle Stature, round Face; had with him when he went away, a Felt Hat half worn, a Kersey Coat and Jacket with brass Buttons, the hinder part of the Jacket is of a piss burnt colour, he has two homespun Shirts, a pair of twill'd Linen Breeches, a pair of Trowsers, a pair of grey yarn Stockings, and a pair of New Shoes.

He took with him a Sickle in order to look for Harvest Work.

Whoever secures the said servant so that his said Master may have him again, shall have *Forty Shillings* Reward, and reasonable Charges,
 paid by me   *Christian Stone.*

The American Weekly Mercury, From Thursday, July 8, to Thursday, July 15, 1736; From Thursday, July 15, to Thursday, July 22, 1736; From Thursday, July 22, to Thursday, July 29, 1736.

RUN away last Night from *Lawrence Reynolds* of this City, Currier, an Irish Servant Man, named *Valentine Clerk*, about 24 Years of Age, tall and slender, raw-bon'd, fresh colour'd, grim visag'd and down look: Had on a Pair of tann'd Trowsers, new ozenbrigs Jacket, new fine and coarse Shirt, blue worsted Stockings and Calfskin Shoes seam'd round the Quarters.

Whoever secures the said Servant so that he may be had again, shall have *Three Pounds* Reward and reasonable Charges
paid by *Lawrence Reynolds. Philadelphia, July* 14, 1736.
The Pennsylvania Gazette, From Thursday, July 8, to Thursday, July 15, 1736; From Thursday, July 15, to Thursday, July 22, 1736; From Thursday, July 22, to August 2, 1736. See *The American Weekly Mercury,* From Tuesday February 4, to Tuesday February 11, 1735

RUN away on the 15th Inst. from *Robert Toms,* of this City, a Servant Lad named *Hezekiah Mills,* born in *Gloucestershire,* about 14 Years of Age, short Stature and sandy Complexion, his Head shaved close: Had on an old Hat with some red Paint about it, ozenbrigs Shirt and Trowsers, and good Pumps or Shoes, has workd at the Taylor's Trade in England, but in this Country at the Shipwright's Business, and pretends to be a Sailor.
Whoever takes up and secures the said Servant so that his Master may have him again, shall have *Forty Shillings* Reward and reasonable Charges paid by   *Robert Toms. Philadelphia, July* 22, 1736.
The Pennsylvania Gazette, From July 15, to July 22, 1736; August 2, 1736.

RAN-away on the 26th of last Month, from *Daniel Kelly* of the Manour of *Moorland,* in the County of *Philadelphia,* an Irish Servant Man named *James Merratty,* about 40 Years of Age, pretty Tall, and well set; he is somewhat Pock-fretten, and has no Hair; he had on an old Felt Hat, a thick Cap, a grey Kersey Jacket lined with blue Duffils, a pair of coarse Linen Breeches, a good Oznabrigs Shirt, old Stockings, and pretty good Shoes.
He is a good Scholar.
Whoever takes up the said Servant, and brings him to his said Master, or secures him so that he may be had again, shall have *Forty Shillings* as a Reward, and all reasonable Charges paid by me   *Daniel Kelly.*
The American Weekly Mercury, From Thursday July 29, to Thursday August 5, 1736; From Thursday August 5, to Thursday August 12, 1736; From Thursday August 12, to Thursday August 19, 1736. See *The Pennsylvania Gazette,* From August 2, to August 7, 1736.

RAN-away on the 15th of *August,* from the Brigantine Meredian, *Samuel Farra,* Master, a Servant Man named *Samuel Caughlan,* about 32 years of Age, Tall, Thin and Raw Bon'd, a Weaver by Trade, but has been a Soldier, can pass for an English, Scotch or an Irish Man; he is very bare of Cloaths, had on an old Frize Jacket and Waistcoat, a speckled Shirt. He is of a dark Complexion and Talks much.

Whoever secures the said Servant so that he may be had again, shall have *Forty Shillings* Reward and reasonable Charges paid by *Evan Bevan*, Merchant in *Philadelphia*.

The American Weekly Mercury, From Thursday August 12, to Thursday August 19, 1736; From Thursday August 19, to Thursday August 26, 1736; From Thursday August 26, to Thursday September 2, 1736.

RAN-away on the 20th of *June* past, from *John Snevely* of the County of *Lancaster*, Yeoman, a Servant Man named *John M'Koy*, about 22 or 23 Years of Age, of midling Stature, Swarthy, Thick and Gross; he had on, or with him, a brown linsey woolsey Jacket with Brass Buttons, a grey linsey woolsey Jacket with Brass Buttons and Pockets at the Sides, a twill'd Jacket, and Trowsers made Dutch fashion.

He took with him an iron Grey Stallion branded on the near shoulder S J, a Star in his Forehead, some Saddle spots, he is about 4 Years old, and a natural Pacer.

Whoever takes up said Man and Horse, and secures them so that the said *John Snevely* may have them again, shall have *Four Pounds* Reward and all reasonable Charges Paid by *John Snevely*.

The American Weekly Mercury, From Thursday August 12, to Thursday August 19, 1736; From Thursday August 19, to Thursday August 26, 1736; From Thursday August 26, to Thursday September 2, 1736.

RUN away on the 26th past, from *Daniel Kelly* of the Mannor of *Moreland*, in this County, an Irish Servant Man named *James Merratty*, about 40 Years of Age, pretty tall but not big, somewhat pock-fretten and has no Hair: Had on an old Felt Hat and a thick Cap, a grey Kersey Jacket lin'd with blue Duffils, coarse linnen Breeches, old Stockings, good Shoes and ozenbrigs Shirt. Whoever secures the said Servant so that he may be had again, shall have *Forty Shillings* Reward and reasonable Charges paid by *Daniel Kelly. Philad. Aug.* 12. 1736.

The Pennsylvania Gazette, From August 7, to August 12, 1736; From August 12, to August 23, 1736; From August 23, to September 2, 1736; From September 2, to September 9, 1736; From September 9, to September 16, 1736. See *The American Weekly Mercury*, From Thursday July 29, to Thursday August 5, 1736.

RAN-away on the 22d of the 6th Month, from *Job Harvey* of *Darby*, in the County of *Chester*, a Servant Lad named *Samuel Mead*, about 18 years of age, of a short Stature, brown Complexion, and a flat Nose. He went away with one *William Barnes* who is since taken.

The said Lad is supposed to have with him, an old Castor Hat, a brown Cloth Coat, an old white Linen Jacket, a pair of new Oznabrigs Breeches with blue and white Buttons, an old pair of dark colour'd worsted Stockings, and a good pair of Neats Leather Shoes, an old linen Shirt, and a Romal Handkerchief. He took a Pistol with him,

Whoever takes up the said Servant, and brings him to his said Master, or secures him so that he may be had again, shall have *Twenty Shillings* as a Reward, and all reasonable Charges
paid by   *Job Harvey.*

The American Weekly Mercury, From Thursday August 19, to Thursday August 26, 1736. See *The American Weekly Mercury*, From Thursday April 28, to Thursday May 5, 1737.

RAN-away on the 28th of *August* past, from his Master *Robert Thomas* of *Lower Dublin* in *Philadelphia* County, an English Servant Lad named *John Williams*, about 18 years of Age, of middling Stature and well set; he has strait light brown Hair, and a pretty smooth Face. He had on a dark colour'd Frize Coat, trimm'd with white metal Buttons, Oznabrigs Jacket and Breeches, gray yarn Stockings, Felt Hat, and good Shoes: He was seen in this City the next day after he left his Master.

N. B. When he works and sweats, he smells as rank as a Negro.

Whoever shall take up said Servant and secure his so that his Master may have him again, shall have *Forty Shillings* Reward, and all reasonable Charges, paid by   *Robert Thomas.*

The American Weekly Mercury, From Thursday August 26, to Thursday September 2, 1736; From Thursday September 2, to Thursday September 9, 1736; From Thursday September 16, to Thursday September 23, 1736.

RAN-away on the 29th of *August* past, from *David Evans* of *Tulpahacca*, an Irish servant Man named *Peter Power*; he is about 35 years of Age, and a Tobacconist by Trade, short of Stature, and of a Pale Complexion; he has short brown curled Hair, and has lost one of Toes: He had on when he went away, a dark brown Pea-Jacket and Breeches, speckled Shirt, Oznabrigs Trowsers, a pretty good Felt Hat, and a pair of old Shoes covered with white Leather.

Whoever secures the said Servant so that he may be had again shall have *Forty Shillings* Reward, and all reasonable Charges
                  paid by   *David Evans.*
The American Weekly Mercury, From Thursday September 2, to Thursday September 9, 1736.

RUN away from Thomas Edwards, *of* Lancaster *County, an Irish Servant Man, named* Thomas Booth *about 21 Years of Age, of a short Stature. some lisping in his Speech, he had on a good homespun linen shirt, Breeches and Waistcoat, a good Pair of Shoes, an old Felt Hat cock'd. Whosoever secures the said Servant so that his Master may have him again, shall have* Forty Shillings *Reward by me.*   Thomas Edwards.
The Pennsylvania Gazette, From August 23, to September 2, 1736; From September 2, to September 9, 1736

RAN-away on the 4th of this Instant from *Thomas Fletcher* of *Abington*, in the County of *Philadelphia*, a servant Man named *William Morgan*, of Welsh Descent, he is about 26 years of Age; of middling Stature and slender, has very long and crooked Teeth, chews much Tobacco, is pretty full Faced, has short black Hair, small Legs, and one Ancle bending much inward; had on a good Felt Hat, Oznabrigs Shirt, a new sute of homespun Cloth Clothes of a light colour, and trimm'd with a dark olive colour, thread Stockings, and good Shoes.

Whoever secures the said Servant so that his Master may have him again, shall have *Forty Shillings* Reward and all reasonable Charges
                  paid by   *Thomas Fletcher.*
The American Weekly Mercury, From Thursday September 9 to Thursday September 16, 1736; From Thursday September 16, to Thursday September 23, 1736.

RAN-away from *William Roe* of *New-Garden*, in the County of *Chester*, on the 12th of this Instant *September*, a Servant Man named *John Mac Doniel*, about 22 years of Age, he was born in *Scotland*, but lately came from *Ireland*; he is of a tall Stature and swarthy Complexion, and has a dull look: He had on a dark colour'd Coat, and blue Sarge Jacket and Breeches, and grey yarn Stockings, his hair being cut off, he took a Wig and woollen Cap.

Whoever secures the said Servant so that he may be had again shall have *Forty Shillings* Reward, and all reasonable Charges
                  paid by   William Roe.

The American Weekly Mercury, From Thursday September 9 to Thursday September 16, 1736; From Thursday September 16, to Thursday September 23, 1736; From Thursday September 23, to Thursday September 30, 1736. See *The Pennsylvania Gazette*, From July 21, to July 28, 1737, for John McDaniel/John MacDoniel.

RAN-away from *William Attwood* of *Philadelphia*, on the 19th of *September*, a Servant Man named *Henry Murphy*, aged about 40 Years; he is a Tall raw-bon'd Man, of a brown Complexion, by Trade a Tanner and Cordwainer; he wears his own Hair, which is short and thin, and curls a little. He had on when he went away, a dark colour'd Frize Coat, with Waistcoat Sleves, brown Sarge Waistcoat and Breeches, light gray yarn Stockings, a Felt Hat half worn, and Shoes without Buckles.

Whoever secures said Servant and brings him to said *William Attwood*, shall have *Forty Shillings* Reward, and all reasonable Charges,
        paid by   *William Attwood.*

The American Weekly Mercury, From Thursday September 16, to Thursday September 23, 1736; From Thursday, September 23, to Thursday, September 30, 1736; From Thursday, September 30, to Thursday, October, 7, 1736; From Thursday, October 7, to Thursday, October, 14, 1736.

RUN away the 23d Instant, from *Joseph Thomson* of *Ridley* Township, *Chester* County, a Servant Man named *Brian M'Manus*, about 36 Years of Age, short of Stature, thin fac'd, brown curl'd Hair and a Roman Nose: Had on when he went away, a coarse homespun Shirt and a fine Shirt, a striped Linsey-wolsey Jacket, Leather Breeches with Brass Buttons, red and blue twisted yarn Stockings and good Shoes. Whoever secures the said Servant so that he may be had again, shall have Forty Shillings Reward and reasonable Charges, paid by   Joshua Thomson.   Philad. Sept. 28. 1736.

The Pennsylvania Gazette, From September 23, to September 30, 1736; From October 7, to October 14, 1736; From October 14, to October 21, 1736; From October 21, to October 28, 1736.

RAN-away from on board the Brigantine Salutation, *John Carrol* Master, lately arrived from *Boston*, two Irish Servant Lads, the one named *Daniel Cremeing*, about 20 years of Age, sore Ey'd, and much mark'd with the Small-Pox; had on when he went away, a dark Pea-Jacket. The other named *Robert Pelican*, full Faced, and round shoulder'd: Took his Chest and Cloaths from on board said Vessel.

Whoever secures said Servants so that their said Master may have them again, shall have *Thirty Shill*ings for each, and reasonable Charges,
           paid by   *John Carrol.*

The American Weekly Mercury, From Thursday October 14, to Thursday October 21, 1736; From Thursday October 21, to Thursday October 28, 1736; From Thursday October 28, to Thursday November 4, 1736; From Thursday November 4, to Thursday, November 11, 1736.

RUN away the 23d Inst. from William Watson *of this City, Shipwright, a Servant Man named* Martin Chard, *an Englishman, by Trade a Weaver, short of Stature, well set, pockfretten in the Face, and wears his own Hair; he lately arrived from Bristol with Capt.* Bromadge. *Had on when he went away, a light coloured Cloth Coat, a striped flannel Wastcoat, and thick Shoes half worn.*

Whoever secures the said Servant so that his Master may have him again, shall have Five Pounds *Reward and reasonable Charges,*
           paid by   William Watson. Philad. Oct. 25. 1736.

The Pennsylvania Gazette, From October 21, to October 28, 1736; From October 28, to November 4, 1736; From November 4, to November 11, 1736; From November 11, to November 18, 1736.

RUN away from John Croker *of this City, an Irish Servant Man named* John Leonard, *by Trade a Taylor, with short black curld Hair, walks stooping, is pretty much pockfretten, has a sly down Look; lived some Time with the Dutch Taylor at* German-town, *and looks somewhat like a Dutchman. Had on when he went away, a snuff-colour'd homespun Coat lin'd with striped linsey-wolsey, a blue Jacket with brass Buttons and no Sleeves, worsted Stockings almost the Colour of his Coat, and good Neats Leather Shoes. Took with him a light-colour'd Drugget Coat not finished, three Yards and a half of Black Shalloon, three dozen double gilt Jacket Buttons, and two Shirts. Whoever takes up and secures the said Servant, so that his Master may have him again shall have* Three Pounds *Reward, and reasonable Charges*
           paid by   John Croker. Philad. Nov. 4. 1736.

The Pennsylvania Gazette, From October 28, to November 4, 1736; From November 4, to November 11, 1736; From November 11, to November 18, 1736.

RUN away on the 7th Inst. from Nathanael Grub *of* Willistown, Chester County, *a Welsh Servant Man named* William Edwards, *aged about 35 Years, thick-set, round shoulder;d, has a down Look, and reddish brown Hair if not* cut off, is pockfretten and professes to be a Miller and a Sailor. Had on a new Felt Hat too little for him, a brown pea Jacket, striped woollen Jacket, grey woollen Stockings, good Shoes, two checker'd Shirts. Also an English Servant Woman named Sarah Sembler, aged 25 Years, fresh Complexion, short of Stature. Had on an old Calico Gown, red quilted Peticoat, lined with blue, and new Pumps.

Whoever secures the said Servants so that they may be had again, shall have Three Pounds Reward for the Man, and Forty Shillings for the Woman, and reasonable Charges
     paid by Nathanael Grub. Philad Nov. 18. 1736.

The Pennsylvania Gazette, From November 11, to November 18, 1736; From November 18, to November 25, 1736; From November 25, to December 2, 1736.

RAN-away on the 29th of November, from Benjamin Armitage of Bristol Township in Philadelphia County, an Irish Servant Man named Thomas Larrance, of low Stature, but slow in Motion; he is about 28 Years of Age, has short Hair, and wears a dark Bob Wig. He had on when he went away, a Felt Hat, a blue gray Cloath Coat and Jacket, old Leather Breeches very open at the Knees, two Shirts, one of them white, the other checkt, a pair of gray yarn Stockings, and double soled Shoes.

Whoever takes up said Servant and returns him to his said Master, or secures him so that his said Master may have him again, shall have Thirty Shillings Reward, and all reasonable Charges
     paid by Benjamin Armitage.

The American Weekly Mercury, From Thursday November 25, to Thursday December 2, 1736; From Thursday December 2, to Thursday December 9, 1736; From Thursday December 9, to Thursday December 16, 1736.

RAN-away on the 5th of this Instant December, from Henry Young, in Arch-street, near the George-Inn, an Irish Servant Man named William Smith, aged about 26 or 28 Years, by Trade a Blacksmith and Farrier: He is a tall fresh colour'd well set Fellow, something mark'd with the Small Pox; has short black Hair, and wears a woollen Cap. He was formerly a Dragoon, and when he ran away had on his Soldier's Coat, red, lin'd with White, and trimm'd with flat Brass Buttons; a short striped Flannen Jacket; two checkt Shirts; a yellow Silk Handkerchief; brown Breeches; yarn Stockings, and a new Felt Hat.

N. B. He lately came from Bristol with Capt. Tough, and ran away in a day or two after his Master bought him.

Whoever secures the said Servant so that his Master may have him again, shall have *Three Pounds* Reward, and all necessary Charges paid by   *Henry Young.*
The American Weekly Mercury, From Thursday December 2, to Thursday December 9, 1736; From Thursday December 9, to Thursday December 16, 1736; From Thursday December 16, to Thursday December 23, 1736.

RAN-away on the 5th of this Instant from *William Fishbourn*, Two Indented Servant Men for four Years each; one named *James Butler*, is a fresh colour'd young Man of middling Stature, his Hair cut off, had on his Head an old Hat and woollen Cap under it, has a dark colour'd Cloth Pea-Jacket lin'd, and striped Flannen Jacket under it, woollen Breeches, blue and white coarse worsted Stockings almost new, his Shoes lately new soled; he is a Carpenter by Trade, an Englishman, and has been used to the Sea for some time; he came in from *Bristol* last Summer with Capt. *Bromadge*.

The other is a short down lookt Fellow, muttering in his Speech, an Irishman, a Plaisterer and Bricklayer; had on an old flapping Hat and woollen Cap, his hair cut off, a light colour'd Cloth Coat and woollen Jacket & Breeches with brass Buttons, and a short red Jacket (belonging to the other Man) brown Oznabrig Shirt; he is much given to Drink, Deceit, and Lying; his Name is *Morris Kerrill.*

Those who take up said Runaways, & secure them, shall have *Four Pounds* Reward for both, or *Forty Shillings* for either, Paid when delivered to me at *Philadelphia*, and reasonable Charges by   *William Fishbourn.*

N. B. An Apprentice Lad named *Thomas Hill* is said to be in Company with them, and a Woman.

The American Weekly Mercury, From Thursday December 2, to Thursday December 9, 1736. See *The Pennsylvania Gazette*, From November 10, to November 17, 1737, for Butler. See *The American Weekly Mercury*, From Thursday June 29, to Thursday July 6, 1738, and *The Pennsylvania Gazette*, From June 29, to July 6, 1738, for Kerrill.

RUN away about the 6th of November *past from* Mathew Clarkson, *a Servant Man named* Johannes Poluck, *born in Switzerland, about Twenty Years of age, of a middle Stature, hath two* Thumbs *on the right Hand, and keeps it bound over with a Rag, came over from Holland, in the Brigt. Prince Frederick,* Joseph Willson, *Master, to* New-York, *about the middle of September last: Had on, a new Felt Hat, a double worsted striped Cap, a double breasted Pea-Jacket with flat brass buttons, two ozenbrigs Shirts, new leather breeches, two pair woollen Stockings, new Shoes & two cotton romal Handkerchiefs. Whoever apprehends the said Servant & delivers him in the Goal of Philadelphia, any Goal in* New Jersey *or at New-York, giving Notice to Mr.* Arent Hassert *of* Philadelphia, Gerardus De Peyster *at* New-Brunswick, *or* Mathew Clarkson *in* New-York *shall receive* Three Pounds *reward and reasonable Charges.*

The Pennsylvania Gazette, From December 2, to December 9, 1736; From December 9, to December 16, 1736; From December 16, to December 23, 1736; From December 23, to December 30, 1736; From December 30, 1736, to January 6, 1737; From January 6, to January 13, 1737; From January 13, to January 20, 1737; From January 20, to January 27, 1737; From February 3, to February 10, 1737.

RAN-away on the 14th of *December,* from *James M'Cra,* of *Northampton* in *Bucks* County, an Irish Servant Man named *John Boyd,* aged about 25 Years, something Pockfretten, of middling Stature, and had dark brown Hair. He had on a good blue Broad Cloth Coat full trimm'd, blue Drugget Jacket and Breeches much worn, an old Felt Hat, white yarn Stockings, and white Mittens with blue and white Fringes: He has a pair of Shoes on which have three Nails in each Heel.

Whoever takes up said Servant and returns him to his said Master, or secures him so that his said Master may have him again, shall have *Forty Shillings* Reward, and all reasonable Charges

paid By   *James M'Cra.*

The American Weekly Mercury, From Thursday December 16, to Thursday December 23, 1736; From Thursday December 23, to Tuesday December 28, 1736; From Tuesday December 28, 1736, to Thursday January 6, 1737.

1737

French-Creek-Iron-Works, in *Chester*-County, *Dec.* 25. 1736.

RAN-away from *Samuel Nutt,* at the Iron-Works aforesaid, a Servant Man named *David McQuatty,* by Trade a Hammerman and Refiner, but formerly followed Shallopping up and down the Bay to *Egg-Harbour.* He is a Scotchman by Birth, but speaks pretty good English, He is a small sized and thin visaged Man, pretty much Pock fretten, with a Roman Nose, and some small blue Spots on the right side of his Face & Nose, occasion'd by Gun-Powder. He is extremely affected with a trembling of the Nerves, so that he can scarcely hold any thing in his hand steadily. He brags much of his Performances, and is quarrelsome when in Liquor. He had on when he went away, a Felt Hat, a cotton or worsted Cap, a reddish colour'd Cloth Coat that had been turned, a very fine new homespun Shirt, a striped flannel Jacket, a pair of Leather Breeches, old pair yarn mill'd Stockings, and a pair of good Shoes.

Whoever takes up the said Servant, and secures him so that he may be brought to his Master, shall have *Three Pounds* Reward and reasonable Charges, if taken up in this Province; or *Five Pounds* and all reasonable Charges, if taken up in any other Province, to be paid directly on delivery of the said Servant, By me   Samuel Nutt.

The American Weekly Mercury, From Tuesday December 28, 1736, to Thursday January 6, 1737; From Thursday January 13, 1737, to Tuesday January 18, 1737; From Tuesday January 18, 1737, to Tuesday January 25, 1737. See *The Pennsylvania Gazette*, From December 30, 1736, to January 6, 1737, *The American Weekly Mercury*, From June 30, to July 7, 1737, and *The Pennsylvania Gazette*, From June 30, to July 7, 1737.

RUN away from Samuel Nutt, *of* French Creek *Iron-Works,* Chester *County, a Servant Man named* David Mc'Quatty, *by Trade a Hammerman and Refiner, but had formerly followed Shalloping up and down the Bay to* Egg Harbour; *he is a Scotchman by Birth, but speaks pretty good English, he is a small-sized and thin-visaged Man, pretty much pockfretten, with a Roman Nose, and some small blue Spots on the right Side of his Face and Nose occasioned by Gun-Powder; he is extremely affected with a trembling of the Nerves, so that he can scarcely hold any thing in his Hand steadily, he brags much of his Performances and is quarrelsome when in Liquor; He had on when he went away, a felt Hat, a cotton or worsted Cap, a reddish-coloured cloth Coat that had been turned, a very fine new homespun shirt, a striped flannel Jacket, Leather Breeches, old yarn mill'd Stockings, and good Shoes. Whoever takes up the said Servant, and secures him so that he may be brought to his Master, shall have* Three Pounds *Reward and reasonable Charges if taken up in this Province, and* Five Pounds *and all reasonable Charges, if taken up in any other Province, to be paid directly on delivery of the said Servant, by me*   Samuel Nutt.   Philad. Jan. 6. 1736,7.

The Pennsylvania Gazette, From December 30, 1736, to January 6, 1737; From January 6, to January 13, 1737; From January 13, to January 20, 1737; From January 20, to January 27, 1737. See *The American Weekly Mercury*, From Tuesday December 28, 1736, to Thursday January 6, 1737, *The American Weekly Mercury*, From June 30, to July 7, 1737, and *The Pennsylvania Gazette*, From June 30, to July 7, 1737.

RAN-away on the 4th Instant from *John Hethcot*, Butcher, of *Philadelphia*, a Servant Girl about 12 Years of Age, commonly known by the Name of *Sarah Boham*: She is fresh colour'd, has light hair, a Sly look, and speaks slow. She had on a new Silk Bonnet, a sad colour'd short Cloak, a brown colour'd Gown, an old white Holland Apron, a linnen and woollen Petticoat, white Stockings, and wooden Heel Shoes with Nails in the Heels.

This is to forewarn all Persons not to entertain her, and also shall oblige me to pay to any Person that shall bring the abovesaid Servant to me *John Hethcot*, the Butcher, *Ten Shillings* upon Demand.

The American Weekly Mercury, From Thursday January 6, to Thursday January 13, 1737; From Thursday January 13, to Tuesday January 18, 1737; From Tuesday January 18, to Tuesday January 25, 1737.

RUN away on the 22d December, last from *George Rice Jones*, of *Philadelphia*, Butcher, a Servant Man, named *John Nutty*, Butcher by Trade, aged about 24 Years, short and well set with dark brown Hair, much disfigur'd with the Small-Pox, and talks broad West-Country. Had on a dark coleur'd Pea-Jacket, and Breeches of the same Stuff, two blue Jackets under the Pea-Jacket Yarn Stockings, and good Shoes, a pair of Seal-Skin Saddle-Bags, and about 6 *l*. in Jersey Money.

Whoever takes up the said run-away, and secures him so that his Master may have him again shall have Three Pounds Reward, and reasonable, Charges baid [sic] by   *George Rice Jones.*

The New-York Weekly Journal, January 17, 1737; January 24, 1737; January 30, 1737; February 6, 1737; February 13, 1737; February 20, 1737.

RAN-away on the 1*st* Day of *Jan* Inst. from *John Wall* of *Lancaster*, a Servant Man named *Samuel Hughs*, small of Stature and round Shoulder'd; he has bandy Legs, and stoops very much in his walk. He had on when he went away, a Felt Hat half worn; a gray linsey-woolsey Coat; coarse Trowsers, and new strong Shoes.

Whoever takes up said Servant and returns him to his said Master, or secures him so that his said Master may have him again, shall have *Thirty Shillings* Reward, and all reasonable Charges paid   By *John Wall*.

The American Weekly Mercury, From Thursday January 13, to Tuesday January 18, 1737; From Thursday January 18, to Tuesday January 25, 1737; From Thursday, February 3, to Tuesday February 8, 1737.

RUN away the 31st of March, *from* James Bennet *of Aston, in* Chester *County, an Irish Servant Man, named* Samuel Henderson, *by Trade a Taylor, about*

20 *Years of Age, low Stature, smooth Fac'd, brown Hair, but perhaps may have cut it off, having taken a Cap with him. Had with him a homespun olive-colour'd cloth Coat and Jacket, leather Breeches with brass Buttons, one fine and one coarse Shirt, a new Felt Hat, brown Stockings, and two pair of Shoes, one new of Calf-skin; took with him also a large Taylors Sheers, and a Gun. 'Tis suppos'd he's gone towards* Donnegal. *Whoever secures the said Servant so that his Master may have him again, shall have* Forty Shillings *Reward, and reasonable Charges paid by* James Bennet.

The Pennsylvania Gazette, From April 7, to April 14; From April 14, to April 21, 1737; From April 21, to April 28, 1737; From April 28, to May 5, 1737.

RAN-away from *Obadiah Johnston* of *Darby*, on the 1st. Instant at Night, an English Servant Man named *John Howlet*, about 20 Years of Age, he is six Foot high, and slender, of a swarthy Complexion, and has short black Hair. He had on when he went away, a small Felt Hat, a striped Worsted Cap, homespun Cloth Coat and Jacket of a light Cinamon Colour, with Brass Buttons, a pair of Linen Breeches, gray Yarn Stockings, a good pair of Shoes, two Shirts, one of Tow Cloth and the other of Flax.
Whoever takes up and secures the said Servant so that his Master may have him again, shall have *Thirty Shillings* Reward, and reasonable Charges,
paid By *Obadiah Johnson.*

The American Weekly Mercury, From Thursday April 28, to Thursday May 5, 1737; From Thursday May 5, to Thursday May 12, 1737; From Thursday May 12, to Thursday May 19, 1737. See below.

RAN-away from *Job Harvey* of *Darby*, on the 1st Instant, an English Servant Lad, named *Samuel Mead*, aged about 19 Years, of brown Complexion, has a large Nose, and short brown Hair. He had on he went away, a brown Cloth Cloath with black Horn Buttons, an Olive colour'd Drugget Jacket with Brass Buttons, old Tow Trowsers, gray Yarn Stockings, Neat Leather Shoes, and a Felt Hat half worn.
He is supposed to be gone away with the above-describ'd Servant of *Obadiah Johnson's.*
Whoever takes up and secures the said Servant, so that his Master may have him again, shall have Forty Shillings Reward, and reasonable Charges,
paid by *Job Harvey.*

The American Weekly Mercury, From Thursday April 28, to Thursday May 5, 1737; From Thursday May 5, to Thursday May 12, 1737; From Thursday May 12, to Thursday May 19, 1737. See *The American*

Weekly Mercury, From Thursday August 19, to Thursday August 26, 1736.

RUN away on Tuesday last from *Joseph Durborow*, Shipwright, an *Irish* Servant Lad named *Thomas Haney,* about 18 Years of Age, of middle Stature, short brown Hair, a little pockfretten. Had on a short blue Jacket, a tarry Frock and Trowsers, a check'd Shirt, a black Jacket over all, an old broken Hat narrow brim'd, Yarn Stockings, pretty good Shoes. He has been something us'd to the sea.

    Whoever takes up and secures the said Servant, so that he may be had again, shall have *Thirty Shillings* Reward, and reasonable Charges,
              paid by   *Joseph Durborow.*
The Pennsylvania Gazette, From April 21, to April 28, 1737; From April 28, to May 5, 1737; From May 19, to May 26, 1737. Last ad shows he ran away "26th of *April*"

RAN-away from my House in *York-Town, Virginia,* on the 6th of *March* past, a Servant Man named *Patrick Burk,* a Saddler by Trade, born in *Virginia,* served his Time in *Philadelphia,* aged about 30, of small Stature, brown Complexion, short black Hair, mark'd with the Small-Pox. He had on when he went away a dark coloured Kersey Coat with Metal Buttons, Fustian Waist-Coat and Breeches. He took with him a dark Bay Horse, mark'd thus ♥ on the near Shoulder.

    Whoever secures the said Servant, so that I may have him again, shall have Three Pistoles Reward, besides what the Law allows,
              paid By   *James Mitchell.*
    The American Weekly Mercury, From Thursday May 5, to Thursday May 12, 1737; From Thursday May 12, to Thursday May 19, 1737; From Thursday May 19, to Thursday May 26, 1737; From Thursday May 26, to Thursday June 2, 1737.

RUN *away last Night from* Thomas Godfrey *of this City, Glazier, an English Servant Maid, named* Elizabeth Barber, *alias* Rugstone, *alias* Burroughs, *about 21 Years of Age, fair Hair, middle Stature. Had on a yellow and red striped worsted homespun Gown, ozenbrigs Apron, muslin Pin[c]ers, silk Handkerchief, blue quilted Petticoat, blue Stockings, and black Shoes. Whoever secures the said Servant so that she may be had again shall have Twenty Shillings Reward and reasonable Charges*
              paid, by   T Godfrey.   Philad. May 18.
    The Pennsylvania Gazette, From May 12, to May 19, 1737.

RAN-away, on the 16th of *May*, from *Thomas Yeardley* of *Bucks* County, a Servant Man named *David Littleford*, a *Herefordshire*-Man, about 40 Years of age; he is Tall, and of a ruddy freckled Complexion; his Hair cut off. He had on an old mealy Hat, an old light colour'd Wig, a thread-bare drab colour'd Coat, gray Kersey Breeches something torn at the Knees, gray Yarn Stockings, and pretty good Shoes.

He professes to be a Miller.

Whoever takes up the said Servant and brings him to his Master, or to *Evan Morgan* in *Philadelphia*, or secures him so that his Master may have him again, shall have *Thirty Shillings* Reward, and reasonable Charges,
        paid By   *Thomas Yeardley.*

The American Weekly Mercury, From Thursday May 19, to Thursday May 26, 1737; From Thursday May 26, to Thursday June 2, 1737; From Thursday June 2, to Thursday June 9, 1737.

BROKE out of the Gaol in *New-Town*, in *Bucks*-County, in the Night between the 19th and 20th of *May*, Two Felons, viz.

Thomas Parker, an Irishman, who was committed for robbing *Jackson's* Fulling-Mill. He is a tall lusty Man, with short dark colour'd Hair, and a sandy Beard. He had on an old dark colour'd Drugget Coat, an old Shirt, old Trowsers, half-worn Neats-Leather Shoes, and an old Felt Hat. And,

Thomas Grant, who is a short slender Fellow, has short black Hair. He had on a yellow Jacket with Brass Buttons, a Beaver Hat half worn, two homespun Shirts, two pair of Trowsers, blue and white yarn Stockings, and a pair of half worn narrow toe'd Shoes.

Whoever takes up the said Felons, or either of them, and brings them to *New-Town* Goal, or secures them in any other Goal, so that they may be had again, shall have *Fifty Shillings* Reward, and reasonable Charges,
        paid by   *Timothy Smith*, Sheriff.

The American Weekly Mercury, From Thursday May 19, to Thursday May 26, 1737; From Thursday June 2, to Thursday June 9, 1737.

RUN away on Sunday the 8th Inst. from *Blakeston Ingledew* of this City, Butcher, an Irish Servant Man named *Thomas Bagg*, aged about 30 Years, of middle size, well set, red fac'd, wears his own black Hair; Had on a blue Coat, black leather Breeches, took with him a little bay Horse, having a slit in one Ear, a Snip and a Star, branded **TN** in one Letter, on the near Shoulder; with a russet Saddle and Bridle. 'Tis suppos'd he's gone towards *New-England*. Whosoever secures the said Servant so that his Master may have him again,

shall have *Three Pounds* Reward, and reasonable Charges,
    paid by   Blakeston Ingledew. *Philad. May* 19.
The Pennsylvania Gazette, From May 12, to May 19, 1737; From May 19, to May 26, 1737. See The American Weekly Mercury, From Thursday May 26, to Thursday June 2, 1737.

RUN away on Sunday the 8th Inst. from *Blakeston Ingledew* of this City, Butcher, an Irish Servant Man named *Thomas Bagg*, aged about 30 Years, of middle size, well set. red fac'd, wears his own black Hair; Had on a blue Coat, black leather Breeches, took with him a little bay Horse, having a slit in one Ear, a Snip and a Star, branded TN in one Letter. on the near Shoulder; with a russet Saddle and Bridle. 'Tis suppos'd he's gone towards *New-England*. Whosoever secures the said Servant so that his Master may have him again, shall have *Three Pounds* Reward, and reasonable Charges,
    paid by   Blakeston Ingledew. *Philada. May* 30.
The American Weekly Mercury, From Thursday May 26, to Thursday June 2, 1737. See *The Pennsylvania Gazette*, From May 12, to May 19, 1737.

RAN-away on the 29*th* of *May* past from their Masters in this City, two Servant Men. One belonging to *Thomas Snooke*, Bricklayer, named *George Jones*, aged 37 Years, of short Stature, black Complexion, and a red Nose; had on when he went away, a dark colour'd Kersey great Coat, Oznabrigs Shirt and Breeches, Flanel Jacket, Yarn Stockings, a Felt Hat, and a white Wig or Cap.

The other belonging to *Joseph Flower*, Joyner, named *John Connal*, aged 23 Years, a tall slim Fellow, with black Hair, and dark Complexion: had on when he went away, a Broadcloth Coat with a Velvet Neck, a black Jacket with new Sleeves, Broadcloth Breeches new seated with a different colour, a pair of Shoes new-soled, a pair of fine gray worsted Stockings & a good Beaver Hat.

Whoever takes up and secures the said Servants, or either of them, so that their Masters may have them again, shall have *Thirty Shillings* as a Reward, for each, and all reasonable Charges, paid by their said Masters.
    The American Weekly Mercury, From Thursday May 26, to Thursday June 2, 1737; From Thursday June 2, to Thursday June 9, 1737; From Thursday June 9, to Thursday June 16, 1737.

RAN-away on the 31*st* of *May* past, from *Edward Annely* of *Philadelphia*, Joyner, a Welch Servant Man named *George Morgan*, talks pretty much in the Welch Tongue, by Trade a Joyner, about 28 Years of age, he is pretty tall and well set, of a fresh Complexion, and has dark brown curl'd Hair; he has the mark of an old Wound on the Pit of his Stomach. He had on when he went away, a good Beaver Hat without Button or Lining, a dark gray Kersey Coat with white metal Buttons, a whitish Linen Jacket, striped homespun Linen Breeches, and a pair of white Trowsers with a large piece down one of the Hips, new Yarn Stockings, and pretty good Shoes.

Whoever takes up the said Servant and secures him so that he may be had again, shall have *Twenty Shillings* if taken within five Miles of this City, and Forty Shillings if taken farther off, as a Reward, and reasonable Charges,

    paid By *Edward Annely.*

 The American Weekly Mercury, From Thursday June 9, to Thursday June 16, 1737; From Thursday June 23, to Thursday June 30, 1737.

WENT from on board the *St. Andrew*, at *New-Castle*, on the 24th of *November* last, a Servant Man named *Nathan MacClure*, belonging to *William Hartley*. He is about 30 Years of Age, of middling Stature; has a broad Face, red Hair (but sometimes wears a Cap or Wig) and is much Pock Fretten. He had on a blue Coat, his other Cloaths unknown.

 Whoever secures the said Servant and brings him to *Walter Denny* in *Lancaster* County and Township of *Dromore*, or to *William Hartley* at *Matthias Alpden's*, Merchant in *Philadelphia*, shall have *Thirty Shillings* Reward and reasonable Charges

    paid By *Walter Denny*, or *William Hartley.*

 N. B. If the said *Nathan MacClure* will come of his own accord, immediately after the publication hereof, to the said *Denny* or *Hartley*, he shall be used with Civility, paying them their just Demands: But if any Persons shall Entertain or Conceal him, they shall be prosecuted according to Law.

 The American Weekly Mercury, From Thursday June 9, to Thursday June 16, 1737; From Thursday June 16, to Thursday June 23, 1737; From Thursday June 23, to Thursday June 30, 1737.

RAN-away from *John M'Comb*, of this City, Taylor, some time in *April* last, an Apprentice named *Samuel Thomas*, in the last year of his Time. He is of middling Stature; had on when he went away, a Drugget Coat and Breeches, of a brownish Colour, and old Felt Hat. It is said that he has been lately seen at *Burlington.*

 Whoever takes him up and brings him to the Work-house, shall have *Thirty Shillings* Reward, and all reasonable Charges

    paid By *John M'Comb.*

The American Weekly Mercury, From Thursday June 9, to Thursday June 16, 1737; From Thursday June 23, to Thursday July 3, 1737.

RUN away on the 5th Instant *June*, from *Owen Evans* of *North Wales*, in *Philadelphia* County, a *Pembrokeshire* Servant Man, named *John Morgan*, speaks some English, aged 24 Years, tall and well set, short, light-brown curl'd Hair, grey Eyes, his Face pockfretten. Had on a felt Hat, a plain woollen grey Coat, strip'd linnen Trowsers, dark colour'd woollen Stockings, old Shoes.

Whoever secures the said Servant so that his Master may have him again, shall have *Forty Shillings* Reward, and reasonable Charges,
   paid by *Owen Evans.*

The Pennsylvania Gazette, From June 2, to June 9, 1737; From June 9, to June 16, 1737; From June 16, to June 23, 1737.

RUN away this Morning from *William Watson* of this City, Shipwright, an Irish Servant Man named *Timothy Somers*, aged about 27 Years, middle Stature, no Hair, dark Complexion: Had on an ozenbrigs Shirt, striped white and red flannel Jacket, ozenbrigs Trowsers and new Shoes.

Whoever secures the said Servant so that he may be had again, shall have *Three Pounds* Reward and reasonable Charges,
   paid by *William Watson.* *Philad. June* 16.

The Pennsylvania Gazette, From June 9, to June 16, 1737; From June 16, to June 23, 1737; From June 23, to June 30, 1737; From June 30, to July 7, 1737.

RUN away on Sunday last, from *Philip Thomas* of *Vincent* Township, *Chester* County, a *Welsh* Servant Man named *Thomas Loyd*, aged about 22 Years, of middle Stature, sandy Complexion, down Look. Had on when he went away, a light cinnamon homespun Vest-Coat, old plush Breeches, old Shoes and Stockings, a new felt Hat, homespun Shirt. He pretends to be a Sailor.

Whoever secures the said Servant, so that he may be had again, shall have *Forty Shillings* Reward and reasonable Charges
   paid by *Philip Thomas. Philad. June* 23. 1737.

The Pennsylvania Gazette, From June 16, to June 23, 1737; From June 23, to June 30, 1737; From June 30, to July 7, 1737; From July 7, to July 14, 1737; From July 14, to July 21, 1737.

RAN-away on the 23d of *June* from *David Davies* of *Goshen* in *Chester* County, an Irish Servant Man, named *James Roult*, aged about 25 Years, of middle stature, swarthy Complexion, a little pockfretten, looks brisk. Had on a good felt Hat, a worsted Cap, a black vest coat, a check shirt, striped breeches, old Trowsers, new round toe'd shoes, with a buckle to one, and a string to the other: He pretends to be a Linen-Weaver by Trade; has been but about three Weeks in the Country, and ran-away once before.

Whoever secures the said Servant so that his Master may have him again, shall have *Twenty Shillings* Reward, and reasonable Charges,
paid By   David Davies.

The American Weekly Mercury, From June 23, to June 30, 1737; From June 30, to July 7, 1737; From July 7, to July 14, 1737. See *The Pennsylvania Gazette*, From June 23, to July 30, 1730.

RUN away on the 23d Inst. from *David Davis* of *Goshen* in *Chester* County, an Irish Servant Man, named *James Roult*, aged about 25 Years, of middle Stature, swarthy Complexion, a little pockfretten, looks brisk. Had on a good felt Hat, a worsted Cap, a black Waste-coat, a check Shirt, striped Breeches, old Trowsers, new round toe'd Shoes, with a Buckle to one, and a String to the other: He pretends to be a Linnen Weaver by Trade; has been but about three Weeks in the Country, and run away once before.

Whoever secures the said Servant so that he may be had again, shall have *Twenty Shillings* Reward, and reasonable Charges
paid by   David Davis.   Philad. June 30.

The Pennsylvania Gazette, From June 23, to June 30, 1730; From June 30, to July 7, 1737; From July 7, to July 14, 1737; From July 14, to July 21, 1737; From July 21, to July 28, 1737. See *The American Weekly Mercury*, From June 23, to June 30, 1737.

RAN-away, on the 3*d* of this Inst, *July*, from *Thomas Mayburry*, of *Poole*, in *Philadelphia* County, an *Irish* Servant Man named *Edward Hamilton*, by Trade a Forgeman, aged about 26 Years, a tall slender Fellow, has a long Neck, black Hair of a middling length, his Beard new shaved, long Visage, large Eyes, a wide Mouth, Teeth larger than common, speaks good *English*, is very forward and apt to swear, and carries a Cudgel. Had on when he went away, an old Garlick Shirt, torn at the Breast and Back, and new mended about the Neck, a pair of Oznabrigs Trowsers, good Shoes, a good Castor Hat with a black Ribbon round the Crown, an Orange colour'd Handkerchief, no Coat nor Jacket.

Whoever takes up and brings the said Servant to his Master, shall have *Five Pounds* if taken up in this Province, or *Seven Pounds* if taken up in any other Province, and reasonable Charges,
   paid By *Thomas Mayburry.*
The American Weekly Mercury, From June 30, to July 7, 1737; From July 7, to July 14, 1737. See *The American Weekly Mercury*, From Thursday September 14, to Thursday September 21, 1732, *The American Weekly Mercury*, From July 14, to July 21, 1737, and *The American Weekly Mercury*, From Thursday August 4, to Thursday August 11, 1737.

RAN-away from *French-Creek* Iron Works in *Chester* County, on the 3d of this Inst. *July*, a Servant Man named *David M'Quatty*, by Trade a Hammerman and Refiner; but formerly followed Shalloping up and down the Bay from *Egg-Harbour*. He is a *Scotchman* but speaks pretty good English, of a middling size, about 28 Years of Age, has a thin Visage small Mouth, thin Lips, Roman Nose, and a few Spots of Gun-Powder under his right Eye, and is something Pockfretten. He is a talkative Fellow, a great lover of Liquor, and when intoxicated very Quarrelsome; and has such a Trembling of the Nerves that he can hold nothing in his Hand steadily. He had on, a new yellowish or Snuff-colour'd Drugget Coat and Jacket, a new fine Shirt, new Castor Hat, a dark silk Handkerchief, Cotton Cap, a pair of new Linen Drawers, or a pair of Oznabrigs Trowsers, and a pair of large carved Brass Buckles in his Shoes.
  Whoever takes up and secures the said Servant so that his Master may have him again, shall have *Three Pounds* if taken up in this Province, or *Five Pounds* if taken up in any other Province, and reasonable Charges,
   paid By *Samuel Nutt.*
The American Weekly Mercury, From June 30, to July 7, 1737; From July 7, to July 14, 1737; From July 14, to July 21, 1737. See *The American Weekly Mercury*, From Tuesday December 28, 1736, to Thursday January 6, 1737; *The Pennsylvania Gazette*, From December 30, 1736, to January 6, 1737, and *The Pennsylvania Gazette*, From June 30, to July 7, 1737; From July 14, to July 21, 1737.

   French-Creek Iron-Works, *Chester* County, *July* 5. 1737.
RUN away from the Iron-Works aforesaid, a Servant Man named *DAVID M'QUATTY*, by Trade a Hammerman and Refiner, but has formerly followed Shaloping up and down the Bay from *Egg-Harbour*; he is a Scotchman but speaks pretty good *English*, middle siz'd, about 28 Years of age, of a thin Visage and a little Pock-fretten, with a Roman Nose and a few spots of

Gunpowder under his right Eye; he is a talkative Man, given to Liquor and then very quarrelsome; he has such a Trembling of the Nerves that he can hold nothing in his Hand steadily; he has a very small Mouth and thin Lips. He had on when he went away, a new Drugget Coat and Jacket of a kind of yellowish or Snuff colour, a good new fine Shirt, a new Castor Hat, a darkish Silk Handkerchief, a Cotton Cap, a pair of new Linen Drawers, or a pair of Ozenbrigs Trowsers, and a pair of large carved Brass Buckles in his Shoes.

Whoever secures the said Servant so that his Master may have him again, shall have *Three Pounds* if taken up in this Province, or *Five Pounds* if taken up in any other Province, and reasonable Charges,
   paid by Samuel Nutt.
The Pennsylvania Gazette, From June 30, to July 7, 1737; From July 7, to July 14, 1737; From July 14, to July 21, 1737; From July 21, to July 28, 1737. See *The American Weekly Mercury*, From Tuesday December 28, 1736, to Thursday January 6, 1737, and *The Pennsylvania Gazette*, From December 30, 1736, to January 6, 1737, and *The American Weekly Mercury*, From June 30, to July 7, 1737.

RAN-away, on the 2*d* of *July*, from the Copper Mines commonly called *Caledonia*, in *Philadelphia* County, two English Servant Men, one of them called *Robert Waye*, aged about 30 Years, small siz'd, black Hair, brown Skin, gray Eyes, thin Visage, and Pockfretten. He had on an old Bever Hat, Oznabrigs Shirt & Trowsers, a striped Flanel Jacket, &c new Shoes. The other named *William Harrison*, aged about 28 Years, middle siz'd, brown Complexion: He had on an Oznabrigs Shirt and Trowsers, and a brown Fustian Frock with metal Buttons. They took with them several Shirts belonging to their fellow Servants.

Whoever takes up and secures the said Servants, or either of them, and gives Notice thereof so that they may be had again, shall have *Forty Shillings* Reward for each, if taken in this Province, or *Three Pounds* if taken in any other Province, and reasonable Charges
   paid. Jonathan Robinson. Nicholas Scull.
The American Weekly Mercury, From July 7, to Thursday July 14, 1737.

RUN on the 3d Instant July, at Night from *Benjamin Paschall*, of this City, Cutler, a Servant Man named *John Creighton*, aged about 25 Years, of middle Stature, a down Look, no Beard, Pockbroken, brown Hair, by Trade a Penknife-Hast-maker, served his Time at *Sheffield*, and has been a Soldier: Had on, a Beaver Hat, a homemade cinnamon colour'd duroy Coat lin'd with Shalloon plain made, striped Vest, and Breeches, brown Vest, blue grey worsted Stockings, old Shoes.

Whoever secures the said Servant, so that his Master may have him again, shall have *Forty Shillings* Reward, and reasonable Charges,
      paid by   *Benjamin Paschall.*
The Pennsylvania Gazette, From July 7, to July 14, 1737; From July 14, to July 21, 1737; From July 21, to July 28, 1737.

RAN-away, on the 15th of this Inst. *July,* from *Thomas Mayburry*, of *Poole*, in *Philadelphia* County, an *Irish* Servant Man named *Edward Hamilton*, by Trade a Forgeman, aged about 26 Years, a tall slender Fellow, has a long Neck, black Hair of a middling length, long Visage, large Eyes, a wide Mouth, Teeth larger than common, speaks good *English*, is very forward and apt to swear. Had on when he went away, a blue Shirt, a pair of Oznabrigs Trowsers, good Shoes, a Jockey Cap, and an Orange colour'd Handkerchief.
    N. B. He ran away a few days before; was taken up, and now (as they were carrying him home in a Waggon) made his escape with him Irons on.
Whoever takes up and secures the said Servant so that his Master may have him again, shall have *Twenty Shillings* if taken within three Miles of *Philadelphia*, or *Thirty Shillings* if taken farther off, and reasonable Charges,
      paid By   *Thomas Mayburry.*
The American Weekly Mercury, From July 14, to July 21, 1737; From July 21, to Thursday July 28, 1737. See *The American Weekly Mercury*, From Thursday September 14, to Thursday September 21, 1732, *The American Weekly Mercury*, From June 30, to July 7, 1737, and *The American Weekly Mercury*, From Thursday August 4, to Thursday August 11, 1737.

RUN away on the 19th of *July* past from *Nathaniel Grubb*, of *Willistown* in *Chester* County, an *Irish* Servant Man named *Richard Barret*, about 20 Years of Age, pretty tall and slender, wears his own Hair, has sore Eyes, and a large Scar on his Cheek caused by a Burn. He had on when he went away, a good felt Hat, homespun cinnamon colour'd Jacket, linnen Trowsers, and good shoes newly mended with strings in them.
    Whoever secures the said Servant so that his Master may have him again, shall have *Forty Shillings* Reward, and reasonable Charges
      paid by   *Nathaniel Grubb.*
The Pennsylvania Gazette, From July 14, to July 21, 1737; From July 21, to July 28, 1737; From July 28, to August 4, 1737; From August 4, to August 11, 1737; From August 11, to August 18, 1737.

ABSENTED himself from the Service of *Richard Pearne*, at *Skuylkill* Mill, in *Blockley* Township, *Philadelphia* County, an indented Man, named *Edward Major*, born in *England* and bred to Gardening; he is small of Stature, with black Hair, grey Eyes and sullen Countenance: had on when he went away, a new ozenbrig Shirt, new Trowsers of Tow Linnen, a new felt Hat and good Shoes. Whoever will secure the said *Servant* , and him safely convey to his Master, shall have *Twenty Shillings* as a Reward if taken in this County, and *Forty Shillings* if in any other, with reasonable Charges
    paid by *Richard Pearne*. *Philad. July* 21. 1737.
The Pennsylvania Gazette, From July 14, to July 21, 1737; From July 21, to July 28, 1737; From July 28, to August 4, 1737; From August 4, to August 11, 1737.

RUN away on *Sunday* last the three following Servant Men, *viz.*
 From *William Roe*, of *New-Garden* in *Chester* County, a *Scotch* Servant Man named *John M'Daniel*, aged about 24 Years, a tall Man with short black curl'd Hair. Had on an old Hat, linnen Jacket and Trowsers, and good Shoes soal'd.
 From *Robert Holiday* of the same Place, one named *Philip Macall*, a Native *Irishman*, of middle Stature, well set, about 24 Years of Age, has black strait Hair. Had on an old Felt Hat, a Tow Jacket, Flax linnen Shirt, ash-colour Kersey Breeches, coarse black worsted Stockings, double soal'd Pumps. Also one *Patrick Tommins*, born in *Dublin*, about 18 Years of age, middle stature, pockfretten, his Hair light brown, but lately shav'd: Has on a tow Shirt and Trowsers, and Leathers Breeches with Leather Buttons at the Knees, a good brown homespun cloth Coat with Brass Buttons, and double soal'd Pumps. 'Tis suppos'd they are all gone together.
 Whoever takes up and secures the said Servants so that their Masters may have them again, shall have *Thirty Shillings* Reward for each, or *Four Pounds Ten Shillings* for them all, and reasonable Charges
    paid, by *William Roe* & *Robert Holiday*. *Philada. July* 28. 1737.
The Pennsylvania Gazette, From July 21, to July 28, 1737; From July 28, to August 4, 1737; From August 4, to August 11, 1737; From August 11, to August 18, 1737. See *The American Weekly Mercury*, From Thursday September 9 to Thursday September 16, 1736, for John McDaniel/John MacDoniel.

RAN-away on the 1st of *August*, from *Thomas Maybery* of *Pool* Forge, an Irish Servant Man named *Edward Hambleton*, aged about 26 Years, speaks good English, a tall slender Fellow, forward in talking and swearing, has a long Neck, black Hair of a middling length, long Visage, large Eyes, a wide

Mouth, Teeth larger than common, his Apparel uncertain, because he stole some Linen and a new pair of Shoes.

With him went another Irish Servant Man named *Faril Crosbe*, belonging to *John Leacock*, he is a thick short Fellow, speaks bad English, blober lipt, hollow ey'd, and of a grim Countenance, has short round Teeth, a dent in the middle of his upper Lip, the mark of a kick by a Horse on one Leg, wears his Shoes crooked or without Heels, has lately cut off his Hair, his Apparel uncertain, he also stole two Garlick Shirts, one double brown holland Cap scollop'd, and a new pair of Oznabrigs Trowsers.

☞ They were both of them catch'd and brought home but a Week before.

Whoever takes them and brings them to their Masters, or either of them, shall have *Forty Shillings* for each, or either, and reasonable Charges, if taken in *Pennsylvania*; and *Fifty Shillings* each, and reasonable Charges, if taken in any other Province, paid by the above, *Maybery* and *Leacock*.

The American Weekly Mercury, From Thursday August 4, to Thursday August 11, 1737; From Thursday August 11, to Thursday August 18, 1737; From Thursday August 18, to Thursday August 25, 1737. See *The American Weekly Mercury*, From Thursday September 14, to Thursday September 21, 1732, *The American Weekly Mercury*, From June 30, to July 7, 1737, and *The American Weekly Mercury*, From July 14, to July 21, 1737, for Hambleton/Hamilton.

RUN away last Monday Morning from *Peter Saunders* of this City, Shoemaker, an *Irish* Servant Man, named *Thomas White*, aged about 18 Years, tall and slender, smooth fac'd, with black Eyes, and no Hair, but wears a Thrum Cap, a felt Hat, a lightish-colour'd drugget Coat, a red napp'd Jacket, with two Rows of Buttons down the Breast, leather Apron and Trowsers.

Whoever takes up and secures the said Servant so that he may be had again, shall have *Twenty shillings* Reward, and reasonable Charges paid by   *Peter Saunders. Philad. Oct.* 6. 1737.

The Pennsylvania Gazette, From September 29, to October 6, 1737; From October 6, to October 13, 1737; From October 13, to October 20, 1737.

RUN away from *Samuel Austin*, of this City, a Servant Man named *Joseph Woore*, by Trade a Joyner, aged about 34 Years, a thin Man with strait dark Hair; had on when he went away a grey Coat with blue Buttons, a Check'd Shirt, ozenbrigs Trowsers, thin Shoes but no Stockings. Whoever secures the said Servant so that he may be had again, shall have *Thirty Shillings* Reward and reasonable Charges paid, by   *Samuel Austin.*

The Pennsylvania Gazette, From September 29, to October 6, 1737; From October 6, to October 13, 1737; From October 13, to October 20, 1737; From October 20, to October 27, 1737.

RUN away from the Sloop *Dolphin*, of *Boston*, *Nathaniel Welsh*, Master, one *John Hamilton*, aged about 25 Years, of middle Stature, slim, pockfretten, and has a pretty high Nose. He robb'd the People on Board, and took from *John Bryan*, a new Rateen long Pea-Jacket, a new blue Rug Pea Jacket shorter, one new slate-colour'd fly Coat, six white Shirts, one dark-colour'd Wig with a large Brow, one pair of Boots little worn; From *William Tally* three new speckled shirts, a new brown Holland Jacket, a new natural Wig.

Whoever secures the said *John Hamilton*, so that he may be brought to Justice; or the said stolen Cloaths, so that the Owners may have them again, shall have *Five Pounds* Reward, paid by
  Philad. Oct. 6. 1737. *John Bryan* and *William Tally*.
The Pennsylvania Gazette, From September 29, to October 6, 1737; From October 13, to October 20, 1737.

RUN away from *Caleb Cowpland* of *Chester* in *Pennsylvania*, on the 21st past, a native Irish Servant Man, named *Patrick Sherradon*, about 16 Years of Age, tall and walks upright, of a thin and brown Complexion, a sharp long Nose, short brown Hair, sometimes wears an old yellowish colour'd Wig, and Felt Hat; took with him a coarse grey Cloth Coat with Black Buttons and no Lineing except the Collar, an old olive-colour'd Jacket, two pair of linnen Breeches, coarse yarn stockings, old shoes; he has likewise taken a Wallet with several Loaves of Bread, and two Cheeses, and 'tis supposed he has changed his Name; has been about three Months in the Country, and stole his Indentures.

Whoever secures the said Servant, so that he may be had again, shall have *Five Pounds* Reward and reasonable Charges
  paid by *Caleb Cowpland*.
The Pennsylvania Gazette, From September 29, to October 6, 1737; From October 6, to October 13, 1737; From October 13, to October 20, 1737; From October 20, to October 27, 1737.

RUN away from *William Crosthwaite*, of this City, Peruke maker, a Servant Lad, named *John Mills*, aged about 18 Years, of middle Stature, with full Eyes: Had on a double breasted blue Coat, with flat metal Buttons, ozenbrigs Jacket, a white Wig, and old Stockings.

Whoever secures him so that he may be had again, shall have *Twenty Shillings* Reward if within 20 Miles of this City, *Thirty Shillings* if within 30 Miles, and *Forty Shillings* if farther off, with reasonable Charges paid by *William Crossthwaite.*

The Pennsylvania Gazette, From October 20, to October 27, 1737; From October 27, to November 3, 1737; From November 3, to November 10, 1737.

RUN away on the 11th Inst. from *John Jones* of *Worcester* Township, *Philadelphia* County, an *English* Servant Man, named *John Hooper*, aged about 21 Years, of middle Stature, well set, darkish Complexion, light brown Hair, and his Hands are full of Warts. Had on when he went away, a felt Hat, a lightish colour'd Kersey Coat lin'd with red, a red and white strip'd flannel Jacket, red white and blue flannel Breeches, a pair of check'd Trowsers, blue worsted Stockings, and new round-toe'd Shoes and a check'd Shirt: He took with him a white Shirt brown Wig, a Gun and Powder-Horn with some Lead.

Whoever secures the said Servant, so that he may be had again, shall have *Forty Shillings* Reward, and reasonable Charges paid by

Owen Owen at the *Indian King*, or by *John Jones.*
Philad. Octob. 20. 1737.

The Pennsylvania Gazette, From October 20, to October 27, 1737; From October 27, to November 3, 1737; From November 3, to November 10, 1737; From November 10, to November 17, 1737.

RAN-away on the 18th of *November* past, from *Henry Smith* of *Tulpahocken*, in *Lancaster* County, the two following Servants, *viz.*

One named *John Impy*, aged about 22 Years, fair Complexion, black Hair, but 'tis supposed he will cut it off and wear a Wig that he has taken with him.

The other is a *Welch* Lad, about 18 Years of Age, speaks good English, and is of a fair Complexion.

They broke open their Masters Store, and took from thence all his wearing Cloaths, two Silk Jackets and Breeches, a good Cloath Coat and Breeches, three or four Holland Shirts, eight or nine Oznabrigs Shirts, two Pair of Stockings, the one pair Silk, the other Worsted, very good Shoes, two Pair of Silver Buckles, a very good Hat, several Yards of Kersey and Stroud, ten or eleven good Skins dress'd and some others in the Hair, two Dozen of Knives, a Pound of Vermilion, with a Parcel of Wampum. They have also taken a bay Horse about 13 Hands high, branded **HS** on the near Buttock, a very small Star in his Forehead, the lower part of his near Forefoot is white. And a brown bay Mare, about 12 Hands high, and has a Fistula on his

Shoulder not quite cured, with two good new Saddles and Bridles, and 'tis thought *John Impy* will take upon him to be a Gentleman, and make the other his Man.

Whoever takes up and secures the said Servants and Goods, so that they may be had again, shall have *Three Pounds* Reward for each Servant, and reasonable Charges paid, by the abovesaid
Henry Smith, or by *Edward Shippen* in *Philadelphia*.
The American Weekly Mercury, From Thursday November 17, to Thursday November 24, 1737; From Thursday November 24, to Thursday December 1, 1737; From Thursday December 1, to Thursday December 8, 1737; *The Pennsylvania Gazette*, December 1, 1737. Minor differences between the papers.

RUN away on the 12th Instant, from William Fishbourn, *an* English *Servant Man, name* James Butler, *a House-Carpenter by Trade, but has been used to the Sea, of middle Stature, smooth Face, fresh colour'd, has a blackish Mark under one of his Eyes (by a blow in the Night) his Hair cut off, and wears a Wollen Cap under an old Hat, (if he has not got another.) Had on, a dark coarse Cloth Pea Jacket lined with blue Woollen Cloth, a dark colour'd Broad Cloth Vest, lined with dark Shalloon, a Linnen Jacket, a pair of Leather Breeches, and has taken another pair of Breeches with him, old check'd Shirts, and a pair of old Shoes and Stockings: he came hither last Year from* Bristol, *with Capt.* Bromadge, *and attempted to run away last Fall for* Cape-Fear.
Whoever secures the said Servant so that his Master may have him again, of within 10 *Miles of this City, shall have Ten Shillings, if* 20, *Twenty Shillings, and if* 40, *Forty Shillings Reward, and reasonable Charges paid by*
William Fishbourn. Philad. Nov. 17. 1737.
The Pennsylvania Gazette, From November 10, to November 17, 1737; From November 17, to November 24, 1737; From November 24, to December 1, 1737. See *The American Weekly Mercury*, From Thursday December 2, to Thursday December 9, 1736.

RAN-away on the 13th of *Decemb*. Inst. from *William Patterson's* Shallop, at *Philadelphia*, a Servant Man nam'd *John McDowell*, about 20 Years of Age, well Set, and fresh colour'd, and has short black Hair. He had on when he went away a double breasted Ratteen Jacket with a brownish one under it, Leather Breeches, coarse Shirt, old Shoes, and a Felt Hat.

Whoever secures the said Servant so that his said Master may have him again, shall have *Thirty Shillings* Reward, and reasonable Charges paid, by *Thomas Williams*, Hatter, in *Philadelphia*, or at *Christiana*,

By *William Patterson.*
The American Weekly Mercury, From Thursday December 8, to Thursday December 15, 1737; From Thursday December 15, to Thursday December 22, 1737; From Thursday December 22, to Thursday December 29, 1737; From Thursday December 29, 1737, to Thursday January 3, 1738; From Thursday January 3, to Thursday January 10, 1738.

RUN away on the 15th Instant from *John Park* of *Fallowfield* in *Chester* County, a Servant Man, named *William Moore*, aged about 20 Years, of short stature, well set, short brown Hair, pale Fac'd. Had with him, a felt Hat, a Bag with a pretty deal of Cloaths in it, a whitish colour'd Broad Cloth great Coat with Brass Buttons, of his Master's, a strait Coat of brown colour, the trimming of a whitish colour, the Collar of it lin'd with red, a Snuff colour'd Jacket and Breeches, grey yarn Stockings new footed, a pair of peek'd toe'd Shoes, a large and small Buckle in them.

He also took with him a large Bay Horse, branded on the off Buttocks thus ▽ Paces pretty fast.

Whoever secures the said Servant, so that he may be had again, shall have *Twenty Shillings* Reward, and reasonable Charges,

paid by   John Park.

The Pennsylvania Gazette, From December 15, to December 22, 1737; From December 22, to December 29, 1737; From December 29, 1737, to January 3, 1738; From January 3, to January 10, 1738; From January 10, to January 17, 1738; From January 17, to January 24, 1738.

1738

RUN away on the 15th of *Decem.* past, from *Joshua Baker* of *Philadelphia*, a Servant Man named *Fernando ONeal*, about 30 Years of Age, of middle Stature, thin Visage, and black Hair: He had on when he went away, a dark colour'd Frise Coat, brown Cloth-Serge Jacket and Breeches, a check Shirt, a pair or yarn Stockings, a pair of new Shoes, and a Felt Hat.

Whoever secures the said Servant so that his Master, or Owen Owen of said City, may have him again, shall have Thirty Shillings Reward, and all reasonable Charges, paid by   *Joshua Baker.*

The Pennsylvania Gazette, From January 3, to January 10, 1738; From January 10, to January 17, 1738; From January 17, to January 24, 1738.

RUN away from Joseph Lynn, *Shipwright, of* Philadelphia, *a Servant Man named* John Boddiscurte, *aged about* 25 *Years, a Shipwright, or Baker by Trade, of middle Stature, with a cast in his Eyes, short brown Hair, and wears a red and white worsted Cap. Had on when he went away, a new Felt Hat, A long brown Pea-Jacket, lin'd with red, a blue and white striped Flannel Jacket, speckled Shirt, black Stockings, and new Shoes. Whosoever takes up and secures the said Servant, so that his Master may have him again, shall have* Forty Shillings *if taken in this Province, and* Three Pounds *Reward, if taken in any other Province, and reasonable Charges,*
        paid by   Joseph Lynn.
    The Pennsylvania Gazette, From January 10, to January 17, 1738; From January 17, to January 24, 1738; From January 31, to February 7, 1738; From February 7, to February 15, 1738; From February 15, to February 22, 1738.

RUN away from *John Hoopes* of *Goshen* in *Chester* County, on the 5th Inst. a Servant Man named *John James*, born in *England*, aged about 20 Years, he is of short Stature, brown Complexion, with dark black Hair, hath been in this Country about 9 Years; he hath with him an old Indenture with several Assignments, the last to *Henry Woodward*, is a very good Hand at dressing Flax, and takes most Delight in that of any Work.
    Whoever shall take up and secure the said Servant , so that his Master may have him again, shall have *Thirty Shillings* Reward and reasonable Charges paid by   John Hoopes.   *Philad. Jan.* 17. 1737, 8.
    The Pennsylvania Gazette, From January 10, to January 17, 1738; From January 10, to January 17, 1738.

RAN-away from *Anthony Noble*, of this City, Glasier and Painter, on the 6th of *February* Instant, an Irish Servant Man named *Morgan Rion*, about 20 Years of Age, short and well set. He had on a dark Coat, short brown Jacket, black Leather Breeches, white woolen Stockings, good Holland Shirt, and an old Hat painted on the Crown.
    Whoever shall take up the said Servant and return him to his said Master, or secure him so that he may be had again, shall have *Thirty Shillings* Reward, and all reasonable Charges, paid   By *Anthony Noble*.
    The American Weekly Mercury, From Tuesday January 31, to Tuesday February 7, 1738.

RAN-away from *Nicholas Castle* of this City, Ship-Joiner, on the 25th of *February*, a Welsh Servant Man named *James Cornish*, by Trade a Joiner, aged about 21 Years, of middling Stature, full Fac'd, has brown bushy Hair, Lisps a little. He took with him two Suits of darkish red Broadcloth, a lightish red Broadcloth Coat lin'd with a shagreen Silk, Scarlet Breeches with shagreen Puffs, a red shag Great Coat, gray worsted Stockings, and several other pair, a pair of old Boots, calf-skin Shoes, two check'd Shirts and a fine white one, a very large pair of carv'd silver Buckles.

Whoever shall take up said Servant and return him to his said Master, or secure him so that he may be had again, shall have *Forty Shillings* Reward and all reasonable Charges paid, By *Nicholas Castle.*

The American Weekly Mercury, From Tuesday February 21, to Tuesday February 28, 1738; From Tuesday February 28, to Tuesday March 7, 1738; From Tuesday March 7, to Tuesday March 14, 1738; From Thursday March 23, to Thursday March 30, 1738. See *The Pennsylvania Gazette*, From February 21, to February 28, 1738.

RUN away on the 6th Inst. from *Henry Clark*, at the Sign of the Coach and Horses in *Chesnut-street*, opposite the State-House, an *Irish* Servant Woman, named *Margaret McClenny*, aged about 40 Years, of a middle Size, pale Complexion, and useth the Word *FAITH* in her common Discourse. Had on a long dark Drab Cloak burnt at one Corner, and towards the Bottom work'd round with an Eylethole, a light colour'd Calimanco Quilt, a black Silk Alamode Bonnet pieced in the Linning of the Cape, and Strings of the same sort, a blue and white check'd Apron, Dun colour'd Gown pretty much worn and darn'd in the Sleeves, pretty good Shoes, and almost new Clogs. Whoever secures the said Servant, so that she may be had again, shall have *Twenty Shillings* Reward and reasonable Charges, paid by   Henry Clark.

The Pennsylvania Gazette, From February 28, to March 7, 1738; From March 7, to March 14, 1738.

RUN away from *Nicholas Castle*, a *Welsh* Servant Man, named *James Cornish*, aged about 21 Years, of middle Stature, full Fac'd, brown bushy Hair, lisps a little when he talks. He was cloth'd when he went away, with two Suits of a darkish red broad Cloth, a lightish red colour'd Coat lin'd with a Shagreen Silk, scarlet Breeches with Shagreen Puffs, grey worsted Stockings, and took with him several other pair, a pair of Calf-Skin Shoes, two check'd Shirts, a fine white one, a very large pair of carv'd Silver Buckels. He also took with him, a red shag great Coat.

Whosoever secures the said Servant, so that his Master may have him again, shall have *Twenty Shillings* Reward, and reasonable Charges,
         paid by   Nicholas Castle. Philadelphia, Feb. 28. 1737,8.

The Pennsylvania Gazette, From February 21, to February 28, 1738; From February 28, to March 7, 1738; From March 7, to March 14, 1738; From March 14, to March 21, 1738. See *The American Weekly Mercury,* From Tuesday February 21, to Tuesday February 28, 1738.

ON the 9th of this Instant *April,* one *Michael Roof,* a Lad about 16 Years of Age, Son to *Coonrade Roof,* near Mount Pleasant Furnace, in *Philadelphia* County, went away from his Father's House, and is not yet return'd Any Person that will return him to his said Father, or to *Thomas Potts* at *Colebrook-dale,* shall be well rewarded, and have all reasonable Charges paid. And all Masters of Vessels, and others, are forewarn'd carrying him off. He is a Palatine, but speaks pretty good English, is pretty short and well set, and was thin cloath'd.   *April* 19. 1738.

The American Weekly Mercury, From Thursday April 13, to Thursday April 20, 1738; From Thursday April 20, to Thursday April 27, 1738; From Thursday April 27, to Thursday May 4, 1738.

RAN-away the 24th of *April* last, from *David Potts* at the Forks of *Delaware,* in *Bucks* County, a Servant Man named *Reese Pritchard,* about 27 or 28 Years of age, tall of Stature and stoops in his walk, he is of a dark Complexion, has black Hair and a Roman Nose; he had on when he went away, a pretty good Felt Hat, an old brown Cloath Jacket, a pair of old Leather Breeches, old gray Yarn Stockings, and his Shoes not Fellows. Whoever takes up and secures the said Servant so that his Master may have him again, shall have *Thirty Shillings* Reward, and reasonable Charges,
       paid by   *David Potts.*

The American Weekly Mercury, From Thursday April 27, to Thursday May 4, 1738; From Thursday May 4, to Thursday May 11, 1738; From Thursday May 11, to Thursday May 18, 1738. See *The Pennsylvania Gazette,* From August 10, to August 17, 1738.

RAN-away the 31st of *March* past, from *Moses Vernon* and *William Lindsay,* of *Providence* in *Chester* County, near *Chester,* two Native Irish Servant Men, *viz.*

From *Moses Vernon,* one named *Peter Ryon,* of middle Stature, blackish strait Hair, thin fac'd and paleish, about 20 Years of Age: Had on a light colour'd Jacket and Breeches of new Cloth, with Brass Buttons, a reddish stripped under Jacket; he also took with him, and old grey wide Coat the Cuffs torn off, and an oldish Beaver Hat. The other from *William Lindsay,* named *Dennis Adogan,* of middle Stature, swarthy Complexion, Black thick

Hair, about 20 Years of Age. He had on, a reddish brown Jacket with Brass Buttons, a cotton and linen Jacket and Breeches with blue striped, white linen Trowsers, a new felt Hat, he took with him an old dark brown wide Coat. Has the Brogue on his Tongue.

 Whoever takes up and secures the said Servants, so that their Masters may have them again, shall have *Three Pounds* Reward for each of them, and reasonable Charges paid By Moses Vernon and William Lindsay.

N. B. *The said Dennis Adogan, was a Redemptioner and it is supposed he has taken his Redemption Bond or Indenture with him.*

 The American Weekly Mercury, From Thursday May 11, to Thursday May 18, 1738; From Thursday May 18, to Thursday May 25, 1738; From Thursday May 25, to Thursday June 1, 1738.

RUN away on the 8th past, from George Stroud, *of* East-Bradford *in* Chester County, *a Servant Man named* Ephraim Callender, American *Born, aged about 30 Years, tall and slender, pale, and thin visag'd, with short yellowish Hair. Had on, an old Felt Hat, new brown Coat with Cuffs, lin'd with white Linsey Woolsey, with Brass Buttons, old Leather Breeches with Brass Buttons, old Yarn Stockings, and good Shoes. Whosoever secures the said Servant so that his Master may have him again, shall have* Twenty Shillings *Reward, and reasonable Charges, paid by* *George Stroud.*

 The Pennsylvania Gazette, From May 11, to May 18, 1738; From May 18, to May 25, 1738; From May 25, to June 1, 1738.

RAN-away about the Beginning of *April* from *Stephen Cole* of *Pequea*, in *Lancaster* County, a Servant Man named *Neil Quin*, about 22 years of age, he is an *Irish* Man and has a great Brogue, he is a lusty Fellow, very Lazy, loves strong Drink, and is a Glutton: He has on when he went away, an Oznabrigs Fly Coat, a green Jacket, he had curl'd black Hair, but we hear he has cut if off and wears a new Cap.

 N. B. He had Liberty to Work out, and was last at *William Branson's* Iron Works, and was to return home once a Month, or oftner, to settle with his Master, but not appearing, he is judg'd to be ran away.

 Whoever beings home the said Servant or secures him so that he may be had again, shall have *Three Pounds* Reward and reasonable Charges,
   paid By *Stephen Cole.*

 The American Weekly Mercury, From Thursday May 4, to Thursday May 11, 1738; From Thursday May 11, to Thursday May 18, 1738; From Thursday May 18, to Thursday May 25, 1738.

RUN away on the 27th of April *past, at Night, from* Samuel Butt *of* Plumsted *Township,* Bucks *County, an* Irish *Servant Man, named* William Cuugh, *short of Stature, bow legged, flat footed, of a dark Complexion, round and full fac'd, much mark'd with the Small-Pox, is watry eyed, and wears a Cap or light colour'd Wig: Had a good Felt Hat, a blue Duroy Coat lin'd with Silk Crape, a pretty good white Dimmity Jacket, and new Breeches of the same, a new fine Shirt and two new homespun ones, two new Muslin Stocks, white Cotton Stockings and a pair of grey yarn ones, old round toe'd Shoes with strings in them. He has taken his own and another Man's Indentures with him.*

Whoever takes up and secures the said Servant, so that his Master may have him again, shall have Forty Shillings Reward, and reasonable Charges, paid by SAMUEL BUTT. Philad. May 1. 1738.

The Pennsylvania Gazette, From May 4, to May 11, 1738; From May 11, to May 18, 1738; From May 18, to May 25, 1738; From June 1, to June 8, 1738.

RUN away on Fryday *last, from* John Parry, *of Chester County, a Servant Man named* William Nichols, *about* 34 *Years of Age, of Middle size, and slender; with a sickly look. Had on, a speckled Shirt, striped flannel Jacket, an old brown plain Coat very greasy: He is by Trade a Brickmaker.*

Whoever secures the said Servant, so that his Master may have him again, shall have Forty Shillings Reward and reasonable Charges paid by JOHN PARRY.

Note, He lately came in with Capt. Chads *from* Bristol, *but has been in this Country before.* Philad. May 23, 1738.

The Pennsylvania Gazette, From May 18, to May 25, 1738; From May 25, to June 1, 1738; From June 1, to June 8, 1738; From June 8, to June 15, 1738; From June 15, to June 22, 1738.

RUN away from William Hamilton, *of* Doe-run, *in Chester County, a Welsh Servant Man, named* William Griffin, *of a middle Stature, coal Black Hair, pale fac'd, much disfigured with Fire, particularly on the right side, sharp Nose. He had on a leather Jacket with brass Buttons, a Shirt and Trowsers pretty much worn, an old felt Hat, a pair of old Brogues.*

Whoever secures the said Servant, so as the Owner may have him again, shall have Three Pounds *Reward, and reasonable Charges paid by* William Hamilton .

The Pennsylvania Gazette, From May 18, to May 25, 1738; From May 25, to June 1, 1738; From June 8, to June 15, 1738; From June 15, to June 22, 1738

MADE his Escape on the 14th Inst. May from the Subscriber, Constable of the Township of Oley, *one* Thomas Gray, *a tall lusty Man, has a Scar near his Nose. He had on when he went away, a light colour'd Drugget Coat. He was committed to* Philadelphia *Goal for Horse Stealing.*

All Persons hereby desired to use their endeavours to apprehend and secure the said Fellon in any Goal, and for so doing shall receive Thirty Shillings *Reward, and reasonable Charges*
    paid by   ROBERT SMITH.
The Pennsylvania Gazette, From May 18, to May 25, 1738; From May 25, to June 1, 1738; From June 8, to June 15, 1738.

RUN away on the 3d. Inst. from Samuel Yarnal *of Edgmont, in* Chester County, *an* English *Servant Man, named* Thomas Onions, *of middle Stature, black Hair, round featur'd, and is by Trade a Bellows-Maker: Had on when he went away a dark mixt colour'd Coat with Mohair Buttons, striped linnen Jacket and Breeches, two homespun Shirts, a pair of old Trowsers, grey yarn Stockings, old Shoes, and a good Felt Hat.*

Whoever takes up and secures the said Servant so that he is had again, shall have Twenty Shillings *Reward and reasonable Charges*
    paid by   Samuel Yarnal.   Philad. May 31. 1738.
The Pennsylvania Gazette, From May 25, to June 1, 1738; From June 1, to June 8, 1738; From June 8, to June 15, 1738.

RUN away from Joseph Lynn *of this City, Shipwright, a Servant Man named* James Bond, *by Trade a Sawyer, he is a well-set stout Fellow, with a down Look and short brown Hair: He had on when he went away a good brown Pea-Jacket lin'd with blue, a white flannel Jacket, a good Felt Hat flopt, Ozenbrigs Shirt and Trowsers, mill'd Yarn Stockings: and good Shoes; he is an Englishman and talks broad West-Country.*

Whoever takes up and secures the said Servant so that he may be had again, shall have Forty Shillings Reward and reasonable Charges
    paid by   Joseph Lynn. Philadelphia,   June 15. 1738.
The Pennsylvania Gazette, From June 8, to June 15, 1738; From June 15, to June 22, 1738; From June 22, to June 28, 1728. See *The American Weekly Mercury*, From Thursday June 15, to Thursday June 22, 1738.

RUN away on the 4th Inst. at Night, from Timothy Scarth, *of the* Northern Liberties, *Tanner, Two Servant Men, viz.*

One named Randal M'Daniel, *an Irishman, aged about* 20 *Years, middle-siz'd, broad made, walks very upright, no Hair, and wears a white Cap. Had on a Felt Hat, dark-colour'd Kersey Coat with close slit Sleeves, and a light-colour'd Cloth Coat, white Linnen Breeches, and blue & white striped homespun Jacket, grey worsted Stockings.*

The other named John Eagen, *an Irishman, and has been a Hatter, about* 20 *Years of Age, tall and stoops as he walks, one of his Ancles turns out and is pretty large, his Cloaths the same with the other, except the light Cloth Coat. And they have taken two pair of new Calf-skin Shoes, two pair of Hide Leather Shoes, one new the other old, and one pair of new Pumps; also two pair of Ozenbrigs Trowsers much dy'd by the Tan; and the Men may be known to be Tanners by their Nails, which are stain'd of a deep Brown by their Business.*

Whoever secures the said Servants so that their Master gets them again, shall have Forty Shillings *Reward for each, and reasonable Charges*
        paid by   Timothy Scarth. Philad. June 15.

The Pennsylvania Gazette, From June 8, to June 15, 1738; From June 15, to June 22, 1738

RAN-away from *Joseph Lynn* Shipwright of *Philadelphia*, a Servant Man named *James Bond*, a Sawyer by Trade, he is a well set stout Fellow, down look, with short brown Hair: He had on when he went away a good brown pea Jacket lin'd with blue, a white Flannel Jacket, a good felt hat flopt, Oznabrigs Shirt and Trowsers, mill'd yarn Stockings, and good Shoes, he is an Englishman and talks broad West-Country.

Whoever takes up and secures said Servant so that his Master may have him again, shall have *Forty Shillings* Reward and reasonable Charges
        paid By   *Joseph Lynn.*

The American Weekly Mercury, From Thursday June 15, to Thursday June 22, 1738; From Thursday June 22, to Thursday June 29, 1738; From Thursday June 29, to Thursday July 6, 1738. See *The Pennsylvania Gazette,* From June 8, to June 15, 1738.

RUN away on *Tuesday* Night, the 13th Instant, from *Joshua Baker*, in *Lancaster* County near *Newtown*, Four Irish Servant Men, *viz.*

Garret Cavannah, a tall slim Fellow, about 26 Years of Age, sandy Complexion, freckled and pockfretten, no Hair; Had on a brown Linen Wastcoat, and a blue broad cloth Wastcoat, and a dark colour'd Frize Coat, and long Trowsers.

Richard Brady, about 22 Years of Age, by Trade a Miller, a lusty Fellow, with a small Hole in his left Cheek; a brown Linen Wastcoat, and a dark Frize Wastecoat with Meal in it, and new long Trowsers.

Patrick Reynolds, a little Fellow, about 30 Years of Age, of a sandy Complexion, with short Hair; had on a striped Ticken Wastcoat and Breeches, and a black Frize Coat, long Trowsers; with one big carv'd Brass Buckle, the other of Iron and plain.

Terence Mc'Dermot, of middle Stature, between 30 and 40 Years of Age, by Trade a Distiller, speaks broken English; Had on a black Frize Coat, coarse Trowsers.

Whoever secures the said Servants so that their Master may have them again, shall have Thirty Shillings Reward for each, and reasonable Charges,

          paid by   *Joshua Baker*. *Philad. June* 9 1738.

The Pennsylvania Gazette, From June 22, to June 29, 1738; From July 6, to July 13, 1738; From July 20, to July 27, 1738; From July 27, to August 3, 1738.

RUN away on Sunday the 25th Inst. from Michael Hillegas, *of this City, Potter, an Apprentice Lad named* Thomas Lancilcus, *about 19 Years old, middle Stature, no Hair; wears a Cap, a Felt Hat, homespun Shirt, two Silk Handkerchiefs one strip'd and the other red, Linsey-woolsey Jacket red and blue striped, whitish Kersey Breeches, two pair of worsted Stockings, one pair olive-colour'd the other whitish, half worn Shoes. Whosoever secures the said Apprentice, so that his Master may have him again, shall have* Forty Shillings *Reward, and reasonable Charges*

          paid by   Michael Hillegas. Philad. June 29. 1738.

The Pennsylvania Gazette, From June 22, to June 29, 1738; From July 6, to July 13, 1738.

RUN away Yesterday from Nathan Lewis *of* Newtown, *in* Chester *County, an* English *Servant Man, named* John House, *aged about 20 Years, of a fair Complexion, full fac'd, short Stature, his Hair shav'd. Had on when he went away, an old Felt Hat, old Fustian Coat, grey Woollen Jacket much worn, with brass Buttons, a coarse Shirt, two pair of Trowsers, and new Shoes with carv'd Buckles in them.*

Whosoever secures the said Servant so that his Master may have him again, shall have Twenty Shillings *Reward, and reasonable Charges, paid by* Nathan Lewis.

N. B. It is supposed he has got an old Indenture of James Ross's, *that serv'd his time with the said Master.*   Philad. June 29. 1738.

The Pennsylvania Gazette, From June 22, to June 29, 1738.

RAN-away, the 20*th* of *June* Inst. from *Samuel Hastings*, a Servant Man named *Thomas Wildeere*, about 22 Years of age, of middling Stature and well-set, of a sandy Complexion and short Hair, much Pock-broken and has a down look; he had on when he went away, an old Felt Hat, a blue Jacket and a striped Flanel Jacket, an Oznabrigs Shirt, a pair of old Oznabrigs Trowsers, new Shoes, and a red Silk Handkerchief,

Ran-away, at the same Time, from *Michael Huling*, a Servant Man named *James Maguire*, an Irishman, about 21 Years of age, he is a tall Man with short sandy Hair, of a brown Complexion, thin Faced and a wide Mouth, generally has Tobacco in his Mouth; he had on a Worsted Cap, a dark gray Kersey Jacket double Breasted with Leather Buttons and Elbow-Pieces like a Sailors Jacket, 2 pair of Flemish Linen Trowsers, a pair of Buckskin Breeches with Buckles at the Knees, several Oznabrigs Shirts, a pair of half worn Shoes, and 2 half worn Castor Hats,

Ran-away at the same Time, from *Bryan Hughes*, a Servant Man named *Thomas Comins*, about 22 Years of Age, an Irish Man and a good Scholar and Writes a good Hand, he is a short Fellow, of a swarthy Complexion and black Hair; he had on when he went away, an old Kersey Jacket of a light colour, and a Olive Russel Jacket Tard, a pair of Cinamon Camblet Breeches with holes in the Knees, an Oznabrigs Shirt, a pair of short Oznabrigs Trowsers and a pair of half worn Shoes.

Whoever secures the said Servants or either of them so that their Masters may have them again, shall have Five Pounds Reward for each, and reasonable Charges

            paid By *Samuel Hastings, Michael Huling, Bryan Hughes*.

The American Weekly Mercury, From Thursday June 22, to Thursday June 29, 1738; From Thursday June 29, to Thursday July 6, 1738.

WHEREAS *Morris Kerril*, House-Plaisterer, my Indented Servant for four Years (who has been a base and wicked Servant in many Respects) makes a frequent Practice to neglect my Business, and works about this City for others, without my leave or Licence (tho' I've often forbid him, and forwarned several Persons not to employ him) by which Practice he gets Money and is very often drunk therewith. Therefore to prevent such vile Doings in him, or others who employ him, I do hereby describe him, (tho' well known in this City.) He is a short down-look'd Irishman, muttering in Speech; wearing a Felt Hat upon a Cap, his Hair cut off, Ozenbrigs Jacket, Breeches and Trowsers, Garlix Shirt, and other Shirts, Shoes and Stockings, and is much given to drink to Excess, Deceit and Lying.

I hereby forbid all Persons to Detain, Entertain, Trust or Imploy him Night or Day in anywise whatsoever, otherwise I will Prosecute them as far as the Law will permit me. WILLIAM FISHBOURN.

The American Weekly Mercury, From Thursday June 29, to Thursday July 6, 1738; From Thursday July 6, to Thursday July 13, 1738; From Thursday July 13, to Thursday July 20, 1738. See *The American Weekly Mercury*, From Thursday December 2, to Thursday December 9, 1736, and *The Pennsylvania Gazette*, From June 29, To July 6, 1738.

WHEREAS *Morris Kerril*, House-Plaisterer, my Indented Servant for four Years (who has been a base and wicked Servant in many Respects) makes a frequent Practice to neglect my Business, and works about this City for others, without my leave or Licence (tho' I've often forbid him, and forwarned several Persons not to employ him) by which Practice he gets Money and is very often drunk therewith. Therefore to prevent such vile Doings in him, or others who employ him, I do hereby describe him, (tho' well known in this City.) He is a short-downlook'd Irishman, muttering in Speech; wearing a Felt Hat upon a Cap, his Hair cut off, Ozenbrigs Jacket, Breeches and Trowsers, Garlix Shirt, and other Shirts, Shoes and Stockings, and is much given to drink to Excess, Deceit and Lying.

I do hereby forbid all Persons to Detain, Entertain, Trust or Imploy him Night or Day in anywise whatsoever, otherwise I will Prosecute them as far as the Law will permit me. WILLIAM FISHBOURN.

The Pennsylvania Gazette, From June 29, to July 6, 1738; From July 6, to July 13, 1738; From July 13, to July 20, 1738; From July 20, to July 27, 1738. See *The American Weekly Mercury*, From Thursday December 2, to Thursday December 9, 1736, and *The American Weekly Mercury*, From Thursday June 29, to Thursday July 6, 1738.

RUN away on the 20th Inst., from *Joseph James* of Cohansey, a Servant Man named *Lazarus Kenny*, is a swarthy Fellow, his Father being a Molatto and his Mother a white Woman, he is pretty tall and well set, his Hair cut off: Had on a Felt Hat, grey Kersey Coat and Vest, old Leather Breeches, an old homespun Shirt, yarn Stockings, round toe'd Shoes and brass Buckles. He took a large white Stallion that trots altogether, with an old black Saddle and good Snaffel Bridle.

Whoever secures the said Servant and Horse so that they are had again, shall have *Forty Shillings* Reward and reasonable Charges,
     paid by Joseph James. *Philad. June* 29. 1738.

The Pennsylvania Gazette, From July 6, to July 13, 1738; From July 13, to July 20, 1738; From July 20, to July 27, 1738.

195

RAN-away on the 13th of this Inst. from the *Calidonia Company*, an *Irish* Servant Lad named *Henry Crawley*, about Sixteen years of Age, of a swarthy Complexion, had on a speckled Shirt, a pair of Trowsers, an old pair of Shoes, a small bundle under his Arm, an old felt Hat cock'd up Tar like, he is a slim Lad and very handy, pretends to be a Sailor, has been seen in and about this City for several Days past.

Whoever brings the said Servant to *John Robinson* in *Philadelphia*, shall have *Twenty Shillings* Reward and reasonable Charges.

The American Weekly Mercury, From Thursday July 13, to Thursday July 20, 1738; From Thursday July 20, to Thursday July 27, 1738; From Thursday July 27, to Thursday August 3, 1738; From Thursday August 10, to Thursday August 17, 1738; From Thursday August 17, to Thursday August 24, 1738. Last two ads show he ran away the "13th of *July*".

RAN-away on the 23 of *July*, two Servant Men. *viz.*

One from *William Overthrow*, named *Philip Dun*, an Irishman, aged about 18 Years, by Trade a Wheelwright and Sawyer, of middle Stature, round Shoulder'd, small Eyes and a down look, a fresh colour, and black Hair or a brown Wigg, his right Leg is shorter than his left, and he Limps; he had on a light colour'd double Breasted Pee-Jacket with some Brass Buttons to it Oznabrigs Jacket, Trowsers, and Shirt, also a fine Holland Shirt, Worsted Stockings, and new Shoes.

The other from *James Kirk*, named *Charles Whitacer*, about 25 Years of Age, an Englishman and speaks West-Country, by trade a Sawyer, of middle Stature and well-set, stoops much in the Shoulders, of a fresh ruddy Complexion, and black Beard and Hair; had on an old Felt Hat, Oznabrigs Jacket and Trowsers, a brown Coat with white Metal Buttons with a Rose on them, an Oznabrigs Shirt, and a fine Garlix Shirt, and good double soal'd Shoes

Whoever secures the said Servants, or either of them, so that their Masters may have them again, shall have *Forty Shillings* Reward for each, and reasonable Charges paid   By *William Overthrow*, and *James Kirk.*

The American Weekly Mercury, From Thursday July 27, to Thursday August 3, 1738; From Thursday August 10, to Thursday August 17, 1738.

RUN away the 12th Inst. the three following Servant Men, viz.

From Thomas Willcox, of Chester County, Paper-Maker, one named James Malone, an Irishman, about 18 Years of Age, short of Stature, round visag'd, and of a black Complexion, stoops in walking. Had on a dark brown Jacket with brass Buttons, new Felt Hat, new homespun shirt, and two pair of Trowsers.

From Nathaniel Ring, of the same County, one named Neal Megloughlin, his speech is much on the French Tongue, well set, sharp visag'd, black curl'd Hair. Had on a dark-colour'd napt Coat with slash sleeves, felt Hat, two pair of Trowsers. He is about 40 Years old, and serv'd a Time about 15 Years ago near Crosswicks.

From Edward Richards of the same County, one named Hugh Burn, an Irishman, well set, no Hair. Had on a sky colour'd blue Coat with Mohair Buttons, homespun shirt, new tow Trowsers, and half worn Hose

Whoever secures the said Servants, so that their Masters may have them again, shall have Three Pounds Reward for each, and reasonable Charges paid by.   Thomas Willcox, Nathaniel Ring, Edward Richards.

The Pennsylvania Gazette, From July 13, to July 20, 1738; From July 13, to July 20, 1738; From July 27, to August 3, 1738; From August 3, to August 10, 1738.

RAN-away on the 9th of *July*, from *Job Harvey* of *Darby*, a Servant Woman named *Mary Jones*, pretty Tall and Slender, had on a strip'd blew and white linen Gown, a new Quilted Petticoat the upper part Linsey Woolsey, & the lower part Worsted Stuff of a brownish Olive colour, a new Straw Hat, and new Calf Skin Shoes: She hath been a Servant some Years ago to *Peter Gardner* over *Schuylkil*, and frequently brought Milk to Town to sell.

Whoever takes up said Servant, and secures her in the Work-House or else where, so that her said Master may have her again, shall have *Twenty Shillings* Reward and reasonable Charges
paid By *Job Harvey*.

The American Weekly Mercury, From Thursday July 6, to Thursday July 13, 1738; From Thursday July 20, to Thursday July 27, 1738; From Thursday July 27, to Thursday August 3, 1738.

RUN away on the 13th Inst. at Night, the two following Servant Men, viz.

From *Samuel Davis* of *Worcester* Township, in this County, one named *John Carawan*, an Irishman, aged about 18 Years, of middle Stature, no Hair, somewhat pockfretten, with a large Scar on one Cheek, and another between his Neck and Breast. Had on a dark Cloth Coat, a white homespun Shirt and Trowsers, and a check'd Shirt, a Felt Hat and good Shoes.

From *Anthony Cunrad*, of the same Place, one named *Rees Pritchard*, aged about 30 Years, tall and of black Complexion, with black Hair lately cut off, and has a large *Roman* Nose: Wears a Cap, a little Felt Hat, striped Jacket, homespun Shirt, Tow Trowsers, and a pair of Pumps on his Feet. He is much given to talking.

James Carawan came in lately in the Brigt. *Hannah, William Tiffin* Master, *from Dublin.*

Whoever takes up and secures the said Servants, so that they are had again, shall have *Thirty Shillings* Reward for each, and reasonable Charges, paid by   Samuel Davis, Anthony Cunrad. *Philad.* Aug. 17. 1738

The Pennsylvania Gazette, From August 10, to August 17, 1738; From August 17, to August 24, 1738; From August 24, to August 31, 1738; From August 31, to September 7, 1738. See *The American Weekly Mercury,* From Thursday April 27, to Thursday May 4, 1738, for Pritchard.

RUN-away the 27*th* of this Instant *August*, from *John White* of this City, a Servant Man Named *William Pullen*, aged about twenty one Years, of middle Stature, and talks West-country: He had on when he went away a brown Fustian-Coat, with flat broad Brass Buttons lin'd with blew Shalloon, a Brown holland Wastcoat, Leather Breeches, grey Stockings, a pair of thin Pumps: Is suppos'd to be conceal'd in some House in or about this City.

Whoever secures him so that he may be had again, shall be rewarded according to the Law of this Province.

N B. All Persons are hereby forewarned not to entertain him.

The American Weekly Mercury, From Thursday August 24, to Thursday August 31, 1738; From Thursday August 31, to Thursday September 7, 1738; From Thursday September 7, to Thursday September 14, 1738. See *The Pennsylvania Gazette,* From August 24, to August 31, 1731.

RUN away about the latter End of June past, from Lewis Lewis *of Richland in the great Swamp,* Bucks County, *a Servant Man, named* John Jones, *aged about 21 Years, of small Stature, short Visage and tann'd with the Sea, no Hair. Has with him a short white Wig, a racoon Hat about half worn and a Felt Hat, a half worn striped Holland Jacket, linnen Shirt, and check'd Trowsers, old pick toe'd Shoes much worn and trod aside, two Holland Caps, and a red and white worsted Cap. He has the Letters* R B *mark'd on his right Hand with Gunpowder. And came in lately with Capt* Chads *from* Bristol, *but has serv'd a Time in the Country before and is well acquainted with it.*

Whoever takes up and secures the said Servant so that he may be had again, shall have Forty Shillings Reward and reasonable Charge

paid by Lewis Lewis. Aug. 10. 1738.
The *Pennsylvania Gazette,* From August 3, to August 10, 1738; From August 10, to August 17, 1738; From August 17, to August 24, 1738; From August 24, to August 31, 1738; From August 31, to September 7, 1738.

RUN away on the 20th *Instant from* Joseph Talbott *of* Middletown, *In* Chester County, *an Irish Servant Man, named* James Welch, *a lusty fresh colour'd Man, about* 25 *Years of Age. Had on when he went away, a new Felt Hat, a white linen Cap, Homespun Kersey Coat, Jacket and Breeches, of a bluish lead colour, without lining, homespun Shirt, old Shoes and Stockings. Whoever secures the said Servant so that his Master may have him again, shall have* Three Pounds *Reward and all reasonable Charges*
    paid by JOSEPH TALBOTT.
The *Pennsylvania Gazette,* From August 17, to August 24, 1738; From August 31, to September 7, 1738.

RUN away on the 27th of this Inst. August, *from* John White, *of this City, a Servant Man named* William Pullen, *about* 21 *Years of Age, of middle Stature, talks West-Country: He had on when he went away, a brown Fustian Coat, with flat broad brass Buttons lin'd with blue Shalloon, a brown Holland Waistcoat, leather Breeches, grey Stockings, a pair of thin Pumps; and is suppos'd to be conceal'd in some House in or about this City.*
    Whoever secures him so that he may he had again, shall be rewarded according to the Law of this Province, and all Persons are forewarn'd not to entertain him.
The *Pennsylvania Gazette,* From August 24, to August 31, 1738; From August 31, to September 7, 1738. See *The American Weekly Mercury,* From Thursday August 24, to Thursday August 31, 1738.

RUN away on Sunday last, from Lancelot Martin *near* Bristol *in* Bucks County, *an Irish Servant Man named* John Mac Hafee, *of small Stature, brown Complexion, long brown Hair. Had on when he went away, an olive green Kersey Coat with flat Pewter Buttons, a good Garlick Shirt, coarse tow Drawers, a pair of black and white yarn Stockings, single soal'd Hogskin Shoes, & a good felt Hat. He is about* 20 *Years of Age.*
    Whoever takes up the said Servant, and secures him so that he may be had again, shall have Forty Shillings Reward, and reasonable Charge
    paid, by Lancelot Martin. Sept. 21. 1738.

The Pennsylvania Gazette, From September 14, to September 21, 1738; From September 21, to September 28, 1738; From September 28, to October 5, 1738.

RUN away from the Brigt. Laurel, John Searle, *Master, an* Irish *Servant Man, aged about* 22 *or* 23 *Years, of middle Stature, fresh Complexion, a little Freckled, & mark'd with the Small-Pox. Had on when he went away, a strip'd flannel Wastecoat, no Stockings, speaks pretty fast, was brought up to Cloth Shearing in* Bristol.
    Whoever secures the said Servant , so that his Master may have him again, shall have Twenty Shillings Reward, and reasonable Charges,
            paid by   JOHN SEARLE.
The Pennsylvania Gazette, From September 7, to September 14, 1738; From September 14, to September 21, 1738; From September 21, to September 28, 1738.

BROKE out of *Lancaster* Jayl the twenty second of *September* last, the following Persons, viz. *David Hickey*, a tall thin Person, a little pock-fretten, Aged about 25 Years, speaks Low-Dutch, as well as English.
    Also *John Murray* a tall Man, Aged about 30 Years of black Complection, wears a Wig; had on when he broke out, a Linnen Coat, Jacket and Trousers. *Joseph Taylor*, Aged about 23 Years of middle Stature, Fresh Colour, and simple Look, had on an Old Blue Cloth Jacket, Old Trowsers, and Coarse Linnen Shirt, by Trade a Miller.
    A Negro Man called *Harry*, about 23 Years of Age, speaks good English, had on a black Wig, an Old striped Jacket and Trowsers. Whosoever secures the said Prisoners, shall have five Pounds Reward, and proportionably for any one of them, on bringing them to
           Richard Lowdon sub. Sheriff at Lancaster.
The American Weekly Mercury, From Thursday October 5, to Thursday October 12, 1738; From Thursday October 12, to Thursday October 19, 1738.

RUN away the 8th of this Instant from *Thomas Blare* of *Bucks County*, near *Durham* Iron-works an Irish Servant Man named *William Garland*, has the Brogue, of middle Stature and slender, a round Visage, fresh Colour and Freckled, dark Hair and hollow Eyes, his upper Lip hanging over the under, he is about 20 Years of Age. He had on an old dark colour'd Coat with Button Holes in each Breast and behind, the Buttons of whitish Cloth, and redish homespun Camlet Lining; a pair of Tow Trowsers, a homespun Shirt, a pair of old Shupaks, and a half-worn Felt Hat.

Whoever takes up the said Servant and secures him so that his Master may have him again, shall have *Forty Shillings* Reward and reasonable Charges.   paid by   Thomas Blare.

The American Weekly Mercury, From Thursday October 12, to Thursday October 19, 1738; From Thursday October 19, to Thursday October 26, 1738; From Thursday October 26, to Thursday November 2, 1738. See *The Pennsylvania Gazette*, From March 15, to April 22, 1739.

RUN away on the 14th *Inst.* Octob. *from* William Miller, *of the Township of* Middletown, Chester *County, an* Irish *Servant Man, named* Peter Kindley, *about* 30 *Years of Age, of a tall Stature, red Complexion, has a little of the Brogue on his Tongue, a Taylor by Trade. Had on when he went away, a dark olive turn'd Coat, an old white Jacket without Sleeves, two fine linnen Shirts, olive green Breeches, yarn Stockings, and a good Hat.*

Whoever takes up and secures the said Servant, so that he may be had again, shall have Forty Shillings *Reward, and reasonable Charges,*   paid by   William Miller.

The Pennsylvania Gazette, From October 12, to October 19, 1738; From October 19, to October 26, 1738; From November 9, to November 16, 1738; From November 16, to November 24, 1738.

RUN away the 15th Instant, the three following *Irish* Servant Men, *viz.*

From *Thomas Wills*, of Middletown in *Chester* County, one named *Philip Dowen*, about 20 Years of Age, of middle Stature, well set, short black Hair, down Look, has a mark Λ between his Eyebrows as in the Margin, but perhaps may cover it with a Patch; had on a reddish Coat lined with darkish Cloth of two Colours, with plain Sleeves and brass Buttons, an old lightish-coloured Great Coat with a large Cape, several Shirts, a pair of Breeches and Trowsers, two pair of Shoes, the one new.

From *Joseph Talbot*, of the same Place, one named *James Welch*, aged about 23 Years, lusty and tall, smooth faced, with several Gunpowder Marks on one of his Hands; had on an old Great Coat of a light Colour, with one of the Cuffs torn off if not both, a Lead-coloured half-worn Kersey Jacket with some brass Buttons on the Breast, black Leather Breeches, old Trowsers, new yarn Stockings, a Pair of Shoes, and wears a Cap.

From *Alexander Hunter* of the same Place, one named *John Benn*, aged about 20 Years, short of Stature, black Hair, swarthy Complexion, pretty much mark'd with the Small-pox, with something like a Wart by the Side of his Nose; had on a brownish Coat with bluish Linning, a greyish Jacket, old Leather Breeches, several Pair of Stockings and Shoes, three good Hatts.

Whoever takes up and secures the said Servants, so that they are had again, shall have *Forty Shillings* Reward each, for the two first, and *Twenty Shillings* for the last mentioned Servant, and reasonable Charges,

paid by *Thomas Wills, Joseph Talbot, Alexander Hunter.*

N. B. 'Tis supposed they'll change both their Names and Cloaths.

The Pennsylvania Gazette, From October 12, to October 19, 1738; From October 19, to October 26, 1738; From October 26, to November 2, 1738. See *The Pennsylvania Gazette,* From August 17, to August 24, 1738, for Welch.

NOTICE is hereby given, That two Men arrived here about the beginning of *July* last, from *Virginia,* but last from *North-Carolina*: one named *Thomas Powel,* tall and slim, black Complexion, curl'd Hair; Had on a fashionable Coat with Waistcoat Sleeves, of a dark cinnamon colour, a striped holland Waistcoat and Breeches, ruffled holland Shirts, and some check'd Shirts, and other Cloaths. The other named *Henry Watkins,* a short Man, pale Complexion, thin Visage, down Look, his Cloaths unknown; they both pretend to be Sawyers, but can do any sort of Plantation Work. *Watkins* about the latter end of *September* was taken up, for Stealing Cloaths from *Thomas Spicer,* Esq; but made his Escape; and has also Stolen from divers Persons; and likewise enticed a Negro Man belonging to *Alexander Morgan* of *Waterford* in *Glocester* County, to runaway, and steal what he could from his Master; accordingly he broke open two Locks of a Writing-Desk, and stole from thence about *Nine Pounds,* in Gold and gave it to them at *Philadelphia,* who receiv'd the said Money, and then runaway, leaving the Negro hid in a Barrack of Hay, which is since taken up and put in the Work-House of *Philadelphia.*

Whoever secures the said Felons in any Goal, so that they may be brought to Justice, shall receive from said *Alexander Morgan* of *Waterford* Township aforesaid, *Four Pounds* as a Reward.

The Pennsylvania Gazette, From October 26, to November 2, 1738; From November 2, to November 9, 1738; From November 9, to November 16, 1738.

RUN away on the 28th *of* November *past, from* Nathan Lewis, *of* Newtown *in* Chester *County, a* Dutch *Servant Lad, named* William Kettsendorff*, aged about* 18 *Years, of a slender Stature, with short black Hair, and a Pimple or Mole on his Nose between his Eyes; had on when he went away an old Linnen Coat, a blue Jacket lin'd with red, with Pewter Buttons, a Leather Apron,* white Sheep-skin Breeches made after the Dutch Fashion, an old Hat, old Shoes, and white yarn Stockings. He is a new Incomer, and can't speak much English.

 Whoever secures the said Servant, so that his Master may have him again, shall have Twenty Shillings Reward, and reasonable Charges, paid by Nathan Lewis.

 The Pennsylvania Gazette, From November 30, to December 6, 1738; From December 6, to December 14, 1738; From December 28, 1738, to January 4, 1739.

WHEREAS a Servant Man named *David Grefith*, belonging to *Alexander Mahone* living near *Daniel Cooksons* at *Pecque*, has several times run away from his said Master, going about the Country stealing Horses, &c. Therefore this may certifie, whom it may concern, that there is now at the Plantation of said *Daniel Cooksons's*, a certain Horse of the above said Servants bringing there, supposed to be stole. Whoever can lay true claim to the said Horse and describe the right Marks thereof, may have him again paying the Charges, and may also prosecute the said Servant Man he being now in *Lancaster Jail*.

 The American Weekly Mercury, From Thursday November 30, to Thursday December 7, 1738.

RUN away on the 16th Instant, from *Daniel Jones* of *Blockley* Township in this County, an Irish Servant Man, named *Dennis Kelly*, a short well-set Fellow, aged about 22 Years, with short black Hair, blinks with his left Eye, has the Brogue on his Tongue and a small Scar in the End of his Nose: Had on when he went away an old dark grey Coat with flat Pewter Buttons, a new blue grey Kersey Jacket with metal Buttons, Leather Breeches with brass Buttons, an ozenbrigs Shirt, light grey Stockings, round-toe'd Shoes, and an old Felt Hat. Whoever takes up and secures the said Servant, so that he is had again, shall have *Twenty Shillings* Reward if taken within Twenty Miles of this City, and *Thirty Shillings* if farther, and reasonable Charges,
    paid by Daniel Jones. Philad. Dec. 21. 1738.

 The Pennsylvania Gazette, From December 14, to December 21, 1738; From December 21, to December 28, 1738; From December 28, 1738, to January 4, 1739; From January 4, 1739, to January 11, 1739.

1739

WENT away on the 13th Inst. from *Samuel Wheler's* at *Miamensin* near *Philadelphia*, one *Edward Lloyd*, an Englishman, about 22 Years of Age, of middle Stature, black complexion'd, black hair'd, has sore Legs, with old brown Leggings and Raggs wrapp'd round 'em: Had on when he went away, an old felt Hat, an old flannel Jacket, old leather Breeches, and old Shoes.

    N. B. He hired himself for a Month, to the said *Wheler*, and set his Barn on fire.

    Whoever takes up and secures the said *Lloyd* so that he may be brought to Justice, shall have *Twenty Shillings* Reward,

          paid by   *Samuel Wheler. Philad. Jan.* 18. 1738,9.

The Pennsylvania Gazette, From January 11, 1739, to January 18, 1739; From January 18, to January 25, 1739; From January 25, to February 1, 1739; From February 1, 1739, to February 8, 1739.

STOLEN on the 15th Instant, by one *William Lloyd*, out of the House of *Benj. Franklin*, an half-worn Sagathee Coat lin'd with Silk, four fine homespun Shirts, a fine Holland Shirt ruffled at the Hands and Bosom, a pair of black broadcloth Breeches new seated and lined with Leather, two pair of good worsted Stockings, one of a dark colour, and the other a lightish blue, a coarse Cambrick Handkerchief, mark'd with an F in red Silk, a new pair of Calfskin Shoes, a Boy's new Castor Hat, and sundry other things.

    N. B. The said *Lloyd* pretends to understand Latin and Greek, and has been a School-Master; He is an Irishman, and 30 Years of Age, tall and slim: Had on a lightish colour'd Great Coat, red Jacket, a pair of black silk Breeches, an old felt Hat too little for him, and sewed on the side of the Crown with white Threat, and an old dark colour'd Wig: but may perhaps wear some of the stolen Cloaths abovementioned.

    Whoever secures the said Thief so that he may be brought to Justice, shall have *Thirty Shillings* Reward and reasonable Charges,

          paid by   *B. Franklin.*   *Philadelphia, Feb.* 22. 1738,9.

The Pennsylvania Gazette, From February 15, 1739, to February 22, 1739.

BROKE out of *Newtown* Goal in *Bucks* County, in the Night between the 27th and 28th of last Month, a Man named *Robert Nailor*, confined on Suspicion of Felony, short and well-set, smooth Faced, thin Beard, short light-brown Hair and wears a Cap. He had on an old light colour'd Jacket double Breasted, Breeches of the same much worn and torn in the seat, Yarn Stockings and old Shoes: he had also an old blue Jacket. He is a Joyner by Trade. It is supposed he will change his Cloaths.

    Whoever secures the said Person so that he may be had again, shall have *Three Pounds* Reward and reasonable Charges,

          paid By   *John Hart* Sheriff.

The American Weekly Mercury, From Thursday March 1, to Thursday March 8, 1739; From Thursday March 8, to Wednesday March 14, 1739; From Wednesday March 14, to Thursday March 22, 1739; From Thursday March 29, to Thursday April 5, 1739

RUN away Yesterday from Thomas Croasdale, of Frankford *near* Philadelphia, *an English Servant Man named* William Ditchett, *about* 24 *Years of Age, short Stature, brown Complexion, with brown Hair, and perhaps he may wear a Cap:* He had on when he went away, an old blue broad-cloth Coat, a blue Jacket with Buttons set on the wrong side, ozenbrigs Shirt, felt Hat, black Stockings and good Shoes.

Whoever secures the said Servant so that his Master may have him again, shall have Forty Shillings *Reward, and reasonable Charges,*
    paid by   Thomas Croasdale. Philad. March 14. 1738,9.
The Pennsylvania Gazette, From March 8, to March 15, 1739; From March 15, to March 22, 1739; From March 29, to April 5, 1739.

RUN away on the 8th of *October* last, from *Thomas Blair* of *Bucks* County, near *Derham* Iron-Works, a Servant Man named *William Garland* (but perhaps may change his Name) an Irishman and has the Brogue on his Tongue, of middle stature, freckled in his Face, has a scar on one of his Legs a little below the Calf, dark colour'd Hair, round Visage, fresh colour'd, and his upper Lip hangs over the under: He was cloath'd when he went away, with an old brown homespun Coat lin'd with a redish stuff, Button Holes of whitish Cloth on each side of the Breast, and three on each side behind, an half worn felt Hat, a pair of two Trowsers, homespun Shirt, &c and old pair of Shoepacks.

Whoever secures the said Servant so that his Master may have him again, shall have *Four Pounds* Reward, and reasonable Charges,
    paid by   Thomas Blair. Philadelphia,   Feb. 22. 1738,9.
The Pennsylvania Gazette, From February 15, to February 22, 1739; From March 1, to March 8, 1739; From March 15, to March 22, 1739; From March 22, to March 29, 1739; From March 29, to April 5, 1739. See *The American Weekly Mercury*, From Thursday October 19, to Thursday October 26, 1738.

RUN away in *February* past, from *Evan Ellis* of *East Town* in *Chester* County, an Irish Servant Man, named *John Kahar*, aged about 24 Years, short of Stature dark brown Hair, and wore a Cap, has on his left Cheek under his Eye, an Issue or Hole, which is sometimes well and breaks out again, he often complains of a sciatick Pain in his Hip. Had on when he went away, a grey colour'd Serge Coat, a Felt Hat, and new Shoes.

Whoever secures the said Servant in any Goal, either in *New-York*, *Pennsylvania*, or *Maryland*, and sends Word to his Master, shall have *Thirty Shillings* Reward and reasonable Charges,
    paid by Evan Ellis. Philad. March 22. 1738,9.
The Pennsylvania Gazette, From March 15, to March 22, 1739; From March 22, to March 29, 1739; From March 29, to April 5, 1739; From April 5, to April 12, 1739; From April 12, to April 19, 1739.

RAN-away on the 22d of *March* from James Daveis, of *Concord*, in *Chester* County, a *French* Servant Man, named *Peter Devoe*, talks very bad English, about 30 Years of Age, of middle Stature, brown Complection, and dark curl'd Hair; he had on when he went away, a white Worsted Coat lined with an Orange colour, and brass Buttons, his Jacket of a lighter colour, the holes wrought with yellow Worsted, the fore part lined with black and white, a new course Shirt, a pair of old Trowsers with a patch on each Thigh, a pair of course white Stockings, good Shoes, and a felt Hat.

Whoever secures said Servant so that his Master may have him again, shall have Three Pounds reward and reasonable Charges
    paid By *James Davies.*
The American Weekly Mercury, From Thursday March 22, to Thursday March 29, 1739; From Thursday March 29, to Thursday April 5, 1739; From Thursday April 5, to Thursday April 12, 1739; From Thursday April 12, to Thursday April 19, 1739.

RUN away on the 2d Inst. from *Isaac Rees* of *Upper Merion* in this County, an *Irish* Servant Man, named *David Punch*, of middle Stature, long black strait Hair, paleish complexion'd, has a large Scar on the back Part of his Head near his Crown, he is a Weaver by Trade: had on when he went away, a light copper-coloured new Drugget Coat, with Buttons of the same, and mohair Button-holes, linnen Jacket, new black and white Hose, light colour'd cloth Breeches much worn, homespun Shirt, new felt Hat, and half worn Shoes.

Whoever secures the said Servant, so that his Master may have him again, shall have *Thirty Shillings* Reward,
    paid by Isaac Rees. Philada. April 5.
The Pennsylvania Gazette, From March 29, to April 5, 1739; From April 5, to April 12, 1739; From April 12, to April 19, 1739. See *The Pennsylvania Gazette*, August 21, 1740.

RUN away on the 3d Inst. from *James Sharples* of *Lower Providence* in *Chester* County, a Servant Lad, named *Henry Bowen*, aged about 17 Years, of small Stature, ruddy complexion, his Hair cut off. Had on when he went away, a light colour'd cloth Jacket, old leather Breeches, yellow Stockings cut above the Shoe.

Whoever secures the said Servant so that his Master may have him again, shall have *Twenty Shillings* Reward, and reasonable Charges,

    paid by *Philad.* James Sharples. *April 5.* 1739.

N. B. He was this Day seen in this City, and it's suppos'd he is now lurking about somewhere therein.

 The Pennsylvania Gazette, From March 29, to April 5, 1739; April 5, to April 12, 1739; From April 12, to April 19, 1739.

RUN away on the 10*th Inst. from* Robert Roberts, *of* Lower Merion, *Malster, an Irish Servant Lad, named* Edward Owen, *aged about 17 Years, of middle Stature, thin visaged, with small Legs: Wore when he went away, an old dark coloured coarse cloth Coat, ragged Leather Breeches, old ozenbrigs Shirt, yarn Stockings footed with Sheeps Black, old Shoes, and old Felt Hat. Whoever takes up the said Servant and secures him so that his Master may have him again, shall have* Thirty Shillings *Reward, and reasonable Charges, paid by* Robert Roberts. Philad. April 12. 1739.

 The Pennsylvania Gazette, From April 5, to April 12, 1739; April 19, 1739. See *The Pennsylvania Gazette*, From April 19, to April 26, 1739.

RUN away on the 12th Inst. from *Edward Collings* of *Cheltenham* Township, in *Philadelphia County*, Mason, an English Servant Man, named *John Gubby*, aged about 35 Years, short of Stature, a down cast Look, and pretends to be a Waterman. Had on when he went away, a dark coloured Pea Jacket and a blue under Jacket, brown Cloth Breeches, speckled Shirt, and good Shoes.

Whoever secures the said Servant so that his Master may have him again, shall have *Forty Shillings* Reward and reasonable Charges,

    paid by *Edward Collings.*

 The Pennsylvania Gazette, From April 12, to April 19, 1739; From April 19, to April 26, 1739.

             PHILADELPHIA.

Monday last the Corps of one *EDWARD OWEN*, a Servant (who was suppos'd to be run away from his Master, and accordingly advertis'd in our last Gazette) was found floating in the River Schuylkill. 'Tis though he laid himself down to sleep in a Canoe, which going adrift, overset in driving over the Rocks at the Falls.

The Pennsylvania Gazette, From April 19, to April 26, 1739. See *The Pennsylvania Gazette*, From April 5, to April 12, 1739,

RUN away on the 5th Inst. from *Henry Huddelston*, of *Plumsted* Township, *Bucks* County, an Irish Servant Man, named *Charles Cambell*, aged about 24 Years, indifferent tall and well set, with long blackish Hair, and long visag'd: had on when he went away, a homespun Coat and Jacket of a yellowish colour mix'd with black, and brass Buttons on both; took with him a pair of old leather Breeches, and white linnen Drawers, two new felt Hats, two pair of new Shoes with peeked Toes, and steel Buckles in one of the pair, two homespun Shirts much worn, white thread Stockings, a Barcelona silk Handkerchief, and a small Gun.

N. B. He is suppos'd to be in Company with one *Martha Bostuck*, a short well-set Woman, with red Hair, and pockbroken; and has a Child with her of about 5 Years old, who has red Hair also.

Whoever secures the said Servant, so that his Master may have him again, shall have *Three Pounds* Reward, and reasonable Charges,

paid by   HENRY HUDDLESTON.

The Pennsylvania Gazette, May 3, to May 10, 1739; From May 10, to May 17, 1739; From May 17, to May 24, 1739; From May 24, to May 31, 1739.

RUN away on the 1st Inst. from *Simon Edgell*, of this City, Pewterer, a Servant Man named *John Spurstew*, by Trade a Refiner in Copper, but can Work at the Smith's or Brazier's Business. Had on when he went away, a felt Hat, woollen Cap, grey Pea Jacket with Mohair Buttons, two speckl'd Shirts, a pair of Breeches very black and greasy, yarn Stockings, and round toe'd Shoes: It's suppos'd he is gone towards *New-York*: he is a lusty round fac'd Fellow, of brown Complexion, and about 30 Years of Age. He came from *Bristol* in the Brigt. *Britannia, John Bond*, Master.

Whoever secures the said Servant, so that his Master may have him again, shall have *Twenty Shillings* Reward, and reasonable Charges,

paid by   SIMON EDGELL.

The Pennsylvania Gazette, From May 3, to May 10, 1739; May 17, 1739.

RUN away on the 12th Inst. from *John Parry*, of *Haverford* Township, *Chester* County, a West-Country Servant Man, named *Philip Brown*, aged about 24 Years, indifferent tall and well set, with no Hair: Had on a new brown Cloth Coat, striped Trowsers, a fine Shirt, and new Calfskin Shoes. 'Tis suppos'd he is gone over in the Jerseys.

Whoever secures the said Servant, so that his Master may have him again, shall have *Forty Shillings* Reward, and reasonable Charges,
     paid by JOHN PARRY.

The Pennsylvania Gazette, From May 10, to May 17, 1739; From May 17, to May 24, 1739; From May 24, to May 31, 1739.

                  Philad. June 14. 1739.
RUN away on the 11*th Inst. from* Samuel Hastings *of this City, Shipwright, an* Irish *Servant Man, named* Thomas Willdear, *well-set, of middle Stature, reddish complexion'd, his Hair cut off, wears a Cap: Had on when he went away, a light colour'd cloth Jacket lin'd with blue, brown Holland Breeches, ozenbrigs Shirt, Felt Hat, grey yarn Stockings, and good Shoes.*

Whoever takes him up and brings him to his said Master or secures him so that he may have him again, shall have Thirty Shillings *Reward, and reasonable Charges,* *paid by* Samuel Hastings.

The Pennsylvania Gazette, From June 7, to June 21, 1739; From June 14, to June 21, 1739; From June 21, to June 28, 1739; From June 28, to July 5, 1739; From July 5, to July 12, 1739. See *The Pennsylvania Gazette*, February 7, 1740, and *The Pennsylvania Gazette*, February 28, 1740.

RAN-away last Night from *Andrew Bradford* a Servant Man named *Ambross Eyre*, about 40 Years of age, a short well set Fellow, fresh Complection, and wears a linnen Cap; he had on when he went away, a dark blew Kersey Jacket, linen Breeches, brown yarn Stockings and old Shoes. He is given to Drink and Swears very much, this not being the first time he has Absented himself by a great Number, so that he must be harboured by some ill Houses in this Town. This is therefore to forewarn all Persons not to Entertain or Harbour said Servant as they will Answer the Contrary at their Peril.

Whoever takes up said Servant and secures him in the Work-House, shall have *Twenty Shillings* Reward and all reasonable Charges
    paid By *Andrew Bradford.*

The Pennsylvania Gazette, From June 14, to June 21, 1739; *The American Weekly Mercury*, From Thursday June 14, to Thursday June 21, 1739. Minor differences between the papers.

RUN away from Perkiomun *Copper Works, an indented Welch Servant Man named* David Haxly, *his Speech discovers his Country, aged near* 40 *Years, well set, common Stature, short black Hair, well complexioned; had with him a black or dark-coloured cloth Jacket, two ozenbrigs Jackets, and ozenbrigs Shirts.*

Whosoever takes up the said Servant and brings him to Joseph Wharton, *at* Philadelphia, *shall have* Four Pounds *Reward.*

The Pennsylvania Gazette, From June 14, to June 21, 1739; From June 21, to June 28, 1739; From June 28, to July 5, 1739; From July 5, to July 12, 1739.

RAN-away on the 24th of *June,* from *David Bush* of *Willing Town,* a Servant Man named *John Christian Travett,* he is a Palatine, and came it the last Fall, in Capt. John Stedman's Ship from Holland: He had on a blew Camblet Coat full trimmed and lined with white, a grey pair of Breeches, white Cotton Stockings, a Felt Hat; black flank Hair, [sic] and a black Cravet on, he is of a middle Stature, a down cast Look, and talks no *English,* had with him two Rasors, one small Looking Glass, two linnen Shirts, two pair of worsted Stockings, one Dutch Bible and Prayer Book, a striped red and white Calimanco Jacket.

Whoever takes up and secures said Servant so that his Master imhave again, shall have *Forty Shillings* Reward and reasonable Charges paid   By *David Bush.*

The American Weekly Mercury, From Thursday June 21, to Thursday June 28, 1739; From Thursday June 28, to Thursday July 5, 1739; From Thursday July 5, to Thursday July 12, 1739; From Thursday July 19, to Thursday July 26, 1739; From Thursday July 26, to Thursday August 2, 1739. See *The Pennsylvania Gazette,* July 5, 1739.

RUN away about the 8th *of* May *past, the two following Servant Men, viz.*

From Ralph Perkenson, *one named* Charles Mosely, *by Trade a Butcher, of middle stature. He was seen going over the Ferry to* Gloucester. *Had on a new cloth Coat and Breeches of a light Colour, a new blue check'd Vest, blue grey Stockings, new Shoes with large brass Buckles in them, and a Felt Hat.*

From Thomas Walker, *of this City, Butcher, one named* Cornelius Fling, *by Trade a Butcher, aged about* 40 *Years, tall, black complexion'd, sour Look, ill humoured, very much given to drink, a small Blemish on one Eye. Had on a very good Hat, an old Wig, a blue cloth Coat, green Jacket, blue Breeches, old white Shirt, very indifferent shoes and stockings.*

Whoever takes up and secures the said Servants so that they are had again, shall have Three Pounds *Reward and reasonable Charges,*
          paid by   Ralph Perkenson, Thomas Walker.
Philad. June 28. 1739.
    The Pennsylvania Gazette, From June 21, to June 28, 1739; From June 28, to July 5, 1739; From July 5, to July 12, 1739.

RUN away on the 25th Inst. from Thomas Marshall, *of Concord, in* Chester County, *an* Irish *Servant Man, named* Charles M'Kenney, *about 24 Years of Age, of middle Stature, thick set, of a sandy Complexion, long chinn'd, a big under Lip, and short Hair: Had on an ozenbrigs Shirt and Waiscoat, a Sea Coat the Coller lin'd with red, good Leather Breeches, coarse Trowsers, strong round toe'd shoes, and a Felt Hat. He is very impudent and will get acquainted with any Body.*
    Whoever takes up and secures the said Servant so that he may be had again, shall have Forty Shillings *Reward and reasonable Charges,*
          paid by   Thomas Marshall.   Philad. June 28. 1739.
    The Pennsylvania Gazette, From June 21, to June 28, 1739; From June 28, to July 5, 1739; From July 5, to July 12, 1739; From July 19, to July 26, 1739; From July 26, to August 2, 1739. See *The Pennsylvania Gazette,* November 22, 1739.

Run away on Sunday Night last, the two following Servants, viz.
    From John Williams, *of this City, Taylor, one named* William Tub, *by Trade a Taylor, aged about 20 Years, short Stature, dark complexion, down Look, no Hair, mark'd on the right Hand with* W T; *Had on a dark colour'd Drugget Coat with Metal Buttons, Breeches of the same, a good fine Shirt, Olive-coloured Stockings. Felt Hat, and old Shoes.*
    From Thomas Williams, *of the said City, Hatter, another named* William Spaggs, *an English Man, aged about 33 Years, short of Stature, pretty well set, fresh complexioned, of a smiling Countenance, and mark'd on his right Arm with* W S; *Had on an old yellow Drugget Coat, A Felt Hat, a linnen or worsted Cap, a white linnen Jacket, Cotton Breeches patched at the Knees, two brown homespun Shirts, a Stock, a Handkerchief, black worsted Stockings, and peek'd toed Shoes.*
    Whoever takes up and secures the said Servants, so that they may be had again, shall have Three Pounds *Reward for both, or* Thirty Shillings *for each, and reasonable Charges,*
              paid by   John Williams *and* Thomas Williams.
    The Pennsylvania Gazette, From July 5, to July 12, 1739; From July 12, to July 19, 1739.

RUN *away on the 24th Inst. from* David Bush *of* Willings-Town, *a Palatine Servant Man, named* John Christian Travatt, *of middle Stature, down Look, and black lank Hair: Had on a blue Camblet Coat full trimm'd and lin'd with white, grey cloth Breeches, white cotton stockings, and a Felt Hat; he also took with him 2 Razors, a small Looking-Glass, 2 linnen Shirts, 2 pair of worsted stockings, a Dutch Bible and Prayer-Book, and a striped Calimanco Jacket. He came in Capt.* Stedman's *Ship last Fall, and talks little or no English.*

Whoever takes up and secures the said Servant so that he may be had again, shall have Forty Shillings *Reward and reasonable Charges,*
   paid by David Bush. *Philad. June* 28. 1739.

The Pennsylvania Gazette, From June 21, to June 28, 1739; From June 28, to July 5, 1739; From July 5, to July 12, 1739; From July 12, to July 19, 1739. See *The American Weekly Mercury*, From Thursday June 21, to Thursday June 28, 1739.

RAN-away from *Richard Ashton* near *Paxton* in *Lancaster*, a West Country Servant Man named *Philip Griffitts*, about 30 Years of Age, he is a tall slim Fellow, of a sandy Complection, red Face, and a long drooping Nose: He had on a light colour'd Pea Jacket half worn, a shipped Linsey Woolsey Vest and Breeches, a new felt Hat, blue yarn Stockings, and new Shoes, his Indenture being not found it's believed the Fellow has taken it with him.

Whoever takes up said Servant and secures him so that his Master may have him again, or Edward Shippen in *Philadelphia*, shall have *Forty Shillings* Reward and all reasonable Charges
   paid By *Edward Shippen.*

The American Weekly Mercury, From Thursday July 12, to Thursday July 19, 1739; From Thursday July 19, to Thursday July 26, 1739; From Thursday July 26, to Thursday August 2, 1739. See *The Pennsylvania Gazette*, From July 12, to July 19, 1739.

RUN *away from* Richard Ashton, *near* Paxton *in* Lancaster *County, a* West Country *Servant Man, named* Philip Griffitts, *aged about* 30 *Years, tall and slim, of a sandy Complexion, red Face and long drooping Nose; he was going* Conestogoe *Road Home. Had on a light-coloured pea Jacket half worn, a striped linsey woolsey Waistcoat and Breeches, a new felt Hat, blue yarn Stockings, and new Shoes; his Indenture being not to be found it's suppos'd he has taken it with him.*

Whoever brings the said Servant to his Master, or to Edward Shippen *of* Philadelphia, *shall have* Forty Shillings *Reward and reasonable Charges paid by* Edward Shippen. Philad. July 19, 1739.

The Pennsylvania Gazette, From July 12, to July 19, 1739; From July 26, to August 2, 1739; From July 2, to July 9, 1739. See *The American Weekly Mercury,* From Thursday July 12, to Thursday July 19, 1739.

STOLEN on the 18th of *July,* at Night, out of the House of *Joseph Webb,* in *Burmingham, Chester* County, a Silver Watch, the out side Case Fish skin studded and hoop'd with Silver, a Calves skin String, with four steel springs and a swivel, two steel Seals and a Key hanging to the String. The Person supposed to commit the Robbery is a pale fac'd Man, talks fast, pretends to be an Indian Trader, and goes by the Name of *James Simmons,* was, some time since, Tried in the Jerseys for Burglary and Burnt in the Hand.

Whoever will bring the said Watch to the Subscriber, shall have *Twenty Shillings* Reward, or if secures the Thief, with the Watch, so that he be brought to Justice, shall have *Forty Shillings*
paid, By *Joseph Webb.*

The American Weekly Mercury, From Thursday July 26, to Thursday August 2, 1739; From Thursday August 2, to Thursday August 9, 1739.

RUN away on the 2d Instant, from *John Eastburn,* of *Norrington* Township, *Philadelphia* County, a Servant Lad, named *John Lipscomb,* aged about 18 Years, of middle Stature and slender, much pockbroken, short brown Hair somewhat curled, and has a large Scar on one side of his Face from the Lip to the Eye: Had on a good narrow brim'd Felt Hat, homespun Shirt and Trowsers, an old brown Camblet Jacket, and old Shoes.

Whosoever secures the said Servant so that his Master may have him again, shall have *Thirty Shillings* Reward, and reasonable Charges,
paid by John Eastburn.

The American Weekly Mercury, From August 2, to August 9, 1739; From August 9, to August 16, 1739; From August 16, to August 23, 1739.

RAN-away, the 26th of this Month, from *Jacob Casdorp* of the City of *Philadelphia,* Shipwright, a Servant Man named *Edmond Howard,* about 18 Years of age, a tall slim Fellow, a little Pockbroken, a stubborn down look, brown Hair lately cut off and wears a white Cap, a Felt Hat, a dark gray Kersey Jacket, a striped homespun Jacket and Breeches, a Linen Shirt, Yarn Stockings, old Shoes, and a pair of Trowsers mark'd with an R on the Wastband.

Whoever takes up and secures the said Servant so that his Master may have him again, shall have *Three Pounds* Reward and reasonable Charges, paid by   *Jacob Casdorp.*

N. B. He is suppos'd to be in Company with *John Griffiths* and *Benjamin Poet*, belonging to *Edward Wyatt*, Taylor, and *Jonathan Chambers* belonging to *Henry Norwood.*

The American Weekly Mercury, From Thursday August 23, to Thursday August 30, 1739; From Thursday August 30, to Thursday September 6, 1739. See *The Pennsylvania Gazette*, From August 23, to August 30, 1739.

RUN away on Sunday Night last, the following Servants, *viz.*

From *Edward Wyatt*, of this City, Taylor, one named *John Griffiths*, aged about 20 Years, of middle Stature, much pock-broken, speaks very thick, and has a Blemish in one Eye: Had on a fine drab cloth Coat with a close Cuff, cloth Breeches made after the Dutch Manner, grey Stockings, half-worn round toed Shoes, a linnen Cap and new Holland Shirt. Also an Apprentice Boy named *Benjamin Poet*, about 16 Years of Age, a Dutch Lad, but speaks very good English: Had on a Duroy Coat lin'd with reddish coloured Silk, a double-breasted scarlet Waistcoat with white horn Buttons, and old Shoes.

From *Henry Norwood, of this City,* one named *Jonathan Chambers*, aged about 19 Years, fair complexion'd and short Hair: Had on a striped Cotton Cap, Felt Hat, dark colour'd Pea Jacket lin'd with red and patch'd at both Elbows with several Colours, coarse Trowsers, white Shirt, and Thread Stockings.

Whoever takes up and secures the said Runaways so that their Masters may have them again, shall have *Thirty Shillings* Reward for each and reasonable Charges, paid by
    Edward Wyatt and *Henry Norwood. Aug.* 30, 1739.

N. B. They are suppos'd to be in Company with one *Edward Howard,* who belongs to *Jacob Casdorp*, of this City, Shipwright, and run away at the same time.

The Pennsylvania Gazette, From August 23, to August 30, 1739; From August 30, to September 6, 1739. See *The American Weekly Mercury*, From Thursday August 23, to Thursday August 30, 1739.

RUN away on the 31st of *July*, past from *James Adams* of *Londongrove* in *Chester* County, a Servant Man, named *Arthur Millholland*, about 30 Years of Age, of middle Stature, fresh colour'd, red Nose, and is shav'd on the Forehead: Had on a double breasted grey Coat, with black Mohair Buttons and slash Sleeves, much like a Sailors Jacket, green Waistcoat, brown

Breeches, check'd Shirt, blue grey worsted Stockings, new Hat and a pair of Shoes. He has been an Indian Trader, and knows the Country very well.

Whoever takes up and secures the said Servant so that he may be had again, shall have *Three Pounds* Reward and reasonable Charges
    paid by *James Adams August* 30 1739.

The Pennsylvania Gazette, From August 30, to September 6, 1739; From September 6, to September 13, 1739; From September 13, to September 20, 1739.

RUN away on the 6th Inst. from Thomas Rees, *of* Heydelburg *Township,* Lancaster *County, a Servant Lad, named* Richard Beddes, *aged about* 17 *Years, has light bushy Hair: Had on an old striped linsey Jacket, old linnen Shirt, new Linnen Breeches and an old Hat, no Shoes nor Stockings. Took with him a smooth Rifle Gun.*

Whoever brings the said Servant to his said Master, or secures him in the County Goal, so that he may be had again, shall *have* Three Pounds *Reward and reasonable Charges,*
    paid by Thomas Rees. September 13, 1739.

The Pennsylvania Gazette, From September 6, to September 13, 1739; From September 13, to September 20, 1739; October 4, 1739.

RUN away on the 8th Instant, from *French Creek* Iron Works, *Chester* County, a Servant Man named *James Coltis*, about 27 Years of Age, pretends to be Carpenter, is low of Stature, dark complexion'd, with thin Hair, the Crown of his Head somewhat inclin'd to be bald, marked on one Hand with I C: Had on an osnabrigs Shirt and Trowsers, a good Felt Hat and Cap, a Seafaring Jacket, grey worsted Stockings, tolerable good Shoes. He also commonly wears a dark coloured Wig. Whoever takes up and secures the said Servant so that he may be had again, shall have *Five Pounds* Reward and reasonable Charges,
    paid by *Samuel Savage.* Philad, Sept. 12, 1738. [*sic*]

The Pennsylvania Gazette, September 6, to September 13, 1739; September 13, to September 20, 1739; From September 20, to September 27, 1739.

RUN away on the 13th Inst. from *John Richey*, of *Makefield*, in the County of *Bucks*, a Scotch Man named *John Morton*, lately from Scotland, a pretty lusty Fellow, about 24 Years of Age, somewhat pockfretten, speaks broad Scotch; Had on when he went away, a blue woollen Jacket very short and cut round the skirts, so that it does not come past the middle of his Thighs, and it is made in the Form of a Coat, with some Holes wrought behind, a check'd Shirt pretty much worn, and old check'd Trowsers patched on the fore parts with old white Linnen, no Stockings, a pair of old Irish Pumps, a Felt Hat with a very narrow Brim, and an old linnen Cap.

Whoever takes up and secures the said Servant so that his Master may have him again, shall have Forty Shillings Reward, and reasonable Charges,
    paid by John Richey. Philad. Sept. 20. 1739.

The Pennsylvania Gazette, From September 13, to September 20, 1739; From September 20, to September 27, 1739; October 4, 1739.

RUN away on the 19th Inst. from *William Crosthwaite*, a Servant Man named *John Johnson*, by Trade a Barber, aged between 20 and 30, small stature; had on an old Bever Hat made for a Boy, light grey bob Wig, double breasted blue Cloth Jacket, Ozenbrigs Trowsers, white Thread Stockings and old shoes. It is known he had a Ten-shilling Bill with him, and 'tis suppos'd he has more. He is of a pale Complexion, down Look, talks thick, and is *Birmingham* Born.

Whosoever takes the said Run away, and secures him so that he may be had again, if within 20 Miles of *Philadelphia* shall have *Twenty Shillings*, and if further, *Forty*, and reasonable Charges
    paid by the said *William Crosthwaite.*

The Pennsylvania Gazette, From September 13, to September 20, 1739; See *The American Weekly Mercury*, From Thursday December 27, to Thursday, January 3, 1740, and *The Pennsylvania Gazette*, March 6, 1740.

RUN away on the 16th Inst. from ANTHONY BRIGHT, of this City, Silversmith, a Servant Man named Stephen Draper, about 27 Years of Age, middle Stature, well set, long Visage, long Nose, and long Chin, has a Scar on the right side of his Cheek: Had on a dark brown Drugget Coat lin'd with brown Shalloon and with mohair Buttons, brown Holland jacket and Breeches, new grey worsted Stockings, good shoes, Felt Hat, and white Cap. Whoever takes up and secures the said Servant so that he may be had again, shall have Three Pounds Reward, and reasonable Charges
    paid by ANTHONY BRIGHT. Philad. Sept. 20. 1739.

The Pennsylvania Gazette, From September 20, to September 27, 1739.

RUN away the 19*th of* August *past, from* Stephen Onion's *Plantation at* Conijohah, *four Miles below Mr.* Wright's *Ferry, over* Susquehannah *River, a Servant Man, named* Abraham Kerslake, *born at* Tiverton *in the* West *of*

England, *aged about 30, of low Stature, brown Complexion, a short round Face, grey Eyes, and pitted a little with the Small Pox, his Hair cut off: Had with him a dark colour'd broad cloth Coat, made with Jacket Sleeves, double breasted, a pair of old blue broad cloth Breeches, hath also an olive colour'd Country cloth Coat the Button Holes made with the blue thread, ozenbrig Shirts and Trowsers, a felt Hat and Country Shoes. He writes tolerable well and its suppos'd hath made himself a Pass, and having been intrusted by me to do some Business hath Money and Letters. He is supposed to be gone away with one* William Green, *an Englishman who laboured in those Parts, the said Green is aged about 23, about six Feet high, ruddy Complexion, his Hair cut off, wears a light colour'd Coat, a pair of check Trowsers, a fine Shirt and* Carolina *Hat. Whoever secures the said* Abraham Kerslake, *and sends intelligence to me at* Patapsco, *shall have* Five Pounds *Currency of the Province where taken as a Reward, or if he is brought to* Patapsco, *shall have* Ten Pounds, Maryland *Currency Reward, and reasonable Charges, paid by* Stephen Onion. Patapsco *in* Maryland, Aug. 23. 1739.

The Pennsylvania Gazette, October 4, 1739; October 25, 1739.

RUN *away on the 28th past from* Stephen Hoopes *of* Westtown, Chester County, *an Irish Servant Man named* John Sulavan, *of short Stature, pretty much pockfretten: Had on when he went away, a light homespun Coat and Jacket with brass Buttons, two pair of coarse Trowsers, two homespun Shirts, a new felt Hat, old worsted Stockings, and good Shoes. Whosoever secures the said Servant so that his Master may have him again, shall have* Twenty-five *Shillings Reward and reasonable Charges*
paid by Stephen Hoopes.

The Pennsylvania Gazette, November 1, 1739; November 8, 1739; November 15, 1739; November 22, 1739; November 29, 1739.

RUN *away on the 28th past at Night, from* William Williams *of* Whitemarsh *in* Philadelphia *County, an English Servant Man, named* William Morgan, *aged about* 29 *Years, tall and slim, of a pale Complexion, long visag'd, and has three Teeth growing together in one side of his Mouth. Had on an old light colour'd Coat, old Trowsers, coarse homespun Shirt, old felt Hat, grey Stockings, and old calfskin sharp toe'd Shoes: has taken with him a dark colour'd old Coat without a Cape, a fine Shirt ruffled at the Hands and Bosom, with several other Things, and perhaps may wear some of them.*

Whoever takes up and secures the said Servant so that his Master may have him again, shall have Forty shillings *Reward and reasonable Charges paid by* William Williams.

The Pennsylvania Gazette, November 1, 1739; November 8, 1739; November 15, 1739; November 22, 1739; November 29, 1739.

RUN away from John Thomas *of* Charlestown *in* Chester *County, a Servant Man, named* John Holt, *aged about 23 Years, middle Stature, fair Complexion, little Beard, light brown Hair, grey Eyes, a Scar over his Eyebrow: Had on when he went away, a light coloured homespun cloth Coat, with flat large carved brass Buttons, dark colour'd Jacket, old leather Breeches, homespun Trowsers, took with him a fine Shirt, and a homespun one, and large round toe'd Shoes.*
Whoever takes up and secures the said Servant so that his Master may have him again, shall have Forty Shillings *Reward, and reasonable Charges,*
paid by John Thomas.
The Pennsylvania Gazette, November 22, 1739; November 29, 1739; December 5, 1739.

RUN away on the 18th Inst. from Thomas Marshal *of* Concord *in* Chester *County, an Irish Servant Man named* Charles Mc'Kennan, *aged about 24 Years, of middle Stature, thick set, sandy Complexion, long Chin, big upper Lip, and short Hair; Had on when he went away, a felt Hat, old greyish Wig or Cap, a dark brown frize Coat the Collar lin'd with red, homespun linnen Jacket, and Shirt, leather Breeches patch'd at the Knees, speckled Trowsers, woollen Stockings, and new double soal'd round toe'd Shoes. He is very impudent, and will get acquainted with any Body.*
Whoever secures the said Servants so that his Master may have him again, shall have Forty Shillings *Reward, and reasonable Charges,*
paid by Thomas Marshal.
The Pennsylvania Gazette, November 22, 1739; November 29, 1739; December 5, 1739. See *The Pennsylvania Gazette,* From June 21, to June 28, 1739.

RAN-away the 9th Instant from *Nathaniel Eavenson* of *Thornbury*, two Servent Men, one a Dutch Man, named *John Mitchel Rode*, aged about 25 years of middle sieze, [sic] by Trade a Cooper, and speaks but poor English; had on when he went away, a blewish colour'd cloth Coat, with brass Buttons, and lined with red, a Leather Jacket and a flower'd one, brown colour'd Cloth Breeches, good Shoes and Stockings.
The other an English Boy of about 17 Years of Age, named *Samuel Parker*, pretty tall and much pock-fretten, had on a felt Hat, a lightish colour'd cloth Coat with brass Buttons, good Shoes and Stockings.

Whoever takes up and secures the said Servants so that they may be had again, shall have *Three Pounds* as a Reward and reasonable Charges,
    paid by *Ralph Eavenson, & John Newlin*, Executors.
The American Weekly Mercury, From Thursday December 6, to Thursday December 13, 1739; From Thursday December 13, to Thursday December 20, 1739; From Thursday December 20, to Thursday December 27, 1739.

RUN away on the 23d Inst. from Samuel Osborne *of* Westtown, *in* Chester County, *an* English *Servant Man named* Christopher Oliver, *about* 20 *Years of Age, short yellow Hair: Had on when he went away, a light colour'd Jacket, lined with red, with some greasy spots on it, and a striped Jacket without sleeves, old Leather Breeches, old Shoes and Stockings, had no Hat, and is a Weaver by Trade.*
 Whoever takes up and secures the said Servant , so that his Master may have him again, shall have Forty Shillings Reward, and reasonable Charges,
    paid by Samuel Osborne.
The Pennsylvania Gazette, December 27, 1739; January 3, 1740; January 10, 1740.

RUN away on 19*th Instant, from* Lodowick Debler *of the Township of* Amity, Philadelphia *County, a* Dutch *Servant Lad, named* John Sedimon, *about 17 Years of Age, of middle size, crook'd Nose, fair Complexion, thick Lips, and short sandy Hair, his Knees bend in, and Feet stand out: Had on when he went away, a good felt Hat, two linsey wolsey strip'd Jackets, one without sleeves, and the other with, leather Breeches, and a pair of Trowsers over them, a good pair of white yarn Stockings, and good Shoes. Took with him a little sorrel Horse, with a russet Hunting Saddle, a good snaffle Bridle, and a hair Halter.*
 Whoever takes up the said Lad, so that his Master may have him again, shall have Three Pounds Reward, and reasonable Charges,
    paid by Lodowick Debler.
The Pennsylvania Gazette, December 27, 1739; January 3, 1740; January 10, 1740; January 15, 1740; January 22, 1740.

1740

RAN-away, the 30th of *December* past, from the Subscriber, a Servant Man named *John Johnson*, by Trade a Peruke-Maker, short of Stature, talks thick and lisping, he had on an old Bever Hat, light Wigg, a good light-colour'd

Broad-Cloth Coat double Breasted, blue double Breasted Broad-Cloth Jacket, green Breeches much worn, grey yarn Stockings, and good Shoes.

Whoever secures said Servant so that his Master may have him again, shall, if taken within Twenty Miles of *Philadelphia*, have as a Reward *Twenty Shillings*, if Thirty, *Thirty Shillings*, and if farther *Forty Shillings*,

        paid By   *William Crosthwaite.*

The American Weekly Mercury, From Thursday December 27, 1739, to Thursday, January 3, 1740; From Thursday January 3, to Tuesday, January 8, 1740; From Tuesday January 8, to Tuesday, January 15, 1740. See *The Pennsylvania Gazette*, From September 13, to September 20, 1739; September 27, 1739, and *The Pennsylvania Gazette*, March 6, 1740.

RAN-away on Sunday the 16th Instant from *Andrew Caldwel* of *Pequay*, in the County of Lancaster, a Servant Man named *Daniel Hagan*, he is an Irish Man, about 23 Years old, of middle Stature, a little round Shoulder'd, a down cast look, very black bushy short curl'd Hair, had on a silver grey Broad Cloth Coat turn'd, and part of it lined with black and white, and trim'd with Black, a new silk Handkerchief about his Neck, a brown Jacket, a pair of leather Breeches, a pair of new grey worsted Stockings, new Shoes, and a felt Hat.

Whoever takes up said Servant and secures him so that his Master may have him again, shall have Three Pounds Reward and reasonable Charges

        paid By   *Andrew Caldwell.*

The American Weekly Mercury, From Thursday December 27, 1739, to Thursday, January 3, 1740; From Thursday January 3, to Tuesday, January 8, 1740; From Tuesday January 8, to Tuesday, January 15, 1740.

RAN-away on the 31st. of *December*, from *Thomas Carvel*, in *Germantown*, a Servant Girl named *Edeth Wolfrys*, aged 17 Years, of a fresh Colour, small in Stature, had on when she went away, a brown Gown and a white Apron.

Whoever takes up and secures said Servant so that her Master may have her again, shall have *Twenty Shillings* Reward and reasonable Charges

        paid By   *Thomas Carvel.*

The American Weekly Mercury, From Thursday January 3, to Tuesday, January 8, 1740; From Tuesday January 8, to Tuesday, January 15, 1740; From Tuesday January 15, to Tuesday, January 22, 1740; From Tuesday January 22, to Tuesday, January 29, 1740.

ON the 8th Instant absented, from his Master *John Pricket*, a Servant Man, named *John Mahany*, purchas'd the Day before of Capt. *Atwood*, a young well-set Man, about 22 tears of Age, with but one Eye, his right Eye being lost by an Accident: He had on a Suit of dark Irish Frize, much worn, old black Plush Breeches, grey worsted Stockings, a speckled Handkerchief about his Head, a Felt Hat, and a pretty good Wig in his Pocket. Whoever takes up the said Servant and brings him to Capt. *Atwood* in this City, shall have Thirty shillings Reward, and all reasonable Charges,
          paid by   *John Pricket.*
The Pennsylvania Gazette, January 10, 1740; January 15, 1740; January 22, 1740.

RUN away the 13th Inst. from *William Blair* of *Middleto*n in *Cheste*r County, a Servant Lad, named *James Odonally*, about 18 or 19 Years of Age, middle Stature, a brisk Blade, short black curl'd Hair, fresh Complexion, a little pock-mark'd: Had on a good Suit of home made Cloaths of a light brown Colour, a good linnen Shirt, a new felt Hat, bluish yarn Stockings, new Shoes with broad brass Buckles, and blue and white spotted Mittins. Whoever takes up and secures the said Servant , so that his Master may have him again, shall have *Forty Shillings* Reward, and all reasonable Charges,
          paid by   *William Blair.*
The Pennsylvania Gazette, January 15, 1740; January 22, 1740.

RUN away last Night, from their Masters, the three following Irish *Servants, viz.*
    From George Rice Jones, *of this City, Butcher, one named* Terrence Toole, *a Butcher by Trade a short thick set fellow, of a brown Complexion: Had on when he went away, a red great Coat, a brown Jacket, a pair of Leather Breeches, with brass Buttons, and strings at the Knees, good grey yarn Stockings, one speckled Shirt, and a white one, a thick blue grey Jacket, good Shoes, and a good Hat with Spots of Paint on it; also a light brown Wig, a worsted Cap and a red Silk Handkerchief.*
    From Samuel Hastings, *of this City, Shipwright, one named* Thomas Wildeer, *of middle stature, red Complexion, down Look, about 25 Years of Age: Had on when he went away, a great Coat of an ordinary dark brown Ratteen, with the Cuff of the right sleeve off, a green Grogram Vest, patch'd under one Arm. and bound down the Button holes with green Bays, an under Jacket of green Bays with two Rows of Button holes, black Mohair Buttons and no lining, a new ozenbrigs shirt, red plush Breeches, the Breeches good*

but the Plush ordinary, a new silk Handkerchief, an old Beaver Hat, light grey yarn stockings, new shoes, and wears a Wig.

From Thomas Sugar, of this City, Carpenter, one named Michael Berry, by Trade a Carpenter, a lusty well-set Fellow, full fac'd, no Hair, but wears a white Cap or Wig: Had on when he went away, a full trimm'd blue cloth Coat, a short homespun linsey woollsey Waistcoat, one Garlix and one Ozenbrigs shirt, leather Breeches half worn, light grey yarn stockings, old Shoes with steel Buckles in them, and a good fine Hat; took with him a new Handsaw of White's, stamped on the Handle in several Places with T S.

Whoever takes up and secures the said Servants, so that their Masters may have them again, shall have Six Pounds Reward, or Forty Shillings for each, and reasonable Charges, paid by

George Rice Jones, Samuel Hastings, Thomas Sugar.
Philad. Feb 4 1739,40.

N.B. *They are supposed to be all gone together, and perhaps may change Apparel.*

The Pennsylvania Gazette, February 7, 1740; February 13, 1740; February 21, 1740. See *The Pennsylvania Gazette,* From June 7, to June 21, 1739, and *The Pennsylvania Gazette,* February 28, 1740, for Wildeer.

Stolen away, the 17th of this Instant *February*, from *Job Harvey* of *Darby*, in *Chester* County, Cloathier, a bright Bay Gelding, about 13 Hands high, with a large Star in his Forhead and a small Snip, a Scar upon the off Hip bone, a natural Pacer and can Trot a little. Likewise from *William Hay* of *Chester*, Inn holder, a half-worn Russet hunting Saddle, a Snaffle Bridle, and a pair of new peaked Toe'd Mens Shoes; which goods 'tis supposed were stolen by a native Irish Man who went by the name of *John Hay*, he hath a hare Mole on the right Cheek, is small of stature, and sometimes wears a gray Wigg. Whoever takes up and secures the said Person in some Goal, and sends Word thereof to the subscribers, shall have *Fifty Shillings* as a Reward and reasonable Charges, paid by   Job Harvey, William Hay.

The American Weekly Mercury, From Tuesday February 19, to Tuesday, February 26, 1740; From Tuesday February 26, to Tuesday, March 4, 1740; From Tuesday March 4, to Tuesday, March 11, 1740; From Thursday March 20, to Thursday, March 27, 1740; From Thursday March 27, to Thursday, April 3, 1740; From Thursday April 3, to Thursday, April 10, 1740.

RUN away Last Night, from Samuel Hastings, *of this City, Shipwright, an* Irish *Servant Man, named* Thomas Wildeer, *of middle stature, red*

Complexion, down Look, about 25 Years of Age: Had on when he went away, a great Coat of an ordinary dark brown Ratteen, with the Cuff of the right sleeve off, a green Grogram Vest, patch'd under one Arm, and bound down the Button holes with green Bays, an under Jacket of green Bays with two Rows of Button-holes, black Mohair Buttons and no lining, a new ozenbrigs shirt, red Plush Breeches, the Breeches good but the Plush ordinary, a new silk Handkerchief, and old Beaver Hat, light grey yarn stockings, new shoes, and wears a Wig.

Whoever takes up and secures the said Servant, so that his Master may have him again, shall have Forty Shillings Reward, and reasonable Charges, paid by Samuel Hastings. Philad. Feb. 4 1739,40.

N. B. *He went in Company with two other Servants, who were taken up at* New-Brunswick, *but he producing two false Passes was let go.*

The Pennsylvania Gazette, February 28, 1740. See *The Pennsylvania Gazette*, From June 7, to June 21, 1739, and *The Pennsylvania Gazette*, February 7, 1740.

RUN away the 3d of this Instant, from the Subscriber, a Servant Man, named *John Johnson*, by Trade a Barber, aged about 30 Years, of small Stature; had on an old Bever Hat, light colour'd Wig, white double breasted broad Cloath Coat, pretty much daub'd with Oyl before, a good Pair of new Breeches made of Irish Beggers Plush or Bird Eye Stuff of blue and red Colour, good homespun Yarn stockings. He was Born in *Birmingha*m, or thereabouts, and talks thick.

Whosoever secures the said Servant, so that he may be had again, shall be well rewarded, by William Crosthwait.

The Pennsylvania Gazette, March 6, 1740; March 12, 1740. See *The Pennsylvania Gazette*, September 27, 1739 and *The American Weekly Mercury*, From Thursday December 27, to Thursday, January 3, 1740.

RAN-away, the seventh of January last, from the Widow *Rutter* in *Market street*, an Irish Servant Girl named *Elinor Caughland*, short Stature but thick, pretty much pitted with the Small-Pox, black Hair, and good Skin, had on when she went away, an ash colour'd Calaminco Gown, blue quilted Petticoat, a red short Cloak, and a red and white silk Handkerchief. Whoever secures the said Servant so that her Mistress may have her again, shall be reasonably Rewarded and all Charges paid.

The American Weekly Mercury, From Tuesday March 4, to Tuesday March 11, 1739,40; From Tuesday March 11, to Thursday March 20, 1739,40; From Thursday March 20, to Thursday March 27, 1740; From Thursday March 27, to Thursday April 3, 1740.

RUN away on the first Day of July last from William Wright, of Lancaster County, *a Servant Man named* Thomas Mc'Swine, *but goes by the Name of* Thomas Mc'Gill, *having with him a Pass that belonged to one of that Name; aged about* 20 *Years, pretty tall, and is purblind, with black Hair; had with him some olive green Camlet, of which he may possibly have made some Cloaths.*

Whoever takes up and secures the said Servant so that his Master may have him again, shall have Forty Shillings Reward and reasonable Charges paid by William Wright.

The Pennsylvania Gazette, March 12, 1740; March 20, 1740.

RAN-away on the 17th Instant, from *William Clare*, Soemaker, [sic] a Servant Man named *John Slack*, by Trade a Shoemaker, of middle Stature, round Shoulders, full Eyes, thick Ankles; had on a redish brown Coat, a blew Jacket, homespun Breeches and new Pumps.

RAN-away also from *Joseph Davis*, Shoemaker, a Servant Man named *Evan Thomas*, by Trade a Shoemaker, of middle Stature, short black Hair, pale Complection, small black Eyes, had on when he went away, a Raccoon Hat, a gray cloth Coat new turn'd, a homespun Stockings and good Pumps.

Whoever takes up said Servants and secures them so that their Masters, may have them again, shall have *Thirty Shillings* Reward for each and reasonable Charges paid By *William Clare* and *Joseph Davis*.

The American Weekly Mercury, From Tuesday March 11, to Thursday March 20, 1740; From Thursday March 20, to Thursday March 27, 1740; From Thursday March 27, to Thursday April 3, 1740.

RUN away on the 2d Inst. from *Samuel Faires* of *Warwick* Township, *Bucks* County, a Scotch Servant Man, named *James Reid*, well set, middle stature, two of his upper Teeth out, speaks very good *Dutch*, and a Fuller by Trade: Had on when he went away, a snuff coloured Coat, brown Jacket and Breeches, blue and white worsted stockings and new shoes. Whoever secures the said Servant, so that his Master may have him again, shall have *Three Pounds* Reward and reasonable Charges paid by *S. Faires.*

The Pennsylvania Gazette, March 27, 1740; April 3, 1740; April 10, 1740.

RUN away about five Weeks ago, from Charles Moor *of this City,* Hatter, *a Servant Women named* Catherine Roach, *aged* 22 *Years; had on when she*

went away, a red, blue and white Callico Petticoat, a green Shalloon Mantle, a speckled Apron, and a good Pair of Shoes; she can speak both Spanish and Portugueze, and is a Roman-Catholick: She has been seen at Well's Ferry, enquiring the Way to New-York, and work'd in that Neighborhood pretending she was free. Whoever takes up and secures the said Servant so that he may have her again, shall have Thirty Shillings Reward and reasonable Charges paid by   Charles Moor.
    The Pennsylvania Gazette, March 27, 1740; April 3, 1740.

RAN-away, the 24th of last Month, from *Edward Brooks* of this City, an English Servant Man named *Robert Driver*, by Trade a Butcher, about 27 years of age, small of Stature, a smooth and thin Vissage, full Eyes, and dark brown Hair a little curl'd; he had on an old Hat, a grayish Coat without Cuffs and a few large Metal Buttons on it, a redish dark Jacket with flat Metal Buttons, a pair of Leather Breeches, gray Yarn Stockings, good Shoes, and a good Oznabrigs Shirt.
    Whoever takes up and secures the said Servant so that his Master may have him again, shall have *Forty Shillings* as a Reward and all reasonable Charges, Paid by   *Edward Brooks*.
    The American Weekly Mercury, From Thursday April 3, to Thursday April 10, 1740; From Thursday April 10, to Thursday April 17, 1740; From Thursday April 17, to Thursday April 24, 1740.

RAN-away, on the 9th of this Instant *April*, from *Hanse Rudulph* near *Willington*, a Servant Man named *Nathaniel Gay*, aged about 21 Years, pretends to be a Seaman, of middle Stature, thin Vissage and a swarthy Complexion; had on when he went away, a light Colour'd Kersey Pea Jacket much tar'd, Breeches of the same, Yarn Stockings, and good Shoes. He also took with him a good blue Cloth Coat very little wore, and two Hats one Bever the other Felt.
    Whoever secures the said Servant in any Goal, so that his Master may have him again, shall have *Three Pounds* Reward, and reasonable Charges,   Paid by   *Hanse Rudulph*.
    The American Weekly Mercury, From Thursday April 10, to Thursday April 17, 1740; From Thursday April 17, to Thursday April 24, 1740.

RUN away on Thursday *last from* Menasses Woods, *of* Maxfield *Township,* Bucks *County, two Servant Men, viz. One a* Londoner, *named* Reuben Shoar, *about 22 Years of Age, short Stature, brown Complexion, black bushy Hair. Had on when he went away, a fine Beaver Hat, a blue duroy Coat, with*

Buttons of the same Colour; a white Birdey'd dimity Jacket, old Leather Breeches, yarn Stockings, old Shoes.

The other an Irishman, named William Que, of low stature, round shoulder'd, stoops in his Gate, fresh Complexion, and black ey'd: Had on when he went away, an half worn felt Hat, a whitish colour'd broadcloth Coat, with plain mohair Buttons of the same Colour, old whitish wollen Jacket, a Pair of homespun Trowsers, coarse yarn Stockings, and round toed Shoes. Whoever takes up and secures the said Servants, so that their Master may have them again shall have Forty Shillings Reward, and reasonable Charges, paid by   Manasses Woods.

The Pennsylvania Gazette, May 8, 1740; May 15, 1740; May 22, 1740.

RAN-away, on Sunday the 11th Instant, from the Ship *Young Neptune*, Robert Winter Master, a Servant Man named *Frederick Perry*, by Trade a Weaver, of a swarthy heavy Complexion, waddles very much in his walking, speaks pretty broad being a *Somerset shire* Man. Had on when he went away, a pair of ragged Trowsers, a check Shirt, a ragged striped Flanel Waistcoat, a Pair of Shoes, but no Stockings.

All Persons are hereby forwarn'd not to harbour or entertain him at their Peril: And whoever brings him to the Subscriber, shall receive *Four Pounds* as a Reward,   Paid by me   *Robert Winter*.

The American Weekly Mercury, From Thursday May 8, to Thursday May 15, 1740; From Thursday May 15, to Thursday May 22, 1740; From Thursday May 22, to Thursday May 29, 1740.

TAken away, on the 10th Instant, by *Anthony Engelbert*, from *Walter Shewell* of *New-Britain*, in *Bucks* County, a gray Horse about 14 Hands high, branded on the near Buttock with **W S** not very plain, Paces very well, trim'd Mane with some Hair hanging on the further side but thin, shod all round. *Engelbert* is a Dutch Man, by Trade a Stone-Cutter, with long black curled Hair, a sort of Dove colour'd Coat with Silver twist Buttons, and a little Silver Plate on the top of the Buttons and red Lining.

He formerly lived in *Philadelphia*, and pretends to have a Commission for enlisting Men.

Whoever secures the said *Engelbert* (and Horse) so that he may be brought to Justice, shall have *Forty Shillings*,
      Paid by me   *Walter Shewell*.

The American Weekly Mercury, From Thursday May 8, to Thursday May 15, 1740.

RAN-away, on the 12th Instant, from *John Holcolm*, near *Wells's* Ferry, a Servant Man named *John* about 22 Years of age, of middle Stature and palish Complexion, with sandy Hair; had on a Felt Hat, a Kersey Coat with Brass Buttons, a striped Jacket, Leather Breeches, no Stockings nor Shoes, but 'tis supposed he has bought some, having Money with him.

Whoever secures him so that his Master may have him again, shall have *Forty Shillings* Reward, and reasonable Charges,
   Paid by   John Holcolm.

The American Weekly Mercury, From Thursday May 8, to Thursday May 15, 1740; From Thursday May 15, to Thursday May 22, 1740; From Thursday May 22, to Thursday May 29, 1740; From Thursday May 29, to Thursday June 5, 1740.

STOLEN last October from *Mary Doharthy* in *Lancaster* County, an Iron-grey Mare, branded on the near Buttock with **MM** and a Flower de Luce above, and on the near Shoulder with a Mark thus ♥ with a Flower de-luce above said Mark, and two slits in the near Ear, paces very well. The said Mare was taken away by one *William Dent*, by Trade a Bricklayer, about 30 Years of Age, of a smooth Face.

Whoever secures the Thief, and returns the Mare to the said *Mary Doharthy* shall have Five Pounds reward, and for the Mare only, Forty-Shillings

The American Weekly Mercury, From Thursday May 22, to Thursday May 29, 1740

RUN away on the 21st of *April* past, from *Nutts* Ironworks in *Chester* County, the following Servants, *viz.*

Patrick Culford, a Carpenter, is a lusty likely Man, of a dark Complexion, black Hair cut off, mark'd on his Hand P C with Gun Powder. He is well cloath'd.

Matthew Reading, of middle Stature, sharp Visage, fair Complexion: Had on an ozenbrigs Jacket and Trowsers.

Edward Morgan, a Taylor, of middle Stature, sandy Complexion, one of his Legs, inclining inwards having been broke, mark'd E M on one of his Hands with Gunpowder; Had on a brown Drugget Coat, striped linnen Jacket and ozenbrigs Trowsers.

They were all seen together, and design'd to go for *New-York*, or the Cedar Swamps in the *Jerseys*.

Whoever secures the said Servants or either of them, so that they may be had again, and gives Notice thereof to the Printer of this Paper, shall have a Pistole Reward for each, or *Five Pounds* for all, and reasonable Charges paid.

The Pennsylvania Gazette, June 5, 1740; June 12, 1740; June 26, 1740.

RUN away on the 9th Inst. from *Thomas Cummings* of *Chester,* Shoemaker, an Irish Servant Man named *Glowd Woods,* of middle Stature, pale Complexion, thin Face and no Hair: Had on when he went away a little Hat, the Brims stitch'd to the Crown, a white Cap, an old whitish Coat, and a pretty good linnen Coat under it, but no Jacket, old waxey leather Breeches, yarn Stockins, and a pair of old Shoes, unless he has taken a pair of new ones, which I suppose he has.

Whoever takes up and secures the said Servant so that his Master may have him again, shall have Twenty Shillings Reward, and reasonable Charges, paid by   *Tho. Cummings.   Chester, June* 13 1740.

The Pennsylvania Gazette, June 12, 1740; June 19, 1740, July 3, 1740.

RUN away on the 25th of June past, from John Williamson, *Fuller at* Nottingham, *in* Chester *County, a Native Irish Servant Lad, named* John Ryan, *aged about* 18 *Years, of middle Stature but slender, round fac'd with black curl'd Hair; Had on when he went away, an half worn felt Hat, a brown Kersey Coat, without Lining, half trim'd and bound round the Neck with red, two homespun Shirts, a pair of coarse Trowsers, and white linnen Drawers, grey worsted Stockings, and old Shoes.*

Whoever takes up and secures the said Servant , so that his Master may have him again, shall have Three Pounds Reward and all reasonable Charges paid by John Williamson.

The Pennsylvania Gazette, July 3, 1740; July 10, 1740; July 17, 1740; July 24, 1740.

RAN-away from *Jacob Kirk* of Lampton Township in *Lancaster* County, a Servant Man named *Roger Ren,* has short Hair, freckels in his Face, white Hair in his Eye-lids, sandy Beard, round Shoulder'd, and can talk English and Irish, had on when he went away, a light colour'd Coat with brass Buttons, old Leather Breeches, dark grey Stockings, good Shoes, and old felt Hat and a Linnen Cap.

Whoever takes up said Servant and secures him so that he may be had again, shall have *Forty Shillings* Reward and reasonable Charges
    paid By   *Jacob Kirk.*

The American Weekly Mercury, From Thursday July 10, to Thursday July 17, 1740; From Thursday July 17, to Thursday July 24, 1740; From

Thursday July 24, to Thursday July 31, 1740; From Thursday July 31, to Thursday August 7, 1740; From Thursday August 14, to Thursday August 21, 1740.

RUN away on the 20th Inst, from *Reese Meredith* a Servant Man named *George Townly*, a Carpenter, has a red Face, and some pimples on it, a short peeked Nose; Had on when he went away, a dark Wigg, a dark brown Wastcoat with Brass buttons, a white or check Shirt, a pair of Leather Breeches, and speaks broad *Cheshire*.

Whoever secures the said Servant, that he may be had again, shall have *Twenty Shillings*, if taken within Five Miles of *Philadelphia*, or *Forty*, if farther off, paid by *Reese Meredith*.

The Pennsylvania Gazette, July 31, 1740; August 7, 1740; August 14, 1740.

RUN away on the 31st of *July* from *Thomas Hartley*, of *Buckingham* in *Bucks* County a Servant Man named *William Center*, aged about 20 Years, middle Stature, fresh Complexion, crooked Leg'd and goes limping, and stooping He had on when he went away, a Pea Jacket, with Leather Buttons and open Sleves, homespun Shirt and Trowsers, Old Shoes, an old Hat without any Brim, he has a very large Scar on his left Wrist.

Whosoever secures the said Servant, so that his said Master may have him again, shall have Forty-Shillings reward
paid by *Thomas Hartley*.

The American Weekly Mercury, From Thursday July 31, to Thursday August 7, 1740; From Thursday August 26, to Thursday September 4, 1740.

Run away from the Subscriber, on the 27th Inst. a Servant Man named *Daniel Dunn*, Aged about 30 Years, well set, bluff Faced, fresh Complexion, speaks good English, he is an *Irishman*: Had on when he went away, a Snuff colour'd Coat, with flat pewter Butons, a pair of Trowsers, and a pair of linnen Breeches, a pair of black Stockings, a homespun Shirt with a very large Patch on the Belly.

Whoever secures the said Servant, so that his Master may have him again, shall have Thirty Shillings Reward, and reasonable Charges
paid by *David Ogden*.

The Pennsylvania Gazette, August 7, 1740; August 14, 1740.

RUN away the 11th Inst. from *James Holmes*, a Servant Man named *William Burrows*, aged about 23 Years; he is about 5 Foot 8 Inches high, reddish Hair, and is pock retten; had with him when he went away, a Dimity Jacket, and an Ozenbrigs Jacket, two Ozenbrigs Shirts, two Ozenbrigs Breeches, thread Stockings, a fine Shirt, and a Felt Hat. Whoever takes up and secures the said Servant, so that he may be had again, shall have *Thirty Shillings* Reward, and all reasonable Charges   paid by   James Holmes.
The Pennsylvania Gazette, August 14, 1740; August 21, 1740; August 28, 1740.

RUN away on the 17th Inst. from Isaac Rees, of Upper-Merion in Philadelphia County, an Irish Servant Man, named *David Punch*, by Trade a Weaver, aged about 20 Years, of middle stature, thick legged and broad-footed, with black bushy Hair; has a Scar on his Head and another on one of his Legs: Had on when he went away, a mixt coloured light blue homespun Cloth Jacket, with Horn-Buttons on it, ozenbrigs shirt, linnen Drawers, good sheep's-black stockings, good shoes and a Felt Hat. Whoever secures the said Servant, so that he may be had again, shall have *Twenty* Shillings Reward, and all reasonable Charges,   paid by   Isaac Rees.
The Pennsylvania Gazette, August 21, 1740; August 28, 1740. See *The Pennsylvania Gazette*, From March 29, to April 5, 1739.

RUN away on the 17th Instant, from Henry Hockley, near *Nutt's* Iron-Works in *Chester* County, an Irish Servant Man, named *Farrel M'Loughlan*, aged about 35 Years, of middle Stature, brown Complexion, large grey Eyes, wide Mouth, has a swelling like in his Throat, and has much of the Brogue on his Tongue: Had on when he went away, a good Felt Hat, diaper Cap, silk Handkerchief, ozenbrigs shirt, homespun dark coloured Coat, striped linnen Jacket, leather Breeches; yarn stockings, and new shoes. Whoever secures the said Servant , so that his Master may have him again, shall have Forty Shillings Reward, and all reasonable Charges,
paid by   Henry Hockley.
The Pennsylvania Gazette, August 21, 1740.

RUN away from *Alexander Crukshank*, of this City, Shoemaker, an Apprentice Lad, named *John Collet*, aged about 19 Years, stoops in his Shoulders, a Scar on his Right Hand, with his Hair: Had with him when he went away, a flesh colour'd duroy Coat with slash Sleeves, striped linnen Jacket and Breeches, and a short blue Jacket, a pair of grey homespun Breeches, new worsted Stockings, and a Pair of yarn Stockings, new narrow toe'd Shoes, two check'd Shirts, and a white Shirt, two pair of Trowsers, a Castor Hat.

Whosoever takes up the said Lad, and secures him, so that his Master may have him again, shall have *Thirty Shillings* Reward

        paid by   *Alexander Crukshank. Philad. Sept.* 14. 1740.

The Pennsylvania Gazette, September 18, 1740; September 25, 1740.

RAN-away on the 23d of Sept. from *Wm. Salkeld*, of *Chester*, Black-smith, a Servant Man named *Peter Brown*, aged about 28 Years, by Trade a Blacksmith, of a Pale Complection with a down look; he took with him a white Camblet Coat, a Corded Fustain Jacket, two homespun Shirts, a pair of Trowsers, good Shoes and a Felt Hat.

Whoever takes up said Servant and secures him so that his Master may have him again, shall have Thrity [*sic*] Shillings Reward and reasonable Charges   paid   By *Wm. Sakeld.*

The American Weekly Mercury, From Thursday September 18, to Thursday September 25, 1740; From Thursday September 25, to Thursday October 2, 1740; From Thursday October 2, to Thursday October 9, 1740; From Thursday October 9, to Thursday October 16, 1740.

RUN away the 15th of this Inst. from *Enoch Anderson* of the City of *Philadelphia*, Innkeeper, an Irish Servant Man named *John Donelan*, of middle Stature, well set, speaks good English but thick; had on when he went away, an old dark Kersey Jacket, and an old Flannen Jacket under it; had also with him two Coats, the one dark Irish Cloth, the other Linnen; two *Germantown* Check linnen Shirts, and four white Shirts, two pair of Stockings, one thread, the other worsted, of a light Colour; good Shoes, three pair of Breeches, the one Ozenbrigs, the other Serge much mended, and the other dark Coarse Kersey. He wears a Wig or linnen Cap and a Felt Hat: he pretends he has been a Tavernkeeper in Dublin. Whoever takes up and secures the said Servant, so that his Master may have him again, shall have *Three Pounds* Reward and reasonable Charges

        paid by   *Enoch Anderson.*

The Pennsylvania Gazette, September 25, 1740; October 2, 1740; October 9, 1740; October 16, 1740. Last ad reads "15th of *September* past".

RUN away from on board the Prince of Orange, Robert Williamson, Master, on the 19th Sept. a Servant Man, named William Ryan, by Trade a

Shoemaker, he is an elderly Man, with Freckles in his Face: He had on him, a light Wigg, speckled Shirt, new frize Jacket split behind, blue waistcoat, shagg Breeches, new brown yarn Stockings, and new Shoes. Whoever secures the said Servant, so that he may be had again, shall have Twenty Shillings Reward, and reasonable Charges,
        paid by   Richard Farmer.
The Pennsylvania Gazette, September 25, 1740; October 2, 1740; October 9, 1740; October 16, 1740.

RAN-away from *John Hyatt* of this City, on the 22d of *September*, a Servant Man named *Lawrance Brimer*, he is a Swede by Birth and a Brasier by Trade, of middle Stature, well set, fresh Complection, short Face and a down look, about 26 Years old: He seems mighty Religious, but on a small Provacation will Curse and Swear, he speaks Swede, High German and English, but so as easily discover'd to be a Foreigner, his Voice low: He had on when he absented himself, an old Hat and Cap, his Hair cut short or shav'd, a course drab colour'd Kersey Pea Jacket, white homespun Shirt, Ozabriggs Trowsers, grey worsted Hose, and Calveskin Shoes, with Brass Buckles. Whoever secures said Servant so that his said Master may have him again, shall have Forty Shillings Reward and reasonable Charges
        paid By *John Hyatt.*
The American Weekly Mercury, From Thursday September 25, to Thursday October 2, 1740; From Thursday October 2, to Thursday October 9, 1740; From Thursday October 16, to Thursday October 23, 1740; From Thursday October 23, to Thursday October 30, 1740.

RUN away last Night, from on board the Sloop Triton, James Hodges, Master, two Indian Men Servants, viz. One named Jeremiah Robin, of middle Stature, well set, flat Nose, strait short Hair, about 30 Years of Age: Had on an homespun Jacket, cotton check'd shirt, and ozenbrigs Trowsers. The other named Nehemiah Robin, something shorter that the other, short Hair, aged about 24; Had on the same sort of Clothing as the other. Whoever takes up and secures said Indians, so that their Master may have them again, shall have Twenty Shillings Reward,   paid by   James Hodges.
The Pennsylvania Gazette, October 2, 1740.

RAN-away on the 19th Instant from the Ship *Hannover*, *Richard Northove*, Commander; now lying at Capt. *Attwoods* Wharfe, two Servant Men, the one named *Timothy Denison*, aged about 25 Years, of a sandy coloured Hair, tall and fresh colour'd, had on when he went away, a dark gray Jacket, check'd

Shirt; had the Irish Brogue on his Tongue. The other named *Daniel Mahegan*, about 25 years old, a short well sett fellow, with light brown Hair, had on when he went away, a light colour'd Jacket & Check'd Shirt.

Whoever Secures both, or either of said Runaways, so as to be delivered safe to the said Master, on board the said Ship, or to Capt. *Attwood*, in Philadelphia, shall have *Thirty Shillings* Reward for each of them & Reasonable Charges paid by, William Attwood.

The American Weekly Mercury, From Thursday October 16, to Thursday October 23, 1740; From Thursday October 23, to Thursday October 30, 1740; From Thursday November 6, to Thursday November 13, 1740. See *The Pennsylvania Gazette*, October 23, 1740.

ABsented himself the 19th Instant from *Edward Evans*, a Prentice Lad named *John Dennis*, of a fair Complection, middle stature, aged about 18 Years, had on when he went away, an old whitish colour'd Kersey Coat, a dirty Oznabrigs Shirt and Trowsers, and an old Hat.

Whoever brings the aforesaid Prentice to his Master shall have *Twenty Shillings* Reward and all reasonable Charges,
paid By Edward Evans.

The American Weekly Mercury, From Thursday October 16, to Thursday October 23, 1740; From Thursday October 23, to Thursday October 30, 1740; From Thursday November 6, to Thursday November 13, 1740. See *The Pennsylvania Gazette*, October 23, 1740.

RAN-away on the 21st of *October* from the Subscribers, the two following Persons, *viz*.

Andrew Aharns, a middle sized Man, of a pale Complexion and thin Visage, about 40 Years of age, and about 5 Foot 7 Inches high, speaks *Low-Dutch* and some broken *English*. Had on when he went away a Seafaring Dress

Alexander Timothy, a well set Man, about 5 Foot 9 Inches high, of a ruddy Complexion and long Visage, speaks inclining thro' his Nose, lame in his right Leg and Foot, which is smaller than the other, and cannot well move his Ancle.

Whoever secures the above-mentioned Persons, in any Goal or otherwise, so that the Subscribers may have them again, shall have *Thirty Shillings* Reward for each Person,
paid by Edward Shippen and Company.

The American Weekly Mercury, From Thursday October 16, to Thursday October 23, 1740; From Thursday October 23, to Thursday October 30, 1740; From Thursday November 6, to Thursday November

13, 1740; From Thursday November 13, to Thursday November 20, 1740.

RUN away the 19th *Inst.* at Night, from the Ship Hanover, Richard Northover Commander; now lying at Capt. Attwoods Wharffe, two Servant Men, the one named Timothy Denison, aged about 15 Years, with sandy coloured Hair, Tall and fresh coloured: Had on when he went away, a dark grey Jacket, and chequ'd Shirt; had the Irish Brogue on his Tongue. The other named Daniel Mohegan, about 25 Years old, a short well set Fellow with light brown Hair: Had on when he went away, a light coloured Jacket, and chequ'd Shirt. Whoever secures both or either of said Run-aways, so as to be delivered safe to the said Master on board the said Ship, or to Capt. Attwood, in Philadelphia, shall have Thirty Shillings Reward for each of them, and reasonable Charges paid by
     William Attwood. Philadelphia, Octo. 22d, 1740.
The Pennsylvania Gazette, October 23, 1740; October 30, 1740. See The American Weekly Mercury, From Thursday October 16, to Thursday October 23, 1740.

RUN away last Night from William Scot, Taylor, of this City, a Servant Man, named Samuel Williams: Had on a blue cloth Coat, with no Lining, nor Flaps, yellow flat metal Buttons: a white Shirt, blue frize Breeches, grey yarn Stockings, old Shoes, and three beaver Hats, one of them old, with a strip'd ticken Jacket.

And from Isaac Morris, of the same Place, Merchant, a Servant Lad, named Harper Mullins, he is a middle siz'd slim Lad: Had on a light colour'd cloth Coat, a red frize Jacket, a new pair of Buck-skin Breeches, new Shoes and Stockings. He is a Painter by Trade, of a pale Complexion, and stoops pretty much in his Walk: He took with him a Castor Hat, a red and yellow India Handkerchief, a blue Pea Jacket, lined with strip'd Flannen.

And from William Maugridge, of the same Place, Ship Joiner, a Servant Man, named George Townly, short of Stature, fresh Complexion, much Pockfretten: Had on when he went away, a Beaver Hat, a mix'd duroy Coat, black Callimancoe Jacket and Breeches, worsted Stockings of a dark grey colour, and new Calf-skin Shoes, he speaks thick, and pretends to be a Carpenter by Trade.

Whoever secures the said Servants so that their Masters may have them again, shall have Three Pounds Reward for each, and reasonable Charges, paid by William Scot, Isaac Norris and William Maugridge.

N. B. They all came over from Bristol with Capt. Richardson, and are supposed to be gone together: They took with them a Wherry belonging to James Wood, Boat-builder. Octob. 13. 1740.
The Pennsylvania Gazette, October 23, 1740; October 30, 1740; November 6, 1740.

ABsented himself the 19th of this Inst. from his Master Edward Evans, an Apprentice Lad, named John Dennis, of a fair Complexion, middle Stature, about 18 Years of Age. Had on when he went away, an old whitish coloured Kersey Coat, a dirty Ozenbrigs Shirt and Trowsers, and an old Hat. Whoever brings the aforesaid Apprentice to his Master, shall have Twenty Shillings Reward, and reasonable Charges,
　　　　　paid by me,　　Edward Evans.
The Pennsylvania Gazette, October 23, 1740; October 30, 1740. See The American Weekly Mercury, From Thursday October 16, to Thursday October 23, 1740.

RUN away about the 19th Inst. from James Agnew, an Irish Servant Man named Alexander Steel, a tall lusty Fellow, of a darkish Complexion, stoops much, and walks ill on his Joints, speaks tolerable English: Had on, an old brown Coat, Jacket and Breeches, of coarse Cloth, a pair of new Pumps, and grey yarn Stockings. Whoever takes him up and brings him to James Agnew, at Mr. Thomas Robinson's, in Front-street, or to Capt. William Blair, in Second-street, shall have Twenty Shillings Reward, and reasonable Charges
　　　　　paid by　　William Blair, James Agnew.
Philadelphia, Octo. 30. 1740.
The Pennsylvania Gazette, October 30, 1740; November 6, 1740.

RUN away the 3d of this Instant from the Subscriber a Dutch Boy named *Christopher Kigler,* sometimes he assumes the Name of *Hans,* about twelve Years old, had on a whitish colour'd Coat with white Mettle Buttons, speaks little English, smooth Fac'd pretty plump. Whoever secures him so as he may be had again, shall have Twenty Shillings Reward, and reasonable Charges
　　　　　paid by　　Samuel Welsh.
The American Weekly Mercury, From Thursday October 30, to Thursday November 6, 1740; From Thursday November 6, to Thursday November 13, 1740; From Thursday November 13, to Thursday November 20, 1740.

RUN away on the 3d Inst from Roger Kirk, in West-Nottingham, a Servant Man, named Dugel or Dennis M' Dowel, aged about 34 Years, of a swarthy Complexion, sour Countenance, and goes Limping, having one Leg thicker than the other; has short Hair, and wears a woollen Cap, Felt Hat, a dark coloured Frize Coat and Vest without Lining, old brown Breeches, white Stockings, and Pumps.

Whoever takes up and secures the said Servant so that his Master may have him again, shall have Twenty Shillings Reward and reasonable Charges paid by   Roger Kirk. *Philadelphia, Nove*mber 5. 1740.

The Pennsylvania Gazette, November 6, 1740; November 13, 1740; November 20, 1740.

A*Bsented himself from Joseph Armit on the 19th Instant, an Apprentice Lad named George Hogg, about 19 Years of Age, of middle Stature, down Look, dark complexion, with a black Beard over his upper Lip: Had on a Kersey Coat and Jacket, with Brass Buttons, and leather Breeches newly wash'd, with Trowsers over them; a good Hat and Stockings and Shoes; also took with him some linnen Cloaths.*

Whoever secures him so that his Master may have him again, shall receive Forty Shillings Reward paid by me   Joseph Armit.

The Pennsylvania Gazette, November 6, 1740.

RUN away from the Subscriber, the 4th Day of November last, a Servant Woman, aged about 28 Years, fair Hair'd, wants some of her Teeth before, a little deafish, named Susannah Wells, born near Biddeford, in England: She had on when she went away, a Callico Gown, with red Flowers, blue Stockings, with Clocks, new Shoes, a quilted Petticoat, Plat Hat. Whoever secures said Servant, and delivers her to said Subscriber at Wilmington, or to Robert Dixson in Philadelphia, shall have Twenty five Shillings Reward, and reasonable Charges paid by   Robert Dixon, or Thomas Downing. Philad. December 4. 1740.

N. B. It's believed the said Servant was carried from New Castle in the Ship commanded by Capt Lawrence Dent, now lying at Philadelphia.

The Pennsylvania Gazette, December 4, 1740; December 11, 1740; December 18, 1740; December 25, 1740; January 1, 1741; January 8, 1740.

RUN away last Night, from on Board the Diana, of Dublin, Richard M"Carty, Master, a Servant Man, named Valentine Handlin, aged about 30 Years, a lusty rawbon'd Fellow small round Visaged, is of a dark Complexion with short Black Hair; Had on when he went away, a brown bob Wig, old Felt Hat, an old lightish colour'd cloth great Coat, a blue grey Waiscoat, old leather Breeches, yarn Stockings, broad square toe'd Shoes; and perhaps may have taken some other Cloaths with him. He is remarkably hollow Footed, and seems crumpfooted when his Shoes are off. Whoever secures the said Servant so he may be had again, shall have Twenty Shillings Reward,
   paid by. William Blair. Philad. December 3. 1740

The Pennsylvania Gazette, December 4, 1740; December 11, 1740; December 18, 1740; December 25, 1740; January 1, 1741.

ABsented herself the 20th of November, from Joseph Canon, of Coventry Township, Chester County, a Girl of about Eleven Years of Age, named Mary Gathen: Had on when she went away, an old striped Cap, linnen Jacket, a good linsey striped Petticoat, a pair of white yarn Stockings, an old pair of Shoes. Whoever takes up the said Mary Gathen, so that she may be had again, shall have Ten Shillings Reward, and reasonable Charges
   paid by Joseph Canon .

The Pennsylvania Gazette, December 11, 1740; December 18, 1740; December 25, 1740.

RAN-away the 14 Instant, from Walter Moore at Abington, an Irish Servant Man named John Lloyd, about 30 years of age, of midle Stature and well set, swarthy Complexion short Hair and wears a Cap; had on a darkish frize Jacket, and a blew flannel one under it, White Plush Breeches, good Woollen stockings, new shoes, Ozenbrigs shirt and a felt Hat.

Whoever takes up said Servant and secure him, so that his Master may have him again shall have Three Pounds as a Reward, and all reasonable Charges.

The American Weekly Mercury, From Thursday December 11, to Thursday December 18, 1740; From Thursday December 18, to Thursday December 25, 1740; From Thursday December 25, to Thursday January 1, 1740-41; From Thursday January 1, to Thursday January 8, 1741; From Thursday January 8, to Thursday January 15, 1741; From Thursday January 15, to Thursday January 22, 1741; From Thursday January 29, to Thursday February 5, 1741; From Thursday February 5, to Thursday February 12, 1741; From Thursday March 12, to Thursday March 19, 1741; From Thursday March 19, to Thursday March 26, 1741.

1741

RUN away from the Subscriber the 3d Inst. a Servant Man named Thomas Wenn, by trade a Barber, appears by his looks to be at least 40 Years old, but pretends he is not 30, middle Stature, well set, sore ey'd, and near sighted: Had on when he went away, a small Hat but good, a small black Wig, but may have taken another of some other colour, a kersey Coat almost new of a mixt colour redish and white, lin'd through with a red half thick or serge, large flat metal Buttons, old white dimity Jacket, a pair of stout Buckskin Breeches almost new with brass Buttons, a pair of new thick mill'd Stockings of a bluish colour, Shoes about half worn. Whoever secures the said Servant so that he may be had again, shall have if twenty Miles off this City Twenty Shillings, if thirty, thirty Shillings, and if forty, forty Shillings Reward,
       paid by   William Crosthwaite. Philad. January 5. 1740, 41.
The Pennsylvania Gazette, January 8, 1741; January 15, 1741; January 22, 1741; January 29, 1741.

STOLEN *on the 12th Inst. from Joshua Thomson, of Ridley township, Chester county, a dark brown Mare, branded on the near side I C, about 13 hands and half high, can both trot and pace, shod before; and had on when she was stolen, a snaffle bridle, a russet leather breasted saddle, with the seat somewhat fallen, about half worn: She was stolen by a Man that goes by the name of John Blowden alias John Williams, a middle-sized man, pale fac'd, brownish hair, short, and wears a linen cap: Had on an old lightish colour'd jacket, cloth breeches of the same colour; darkish colour'd stockings. He says that he liv'd a considerable time in Philadelphia, and is well acquainted there; and has, since he was guilty of the theft aforesaid, been detected in the aid [sic] city for a crime of the like nature, and left his great coat, and made his escape, on the mare above described.*

    Whoever takes up and secures the mare, saddle and bridle, so that the Owner may have them again, and the thief that he may be brought to justice, shall have Forty Shillings reward, or the same reward for the bridle and saddle paid by Joshua Thomson.

    Note, the said Thief pretends to be a Shoemaker, and sometimes a doctor.

    The Pennsylvania Gazette, January 29, 1741; February 5, 1741; February 12, 1741; February 19, 1741; February 26, 1741. See *The American Weekly Mercury*, From Thursday July 3, to Thursday July 10, 1729; *The Pennsylvania Gazette*, From March 4, to March 11, 1731;

The American Weekly Mercury, From Tuesday March 13, to Tuesday March 20, 1733; *The Pennsylvania Gazette*, From March 8, to March 15, 1733; *The American Weekly Mercury*, From Thursday October 4, to Thursday October 11, 1733; *The Pennsylvania Gazette*, From September 28, to October 11, 1733, and *The Pennsylvania Gazette*, From November 13, to November 20, 1735.

BROKE out of the Goal in Philadelphia, on the 4th Instant, one John Williams, alias Henry Welch, being used to change his Name, a short set fellow, has two brands or marks over each Eyebrow about as big as a large Kidney Bean, fresh Vissage, hollow nosed, and down look'd, generally covering his Brands with his Hat, supposed to have Stolen from Thomas Chalkley of Frankford, a dapple grey Horse, better than 14 Hands high, a natural Pacer, and Branded on the near Thigh **TC** also a ruset hunting Saddle almost new, with a Buck Skin Seat, a Male-Pillion to a Housen. Also took from Thomas Crosdale, Vintner, in said Place, two Beaver Hatts almost new, a white Dimity Jacket and Breeches, a new white and two chex Shirts, a pair of good round toe'd Boots, with sundry other Things. He wears a blue broad Cloth Coat with slash'd Sleeves, a light colour'd Jacket, a pair of Leather Breeches with round white Buttons, and is made Dutch Fashion with a flap before.

Whoever takes up and secures him so that he may be brought to Justice, with the Horse, &c. so that the Owners may have them again, shall have three Pounds paid them by

Thomas Chalkey and Thomas Crosdale, with reasonable Charges.

The American Weekly Mercury, From Thursday January 29, to Thursday February 5, 1741; From Thursday February 5, to Thursday February 12, 1741; From Thursday March 12, to Thursday March 19, 1741.

RAN-away the 17th of February, from John Hibberd, of Willis-Town, Chester County, an Irish Lad named Edward Swane, aged about 16 Years, well set, short dark Hair, had on a light colour'd Cloth Coat, and Jacket, Buck skin Breeches, good Shoes and Yarn Stockings of two colours, a homespun Shirt, and a felt Hat about half worn.

Whoever takes up said Servant and secures him so that his Master may have him again, shall have Twenty Shillings Reward and reasonable Charges paid By John Hibberd

The American Weekly Mercury, From Thursday February 12, to Thursday February 19, 1741; From Thursday February 19, to Thursday

February 26, 1741; From Thursday March 12, to Thursday March 19, 1741.

RUN away on the 25th Instant, from Jonathan Peasley, Chocolate Grinder, near the Church, Second-Street, Philadelphia, a Servant Man named George Harris, a West-Countryman, about 26 Years of Age, small Stature, pale Complexion, has his Name in blue Letters on both Arms, and several other Letters besides: Had on when he went away, a Felt Hat, a plad Jacket, a striped linsey woolsey Jacket and a pea Jacket, a new check'd Shirt, homespun cloth Breeches, and very large Buckles, a pair of yarn Stockings, and a pair of black and white worsted Stockings, and old Shoes. 'Tis supposed he will wear a coal black Wig, and a worsted Cap. Whoever takes up and secures the said Servant so that his Master may have him again, shall have Forty Shillings Reward, and reasonable Charges
        paid by   Jonathan Peasley. Philadelphia, March 26. 1741.
The Pennsylvania Gazette, March 26, 1741; April 2, 1741; April 9, 1741; April 16, 1741.

RAN-away, the 31st of March last from John Woodward of Thornbury, in Chester County, a Servant Man named Thomas Hadley, about, 21 Years of age, short and slender, with short black Hair; had on when he went away, an old lightish coloured Cloth Jacket, a course homespun Shirt, an old Felt Hat, old Trowsers, course redish coloured Woollen Stockings, and good Shoes well Nail'd.
    Whoever secures the said Servant so that his Master, may have him again, shall have Twenty Shillings Reward and reasonable Charges,
        Paid By   John Woodward.
The American Weekly Mercury, From Thursday March 26, to Thursday April 2, 1741; From Thursday April 2, to Thursday April 9, 1741; From Thursday April 16, to Thursday April 23, 1741.

RAN away last January, from Henry Smiths Plantation at Tulpehocken, a Servant Man named Benjamin Hicks, a West Countryman, about 26 Years of Age, he is a stout well set fellow, full Fac'd, swarthy Complexion, had on when he went away a striped Blanket, a brown Duroy Coat, Oznabrigs Shirt, Leather Breeches, white half thick Indian Stockings and Indian Shoes, a Worsted Cap and a Felt Hat. His Master sent him to Allegheny to the Indians with a Horse Load of Goods, such as white Duffels white half Thicks, small Looking Glasses, clasp Knives, Worsted Caps, narrow red Ribbon, Awl

Blades, small white Beades, Sissars and Gartering, all which he took with him. It is but lately since his Master discovered he was run away.

Whoever brings the said Servant to Philadelphia, shall have Three Pistoles Reward and reasonable Charges

paid by the said Master, or Edward Shippen of the said City.

The American Weekly Mercury, From Thursday March 26, to Thursday April 2, 1741; From Thursday April 9, to Thursday April 16, 1741; From Thursday April 16, to Thursday April 23, 1741; From Thursday April 30, to Thursday Mat 7, 1741. See *The Pennsylvania Gazette*, April 2, 1741.

RUN away last January, from Henry Smith's Plantation, at Tulpahocken, a Servant Man named Benjamin Hicks, a West- Countryman, about 26 Years of Age, he is a stout well set Fellow, full fac'd, swarthy Complexion: Had on when he went away, a striped Blanket, brown Duroy Coat, Ozenbrigs Shirt, Leather Breeches, white half thick Indian Stockings, Indian Shoes, worsted Cap, Felt Hat: His Master sent him to Allegheny to the Indians with a Horseload of Goods, such as white Duffels, white half thick, small Looking Glasses, clasp Knives, worsted Caps, narrow Ribbon, Awl Blades, small white Beads, Scizzers and Gartering, all which he took with him, it is but lately since his Master discovered he was run away. Whoever brings the said Servant to Philadelphia, shall have three Pistoles Reward, and reasonable Charges paid, by his said Master, or Edward Shippen of Philadelphia.
N. B. It is said he had a Companion with him.

The Pennsylvania Gazette, April 2, 1741; April 9, 1741; April 16, 1741. See *The American Weekly Mercury*, From Thursday March 26, to Thursday April 2, 1741.

RUN away last Summer from Abraham Emmit of New London Township, Chester County, a Servant Man, named Peter Willy, an Irishman about 20 Years of Age, pale Complexion, long sandy Hair, and a Glover by Trade. He was heard of last Week, and supposed to be some where in Bucks County.

Whoever takes up and secures the said Servant so that his Master may have him again, or brings him to Benjamin Davis, Esq; in Chester, shall have Twenty Shillings Reward, and reasonable Charges,

paid by   Abraham Emmit.   Philad. April 2, 1741.

The Pennsylvania Gazette, April 2, 1741; April 16, 1741.

RUN away on the 6th Inst. from William Branson's Furnace, called Reading, in the Township of Nantmel, Chester County, a Native Irish Servant Man, named Matthew Burn, well set, of middle Stature, likely and full fac'd, fresh Complexion, fair hair'd but wears a red and white cotton Cap: Had on when he went away, a felt Hat, a bluish grey double breasted Jacket, with brass Buttons, black callimancoe Jacket and Breeches, ozenbrigs Shirt, yarn stockings, and new Shoes.

Whoever takes up and secures the said Servant, so that his Master may have him again, shall have Three Pounds Reward, and reasonable Charges paid by   Francis M'Connal.   Phila. April 9, 1741.
N. B. He is supposed to be in Company with one Bryan Kennedy, pockfretten, a native Irishman, a Servant to George Lion, of the same Township.

The Pennsylvania Gazette, April 9, 1741; April 16, 1741; April 23, 1741; May 7, 1741.

STOLEN from the Plantation of John Clevet, of Bristol Township, Philadelphia County, on the 12th of April, a Sorrel Horse, Branded with a Bloch or Mark on the near Shoulder. It is supposed he is stolen by two idle Persons, their Names not certainly known, the one is a short Man, fair shin'd, brown Hair, and brown Cloaths, and has for some Years past been about Colebrookdale Iron Works, where he gave out that his Name was John Jones, but has since called himself by the Name of Morgan Morgan. The other is a tall Man, black skin'd, short black Hair, and a light colour'd Coat, his Name unknown. It is supposed they have taken another Horse of a gray colour, a natural Pacer, and has no Brand Mark, belonging to John Cunrod of Germantownship, in said County.

Whoever takes up and secures said Thives and Horses shall have Five Pounds Reward, or Three Pound for the Horses paid by John Clevet.

N. B. There was left in the room of the said Horses two old black Horses, the Owner describing the Marks, &c. may have them again.

The American Weekly Mercury, From Thursday April 9, to Thursday April 16, 1741; From Thursday April 16, to Thursday April 23, 1741.

RUN away from the Subscriber hereof, last Sunday night the twelfth of this Instant April, two servant men, one named Charles McGlachon, a tall lusty fellow, a Hilandman born, he speaks good english, much pock marked, with short black hair, a pretty good carpenter and professes to be a sailor: Had on when he went away, a duroy coat patched at the elbow, a camlet Jacket double breasted of a bluish colour, and a homespun Jacket of sky blue, two ozenbrigs shirts, one pair of striped holland trowsers, a pair of camlet breeches of a greenish colour, one pair of new calfskin shoes peaked toe'd, and one pair of oval toe'd shoes, half soled, a pair of yarn stockings ragged and furow'd, a castor hat half worn, a check shirt half worn. He was whipt at Dover for stealing a sheep, and listed with Captain Jenkins at New-Castle.

The other an Irishman born, named Thomas Oungess, he speaks much with the brogue upon his tongue, a thick short fellow of a swarthy complexion, down look, high eye brows, he can write pretty well, and we suppose that he has forged a pass for themselves; he came in last fall to Messrs. Davy and Carson: Had on when he went away, a brown cloth coat with yellow lining, a red jacket, a fine linnen shirt, homespun trowsers, pretty good shoes, a new beaver hat, yarn stockings, with bushy hair. Whoever takes up and secures the said servants, so that their masters may have them again, shall have Five Pounds as a reward, and reasonable charges, paid by
Charles White and Robert Gray. Phila. April 23. 1741.
The Pennsylvania Gazette, April 23, 1741; April 30, 1741; May 7, 1741.

RUN away on the 20th of March from James Baldwin, Bristol township, Philadelphia county, a servant man, named Thomas Holt, an Irishman, aged about 28 years, by trade a joiner, of middle stature, well set, bow leg'd, and walks wide between his knees, and wears his own hair: Had on when he went away, a lightish colour'd coat with mohair buttons, and lin'd with lightish shalloon, small striped woolen Wastcoat, without sleeves, leather breeches, homespun shirt, blue worsted stockings, half worn shoes, half worn castor hat. Whoever takes up the servant, so that his Master may have him again, shall have Twenty-shillings reward, and reasonable charges
paid by   James Baldwin. Phila. April 23. 1741
The Pennsylvania Gazette, April 23, 1741; April 30, 1741; May 7, 1741.

RUN away on the 26th Inst. from Thomas Rogers of Nottingham, in Chester County, a servant man named John Robison, an Irishman, of middle stature, about 18 years of age, fresh colour'd, light colour'd long hair, a weaver by trade: Had on a blue drugget coat and jacket lined with blue shalloon, breeches of the same, a half worn felt hat, white shirt, blue grey worsted stockings, midling shoes.

Whoever takes up and secures the said servant so that his master may have him again, or brings him to Owen Owen, Esq; at the sign of the indian king in Philadelphia, shall have Forty Shillings reward, and reasonable charges paid by   Thomas Rogers.   Phila. April 30. 1740. [sic]
The Pennsylvania Gazette, April 30, 1741; May 7, 1741; May 14, 1741.

RUN away on the 18th of April past, from William Hall, living in Chesnut-street, Philadelphia, an Irish servant woman, named Margaret Dampsey, aged about 18 years, short and slender, pockbroken, a fair complexion, brown hair, has a scar on her forehead, and halts a little in her walking: Had on and took with her a brown holland gown cuff'd and rob'd with red and white calico, old yellow quilted petticoat, an old white quilted petticoat, a brown serge petticoat, a brown stuff gown, blue worsted stockings with white clocks, and good shoes, with some silver. Whoever takes up and secures the said servant, so that she may be had again, shall have Forty shillings if taken within Forty miles of this City, and Three Pounds if farther, and reasonable charges
    paid by William Hall.
The Pennsylvania Gazette, May 7, 1741; May 14, 1741; May 21, 1741.

RUN *away from Stephen Vidal, School-master in Philadelphia, on the 30th of April last, a servant Lad named* James Mansfield, *about* 18 *or* 19 *Years of age, of low stature, and well set: Had on when he went away a brown broad cloth coat broke at the button holes, and pieced at the elbows with some cloth of the same, a dark Olive colour'd Jacket, a pair of good light colour'd fustian breeches, a pair of blue and white mottled stockings, but not fellows, an old pair of narrow square toed shoes, a bever hat, and a brown wig; took with him a pair of brown yarn stockings, a pair of new round toe'd shoes, a pair of blue rib'd stockings, but not exact colour nor fellows; a Worsted cap, large new speckled yellow and red silk handkerchief.*

Whoever secures the said servant so that he may be had again, shall have Forty Shillings reward and reasonable charges,
    Paid by the said *Stephen Vidal.*
The Pennsylvania Gazette, May 7, 1741; May 14, 1741; May 21, 1741.

STOLEN *on Sunday Night last, from Jonathan Potts, of Plymouth Township Philadelphia County, a bay horse, with a switch tail, some saddle spots on his back, is a natural paces, shod before, branded on the near shoulder with a small* **O** *and on the near buttock with* **TP** *not very plain. He is supposed to be taken by a person that was seen lurking about the Neighbourhood, who is of a swarthy complexion, and had on a blue great Coat, cinnamon or snuff colour'd Coat and jacket, red Puffs to his breeches, and a red silk handkerchief, with white spots on it, about his neck*

Whoever secures the said thief and horse so that he may be brought to justice and the horse had again, shall have Five Pounds reward, or Forty Shillings for the horse, and reasonable Charges
    paid by *Jonathan Potts,*

N. B. *There was left in the pasture where the said horse was taken from, an old bay mare much tir'd with riding; the owner describing her marks and paying the Charges, may have her again.*
The Pennsylvania Gazette, May 7, 1741; May 14, 1741; May 21, 1741.

RUN away from Joseph Williams, of Merion, in Philadelphia County, a servant man named William Williams, a Welch man, about 50 years of age, with a blemish in the right eye, that darkens his sight, which with good notice may be seen somewhat reddish and lesser than the other, he goes something with face sidewards, by reason of his weak eye: Had on a darkish old coarse cloth coat without patches, and patch'd breeches of the same, old striped jacket, two speckled Shirts, half worn felt hat, and worsted cap, ordinary shoes and Stockings.

Whoever takes up and secures the said servant so that his master may have him again, or brings him to Richard Hughes, Innkeeper, Philadelphia Road, shall have Forty Shillings reward, and reasonable charges
paid by   Joseph Williams.   Philad, May 7. 1741
N. B. he was seen going thro' Lancaster, and pretended to have a Wife and Children in North Carolina; he wears his beard, and perhaps that and his old age, and lies, may help him off.
The Pennsylvania Gazette, May 7, 1741, May 14, 1741; May 21, 1741; June 25, 1741. Last ad begins "RUN away on the 19th of April past...."

RUN away from Robert Macky, on the 17th of July 1740, an Irish Servant Man, named Robert Norry, about 20 Years of Age, a fat chunky Fellow, long Visaged, tawny Complexion, walks with one Foot outwards, and speaks scotchify'd: Had on when he went away, a Suit of brown homespun Cloth Cloaths, full trim'd. He may pass for Pewterer and make Spoons.

Whoever takes up the said Servant, and brings him to James Macky, Merchant, in Front-street, Philadelphia, shall have (if within Forty Miles of this City) Forty Shillings, and if farther, Three Pounds Reward, and reasonable Charges, paid by   James Macky.
The Pennsylvania Gazette, May 7, 1741; May 21, 1741; June 25, 1741.

RAN away the 10th Instant from John Dabbin, of this City Blacksmith, an Irish Servant Man, named Nicholas Ingray, by Trade a Black-smith, aged about 26 Years, a well set Fellow, full fac'd and red Complexion, had on when he went away, a Suit of brown Duroy, white Stockings, new Pumps, a Beaver Hat, white Wigg or Cap, and a white Shirt.

Whoever takes up and secures said Servant so that his Master may have him again, shall have Five Pounds Reward and reasonable Charges paid   By John Dabbin

The American Weekly Mercury, From Thursday May 7, to Thursday May 14, 1741; From Thursday May 21, to Thursday May 28, 1741. See *The Pennsylvania Gazette*, May 14, 1741.

RUN away on Monday last, from Edward Woodward of Newtown, in Chester County, an Irish servant man, named Darby Bradley, aged about 18 *years, of middle stature, swarthy complexion, surly down look, mark'd on one side of his nose, speaks bad english, his hair is cut to his ears and over his forehead: Had on when he went away, a black rateen coat, with a green collar to it, black buttons, lin'd with black shalloon, linnen jacket, pair of blue shag breeches, lin'd with shammy, a homespun and fine shirt, three pair of trowsers, two coarse and one check, lightish brown stockings, two pair of round toe'd shoes, tied with strings, felt hat, an half worn wig, two striped worsted caps, and an old grey coat, that was broke on the back, and sewed up in the shape of a C, with some brass buttons on it, Whoever takes up and secures the said servant, so that his Master may have him again, shall have Forty Shillings reward, and reasonable charges*
paid by   Edward Woodward. Phila, May 13. 1740. [sic]
The Pennsylvania Gazette, May 14, 1741; May 21, 1741.

RUN away last Night, from John Dabbin, of this City, Blacksmith, an Irish servant man named Nicholas Ingray, *by Nicholas M'Gray, aged about 26 years, a well set fellow, full fac'd, and red complexion: Had on when he went away, a suit of brown duroy, white stockings, new pumps, beaver hat, white wig or cap, and white shirt. Whoever secures the said servant so that his master may have him again, shall have Five Pounds reward, and reasonable charges paid by*   John Dabbin.   Phila. May 11. 1740. [sic]
The Pennsylvania Gazette, May 14, 1741; May 21, 1741. See *The American Weekly Mercury*, From Thursday May 7, to Thursday May 14, 1741.

RUN-away on the 19th of May from Samuel Osburn, of Westown Chester County, an English Servant Man named Christopher Oliver, he had on a good felt Hat, a blewgray Cloth Coat lin'd with brown Cloth and a new Shirt, a good pair of Leather Breeches a new pair of Shoes he is about 22 Years of age short of Stature, with light or yallowish Hair.

Whoever takes up and secures the said Servant so that his Master may have him again shall have Forty Shillings Reward, and reasonable Charges, paid by   Samuel Osburn.
The American Weekly Mercury, From Thursday May 14, to Thursday May 21, 1741; From Thursday May 21, to Thursday May 28, 1741.

RAN-away on the 10th of May from Frederick Wamburg, of Skippack, a Dutch Servant Man named Blasius Bare, aged about 21 Years, of middle Stature, well set, black curl'd Hair: Had on when he went away, a new felt Hat, wears a black Stock, brown homespun cloth Jacket with Dutch fashion'd Buttons, red Jacket under it, with white linen metal Trowsers, new Shoes with brass Buckles, and no Stockings.

Whoever takes up and secures the said Servant, so that his Master may have him again, shall have Five Pounds Reward and reasonable Charges paid Frederick Wamburg.

He has Stolen his Indenture and pretends to be a free Man, his Master thinks he will change his Name; he has the Mark of a Bullet in his right Leg.

The American Weekly Mercury, From Thursday May 14, to Thursday May 21, 1741; From Thursday May 21, to Thursday May 28, 1741.

RAN-away, on the 24th of May from Francis Trimble, of this City, Joyner, a Palatine Servant Man named George Keifer by Trade a Joyner, about 33 Years of age, a stout well-set Man, of middle Stature, ruddy Complexion and Pockfretten, has a Scab on one side of his Nose and several Scars on his Head. Had on when he went away a narrow brim'd Hat without loops, a white nap'd Cap, a plain light-colour'd Cloth Coat, a pair of good Buckskin Breeches and newcheck Trowsers, blue gray Worsted Stockings, and round to'd Shoes. He took with him one fine white Shirt, a Holland Cheat [*sic*] and a pair of Muslin Sleeves, two white and two check Handkerchiefs, also several small Joyners Tools, and some Powder and Shot.

Whoever secures the said Servant so that his Master may have him again, shall have *Forty Shillings* Reward and reasonable Charges,
         paid by   Francis Trimble.
The American Weekly Mercury, From Thursday May 21, to Thursday May 28, 1741; From Thursday May 28, to Thursday June 4, 1741; From Thursday June 4, to Thursday June 11, 1741.

RAN-away the 22d of May from the Ship Adriatick, Christopher Huddy, Master, a Servant Man, named Thomas Rogers, about 21 or 22 Years of age, by Trade a Taylor, he is tall and thin, of a pale Complexion, short Hair, his right Arm shorter than his left; he had on when he went away, a canvass close bodied Frock, a pair of Trowsers, and new Soes without Buckles.

Whoever takes up brings him to Thomas Lloyd, shall have *Thirty Shillings* Reward and reasonable Charges.

N. B. All Masters of Vessels and others are hereby cautioned not to entertain him.

The American Weekly Mercury, From Thursday May 21, to Thursday May 28, 1741; From Thursday May 28, to Thursday June 4, 1741. *See The Pennsylvania Gazette*, May 28, 1741.

RUN away the 22d Inst. from the Ship Adriatick, Christopher Huddy, Master, a Servant Man, named Thomas Rogers, about 21 or 22 Years of Age, a Taylor by Trade, he is tall and thin, of a pale Complexion, short Hair, his left Arm longer than his right: Had on when he went away, a canvas close body'd Frock, a pair of new Shoes without Buckles.

Whoever brings him to Thomas Loyd, shall have Thirty Shillings Reward and reasonable Charges allow'd them.

N. B. All Masters of Vessels and others are hereby caution'd not to entertain him.

The Pennsylvania Gazette, May 28, 1741; June 4, 1741; June 11, 1741; June 25, 1741. See *The American Weekly Mercury*, From Thursday May 28, to Thursday June 4, 1741.

RUN away on Sunday last, from Thomas Mullan, of this City, an English servant man, named John Goodenough, of low stature, swarthy complexion, large black eye-brows, had a small new hat, a good short bob wig, a whitish fustian frock coat with brown linnen lining, a blue and white strip'd ticken jacket and linnen breeches, good thread stockings, good shoes, a broad square copper pair of buckles.

Whoever takes up the said servant, so as his master may have him again, shall have Thirty Shillings reward, and reasonable charges
           paid by   Thomas Mullan.

The Pennsylvania Gazette, June 4, 1741; June 11, 1741; June 18, 1741; June 25, 1741; July 2, 1741.

RUN away from John Bleakley, of Philadelphia, an Irish servant man called Patrick M'Guire, aged about 22 years, of a swarthy complexion: had on a Cap and dark frize coat. Whoever takes up the said servant and brings him to John Bleakley, in Water Street, shall have, if within ten miles ten shillings, twenty miles, twenty shillings, thirty miles, thirty shillings, forty miles, forty shillings, fifty miles, fifty shillings, sixty miles, sixty shillings, and so on, reward, and reasonable charges

          paid by   John Bleakley.

The Pennsylvania Gazette, June 4, 1741; June 11, 1741; June 25, 1741.

RAN-away, the 6th Instant from Capt. Richard Chapman, of Philadelphia, an Irish Servant Man named James Carne, about 24 Years of age, of Middle Stature, brown Complexion, and has a small Lisp in his Speech. He had on when he went away, a Felt Hat, a brown Wigg, a light colour'd Duroy Coat, a double Breasted red Waste-Coat mended under the right Arm with a Piece of Cloth of a litish purple colour, a Silk Handkerchief with Porto-Bello and Ships in it, and Yarn Stockings.

Whoever secures the said Servant so that his Master may have him again, shall have Twenty Shillings Reward if taken in this City, and if taken in the Country Three Pounds , and all reasonable Charges,

          Paid by   Richard Chapman.

The American Weekly Mercury, From Thursday June 4, to Thursday June 11, 1741; From Thursday June 11, to Thursday June 18, 1741; From Thursday June 25, to Thursday July 2, 1741.

RUN away on Tuesday Night last, from Robert Miller, of Caln Township, Chester County, an English servant man, named Roger Noble, a short well set fellow, about 30 years of age, black complexion, down look: Took with him when he went away, a light colour'd broad cloth Coat & Jacket, with white metal buttons, 2 pair of leather breeches two pair of trowsers, two felt hats, several pair of stockings, and good shoes. Whoever takes up and secures the said servant, so that his Master may have him again, shall have Thirty Shillings Reward, and reasonable Charges

          paid by   Robert Miller. Philad. June 18. 1741.

The Pennsylvania Gazette, June 11, 1781; June 18, 1741; July 2, 1741.

RAN-away the 15th Instant from David Rees and John Moor, of Radnor, Chester County, an Irish Servant Man named John Hicky, by Trade a Black-Smith and Nailor, aged about 40 Years, he had on when he went away a Broad Cloth Jacket of a dark brown colour, Leather Breeches, good Shoes and Stockings. He has been in this Country several Years and has lived in Boston.

Whoever takes up and secures said Servant so that he may be had again shall have Thirty Shillings Reward and reasonable Charges

          paid   By David Rees and John Moor.

The American Weekly Mercury, From Thursday June 18, to Thursday June 25, 1741; From Thursday June 25, to Thursday July 2, 1741; From Thursday July 2, to Thursday, July 9, 1741. See *The Pennsylvania Gazette*, June 25, 1741.

RUN away from David Rees and John Moore, of Radnor, in Chester County, a Servant Man named John Hickay, by Trade a Blacksmith, a middle aged Man: Had on when he went away, a dark brown cloth Jacket, a fine Shirt, a good beaver Hat, white yarn Stockings, strong peeked to'd Shoes, leather Breeches, and wears a linnen Cap.
Whoever takes up and secures the said Servant so that his Master may have him again, shall have Thirty Shillings Reward, and reasonable Charges
        paid by   David Rees, and John Moore.
The Pennsylvania Gazette, June 25, 1741; July 2, 1741; July 9, 1741. See *The American Weekly Mercury*, From Thursday June 18, to Thursday June 25, 1741

RAN-away on the 1st of July from Jonathan Fishar, an Irish Servant Man named Thomas Bennet, aged about 19 Years, freckles in his Face, red Hair, had on when he went away, a coarse Shirt, an old calimanco Jacket, coarse Thread Stockings, and his Knees knocks together.
    Whoever takes up and secures said Servant so that his Master may have him again shall have *Forty Shillings* Reward and reasonable Charges
        paid   By *Jonathan Fishar.*
The American Weekly Mercury, From Thursday June 25, to Thursday July 2, 1741; From Thursday July 2, to Thursday July 9, 1741; From Thursday July 9, to Thursday July 16, 1741.

RUN away from William Maugridge, of this City, Ship-Joiner, an English Servant Man named George Townly, aged about 24 years, of short stature, fresh colour'd, and pock-fretten; his hair newly cut off with scissars: had on a beaver hat, a white linnen cap, mixt duroy coat, ozenbrigs trowsers, worsted stockings, and new shoes.
Whoever takes up and secures the said Servant, so that his Master may have him again, shall have Forty Shillings Reward, and reasonable charges
        paid by   William Maugridge.
The Pennsylvania Gazette, July 2, 1741. See *The New-York Weekly Journal*, July 6, 1741.

RUN away from *William Maugridge*, of this City, Ship-Joiner, an *English* Servant Man named *George Townley*, aged about 24 years, of short stature, fresh colour'd, and pock-fretten; his hair newly cut off with Scissars. had on a Bever hat, a white linnen cap, mixt duroy coat, ozenbrigs Trowsers, worsted Stockings, and new shoes.

Whoever takes up and secures the said Servant, so that his Master may have him again, shall have *Forty Shillings* Reward, and reasonable charges
              paid by   *William Maugridge.*
The New-York Weekly Journal, July 6, 1741. See *The Pennsylvania Gazette*, July 2, 1741.

RUN away the 6th of July Instant, from Belchior Preston, of this City, a servant woman, named Susannah Lewis, can speak Welsh fluently, about 20 Years of Age, middle stature, fresh complexion, dark brown hair: Had on when she went away, a double gown, one side olive colour'd shalloon, the other side a brown and yellow poplin, a strip'd linsey woolsey petticoat of divers colours, a pair of blue stockings with white clocks, a pair of new shoes. Whoever brings her to Joseph Scull, in Philadelphia, shall receive Ten Shillings reward if taken in Philadelphia, if ten miles farther, Twenty Shillings, and reasonable charges,
              paid by   Belchior Preston. Phila. July 9. 1741.
The Pennsylvania Gazette, July 9, 1741; July 16, 1741; July 23, 1741.

STolen from William Harbert, out of the Alms House, last Friday Night, the following particulars, viz.

A new lead colour'd camlet Coat, a small striped callimanco Jacket and Breeches, a green olive colour'd duroy Coat lined with green shalloon, with round brass buttons, and a Jacket of the same, a pair of spanish colour'd cloth Breeches, with crimson china Puffs, a callico Gown robed with blue silk, and a linnen border round the bottom, a coarse holland loose Gown with blue and white stripes, lined with Ozenbrigs, a fine holland Gown with blue and white stripes, fit for a Girl of about 9 Years old, a loose double Gown one side light colour'd Calimanco, the other side an olive colour'd Serge, a pair of silver Shoe Buckles, a pair of silver Knee Buckles, a set of silver sleeve Buttons, and divers things too tedious to mention. The Goods aforesaid, are supposed to be stolen by one James Symmonds, alias Cyrcus Symmonds, born in Somersetshire in England, above 60 Years of age, long visag'd, large grey Eyes, much pockfretten, large open Fore-Teeth, burnt in the Hand at Burlington, and has been whipt in most Towns in Pensylvania, the Jerseys &c. Had on a close bodied homespun Coat without lining, long Pockets in it always stuff'd full; a Belt round his middle with Bags tied to it, wears a Cap, and Hat much over his Forehead. When he is detected in theft, he alters his Voice and squeaks.

Whoever takes up the said Thief, so that he may be brought to Justice, and secures the Goods so the Owner may have them again, shall have Thirty Shillings reward, and reasonable Charges, paid by   William Harbert.
The Pennsylvania Gazette, July 9, 1741.

RUN away the 7th Inst. from his Bail James Sill, of Chester County, an Irish Man named Samuel Henderson, who was taken on suspicion of Theft, a Taylor by Trade, fresh colour'd, short Stature, sandy Complexion, brown sandy Hair; Had on when he went away, a felt Hat, white Shirt, pale blue broad cloth Coat, thin stuff or linnen Jacket & Breeches, blue worsted Sockings, good Shoes. Has taken with him, an old bay Horse with a Star in his Forehead, and a Snip, with a new russet Saddle: It is suppos'd he is gone towards the Jerseys or New-York.

Whoever brings said Runaway to his said Bail, or secures him in any Goal, shall have Forty shillings Reward, and reasonable Charges,
           paid by   James Sill.
The Pennsylvania Gazette, July 9, 1741; July 16, 1741; July 23, 1741.

RUN away from the Snow Lancashire Witch about 14 days ago, a Spanish indian man about 30 years of age, low stature, a very yellow Complexion, and speaks but few words of English; He is now skulking about Town, and is entertain'd by some persons unknown. whoever secures him, and brings him to Emerson and Graydon, shall have 20 shillings Reward.
N. B. All persons are forwarn'd from entertaining him.
           Emerson & Graydon.
The Pennsylvania Gazette, July 9, 1741; July 16, 1741; July 23, 1741.

RUN away on Monday the 13th Inst. from on board James Gorrel's Shallop, then at Philadelphia, an Irish servant lad, named Larke Londergan, about 18 years of age, darkish complexion, short brown hair; has the brogue on his tongue: Had on, a brown kersey pea jacket, a checkshirt with ozenbrigs frock over it, old shoes, no stockings, an old felt hat. Whoever takes up and secures the said servant, so that his master may have him again, shall have Twenty Shillings Reward, and reasonable charges,
           paid by   James Gorrel.   Philad: July 16. 1741.
The Pennsylvania Gazette, July 16, 1741; July 23, 1741; July 30, 1741.

RUN away on the 17th Instant, from Ellis Davies, of Goshen, Chester County, a servant man, named Edward Whitehead, by trade a fuller, and understands plantation work, aged about 30 years, middle stature, fresh complexion, black curl'd hair, black beard when grown: Took with him, two felt hats, a good light colour'd cloth coat and breeches pretty much worn, and old striped Jacket, two homespun shirts, silk handkerchief, two pair of trowsers, white thread stockings, new round toe'd shoes, a sickle, and a pillow case supposed to put his things in. Whoever takes up and secures the said servant, so that his master may have him again, shall have Forty Shillings reward, and reasonable charges
    paid by Ellis Davies. Philada. July 23. 1741.
 The Pennsylvania Gazette, July 23, 1741; July 30, 1741; August 6, 1741.

RUN away on the 18th Instant, from Samuel Patterson, of Pequa Creek, Lancaster County, near John Varner, Tavernkeeper, a servant man, named John FitzGerrald, about 24 Years of Age, a tall fellow, with black curl'd hair: Had on, a felt hat, an old whitish Jacket lin'd with old grey cloth, a coarse shirt, and broken trowsers, took with him a new sickle. Whoever takes up and secures the said servant, so that his Master may have him again, shall have Twenty Shillings Reward, and reasonable charges
    paid by Samuel Patterson.
 The Pennsylvania Gazette, July 23, 1741; July 30, 1741; August 6, 1741.

RUN away the 24th Inst. from David Linsey, of Northampton Township, in Bucks County, an Irish Servant Man, named Dennis Macarty, about 30 Years of Age, of a middle Stature and well set, a dark Complexion, no Hair, his Head shaved before, and has two large Holes, one on each side of his Forehead under his Cap. He had on when he went away, a new felt Hat, a striped Cap, a dark colour'd frize Coat, a blue Jacket trim'd with black, blue plush breeches, grey yarn Stockings, new Shoes with pewter Buckles in them, and a check Shirt.
 Whoever takes up the said Servant, and brings him to his Master, or secures him so that he may be had again, shall have Ten Shillings if taken within ten Miles of Home, Twenty Shillings if within twenty Miles, and Forty Shillings if taken farther off, and all reasonable Charges,
    paid by David Linsey.
 The Pennsylvania Gazette, July 30, 1741; August 6, 1741; August 13, 1741.

RAN-away the 29th of last month, from *Jacob Neglee* of *Oley* Township in *Philadelphia* County, a Dutch Servant Man named *Michael Reichard*, aged about 19 Years, of middle Stature and fresh colour, with yellow Hair; had on when he went away, an old Felt Hat, a short blue Jacket without Sleeves and another blue jacket over it, a pair of Leather Breeches, black Wollen Stockings, old Shoes with Steel Buckles, and a homespun Shirt.

He took with him a Roan Horse about 13 Hands high, 8 Years old, branded on the off Buttock with a Figure 8, a thin Neck and little Mane; a breasted Russet Saddle, and a new Snaffle Bridle with a Strap to the Headstall to buckle round the Neck. He has taken some Money with him. Whoever takes up the said Servant and brings him to his Master, or secures him and gives Notice thereof to the Subscriber, or to *John Wister* in *Philadelphia*, shall have *Three Pounds* as a Reward, and all reasonable Charges
           Paid by   *Jacob Neglee.*

The American Weekly Mercury, From Thursday July 30, to Thursday August 6, 1741; From Thursday August 13, to Thursday August 20, 1741; From Thursday August 20, to Thursday August 27, 1741.

TAKEN away the 22d past, from Edward Waldron, Scyth-Maker in Darby, Chester County, a roan Gelding, 5 Years old, about 14 hands high, his Tail is drawn much aside towards the near Buttock, occasioned by the Itch, with Scars near his Tail and no hair growing thereon; he's a natural pacer, and goes pretty well: Also a russet hunting Saddle with several cuts or scratches near the Pummel, and a snaffle Bridle. They were taken by one Benjamin Harvey, an English Man, some what tall, and pretty much pitted with the Small-Pox, a downish look, a brownish coloured Coat, and striped Jacket and Breeches. Any Person or Persons that will take up and secure the said Man, so that he may be brought to Justice, and the said Gelding so that the Owner may have him again, shall have Forty Shillings (if the Horse, Saddle and Bridle only, then Twenty Shillings) Reward, and reasonable Charges,
           paid by   Edward Waldron.   August 6, 1741.

The Pennsylvania Gazette, August 6, 1741; August 13, 1741; August 20, 1741.

RUN away the 27th of July at Night, from his Master William Lynch, near the Crooked-Billet, on York Road, in the County of Philadelphia, an Irish Servant Man named John Oliver, but is supposed to have taken on himself the name of Oliver Jones, about 25 Years of Age, fair Complexion, light sandy Hair, middle size, pretty long Nose, and talks good English: Broke open his Master's Chest, and took out four white Garlix Shirts; Thirty two Shillings of Pennsylvania Money and Five Shillings in Copper; a Silver

Clasp, and two Muslin Stocks; left his own Cloaths, and took of his Master's a new Coat and Jacket of brown Camlet, made plain, with slash Sleeves, and lined with green Shalloon, a great Coat of white colour'd Cloth, pretty much worn, two pair of white worsted knit Stockings, two pair of thread ditto, two pair of speckled Trowsers, one of them new; all which Cloaths are something too short for him, but he may have some old Trousers, Stockings and Shirts of his own along with him: He also stole out of the Pasture, a swift natural pacing Mare, about 13 Hands and a half high, well-set and in good Order, no Shoes on when he took her; she has a bald Face, both hind Feet white, and seems to have something of the Scratches, also a small scratch on the near Hip, that the Hair does not grow on, but may be cover'd by the Housing of the Saddle; she's about 7 Years old, and of a chesnut bay colour: Took a new Holland Jacket double breasted, a check shirt, and a small silk Handkerchief belonging to another Man; and took a new kirb Bridle of Russet Leather, and a hunting Saddle of the same, but much worn.

Whoever secures the said Servant, Mare, and other Goods, so that his Master may have them again, shall have Five Pounds Reward, and all reasonable Charges; or if taken separately, Three Pounds for the Man, Twenty Shillings for the Mare, and Twenty Shillings for the rest of the Effects, paid by William Lynch.

The Pennsylvania Gazette, August 6, 1741; August 13, 1741; August 20, 1741.

RAN-away the 9th of this Instant, from William Peters, of Concord Township in Chester County, an Irish Servant Man named Timothy Conner, about 19 years of age, a raw-bone slender Fellow of middle Stature, a pale Complexion and lightish curl'd Hair. Had on when he went away, a Felt Hat, a red Silk Handkerchief with white spots and a blue and white Linen Handkerchief, a new Copper colour'd Coat with Pewter Buttons & no Lining, a gray Jacket if any, course Shirt and Trowsers, and old tap'd Shoes.

Whoever takes up and secures the said Servant so that he may be had again, shall have Five Pounds as a Reward, and all reasonable Charges Paid by William Peters.

The American Weekly Mercury, From Thursday August 6, to Thursday August 13, 1741; From Thursday August 13, to Thursday August 20, 1741; From Thursday August 20, to Thursday August 27, 1741.

RUN away last Night, from Lewis Williams, of North-Wales, a Servant Man, named Robert Anderson, about 30 *Years of Age, of middle Stature, well set, black Complexion, short black curled Hair: Had on when he went away, an Ammunition Coat with slash Sleeves, a green short Jacket, short sail cloth*

Trowsers, and old red plush Breeches, two white Shirts and a speckled Shirt, grey yarn Stockings, peaked toe'd Shoes, and an old beaver Hat. Whoever takes up and secures the said Servant, so that his Master may have him again, shall have Thirty Shillings Reward, and all reasonable Charges,
    paid by Lewis Williams. August 13. 1741.
The Pennsylvania Gazette, August 13, 1741; August 20, 1741.

RUN away the tenth Inst. from Robert Christie, of Philadelphia, an Irish Servant Man named John Green, by Trade a Barber (of the late John Gilbert's, Barber, deceas'd) about 24 Years of Age, down Look, middle Stature, pale Complexion, and much pockfretten, had on when he went away, a Castor Hat, a black Wig, a red and white yellow India Handkerchief, an Olive colour'd broad Cloth Coat, and lined with the same, a check Shirt with a white one under it, a pair of Breeches of the same of the Coat, a white Linnen Jacket shagg'd round the tail, a dark grey pair of Stockings, a new pair of brass Buckels, a pair of Pumps, soaled; carried away a pair of Ozenbrigs Trowsers, a pair of shoes almost new, and Instruments to draw teeth. Whoever takes up and secures the said Servant so that he may be had again, shall have Forty Shillings reward and reasonable Charges
    paid by Robert Christie,
N. B. *It is suppos'd he had a false Pass; he can bleed and draw Teeth.*
The Pennsylvania Gazette, August 20, 1741; August 27, 1741; September 3, 1741.

RUN away the 24th Instant, from Robert Lamborn, of London-grove Township in Chester County, an Irish Servant Man named Darby Morgan, aged about 18 or 20 Years, has very short sandy colour'd Hair; had on a felt Hat about half worn, a dark colour'd Cloth Coat with linsey Lining, short dark colour'd Jacket without Lining, new homespun Shirt with 3 Button-holes in the Collar and no Buttons, Two Trowsers with a broad Hem at the Bottom, new strong Shoes with single Soles and large square steel Buckles.

 Whoever secures the said Servant, so that his Master may have him again, shall have Twenty Shillings Reward, and reasonable Charges,
    paid by Robert Lamborn.
The Pennsylvania Gazette, September 3, 1741; September 10, 1741.

RUN away the 21st of August, from the Subscribers, of Kingsess, Philadelphia County, a White Man and a Negro, it is supposed they are gone together; the White Man's Name is Abraham Josep, a Yorkshire Man, a Shoemaker by Trade, aged about 24 Years, of middle Stature: Had on, a ratteen Jacket and Breeches of a light colour, a castor Hat pretty much worn, a check Shirt with white patches on the Back, two pair of yarn Stockings, one pair of a grey colour and t'other pair blue, a pair of thin Shoes round toed, and a pair of Boots.

The Negroe's Name is Tom, of a yellowish colour, pretty much pitted with the Small Pox, thick set: Had on, a light coloured cloth Coat, a linnen Jacket and Breeches, a pair of check Trowsers, good Shoes sharp toed.

Two Nights before there were several things Stolen, and it's supposed they have them, a List whereof follows, viz. a suit of Drugget of a snuff colour half trim'd, a light coloured cloth Coat, two linnen Jackets, a pair of leather Breeches, two pair of check Trowsers, two Hatts, a drab coloured broad cloth Coat pretty much worn, a Jacket of the same colour of the first mentioned Suit, a dark brown Wig, two napt Caps, a Gun, and a Pocket Book with two Bonds in it, one of Ten Pounds, the other of Eight Pounds, with a Note written at the end for Sixteen Shillings, with several other small things.

Any Person or Persons that will take up and secure the said Men, so that they may be had again, shall have for the White Man Three Pounds, and for the Negro Five Pounds Reward, and reasonable Charges,
paid by   James Hunt,   Peter Elliot.

N. B. They took a Cedar Canoe with them, broken at the Stern and spit at the Head.

The Pennsylvania Gazette, September 10, 1741; September 17, 1741.

STOLEN *on the 6th Instant, from Jenkin Hugh, of Trediffryn, in Chester County, a white Mare, about 9 Years old, 12 or 13 Hands high, shod before, with Saddle marks on her Back, a half-penny Cut under the near Ear not plain to be seen, and a new russet hunting Saddle and Bridle: Stolen with the Mare, a pair of new leather Breeches with brass Buttons, a pair of new black and blue woollen Stockings, a red Pocket Book with Sixteen Shillings in it, and several other things. The Person that stole the Mare and Goods, goes by the Name of William Evan, speaks good Welch and English, about 27 Years of Age, short and slender, thin visaged, thin sandy curled Hair, sharp thin crooked Nose stands much a-wry: He wears a old light coloured Coat with pewter Buttons, and lined with linsey woolsey, check Trowsers, a small trim'd fur Hat.*

Whoever takes up the said Thief and Goods, and secures him, shall have Forty Shillings Reward, and reasonable Charges,
paid by   Jenkin Hugh.   Phila. September 10, 1741.

The Pennsylvania Gazette, September 10, 1741; September 17, 1741; September 24, 1741.

RUN away an English Servant Girl, named Hannah Tompson, short and thick, with grey Eyes, brown thick Hair, a full Face, and fair if it be clean, she speaks very quick and in the Bristol Fashion: Had on when she went away, a yellow bird ey'd Callimanco Gown and muslin border'd apron. Whoever takes her up, and brings her to the Printer hereof, shall have Twenty Shillings Reward.
N.B. If she returns Home she shall be forgiven.
The Pennsylvania Gazette, October 8, 1741; October 15, 1741; October 29, 1741.

RUN away the 5th of this Instant, from James Casey, of Marcus Hook, Chester County, an Irish Man, named Michael Bryan, by Trade a Sawyer, aged about 26, short Stature, round visaged, short Nose; had on, a Suit of brown broad Cloth, check Shirt, an old felt Hat, worsted Cap, bluish worsted Stockings, an old pair of peaked toe'd Shoes, with brass Buckles. Whoever takes up and secures said Servant, so that his Master may have him again, shall have Forty Shillings Reward, and reasonable Charges,
            paid by   James Casey.
The Pennsylvania Gazette, October 15, 1741; October 22, 1741; October 29, 1741; November 5, 1741.

RUN away on the 19th Inst, from the Subscribers, in Charles-Town, Chester County, two Native Irish Servant Men, viz.

One named Andrew Sullivan, about 21 Years of Age, speaks very broken English; had on when he went away, a dark coloured Coat lined with blue Flannel, a blue flannel Jacket, good Shoes, old felt Hat, a Coat and Breeches of a whitish colour, striped linnen Waistcoat, three Shirts, one fine and two coarse, three pair of grey yarn Stockings, two or three pair of Trowsers one of which is Check.

The other named Edward Looney, speaks very broken English, about 16 Years old, his fore Teeth stick out very much, short black Hair; had on when he went away, a new homespun Coat with small brass buttons, lined with blue Shaloon, a pair of worsted Stockings, good Shoes, and some other Cloathing. Whoever takes up and secures the said Servants, so that their Master may have them again, shall have Thirty Shillings as a Reward for each, and reasonable Charges
            paid by us Llewelling Davis, Job Harvey.
The Pennsylvania Gazette, October 22, 1741; October 29, 1741.

RUN away on the 22d Inst from Samuel Hill, of New-Garden, in Chester County, an English Servant Man, by Trade a Wool Comber, named William Kemp, about 27 Years of Age, a poor-looking pale-faced Fellow, of middle Stature, with short brown Hair: Had on when he went away, a felt Hat, a grey Coat without Buttons, a blue and white striped woollen Jacket, white Trowsers, brown Stockings, Shoes with Nails in the Soals. Whoever takes up said Servant and secures him, so that his Master may have him again, shall have Forty Shillings Reward, and all reasonable Charges,
         paid by   Samuel Hill.   October 29. 1741.
The Pennsylvania Gazette, October 29, 1741; November 12, 1741.

WHereas a certain Person was committed to *Philadelphia* Goal, by *Jonathan Robeson*, Esq; on suspicion of being a Run-a-way Servant, and goes by the Name of *William Smith*, and says he came from *Ireland* to *New-York* about Ten Weeks ago. He is of small Stature and about 20 Years of age: His Apparel is a course grey Bays Coat, a blue Jacket and Breeches half worn & Buttons of the same, an old check Shirt, and old Stockings and Shoes. Any Person appearing and producing an Indenture against the said *Smith*, may have him again, paying the Charges to
         Thomas Croasdale, S. Sheriff.
The American Weekly Mercury, From Thursday November 5, to Thursday November 12, 1741; From Thursday November 12, to Thursday November 19, 1741.

ON the 15th of last Month, in the Night, the Store of *John Harris*, at *Paxton*, was broke open, and the following Goods, belonging to *Peter Shaver*, were Stolen, *viz.* A new Gun, some Powder and Lead, 9 Garlix Shirts, five Pounds worth of Silver Broaches, seven Yards of red Stroud, 24 Pounds worth of Wampum, a pair of new Shoes, four Razors, a Case of Horse-Flemes, and sundry other Goods. The above Things were Stolen by two Servant Men belonging to the said *John Harris*, at *Sasquehanna* Ferry, who are Run away, the one named *Timothy*, a well-set Man, of a swarthy Complexion, had on a light colour'd Coat with Brass Buttons, and Buckskin Breeches with Brass Buttons. The other named *Thomas*, (neither of their Sir-Names known to the Messenger) a tall slender Man, of a thin Vissage, a swarthy Complexion and Pock-broken, had on a brown Irish Cloath Coat Jacket and Breeches. They are both Irish Men and very good Scholars.

Whoever takes up and secures the said Servants so theat their Master many have them again, shall have Five Pounds Reward for each, and reasonable Charges, paid by   John Harris.
The American Weekly Mercury, From Thursday October 25, to Thursday November 5, 1741; From Thursday November 5, to Thursday November 12, 1741; From Thursday November 19, to Thursday November 26, 1741; From Thursday November 26, to Thursday December 3, 1741.

ABsconded from the Brigantine Lucy, John Lindsay, Master, two Men, Sailors, viz. Thomas Newton, a tall Man, about 35 Years old, with a blue great Coat, and red Plush Breeches, an old duffeld Great Coat: The other a Genoa Man, named John Domingo, can speak but broken English, of a swarthy Complexion. Whoever takes up the said Men, or either of them, and brings them to John Abraham Denormandie at Bristol, or to John Bard in Philadelphia, shall have Twenty Shillings for each, besides reasonable Charges,   paid by   John Abraham Denormandie,   or John Bard.
The Pennsylvania Gazette, December 3, 1741.

RAN-away, last Night from *Thomas Griffiths*, of the City of *Philadelphia*, an English Servant Man named *David Hearcoat*, of middle Stature and well set, a large Face and a down Look, has a large Scar on the left side of his Head a little about the Temple; he speaks broad English. Had on when he went away, an Irish-gray Cloath Coat, a Flannel Jacket, Leather Breeches, black Stockings, and old Shoes. He also took an old Bever Hat which was sent to my Shop to be dressed and sodl [*sic*] it: this is therefore to desire them that bought it, or those that had any Hand in helping him to sell it, that they immediately return the same to prevent a Prosecution. Whoever takes up the said Servant and brings him to the Work-House, or secures him so that he may be had again, shall have *Ten Shillings* if taken in this City, or if taken Ten Miles off *Twenty Shillings*, and all reasonable Charges,
              paid by   *Thomas Griffiths*.
N. B. All Persons are hereby forwarned not to entertain the said Servant as they will answer the same at their Peril.   *Philadelphia, Nov.* 10. 1741.
The American Weekly Mercury, From Thursday December 3, to Thursday December 10, 1741; From Thursday December 10, to Thursday December 17, 1741; From Thursday December 17, to Thursday December 24, 1741; From Thursday December 24, to Thursday December 31, 1741.

RUN away on the first of December, from Joseph Bond, of the Great Swamp, Bucks County, an Irish Servant Man, named Timothy Shoogle, a short set Fellow, black short Hair, about 16 Years of Age; had on, a grey coarse Cloth Coat, blue Jacket, blue shag Breeches, lately mended with white Cloth, round toe'd Shoes, coarse yarn Stockings, a coarse Felt Hat daub'd with Pitch on Top. Whoever secures the said Servant, so that his Master may have him again, shall have Twenty Shillings Reward, and reasonable Charges,
   paid by me Joseph Bond.

The Pennsylvania Gazette, December 10, 1741; December 17, 1741; December 24, 1741.

1742

RUN away the 3d Inst. from, Moses Coates, of Charlestown, in Chester County, an Irish Servant Man, named Cornelius Cannor, Alias Cheribly, a tall young Man, aged about 21 Years; had on an old lightish colour'd fashionable Coat, green double breasted jacket, old black Breeches, grey yarn Stockings, round toe'd Shoes with brass Buckles, an old Felt Hat. Whoever secures the said Servant, so that he may be had again, shall have Three Pounds Reward, and reasonable Charges,
   paid by me Moses Coates.

The Pennsylvania Gazette, January 6, 1742; January 13, 1742; January 20, 1742.

RUN away from Francis Jodon, of Warminster Township, Bucks County, an Irish Servant Man, named Arthur M'Donald, of middle Stature, full visaged, strong and well set, about 21 Years of Age, brown Hair: Had on when he went away, an old Coat, with some leather and some mohair Buttons, a lightish coloured old Jacket with brass Buttons, an old pair of patch'd leather Breeches, new Shoes and Stockings, and an old castor Hat, white homespun Shirt. Whoever takes up and secures the said Servant, so that his Master may have him again, shall have Forty Shillings Reward, and reasonable Charges,
   paid by *Francis Jodon.*

The Pennsylvania Gazette, February 10, 1742; February 17, 1742; February 24, 1742.

ABsented from the School-House, in *Solebury* Township in *Bucks* County, from under the care of *Manuel Coryell, Benjamin Canby* and *Jonathan Ingham*, with several others; a Servant Man, named *Thomas Dyck*, a Schoolmaster, belonging to *Edward Barber* and *Miner Johnson*, both of *West-*

Jersey, in the County of *Hunterdon*, he is a man may be well known for he is very much Pock-broken, with a large Nose, and speakes as though his Mouth was full of Plums; had on a Light Colour'd new Kersey Coat without Lining, wears a cock'd Hat and a black Wigg, and walks upright, with Leather Breeches, gray Yern Stockings and pecked toe'd Shoes. Whoever takes up said Servant and secures him so that his Masters may have him again, or the Subscribers abovesaid, shall have Thirty Shillings reward, and Reasonable Charges, paid by   *Benjamin Canby*, or *Jonathan Ingham*.

The American Weekly Mercury, From Thursday February 4, to Thursday February 11, 1742; From Thursday February 11, to Thursday February 18, 1742; From Thursday February 18, to Thursday February 25, 1742.

RAN-away, on the 16th day of this Instant, from *William Richards* of *Oley*, in the County of *Philadelphia*, a Servant Man named *Michael Rikard*, but it's supposed he will change his name, a High-Dutcher, slow of Speech, about 20 Years old, of middle Stature, fresh Complexion, light coloured Hair pretty long and thick, had on a whitish coloured Coat half worn, of homespun Cloth with Brass Buttons and slash Sleeves, two blue Cloth Jackets, and others, old Leather Breeches with Brass Buttons, something too small for him and greasy, a half worn Felt Hat with a small Cord instead of a Hatband, a white Shirt and a speckled one, course white Yarn Stocking; He is supposed to be flush of Money.

He took with him a likely trotting Horse about 11 Years old, of a bay colour, a small Reach down his Face, a trim'd Mane, branded on the Shoulder and Thigh of the near side with **WR**, but much plainest on the Thigh.

Whoever secures the said Servant and Horse so as the Owner may have them again, shall have *Five Pounds* Reward, and all reasonable Charges, paid by   *William Richards*.

The American Weekly Mercury, From Thursday February 18, to Thursday February 25, 1742; From Thursday March 4, to Thursday March 11, 1742.

RAn-away, the 2d of this Instant *March*, from *George Sheed* of *Philadelphia*, Barber and Perriwig-Maker, a Servant Man of the same Trade, named *George Tanner*, a short well-set Fellow with short Leggs, short clumsey Hands full of Warts, a pretty broad Face and pretty much Pockfretten, and waddles in his Gate; a very lying talkative Fellow, is sometimes English sometimes Irish as it may suit his Purpose, & pretends to have been a great Traveller. He had on when he went away, a dark brown Jacket and an old blue one under it, old Duroy Breeches, a white Shirt, gray Yarn Stockings peaked Toed Shoes, an old Felt Hat, and a brown bobb Wigg. He is of a fresh Complexion.

Whoever takes up the said Servant and brings him to his Master, shall have, it taken in or near this City *Ten Shillings*, if Ten Miles off *Twenty Shillings*, and if farther off *Forty Shillings* Reward, and reasonable Charges.

      Paid by me George Sheed.

The American Weekly Mercury, From Thursday February 25, to Thursday March 4, 1742. See *The American Weekly Mercury*, From Thursday August 5, to Thursday August 12, 1742.

RUN away, about two Months ago, from on board the Rundle Galley, Robert Nutt, Mast. an Irish servant Girl named Ann Boyd, a tall likely fair complection'd Girl about Twenty two Years of Age. Whoever takes up the said Run-away, and brings her to Redmond Cunningham, at the Widow Harper's, in Gray's Alley, shall have 30*s*. Reward, and reasonable Charges

    paid by Redmond Cunningham.

The Pennsylvania Gazette, March 3, 1742; March 10, 1742; March 17, 1742; March 25, 1742.

RUN away from the Subscriber in the Town of Lancaster, on Sunday last, an English Servant Man, named Mathew Burrass, about 30 Years of Age, short Stature, but well set, pretty bold and fresh countenanced; he pretends to be something of a Brick-maker, but is by Trade a Baker; he had on when he went away, a Leather Cap, a Kersey Jacket, and a red Vest without Sleeves, an old pair of Shoes, and old blue Stockings. He has his Wife along with him, who wears a brown Camblet Cloak. Whoever takes up the said Servant, and secures him, so that his Master may have him again, shall have 40*s*. Reward, and all reasonable Charges, paid by Thomas Brown.

The Pennsylvania Gazette, March 17, 1742; March 25, 1742; March 31, 1742; April 8, 1742.

DEserted from on board the Brigt. Vernon, Arthur Burrows, Master, bound to Jamaica, one Arthur Flemming, an Irishman, of a middling Stature, fresh Complexion, sandy colour'd Hair, has the Brogue; he appears to be a brisk active Man, and has sail'd out of this Port some Years: He has received Three Pounds Ten Shillings advanc'd Money. Whoever takes up the said Deserter, and brings him to Thomas Lloyd, of this City, shall have Twenty Shillings Reward, besides what the Law allows.

Note, 'Tis hoped that all Masters of Vessels and others, to prevent and discourage such Practices (which has increas'd very much of late in this City) will give Information, if he offers to ship himself; and hereby forwarn'd, at their Peril, to carry him off, he having been aboard but two Days.

The Pennsylvania Gazette, March 31, 1742. See *The American Weekly Mercury*, From Thursday March 25, to Thursday April 1, 1742.

Deserted on the 28th of *March*, from on board the Brigg *Vernon*, Arthur Burrows Master, for *Jamaica*, *Arthur Flemming*, an Irishman, of a middling Stature, (who has sail'd out of this Town some Years) having a fresh Complexion, and short sandy-colour'd Hair, appears to be a brisk active Man, and has the Brogue. He has received 3 *l.* 10 *s.* advance Money. Whoever takes up the said Deserter, and brings him to *Thomas Lloyd* in *Philadelphia*, shall have *Twenty Shillings* Reward, besides what the Law allows.

N B. It is hoped that all Masters of Vessels, and others, in order to prevent and discourage such Practices (which are increased very much of late in this Town) will give Information if he offers to ship himself; and are hereby forwarn'd carrying him off at their Peril, to carry him off, he having been but 2 Days on Board.

The American Weekly Mercury, From Thursday March 25, to Thursday April 1, 1742. See *The Pennsylvania Gazette*, March 31, 1742.

RAN-away, on the 4th of this Instant, from *Jacob Leech* of *Chiltinham* Township, in *Philadelphia* County, a Servant Man camed [sic] *Thomas Thomson*, about 20 Years of age, of middle Stature, and dark curl'd Hair, he was born in *Westmoreland* in *Great-Britain*, and talks thick. He had on when he went away, a light-blue Cloth Coat that has been turned and has flat Pewter Buttons on it, a striped Linsey Jacket, Buckskin Breeches with roundish Pewter Buttons, an Oznabrigs and a good white Shirt, Yarn Stockings, half-worn Shoes, and a good Felt Hat.

Whosoever takes up the said Servant and secures him so that his Master may have him again, shall have *Twenty Shillings* Reward and all reasonable Charges, paid by me   Jacob Leech.

The American Weekly Mercury, From Thursday April 1, to Thursday April 8, 1742; From Thursday April 8, to Thursday April 15, 1742; From Thursday April 15, to Thursday April 22, 1742.

RUN away on the 4th Instant, from David Wiley, of New London Township, Chester County, a Servant Man, named Robert Hamilton, an Irishman, of the Age of 24, middle Stature, fair Complexion, red Hair, and wears a black Wig; had on when he went away, a grey Kersey Jacket almost new, Breeches of the same, and a pair of coarse linnen Trowsers, and shirt of the same, old

Stockings, and a pair of new Shoes, a whitish coloured Great Coat, and cock'd Hat. Whoever takes up an secures the said Servant so that he may be had again, shall have Forty Shillings Reward, and reasonable Charges,
     paid by David Wiley.
 The Pennsylvania Gazette, April 8, 1742; April 15, 1742; April 22, 1742; April 29, 1742; May 6, 1742.

RUN away from the Subscriber, two Irish Convict Servant Men, the one named Thomas M'Quire, who ran from Peter Worrial, in Lancaster Town, in Pennsylvania; he is of low Stature, dark brown Hair, much broken with the Small Pox; Had on when he went away, a whitish close bodied Coat which he stole from the said Worrial's, a red Great Coat with Brass Buttons stamp'd with the Castle of Porto Bello, (commonly call'd Vernon's Buttons.) The other named Daniel Hern, but 'tis suppos'd he will change his Name, of middle Stature, much broken with the Small Pox, has the Brogue on his Tongue, meanly apparel'd, but 'tis suppos'd he has Stolen better Cloaths than he had on when he went off; he was lately taken up at Alexander Osbourn's, at Quittipehilla, in Lancaster County, where he had married, and has since made his escape from Prince William's County, in Virginia.
 Whoever apprehends the said Servants, or either of them, and gives Notice to Peter Worrial, in Lancaster, or to me at Goose Creek, in Prince William's County aforesaid, shall for each, so that I may have them again, have Forty Shillings Reward above what the Law allows,
     paid by John Awbrey.
 The Pennsylvania Gazette, April 8, 1742; April 15, 1742; April 29, 1742; May 6, 1742.

RAn-away, on the 19th of this Instant, from *Thomas York* of *Germantown*, in *Philadelphia* County, an Irish Servant Man named *Cobernelius Donnever*, aged about 20 Years, of low Stature but well-set, a fresh Complexion and black bushy Hair, takes much delight in playing Hussel-Cap, he had on when he went away, a new Felt Hat, a black Frize Coat, an Oznabrigs Shirt, Leather Breeches, new Shoes and Stockings. Whoever apprehends the said Servant and brings him to his Master, or secures him in some Goal, shall have *Twenty Shillings* Reward and reasonable Charges, from *Thomas York.*
 The American Weekly Mercury, From Thursday April 15, to Thursday April 22, 1742; From Thursday April 22, to Thursday April 29, 1742; From Thursday April 29, to Thursday May 6, 1742; From Thursday May 6, to Thursday May 13, 1742. See *The Pennsylvania Gazette*, April 22, 1742.

RAn-away, the 18th of this Instant; from *Edward Farmer* of *Whitemarsh*, in the County of *Philadelphia*, a lusty Servant Man near 6 Foot high, of a ruddy Complexion, short brown curl'd Hair or a Cap, an old Hat, a yellow Silk Handkerchief round his neck, a check or a white shirt, a green figur'd Fustian Jacket with cross Pockets and lined with homespun Linen, a pair of gray Cloth Breeches lined with white Linsey, a pair of white home made Yarn Stockings and a pair of pach'd Shoes. He served some time in the *Jerseys*.

Whoever takes up the said Servant and brings him to his Master, shall have *Forty Shillings* Reward and reasonable Charges,
   paid by *Edward Farmer.*

The American Weekly Mercury, From Thursday April 15, to Thursday April 22, 1742; From Thursday April 22, to Thursday April 29, 1742; From Thursday May 6, to Thursday May 13, 1742. See *The Pennsylvania Gazette*, April 22, 1742.

RUN away on Monday the 9th of this Instant, from Thomas Yorke, of Germantown, in the County of Philadelphia, Province of Pennsylvania, an Irish Servant Man; named Cornelius Donnevan, aged about 20 Years, of fresh Complexion, and has black bushy curl'd Hair, of low Stature, but well set: Had on when he went away, a new felt Hat, black frize Coat, oznabrigs Shirt, leather Breeches, and new Shoes and Stockings. He delights very much in Playing Hustle-Cap. Whoever apprehends the said Servant , and brings him to the said Thomas Yorke, in Germantown, or otherwise puts him in the Goal nearest to the Place he is taken, shall receive Twenty Shillings Reward, and reasonable Charges, from Thomas Yorke.

The Pennsylvania Gazette, April 22, 1742. See *The American Weekly Mercury*, From Thursday April 15, to Thursday April 22, 1742.

RUN away the 19th Inst. from the Subscriber, of the Township of Solsbury, in Lancaster County, an Irish Servant Man, named Robert Turner, of a swarthy Complexion, near six Foot high; had on when he went away, a coarse copper-coloured Coat, with brass Buttons, a Scotch plad Jacket and Breeches, coarse Trowsers, blue worsted Stockings, old Shoes, old felt Hat, also by Supposition, a drab-colour'd Great Coat. Whoever secures said Servant, so that the Owner may have him again, shall have as a Reward, Three Pounds Pennsylvania Currency, and reasonable Charges,
   paid them by me James M'Conoll.

The Pennsylvania Gazette, April 29, 1742; May 13, 1742; June 3, 1742.

BROKE out of Chester Goal, an Irishman, named Thomas Maloughlan, a short well set Fellow, black curl'd Hair, and black full Beard, brisk lively look: Had on a blue broad cloth Coat, Jacket and Breeches, an Ozenbrigs Shirt, old Stockings and Shoes, an old Beaver Hat, all his Cloaths much worn.

Whoever takes up the said Fellow, shall have Forty Shillings Reward, and reasonable Charges, paid by   Benjamin Davis, Sher.

The Pennsylvania Gazette, April 29, 1742.

RUN away, on the 5th Inst. from John Haines, of this City, Joiner, a Scotch Servant Man, named James Robertson, by Trade a Joiner, and understands something of the Carpenters Trade, aged about 25 Years, a lusty well set Fellow, full-faced, fresh complexion'd, no Hair, and speaks broad Scotch. Had on, a blue Camlet Coat, pretty much worn, a Plad Waistcoat, patch'd on one of the Hind Skirts with light Broad Cloth, old Leather Breeches, new blue grey worsted Stockings, new Shoes, new felt Hat, cotton Caps; and has with him two striped cotton Shirts, mended at the Neck with check'd Linnen, and two white Shirts.

Whoever takes up and secures the said Servant so that his Master may have him again, shall have Three Pounds Reward, and reasonable Charges,   paid by   John Haines.

The Pennsylvania Gazette, April 29, 1742; May 6, 1742; May 13, 1742; June 3, 1742.

RUN away last Night, from James Bennett, near Concord, Chester county, three servants, One named Patrick M'Guire, (who lived sometime ago with one Jones, a shallop-man, at Apoquiminy,) aged about 21, a lusty fellow, swarthy complexion, without hair, speaks bad english; had on when he went away, a dove-colour'd homespun coat, trim'd with mohair buttons, but almost wore out, a brown kersey jacket with brass buttons, leather breeches, and new shoes; he has a large scar on one of his legs cut with an ax. The other named John Fowler, an irish man, by trade a taylor, aged about 21, of low stature, and limps very much, caused by a weakness in his knee; had on a new felt hat, an old brown coat, striped linnen jacket, leather breeches and trowsers, good shoes, speaks but indifferent english.

The third a servant woman, named Margaret M'Collister, aged about 25, of low stature, brown hair, swarthy complexion; took with her two gowns, one a brown linsey, pretty good; the other an old lead-colour'd stuff gown, and an old brown drugget quilted petticoat. Whoever secures the said Runaways, so that their master may have them again, shall have Twenty Shillings reward for each, and reasonable charges,

paid by James Bennett.
The Pennsylvania Gazette, May 20, 1742; May 27, 1742.

RUN away on the 16th of May, from John M'Machin, of Buckingham township, Bucks county, Henry Blakely, an Irish servant lad, aged about 17 years, is lusty and well set, full fac'd and freckled, with short brown hair, a little curl'd, a little out mouth'd and thick lip'd; had on, a felt hat, half worn, with a hole burnt in the brim; a white linnen jacket, broke under the arms, about half worn, with some pewter buttons on the lower part, and a blue woollen one under it, without sleeves or lining, coarse tow trowsers that scarce reach his ancles, and coarse half worn Shoes, with thongs in 'em. a white shirt, with brass sleeve buttons, and pinn'd at the collar, made of about ten hundred linnen. Whoever secures the said servant, so that his master may have him again, shall have Forty Shillings reward, and reasonable charges, paid by John McMachin.
The Pennsylvania Gazette, June 10, 1742; June 17, 1742; June 24, 1742.

DEserted from on board the Ship Mary, George Davis, Master bound to London: One George Turner, a lusty well-set man: Had on when he went away, a red jacket, black leather cap, and short wig. Michael Quin, an Irishman, tall, with black bushy hair, dark complexion, and thin visage, generally wears a green jacket. And Dennis Burne, an Irishman, a big mouth'd Fellow, with the brogue on his tongue, a stout lusty man; each of them have receiv'd four pounds advance. Whoever takes up the said deserters, and brings them or either of them to John Reynolds, in Philadelphia, shall have FORTY SHILLINGS reward for each, besides what the law allows.

N. B. *'Tis hoped all masters of vessels and others, to prevent and discourage such wicked practices, (which have increas'd very much of late) with give information if they offer themselves, and hereby forwarned at their peril to carry them off.*
The Pennsylvania Gazette, June 10, 1742.

WHEREAS Jacob Ebberman, of Germantown township, in Philadelphia county, did on the 3d of this inst. make his escape from Christopher Ottinger, constable of Springfield precinct, as he was conveying him to the Goal of this City, for falsifying several bills of credit of this Province, New Jersey, New Castle, &c. by altering the smaller bills of New Jersey into higher denomination, and the Two Shilling bills of New Castle, &c. into Twenty Shilling bills, and then passing them. This is therefore to give Notice, that whoever takes up and secures the said Jacob Ebberman in some goal, so that he may be brought to Justice, shall have FIVE POUNDS as a reward, and reasonable charges, paid by Christopher Ottinger.

N. B. *The said Jacob is a German or Palatine, and has followed the butchering business; he is short of stature, with jet black hair, and a pale look, a very large mouth, and his teeth wide set in the fore part; he had on when he made his escape, a linnen jacket and trowsers, and a felt hat, but it is supposed he has since got a coat of linsey woolsey, of a cinnamon or brown colour.* Philad. June 10. 1742.

The Pennsylvania Gazette, June 10, 1742; June 17, 1742; June 24, 1742.

RUN away on the 5th Inst. from Richard Waln, jun. near this City, a servant lad, named John Barker, aged about 18 years, he us a short thick well-set fellow, something freckled, born in London, and brought up in Ireland: Had on when he went away, an old brown cloth jacket, with brass buttons, new ozenbrigs shirt, a new pair of tow trowsers, and a good pair of strong shoes, with steel buckles, a good felt hat, and white cap. Whoever takes up and secures the said servant so that his master may have him again, shall have Forty Shillings as a reward, and all reasonable charges,

paid by   Richard Waln, jun.

The Pennsylvania Gazette, June 10, 1742; June 17, 1742; June 24, 1742.

RUN away from Benjamin Mifflin, of Philadelphia, a servant man, named Henry Carpenter, by trade a carpenter, of dark complexion, black hair, and tall, drawls in his talk, and is a great boaster; had on when he went away, a blue-grey coat, dark colour'd flower'd fustian jacket, lined with blue, homespun shirt and trowsers, and a garlick shirt, new soal'd Shoes. Has a son with him of his own name, about 13 years old, pale look'd and thin.

Whoever secures the said Servant so that his Master may have him again, shall have FORTY SHILLINGS Reward and reasonable Charges,

paid by   Benjamin Mifflin.

The Pennsylvania Gazette, June 17, 1742.

WIlliam Mathewson absented himself, June the 6th, from William Clarke, Master of the Brigantine Revolution: He is a Scotch Man, with a red Face, with reddish Hair, his Ancles grown over his Shoes: had on when he went away, a brown holland Coat, a white dimmity Waistcoat and Breeches, speckled Shirt, and felt Hat. He understands Husbandry Work. He served his Apprenticeship to Samuel Parr, of New-Jersey.

Whoever shall bring the said William Mathewson, to William Clarke, or to Mr. Edward Durey, shall receive Twenty Shillings Reward, and all reasonable Charges, paid by William Clarke.

The Pennsylvania Gazette, June 24, 1742; July 1, 1742; July 8, 1742.

RUN away on Sunday Night, the 27th Instant, from Richard Jerrard, of Spring-Garden, near Philadelphia, Wheelwright, an Irish Servant Man, named Patrick Allen, a House-Joiner by Trade, about 30 Years of Age, of middle Stature, no Hair, brownish Complexion, speaks English with great Difficulty, and Irish readily, walks very stiff, by reason of a Fistula: Had on when he went away, an old Pisburnt Wig, or a Cap, homespun Shirt, good blue Cloth Coat and Jacket, black Plush Breeches, half worn, with new black Plush Pieces put down the out-side of the Thigh for to widen them, blue yarn Stockings, and old Shoes. He is a Roman Catholick.

Whoever secures the said Servant so that his Master may have him again, shall have Twenty Shillings Reward, and all reasonable Charges, paid by Richard Jerrard. Philadelphia, July 1, 1742.

The Pennsylvania Gazette, July 1, 1742; July 8, 1742; July 15, 1742; July 22, 1742.

RUN away on the 1st Inst. from Wm. Noble, of Fallowfield Township in Chester County, an Irish Servant Man, named Cornelius Murley, aged about 35 years, a thickset Man, dark Complexion, black bushy Hair, and grim look'd. Had on when he went away an old blackish Kersey Coat, patch'd on one Sleeve with whitish colour'd Cloth, an old Hat, new coarse shirt, patch'd Trowsers half worn, Shoes with latchets, and had a Sickle along with him.

Whoever takes up and secures the said servant so that his Master may have him again, shall have Forty Shillings reward and all reasonable charges, paid by William Noble.

The Pennsylvania Gazette, July 8, 1742; July 22, 1742.

RUN awaay [sic] last Night, from David Kennedy, of London-derry Township, Chester County, a Servant Man, named Thomas M'Atee, a Weaver by Trade for fine Work, but not so good for coarse, low of Stature, black Complexion, about 30 Years of Age, his Hair cut off, but sometimes wears a Cap and sometimes a Wig, and is remarkable for having few Hairs on his Eye-brows. Had on an old blue Coat without Lining, and took with him a new brown homespun Coat and Jacket, lin'd with an olive colour'd Linsey and trimm'd with Mohair, two Pair of linnen Trowsers one being check'd, the other plain, new Buckskin Breeches with Buttons of the same, good Shoes with Buckles, and had a Sickle with him.

Whoever secures the said Servant so that his Master may have him again, shall have Five Pounds Reward,
    paid by David Kennedy. Phila. 8 July 1742.

The Pennsylvania Gazette, July 8, 1742; July 15, 1742, July 22, 1742; July 29, 1742; August 5, 1742.

A CAUTION to the Publick

TO beware of a Person who has lately passed under the Name of Ebenezer Willson, but formerly called himself Lloyd; he goes up and down the Country undertaking to keep School, and sometimes to preach, canting most egregiously, and assuming all Professions of Religion at different Times and Places, pilfering and robbing every House that entertains him; when apprehended for his Thefts he pretends great Contrition, and moving the Compassion of those that have him in Custody, by that means frequently escapes Punishment. He was last Week in Philadelphia Goal, for a Felony in Chester County, but counterfeiting extream Sickness, was suffered to be taken out in order to be nursed; and being discovered at his Lodging to be the Person who had robbed a neighbour's House some time since, he immediately fled. He is a tall spare Man, of black Complexion, black Hair and Eyes, his Nose sharp and thin, had a narrow brim'd stopt Hat, a white Cap, plad Jacket and Breeches, white shirt, blue Stockings, and brass Buckles in his Shoes.

The Pennsylvania Gazette, July 8, 1742; July 15, 1742.

RUN away last Night, from David Kennedy, of London-derry Township, Chester County, a Servant Man, named Thomas M'Atee, a Weaver by Trade for fine Work, but not so good for coarse, low of Stature, black Complexion, about 30 Years of Age, his Hair cut off, but sometimes wears a Cap and sometimes a Wig, and is remarkable for having few Hairs on his Eye-brows. Had on an old blue Coat without Lining, and took with him a new brown homespun Coat and Jacket, lin'd with an olive colour'd Linsey and trimm'd with Mohair, two Pair of linnen Trowsers one being check'd, the other plain, new Buckskin Breeches with Buttons of the same, good Shoes with Buckles, and had a Sickle with him.

Whoever secures the said Servant so that his Master may have him again, shall have Five Pounds Reward,
    paid by David Kennedy. Phila. 8 July 1742.

The Pennsylvania Gazette, July 22, 1742; August 5, 1742. See *The Pennsylvania Gazette*, July 8, 1742.

ABsented from the Service of his Master, Benjamin Betterton, of this City, Cooper, an Apprentice Lad, named John Pugh, about 18 Years of Age and well set: Had on when he went away, a tufted fustian, Coat, check'd Shirt, a pair of leather Breeches, dark grey worsted Stockings, a pair of square toe'd new Pumps, a linnen Cap and a new castor Hat. Whoever secures the said Apprentice, so that he may be had again, shall have 20 *s*. Reward, and reasonable Charges, paid by
                    Benjamin Betterton. Philadelphia, July 20. 1742.
The Pennsylvania Gazette, July 22, 1742; July 29, 1742; August 5, 1742.

Run-away on the 25th of this Instant a Servant Man who went by the Name (while in these Parts) of James Ogleby he has been taken out of Prison about a Fortnight since and is accustomed to absent himself. He had on a half worn Beaver Hat a light colour'd Wig, an old brown colour'd Broad-Cloth Jacket the Buttons wore off and the Lining much wore, a speckled Linen Shirt, old dark colour'd plush Breeches, gray worsted Stockings, good Calf-Skin Shoes and large Metal Buckles. 'Tis sermis'd he will endeavour to change his Cloaths; his Person is thus describ'd, a slender visag'd Fellow about six Feet in Stature and dark Complexion, *came from Ireland*. Whoever secures the said Servant in the nearest Goal and brings or sends Tidings to *Thomas Croasdale* of *Philadelphia*, or *John Harry* of *Whitemarsh* in the County of *Philadelphia*, shall have Forty Shillings Reward, and reasonable Charges,
                    paid by   John Harry.
The American Weekly Mercury, From Thursday July 22, to Thursday July 29, 1742; From Thursday July 29, to Thursday August 5, 1742; From Thursday August 5, to Thursday August 12, 1742.

RUN away on Sunday last, the 25th Inst. from Joseph Grove, of Frederick Township, Philadelphia County, an Irish Servant Lad, named Hugh Rouke, about 18 Years of Age, tall and slender, fair complexion'd, with yellowish Hair, cut off: Had on when he went away, a new felt Hat, lightish blew homespun Jacket, with blue Stripes wove in it, new pair of Trowsers, a good Shirt, an old pair of Shoes, and an Handkerchief, half Silk.
    Whoever secures the said Servant so that his Master may have him again, if fifty Miles from home, shall have Three Pounds, and if farther Five Pounds Reward, and all reasonable Charges,
                    paid by   Joseph Grove.
The Pennsylvania Gazette, July 29, 1742; August 5, 1742; August 12, 1742; August 19, 1742.

STOLEN on Sunday last, the first Inst. out of the House of Bartle Bartleson, in the Township of Norrington, Philadelphia County, a Silver Watch, engrav'd in and out-side *LONDON, Stanton*, with a Silver Chain, and glass Seal, silver Case, a silver Shutter over the Key-hole, fasten'd with a brass Pin. It's suspected to be stolen by one John Ashbrook, who absented himself from the Neighbourhood on Enquiry for it. He is a short Man, with dark colour'd Hair, lately shav'd; had on when he absented himself, a blue Jacket, two check'd Shirts, leather Breeches, with brass Buttons, the button Holes work'd with red silk, check'd Trowsers, yarn stockings of Walnut colour, round toed Shoes, and Beaver Hat, half worn.

Whoever apprehends the said Thief, so that he may be brought to Justice, and secures the Watch, so that the Owner may have it again, shall have Forty Shillings Reward, or for the Thief only, Twenty Shillings, and reasonable Charges   paid by   Bartle Bartleson.

The Pennsylvania Gazette, August 5, 1742; August 19, 1742.

RAN-away, on the 25th of last Month, from Joseph Groves, *of Frederick Township,* Philadelphia *County, an Irish Servant Lad named* Hugh Rourke, *about 18 Years of age, tall and slender, fair complexion'd, with yellowish Hair cut off: Had on when he went away, a new Felt Hat, a lightish blue homespun Jacket with blue stripes wove in it, new Trowsers, a good Shirt, old Shoes, and a half silk Handkerchief.*
N. B. It is supposed to be gone towards Esopus.

Whoever secures the said Servant so that his Master may have him again, if 50 Miles from home, shall have Three Pounds, and if farther Five Pounds Reward, and all reasonable Charges,
             paid by   Joseph Grove.

The American Weekly Mercury, From Thursday August 5, to Thursday August 12, 1742; From Thursday August 19, to Thursday August 26, 1742; From Thursday September 2, to Thursday September 9, 1742. See *The Pennsylvania Gazette*, July 29, 1742.

RAN-away, on the 7*th of this Instant, from* Francis Garriques, *Carpenter, in* Philadelphia, *an Irish Servant Man named* John Murphy, *about* 32 *Years of age, well-set; and has a Scar over his right Eye. Had on when he went away, a dark colour'd frize Coat lined with a light colour'd Duroy, slash Sleeves, and Brass Buttons, an old check Shirt, new Oznabrigs Jacket, Breeches and Trowsers, dark Iron gray Stockings, and a pair of Shoed too big for him and newly soal'd.*

Whoever secures the said Servant so that his Master shall have him again, shall have Forty Shillings *Reward, and all reasonable Charges,*
          paid by   Francis Garriques.

RAN-away, the 7th of this Instant, from *George Sheed* of the City of *Philadelphia*, Barber and Perriwig-Maker, a Servant Man of the same Trade, named *George Tanner*, a short well-set Fellow with short Leggs, short clumsey Hands full of Wharts, a pretty broad Face and much Pockfretten, and waddles in his gate. He is a very lying talkative Fellow, is sometimes English and sometimes Irish as it may suit his Purpose and pretends to have been a great Traveller. He had on when he went away, a light colour'd Fustian Frock with a Collar and broad Brass Buttons, an old white Shirt, old Oznabrigs Breeches, old gray Yarn Stockings, a new pair of Duck-bill'd Shoes, an old brown Wigg, he had no Hat when he went away,

Whoever takes up the said Servant and brings him to his said Master, shall have, if taken in or near the City *Ten Shillings*, if 10 Miles off Twenty, if farther *Forty Shillings* Reward, and reasonable Charges,
          paid by me   *George Sheed.*

N. B. 'Tis supposed he is in Company with *John Murphy*, above mentioned, *The American Weekly Mercury*, From Thursday August 5, to Thursday August 12, 1742; From Thursday August 12, to Thursday August 19, 1742; From Thursday August 19, to Thursday August 26, 1742. See *The American Weekly Mercury*, From Thursday February 25, to Thursday March 4, 1742, for Sheed.

RUN away on the 1st Instant, from Caspar Ullrich, of this City, Baker, a Dutch Servant Lad, named Anthony Coes, about 16 Years of Age, well set, black Complexion, no Hair, and has a Scar on his right Cheek: Had on when he went away, a brown broad-cloth Jacket, and striped Jacket, fine Shirt, new brown linnen Breeches, coarsethread Stockings, Calf-skin Shoes, felt Hat, and several Caps. Whoever brings the said Servant to his Master, or secures him so that he may be had again, shall have THREE POUNDS Reward, and reasonable Charges,
          paid by   Caspar Ullrich. Philad. August 12. 1742.

The Pennsylvania Gazette, August 12, 1742; August 19, 1742; August 26, 1742; September 2, 1742.

RUN away the 17th Instant, from Joseph Wright, Taylor, of Pequea, in Lancaster County, a Servant Man named Edward Sampson, aged about 23 Years, of a swarthy Complexion, short neck'd, hump'd back'd, and his Hair cut off, wore a worsted Cap, but perhaps may wear a white Wig: He had on when he went away, a new homespun Shirt, a coarse linnen Jacket, with

neither Buttons or Button-Holes to it, Trowsers of the same, old Shoes, and no Stockings, the Hat he wore had been a Woman's Hat, and without Lining, he had also a large silk red Handkerchief with Spots in it: He can do something at the Taylor's Trade; and has taken a Wallet with him. Whoever takes up and secures the said Servant so that his Master may have him again, shall have Forty Shillings Reward, and reasonable Charges,
    paid by Joseph Wright. Phil. August 24.
The Pennsylvania Gazette, August 26, 1742.

RUN away on the 29th past, from Samael M'Alhany, of Fallowfield Township, Chester County, an Irish Servant Man, named John Shields, a squat well- set Fellow, reddish Complexion, short black curled Hair, black Eyes: Had with him when he went away, a black Frize Coat, old green Jacket, Buckskin Breeches, check Trowsers, coarse yarn Stockings, brown great Coat, brown streight body'd Coat with mohair Buttons, three fine Shirts, coarse Shirt and Trowsers, fine Hat, peak-toed Shoes, and had about Twenty Shillings with him. Whoever secures the said Servant , so that his Master may have him again, shall have Forty Shillings Reward, and reasonable Charges,
    paid by *Samael M'Alhany.*
N. B. He ran away in Company with Thomas Vaughan, a Servant to James Shields.
 The Pennsylvania Gazette, September 2, 1742; September 9, 1742.

RUN away on Sunday Night last from James Shields, of New-Lynn, in Chester County, an Irish Servant named Thomas Vaughan, about 23 Years of Age, of middle stature, thin visage, black Complexion, and black Hair, a large Wart on his Fore-Finger: Had on, an old dark colour'd Rateen Coat, with slash Pockets and a Collar lin'd with black Plush, buttoning with two Buttons; a light colour'd broadcloth Jacket, the button-moulds cover'd with Shalloon, a grey cloth Jacket with brass Buttons, strong double soal'd Shoes, with Buckles, three coarse Shirts and one fine, two silk and one cotton Handkerchief, yarn Stockings, and half worn felt Hat with a narrow Brim, one pair tow Trowsers, one pair linnen ditto, one pair of check ditto. 'Tis suppos'd he has taken Money with him.
  Whoever takes up said Servant, or secures him so that his Master may have him again, shall have Forty Shillings Reward, and reasonable Charges,
    paid by James Shields.
 The Pennsylvania Gazette, September 2, 1742; September 9, 1742.

Philadelphia, September 15. 1742.
YESTERDAY was committed to the Goal of this County, a Person taken upon Suspicion of being a Run-away Servant: He goes by the Name of Hugh Templeton; of middle Stature, thin Visage, grey ey'd, with short brown Hair: Has on an old broad-cloth Jacket, the Skirts lin'd with red, old black ratteen thread-bare Breeches, old felt Hat, old dowlass Shirt, old grey worsted Stockings, old Shoes, with brass Buckles not fellows.

Any Person producing an Indenture against the said Templeton, before the Sixteen of October ensuing, and paying the Charges, may have him again.   JOHN HYATT, Sheriff.

The Pennsylvania Gazette, September 16, 1742; September 23, 1742; September 30, 1742; October 7, 1742.

RUN away on the 11th of this Inst. from Jonathan Potts, of Plymouth Township, in Philadelphia Country, a Servant Man, named Matthew Mulloan, aged about 20 Years, of short stature, thin Face, swarthy Complexion, brown Hair, is an native Irishman, particularly remarkable for ill Manners, and an audacious Behaviour wherever he comes: He had on when he went away, a linnen Jacket and Breeches, wove calliminco fashion, a blue under Jacket, two check'd Shirts, blue woolen Stockings, and pretty good Shoes. Whoever takes up and secures the said Servant so that his Master may have him again, shall have, if taken 15 Miles from Plymouth aforesaid, Twenty Shillings, and if above 60 Miles from thence, Three Pounds Reward, with reasonable Charges,

paid by   Jonathan Potts. Philad. Sept. 16. 1742.

The Pennsylvania Gazette, September 16, 1742; September 23, 1742; September 30, 1742; October 7, 1742.

LAST Night made his Escape from the Prison of this City, one John Brown, a Sailor, lately belonging to the Ship Hanover Pink, Richard Northover, Master, a likely well set Man, black Complexion, black Eyes, about five Foot eight Inches high: Had on a specked Shirt, blue Jacket, blue Breeches, a pair of Pumps, and Buckles with small Rims, a good Hat, and cotton Cap.

Whoever secures the said Brown, that he may be had again, shall have Twenty Shillings Reward, paid by

Thomas Croasdale, Dep. Sheriff. Phi. Oct. 7. 1742.

The Pennsylvania Gazette, October 7, 1742.

RUN-away, the 28th of *September*, from *Jacob Slough*, of *Manheim* Township in *Lancaster* County, a Dutch Servant Man named *Leonard*

Pombark, about 24 Years of age, by Trade a Shoemaker, a pretty tall Man, of a brown Complexion with Scars in his Face, and stoops a little, a Man of very few Words, and speaks no English. Had on when he went away, a gray Kersey Coat lined with white flannel and brass Buttons to it, a Linsey-Wolsey Jacket without Sleeves, a pair of white Linen Trowsers, a Felt Hat, a pair of Shoes pretty well worn and Brass Buckles, and a black Leather Stock about his Neck ty'd with a Leather String.

Whoever takes up and secures the said Servant so that his Master may have him again, shall have *Forty Shillings* Reward and reasonable Charges,
   Paid by *Jacob Slouch,*
The American Weekly Mercury, From Thursday October 7, to Thursday October 14, 1742; From Thursday October 14, to Thursday October 21, 1742; From Thursday October 21, to Thursday October 28, 1742. In the second and third ads the name appears as Slouch twice.

          Philadelphia, October 11, 1742.
RUN-away, last Night, from *William Walker*, at the Forks of *Neshameny* in *Bucks* County, a native Irishman (but speaks indifferent good English) about 22 Years of age, calls himself *Roger Moor*, a well-set Fellow, of middle Stature, a fresh Complexion and short redish Hair, he chews much Tobacco; had on when he went away, a blackish colour'd Coat with slash Sleeves and two Button-holes on each side behind, the back dawb'd with Tar, two short blue Jackets with black Buttons, dark colour'd Woollen Breeches lined with Linen, two Check and two course white Shirts, old blue Yarn Stockings, a pair of 3 Sole'd Shoes with 3 rows of Hob-nails in each and ty'd with Strings, and a half worn Felt Hat.

Whoever takes up and secures the said Servant so that his Master may have him again, shall have *Thirty Shillings* if taken within 40 Miles of home, if farther off *Three Pounds* Reward and reasonable Charges,
   Paid by *William Walker.*
The American Weekly Mercury, From Thursday October 7, to Thursday October 14, 1742; From Thursday October 14, to Thursday October 21, 1742; From Thursday October 21, to Thursday October 28, 1742. See *The American Weekly Mercury*, From Thursday November 4, to Thursday November 11, 1742, and *The Pennsylvania Gazette*, July 7, 1743.

RUN away from John M'Mackin, of Buckingham Township, Bucks County, an Irish Servant Lad, about eighteen Years of Age, five Foot four Inches high, named Henry Bleakly, but he has changed his Name to John Sempell, and pretends to be looking for Creatures, or to be lost: Had on when he went away, an old felt Hat with a Hole burnt in the Brim, old linnen Cap, or else very short Hair, an old greasy Jacket much patch'd with Cloth almost of the same Colour, an old coarse Shirt very much patch'd, Buckskin Breeches had no Buttons at the Knees, light blue Stockings broke at the Heels, old Shoes with Thongs in them; a full Face, and a little out-mouth'd, thick Lips, and holds his Face very high. Whoever takes up and secures the said Servant, so that his Master may have him again, shall have Twenty Shillings Reward, and reasonable Charges, paid by   John M'Mackin,

The Pennsylvania Gazette, October 28, 1742; November 4, 1742; November 11, 1742; November 18, 1742; November 25, 1742. See *The Pennsylvania Gazette*, February 2, 1743.

RUN-away, the 10th of last *October*, from *William Walker*, at the Forks of *Neshameny* in *Bucks* County, a native Irish Servant Man (but speaks indifferent good English) about 22 Years of age, calls himself *Roger Moor*, a well-set Fellow, of middle Stature, a fresh Complexion, short redish Hair and a very red and thick Beard, he chews much Tobacco; and is very mannerly, uften osing [sic] the Word *Sir* in his Discourse; had on when he went away, a blackish colour'd Coat with slash Sleeves and two Button-holes on each side behind, the back dawb'd with Tar, two short blue Jackets with black Buttons, dark colour'd Woollen Breeches lined with Linen, two Check Shirts without Buttons at the Collar, old blue Yarn Stockings, a pair of 3 Sole'd Shoes with 3 rows of Hob-nails in each and ty'd with Strings, and a half worn Felt Hat.

N. B. 'Tis suppos'd he has chang'd his Cloths, and his Name also. He took with him a large gray Dog who answers to the Name of Captain.

Whoever takes up and secures the said Servant so that his Master may have him again, shall have *Five Pounds* Reward and reasonable Charges,   Paid by   *William Walker.*

The American Weekly Mercury, From Thursday November 4, to Thursday November 11, 1742; From Thursday November 11, to Thursday November 18, 1742. See *The American Weekly Mercury*, From Thursday October 7, to Thursday October 14, 1742, and *The Pennsylvania Gazette*, July 7, 1743.

RUN away from Alexander Hickinbottom of Philadelphia, Bricklayer, a Servant Man, named Anthony Hill, of middle stature, and Visage comely when dress'd, with short black Hair; both his Legs sore, the right Leg occasion'd by the Wheel of a Cart running over it, and the other by an Anchor of a Ship, his right Hand has been burnt, and he has a Band over it. Had on when he went away, a Castor Hat, an old camblet Coat the Sleeves ripped up,

a good Homespun striped Jacket and Breeches, and Oznabrigs Trowsers over them, new Shoes. He was imployed in sweeping of Chimnies, and is well known about the City of Philadelphia. Whoever takes up and secures the said Servant so that his Master may have him again, shall have Twenty Shillings Reward and reasonable Charges paid by Alexander Hickinbottom.
N. B. 'Tis supposed he went towards New-York.

The Pennsylvania Gazette, November 18, 1742; November 25, 1742; December 2, 1742; December 7, 1742; December 14, 1742.

BRoke out of the Work-House of Philadelphia, about 3 Weeks ago, a Servant Man named John Smith, by Trade a Naylor, about five Foot eight Inches high, a slender Fellow, yellow Skin, small Face, black Eyes, and black Hair, full breasted, walks very upright & appears in Sailor's Dress: Whoever secures the said Servant, so that his Master may have him again, shall have Forty Shillings Reward, and reasonable Charges, paid by John Naylor. All Captains and others, are forewarned not to Entertain or carry him away, as they shall answer the same at their Peril.

The Pennsylvania Gazette, November 25, 1742; December 2, 1742; December 7, 1742; December 14, 1742.

RUN away from the Ship Lucea, Thomas Smith, Master, from Jamaica, two Servant Men, one named John Bryant, about 29 or 30 Years of Age, of middle Stature, thin visaged, of a brown Complexion, he stoops in his Walk, and has a remarkable Gait: Had on when he went away, a check Shirt, a blue kersey Waistcoat, and sometimes wears a linnen Frock, and red plush Cap, The other named Lewis Wilson, about 22 Years of Age, of low Stature and well set, black eye'd, wears his own Hair, cut short, and under a Cap: Had on, a check Shirt, striped swanskin Waistcoat, laced, a blue Pea Jacket; also a Servant's small round common Jacket, striped ticken Trowsers, blue Stockings, and a large flapped Hat; he is by Trade a Joiner or House Carpenter, and speaks Welch. Whoever secures the said Servants or either of them, so that they may be had again, shall have Forty Shillings Reward for each, and reasonable Charges, paid by   Charles Willing.

The Pennsylvania Gazette, December 2, 1742; December 7, 1742.

This is to give NOTICE,
THAT there is one Daniel Horley in the Work-House of Philadelphia, that owns himself to be a Servant, to Nathaniel Lightle, in the Township of Donnigall; he was taken up, and put in there about three Weeks ago, since which I have wrote and sent by several Hands to his said Master, but have

receiv'd no Answer. The Owner of the said Servant, or his Order, is desired to come or send for him to Abraham Shelley Keeper of the Work-House. Phil. Nov. 30. 1742.
The Pennsylvania Gazette, December 2, 1742; December 7, 1742; December 14, 1742; December 21, 1742; January 13, 1743.

RUN away last Night, from William Rush, in Front-street, Philadelphia, an Irish Servant Man, named Garrat Condon, round shoulder'd: Had on when he went away, a good felt Hat, worsted Cap, or white Wig, an olive colour'd drugget Coat, new kersey Jacket, lead colour'd, with flat mettal Buttons, white Shirt, light broad-cloth Breeches, new yarn Stockings, and good Shoes.
Whoever takes up and brings the said Servant to his Master, or secures him so that he may be had again, shall have Three Pounds Reward, and reasonable Charges,
   paid by William Rush. Nov. 23. 1742.
The Pennsylvania Gazette, December 2, 1742; December 7, 1742; December 14, 1742; December 21, 1742; December 30, 1742.

RUN away the 30th of November from Joseph Jackson *of* London-Grove *in* Chester *County, a Servant Man named* William M'Crackan, *of a large Stature, thick set, pock marked dark colour curled Hair, had on a litish coloured Coat, Jacket and Breeches of the same, all with Brass Buckles, a Castor Hat half wore, somewhat meally: He had taken a Mare, old Bridle and Saddle, (but the Mare is come back and he supposed to have stolen another.) Whoever take up and secures the said Servant so that his Master may have him again, shall have forty Shillings Reward, and reasonable Charges paid by* Joseph Jackson.
The Pennsylvania Journal, or, Weekly Advertiser, December 2, 1742; December 9, 1742; December 21, 1742.

RUN away on the 13th of December Inst. from John Bleakley of Philadelphia, from on board the Sloop Speedwell, an Irish Servant Man named Patrick Dennison, Aged about 35 Years, high Stature, and slim Legs, a little pitted with the small Pox, writes a good Hand: Had on when he went away, a coarse brown Coat Jacket and Breeches, a check shirt, and new Shoes. Whoever secures the said Servant, so that his Master may have him again, shall have Forty Shillings Reward and reasonable Charges,
   paid by John Bleakley.
The Pennsylvania Gazette, December 21, 1742; December 30, 1742; January 13, 1743.

WHEREAS Charles and John Morrow, two Brothers that came from Ireland in the Ship Linnen Draper, which arrived at Philadelphia the 29th of May last, both indented Servants to the Subscriber, they are both Black Smiths by Trade: Charles is a lusty well-made Man, about five Foot ten Inches high, aged about 28 Years, and John is aged about 26 he is thick and well set, and somewhat hollow-faced, about five Foot eight Inches high. This is to give Notice, that any Person or Persons who will apprehend the said Charles and John after the first Day of January, shall have Five Pounds Reward for both, or Three Pounds for either, and all reasonable Charges, paid at the Delivering them at Philadelphia, by   John Bleakley.   Phil. Dec. 21. 1742.
The Pennsylvania Gazette, December 21, 1742; December 30, 1742.

RUN away from Francis Pearson, of Goshen, in Chester County, on the 19th of Dec. an Irish Servant Man, named Michael Barry, aged about 24 Years, middle Stature, fresh Complexion, smooth Face, short black Hair; a Weaver by Trade: Had on when he went away an old felt Hat, a good drab colour'd Coat, Jacket and Breeches of the same, pretty much worn, large flower'd Handkerchief, old coarse Shirt, good yarn Stockings, and new Shoes. Whoever takes up and secures the said Servant, so that his Master may have him again, shall have Thirty Shillings Reward, and reasonable Charges,
paid by   Francis Pearson .
The Pennsylvania Gazette, December 30, 1742; January 4, 1743; January 13, 1743.

1743

RUN away, on the 11th Instant, from Samuel Hill, of New Garden, in Chester County, an Irish Servant Man, named William Gould, about 20 Years of Age, of middle Stature, pale complexion'd, thin visaged, down look'd, with light Hair: Had on when he went away, a frize Sea Jacket, with Patches of light Cloth on the Hips, Breeches of the same Cloth, old Shoes and Stockings. Whoever takes up and secures the said Servant, so that his Master may have him again, shall have, if taken 20 Miles from Home, Twenty Shillings Reward, if farther, Forty Shillings, and reasonable Charges,
paid by   Samuel Hill.
The Pennsylvania Gazette, January 18, 1743; January 27, 1743; February 2, 1743.

RUN away last Night, from John Dabbin, Blacksmith, an English Servant Man, named William Corbie, aged almost 24 Years, by Trade a Blacksmith, about five Foot eight Inches high, thin Visag'd, and redish Hair: had on when he went away, a white Shirt, two Jackets, an old Great Coat of a whitish colour, coarse yarn Stockings, old felt Hat, old worsted Cap. Whoever takes up and secures the said Servant, so that his Master may have him again, shall have Three Pounds Reward, and reasonable Charges,
        paid by   John Dabbin.
The Pennsylvania Gazette, January 27, 1743; February 2, 1743.

RUN away the 23d of Jan. from Peter Grubb's Ironworks, Lancaster County, two English Servant Men, One named Charles Smith, aged about 20 Years, of middle Stature, square Shoulders, small Waist, short brown Hair, one Eye something less than the other, midling wide Mouth, with sound Teeth before, has had the Small Pox, he is no Scholar, and pretends to be a Blacksmith or Bloomer: Had on when he went away, a half worn felt Hat, worsted Cap, a fad-colour'd Coat, with white metal Buttons, new ozenbrigs Shirt, old pair of leather Breeches, with brass Buttons, white yarn Stockings, good pair of peaked toe'd Shoes. The other named Thomas May, about 30 Years of Age, but looks older, well set, flat faced, dimple in his Chin, thick Lips, brown Hair, sandy Beard; he came from Cornwall, and may go by the Name of a Miner, reads pretty well: Had on when he went away, an old felt Hat, old Cap, blue duffil Jacket, close body'd Coat (or it may be call'd a Jacket) it is short, of a fad or lead colour, lined with white and blue linsey, with flat metal Buttons, new ozenbrigs Shirt, leather Breeches, white yarn Stockings, and half worn Shoes. Whoever takes up the said Servants and secures them, so that their Master may have them again, shall have Five Pounds Reward, or Fifty Shillings for either of them, and reasonable Charges,
        paid by me   Peter Grubb.
The Pennsylvania Gazette, February 2, 1743; February 10, 1743; February 17, 1743.

RUN away on the 20th of October last, from John M'Mackin, of Buckingham Township, Bucks County, Province of Pennsylvania, an Irish Servant Lad, named Henry Bleakly, but has changed his Name to John Sempell (and it's supposed will often change his Name) full fac'd, a little out-mouth'd, thick Lips, Legs and Feet, carries his Head very high, and in Discourse, when sitting, is attentive with open Mouth; he says he came from Mirock or Mackerlin, in Ireland, and has a little of the Brogue on his Tongue: Had on when he went away, an old greyish Jacket, much patch'd with Cloth almost of the same Colour, an old coarse Shirt; Buckskin Breeches, had no Buttons

at the Knees, light blue Stockings, broke at the Heels, old Shoes, with Thongs in them. Whoever takes up and secures the said Servant, so that his Master may have him again, shall have Three Pounds Reward, and reasonable Charges,   paid by   John M'Mackin.
The Pennsylvania Gazette, February 2, 1743; February 10, 1743; February 17, 1743; February 24, 1743; March 10, 1743. See *The Pennsylvania Gazette*, October 28, 1742.

WHEREAS Margaret, the Daughter of James Dickson, of the Township of Little Britain, in Lancaster County, a Child about three Years of Age, has been missing from her Father's House ever since the 26th of December past; diligent Search and Enquiry having been made after her, and not being yet heard of, 'tis suspected she is stolen and carried away: She is a Child of fair Complexion, with long pale Hair, round fat Face, grey Eyes, a black Mole on the right Side of her Neck, a Place above her Forehead without Hair, her right Hand and Foot bigger than the left, of a pleasant Countenance, and speaks plain: Had on when she was miss'd, a pair of Stays, and a blue quilted Petticoat. Now whoever gives Intelligence where she is, or what become of her, to her Father aforesaid, Chester County, or to Mr. George Gibson, in Lancaster Town, shall receive Ten Pounds Reward,
   paid by   James Dickson.
The Pennsylvania Gazette, February 10, 1743; February 17, 1743; February 24, 1743; March 3, 1743.

LAtely taken up, and commited to the County Goal of Lancaster, one David Griffith, who has several Times been convicted of Horse-stealing, and had in his Possession, at the Time of his being taken up, a young bay Stallion, with black Mane and Tail, a small Star in his Forehead, branded on the left Buttock, but so dull as not be made out, and also a new russet leather hunting Saddle, with blue cloth Housings, and a blue Saddle-cloth, an old snaffle Bridle; which are suppos'd to be stolen. Whoever can lay any just Claim to the Horse and Saddle above, may apply to the Subscriber at Lancaster.
   Francis Reynolds, Sub-Sheriff.
The Pennsylvania Gazette, February 10, 1743; February 17, 1743. See *The American Weekly Mercury*, From November 17, to November 24, 1743, and *The Pennsylvania Gazette*, May 30, 1745.

ABsented from on board the Snow Prince of Orange, on Thursday last, a Sailor, named Charles Crane, an Irishman, aged about 26 Years, tall and well proportion'd, fresh complexion'd, large Mouth, and has a good Set of Teeth:

Had on when he went away, a good Hat, worsted Cap, light ratteen Great Coat, light double breasted Jacket with brass Buttons, worsted Stockings, new Shoes, with large plain Silver Buckles in them.

Whoever takes up and secures the said Sailor in any County Goal, and gives Notice thereof to Messrs. Davey and Carson, Merchants, in Philadelphia, or to Ann Baird, at the Sign of the Bowling-Green, in Water-street, near Arch-street, shall receive Forty Shillings Reward, and reasonable Charges.

The Pennsylvania Gazette, February 17, 1743; March 10, 1743.

RUN away this Morning from William Hartley, of Charlestown, Chester County, two Servant Men viz. one named Jenkin Lewis, this County born, a lusty likely young Fellow, about 23 Years of Age, speaks both Welch and English: Had on when he went away, a brownish Jacket, old leather Breeches, old brown Stockings, old Shoes, half worn beaver Hat, and a homespun Shirt, he served his Time with David Jenkin, of Uwchland, in Chester County; but for Sheep stealing and other Theft was made a Servant of.

The other named Peter Fowler, an Irish Lad about 20 Years of Age, a short thick well set Fellow, with dark brown Hair: Had on a brown lincey Jacket and Breeches, with flat pewter Buttons, coarse brown Stockins, and good Shoes drove round with Nails, felt Hat, and Cap.

Whoever secures the said Servants, or either of them, so that their Master may have them again, shall have Fifty Shillings for each of them, and reasonable Charges

        paid by   William Hartley. Feb. 18. 1742,3.

N. B. Its supposed they have plenty of Money, they having robb'd their Master of a considerable Sum about two Weeks ago.

The Pennsylvania Gazette, February 24, 1743; March 3, 1743; March 10, 1743. See *The Pennsylvania Gazette*, June 27, 1745, *The Pennsylvania Journal, or, Weekly Advertiser*, June 27, 1745, *The Pennsylvania Gazette*, March 3, 1747, and *The Pennsylvania Gazette*, April 9, 1747, for Fowler.

MADE his escape from the common Goal of this City, a young Man of middle Stature, named *George Brown*, and Englishman, about 26 Years of Age: Had on when he went away, a Frize copper colour'd Coat with slash Sleeves, a light broad Cloth old Jacket, and a pair of blewish colour'd Breeches, made of what is call'd Everlasting, a white Coarse Shirt, a pair of blewish worsted Stockings, an old felt Hat, a Cotton Cap, and a red Bir'd-Ey'd silk Handkerchief.

Whoever shall apprehend the aforesaid Prisoner, and secure him so that he may be had again, shall have three Pounds Reward and reasonable Charges, Paid by Thomas Crosdale, sub. Sher.

N. B. He is a Baker by Trade, and serv'd most of his Time with Mr. *Henry Wormley* in this City.

All Masters of Vessels are hereby forwarn'd to carry him off, as they will answer it at their Peril. *Philadelphia, March 4.*

The Pennsylvania Journal, or, Weekly Advertiser, March 8, 1743; March 15, 1743; March 22, 1743; March 24, 1743; March 31, 1743.

STolen about 9 Weeks ago, from Mary M'guire Widow, of Shanandore, a blue broad cloath Great Coat, a brown mixt double breasted Jacket, with brass Buttons, a new Beaver Hat, 15 Pistoles, and 14 Pounds in Pennsylvania Money, seven Pounds in Silver and a 4l. 10s. Piece of Gold; also a black Horse. He took also from Charles Hart of the same Place, a bay Horse, his off fore Leg crooked as if it had been broke. The above were Stolen and carried away by one John M'guire, a full-faced fresh colour'd Man, of middle Stature, with dark curled Hair, full of Talk, and pretends to be an Indian Trader. He has since sold the black Horse in Philadelphia, and went over the River into the Jerseys. Whoever secures him and gives Notice to Roger Hunt in the Great Valley, Pensylvania, shall have Five Pounds Reward, and reasonable Charges, paid by Charles Hart.

The Pennsylvania Gazette, March 10, 1743; March 17, 1743.

RUN away from Thomas Pierce, opposite to the Work-House, in Third-street, Philadelphia, a Servant Woman, named Sarah Brookman, about 20 Years of Age, she has large Eyes, a small Nose, a Wound on her right Shoulder about an Inch deep, and Snuffles very much through her Nose. She has a Bundle of Cloaths under her Arm, and had on a coarse homespun Gown. Whoever takes up said Servant, and brings her back to the Owner, shall have a reasonable Reward, and reasonable Charges
paid by. Thomas Pierce.

N. B. She serv'd Part of her time in Maryland.

The Pennsylvania Gazette, March 31, 1743; April 7, 1743; April 14, 1743.

RUN away on the first of March past, from Benjamin Armitage, of Philadelphia, an Irish Servant Woman, named Ann Strawbridge, of middle stature, fair Complexion, long Visage, high Forehead, and is about 20 Years of Age. Had on a brown Stuff Gown, and an old red Cloak bound with Yellow.

Whoever secures the said Servant, so that she may be had again, shall have Twenty Shillings Reward,
paid by   Benjamin Armitage.
'Tis suppos'd she is conceal'd somewhere in Town.
The Pennsylvania Gazette, April 14, 1743; April 21, 1743; April 28, 1743; May 5, 1743.

RUN away on the 29th of March past, from Morgan Evans, of Carnarvon Township, Lancaster County, an Irish Servant Man, named Charles M'Onagel, about 20 Years of Age, with short curled Hair: Had on when he went away, a new felt Hat, brown homespun Waiscoat, old woollen Breeches, black Stockings, round toed Shoes. Whoever takes up and secures the said Servant, so that his Master may have him again, shall have Thirty Shillings Reward,   paid by   MORGAN EVANS.
The Pennsylvania Gazette, April 14, 1743; April 21, 1743; April 28, 1743; May 5, 1743.

RUN away from his Bail, at Chester Court, in February last, a sizable young Man, named Thomas Canadey, about 23 Years of Age, swarthy Complexion, four Look, dark brown coffee olive colour'd Jacket, with large pewter Buttons, leather Breeches, white Stockings. Whoever takes up and secures him, so that he may be had again, shall have Three Pounds, and reasonable Charges,
paid by   John Jones, of Charles Town, Chester County.
The Pennsylvania Gazette, April 21, 1743; May 5, 1743.

RUN-away, on the 24th past, from *Joseph Allison*, of *New-London* Township, *Chester* County, an Irish Servant Man, named *Cornelius Sweney*, aged about 24 Years, of middle Stature, well set, black curl'd Hair, and round full Face. Had on when he went away, a brown Cloth Coat with slash Sleeves, patch'd near the Armpits with light-colour'd Cloth and the Lining somewhat torn, check'd Shirt and Drawers, coarse new Trowsers, strong Neat's Leather Shoes, soaled, halfworn Felt Hat, and Barcelona Handkerchief. He took with him a riding Wallet with some Cloaths and other Things in it.

Whoever takes up and secures the said Servant, so that he may be had again, shall have *Thirty Shillings* Reward and reasonable Charges
paid, by   *Joseph Allison.*

N. B. He went in Company with one David Condon, who is likewise a Servant and run away.

The American Weekly Mercury, From April 28, to May 5, 1743; From May 5, to May 12, 1743; From May 19, to May 26, 1743.

RUN away from William Gardiner & Adam Farquhar, of Nutt's Iron-Works, Chester County, a Servant Man, named Peter M'Kenny, low stature, well set, black Complexion and round faced: Had on when he went away, a felt Hat, cotton Cap, new striped Silk Handkerchief, a light colour'd French Drugget Coat and Jacket, the Jacket without Sleeves, coarse homemade Trowsers, thread Stockings, new peeked toed Shoes.

Whoever takes up and secures said Servant, so that his Master may have him again, shall have Three Pounds Reward, and reasonable Charges paid by WILLIAM GARDINER, or ADAM FARQUHAR.

The Pennsylvania Gazette, May 5, 1743; May 12, 1743; May 19, 1743; May 26, 1743; June 2, 1743.

ON the 14th of September past absented himself (but suppos'd was entic'd away) from his Master's Service, an Apprentice Lad, named Macaja Carman, about 19 or 20 Years of Age, tall, pale and slim, and often indisposed from a Bruise on the Head. He has been seen at his Brother's Joseph Carman, near the Head of Sassafras River, in Maryland. Now whoever apprehends him, and brings him to the Subscriber, living in the City of Philadelphia, shall have Three Pounds Reward, and reasonable Charges: And whoever gives me Intelligence of the person who carried him off, so that I may obtain Justice, shall have Forty Shillings Reward. And I do hereby forwarn all Persons from harbouring and concealing the said Apprentice, as they will answer the same at their Peril.   JOHN READ.   Philadelphia, May 24. 1743.

The Pennsylvania Gazette, May 26, 1743; June 2, 1743; June 9, 1743; June 16, 1743.

ON the 7th and 8th of this Instant June was stolen from the Subscriber, living at Billens-Port, Gloucester County, West-New-Jersey, the following Goods, &c. viz. a brown colour'd Cloth Coat, with Metal Buttons, a double breasted Jacket of the same, with Brass Buttons on one side and Pewter on the other, a new Raccoon Hat, a Pocket Book with a Bond for six Pounds, a Fifteen Shilling Bill, a five Shilling Bill, and several other small Bills in it. They were stolen by one David Howell, an Englishman, aged about 25 Years, short of Stature, ruddy Complexion, light Hair, and battel-knee'd: He had on a Cinnamon-colour'd Jacket, Ozenbrigs Shirt, new Leather Breeches, bluish

Worsted Stockings, and old Shoes, with Part of the Toe of one of them burnt off. He served his Time with one Samuel Sellers, near Darby in Chester County.

Whoever takes up and secures the said Thief, so that he may be brought to Justice, shall have Forty Shillings Reward, and reasonable Charges,
>paid by   BARTHOLOMEW SAPLES.

The American Weekly Mercury, From June 9, to June 16, 1743; From June 16, to June 23, 1743; From June 30, to July 7, 1743; From July 7, to July 14, 1743.

RUN away, on the 12th Instant, from William Thomas, of Canarvon Township, Lancaster County, a Servant Lad, named John Smith, aged about 19 Years, a thin slender Lad, with blackish short Hair, a grey cloth Coat, with brass Buttons, a strip'd Linen Jacket, check Trowsers, a good Felt Hat, and old Shoes; he took with him a Horse and Saddle, and 40 or 50 Shillings in Money, as it is supposed. Whoever takes up said Servant, and secures him so that his Master may have him again, shall have Five Pounds Reward, and reasonable Charges,
>paid by   William Thomas.   June 16.

The Pennsylvania Gazette, June 16, 1743.

RUN away on the 8th Instant, from the Subscriber, a Convict Man, named Thomas Overton, a Weaver by Trade, of middle Stature, pittied with the Small-Pox, dark hazle Eyes, and dark brown Hair, but 'tis supposed he has cut it off, about 30 Years of Age: Had on, a felt Hat, green-like colour'd linsey woolsey Jacket, mix'd with white, the Skirts lin'd with striped Stuff, an old flannel strip'd Jacket, two Country linen Shirts, cotton Breeches, grey yarn Stockings, Country-made Shoes, cotton blue and white Handkerchief, and double worsted Cap. It is supposed he has taken with him, a Negro Fellow, belonging to Antil Deaver, at the Head of Bush-River; which Negro has been advertised in the News-Paper; but may since have chang'd his Apparel. Whoever takes up the said Servant or Slave, and brings them to their Masters, shall have Three Pounds Reward for each, and reasonable Charges paid by
>MICHAEL LAWLESS. ANTIL DEAVER. June 13. 1743.

The Pennsylvania Gazette, June 16, 1743; June 23, 1743; June 30, 1743; July 7, 1743; July 21, 1743.

RUN away from Benjamin Davis, of Chester, in the Province of Pennsylvania, in April last, a Servant Man, named John Taylor, of low Stature, brown Hair: Had on, leather Breeches, brown yarn Stockings,

ozenbrigs Shirt, and an old felt Hat; no Coat or Jacket. He was Servant sometime ago to William Ellis, near Gloucester, is much addicted to Drinking and Singing, and in Behaviour very forward. Any Person who secures him so that his Master may have him again, shall, besides reasonable Charges, have Twenty-five Shillings Reward,
   paid by BENJAMIN DAVIS.
The Pennsylvania Gazette, June 16, 1743; June 23, 1743.

RUN-away on the 13th of this Instant, from Henry Smith of Tulpehacken, two Servant Men, one named Joseph Wall, the other Edward Colson; Wall is of a middle Stature, his Hair cut off; had on an ash-colour'd Kersey Jacket, and Oznabrigs Trowsers. Colson had on a blue Jacket, and Oznabrigs Trowsers, he has black curl'd Hair. They stole two Mares, one a large Bay with a black List down her Back, branded **H 8**; the other a small bright Bay with a white Face, branded on her Buttocks, **TT HS**. They also carried with them, a blue and white striped Jacket, a grey Kersey Jacket, a Pair of Silk Breeches, two Saddles, one with a Plush Seat faced with red, the other a black carrying Saddle, Paper Money and Silver to the Value of Ten Pounds, two pair of Silver Buckles, a Gold Ring, 20 Shirts, two Bever Hats, and a parcel of Shoes and Stockings.

Whoever takes up the said Servants, with Creatures and Goods, so that their Master may have them again, shall have Ten Pounds Reward, and reasonable Charges,
   paid by HENRY SMITH. June 21. 1743.
The American Weekly Mercury, From June 16, to June 23, 1743; From June 23, to June 30, 1743; From June 30, to July 7, 1743; From June 30, to July 7, 1743; From July 7, to July 14, 1743; From July 28, to August 4, 1743. See *The Pennsylvania Gazette*, June 23, 1743.

RUN away on the 13th of June, from Henry Smith of Tulpehocken, two Servant Men, one named Joseph Wall, the other Edward Colson; Wall is of middle Stature, has his Hair cut off: Had on an ash colour'd Kersey Jacket, ozenbrigs Trowsers. Colson had on a blue Jacket, ozenbrigs Trowsers, and has black curled Hair. They stole two Mares, one a large Bay, with a black List down her Back, branded **H 8**. The other a small bright Bay, with a white Face, branded on her Buttocks, thus, **TT, HS**. They also carried with them, a blue and white striped Jacket, a grey Kersey Jacket, a pair of silk Breeches, two Saddles, one with a plush Seat, faced with red, the other a black carrying Saddle, Paper-Money and Silver to the Value of Ten Pounds, two pair of Silver Buckles, a Gold Ring, 20 Shirts, 2 Beaver Hats, and a parcel of Shoes and Stockings. Whoever takes up the said Servants, with Creatures and

Goods, so that their Master may have them again, shall have Ten Pounds Reward, and reasonable Charges,
   paid by HENRY SMITH.
The Pennsylvania Gazette, June 23, 1743; June 30, 1743; July 7, 1743; July 14, 1743; July 21, 1743; July 28, 1743; August 4, 1743; August 11, 1743. See *The American Weekly Mercury*, From June 16, to June 23, 1743.

            Philadelphia, June 16, 1743.
BROKE out of Prison on the 11th Instant, at Night, the Noted and Notorious TOM BELL, born in New-England, generally known by his Rogueries throughout the Colonies, and some Part of the West-Indies, and often changes his Name and Cloaths; he is a slim Fellow, and thin Visage, and pale Complexion: Had on when he broke Prison, a dark blue cloth Coat, black silk Jacket, black cloth Breeches, black silk Stockings, new Pumps, with black steel Buckles, and 'tis supposed he'll wear a new castor Hat or velvet Jockey-Cap and grey Wig; he stole a Great Coat of lightish brown Colour, with brass Buttons.

 Whoever apprehends the said Bell, and secures him, in any Goal, so that he may be brought to Justice, shall have Five Pounds Reward, and reasonable Charges, paid by THOMAS CROSDALE, Sub-Sher.

 N. B. Among his other Tricks and Villianies he is very dexterous in Picking of Locks, having obtain'd his Liberty from Confinement by this Means. He was seen going towards New-York.
 The Pennsylvania Gazette, June 23, 1743; June 30, 1743; July 7, 1743.

RUN away from Thomas Cockran, of Earl-Town, in Lancaster County, an indented Irish Servant Man, named Alexander Laverdy, something of a Scholar, about 22 Years of Age, a Weaver by Trade, tall and slender Stature, fair Complexion, long streight black Hair: Had on a linen Coat, grey Waistcoat, old Trowsers and linen Drawers, old Shoes, old felt Hat, he took two or three good Shirts, a Bible, and several other Books. Whoever secures the said Servant, so that his Master may have him again, shall have Forty Shillings, paid by Thomas Cockran.
 The Pennsylvania Gazette, June 23, 1743

RUN away last Night, from John Hughes, of Upper-Merion, Philadelphia County, an Irish Servant Lad, named Daniel Brothers alias Broderick, about 19 Years of Age, middle siz'd and well-set, ruddy Countenance, and strait brown Hair: Had when he went away, a dark frize Coat with slash Sleeves, and 3 Buttons, Breeches of the same, white frize Jacket, such as Servants

have from the Captains, good homespun Shirt, and check Shirt, two pair of tow Trowsers, two pair of Stockings, one pair blue the other palish blue, two pair of Shoes, and two felt Hats. Whoever secures the said Servant, so that his Master may have him again, shall have Forty Shillings Reward, and reasonable Charges,
     paid by John Hughes. Philadelphia, June 25. 1743.

The Pennsylvania Gazette, June 30, 1743; July 7, 1743; July 14, 1743; July 21, 1743; July 28, 1743; August 4, 1743; August 11, 1743.

RUN away last Night, the two following Servant Men, viz.

From John Naylor, of this City, an Englishman, named John Smith, by Trade a Nailor, about five Feet 8 Inches high, full breasted, yellow Skin, black Hair, black Eyes, and is lame of his right Hand: Had on, a brown camblet Coat, lined with blue, with a small Cape, ozenbrigs Shirt, worsted Stockings, linen Breeches, old Pumps, and old Hat.

From John Dabbin, of this City, Blacksmith, an Englishman, named William Corby, about five Feet Inches, thin and reddish Complexion: Had on, an old brown duroy Coat and Jacket, check Shirt, racoon Hat, white Cap, Buckskin Breeches, old Shoes and Stockings.

Whoever takes up and secures the said Servants, so that their Masters may have them again, shall have Three Pounds Reward for each, and reasonable Charges, paid by
    John Naylor, and John Dabbin. Philadelphia, July 3, 1743.
N. B. All Captains and others, are forbid to entertain them at their Peril.

The Pennsylvania Gazette, July 7, 1743; July 14, 1743; July 21, 1743.

RUN away on the 29th of June, last, from James Whithill, of Lancaster County, an Irish Servant Man, named Patrick Makseron, aged about 50 Years, talks Scotch, has been a Soldier, and pretends to understand the Exercise: Had on when he went away, a light colour'd frize Coat with a Cape, leather Breeches, yarn Stockings, and old Shoes, has lost his fore Teeth, and is much stoop shoulder'd. Whoever takes up the said Servant and brings him home, or secures him, so that his Master may have him again, shall have Twenty Shillings Reward, paid by James Whithill.

The Pennsylvania Gazette, July 7, 1743; July 14, 1743; July 21, 1743; July 28, 1743; August 11, 1743; August 18, 1743. See *The Pennsylvania Gazette,* July 28, 1743.

RUN away on the 4th, Inst. from William Walker, at the Forks of Neshaminy, in Bucks County, a native Irish Servant Man, but speaks indifferent good

English, calls himself Roger Moor, but 'tis suppos'd he will change his Name, having done so before, about 23 Years of Age, of middle Stature and well set, fresh Complexion, short redish Hair, and a very red thick Bear: close Cuffs, the Button holes of the Sleeves work'd with Thread, the Buttons new, and not well fitted to the Colour, the Coat has been turn'd, and the wrong side of the Button holes of the Sleeves are out, and is lined with blackish Woollen which does not come to the bottom, old Shoes open in the Quarters, old black Legings, an old felt Hat, homespun tow Drawers, sew'd at the Knees without Puffs, two Shirts, with Ilet holes at the Wristbands, a brown linen Jacket, wash'd almost white, lined with Linen and broke in the fore Skirts, with small thread Buttons. 'Tis suppos'd he took with him a middle size black Mare, with a large Blaze in her Forehead, branded with **IL** on the near Shoulder and near Buttock, shod before, trots well, about 8 Years old, and is very shy about the Ears. Whoever takes up and secures the said Servant, so that his Master may have him again, shall have Five Pounds Reward, and reasonable Charges,
   paid by William Walker.
The Pennsylvania Gazette, July 7, 1743. See *The American Weekly Mercury*, From Thursday October 7, to Thursday October 14, 1742, and *The American Weekly Mercury*, From Thursday November 4, to Thursday November 11, 1742.

RUN away on the 13th of June last, from Isaac Baker, of Cunnecocheg, a Servant Man, named John Haygen, is a short Fellow, dark Complexion: Had on a leather Jacket with brass buttons, and a whitish stuff Jacket, old check Trowsers, felt Hat; he is an Irishman and has a smooth Tongue. Whoever takes up the said Servant , and secures him, so that he may be had again, shall have Forty Shillings Reward, and reasonable Charges,
   paid by the said Isaac Baker, or Joshua Baker, near Lancaster.
The Pennsylvania Gazette, July 14, 1743; July 21, 1743.

RAN-away on the 26th of June, from John Fareis, of Philadelphia, Cordwinder, a Servant Man named William Morris, of low Stature, about 28 Years of Age, Had on when he went away a white Linen Cap, a new check Shirt, a brown Pea Jacket, a white Linen Frock, worsted Stockings, and a pair of Duck Bill'd Shoes, with pretty large carv'd Buckels. Whoever takes up and secures the said Servant so that his Master may have him again, shall have *Twenty Shillings* Reward, if found within Ten Miles of Philadelphia, if further *three Pounds*, and reasonable Charges
   paid By *John Fareis.*
The Pennsylvania Journal, or, Weekly Advertiser, July 14, 1743; July 21, 1743; July 28, 1743; August 4, 1743.

RUN-away, on the 4th of this Instant, from Samuel Tamplan, Hammerman at Spring Forge, near Oly Township, in Philadelphia County, an Irish Servant Man named James Murfy, about 20 Years of Age; he is a well-set thick Fellow, of middle Size and pretty fresh Complexion, somewhat mark'd with the Small-Pox, and black Hair lately cut off; he is slow in Speech and smooth tongued, talks both Irish and English pretty well. Had on when he run away, a light colour'd Kersey Coat, a fine Shirt, a yellowish colour'd Silk Handkerchief, a new Castor Hat, a Linnen Cap, a Pair of check Linnen Trowsers with Brass Buttons, a Pair of Thread Stockings, new strong Shoes and a Pair of large Brass Buckles somewhat carv'd or figur'd at the Corners. He pretends to be something of a Hammerman, but knows very little of it.

  N. B. The said Servant stole his Indentures, which 'tis suppos'd he makes use of for a Pass.

  Whoever takes up and secures the said Servant so that his Master may have him again, shall have Four Pounds Reward and reasonable Charges,
    Paid by me SAM. TAMPLAN.

The American Weekly Mercury, From July 14, to July 21, 1743; From July 21, to July 28, 1743; From July 28, to August 4, 1743; From August 4, to August 11, 1743; From August 11, to August 18, 1743. Third, fourth fifth 5th ads show he ran away "on the 4th of *July* past...."

Two Men suppos'd to be Servants runaway, the one from William Walker at the Forks of Neshaminy, the other from James Whitehill of Lancaster County, are taken up and committed to Burlington Goal; but will soon be discharged if their Masters do not appear.

The Pennsylvania Gazette, July 28, 1743. See *The American Weekly Mercury*, From Thursday October 7, to Thursday October 14, 1742, *The American Weekly Mercury*, From Thursday November 4, to Thursday November 11, 1742, and *The Pennsylvania Gazette*, July 7, 1743, for Walker's servant. See *The Pennsylvania Gazette*, July 7, 1743, for Whitehill/Whithill's servant.

RUN away on the 14th Instant, the two following Servants, viz. The one named William Ragan, from Joseph Harlen, of Kennet Township, Chester County, of middle Stature, well set, pale Complexion, round shoulder'd, straddles in his Gate, no Hair: Had on an old felt Hat, brown worsted Coat, linnen Shirt, a pair of old linen Trowsers, peaked to'd Shoes.

  The other named John Beddall, from Ruth Harlen, of Kennet Township, Chester County, short of Stature, with black Hair and Beard, dark Complexion: Had a fur Hat, grey cloth Coat, linen Shirt, Pair of Trowsers,

peaked to'd Shoes. Whoever secures the said Servants, so that their Owners may have them again, shall have Forty Shillings Reward, and reasonable Charges, paid by   Joseph Harlen, Ruth Harlen. August 16, 1743.
N. B. 'Tis supposed they have changed their Names.
    The Pennsylvania Gazette, August 18, 1743; August 25, 1743; September 1, 1743; September 8, 1743; September 15, 1743.

RUN away the 17th Instant, from John Michener, of the Mannor of Moreland, Philadelphia County, an Irish Servant Lad, named John Cogdill, about 17 or 18 Years of Age, short of Stature, well set, swarthy Complexion, brownish Hair, much pockfretten: Had on, a felt Hat, lead-colour'd cloth Coat, without Lining, Jacket Sleeves, and pewter Buttons, ozenbrigs Jacket, two Shirts, one ozenbrigs, the other coarse Linen, a Pair of leather Breeches, two Pair of Trowsers, one check line, the other tow, two Pair of Stockings, one olive green Yarn, the other Thread, a Pair of Neat's leather Shoes, soal'd, with brass Buckles. Whoever takes up and secures the said Servant, so that his Master may have him again, shall have Thirty Shillings Reward, and reasonable Charges,
        paid by   John Michener. August 18. 1743.
    The Pennsylvania Gazette, August 18, 1743; August 25, 1743; September 1, 1743.

RUN away from Robert Boyle, Tanner, of Fallowfield, Chester County, an Irish Servant Man named Michael Vachen, about 26 Years of Age, a short thick Fellow, swarthy Complexion, Pock-mark'd, two of his Teeth out before, his Head shaved and many Cuts on it: Had on an old felt Hat, two Shirts, one an old coarse homespun, the other half worn Linen, brown coloured Coat, with slash Sleeves, mohair Buttons and linsey woolsey lining of a Moss colour, brown Breeches, grey Stockings, a pair of sharp toed Shoes, carved pewter Buckles, striped silk Handkerchief, muslin Stock: He took with him eight Pounds in Money. Whoever takes up and secures the said Servant, so that his Master may have him again, shall have Forty Shillings Reward, and reasonable Charges
        paid by   Robert Boyle. Phila. August 24.
N. B. All Masters of Vessels are forwarn'd not to entertain him or carry him off, at their Peril.
    The Pennsylvania Gazette, August 25, 1743; September 1, 1743; September 8, 1743; September 15, 1743.

STOLEN from Alice Wilkins of the City of Philadelphia, the following good, viz. a blue Poplin Gown cuff'd with blue Taffaty, a Petticoat of the same, a good Holland Shift, and several other Shifts, a Muslin Apron and several other Aprons, several Caps and Silk Handkerchiefs, and some other Wearing Apparel, and about Three Pounds Ten Shillings in Money: The above Goods were stolen last Friday Morning (as supposed) by one John Hall, a likely well set Man, with black curl'd Hair, a light-colour'd Jacket and Ozenbrigs Trowsers; he has a Boy of about 6 or 7 Years of Age with him, whose Head was lately shaved.

Whoever takes up and secures the said Thief so that he may be brought to Justice, and the Goods had again, shall have Thirty Shillings Reward and reasonable Charges,
    paid by ALICE WILKINS. Sept. 8. 1743.

The American Weekly Mercury, From September 1, to September 8, 1743; From September 8, to September 15, 1743; From September 15, to September 22, 1743; From October 6, to October 13, 1743.

RUN away on the 23d. Instant from John Hamilton, Tanner, near Lancaster, a Bristol Servant Girl named Rebecca Fling, aged about 25 Years, short and well set, mild Countenance, light Hair, much Pock-mark'd: Had on a bluish stuff Gown, old Shoes, red Stockings. Sometimes calls her self Rebecca Huffey.

Whoever secures the said Servant, so that her Master may have her again, shall have Twenty Shillings Reward, and reasonable Charges
    paid by John Hamilton.

The Pennsylvania Gazette, September 29, 1743; October 6, 1743; October 13, 1743; October 20, 1743.

RUN away on the 25th of September, from Jacob Bouman, of Germantown, a Dutch Servant Boy, named Henry Wolff, about 18 Years of Age: Had on when he went away, a blue and white striped Jacket and Breeches, blue worsted Stockings, old Shoes, an old Hat, speckled Shirt. Whoever takes up and secures the said Servant, so that his Master may have him again, shall have Forty Shillings Reward, and reasonable Charges
    paid by Jacob Bouman.

The Pennsylvania Gazette, September 29, 1743; October 6, 1743; October 13, 1743; October 20, 1743; October 27, 1743.

RUN away from the Ship Neptune, four Sailors; one named Daniel Fox, of middle Stature, much pock-mark'd; one named John Guy, of middle Stature,

round shoulder'd, thin visage; one named John Margison, of middle Stature, has a Cast in his right Eye; one named Mundo M'Kinsey, a Scotch Man, of middle Stature, and has a little Impediment in his Speech. Whoever secures the said Sailors, and brings them to Philadelphia, shall have Three Pounds Reward, and reasonable Charges,
    paid by George Okill. *Phila. Octo.* 12. 1743.
 The Pennsylvania Gazette, October 13, 1743; October 20, 1743; October 27, 1743; November 3, 1743; November 10, 1743; November 16, 1743; November 24, 1743.

RUN away from his Bail, John Leik, of Middletown, Chester County, an Irishman, named John Homer, by Trade a Shoemaker, (and has his Tools with him) he us a thick set short Man, wears his own Hair, is lame in both Feet, half of one Foot being cut off, and some Toes off the other; his Leg has been broke and is a little crooked: Had on when he went away, a light coloured homespun Coat, Jacket and Breeches, and it is supposed he has several others with him. Whoever takes up the said Homer and brings him to his said Bail, or secures him so that he may be had again, if in this Province, shall have Twenty Shillings, if in any of the neighbouring Provinces, Forty Shillings Reward, paid by John Leik.
Note, *'Tis suppos'd he was seen in Lancaster, with an old blue Coat on.*
 The Pennsylvania Gazette, October 27, 1743; November 3, 1743; November 10, 1743; November 16, 1743.

RUN away the 30th of October last, from Joseph Bartholomew, in Whiteland, Chester County, an Irish Servant Man, named Henry Raffardy, about 22 Years of Age, middle Stature, well set, swarthy Complexion, down look, black strait Hair: Had on when he went away, an half worn felt Hat, dark cinnamon colour'd duroy Coat, with square narrow Sleeves turn'd up, white cloth Jacket with Buttons of the same, leather Breeches, homespun linnen Shirt, light blue yarn Stockings, old peaked to'd Shoes with brass Buckles. Whoever takes up and secures the said Servant, so that his Master may have him again, shall have *Thirty Shillings* Reward, and reasonable Charges,
    paid by Joseph Bartholomew.
 The Pennsylvania Gazette, November 3, 1743; November 10, 1743; November 16, 1743; November 24, 1743.

RUN *away on the 6th Inst from on board the Ship Phoenix, William Wilson, Master, three Sailors, viz. one named James Sutherland, a Yorkshire Man, is* a lusty Man, by Trade a Ship's carpenter; one named Gray Patterson, and the other named William Finch.

Whoever secures the said Sailors, or either of them so that the said Captain may have them again, shall have Twenty Shillings Reward, for each, and reasonable Charges, paid by   William Wilson.

N. B. *All Masters of Vessels are hereby desired not to Entertain them at their Perril.*

The Pennsylvania Gazette, November 3, 1743; November 10, 1743; November 16, 1743; November 24, 1743.

RUN away from the Subscriber, an Irish Lad, named Peter Fulham, by Trade a Taylor, a short well set Land, having a down look, strait light brown Hair: Had on when he went away, a light-colour'd camlet Coat, lined with green shalloon, a new dowlais Shirt, dark-coloured Breeches, grey worsted Stockings, an old pair of Shoes, and an old Beaver Hat. Whoever takes up and secures him, so that he may be had again, if within five Miles of Philadelphia, shall have Ten Shillings, if farther Twenty Shillings Reward, and reasonable Charges, paid by   William Craddock.

The Pennsylvania Gazette, November 3, 1743; November 10, 1743; November 16, 1743; November 24, 1743.

RUN away the 7th Instant, from John Mackey, of Fallowfield Township, Chester County, an Irish Servant Lad, named John Hughes, about 18 Years of Age, middle Stature, pockfretten: Had on when he went away, an old Hat, and muslin Cap, a lightish colour'd broadcloth great Coat, tore up the Back, but has been sown down again, blue Jacket, London brown Breeches, and Stockings of the same, tow Shirt, and Country made Shoes. Whoever takes up and secures said Servant, so that his Master may have him again, shall have Twenty Shillings Reward, and reasonable Charges,
        paid by   John Mackey.

The Pennsylvania Gazette, November 10, 1743; November 16, 1743; November 24, 1743; December 1, 1743; December 6, 1743; December 15, 1743.

RUN away on the 15th Instant from *Roger Conner*, of *Lancaster* Town, an Irish Servant Man, named *Patrick Doller*, by trade a Hatter, aged about 30 Years, a lusty well set Fellow, broad faced, down Look, brown Complexion, has lately had a Cut near his right Eye, which looks very Fresh, with a red Spot very plain, has the Picture of a Man on his Breast and in the Head of the Picture these Letters, INREE, and on his right Hand P D. Had on when he went away, a tufft Fustian Coat, a worsted Damask Jacket and Breeches, two check and one white Shirt, a Kersey Jacket with brass Buttons and no Lining, blue worsted, and Sheep grey Stockings, new Shoes, with large brass Buckles, one plain and the other carved, a brown Wig, and cotton Cap, and felt Hat.

Whoever takes up the said Servant, and secures him so that his Master may have him again, shall have three Pounds if taken in the Province of Pennsylvania, and four Pounds if in any other Colony,
        paid by   Roger Conner. *Nov.* 17. 1743.

The Pennsylvania Journal, or, Weekly Advertiser, November 17, 1743; November 24, 1743; December 1, 1743; December 8, 1743; December 15, 1743; December 20, 1743; December 29, 1743; January 3, 1744; January 12, 1744. See *The Pennsylvania Gazette*, November 24, 1743, and *The Pennsylvania Gazette*, January 3, 1744.

        Lancaster County, in Pennsylvania, November 4. 1743. STolen out of George Gibson's Yard, in Lancaster, on the 2d Instant, a black natural pacing Mare, of three Years old, (the property of James Smith, near Mill-creek, in the said County) with Saddle, Bridle and Saddle-Bags, branded on the near Buttock IS, a Star in her Forehead, a small Snip on her Nose, both hind Feet white, and is ring'd. She was stolen by one David Griffith, a noted Horse Thief, who has been frequently convicted of Horse-stealing; he is a fair faced Person, and had dark colour'd Cloaths on.

Whoever takes up and secures the said Mare and Thief, so as the Owner may have his own again, shall have Forty Shillings Reward and reasonable Charges,   paid by   James Smith.

The American Weekly Mercury, From November 17, to November 24, 1743; From November 24, to December 2, 1743; From December 8, to December 15, 1743; From December 15, to December 21, 1743; From December 21, to December 28, 1743. See *The Pennsylvania Gazette*, February 10, 1743, and *The Pennsylvania Gazette*, May 30, 1745.

RUN away on the 15th Instant from Rodger Conner, of Lancaster Town, an Irish Servant Man, named Patrick Dollar, by trade a Hatter, aged about 30 Years, a lusty well set Fellow, broad faced, down look, brown Complexion, has lately had a Cut near his right Eye, which looks very fresh, with a red Spot very plain, has the Picture of a Man on his Breast, and in the Head of the Picture these Letters, I.N.R.I. and on his right Hand P D. Had on when he went away, a tufft Fustian Coat, a worsted damask Jacket and Breeches, two check and one white Shirt, a kersey Jacket with brass Buttons and no lining, blue worsted, and Sheep grey Stockings, new Shoes, with large brass

Buckles, one plain the other carved, a brown Wig, and cotton Cap, and felt Hat. Whoever takes up the said Servant, and secures him so that his Master may have him again, shall have three Pounds if taken in the Province of Pennsylvania, and four Pounds if in any other Colony, paid by Roger Connor. *The Pennsylvania Gazette,* November 24, 1743; December 1, 1743; December 6, 1743; December 15, 1743. See *The Pennsylvania Journal, or, Weekly Advertiser,* November 17, 1743, and *The Pennsylvania Gazette,* January 3, 1744.

ABsconded the 24th of November, from Mathias Lamy, of Whiteland, Chester County, an English Apprentice Lad, named William Thomas, by Trade a Taylor, about 14 Years of Age, well set, fair Complexion, dark Hair, squints very much, has a Scar on his Face: Had on when he went away, a half worn felt Hat, grey Country cloth Jacket, blue Breeches, but has a Pair of short Trowsers over them, coarse Shirt, old yarn Stockings, new Shoes ty'd with Strings. Whoever takes up and secures said Apprentice, so that his Master may have him again, shall have Twenty Shillings Reward, and reasonable Charges, paid by Mathias Lamy.

The Pennsylvania Gazette, December 15, 1743; December 20, 1743; December 29, 1743; January 3, 1744. See *The Pennsylvania Gazette,* November 21, 1745.

1744

RUN away on the 15th of Nov. from Roger Connor, of Lancaster Town, an Irish Servant Man, named Patrick Dollard, by trade a Hatter, aged about 30 Years, a lusty well set Fellow, broad faced, down look, brown Complexion, has lately had a Cut near his right Eye, which looks very fresh, with a red Spot very plain, has the Picture of a Man on his Breast, and in the Head of the Picture these Letters, I.N.R.I. and on his right Hand P D. Had on when he went away, a tufft Fustian Coat, a worsted damask Jacket and Breeches, two check and one white Shirt, a kersey Jacket with brass Buttons and no lining, blue worsted, and Sheep grey Stockings, new Shoes, with large brass Buckles, one plain the other carved, a brown Wig, and cotton Cap, and felt Hat. Whoever takes up the said Servant, and secures him so that his Master may have him again, shall have three Pounds if taken in the Province of Pennsylvania, and four Pounds if in any other Colony, paid by Roger Connor. P. S. *If the said Dollard is taken after the Date hereof, I will give* Five Pounds Reward. *I suppose the will try to get away in some of the Privateers; but as he is a Fellow that knows the Country well, may be lurking in some Part of it: It is mostlikely he is gone towards New-England.*
Lancaster, Dec. 12. 1743.

The Pennsylvania Gazette, January 3, 1744; January 11, 1744; January 19, 1744. See *The Pennsylvania Journal, or, Weekly Advertiser*, November 17, 1743, and *The Pennsylvania Gazette*, November 24, 1743.

RUN away, about the middle of Dec. past, an Irish Servant Woman, named Eleanor Cavenough, alias Plunkett, about 35 Years of Age, very short and little, cole black Hair, swarthy Complexion, small Hands and Feet, has E P in Blue, wrote with Gun Powder on the back of her left Hand, she is a good Spinner: Had on when she went away, two new Shifts, blue worsted Stockings with white Clocks, leather Pumps, white shaloon Gown, and blue shaloon Pettycoats. Whoever secures her, and brings her to to the keeper of the Work -House in Philadelphia, shall have Twenty Shillings Reward,
   paid by Abraham Shelly.
N. B. Said Shelly has a likely Servant Lad's Time to dispose of for four Years.
The Pennsylvania Gazette, January 26, 1744; February 2, 1744; February 16, 1744; February 22, 1744; March 1, 1744; March 9, 1744; March 15, 1744.

RUN away, on the 8th Instant, from William Baker, in Chesnut Street Philadelphia, a Dutch Servant Woman, named Catherine Vernon, lusty and well set. fair Complexion, drest after the Dutch Fashion, dark Petticoat, short calico Jacket, dutch Cap, white Apron and Handkerchief, dutch Shoes with Nails in them; the said Servant can talk pretty good English, and has been in this Country about three Years. Whoever takes up the said Servant, and secures her so that her Master may have her again, shall have Forty Shillings Reward, and reasonable Charges
   paid by William Baker.
The Pennsylvania Gazette, February 2, 1744; February 8, 1744; February 16, 1744; February 22, 1744.

RAN-away on the 18th of February, from Edward Farmar, *of Whitemarsh, in Philadelphia County, a Servant Man named* Timothy Brennan, *about 26 Years of age, and short thick bushy Hair; had on when he went away, a brown Coat, a brown holland Jacket lined with white linen, a pair of light blew stockings sotted in the small with white; he served for 5 Years about Pequea, in Lancaster County, He stole out of the House a holland shirt, a fine homespun Womens shift, with holland sleeves, and several other Things.*

 Whoever takes up said Servant and secures him so that he may be had again, shall have three Pounds

paid By   Edward Farmar.
The Pennsylvania Journal, or, Weekly Advertiser, February 21, 1744; February 29, 1744; March 6, 1744; March 15, 1744; March 21, 1744; March 29, 1744; April 12, 1744; April 17, 1744; April 26, 1744.

RUN away on the 10th of Jan. from the Subscriber, a Servant Man named Richard Gregory, about 30 Years of Age, of middle Stature, a Joyner by Trade; had on when he went away, a white drab double breasted Coat with a large cape, new castor Hat, leather Breeches, a light coloured cloth Jacket. Whoever takes up and secures the said Servant so that his Master may have him again, shall have Five Pounds Reward,
      paid by   Nathan Rigbie.
The Pennsylvania Gazette, February 22, 1744; March 1, 1744; March 9, 1744; March 15, 1744; March 21, 1744; March 29, 1744; April 5, 1744.

RUN away from William Foster, of Paxton, in Lancaster County, an Irish Servant Man, named Thomas Gallachar, short Stature, round shouldred, has two moulds on his left Jaw about an Inch apart: Had on when he went away, a course cloth Jacket with yellow Buttons, lined with course linen, old Trowsers tied about his Thighs, blue Stockins, old Shoes or Indian Mokisins, wore his own Hair, old beaver Hat, took with him a Wallet and a large branet Dog with a long Tail, its supposed the said Servant is gone towards New-York, or to Sopus, or Albany.
Whoever secures said Servant, so that his Master may have him again, shall have Forty Shillings Reward, and reasonable Charges
      paid by   William Foster.
The Pennsylvania Gazette, March 15, 1744; March 21, 1744; March 29, 1744; April 5, 1744.

RUN away on the 27th Instant, from *Benjamin Town*, of *Bristol* Township, *Bucks* County, a Servant Man named *Scilis Adder*, low statur'd, dark brown Hair. Had on when he went away, a new Felt Hat, new dark colour'd Kersey Coat with Mohair Buttons, Serge Jacket, lin'd with Orange colour'd Shaloon, with Mohair Buttons, ozenbrigs Shirt, lin'd Sheep skin Breeches with cover'd Buttons, light blue woollen Stockings, new Shoes with round Toes.
   Whoever takes up the said Servant and brings him to his Master or secures him so that his Master may have him again, shall have Thirty Shillings Reward,   paid by   Benjamin Town.

N. B. The said Servant understands Baking, and it's suppos'd he aims to get into that Business.
The Pennsylvania Gazette, March 29, 1744; April 5, 1744; April 12, 1744.

RUN away, on the 23d of March from George Marpole, of Bristol, an Irish Servant Lad named Nicholas Coging, about 18 Years old: Had on when he went away, an old worsted Cap, a light colour'd Jacket with brass Buttons, leather Breeches, with brass Buttons, dark coloured Stockings, round to'd Shoes, ozenbrigs Shirt, felt Hat.
Whoever takes up said Servant and brings him to his Master, or to Joseph Rush, in Philadelphia, shall have Forty Shillings Reward,
   paid by George Marpole.
The Pennsylvania Gazette, April 5, 1744; April 12, 1744.

RUN away on the 2d of April from William Gray, Bisket Baker, in Philadelphia, a Servant Lad, named William Goddin, short statur'd, wears his own Hair, has but one Eye; Had on when he went away, a light coloured kearsey Coat, a thick flannel Jacket, Yarn Stockings, leather Breeches, and good Shoes. Took with him a Pair of strip'd ticken Breeches, blewish worsted Stockings, and blue and red silk Handkerchief.
Whoever secures the said Servant, so that his Master may have him again shall have Forty Shillings Reward, and reasonable Charges,
   paid by William Gray.
The Pennsylvania Gazette, April 12, 1744; April 19, 1744; April 26, 1744; May 3, 1744.

RUN away from Marcus Kühl, Baker of Philadelphia, a Dutch Servant Man named John Barnhard Biederey, about 20 years of Age, tall and slender, pale Complexion, red Hair, but lately shav'd. He had on, a blue cloath Coat, with white Mettal Buttons, Ozenbrigs Jacket and Trowsers, blewish Worsted Stockings, Shoes new soal'd, a good Racoon Hat. Whoever takes up the said Servant, so that his Master may have him again, shall have Three Pounds Reward, and all reasonable Charges
   paid by Marcus Kühl:
The Pennsylvania Gazette, April 26, 1744; May 10, 1744; May 24, 1744; May 31, 1744; June 7, 1744; June 14, 1744; June 21, 1744; June 28, 1744.

RUN away, from the Ship *Agnes* and *Betty*, John Brame Master, 4 Sailors, viz. *John Godsel*, about 30, middle Stature, thin Body and Pock-fretten, wearing a Wig. *James Bond*, of short Stature, fair Complexion, full faced, aged about 25, wears a Wig. William Bag, a *Liverpool* Man, aged 23, of middle Stature, freckled and sandy Complexion. *Edward Harding*, aged 16 or 17, short Stature, wearing his own Hair.

   Whoever apprehends and brings them to said Ship, shall have 40s Reward for each,   paid by   *John Brame.*
The Pennsylvania Gazette, April 26, 1744.

RUN away the 14th Instant, from Nathan Yarnall, of Edgmont Township, Chester County, a Welsh Servant Man, named David Jones, about 21 Years of Age, middle Stature, dark Complexion, short black Hair, high-nos'd, can read and write both Welsh and English. Had on when he went away, a new felt Hat, new Cloth Coat of a lightish brown Colour, with brass Buttons, homespun Shirts and Trowsers, old Shoes. Whoever takes up and secures said Servant, so that his Master may have him again, shall have Thirty Shillings Reward, and reasonable Charges,
    paid by   Nathan Yarnall.
The Pennsylvania Gazette, May 17, 1744; May 24, 1744; May 31, 1744; June 7, 1744; June 14, 1744.

RUN away on the 14th Instant, from Christian Warner, Blacksmith, in Germantown, a Servant Boy, named Ludowick Katts, thick well set, about 19 Years of Age, thin jaw'd, bow leg'd, his Feet turning inwards: Had on when he went away, a homespun shirt, Linsywoolsy Breeches.

  Whoever secures the said Lad so that his Master may have him again, shall have Twenty Shillings Reward, and reasonable Charges,
    paid by   Christian Warner.
The Pennsylvania Gazette, May 17, 1744; May 24, 1744; May 31, 1744; June 7, 1744; June 14, 1744.

RUN away the 19th Instant, from William Bonar, an Irish Servant Man, named John Cardiff, about 40 Years of Age, dark Complexion, grim Countenance, talks thick, short black Hair, with some grey Hairs, broad Shoulders, and stoops a little; he has been but 5 Months in the Country. Had on when he went away, an old felt Hat, a great Coat of walnut colour, with Buttons of the same, a white woolen Jacket, a Pair of good tow Trowsers, check Shirt. He may have chang'd some of the said Cloaths. Whoever takes

up said Servant, either by Sea or Land, and secures him, so that his Master may have him again, shall have Thirty Shillings Reward, and reasonable Charges,   paid by   William Bonar.
The Pennsylvania Gazette, May 24, 1744; May 31, 1744; June 7, 1744; June 14, 1744. Third and fourth ads show he "RUN away the 19th of May...."

RUN-away, on the 29th of May past, from Matthias Kairlin, of Concord Township, Chester County, an English Servant Man, named John Licet, (but commonly went by the Name of Twig) aged about 21 Years, by Trade a Brass-Founder, or Brasier, short of Stature, thin visag'd, pitted with the Small Pox, no Hair; Had on, a light colour'd Homespun Drugget Coat, with white Metal Buttons and slash Sleeves, linen Jacket, fine white Shirt, Leather Breeches, worsted Stockins, calf-skin Pumps, linen Cap, flag silk Handkirchief, and half-worn Castor Hat. Whoever takes up and secures the said Servant, so that his Master may have him again, shall have Twenty Shillings Reward and reasonable Charges,
paid by   MATTHIAS KAIRLIN.
The American Weekly Mercury, From May 31, to June 7, 1744; From June 7, to June 14, 1744; From June 14, to June 21, 1744; From June 21, to June 28, 1744.

RUN away the 24th of May, from *Wm. Noblit* of *Middletown* in *Chester* County, an Irish Servant Man named *John McColbem*, about 26 Years of Age, a likely Man, fair and fresh colour'd straight brown Hair, has little smiling Eyes, a sharp Nose and broad Chin, a sober modest young Man, but in Company he is apt to sing, has a soft womanly Voice, he whistles well, with little Alteration of his lips. Had on when he went away, a Jockey Coat of blue broad Cloath, with white mettal Buttons, a light coloured Jacket with a double Breast, a check Shirt and a white one, blue Plush Breeches, flowered Garters green and yellow, and wears them commonly below his Knees.

Whosoever takes up and secures the said Servant, so that his Master may have him again, shall have *Three Pounds* Reward and reasonable Charges   paid by   *William Noblit.*

N. B. It is supposed that he either went with or followed a *New-England* Man, named *John Hoyet*, to some of the Iron-works. It is likewise supposed that he may have changed his Apparel.
The Pennsylvania Gazette, June 7, 1744; June 14, 1744; June 21, 1744; June 28, 1744.

RUN away from Edward Woodward, of Middletown, Chester County, an Irish Servant Lad, about 17 Years of Age, named Edward Wilson, of short Stature, yellowish Complexion, and his Hair cut off, can talk good English, and tolerable good Dutch. Had on when he went away, a lightish colour'd homespun cloth Coat, a Copper colour'd Jacket, both with brass Buttons, check Trowsers, a fine Shirt, a felt Hat almost new, a new coarse Shirt, and Trowsers, a pair of strong toed Shoes almost new, two silk Handkerchiefs, the one red, the other striped, a tow Wallet, he also took Provision with him. Whoever takes up and secures the said Servant, so that his Master may have him again, shall have Thirty Shillings Reward and reasonable Charges,
   paid by Edward Woodward .
The Pennsylvania Gazette, June 14, 1744; June 21, 1744; June 28, 1744.

RUN away on Saturday last, from Joseph Clark, of this City, Baker, an Apprentice Lad named Thomas Edwards, aged about 15 Years, this Country born, of a fair Complexion, and brown bushy Hair: Had on a blue Frize Coat with a Cape, white Shirt, half-worn linen Breeches, good calfskin Shoes, and Racoon Hat. Whoever takes up and secures the said Apprentice, so that his Master may have him again, shall have Twenty Shillings Reward and reasonable Charges paid by Joseph Clark.
N. B. It is supposed he is about Abington. Philadelphia, July 19, 1744.
The American Weekly Mercury, From July 12, to July 19, 1744. See *The American Weekly Mercury*, From May 30, to June 6, 1745.

RUN away the 16th Instant, from *James Keimer*, an *English* Servant Man, named *Joseph Waln*, speaks *Dutch* and *Welsh*, he lived formerly with *Peter Shaver*, is of middle Stature, fair Complexion, short Hair, about 20 Years of Age. Had on when he went away, a greenish colour'd silk camlet Coat, lin'd with Fustian, a Dimity double-breasted Jacket with white Buttons, a blue and green Jacket, the Green had no Sleeves, double breasted with metal Buttons. Also an *Irish* Servant Lad, named *Charles Dunevan*, a short squat Fellow, full faced, short thick Legs, speaks much on the Brogue, short dark colour'd Hair. They took a broad cloth Coat full trim'd, and several fine and coarse Shirts, which they stole.
  Whoever takes up or secures them, so that *James Keimer*, of *East-Nantmel*, or *Samuel Flower*, at *Reading*, may have them again, shall have *Forty Shillings* Reward for each, and reasonable Charges
   paid by *Samuel Flower*, or *James Keimer*.
The Pennsylvania Gazette, June 21, 1744; June 28, 1744; July 5, 1744. The July 5 ad also lists William Branson as an advertiser.

RUN away from *William Bird*, of *Amity* Township, and County of *Philadelphia*, the following *Irish* Servant Men; one named *Dennis Dailey*, aged about 22 Years, down Look, has a Stoppage in his Speech. Had on when he went away, a homespun Jacket of a Cinnamon Colour, an old Check Shirt, ozenbrigs Trowsers, patched with homespun Linnen, old felt Hat, strong Shoes, with Hobnails in them.

The other named *Edward Rannels*, about 21 Years of Age: Had on when he went away, a pretty good homespun Jacket of a light colour, supposed to have an old fustian Coat, felt Hat, ozenbrigs Trowsers patched, old Shoes, good cotton Cap. They are both supposed to have Guns with them.

Whoever takes up and secures the said Servants in some Goal, or brings them to their Master, shall have *Three Pounds* Reward, and reasonable Charges paid by *William Bird.*
N. B. They took a small grey Dog.
The Pennsylvania Gazette, June 21, 1744; June 28, 1744.

RUN away from *George Kastner*, of *Whitpin* Township, the 17th of this Instant, a dutch Servant Man named *Connerd Wead*, aged about 30 Years, a middle siz'd Man well set, full fac'd fresh Complexion; had on when he went away, a purple brown Waistcoat, brown linsey Breeches, a good home spun tow Shirt, a pair of Shoes, drover all round with Nails, a tow Wallet, a new Shirt and Trowsers, his Waiscoat is lin'd with Linsey of three or four different Stripes; also a felt Hat half worn, with other Things. Whosoever takes up and secures the said Servant, so that his Master may have him again, shall have *Forty Shillings* Reward, and reasonable Charges
paid by *George Kastner.*
The Pennsylvania Gazette, June 21, 1744; June 28, 1744; July 5, 1744.

RUN away from the Subscriber, on the Twenty Eighth of *May* last, a Servant Man named *Adam Redman*, an Irishman, of a low Stature, about Twenty Years of Age, a down looking Fellow pretty much pitted with the Small Pox, had on when he went away, a whitish colour'd Coat with Buttons of the same, Ozenbrigs Shirt and Trousers, an old Felt Hat with two Holes in the Crown, a whitish fulled Linen Cap, pretty good Shoes, no Stockings that is known of, very apt to put out his Tongue as walks. Whosoever takes up or secures the said Servant, so that his Master may have him again, shall have Forty Shillings as a Reward, and reasonable Charges
paid by *Derick Clever. Pine Forge*, June 14. 1744.
The Pennsylvania Journal, or, Weekly Advertiser, June 21, 1744; June 28, 1744; July 4, 1744; July 11, 1744; July 19, 1744; July 26, 1744.

RUN-away on the 25th of this Instant from Thomas Yeardley of Bucks County an Irish Servant Man, named John Singin, aged about 25 Years, a well set down looking Fellow, black Beard, his Hair cut off: Had on when he went away a light colour'd Camblet Vest, Oznabrigs Shirt, Trowsers and Frock, new Shoes, and a good Caster Hat.

Whoever takes up said Servant and secures him, or gives Inteligence to his Master, or to Thomas Howard of this City, so that he may be had again, shall have Forty Shillings Reward and reasonable Charges paid by Thomas Yeardly. *Philadelphia June* 26. 1744.

The Pennsylvania Journal, or, Weekly Advertiser, June 28, 1744; July 11, 1744; July 19, 1744; July 26, 1744.

RUN-away from the Subscriber on the 1st of this Instant (July) two Irish Convict Servant Men, one named Thomas Goodwin, an elderly man; had on a Pea Jacket, piched in the Back with two Breadths behind, part white and part gray, and is suppos'd to have stolen a Sailors Oznabrigs Frock, and may, upon Examination, be found to have attempted to cut his Threat, but healed up with a large Scare. [*sic*] The other named John Nowlan, aged about 23 Years, with short black Hair; had on a Pea Jacket of gray Cloth, bad shoes, Oznabrigs Shirt white Cotten Breeches, pale Complection, broad Shoulders, and swings in his Gate.

Whoever takes up said Servants, or either of them, and secures them so that their Master may have them again shall have Twenty Shillings Maryland Money besides what the Law allows. John Jackson.

The Pennsylvania Journal, or, Weekly Advertiser, June 28, 1744; July 11, 1744; July 19, 1744; July 26, 1744.

RUN away from Capt. Thomas Anderson, a Servant Man, named Patrick Cunningham, about Thirty Years old, has a scabby Head. Had on when he went away, a blue great Coat, a red Jacket.

Whoever takes up and secures the said Servant, so that his Master or Samuel Welsh may have him again, shall have Twenty Shillings Reward, and reasonable Charges paid by Samuel Welsh.

The Pennsylvania Gazette, July 5, 1744; July 12, 1744; July 19, 1744.

RUN-away on the 8th of this Instant the following Persons, viz. From James Davis, of this City, Carpenter, an Apprentice Lad, named John Jones, thick set, fair Complexion, and wears a Cap: Had on when he went away, a light colour'd Coat and Jacket, a fine Shirt, and a Oznabrigs one, striped

Breeches, with Oznabrigs Trowsers over them, worsted Stockings and new Shoes.

Also from George Emlin, of this City, a Welch Servant Lad, named Morgen Jones, about 20 Years of Age, short stature, well set, fresh Complection, flat Face, bow Legs, speaks thick, and has his Hair cut off: Had on when he went away, a Beaver Hat, brown Broad Cloth Coat, Duroy Jacket, worsted Stockings, thin Shoes, and Cloth Breeches under a Pair of Trowsers.

Also from Timothy Matlock, of Hadonsfield, Gloucester County, an English Servant Man, named Andrew Goodson, looks pale, having had the Fever and Ague: Had on when he went away a blew Cloth Coat, Oznabrigs Jacket and Trowsers, thread Stockings, felt Hat and no Hair, and a Ven on his right Shoulder.

Also from Abraham Carlisle, of this City, a Servant Man, named William Collemore: Had on a Bever Hat half worn, Oznabrigs Shirt, Jacket and Breeches, blue worsted Stockings, and new Pumps.

Whoever takes up and secures either of them, so that their Masters may have them again, shall have three Pounds Reward, for each and reasonable Charges paid by

        James Davis,   George Emlin,
        Timothy Matlock,   Abraham Carlisle.

N. B. They have taken with them a Boat of 17 Feet Keel, lately trim'd, Part of her Gunnel new, with a Mast, and old Sprit Sail, a new Pine Rudder painted black on the Top. Whoever brings the Boat, shall have Twenty Shillings Reward.

The Pennsylvania Journal, or, Weekly Advertiser, July 11, 1744; July 19, 1744; July 26, 1744; August 2, 1744; August 9, 1744; August 16, 1744; August 23, 1744. *The American Weekly Mercury*, From July 5, to July 12, 1744, and *The Pennsylvania Gazette*, July 12, 1744.

RUN away on the 8th of Inst. the following Persons, viz.

From James Davis, of this City, Carpenter, an Apprentice Lad, named John Jones, thick set, fair Complexion, and wears a Cap: Had on when he went away, a light Coat, red Jacket, a fine Shirt, and a ozenbrigs one, striped Breeches, with ozenbrigs Trowsers over them, worsted Stockings, and new Shoes.

From George Emlen, of this City, a Welsh Servant Lad, named Morgan Jones, about 20 Years of Age, short of Stature, well set, fresh colour'd, flat Face, bow Legs, speaks thick, and has his Hair cut off: Had on when he went away, a Beaver Hat, brown Broad Cloth Coat, Duroy Jacket, worsted Stockings, thin Shoes, and Cloth Breeches under a Pair of Trowsers.

From Timothy Matlack, of Haddonfield, Gloucester County, an English Servant Man, named Andrew Goodson, has a Wen upon his right Shoulder, looks Pale, having had the Fever and Ague: Had on when he went away, a blue Cloth Coat, ozenbrigs Jacket and Trowsers, Thread Stockings, Felt Hat and no Hair.

From Abraham Carlisle, of this City, a Servant Man, named William Collemore. Had on when he went away, an half worn Beaver Hat ozenbrigs Shirt, Jacket and Breeches, blew worsted Stockings, new Pumps.

Whoever takes up and secures any of the said Runaways, so that their Masters may have them again, shall have Three Pounds Reward, for each and reasonable Charges paid by Philadelphia,

   James Davis George Emlen
   Timothy Matlack Abraham Carlisle.   July 12. 1744.

N. B. They have taken with them a Boat of 17 Feet Keel, lately trimm'd, part of her Gunnel new, with a Mast and old square Sprit-Sail, a new Pine Rudder painted black on the Top, Whoever brings the Boat, shall have Twenty Shillings Reward.

The American Weekly Mercury, From July 5, to July 12, 1744; From July 19, to July 26, 1744; From August 2, to August 9, 1744; From August 9, to August 16, 1744; From August 16, to August 23, 1744; From August 23, to August 30, 1744. See *The Pennsylvania Journal, or, Weekly Advertiser*, July 11, 1744, and *The Pennsylvania Gazette*, July 12, 1744.

RUN away on the 8th of July, the following Persons, viz. from James Davis, of this City, Carpenter, an Apprentice Lad, named John Jones, thick set, fair Complexion, and wears a Cap: Had on when he went away, a light Coat, red Jacket, fine Shirt, and ozenbrigs one, strip'd Breeches, with ozenbrigs Trowsers over them, worsted Stockings, and new Shoes.

Also from George Emlen, of this City, a Welsh Servant Lad, named Morgan Jones, about 20 Years of Age, short statur'd, well set, fresh, flat Face, bow Legs, speaks thick, and has his Hair cut off. Had on when he went away, a Beaver Hat, brown Broad Cloth Coat, Duroy Jacket, worsted Stockings, thin Shoes, and cloth Breeches under a pair of Trowsers.

Also from Timothy Matlack, of Haddonfield, Gloucester County, an English Servant Man, named Andrew Goodson, looks pale, having had the Feaver and Ague, has a Wen upon his right Shoulder. Had on when he went away a felt Hat and no Hair, a blue cloth Coat, ozenbrigs Jacket and Trowsers, thread Stockings.

Also from Abraham Carlisle, of this City, a Servant Man, named William Collemore. Had on when he went away, a Beaver Hat half worn, ozenbrigs Shirt, Jacket, and Breeches, blew worsted Stockings, new Pumps. Whoever takes up and secures any of the said Runaways, so that their Masters

may have them again, shall have Three Pounds Reward, for each and reasonable Charges paid by
   James Davis, George Emlen,
   Timothy Matlock, Abraham Carlisle.
N. B. They have taken with them, a Boat of 17 Foot Keel, with an old Square Sprit-sail, a new Pine Rudder, painted black on the Top, and lately trim'd, part of her Gunnel new. Whoever brings the Boat, shall have 20s Reward.
 The Pennsylvania Gazette, July 12, 1744; July 19, 1744; July 26, 1744; August 2, 1744; August 9, 1744; August 16, 1744; August 23, 1744; August 30, 1744. See *The Pennsylvania Journal, or, Weekly Advertiser*, July 11, 1744, and *The American Weekly Mercury*, From July 5, to July 12, 1744.

RUN away, from Joseph Baker and Stephen Beakes, both of Goshen in Chester County, two Irish Servant Men; one named Michael Linsey, about 25 Years of Age, of middle Stature, fresh Complexion, short brown Hair. Had on when he went away, a mixt coloured Kersey Coat with white metal Buttons, an old beaver Hat, a holland Shirt and two ozenbrigs Shirts, a pair of homespun Trowsers made Sailor fashion, old Shoes, tied with Thongs. The other named Timothy Riley, aged about 30 Years, a short slim Man, having several remarkable red Spots on his Nose and Forehead: Had on when he went away, an old Hat, two coarse and one fine Shirt, a yellow mixt-coloured tammey Jacket, the Buttons covered with the same; new worsted Stockings and new Shoes. Whoever shall apprehend the said Servants, and secure them so that their said Master may have them again, shall have Three Pounds Reward, or Thirty Shillings for either of them, with reasonable Charges,
   paid by Joseph Baker, Stephen Beakes,
 The Pennsylvania Gazette, August 2, 1744; August 9, 1744; August 16, 1744.

RUN away on the 6th Inst. from John Cuthbert, of Whiteland, in Chester County, an Irish Servant Man, named John Roney, alias John Fleming, short and thick set, sandy short Hair, talks broken English. Had on when he went away a homespun grey Coat, with Buttons of the same, felt Hat, checked Shirt, tow Trowsers, and old Shoes. Whoever takes up and secures him again, shall have Forty Shillings Reward and reasonable Charges,
   paid by John Cuthbert.
 The Pennsylvania Gazette, August 9, 1744; August 16, 1744; August 23, 1744.

MADE an Escape from the Goal of Lancaster, on the 17th of this Instant, a Prisoner, named John Dennis, a native Irishman, about 25 Years of Age, a pretty lusty Fellow, cannot talk plain English, his Hair cut or shaved close off, when grown of a blackish Colour. He had on a brownish coloured Coat not half worn, trim'd with flat metal Buttons and small Ditto on the Sleeves, and an old Jacket the same as the Coat, but more worn. Whoever secures the said Prisoner, and brings him to Lancaster Goal, shall have *Forty Shillings Reward*, paid by   Francis Reynolds, Sub-Sheriff.
   The Pennsylvania Gazette, August 23, 1744; August 30, 1744.

RUN away from Edmund Briggs, of Bucks County, a English Servant Man, named Richard Price, of middle Stature, black Complexion, black Eyes, he is much given to drink. Had on when he went away, an old felt Hat, linnen Cap, brown Jacket, linnen Drawers, old blue grey Stockings, sharp toed Shoes. Whosoever takes up and secures the said Servant, so that his Master may have him again, shall have Twenty Shillings Reward, and reasonable Charges paid by   Edmund Briggs, or William Briggs.
   The Pennsylvania Gazette, August 30, 1744; September 6, 1744.

RUN away the 23d of August last, from John Peters of Plymouth, in the County of Philadelphia, a Servant Man named Robert Anderson, he is adicted to change his Name: He's of a remarkable dark Complection, immoderately given to strong Drink, to swearing, and accompanying himself with Women of any Colour. His Apparel when he went away was as follows, an almost new Felt Hat. a Linsey Woolsey Jacket of a brown Colour, two pair of Trousers, one check'd the other white, a pair of strong double soald Shoes. Whoever secures the said Servant in any Goal, and send Notice thereof to his said Master, shall have Thirty Shillings Reward, and reasonable Charges   paid by   John Peters.   Septem. 2, 1744.
   The Pennsylvania Journal, or, Weekly Advertiser, September 6, 1744; September 13, 1744; September 20, 1744; September 27, 1744.

RUN away the 11th of September, from William Branson's Ironworks, at Reading Furnace, an Irish Servant Lad, named Robert Murphy, a short squat Lad, thick set, fresh Complexion, and short black Hair, full of talk, writes a good Hand, and ready at Accompts: Had on when he went away, a blew cloth Coat, lined with red shaloon, a check'd Shirt, and Trowsers. Also went with him one John Smith, a slender tall Lad, about 18 or 19 Years of Age, thin Visage, black Eyes, and a yellowish Complexion, born near Stratten Island: Had on when he went away, a blue and white linsy Jacket, and another Jacket of flowered stuff, a large black, red and yellow, silk Handkerchief, a pair of large carved Buckles; they have taken with them other Cloathes, and it's supposed they will change them, they also took 4 Pieces of Eight, and a Ten Shilling Bill, and it is supposed they have taken with them a large bay Horse, branded on the near Buttock with C, Trots and Paces. Whoever takes up and secures the said Servants, or brings them to William Branson in Philadelphia, or Samuel Flower, at Reading Ironworks, shall have Five Pounds Reward, and reasonable Charges,

    paid by William Branson, or Samuel Flower.
The Pennsylvania Gazette, September 13, 1744; September 20, 1744; September 27, 1744.

STolen away from Hugh M'Clelan of Salisbury-Township in Lancaster County, by Patrick Dudy and Margaret Breuster; sundry Sorts of Goods, viz. One Rug and new Blankets, one Webb of white Linen Cloth, a quantity of Worsted Yarn; five or six Gowns, one of English Pladd, one of yellow Worsted, one of twill'd Silk, &c. a small Box or Chest with Pewter, and many other small and valuable Goods. Margaret Breuster is small of Stature with low black Hair, a Mark on her left Cheek, something red Faced, and generally wears a black Bonnet or an old Hat. Patrick Dudy is a tall fair faced Man, with light-brown Hair, a brown Coat and a blue Jacket. They also took with them a natural paceing sorrel Mare, an old Buckskin Saddle, and a roan Horse.

 Whoever takes up and secures the said Man and Woman with the above Goods so that the owner may have them again, shall have Forty Shillings Reward and reasonable Charges,

    Paid by me HUGH M'CLELAN.
The American Weekly Mercury, From September 13, to September 20, 1744; From September 20, to September 27, 1744; From September 27, to October 4, 1744; From October 4, to October 11, 1744; From October 11, to October 18, 1744.

RUN away last Night from Robert Lewis, of Kennet, in Chester County, two Servant Lads, viz. James Mundle, aged about 20 Years, of short Stature, thick Lips, and very rough Complexion, slow of Speech, one Ancle bone out of Joint, so that his Foot stands out. Had on when he went away, a half-worn Felt Hat, a light-coloured Cloth Serge Coat with cross Pockets and Vest Sleeves and large white metal Buttons; cotton-and-linnen jacket and Breeches, a Pair of mixt thread Stockings, gray woollen Stockings; and good Shoes. Edmond Roach, about 16 Years of Age, a short well set Lad, speaks a little Broguish, served some Time with Joshua Littler at Wilmington, is a

Scholar and may write himself a Pass. Had on a half-worn Felt Hat, a brown Coat with cross Pockets, slash Sleeves, and (I think) brass Buttons, striped Linnen Vest, Buckskin Breeches, grey Yarn Stockings and good Shoes. Whoever secures the said Servants, so that they may be had again, shall have Fifty Shillings Reward for Each, and reasonable Charges
    paid by Robert Lewis.
N. B. It is supposed they will change their Names, and that Mundle may pass for a Miller.

  The Pennsylvania Gazette, October 4, 1744; October 11, 1744; October 18, 1744.

  RUN away on Sunday Night last, from Peter Matson, of Upper Merion, an Irish Servant Man, named Cornelius Calaghan, having somewhat of the Brogue on his Tongue, long visag'd, and very red in the Face, short, thick, and well set, long thick yellowish Hair: Had on when he went away, a Leather Jockey Cap, an old darkish Coat, with Jacket sleeves, a thick brownish woolen Jacket, with metal Buttons and a white Linnen Jacket, two shirts, buckskin Breeches, grey broken stockings, sharp toed shoes, broke at the Toes. He has taken his Indentures with him. Whoever takes up and secures the said Servant, so that his Master may have him again, shall have Thirty Shillings Reward, and reasonable Charges,
    paid by Peter Matson.

  The Pennsylvania Gazette, November 1, 1744; November 8, 1744; November 15, 1744.

  RUn-away, on the 22d of October, 1744, from Thomas Maybury, of Greenlane Forge, in Philadelphia County, a Servent Man named Thomas Dyke, about 27 Years of age, long pale pock-fretten Vissage, very apt to get Drunk, and pretends to be a School-Master, speaks thick as if his Tongue was too large for his Mouth, light Hair, and very short Nails on his Fingers. Had on when he went away, an old blue Coat, an ash-colour'd Drugget Coat, Ozenbrigs Jacket and Trowsers, good Shoes and Stockings, and a small Castor Hat. He was born in England.

  Run-away, on the 29th of the same Month, from the above-said Maybury, an Irish Servant Man named Francis Shae, about 26 Years of age, long Vissaged, blind of his right Eye, hard of hearing, stoops in his walk and is round Shoulder'd. Had on when he went away, a light-colour'd home-made Cloth double-breasted Jacket lined with red Shalloon, Breeches of the same with red Shalloon Puffs, and an old white Fustian Jacket under the Cloth Jacket.

Whoever takes up the said Servants, or either of them, and secures them in any Goal, so that their Master may have them again, shall have, if taken in the Province of Pennsylvania Forty Shillings for each, if taken in any other Province Three Pounds for each, and reasonable Charges.

          Paid by   THOMAS MAYBURY.

The American Weekly Mercury, From November 1, to November 8, 1744; From November 8, to November 15, 1744; From November 15, to November 22, 1744; From November 22, to November 29, 1744; From November 26, to December 6, 1744; From December 6, to December 14, 1744; From December 14, to December 20, 1744; From December 20, to December 28, 1744; From December 28, to January 1, 1745; From January 1, to January 9, 1745; From January 23, to January 29, 1745; From January 29, to February 5, 1745; From March 5, to March 12, 1745; From March 26, to April 4, 1745; *The New-York Weekly Journal,* January 28, 1744; February 4, 1744. [*sic*] Minor differences between the papers.

RUN away the 14*th Instant Decem. from Michael Cario (Jeweller) in Philadelphia, a Servant Man, named Thomas Dean, aged about 21 Years, short Stature, well set, much pockbroken, his Hair cut off: Had on when he went away a brown Frieze Coat and Jacket, Leather Breeches, Yarn Stockings, Brass Buckles, his Hat has been laced, new speckled Shirt, Silver Buttons in his Sleeves, one pair of which have lost one of the Stones that were in them. Whoever takes up the said Servant, and secures him, so that his Master may have him again, shall have Twenty Shillings Reward, and reasonable Charges, paid by Michael Cario .*

The Pennsylvania Gazette, December 18, 1744; December 25, 1744; January 1, 1745.

1745

RUn away on the 25*th of December last, from Thomas Hanaway, of Sadsbury, Lancaster County, Cooper, an English Servant Man, named Richard Gamble, about 26 Years of Age, has been 10 Years in the Country, and can Work at most Sorts of Country Business, and was mostly us'd to Horse Racing, &c. in England, pretends to be a Farrier, and can play many Tricks in Legerdemain, or Hocus Pocus; he is a well set Fellow, midling Stature, broad flat Face, and a small Mouth: Had on when he went away, a Cotton Cap, an old Hat, a yellowish coloured Cloth Coat, with flash Sleeves and Brass Buttons, blue and white Bird Eye double Breasted Jacket, Oznabrigs Shirt, a Pair of striped Cotton and Linnen Trowsers, old dark Yarn Stockings, and a Pair of Pumps; he has been some Time among the Dutch,* *and pretends to speak that Language. Whoever takes up and secures the said Servant, so as his Master may have him again, shall have Forty Shillings Reward, and reasonable Charges, paid by Thomas Hanaway.*

The Pennsylvania Gazette, January 8, 1745; January 15, 1745; January 22, 1745.

RUN away, on the 2d Instant, a Servant Woman, named Sarah Butler: *Had on a Homespun yellowish Petticoat, a short Stuff Bed-Gown, of a Purple Cast. She is a middle sized Woman, of a swarthy Complexion, and ill favoured. Whoever will bring her to her Master,* John Cottinger, *Taylor, the Corner of* Arch-Street, *over against the Sign of the* George, *shall have* Forty Shillings *Reward, and reasonable Charges.*
N. B. *The said Servant run away in* May *last from one* Delaplane, *in* Bucks County. *She was seen on the Road to* Bristol.

The Pennsylvania Gazette, January 15, 1745; January 22, 1745; January 29, 1745.

RUN away on the 12th of this Inst. January, from the Subscriber's Plantation, in the Northern Liberties of this City, a Dutch Servant Man, and his Wife; the Man's Name Harmon Frivall, *a hardy smart Fellow, of middle Stature, brown Complexion about* 24 *Years of Age, talks much, but little English, as being a New comer, had a Scar on his Neck, as it were from an Evil. Had on a Beaver Hat half-worn, a grey or black Wig, a new Pair of Shoes grey yarn Stockings, his other Cloathing uncertain, as having some Changes. The Woman of middle Stature, and well set, of brown Complexion, is big, and near her Time; and has among other Cloaths, a black Jacket with Gold-lace on the Sleeves. They had some Bags with Cloaths, &c. It is supposed they got off in a Dutch Waggon. Whoever takes up and secures the said Runaways, so that their Master may have them again, shall have* Three Pistoles *for the Man, and for both* Four Pistoles *Reward,*
         paid by   Robert Meade.

The Pennsylvania Gazette, January 22, 1745; January 29, 1745; February 5, 1745.

RUN-away, on the 18th Instant, from John Jackson, of East-Caln, in the Great Valley, Chester County, a Servent Man named William Finly, about 26 Years of Age, a middle siz'd fresh colour'd Man, with short Hair, and blind of the right Eye, but not easily discour'd. [sic] He had on when he went away, an old Felt Hat, brown Cloath Jacket and Breeches, a home-made Olive coulour'd Stuff Jacket, brown Yarn Stockings, strong picked-toe'd Shoes a fine and two homespun Shirts.

Whoever takes up and secures the said Servant so that his Master may have him again, shall have Three Pounds Reward, and reasonable Charges,
    Paid by John Jackson.
The American Weekly Mercury, From January 15, to January 23, 1745.

            Lancaster, January 26, 1744-5.
RUN away from the Subscriber, in Hempfield Township, Lancaster County, on the 22d Instant, an Irish Servant Man, named William Hamilton, aged about 20 Years, a short, thick Fellow, down looking Countenance, red haired: Had on when he went away two Jackets, the outward a brown Lindsey one, patched with Cloath of the same Colour, the other a blue and white Damask one, brown Breeches, half worn, with Brass Buttons. 'Tis supposed he will go to Philadelphia, in order to get on board a Privateer. Whoever secures the said Servant, so as his Master may have him again, if taken up in this County, shall have Twenty Shillings Reward, and reasonable Charges; and if out of this County, Forty Shillings, and reasonable Charges,
    paid by John Brandon.
The Pennsylvania Gazette, January 29, 1745; February 5, 1745; February 12, 1745.

ABsconded from his Bail in Northampton Township, Bucks County, the 16th of January, one John Humphreys, Country-born, about 23 Years of Age, midling Stature, down Look, short black curl'd Hair, and one Ancle larger than the other: Had on a Castor Hat, light coloured Great and Jockey Coats, white Shirt, Leather Breeches, and Boots patch'd behind. Whoever secures the said Humphreys, so that his Bail may have him again, shall have Six Pounds Reward,
    paid by *John or Bernard Vanhorn, jun.*
N. B. 'Tis suppos'd he is gone towards Potomack in Virginia.
The Pennsylvania Gazette, January 29, 1745; February 5, 1745.

WHereas Thomas Cavenaugh, a Servant to George Kelly, of Philadelphia, Blacksmith, absented from his Master on Monday the eleventh Instant, and keeps incognito ever since; These are to forewarn all Persons from harbouring or entertaining him, as they will answer for it as the Law directs; and all Commanders and Masters of Vessels are desired not to harbour or receive him on board.

The Pennsylvania Gazette, February 19, 1745; February 26, 1745. See *The New-York Weekly Journal,* April 1, 1745.

RUn away, on the 15th Instant, from Joseph Gilbert, of Biberry, Philadelphia County, a Servant Lad, named Samuel Cook, Country-born, about 18 Years of Age, thin Visage, light Hair: Had on a Felt Hat, reddish brown Coat, turned, with Pewter Buttons, new brown Jacket, with Pewter Buttons, Ozenbrigs Shirts, tanned Sheepskin Breeches, with Pewter Buttons, brown Yarn Stockings, and a light Worsted Pair, two Pair of Shoes. Whoever secures said Lad, so that his Master may have him again, shall have Forty Shillings Reward,
          paid by   Joseph Gilbert.
The Pennsylvania Gazette, February 19, 1745; February 26, 1745; March 5, 1745; March 19, 1745; March 26, 1745. See *The Pennsylvania Gazette,* March 11, 1746.

RUN away, on the 6th Instant, from Mary Lownes, of Myomenson, a Welsh Servant Man, named William Dollaha, about 30 Years of Age, middle Stature, down Look, thin Face, and greyish Hair: Had on an old blue Coat, grey Stockings, and good Shoes. Whoever secures said Runaway, so that he may be had again; shall have Thirty Shillings Reward,
          paid by   Mary Lownes.
The Pennsylvania Gazette, March 12, 1745; March 19, 1745; March 26, 1745; April 4, 1745.

NOtice is hereby given to all good People to whom these Presents shall come, of a strolling Woman, who goes under the Name of *Elizabeth Castle,* alias *Morrey.* She pretends to be a School Mistress, Tayloress and Staymaker, Embroiderer and Doctoress. She is of little Stature, high Shouldered, grey Eyed, and very well qualified in Lying, Cheating, Defrauding, Cursing, Swearing, Drunkenness, Tale-bearing, Backbiting, Mischief making among Neighbours, and is reported to be a Thief. She carries with her a Quantity of Pieces that shine like Gold, by which Means she hath deceived several Women and Children to their great Prejudice. She squeaks when she speaks, and hath done Damage in Newtown, Chester County. This is but little to what might be said within Bounds of Truth.   *Thomas Thomas.*
The Pennsylvania Gazette, March 19, 1745; March 26, 1745; April 4, 1745.

RUn away, the 11*th Instant, from* Thomas M'Mollin, *of* East Nantmell, *in* Chester *County, an* Irish *Servant Woman, named* Mary Sullivan, *a smooth faced young Woman, pretty fresh coloured, and about Twenty Years of Age: Had on when she went away, a short Cloak of blue Cloath, no Cap, an old striped Gown, faced with old stamped Callicoe, 3 Petticoats, one of which is new, the Filling whereof is blue, the Fore-part of a much paler blue than the rest, a Pair of new Wooden heel'd Shoes, a great deal too large for her, and a darkish coloured half-worn Silk Handkerchief. Whoever secures said Servant, so as her Master may have her again, shall have Ten Shillings Reward, and reasonable Charges,*
    paid by Thomas M'Mollin.
The Pennsylvania Gazette, March 26, 1745; April 4, 1745; April 12, 1745.

RUN away from *George Kelly* Black Smith of *Philadelphia,* a Servant Man, named *Thomas Cavenaugh,* an *Irishman* aged about 22 Years, wears a Cap and a Brownish Westcoat, he has been in the Work House at *New-York* and was taken out, but made his escape in the Evening. Whoever secures the said Servant, so that his said Master may have him again, shall have *Forty Shillings* Reward, and all reasonable Charges
    paid by the said,   *George Kelly,*
The New-York Weekly Journal, April 1, 1745; April 8, 1745. See *The Pennsylvania Gazette,* February 19, 1745.

RUN away from *Richwelly* in *Bucks* County, Province of Pennsylvania, John Fry, a Sweitzer by Nation, middle Stature, black curled Hair and speaks but little English; he took with him his Wife and three Children, the eldest about 14 Years of age the Wife is a Palatine by Birth and very talkative.—Whoever secures the said John Fry, or gives Intelligence where he may be secured, shall receive *Five Pounds* Reward and all reasonable Charges of *John George Cook,* Stocking Weaver, at his Lodging at the House of
    John Peter Zenger, Printer.
The New-York Weekly Journal, January 28, 1745; February 4, 1745; April 1, 1745; April 8, 1745.

RUN away from James Dougherty, of Nottingham, Chester County, on the 17th of March last, a Native Irish Servant Man, named John Greevy, or Reeves, about 5 Foot high, has a Cast with his Right-eye, as if it were blind,

35 Years of Age, or thereabouts, speaks much on the Brogue, a little pitted with the Small-pox, short black Hair, and is an ill looking Fellow: Had on when he went away, a whitish coloured Suit of Cloathes, Brass Buttons on the Coat, and slash Sleeves, the Jacket and Breeches trimmed with black Mohair, an old Shirt, new Shoes, blue Stockings, and new Felt Hat: He also took with him a Suit of blue Home-made Cloaths, very good, and made for a Man about 6 Feet high. Whoever takes up said Servant, and secures him in any County Goal in America, and gives Notice thereof to his said Master, in the publick Prints, or otherwise, so that he may have again, shall have Five Pounds Reward, and reasonable Charges,
    paid by James Dougherty.
The Pennsylvania Gazette, April 4, 1745; April 12, 1745; April 18, 1745; April 25, 1745; May 9, 1745.

RUN away from the Subscribers, in Amity Township, Philadelphia County, the two following Servants, viz. An Irish Servant Man, named Dennis Daley, *about 22 Years of Age, has the Brogue on his Tongue, a great Stoppage in his Speech, and very much addicted to Drinking and Swearing; Had on when he went away, a coarse Kersey Coat, black Callimancoe Jacket, new Ozenbrigs Trowsers, and Leather Breeches under them, white Yarn Stockings, and good Shoe, with Hobnails in them.*

The other an Englishman, named Thomas Jennings, *and can talk the Swedish Language: Had on an old Orange coloured Coat, old brown Breeches, and Shoes new soaled.*

Whoever secures said Servants, and brings them to their Masters, shall have Forty Shillings *Reward for* Daley, *and* Twenty Shillings *for* Jennings, *with reasonable Charges,*
    paid by William Bird *and* Marcus Hulings.
The Pennsylvania Gazette, April 18, 1745; April 25, 1745; May 2, 1745.

            Philadelphia, April 22. 1745.
RAn-away, on the 14th Instant, from Isaac Vanhorne, of Salisbury Township in Bucks County, a Servant Lad named William Crotty, about 18 or 19 Years of Age, short of Stature and well-set, fresh colour'd and brownish Hair, has a small cast in his Eyes and a down Look; had on when he went away, a half worn Felt Hat, a brownish Drugget Coat with white Metal Buttons, a Jacket of the same with Brass Buttons, Leather Breeches with Brass Buttons, lightish colour'd Worsted Stockings, new Shoes with Brass Buckles, a fine white Shirt and a red Silk Handkerchief about his Neck.

Whoever takes up the said Servant and secures him so that his Master may have him again, shall have Twenty Shillings Reward and all reasonable Charges, paid by   ISAAC VANHORNE.
The American Weekly Mercury, From April 18, to April 25, 1745; From April 25, to May 2, 1745; From May 2, to May 9, 1745; From May 9, to May 16, 1745; From May 16, to May 23, 1745; From May 23, to May 30, 1745; From May 30, to June 6, 1745.

RUn away; on the 5th Instant, from *Thomas Bate*, of *Montgomery*, in *Philadelphia* County, a Servant Man, named *Lewelin Williams*, a *Welshman*, about 20 Years of Age, short and well-set, short dark brown Hair, round full Face, fresh coloured, wide Mouth, thick Ancles, and chaws Tobacco: Had on when he went away, a Drugget Olive Green Coat, an old white Linen Jacket, good Leather Breeches, with Brass Buttons, a large new Felt Hat, dark brown Stockings, and good Shoes: He took with him a Wallet, and two good Linen Shirts, a Loaf of Bread, and 'tis supposed a Cheese, and a Bible bound with Harness Leather.
Whoever takes up and secures said Servant, so that his Master may have him again, shall have *Fifty Shillings* Reward from
THOMAS BATE.
The Pennsylvania Gazette, May 9, 1745; May 16, 1745; May 23, 1745; May 30, 1745.

RUn away, on the 28th of last Month, from *Richard Loyd*, of *Derby*, *Chester* County, an *Irish* Servant Man, named *William Goodman*, about 30 Years of Age, a short, thick, well-set Fellow, with strait brown Hair: He took with him one Fur and one Felt Hat, about half worn, two Garlix and two Ozenbrigs Shirts, a good Duroy Coat, an old Kersey Coat, a Linen Jacket, several Pairs of Breeches and Trowsers, a Pair of Yarn and a Pair of Thread Stockings, and two or three Pairs of Shoes. Whoever secures said Servant, so that his Master may have him again, shall have *Thirty Shillings* Reward,
paid by   RICHARD LOYD.
The Pennsylvania Gazette, May 9, 1745; May 16, 1745; May 23, 1745.

Philadelphia, May 22. 1745.
RUN-away, on the 12th of January last, from the Subscriber's Plantation, in the Northern liberties of this City, a Dutch Servant Man and his Wife: The Man's Name John Harmon Fretzel, a hardy smart Fellow, of middle Stature, brown Complexion, about 24 Years of Age, talks much, but little English, as being a New-comer, had a Scar on his Neck, as it were from an Evil. Had on

when he went away, a Beaver Hat half-worn, a gray or black Wig, a new Pair of Shoes, and gray Yarn Stockings; his other Cloathing uncertain, as having some Changes. The Woman named Gertrude, of middle Stature and well-set, brown Complexion, was big and near her Time, and had some other Cloaths, a black Jacket with Gold Lace on the Sleeves. They had some Bags with Cloaths, &c. It is supposed they got off in a Dutch Waggon.

Whoever takes up and secures the said Runaways so that their Master may have them again, shall have TEN Pounds Reward, and reasonable Charges.   Paid by   ROBERT MEADE.

The American Weekly Mercury, From May 16, to May 23, 1745; From May 23, to May 30, 1745; From May 30, to June 6, 1745; From June 13, to June 20, 1745; From June 20, to June 27, 1745; From June 27, to July 5, 1745; From July 11, to July 18, 1745; From July 18, to July 25, 1745. See *The Pennsylvania Gazette*, November 27, 1746.

Lancaster, May 21. 1745.
THIS Day escaped from the Goal of Lancaster, one David Griffith, often times convicted of Horse-stealing, fair Complexioned and well Featured, and wears short black Hair: Had on when he made his Escape, a Cloth Jacket, of a lightish Colour, without Sleeves, and one Linen Jacket over the same, white Linen Trowsers, Linen Stockings, and good Shoes. Also one Michael Trone, a native Irishman, convicted of Felony: He is a short well set Fellow, with red Hair: Had on when he made his Escape, a red Worsted Cap, Linen Coat, with Brass Buttons, an Olive green Jacket, Leather Breeches, Linen Stockings and old Shoes.

Whoever takes up and secures the said Prisoners in any County Goal, so that I may receive them again, shall have Four Pounds Reward, or Forty Shillings for each, and reasonable Charges paid by me.

Joseph Pugh, Sub-Sheriff, of Lancaster County.

The Pennsylvania Gazette, May 30, 1745; June 6, 1745; June 13, 1745. See *The Pennsylvania Gazette*, February 10, 1743, and *The American Weekly Mercury*, From November 17, to November 24, 1743.

Philadelphia, *May* 30, 1745.
R*UN away, Yesterday, from Daniel Cooper, a Servant Lad, about* 18 *or* 19 *Years of age, called John Davis: He is pretty well-set, and had on when he went away, a short coarse Kersey Jacket, of a greyish Colour, an Ozenbrigs Shirt, a Pair of Dutch Tow Cloth Trowsers, and goes limping with his Right foot or Ancle, and has a little Impediment in his Speech. Whoever takes up the above Servant , and brings him to Peter Brown's, at the Ferry-House, in*

Philadelphia, shall have Three Pounds Reward, and reasonable Charges, paid by   Daniel Cooper.
The Pennsylvania Gazette, May 30, 1745.

Philadelphia, June 4. 1745.
RUN-away, on Sunday last, from Joseph Clark, of this City, Baker, an Apprentice Lad named Thomas Edwards, about 16 Years of Age, of a fair Complexion when clean, but generally wears a dirty Face. He had on when he went away, a light coloured Cloath Jacket double Breasted with Brass Buttons, a Pair of Linen Breeches, a white Shirt, bluish Stockings with large Clocks, a Pair of Calf-Skin Shoes with Steel Buckles, a Rackoon Hat, a Worsted Cap and short Hair, and had a speckled Handkerchief about his Neck.

Whoever takes up and secures the said Apprentice, so that his Master may have him again, shall have Twenty Shillings Reward, and reasonable Charges, Paid by   JOSEPH CLARK.

The American Weekly Mercury, From May 30, to June 6, 1745; From June 6, to June 13, 1745; From June 13, to June 20, 1745; From June 20, to June 27, 1745; From June 27, to July 4, 1745; From July 11, to July 18, 1745; From July 18, to July 25, 1745; From July 25, to August 1, 1745; From August 1, to August 8, 1745; From August 8, to August 15, 1745; From August 15, to August 22, 1745; From August 29, to September 5, 1745; From September 5, to September 12, 1745; From September 12, to September 19, 1745. See *The American Weekly Mercury,* From July 12, to July 19, 1744.

RUN-away, on the first of this Instant June, from Nicholas Fenuel, of the City of Philadelphia, Cordwainer, an Irish Apprentice Lad named James Bryan, about 18 Years of Age, low of Stature, hump-back'd and bandy-leg'd. Had on when he went away, blue Drugget Coat, Jacket and Breeches, check Trowsers, several check Shirts, black Worsted Stockings, old Shoes with Brass Buckles, a Felt Hat and a Worsted Cap.

Whoever brings the said Apprentice to his Master, or secures him so that his Master may have him again, shall have, if taken within 20 Miles of said City Twenty Shillings, if 40 Miles Forty Shillings, or if taken in any other Part of America, a suitable Reward, and reasonable Charges,
Paid by   NICHOLAS FENUEL.

The American Weekly Mercury, From May 30, to June 6, 1745; From June 6, to June 13, 1745; From June 13, to June 20, 1745; From June 20, to June 27, 1745; From June 27, to July 4, 1745.

RUN away June 4, from the Subscriber, a Servant Man, named William Vepon, about 50 Years of Age, short of Stature, had his Head shaved, a large red Nose, and when he drinks there seems to be a Stoppage in his Throat; by Trade a Weaver: Had on a Cloth Coat, with white Metal Buttons, and a brown Serge Coat too long for him, Leather Breeches, checked Trowsers. Whoever takes up and secures said Servant, so that his Master may have him again, shall have Thirty Shillings Reward, paid by Anthony Lee, or Joseph Gray, at the Conestogo Waggon, Philadelphia.
The Pennsylvania Gazette, June 6, 1745; June 13, 1745; June 20, 1745.

RUn away, on the 22d of May last, from William Williams, of Radnor Township, Chester County, an Irish Servant Man, named John Carrel, about 26 Years of Age, short, thick, and well set, and mark'd on the Left hand with Powder: Had on when he went away, a white Cloth Coat, white Cotton Jacket, Check Drawer, blue Stockings, and peek Toed Shoes. He has taken his Wife with him, an Irish Woman; she is short, thick, and of a dark Complexion; and had on when she went away, a brown Linsey Wolsey Gown, and a black Hat, shagg'd below with blue. Whoever secures the above Runaways, so that the Subscriber may have them again, shall have Five Pounds Reward for both, and reasonable Charges,
   paid by WILLIAM WILLIAMS.
N. B. The Woman perhaps may go either by the Name of Mary Umphrey, Cochran, or Carrel.
The Pennsylvania Gazette, June 6, 1745; June 13, 1745; June 20, 1745.

RUN away on the 11th Instant, from Henry Fagan, of Marple Township, Chester County, an English Servant Man, named William Morgan, aged about 37 years, middle Stature, dark Complexion, full Mouth, broken Teeth, and black Beard: Had on an old brown Jacket, Homespun Shirt, new Worsted Cap, old Hat, Homespun Trowsers, new blue Worsted Stockings, old Shoes. Whoever secures the said Servant, so that his Master may have him again, shall have Three Pounds Reward and reasonable Charges,
   paid by Henry Fagan.
N.B. He lately followed Flatting up Delaware.
The Pennsylvania Gazette, June 6, 1745; June 13, 1745. See *The Pennsylvania Gazette*, January 21, 1746.

Philadelphia, June 3 1745.
RUN-away this Day from Augustin Stillman, an Apprentice Lad named John Turner, a Shoemaker by Trade, and speaks thro' his Nose, he is a little short, thick set Fellow, about 18 Years of Age, of a Brown Complexion, and his Hair off: Had on when he went away a light blue Drugat Coat, with broad metal Buttons, brown linnen Jacket and Breeches, blue and white worsted Stockings, old Shoes, a Garlix Linnen Shirt, and a felt Hat. Whoever takes up and secures the said Apprentice so that his Master may have him again, shall receive Twenty Shillings reward from   Augustin Stillman.

The Pennsylvania Journal, or, Weekly Advertiser, June 6, 1745; June 13, 1756; June 20, 1745; June 27, 1745; July 11, 1745; July 25, 1745; August 1, 1745; August 8, 1745; August 15, 1745; August 22, 1745; August 29, 1745; September 5, 1745; September 12, 1745.

Philadelphia, June 15. 1745.
RUN away on Thursday last, from Joseph Beaks, *of this City, Drayman, an English Servant Man, named* Richard Daniels. *He is a short thick, downlooking, well set Fellow, much pitted with the small Pox, his Hair cut off, chews Tobacco, goes a little Limping, occasion'd by the Kick of a Horse, is given to Drinking, and may have chang'd his Name. Had on when he went away, an old Pea Jacket, old Hat, Ozenbrigs Shirt and Trowsers, and good Shoes. Whoever takes up and secures the said Servant, so that his Master may have him again, shall have* Three Pounds *Reward, and reasonable Charges, paid by*   Joseph Beaks.

The Pennsylvania Gazette, June 20, 1745; June 27, 1745; July 4, 1745; July 11, 1745; July 18, 1745; July 25, 1745.

RUN away the 16th Instant, from Thomas Shipley, of Ridley Township, Chester County, an Irish Servant Man, named Lawrence Soward, about 20 Years of Age, a thick, well set, clumsey Fellow, smooth fac'd, no Beard, fresh coloured, and wears short blackish curled Hair. He run away once before, and went on board a Privateer, but proving cowardly, only got some French Cloaths, which he has taken with him; also a Fur Hat half wore, two Caps, one Cotton, and the other Worsted, some ordinary thin Shirts, a blue Linnen Coat, with Slash Sleeves, striped Jacket and Trowsers, with several other thin Cloaths, such as Sailors use, four or five Pair of Stockings, and good Peektoed Shoes. Whoever takes up said Servant, and secures him, so that his Master may have him again, shall have Fifty Shillings Reward, and reasonable Charges, paid by   Thomas Shipley.

The Pennsylvania Gazette, June 20, 1745; June 27, 1745; July 4, 1745.

RUN away the 18th of June last, from Joseph James, of Willistown, in Chester County, an Irish Servant Man, named John Whellen; he is a tall slender Fellow, somewhat marked with the Small -ox, and has light brown Hair: Had on when he went away a brown Jacket, with Brass Buttons, a striped Linnen Jacket, and a new Pair of Shoes, seamed round the Quarters. Whoever secures the said Servant, so that his Master may have him again, shall have THREE POUNDS Reward, paid by me JOSEPH JAMES.

N. B. he passed over the River into the Jerseys, at Cooper's Ferry, the 19th Instant.

The Pennsylvania Gazette, June 27, 1745; July 4, 1745; July 11, 1745.

RUN away the 17th of June last, from William Hartley, living in Charles-Town, Chester County, a Servant Man, named Peter Fowler, aged about 22 Years, and born in Ireland: Had on when he went away a brown Linsey Coat, with Pewter Buttons, homespun Trowsers and Shirt, new strong Shoes, his Hair black and short, if not cut off. Whoever takes up and secures the said Servant, shall have THREE POUNDS Reward, and reasonable Charges, paid by said William Hartley, or Joseph Goodwin, Bookbinder, in Black-Horse-Alley, Philadelphia.

N. B. the said Servant hath been in the Province near 4 Years, but by running away, and other Misdemeanours, hath yet upwards of 4 Years to serve, before this Charge.

The Pennsylvania Gazette, June 27, 1745; July 4, 1745. See *The Pennsylvania Gazette*, February 24, 1743, *The Pennsylvania Journal, or, Weekly Advertiser*, June 27, 1745, *The Pennsylvania Gazette*, March 3, 1747, and *The Pennsylvania Gazette*, April 9, 1747.

RUn away on the 17th Instant from William Hartley, living in Charlestown, Chester County, a Servant Man, named Peter Powler, aged about 22 ears, and born in Ireland: Had on when he went, a brown Linsey Coat, with Pewter Buttons, Homespun Trowsers and Shirt, new Strong Shoes, his Hair black and short, if not cut off.

Whoever takes up and secures the said Servant, shall have Three Pounds Reward, and reasonable Charges paid by said William Hartley, or Joseph Goodwin, Bookbinder in Black Horse Alley, Philadelphia.

N. B. The said Servant hath been in the Province near 4 Years, but by running away, and other Misdemeanours, hath yet upwards of 4 Years to serve, before this Charge.

The Pennsylvania Journal, or, Weekly Advertiser, June 27, 1745; July 4, 1745; July 11, 1745; July 18, 1745; July 25, 1745; August 1, 1745.

See *The Pennsylvania Gazette*, February 24, 1743, *The Pennsylvania Gazette*, June 27, 1745, *The Pennsylvania Gazette*, March 3, 1747, and *The Pennsylvania Gazette*, April 9, 1747, for Fowler.

RUN away, on the 6th Instant, from John Nelson, of Philadelphia, a Scotch Servant Man, named William M'Call, about 40 Years of Age, of a red Complexion, tall and well-set, by Trade a Carpenter: Had on when he went away greyish Apparel, and a Worsted Cap. Whoever takes up and secures said Servant, so that his Master may have him again, shall have Twenty Shillings Reward, and reasonable Charges,
    paid by *JOHN NELSON.*
The Pennsylvania Gazette, July 18, 1745.

RUN away, on the 22d of January last, from Joel Bailey, of West Marlborough, Chester County, an Irish Servant Lad, named Dennis Crowley, about 16 Years of Age, of low Stature, sandy Complexion, much freckled, Down-look'd, pretty well set, and has a good deal of the Brogue: Had on when he went away an old Freeze Coat, too big for him, a Flannel Jacket, Tow Shirt and Trowsers, old Stockings, good Shoes, and a Felt Hat. Whoever takes up and secures said Servant, so that his Master may have him again, shall receive Four Pounds Reward Currency of the Province where taken, and reasonable Charges, from JOEL BAILEY.
N. B. 'Tis supposed he is gone on board a Privateer.
The Pennsylvania Gazette, July 25, 1745; August 1, 1745.

RUN away from Samuel Butcher, of Moreland, Philadelphia County, the 19th of July last, a Servant Lad, named John Hughs, about 15 Years of Age, of brown Complexion, has short Hair, and is small of Stature: Had on when he went away a homespun Shirt and Trowsers, and old Hat. Whoever takes and secures said Lad, so that his Master may have him again, shall have *Thirty Shillings* Reward, and reasonable Charges,
    paid by *Samuel Butcher* and *Joseph James.*
The Pennsylvania Gazette, August 1, 1745; August 8, 1745; August 15, 1745.

STole, the 28th of July last, from Benjamin Harvey, of Maxfield Township, Bucks County, sundry Sorts of Goods, viz. a Coat and Vest of Woollen Drugget, lightish Colour; a Worsted Drugget Coat, of two Colours, blue and Sassafrass, half trimmed; a brownish Great-coat, pretty much wore, with

Brass Buttons; also a Hunting-saddle and Bridle, the Saddle had white Plush Housings, with blue Orris; also a Pocket-book of red Turkey Leather, with Philadelphia writ on it, and Twenty Shillings in it; and a Pair of Buckskin Breeches, with Brass Buttons.

And from Anthony Tate, of Newtown, was stole at the same Time, a sorrel pacing Horse, about 14 Hands high, a Star in his Forehead longer than common, has a Lump on the near side of his Pole much like a Pole-Evil, his Hind-feet white, shod before, branded I R on his near Thigh, and delights to Gallop rather than Pace. 'Tis supposed the above Goods and Horse are stole by a Man who calls himself John Righby, and says he came from Cheshire, in England; he's about 5 Feet 9 Inches high, slender Body, long Nose, fresh Complexion, pretty much given to Drinking, and says he was lately taken by the Spaniards.

Whoever secures the Thief so that the Owners may have their Things again, shall have Four Pounds Reward,

     paid by *Benjamin Harvey*, and *Anthony Tate*.

The Pennsylvania Gazette, August 1, 1745; August 8, 1745. See *The Pennsylvania Gazette*, August 15, 1745, and *The Pennsylvania Gazette*, May 8, 1746.

RUN away from on board the Brigantine Rebecca, William Childs Commander, on the 27th of July last, one John Thompson, a lusty thick Fellow, about 5 Feet 8 Inches high, smooth and full faced, and very talkative: Had on when he went away a dark brown Wig, a blue Waistcoat, a Pair of Check Trowsers, with Fringes, and pretends to be a Surgeon. Whoever takes up and secures said John Thompson, and brings him to Charles Edgar, Joseph Marks, or Archibald Montgomery, shall have Five Pounds Reward, and reasonable Charges.

The Pennsylvania Gazette, August 1, 1745; August 8, 1745; August 15, 1745; *The Pennsylvania Journal, or, Weekly Advertiser*, August 1, 1745; August 8, 1745; August 15, 1745; August 22, 1745; August 29, 1745; September 5, 1745; September 12, 1745; September 19, 1745. Minor differences between the papers.

RUN away the 27th of July last, from John Harper, of the Mannor of Moreland, Philadelphia County, a Servant Man, named Francis Kanton, about 22 Years of Age, middle sized, smooth faced, and little Beard: Had on when he went away a red Jacket, home spun new Shirt, Trowsers, patched on the Knees, Peek-toed Shoes, with Buckles of different Sorts, an old Felt Hat,

and old Linnen Cap. Whoever takes up and secures said Servant, so that his Master may have him again, shall have *Thirty Shillings* Reward, and reasonable Charges,
           paid by   JOHN HARPER.
The Pennsylvania Gazette, August 1, 1745; August 8, 1745; August 15, 1745.

RUN away, the 17th of July last, from William Macarslon, in the Township of Laycock, Lancaster County, an Irish Servant Man, named William Carmichael, about 30 Years of Age, or upwards, five Foot ten Inches high, and stoops a good deal, is much pitted with the Small-pox, of a fair Complexion, very talkative, and will probably change his Name; he pretends to know something of several Trades, but knows nothing of any, and is very much addicted to Lying and Swearing: had on when he went away an old brown Coat, coarse Trowsers and Shirt, old Shoes, an old Felt Hat, and wears his own Hair. Whoever takes up and secures said servant, so that his Master may have him again, shall have Forty Shillings Reward, and reasonable Charges, paid by   WILLIAM MACARSLON.
The Pennsylvania Gazette, August 1, 1745; August 8, 1745; August 15, 1745.

RUN away, on the 20th of July last, from Samuel Richey, of Philadelphia, Weaver, an Irish Servant Man, named James Davis, by Trade a Weaver, tall of Stature, between 30 and 40 Years of Age, thin and pale, of a yellowish Complexion, having lately been sick: Had on a pale Wig, a blue Coat daubed with Tar, Fustian Breeches, coarse Yarn bluish Stockings, and thick Shoes, new soal'd.
    Whoever takes up and secures said Servant, so that his Master may have him again, shall have Forty Shillings Reward, and reasonable Charges,
           paid by   SAMUEL RICHEY.
The Pennsylvania Gazette, August 1, 1745; August 8, 1745; August 15, 1745. The second ad only begins "RUN away, on Saturday the 20th Instant...."

RUN away, on the 12th Instant, from Enos Lewis, of the Township of North-Wales, Philadelphia County, an Irish Servant Lad, named John Macmullen, about 17 years of Age, pitted with the Small-pox, of slender Stature, and has short black Hair: Had on when he went away, an old brownish Linsey Coat, Home spun Breeches and Shirt, Stockings, and old Shoes, torn behind, an old Hat, with little Brim, and sometimes wears a Cotton Handkerchief about his

Head. Whoever takes up the said Servant, and brings him to Master, or secures him in any Goal, so that he may be had again, shall have Forty Shillings Reward, and reasonable Charges,
          paid by   ENOS LEWIS.
The Pennsylvania Gazette, August 15, 1745; August 22, 1745; August 29, 1745.

MAde his Escape, on the 7th Instant, in the Evening, from Anthony Tate, near Newtown Goal, Bucks County, one John Ridgway, born in Cheshire, about 40 Years of Age, 5 Feet 9 Inches high, well-set, black curled Hair, ruddy Complexion, long Visage, high Nose, and a Learing Down Look, is pretty much given to Drinking, and says he was lately taken by the Spaniards: Had on when he went away an old Hat, Oznabrigs Jacket, Home-spun Shirt and Trowsers, and Peek-toed Shoes, almost new. Whoever secures said Ridgway, so as he may be brought to Justice, shall have Fifty Shillings Reward,   paid by   ANTHONY TATE.
N. B. He was lately advertised in the Pennsylvania Gazette for Felony, and taken, but since made his Escape.
The Pennsylvania Gazette, August 15, 1745; August 22, 1745. See *The Pennsylvania Gazette*, August 1, 1745, and *The Pennsylvania Gazette*, May 8, 1746.

                        Philadelphia, August 22. 1745.
TAken up on Suspicion, and now in the Workhouse, a tall slim Fellow, who calls himself John White; he is six Feet and one Inch high with his Shoes on, pitted with the Small pox, between 20 *and* 30 *Years of Age, is a very great Liar, tells many different Stories, and will not tell from whence he came, nor to whom he belongs; his Hair has been lately cut, and is of a dark brown Colour. His Master is desired to come or send for him in one Month after the Date hereof.*   ABRAHAM SHELLEY, *Keeper.*
The Pennsylvania Gazette, August 22, 1745; August 29, 1745; September 5, 1745.

RUN away on the 19th Instant, from Arthur Murphy, of Bucks County, in the Falls Township, at Pensbury, a Servant Man, named Richard Loyd, about 26 Years of Age, and says he is a Welshman, he is a short Fellow, with a sharp Nose, has a Downlook, and Warts on his Left-hand: Had on when he went away an old Coat, very much patched, with Leather Buttons, a brown Holland Jacket, cut under the Arms, with a short Flannel Jacket, laced, a Homespun Shirt, and Oznabrigs Drawers, new Shoes, and a Pair of Worsted Stockings, an old Hat, and a Linnen Cap. Whoever takes up the said Servant,

and secures him, so that he may be had again, shall have Three Pounds Reward, and reasonable Charges,
        paid by   ARTHUR MURPHY.
The Pennsylvania Gazette, August 22, 1745; August 29, 1745; September 5, 1745.

                                Philadelphia, September 12, 1745.
RUN away, on Monday last, from Aylmer Grevill, on Society Hill, a Country-born Servant Man, named Philip Myers, well set, short stature, full Faced, and fair Complexion: Had on a blue Coat, with round Sleeves, white Shirt, fine homespun Trowsers, and good Yarn Stockings, good Shoes, and small castor Hat. Whoever secures said Servant in any County Goal, shall have Forty Shillings Reward, and reasonable Charges,
        paid by   ALYMER GREVILL.
The Pennsylvania Gazette, September 12, 1745; September 19, 1745; September 26, 1745.

RUN away on the 10*th Instant from the Subscriber, in New Hanover Township, Philadelphia County, a Dutch Servant Man, named Caril Witt, a Smith by Trade, between Thirty and Forty Years of Age, middle sized, well set, and fair Complexioned: Had on a bluish coloured Coat, homespun striped Jacket, a fine white Shirt, and Shoes and Stockings. Whoever secures said Servant, so as his Master may have him again, shall have Forty Shillings Reward, and reasonable Charges,*
        paid by   *PETER CONRAD.*
N. B. He has taken with him a Boy about Fifteen Years of Age.
The Pennsylvania Gazette, September 12, 1745; September 19, 1745.

RUn-away, on the 12th of this Instant from Henry Teringer, of Hanover Township in Falconar Swamp, Pennsylvania, a Dutch Servant Man named Rudolph Mick, about 35 Years of age, of middle Stature and brown Complexion, his Right Hand lamed by a former Wound. He had on when he went away, a Linsey-Woolsey brownish Jacket, a short red Jacket without Sleves, good Leather Breeches, and a Felt Hat. He came in last Fall, and speaks little or no English.
Whoever takes up and secures he said Servant so that his Master may have him again, shall have Four Pounds Reward, and all reasonable Charges,
        paid by   HENRY TERINGER.   Sept. 17. 1745.
The American Weekly Mercury, From September 12, to September 19, 1745; From September 19, to September 26, 1745; From September 26,

to October 3, 1745; From October 3, to October 10, 1745; From October 10, to October 17, 1745; From October 24, to October 31, 1745.

RUN away on the 28th of September, a Servant Girl, named Hannah Hollington, about 16 Years of Age, fair Complexion, some what slim, with curled flaxen Hair, has a small cut upon her Chin: Had on a blue quilted Stuff Petticoat, no Gown, Shoes, nor Stockings: Says she was born in Spain, but came from Dublin, in the Draper, Capt. Basnet. Whoever secures the said Servant, so that she may be had again, shall have Twenty Shillings Reward,
paid by   JOHN DOUGLAS.
N. B. All Persons are forewarn'd to entertain her at their Peril.
The Pennsylvania Gazette, October 3, 1745.

RUN away the 1st of October, 1745, from Peter Browne, at the Old Ferry, in Philadelphia; two Servant Lads, the one named William Millord, about 20 Years of Age, fresh Complexion, down Look, well set, and of middle Stature: Had on when he went away, a green Jacket, Oznabrigs Shirts and Trowsers, new Stockings, and a Pair of Pumps, with large Buckles. The other named John Curtis, about Seventeen or Eighteen Years of Age, Five Feet high, brown Complexion, pitted with the Small Pox, down Look, and stoops a little in his Shoulders: Had on when he went away, the same Sort of Apparel as the other. Whoever takes up and secures the said Runaways, that their Master may have them again, shall have Forty Shillings Reward, for each, and reasonable Charges , paid by   PETER BROWNE.
N. B. They are both gone in Company, and took with them 2 blue Duffield Jackets, lined with red, and Brass Buttons; with sundry other Sorts of Apparel, and may alter their Dress.
The Pennsylvania Gazette, October 3, 1745.

RUN-away on the 16th Instant from Daniel Hister of old Cusaphen, a Servant Man named *John Murphy*, aged about 20 Years, of middle Stature, black short Hair, but wears a white Whig: Had on a blue great Coat, a red Jacket, and a white and blue Woolen Jacket under that, a check'd Shirt, Kersey Breeches very Greasy, grey Stockings, and good Shoes.
Whoever takes up and secures the said Servant so that his Master may have his again shall have Forty Shillings Reward and reasonable Charges
paid by   Daniel Hister.
The Pennsylvania Journal, or, Weekly Advertiser, October 10, 1745; October 24, 1745; October 31, 1745; November 7, 1745; November 14, 1745; November 21, 1745; November 28, 1745; December 12, 1745;

December 19, 1745; December 24, 1745; December 31, 1745; January 7, 1745.

October 10. 1745.
RUN-away, on the 7th of this Instant, from Francis Morgan of Carnarvon, in Lancaster County, a Servant Man named John Cook, about 19 Years of Age, had on when he went away, a bluish colour'd Linsey Coat, blue Cloth Breeches, and white Stockings.

Whoever takes up the said Servant and brings him to his Master, shall have Thirty Shillings and reasonable Charges,
         paid by   Francis Morgan.

The American Weekly Mercury, From October 10, to October 17, 1745; From October 24, to October 31, 1745; From November 14, to November 21, 1745; From November 21, to November 28, 1745; From November 28, to December 5, 1745; From December 5, to December 10, 1745; From December 17, to December 24, 1745; From December 24, to January 1, 1745; From January 8, to January 15, 1745.

RUN away on Sunday the sixth Instant, from Joseph Rogers, of Vincent Township, Chester County, an Irish Servant Lad, named James Ray, about 18 Years of Age, red Complexion, much pitted with the Small pox, and very black curled Hair: Had on when he went away, an old Felt Hat, Linsey Woolsey Cinnamon coloured Coat, with Brass Buttons, and Slash Sleeves lined with Tow Cloath, Tow Trowsers, Flax Shirt, and Silver Buttons in his Sleeves, old Shoes, and white Stockings. Whoever secures said Servant, so as his Master may have him again, shall have Thirty Shillings Reward, and reasonable Charges,   *paid by*   *JOSEPH ROGERS.*

The *Pennsylvania Gazette*, October 17, 1745; October 24, 1745; October 31, 1745. See *The Pennsylvania Gazette*, July 10, 1746, and *The Pennsylvania Gazette*, November 24, 1748.

ABsented himself last Night, from John Howell, of the City of Philadelphia, Tanner, a Servant Man, named James Gardner, about Thirty Years of Age, a Skinner or Leather Dresser by Trade: He is of a pretty fresh Complexion, middle Stature, and round and full bodied: He had on, and with him, a dark homespun Coat, with flat Metal Buttons, a half worn Hat, a Worsted Cap, a light coloured Cloth Jacket, with Pewter Buttons, and dark dyed Leather Breeches, half worn, with metal Buttons, covered with Leather, new black and white Yarn Stockings, good Shoes, two homespun Shirts, and a Pair of short Trowsers. Whoever takes up said Servant, and brings him home, or

secures him any Goal, so that his Master may have him again, shall have Five Pounds reward, and reasonable Charges,
    paid by JOHN HOWELL. Nov. 11. 1745.
The Pennsylvania Gazette, November 14, 1745; November 21, 1745; November 28, 1745; December 6, 1745; December 10, 1745; December 17, 1745; December 24, 1745; December 31, 1745; January 14, 1746.

RUN away from John Hackett, of New-garden, Chester County, on the 24th of October last, an Irish Servant Man, named Daniel Ryan, about 26 Years of Age, a lusty, well-set Fellow: Had on when he went away, a Cloth coloured Cotton and Linnen Coat, a fine white Shirt, a Pair of fine white Drawers, brown Yarn Stockings, new Shoes, a half worn Castor Hat; he has brown bushy Hair, and a little of the Brogue on his Tongue. Whoever takes up and secures said Servant, so as his Master may have him again, shall have Forty Shillings Reward, and reasonable Charges. All Masters of Vessels are forbid taking him away at their Peril. *JOHN HACKETT.*
The Pennsylvania Gazette, November 14, 1745; November 21, 1745; November 28, 1745.

           Philadelphia, November 21, 1745.
RUN away on Sunday Morning, last, from Matthias Lamey, of Whiteland, in Chester County, an English Servant Lad, named William Thomas, about 17 Years of Age, well set, but of middle Stature, squint-eyed, and dark Hair. Had on a grey homespun Cloth Jacket and Breeches, Tow Cloth Shirt, new Shoes with Strings in them, grey Yarn Stockings, and a red Cotton Handkerchief. Whoever takes up and secures the said Servant, so that his Master may have him again, shall have Twenty Shillings Reward, and reasonable Charges,
    paid by MATTHIAS LAMEY.
The Pennsylvania Gazette, November 21, 1745; November 28, 1745; December 6, 1745; December 10, 1745; December 17, 1745. See *The Pennsylvania Gazette*, December 15, 1743.

RUN away November 17, 1745, from Ann Burn, an Irish Servant Man, named Bartholomew Durham, about 20 Years of Age, of middle Stature, fair Complexion, and has a Scar on one of his Hands just above his Thumb, with a Dimple in his Chin: Had on when he went away, a Felt Hat, light coloured Wig brown Holland Shirt, light coloured Kersey Coat, green Plush Jacket, and a blue Serge Jacket under it, with light coloured Plush Breeches, white Cotton Stockings, and old Shoes; his Buckles are of different Sorts, and his Studs in his Sleeves are not Fellows. Whoever secures the said Servant , and

brings him to the Indian King, in Philadelphia, shall have Five Pounds Reward, and reasonable Charges,
        paid by   Ann Burn, or Peter Robeson.
N. B. He is a pretty good Scholar, and understands the Seafaring Business, and probably may get off by Sea.
The Pennsylvania Gazette, November 21, 1745.

RUN away from the Brigt. Kouh Kan, on Monday the 18th Instant, a Welsh Servant Man, named Francis Williams: Had on when he went away, a brown Coat of Country Cloth, a blue Jacket and Breeches, check'd Shirt, new Shoes, new Hat, and a brown Wig: He speaks very bad English, laughs when he speaks, and was marked under the Chin with an Evil when young; about 5 Foot 9 Inches high: He carried with him, a new Bible, and sundry other Things. Any Person that brings him to James Templeton, at Mr. Alexander Lang's Store, shall have Forty Shillings Reward, and reasonable Expences,
        paid by   JAMES TEMPLETON.
The Pennsylvania Gazette, November 21, 1745. See *The American Weekly Mercury*, From December 10, to December 17, 1745.

RUN away on the Twentieth Instant, from Richard Naylor, of Montgomery, Philadelphia County, a Scotch Servant Lad, named John Kensey, aged about 19 Years, of middle Stature, Pock-marked, with long thick brownish Hair, and speaks good English. Had on when he went away, a double breasted Cloth Serge Jockey Coat, with Jacket and Breeches of the same, the Clothes of a sort of Lead Colour, a good new Castor Hat, two Pairs blue Stockings, one Yarn, the other Worsted, two Pairs Shoes, one Peek-toed, the other Cowmouth, a fine Shirt, and Silver Studs in his Sleeves, a Stock with a Silver Buckles in it, also a red Handkerchief, with Spots in it. Whoever secures said Servant, so that his Master may have him again, shall have Twenty Shillings Reward, and reasonable Charges,
        paid by   *RICHARD NAYLOR.*
The Pennsylvania Gazette, November 28, 1745; December 6, 1745; December 10, 1745. See *The Pennsylvania Gazette*, December 17, 1745. Later ads show he ran away "*on the 20th of last Month....*"

RUN away, the 26th of October last, from Isaac Whitelock, of the Borough of Lancaster, an Irish Servant, named Roger Farrall, aged about Forty-five Years, and is Five Feet Six Inches high, of a ruddy Complexion, thick Lipped, speaks pretty fast, wears his own Hair, of a brownish Colour, and short, and is much addicted to Drinking: Had on when he went away, a brown Cloth

Coat, and red Jacket, a Pair of Buckskin Breeches, and black Yarn Stockings. Whoever takes up said servant, and secures him, so that his Master may have him again, shall have Twenty Shillings Reward, and reasonable Charges, paid by   ISAAC WHITELOCK.
The Pennsylvania Gazette, December 6, 1745; December 10, 1745; December 17, 1745; December 24, 1745; December 31, 1745.

Philadelphia, December 6, 1745.
*RUN away, on the 27th of last Month, from the Ship Catharine, Joseph Smith, Master, John Mullin, an Apprentice Irish Lad, about 17 Years of Age, of low Stature, but well set, very thick Legg'd, and much freckled: Had on when he went away, a Half-worn brown Kersey Jacket, Breeches of the same, Trowsers, an old Felt Hat, and worsted Cap, Check Shirt, grey Stockings, and good Shoes. Whoever takes up and secures said Apprentice Lad, so that he may be had again, shall have Fifty Shillings Reward, and reasonable Charges, paid by   Cunningham and Gardner,
Merchants in Philadelphia.*
N. B. As he is a Sailor, 'tis probable he may offer his Service to some Ship master; therefore all Masters of Vessels are forbid carrying him off at their Peril.
The Pennsylvania Gazette, December 6, 1745; December 10, 1745; December 17, 1745; December 24, 1745; December 31, 1745.

RUN-away, on the second of this Inst. from Joseph Rogger, of Vinsent Township, in Chester County, a Servant Lad named James Rea, about 18 Years of age, small of Stature, with curled Hair. He had on when he went away, a light colour'd Coat with hardly any Buttons on it, old torn Trowsers, no Stockings, old stitch-toed Shoes, and an old Hat. He took some Womens Apparel with him, which it is supposed he will offer to sale. [*sic*]
Whoever takes up and secures the said Servant so that his Master may have him again, shall have Thirty Shillings Reward and reasonable Charges, paid by   Joseph Rogger. December 10. 1745.
The American Weekly Mercury, From December 5, to December 10, 1745; From December 10, to December 17, 1745; From December 17, to December 24, 1745; From December 24, to January 1, 1745.

RUN away, the 20th of November last, from William Clayton, of Chichester, Chester County, an Irish Servant Man, named William Reardon, aged about Twenty-five Years, is a thick, well-set Fellow, full Fac'd, fresh Complexion, stutters in his Speech, and has much of the Brogue: He has been out on a

Privateering Cruize from Philadelphia; and had on when he went away, an Olive coloured Coat and Jacket (the Coat very greasy along the fore Part) Leather Breeches, with a Piece of the Fore-part sewed in with a waxed Thread or End, Cotton Cap or Wig, and a good Beaver Hat. He endeavoured to procure a Pass, and may have a false One, and is supposed to have gone towards Susquahannah. Whoever secures said Servant, so that his Master may have him again, shall have Forty Shillings Reward, and reasonable Charges, paid by WILLIAM CLAYTON.
The Pennsylvania Gazette, December 10, 1745; December 17, 1745; December 24, 1745; December 31, 1745. See *The Pennsylvania Gazette*, December 16, 1746, *The Pennsylvania Gazette*, June 4, 1747, and *The Pennsylvania Gazette*, July 30, 1747.

RUN away from *John M''Queen* in *Derry* Township, *Lancaster* County, an Irish Servant Man named Barnaby Grady, about seventeen Years of Age well set, smooth round Face, some what of a heavy Countenance, hath much of the Brogue. Had on when he went away a brown Coat, blue Jacket and Breeches, check Shirt, white Stockings, good Shoes with Buckles, he wears a dark brown Wigg, some what like his own Hair, with a felt Hat. Whoever takes up the said Servant, so that his Master may have him again shall have Thirty Shillings Reward
paid by John M''Queen.
The Pennsylvania Journal, or, Weekly Advertiser, December 12, 1745; December 19, 1745; December 24, 1745; January 14, 1745.

RUN-away, on Sunday the 15th Inst. from the Subscriber, a Welch Servant Man named Francis Williams; had on when he went away, a brown Country Cloth Coat, blue Jacket and Breeches, a check Shirt, new Hat and Worsted Cap, new Shoes and grey Worsted Stockings. He speaks very bad English and always Laughs when he speaks; he is about five Feet nine Inches high, and is marked under the Chaps [sic] with an Evil when young. It is suppos'd he was advis'd away by a Waterman, as he was seen in Company with a strange Man who had on a red Great Coat and Trowsers Seaman like.
Whoever takes up and secures the said Servant so that he may be had again, or gives Notice to Mr. Alexander Lang, Merchant, in Philadelphia, shall have Forty Shillings Reward and reasonable Charges,
paid by James Templeton. Philadelphia, December 17. 1745.
The American Weekly Mercury, From December 10, to December 17, 1745; From December 17, to December 24, 1745. See *The Pennsylvania Gazette*, November 21, 1745.

This is to inform Richard Naylor, of Montgomery Township, Philadelphia County, that his Servant Man, lately advertised in this Paper, is in Custody at Annapolis.

    Pennsylvania Gazette, December 17, 1745. See *The Pennsylvania Gazette*, November 28, 1745.

1746

    Philadelphia, January 7, 1745,6.
RUN away, the 28th of December last, from Samuel Morris, of Whitemarsh, Philadelphia County, a Servant Man, named John Codgdill, a short Fellow, down looked, and coarse Complexion: Had on a Great Coat, a homespun Cloth Vest, with flat Metal Buttons, and it is probable he may change his Name: His Employment was driving a Team of Horses. He has taken with him one of the Horses, of a brown Colour, with a Star in his Forehead, a good Draught Horse, a natural Pacer, and shod before.

    Whoever takes up the said Servant, and secures him, so that his said Master may have him again, shall have Forty Shillings Reward, and if the Horse likewise, Three Pounds,
          paid by   SAMUEL MORRIS.

    The Pennsylvania Gazette, January 7, 1746; January 14, 1746; January 21, 1746; January 28, 1746. See *The Pennsylvania Journal, or, Weekly Advertiser*, January 7, 1746, and *The American Weekly Mercury*, From January 1, to January 8, 1746.

RUN-away, on the 28th of this Instant, from Samuel Morris at Whitemarsh in Philadelphia County, a Servant Man, named John Cdgdill, a short little siz'd Fellow, down look and Coarse Complexion, had on when he went away an old felt Hat, a great Coat, a homespun Cloath Vest with flat mettle buttons, probably he may change his Name, his Imployment was driving a Team of Horses, he has also taken one of the Horses of a brown Colour, with a Star in his Forehead, a good draft Horse, natural Pacer, and shod before. Whoever will take up the said Servant and secures him so that his said Master may have him again shall have Forty Shillings, and if the Horse likewise, Three Pounds Reward
          paid by   Samuel Morris. *Philad. December* 31. 1745.

    The Pennsylvania Journal, or, Weekly Advertiser, January 7, 1746; January 14, 1746; January 21, 1746; January 28, 1746; February 4, 1746; February 11, 1746; February 18, 1746; February 26, 1746; March 4, 1746; March 11, 1746; March 25, 1746; March 27, 1746. All but the first ad show the name as "Codgdill". See *The Pennsylvania Gazette*,

January 7, 1746, and *The American Weekly Mercury*, From January 1, to January 8, 1746.

December 31. 1741.
RUn-away, on the 28th of this Instant, from Samuel Morris of White-Marsh, a Servant Man, named John Codgdill, a short little-sized Fellow, down look'd, and course Complexion. Had on when he went away, an old felt Hat, a great Coat, a Cloth Vest with flat Metal Buttons. It is probable he may change his Name. His imployment was driving a Team of Horses; he has also taken one of the Horses of a brown Colour, with a Star in his Forehead, a good draft Horse, a natural Pacer, and shod before.

Whoever will take up the said servant and secures him, so that his said Master may have him again, shall have Forty Shillings Reward and if the Horse likewise Three Pounds Reward,
       paid by   Samuel Morris.
The American Weekly Mercury, From January 1, to January 8, 1746; From January 8, to January 15, 1746; From January 15, to January 21, 1746; From January 21, to January 29, 1746. See *The Pennsylvania Gazette*, January 7, 1746, and *The Pennsylvania Journal, or, Weekly Advertiser*, January 7, 1746.

Philadelphia, January 14. 1745. [*sic*]
RUN away the 7th Instant from the Subscriber, in East Marlborough, a Servant Lad, named Joseph Orin, about 16 Years of Age: Had on when he went away, a brown coloured Jacket, a Pair of half-worn Buckskin Breeches, Yarn Stockings, footed with yellow above the Shoes, round Toed Shoes, and a Felt Hat. Whoever takes up and secures said Servant, so as he may be had again, shall have Thirty Shillings Reward, and reasonable Charges,
       paid by me   DANIEL MERCER.
N. B. *he has a false Pass, and has carried with him a Pillow Case or Wallet, with a Bible in it.*
The Pennsylvania Gazette, January 14, 1746; January 21, 1746; January 28, 1746.

STOLEN on the first of January, from Hezekiah Bye of Solebury in Bucks County, a Suit of dark brown Clothes, Coat, Jacket, and Breeches; a pair of Worsted Stockings of the same Colour; a fine Shirt, fine Hat, and some Money. One Lawrence Davis, has since been seen drest in the said Clothes; He is a little Man, with short black Hair, no Beard, about 24 Years of Age, born in England. Whoever secures the Thief, so that he be brought to Justice, shall have Thirty Shillings *Reward, and reasonable Charges,*
       paid by   HEZEKIAH BYE.

The Pennsylvania Gazette, January 14, 1746; January 21, 1746.

ON the 30th Day of November last, was committed to the Goal of this City, two persons, supposed to be Servants, both Irishmen: The one short and well-set, with short sandy Hair, wears a Wig, fresh Complexion, about 35 Years of Age. Had on, an old brown Cloth Waistcoat, a strip'd Holland one under it, Check Shirt, leather Breeches, Yarn Stockings, and old Shoes; he goes by the Name of John Basker. The other a slender Man, short black Hair, dark Complexion, about 21 Years of Age. Had on, a French Frize Coat, a light colour'd Drugget Waistcoat and Breeches, blue rib'd Stockings, and good Shoes; and goes by the Name of Thomas Butler.
    JOSEPH SCULL, Keeper.

The Pennsylvania Gazette, January 7, 1746; January 14, 1746; January 21, 1746.

Philadelphia, January 21, 1745-6.
RUN away, the 7th of December last, from the Privateer Ship Marlborough, Christopher Clymer, Commander, the seven following Sailors, who have each of them received Four Pounds Bounty Money, and Four Pounds Advance, and signed the Articles to go the Cruize, viz.

    WESTLOCK MACKENNY, Carpenter, a middle sized Fellow, smooth faced, thin Visage, and down looked, about Thirty-two Years of Age, and had on a light coloured Coat, and black Wig.

    JAMES GANTHONY, a tall, slim, round shoulder'd, ill looking Fellow, about Thirty-five Years of Age, and had on a green Jacket, and either Cap or Wig, the rest of his Clothes unknown.

    JOSEPH BRYAN, a tall swarthy Fellow, lame in his Left-hand, about Forty Years of Age, and had on a brown Greek Great Coat.

    FRANCIS HICKEY, short, and well set, Pock-pitted, about Twenty-four Years of Age, and had on a blue Coat, with Silver work'd Buttons, laced Hat, ruffled Shirt, and black Wig.

    THOMAS HUSBANDS, middle sized, and slender, swarthy Complexion, small black Eyes, very talkative, and speaks hoarse, about Twenty-three Years of Age, and commonly wears a brown Jacket and brown Wig.

    JOHN HAZELY, about Thirty Years of Age, is tall, generally wears a brown Jacket, and a Cap, and has lost two of his upper Fore-teeth.

    ROBERT HARRIS, about Forty Years of Age, is tall and lusty, very talkative, and has a large black Beard, his Clothes unknown.

    Whoever secures said Fellows, or any of them, in any Goal, so that the Owners of said Ship may have Satisfaction, or brings them to Philadelphia,

shall receive Three Pounds Reward for each Man, and reasonable Charges,
paid by   PETER BARD or JOHN HOWELL.

N. B. Mackenny and Ganthony are supposed to have gone towards Maryland; the others, we are well assured, are gone towards New York.
The Pennsylvania Gazette, January 21, 1746; January 28, 1746; February 4, 1746. See *The Pennsylvania Journal, or, Weekly Advertiser*, January 21, 1746.

RUN away Jan. 16, 1745-6, *from John Leadlie, of Bristol Township, Philadelphia County, a Servant Woman named Margaret Brown; she has large staring Eyes, has had four or five Children, and has left two behind her:* Had on when she went away, a dark coloured Bed Gown of Linsey, streek'd quilted Petticoat, paned one Pane Yellow and the other check'd with a large Check; a blue and white strip'd Apron, a Pair of Leather heel'd Shoes half worn, a Pair of blue Stockings new footed with Blue, a little brown Cloak without a Cape, a Cotton check'd Handkerchief, ty'd on her Head. Whoever takes and secures the said servant, so as her Master may have her again, shall have Twenty Shillings Reward, and all reasonable Charges,
paid by   JOHN LEADLIE.

The Pennsylvania Gazette, January 21, 1746; January 28, 1746; February 4, 1746. See *The Pennsylvania Gazette*, May 25, 1749.

Philadelphia, January 21, 1745-6.
RUN away, on the 8th Instant, from the Subscriber, in Marpole Township, Chester County, an English Servant Man, named William Morgan, aged 29, middle Stature, black, swarthy Complexion, full Mouth, Buck-tooth'd, is very apt to laugh at his own Discourse, and can talk the Welsh Language. Had on when he went away, an old Felt Hat, and Worsted Cap, a homespun brown Coat, with flat carved Metal Buttons, a Jacket much of the same Colour, with Brass Buttons, old Buckskin Breeches, old light coloured Yarn Stockings, and half worn Shoes, but had Boots, and may wear them.

Whoever takes up and secures said Servant, so that his Master may have him again, shall have Forty Shillings Reward, and reasonable Charges,
paid by   HENRY FAGAN.

N. B. 'Tis supposed that he is either gone over Brandywine, or into West-Jersey, and has a former Indenture with him, by which he may appear to be a free Man, but has been since bound by another.
The Pennsylvania Gazette, January 21, 1746; January 28, 1746. See *The Pennsylvania Gazette*, June 6, 1745.

RUN away, the 7th of December last from the Privateer Ship Marlborough, *Christopher Clymer*, Commander, the Seven following Sailors, who have each of them received Four Pounds Bounty, and Four Pounds advance, and signed the Articles to go the Cruize, *Viz.* WESTLOCK MACKENNY, Carpenter, a middle sized Fellow, smooth Face, thin Vissag'd, and down look'd, and about 32 Years of Age; and had on a light colour'd Coat and black Wigg JAMES GANTHONY, a tall slim round shoulder'd ill looking Fellow, about 35 Years of Age, had on a green Jacket, and either a Cap or a Wigg, the rest of his Cloaths unknown. JOSEPH BRYAN, tall and swarthy, aged about 40 Years, lame in his left hand, and had on a brown Greek great Coat. FRANCIS HICKEY, short, and well set, pock pitted, aged about 24 Years, had on a blew Coat, with Silver work'd Buttons, lac'd, a ruffled Shirt and black Wigg. THOMAS HUSBANDS, middle siz'd and slender, swarthy Complexion, small black Eyes, very talkative and speaks Hoarse, aged about 23 Years, generally wears a brown Jacket and brown Wigg. JOHN HAZEEY, about 30 Years of Age, tall, generally wears a brown Jacket and Cap, and has lost two of his upper fore Teeth. ROBERT HARRISS, aged about 40 Years, tall and lusty, very talkative, and has a large black Beard, his Cloaths unknown.

Whoever takes up and secures the said Fellows, or any of them, in any Goal, so that the Owners of said Ship may have Satisfaction, or brings them to Philadelphia, shall receive Three Pounds Reward for each Man, and reasonable Charges,
    paid by PETER BARD, JOHN HOWELL.

N. B. Mackenny and *Ganthony* is supposed to have gone towards *Maryland*, the others we are well assured are gone towards *New-York*.

The Pennsylvania Journal, or, Weekly Advertiser, January 21, 1746; January 28, 1746; February 4, 1746; February 11, 1746; February 18, 1746; February 25, 1746; March 4, 1746; March 11, 1746; March 25, 1746. See *The Pennsylvania Gazette*, January 21, 1746.

          Philadelphia, January 28. 1745-6.
RUN away, the 24th Instant, from George Walker, of Pykes's Land, Chester County, an Irish Servant Lad, named Bryan Ryley, about 18 Years of Age, full faced, short and well-set, has black Hair, and speaks very bad English: Had on when he went away, a blue grey Drugget Jacket, and a striped Linsey One under it, brown patched Breeches, brown Stockings, one of which has a blue Foot sewed to it, which comes up almost to the Calf, old round toed Shoes, and old Hat, cut like a Hunting Cap. Whoever takes up and secures said servant, so that his Master may have him again, shall have Twenty Shillings Reward, and reasonable Charges,
    paid by *GEORGE WALKER.*

The Pennsylvania Gazette, January 28, 1746; February 4, 1746; February 11, 1746.

Philadelphia, February 4. 1745-6.
RUN away on the 2d Instant, from George Correy, of New-London Township, Chester County, a Servant Man from Darbyshire in England, named John Carhalt. He talks North-country English, about 23 Years old, middle Stature, well set, short brown Hair, and fresh coloured: Had on when he went away, a light grey Broad-cloth Coat, red Jacket, new Leather Breeches, black die'd Stockings, and new Shoes. He has taken a Pocket Book with Thirty Pounds in Money, and other Papers. Whoever takes up and secures said servant, so that his Master may have him again, shall have Three Pounds Reward, and reasonable Charges,
    paid by *George Correy.*
N. B. The Clothes are almost new.
The Pennsylvania Gazette, February 4, 1746; February 11, 1746; February 18, 1746.

   Charles Town, Chester County, Pensilvania, February 10. 1745-6.
MAde his Escape, on Friday last, from the Constable in Donnegall, Lancaster County, one Samuel Prichard, taken for Forgery, counterfeit and most fraudulent Dealing; he lived some time past in this Township, but now had his Dwelling about eight Miles from John Harris's Ferry, on Susquehannah; he is of short Stature, well set, dark Complexion, large, black Eyebrows, ill look'd, rough Voice, and had with him a considerable Sum of Money, he got by his Forgery and Fraud; he had on when he made his Escape a new white Cloth Jockey Coat, with broad Metal Buttons, an old Pair of Boots, with the Feet covered, his Hair cut, and wears a white Cap. Whoever takes up and secures said Prichard , so as he may be brought to Justice, shall have TEN POUNDS Reward, paid by the Subscriber, living near James Trego's.
   JOHN DAVID.
N. B. He has a Bond from me for Twenty-two Pounds Ten Shillings, bearing Date, February 1. 1745-6. All Persons are hereby desired not to take an Assignment of it, it being obtained in the most fraudulent Manner.
The Pennsylvania Gazette, February 4, 1746; February 11, 1746; February 18, 1746; February 24, 1746. See *The American Weekly Mercury*, From February 11, to February 18, 1746.

   Charles-Town, Chester County in Pennsylvania, February 10. 1745,6.

Philadelphia, February 11, 1745-6.
RUN away, on the 4th of this Instant, from his Bail in Chester, an Irishman, named Edward Brogden, a House Carpenter by Trade, and about 25 Years of Age; he is low of Stature, well set, fair Complexion, has brown curl'd Har [*sic*] or a Wig: Had on a whitish Cloth Great-coat, with Brass Buttons, a blue Camblet Body coat, an old Diaper Jacket, with Leather Breeches, and a new Beaver Hat; his Shoe and Knee Buckles are Silver, and has Gold Sleeve Buttons; he rode on a white Stallion, about 14 hands High, in good Case, [*sic*] and a natural Pacer; and took with him a Bundle of Flesh coloured Broad cloth, and black Stuff for a jacket, besides Saddle Bags.

Whoever secures him, so that his Bail, the Subscriber, may bring him to Justice, shall have TEN POUNDS Reward, and reasonable Charges,
paid by   *JOHN HANLY.*

The Pennsylvania Gazette, February 11, 1746; February 18, 1746; February 25, 1746. See *The Pennsylvania Gazette*, March 15, to 27, 1746.

MAde his Escape, on Friday last, from the Constable in Donnegall, Lancaster County, one Samuel Prichard, taken for Forgery, Counterfeit and most fraudulent Dealing. He lived some time past in this Township, but now had his Dwelling about eight Miles from John Harris's Ferry on Susquehannah. He is of short Stature, well set, dark Complexion, large black Eyebrows, has an ill look, and his Voice course. He had with him a considerable Sum of Money, which he got by his Forgery and Fraud. Had on when he made his Escape, a new white Cloth Jockey Coat with broad Metal Buttons, an old pair of Boots with the Feet covered, his Hair cut off and wears a white Cap.

Whoever takes up and secures him, so as he may be brought to Justice, shall have Ten Pounds Reward, paid by the Subscriber, living near James Trego's.   JOHN DAVID.
P. S. He has a Bond from me for Twenty two Pounds Ten Shillings, bearing Date, Feb. 1. 1745,6. All Persons are hereby warn'd not to take an Assignment of it, it being obtain'd in the most fraudulent Manner.

The American Weekly Mercury, From February 11, to February 18, 1746; From February 11, to February 18, 1746; From February 18, to February 25, 1746; From February 25, to March 4, 1746; From March 4, to March 11, 1746; From March 11, to March 18, 1746; From March 18, to March 27, 1746. See *The Pennsylvania Gazette*, February 4, 1746.

RUN away from the Ship Westmoreland, John Dod Bonell, Commander, Richard Edwards, George Todder, John Pipe, Samuel Fields, John Jackson, William Gesson, and James Carroll, Mariners. The above Persons have all received advanced Wages, and absented themselves (as it is supposed) to go out in the Privateers. Whoever takes up the above named Mariners, and secures them in any Goal in this Province, shall have Three Pounds for each,
        paid by   WILLIAM PLUMSTED.
The Pennsylvania Gazette, February 25, 1746; March 4, 1746; March 11, 1746.

RUN-away the 24th Instant from *Hugh Mc'Mahon*, Cooper, of this City, a Servant Lad, named *Moses Horrom*, about 16 Years of Age, long visag'd, a little Freckel'd, and pitted with the Small Pox, with brown Hair; had on when he went away and old felt Hat, a light colour'd Duroy Coat much wore, a dark colour'd Jacket, with flat white mettal Buttons, Buck-skin Breeches with Brass Buttons, grey Yarn Stockings, and large Shoes with Buckles. If in a Hurrey he has a Stoppage in his Speech.
    Whoever takes up and secures the said Servant so that his Master may have him again, shall have Ten Shillings if taken within Ten Miles of this City, and if further Twenty Shillings, Reward and reasonable Charges
        paid by me   Hugh Mc'Mahon. *Philadelphia, Feb.* 25th. 1746.
The Pennsylvania Journal, or, Weekly Advertiser, February 25, 1746.

                      Philadelphia, March 8, 1745-6.
RUN away on the 6th Instant, from the Subscriber, an Irish Servant Man, named William Steuart, about 37 *Years of Age, by Trade a Shoemaker, of short Stature, has very short Thumbs, sandy Complexion, grey Eyes, red Beard, a large dimple in his Chin, his Nose mark'd with wearing Spectacles, a stern impudent looking Fellow, is much given to talk when in Drink, and pretends to be a Scholar. Had on when he went away, a Worsted Cap, light Camblet Jacket, Leather Breeches, white Shirt, mill'd Stockings and high heel'd Shoes, but may have chang'd his Clothes. Whoever takes up the said Servant , so that his Master may have him again, shall have Three Pounds Reward, and reasonable Charges*
        paid by   William Moode.
The Pennsylvania Gazette, March 11, 1746; March 15, 1746; March 15 to March 27, 1746. *The Pennsylvania Gazette*, May 15, 1746

RUN away the 8th Instant, from Joseph Gilbert, of Biberry, Philadelphia County, a Servant Lad, named Samuel Cook, Country born, about 19 Years

of Age, thin Visage, light Hair: Had on a Felt Hat, new light colour'd Cloth Coat and Vest, with Small Pewter Buttons; two Pair of Breeches, one Pair lin'd with fustian about half worn, Coat and Vest half worn, of a reddish Brown; three Shirts, one fine; two Pair Yarn Stockings, of a brown Colour. He has taken a new Bag, with one of the Suits of Clothes in it. Whoever takes up and secures said Lad, so that his Master may have him again, shall have Forty Shillings Reward, and reasonable Charges,
    paid by   Joseph Gilbert.

 The Pennsylvania Gazette, March 11, 1746; March 15, 1746; March 15 to March 27, 1746; April 3, 1746; April 10, 1746. Last ad has "Philadelphia, March 27, 1746." at the top. See *The Pennsylvania Gazette*, February 19, 1745.

      TWENTY PISTOLES Reward.
RUN away on the 4th Day of February last, from his Bail in Chester County, Pennsylvania, one Edward Brogden, an Irishman, about 27 Years of Age, by Trade a House Carpenter. He is a part little Fellow, about five Feet four Inches high, well set, flat footed, smooth faced, fair Complexion, grey Eyes, thin whitish Beard, a small Chin, curl'd brown Hair, if not cut off. He had been advertis'd in this Paper already, also in New York and Boston Papers, to wear a blue Camblet Coat, &c. but then he lay secreted by those to whom he made over his Effects, in order to defraud his Creditors, until they procur'd him other Cloaths than was advertis'd. He may have with him a Silk Damask Jacket, and a black Russel one, and blue Plush Breeches. He may be flush of Money; but no Spender nor Drinker. He is mighty apt to make Bargains; and full of Law in his Discourse. Whoever secures him, so that the Subscriber his Bail may have him again, and reasonable Charges, for bringing him to Chester, paid by *JOHN HANLY*.

 N. B. All Masters of Vessels are charg'd at their Peril not to carry him off. And if any Master of a Vessel has already taken him, for their Information where they landed him, whereby he is found again, shall have FIVE PISTOLES Reward, and no Advantage taken for carrying him away.

 The Pennsylvania Gazette, March 15, to 27, 1746; April 3, 1746; April 10, 1746. See *The Pennsylvania Gazette*, February 11, 1746.

RUN away on the 26th of March last, from Hugh Patrick, of Little-Britain township, in Lancaster county; two servant men, one named Edward Purcell, of about twenty years of age, a reddish fair complexion, much freckled, wears a worsted cap, double breasted coat half worn, of a light colour, a Jacket much the same, grey worsted stockings, pretty good shoes, and a new felt hat. The other named John Rogharty, about 20 years of age, red face, down look,

short black hair, but wears a cap, a brown strait-body'd coat, with light blue lining, green jacket, cloth breeches of an olive colour. It is supposed they intend to come to Philadelphia, in order to go on board some ship there, and that they have some confederates, that will assist them in getting off. Whoever takes up and secures said servants, so that their master may have them again, shall have Five Pounds reward for each, paid by Hugh Patrick.
    N. B. Edward Purcell was bought of John Clare, and the other of Charles Moor, hatter, in Philadelphia, in February last.
    The Pennsylvania Gazette, April 3, 1746; April 10, 1746; April 17, 1746. Third ad has "*Philadelphia, April* 3, 1746." at the top.

RUN away the 23d of February last, from George Correy, of New-London township, Chester County, an English servant man, from Darbyshire, named John Carnell; he speaks the North-country dialect, is middle stature, about 23 years of age, short lightish coloured hair, but 'tis supposed he will cut it off; full faced, fresh sandy complexion, heavy eye brows with a scar between them, and a scar across the small of one of his legs, and a scar in his Forehead amongst the hair; he goes with the side of the left foot partly foremost: Had on when he went away, an old dark coloured coat, with a sleeve of a different colour from the body, and one shirt patched with a different colour, an old blue jacket and breeches, the breeches patched at the knees, check'd shirt, coarse stockings, and old shoes. He ran away the second day of February, and took with him a suit of new clothes, and 30 £. of money with him, and called himself by the name of White, and passed for a privateer's man, but was taken up, and made his escape again, in the dress above described. Whoever takes up and secures said servant, and gives notice thereof to his master, or to John Correy in Philadelphia, shall have Fifty shillings reward, and reasonable charges,
          paid by   George Correy.
    The Pennsylvania Gazette, April 3, 1746; April 10, 1746; April 17, 1746. Third ad has "*Philadelphia, April* 3, 1746." at the top.

                      Philadelphia, April 10. 1746.
RUN away from Thomas James and Robert Murray, of Lancaster, in the Province of Pennsylvania, about the Middle of March, a Servant Man, named David Wood, by Trade a Mill-wright. He is of short Stature, well set, smooth flat faced, his upper Teeth broad before, and somewhat rotten, wears light brown Hair, or a Cap, and is about 23 Years of Age: Had on when he went away, a new light coloured Broadcloth Surtout Coat, with flat eight Square yellow Metal Buttons, red Jacket, trimmed with Silver Twist Buttons and Button Holes, a new Beaver Hat, a Pair of Half-boots, laced, a large Pair of

Silver Shoe Buckles, marked IL, and Knee Buckles of the same, and has taken with him a small Silver Watch, of Somerset's Make, with a dull Chrystal, pretty much scratched. He was seen in New-York on Easter Sunday in the same Dress as herein described, and 'tis supposed he is secreted there, until he can ship himself for some other Port: Therefore this is to forewarn all Persons not to entertain him, or Masters of Vessels to ship him on board, lest they suffer by it; for he has been guilty of some Misdemeanors not mentioned here; but if any have entertain'd him before this Notice, and can apprehend him, and bring him to Philadelphia Goal, shall have Six Pounds Reward, and reasonable Charges, and if the Watch is got again, 40 Shillings more, paid by *Thomas James* and *Robert Murray.*
The Pennsylvania Gazette, April 10, 1746; April 17, 1746; April 24, 1746.

hiladelphia, April 14. 1746.
RUN away last night, from Thomas Morgan, of the Burrow of Chester, in Chester County, a servant man named John Leycet, by trade a brass button and buckle maker, or a middling stature, and pretty slender, stoops a little in his shoulders as he walks, fresh complexion, pretty much pitted with the small pox, talks pretty freely, and a lover of drink: Had on when he went away, a sort of a snuff coloured brown coat, pretty much worn, and ript and tore in several places, with brass buttons on it, a pair of old leather breeches with brass buttons, old brown yarn stockings, and a pair of thread ones, good new shoes, with one brass buckle and another of a different sort, has also with him a pair of silver buckles, a oznabrigs shirt, and an old fine white shirt, he has thick sandy or greenish colour'd hair.

Whoever takes up said servant, and brings him to his master at Chester, shall have twenty shillings reward, and reasonable charges, or secures him in any goal, so his master may have him again, shall have the above reward paid by THOMAS MORGAN.
The Pennsylvania Gazette, April 17, 1746; April 24, 1746; May 1, 1746.

Philadelphia, April 17. 1745.
RUN away, the 12th Instant, from Thomas Maule, Joiner in Front-Street, Philadelphia, an Apprentice Boy, about 16 Years of Age, named William Holland: Had on when he went away, a Racoon Hat, blue Cloth Coat, blue flower'd Worsted Jacket, brown Cloth Breeches, brown Worsted Hose, and Silver Buckles in his Shoes, Whoever takes up said Apprentice, and brings him to his Master, shall have Twenty Shillings Reward, and reasonable Charges, paid by Thomas Maule.
The Pennsylvania Gazette, April 17, 1746; April 24, 1746; May 1, 1746.

RUN away on the 25th of March, 1746, from the house of Arthur Foster, of Paxton township, in the county of Lancaster, a prisoner woman, named Mary Porter; is low and slender, heavy brow'd, squints a little, thin face, and black hair: Had on a lead coloured diamond rais'd stuff gown, a blue petticoat with black pains in it; she stole a callicoe gown, a striped blue and white petticoat with a callicoe border, a black callimancoe petticoat, a white flannel petticoat, a red short cloak, a felt hat, two pair of womens shoes, several womens and babies caps, a woman's shift with silver buttons on the sleeves, and aprons. Whoever takes up the said Runaway, so that the said Foster may have her again, shall have Forty shilling reward, and reasonable charges,
    paid by me ARTHUR FOSTER.
The Pennsylvania Gazette, April 24, 1746; May 1, 1746; May 8, 1746.
See *The Pennsylvania Gazette,* July 3, 1746, and *The Pennsylvania Journal, or, Weekly Advertiser,* July 3, 1746.

            Philadelphia, May 1. 1746.
RUN away on the 27th of April last, from James Payne, Cooper, living on Society Hill, a servant Lad, named Michael Woldridge, of middle Stature, dark Complexion, bushy Hair, between 17 and 18 Years of Age: Had on, a Felt Hat, a silk Barcelona handkerchief, a brownish colour'd jacket lin'd with blue, a pair of buckskin breeches with brass buttons, ozenbrigs shirt, mix'd yarn stockings, and a pair of double soal'd shoes. Whoever takes up and secures said servant, so that his master may him again, shall have Twenty shillings reward, and reasonable charges,
    paid by *JAMES PAYNE.*
The Pennsylvania Gazette, May 1, 1746; May 8, 1746; May 15, 1746.

            Philadelphia, April 24, 1746.
ABsconded from the Ship Ballance (now at Philadelphia) Richard Gill, Master the three following Men, viz.
 JAMES WORTHINGTON, a fat, lusty, slovenly Fellow; had on a blue Jacket, and otherwise clothed as a Sailor; he pretends to be a Carpenter, and says he served his Time in Liverpool.
 The other two, HUGH CLEMMONS, and ARCHIBALD HALL, are both Irishmen, of middle Stature, and clothed as Sailors, but particularly have on brown Jackets.
 Whoever takes up and secures the above Men, or either of them, shall have Two Pistoles Reward for each,
    paid by *RICHARD GILL.*
The Pennsylvania Gazette, May 1, 1746; May 8, 1746.

Dover, April 27. 1746.

NOTICE is hereby given, that there is in this goal, a man that goes by the name of James Young, an Englishman, is about 5 feet 9 inches high, of a ruddy complexion, well set, has black curl'd hair, long visage, high thin nose, a learing down look, and is about 40 years of age. 'Tis thought he is the person that made his escape in August last, from Anthony Tate, near Newtown goal, Bucks county, as he has confessed he had an ax with him, when he made his escape some time ago, from some body in Bucks county, but does not know from whom. If he is the person, it is desired he should be speedily taken away.   THOMAS GREEN, Sheriff.

The Pennsylvania Gazette, May 8, 1746; May 15, 1746; May 29, 1746.
See *The Pennsylvania Gazette*, August 1, 1745, and *The Pennsylvania Gazette*, August 15, 1745.

Philadelphia, May 8, 1746.

RUN away on the 3d inst. from the subscriber, an apprentice lad, named James Jacobs, about 18 or 19 years of age, tall and slender, of a pale complexion, long visage, long nose, long dark hair, if not cut off, by trade a carpenter, and was born at New-York. Had on when he went away, a brown kersey Coat, with large brass buttons, a brown linnen vest, both leather and linnen breeches, grey worsted stockings, and cotton ditto, new shoes, large silver buckles, with brass anchors, a pair of wrought brass buckles, and a good castor hat. Whoever takes up said apprentice, and brings him to the subscriber, or secures him in any goal in Pennsylvania government, shall have Three Pounds reward, and reasonable charges; or if taken in any other government, Ten Pounds, and reasonable charges,
     paid by   ISAAC TAYLOR.
N. B. 'Tis probable he may change his clothes.

The Pennsylvania Gazette, May 8, 1746; May 15, 1746; May 29, 1746.

Philadelphia, May 15, 1746.

RUN away, the 6th of March last, from the Subscriber, an Irish Servant Man, named William Stuart, about 37 Years of Age, by Trade a Shoemaker, about five Foot high, has a Scar on his Throat, short Thumbs, sandy Complexion, large eyebrows, grey Eyes, red Beard, a large Dimple in his Chin, his Nose marked with wearing Spectacles, is a stern, impudent looking Fellow, much given to Talk when in Liquor, writes a good Hand, and pretends to be a Scholar. Had on when he went away, a Worsted Cap, light Camblet Jacket, Leather Breeches, white Shirt, mill'd Stockings, and high Heel'd Shoes, but may have changed his Name and Clothes. Whoever takes up said Servant ,

and secures him, so that his Master may have him again, shall have FIVE PISTOLES Reward, and reasonable Charges,
    paid by *WILLIAM MOODE.*
 The Pennsylvania Gazette, May 15, 1746; May 29, 1746; June 5, 1746.
See *The Pennsylvania Gazette,* March 11, 1746.

              Chester, May 14. 1746.
MAde his escape from the sheriff of Chester County, this morning, one Simon Connoly, who served his time in the upper part of the said county, near James Way's; he is of middle stature, slender, dark short curled hair, about 24 years of age, a native Irishman, and hath been a privateering one voyage: Had on a homespun shirt, leather breeches, with brass buttons to the knees, and leather buttons to the pockets; a brown cloth coat, an old beaver hat, lined with white linen, and the crown sewed on to the other part. Whoever takes up the said Simon Connoly, and brings him to Chester goal, or to the said sheriff, shall have Forty Shillings reward, and reasonable charges, paid by *JOHN OWEN,* Sheriff.
 The Pennsylvania Gazette, May 22, 1746; June 5, 1746; June 12, 1746.

RAN-away on the 21st Instant, from *John Smith* of *Donagaul, Lancaster* County, two Servant Men, the one named *John Codgall,* an Englishman, formerly belonging to *Samuel Morris,* Miller in Whitemarsh, and was generally employed in driving Morris's Team to Town, a short down looking Fellow, fair Complection, with his Hair off, between 20 and 21 Years old, and can talk the Dutch Tongue: Had on when he went away, a whiteish colour'd Cloth Jacket, with flat white Mettal Buttons, tow Trowsers, no Stockings, Shoes almost new, steal Buckles, [*sic*] felt Hat, and Linnen Cap. Also one *George Hill,* an Irish Man, about 19 or 20 Years of Age, dark Complection, middle sized, down looking Fellow: Had on an Olive green Cloth Jacket, tore in two Places on the left Skirt, and is darn'd with green Worsted, Buckskin Breeches, and tow Trowsers, coarse brown yarn Stockings, old Shoes, half Soal'd, with large Steel Buckels, an old Beaver Hat, a linnen Cap, and light colour'd Wigg.
 N. B. They have six Shirts, three fine and three coarse, and is supposed to be together, and come into this City; it is not unlikely but they will change their Names.
 Whoever takes up both, or either, of the said Servants, and secures them so that their Master may have them again, shall have Four Pounds for both, or Forty Shillings for each paid By *John Smith.*
 The Pennsylvania Journal, or, Weekly Advertiser, May 29, 1746; June 5, 1746; June 12, 1746; June 19, 1746; June 26, 1746; July 3, 1746.

Philadelphia, June 5. 1746.
RUN away from Alexander Cruikshank, of Philadelphia, Shoemaker, an Irish Servant Man, named John Brooks, a short, thick, set Fellow, by Trade a Shoemaker: Had on when he went away, a large Jacket, of a light Colour, a blue Waistcoat and Breeches, blue Stockings, old Shoes, and black Wig. Whoever secures the said Servant, or brings him to his said Master, shall have *Thirty Shillings* Reward, and reasonable Charges,
    paid by *ALEX. CRUIKSHANK.*
 The Pennsylvania Gazette, June 5, 1746; June 12, 1746; June 19, 1746.

Philadelphia, June 12, 1746.
RUN away from the Snow Entwistle, Capt. William Davison, on William Ramsey, a Sailor; a tall Fellow, about 5 Feet 9 Inches high, stoops in his Shoulders much, mark'd with the Small Pox, and splaw footed: Had on when he went away, a brown Cloth Jacket, blue Shag Breeches, and a red and white striped Waistcoat.—Also a Servant Man, named David Young; he is about 5 Feet 10 Inches high, strait, well limbed, and a fresh Complexion: Had on a brown Jacket and Breeches. They both came from Londonderry. Whoever takes them up and brings them to Mr. George Okill, Merchant in Philadelphia, shall have Three Pounds Reward, and reasonable Expenses
    paid by George Okill.
 The Pennsylvania Gazette, June 12, 1746.

Philadelphia, June 19. 1746.
RUN away the 15th Instant, from Rees Price and Henry Glasford, of London Britain Township, Chester County, two Irish Servant Men; the one named Michael Ohare, about Twenty Years of Age, of middle Stature, is a bold looking Fellow, much freckled, and has a good deal of the Brogue: Had on a new brown homespun Cloth Coat, two homespun Jackets, one brown, the other of a whitish Colour, new Trowsers, and Leather Breeches, new Shoes, with large Brass Buckles, new Felt Hat, and brown Wig. The other named William Martin, about 6 Foot high, well made, and about 20 Years of Age, short necked, and has short black Hair: had on when he went away a good homespun blue Coat, lined with blue Shalloon, a Cotton tuft Jacket, double breasted, much wore, new white Shirt, Leather Breeches, with Brass Buttons, brown Woollen Stockings, old Shoes, and an old Castor Hat. Martin has an Indenture with him, and will probably alter the Date, so that he may appear to be free. He has also with him a new Gun, and some other Things. Whoever takes up and secures said servants, so that they may be had again, shall have Five Pounds Reward for both, or Fifty Shillings for either of them, and reasonable Charges, from Rees Price *or* Henry Glasford.

The Pennsylvania Gazette, June 19, 1746; June 26, 1746; July 3, 1746.

RUN away the 28th of April last, from James Davis, of Tredyffryn, a Scotch Servant Man, named Malchum Robeson, of short Stature, round Visage, has a large Scar on one of his Cheeks, wears his own Hair, and can talk Welch. Had on when he went away, a blue Cloth Jacket, fine Homespun Shirt, Tow Trowsers, old Shoes, and old Hat. Whoever takes up the said Servant, and brings him to his said Master, shall have Twenty Shillings Reward,
   paid by JAMES DAVIS.
N. B. Any Person that shall be found guilty of Imploying, Harbouring, or Concealing the said Servant, may expect to be prosecuted as the Law directs.
The Pennsylvania Gazette, June 19, 1746; June 26, 1746; July 3, 1746.

Philadelphia, July 3. 1746.
ON Tuesday Night, the 24th of June, broke out of the County Goal of Lancaster, the three following Women, viz. Jane M'Coun and Ann Guttery, committed for Murder. Jane M'Coun is about 20 Years of Age, wears a blue Linsey or Callico Gown; took with her a red Mantle; is a likely slender Woman. Ann Guttery, about 13 Years of Age: Had on a blue and white striped Gown. Mary Porter, she is a bold, talkative and impudent Woman; has on a Bird-Eye Gown, of a darkish brown Colour, a short Callico Bed Gown, lined with Linnen, a blue Stuff Petticoat, and blue Stockings, with white Clocks; she was convicted of Felony on several Indictments at last May Court. Whoever secures the said Women, so that they may be brought to the County Goal aforesaid, shall receive FIVE POUNDS for Jane M'Coun and Ann Guttery, and for Mary Porter, Thirty Shillings, with reasonable Charges,
   paid by JOSEPH PUGH, Sub-sheriff.
N. B. They were assisted by some vile Persons to break the aforesaid Goal.
 The Pennsylvania Gazette, July 3, 1746; July 10, 1746; July 17, 1746;
 July 24, 1746. See *The Pennsylvania Gazette*, April 25, 1746, for
 Porter, and *The Pennsylvania Journal, or, Weekly Advertiser*, July 3,
 1746.

Philadelphia, July 3. 1746.
MADE his Escape from Newtown Goal, Bucks County, on the 18th of June last, John Warren, a Felon, who was confined for his Fine and Charges. he is a Westcountryman, between 50 and 60 Years of Age. Had on when he went away, a blue Duroy Coat, with Mohair Buttons, two Linnen Shirts, one Pair of Trowsers, a Pair of good Shoes, with Steel Buckles, two Caps, one Linnen, and the other Cotton, a fine Hat, much worn, his Heels a little gaulled with wearing of Irons.

Whoever takes up and secures said Felon, so that he may be had again, shall have Three Pounds Reward, and reasonable Charges
    paid by JOHN PENQUITE.
The Pennsylvania Gazette, July 3, 1746; July 10, 1746; July 17, 1746; July 4, 1746. See *The Pennsylvania Gazette,* November 20, 1746.

            Philadelphia, July 3. 1746.
RUN away, the 29th of June last, from the subscriber, two servants, one named Thomas Warde, an English lad, of a short stature, fresh colour'd, well set, about 19 years of age: Had on when he went away, a good hat, brown duroy coat and jacket, of a lightish colour, a pair of half worn shoes, and oznabrigs shirt. The other a Dutchman, named Barnet Ward, about 24 years of age, of a pale complexion and has short brown hair: Had on an oznabrigs shirt, a good hat, and a pair of half worn shoes. Whoever takes up and secures the said servants, so that their Master may have them again, shall have Forty Shillings Reward for each, and reasonable Charges,
    paid by GEORGE EMLEN.
The Pennsylvania Gazette, July 3, 1746.

ON Tuesday Instant broke out of the County of Lancaster, [*sic*] the three following Women, *viz.*
 Jane Mc.Cown and *Ann Guttery,* committed for Murder. *Jane Mc.Cown,* is about Twenty Years of Age, wears a blue Linsey or Callico Gown; took with her a red Mantle; she is a likely slender Woman.
 Ann Guttery, about Thirteen Years of Age; had on a blue and white striped Gown.
 Mary Porter, she is a bold talkative and impudent Woman; has on a Bird-Eye Gown of a darkish brown Colour, a short Callico Bed Gown, lined with Linnen, a blue Stuff Petticoat, and blue Stockings with white Clocks. She was convicted of Felony on several Indictments at last May Court.
 Whoever secures the said Women, so that they may be brought to the County Goal aforesaid, shall receive Five Pounds for Jane Mc'Cown and Ann Guttery, and for Mary Porter Thirty Shillings, with reasonable Charges,
    paid by *Joseph Pugh,* sub. sheriff.
They were assisted by some vile Persons to break the aforesaid Goal.
The Pennsylvania Journal, or, Weekly Advertiser, July 3, 1746; July 17, 1746. See *The Pennsylvania Gazette,* April 25, 1746, for Porter, and *The Pennsylvania Gazette,* July 3, 1746.

Philadelphia, July 10. 1746.
Made his Escape from the Goal of this City, on the 5th Instant, one James Ray, a Felon, about 19 Years of Age, short and well set, and has black curled Hair: Had on when he went away, an ozenbrigs Shirt, wide Sailor's Trowsers, and old Felt Hat, old Shoes, no Stockings, and it is supposed he has taken with him a blue Stuff Waistcoat. He was sometime ago Servant to Abraham Underhaven in New Providence, and since to Joseph Rogers of Chester County, and having Committed a Felony was convicted of the same last March Sessions. Whoever takes up and secures said Felon, so that he may be had again, shall have Fifty Shillings Reward, and reasonable Charges,
        paid by   Joseph Scull.
N. B. Any Person that shall be found guilty of the imploying, harbouring or concealing the said Felon, may expect to be prosecuted as the Law directs.
    The Pennsylvania Gazette, July 10, 1746; July 17, 1746. See *The Pennsylvania Gazette*, October 17, 1745, and *The Pennsylvania Gazette*, November 24, 1748.

Philadelphia, July 10. 1746.
RUN away from Benjamin Davis of Upper Merion, Philadelphia County, an Irish Servant Man, named John M'Cormick: A well set Fellow, between Thirty and Forty Years of Age, and bushy Hair. Had on when he went away a Felt Hat, striped Jacket, Linen Drawers, blue Stockings, new Shoes; and had with him three Homespun Shirts. Whoever takes up and secures said Servant, so that his Master may have him again, shall have Three Pounds Reward, and reasonable Charges
       paid by   Benjamin Davis.
   The Pennsylvania Gazette, July 10, 1746; July 17, 1746; July 24, 1746.

Philadelphia, July 18. 1746.
RUN away from John Philips, of this City, House-carpenter, an English Servant Man, named Thomas Fairbrother, about 27 Years of Age, five Feet high, his Hair cut off, sandy Complexion, well set, and has T F mark'd with Gunpowder on the Back Part of the Root of his Thumb: He is a Carpenter by Trade, but can Work at most sorts of Plantation Work. Had on, an old Beaver Hat, without Lining, two Jackets, one blue Kersey with striped Lining, the other brown Holland with Brass Buttons, a Pair of white Trowsers pretty much worn, Thread Stockings, Half worn Shoes, Brass Buckles. Whoever takes up said Servant, and secures him in any Goal, so that his Master may have him again, shall have Twenty Shillings Reward, and reasonable Charges,   paid by   JOHN PHILIPS.

The Pennsylvania Gazette, July 24, 1746; July 31, 1746; August 7, 1746; August 14, 1746.

Philadelphia, July 28. 1746.
RUN away last Night, from Elizabeth Jefferis, of East-Bradford Township, Chester County, a Servant Man, named William Cole, about 20 Years of Age, of middle Stature, fair Complexion, has his Hair cut off, and limps a little with his Right Knee: Had on when he went away, an old Felt Hat, a mixt coloured Worsted Coat with Slash Sleeves, coarse Linnen Shirt, Tow Trowsers, an old Pair of Shoes tied with Strings. He stole and took with him a light brown Horse, branded on the near Shoulder and Buttock with a 3, his Mane hangs to the near Side, is shod before, and his off Hind Foot a little White; also a Double breasted Saddle, without a Crupper. Whoever takes up said Servant, and secures him so that his master may have him again, shall have Forty Shillings Reward, and if the Horse is taken and sent to Joseph Gray's in Philadelphia, Three Pounds Reward for the Horse, and reasonable Charges, paid by   ELIZABETH JEFFERIS.

The Pennsylvania Gazette, July 31, 1746; August 7, 1746; August 14, 1746.

Philadelphia, July 31. 1746.
RUN away from David Sheerer, of Nantmill township, Chester county, on the 20th of this instant, a servant man, named Patrick O Durish, a thick set fellow, of a dark complexion, heavy black brows, a down look, a black bushy hair. Had on when he went away, a whitish cloth jacket, with brass buttons, and blue and white lining in the foreskirts, a coarse shirt and trowsers, old felt hat, and new shoes. Whoever takes up said servant, and secures him, so as he may be had again, shall have forty shillings reward, if taken within 40 miles of Nantmill, and 3 pounds if farther, with reasonable charges,
from   DAVIS SHEERER.

The Pennsylvania Gazette, July 31, 1746; August 7, 1746; August 21, 1746.

Philadelphia, August 7. 1746.
FROM Thomas Clemson ran away,
One Evening on a Saturday,
The Six and Twentieth Day of July,
If that I am informed truly;
A Man, one Joseph Willard call'd,
His Hair is brown, he is not bald;
His Visage long, and wou'd you know
His Colour, it is swarthy too;
His Hat, it is of an antient Date,

Which keeps the Weather from his Pate;
A yellow Jacket, old and torn,
His wretched Carcase doth adorn;
A Homespun Shirt, and look below,
You'll find his Trowsers made of Tow,
And also coarse; and for his Shoes,
He did the same this six Months use;
They ragged are: He with him took
(If that you will be pleas'd to look)
A Handsaw, made of London Steel,
And stamped with White, near to the Heel;
A Broad-ax, of an ugly Shape,
A Justice made it, near to Gap;
And other Clothes, perhaps may have,
That he may better play the Knave.
By Calling, he pretends to be
A Person used to the Sea,
A Millwright, Carpenter, and all
The Crafts which you to Mind can call.
If you shou'd happen for to be
By Chance drawn into his Company,
You'll find him lye at such a Rate,
You can't conceive it in your Pate.
His Birth Bucks County did adorn.
To all his Friends he is a Scorn;
His Father left him an Estate
Enough, with Care, to make him great;
He wasted it, and then he went
To Lancaster, with Intent
His ragged Fortune to repair,
And soon was made a Servant there.
If you'll expect to have a Fee
For taking up this Man for me,
Full TWENTY SHILLINGS I will give,
And truly pay it, as I live;
Provided, that you will not fail,
To cast him in the nearest Goal,
And send me Word, you need not doubt,
I'll quickly lug the Money out:
In Christine Hundred, there you may
Soon find me out, on any Day;
I at John Heath's doth make my Home.
It will please me, if you hither come;

Pray use your Skill, to help your Friend,
And I'll conclude, and make an End.
THOMAS CLEMSON.
The Pennsylvania Gazette, August 7, 1746; August 14, 1746.

Philadelphia, August 14. 1746.
RUN away from the Subscriber, at the sign of the Bear, in Frankford, on Wednesday the 30th of July, a servant lad, named William Goodfellow, about 15 years of age. Went off in his shirt and trowsers only, without hat, shoes or stockings. He is an old offender, having ran away seven times since January last, and very cunning to frame a story for his purpose. It is thought he may have stolen some cloaths to travel with. He is of short stature, lank black hair, and squints a little; he belong'd to a tinman about a year and an half ago, who employ'd him to travel distant parts of the country with his ware. Whoever secures said servant, so that he may be had again, shall have Twenty Shillings, if taken within ten miles; if further, Thirty, Money of this Province, with reasonable charges.   JAMES CLAXTON.
The Pennsylvania Gazette, August 14, 1746; August 21, 1746; September 4, 1746.

RAN-away the 7th of August from *Joseph Farmar*, an Irish Servant Man, named *Joseph Bryant*, about 20 Years of age, middle Stature and well set, has a Scar on the fore Finger of his left Hand, his little Finger is stiff, occasioned by a cut, has short brown hair, yet wears a Cap. Had on when he went away, a brown double breasted Waistcoat, wide Sailors Trowsers, from which 'tis imagined he will endeavour to pass for one, has old Shoes but no Stockings. Whoever takes up and secures him so that his Master may have him again, shall have Forty Shillings Reward and reasonable Charges
     paid By   Joseph Farmar.
The Pennsylvania Journal, or, Weekly Advertiser, August 21, 1746.

Philadelphia, August 23. 1746.
RUN away the 6th Instant from James Maxwell of Chester County, Township of Londongrove, an Irish Servant Man, named Thomas Hanraty, of low Stature, sandy Complexion, about 19 Years of Age, speaks with the Brogue, and took with him a lightish coloured Rateen Coat, black Broad Cloth Jacket, a Pair of striped Ticken Breeches, blue gray Stockings, check Trowsers patched on the Knees, old Pumps, a fine and coarse Shirt. Whoever takes up and secures said Servant, so that his master may have him again, shall have Forty Shillings Reward, and reasonable Charges

paid by   JAMES MAXWELL.
The Pennsylvania Gazette, August 28, 1746; September 4, 1746; September 11, 1746.

Philadelphia, August 28. 1746.
RUN away the 24th Instant, from the Subscriber, of Bensalem in Bucks County, an Apprentice Lad, named Joseph Rue, aged about 19 Years, by Trade a Shoemaker, of middle Stature, full faced, a narrow Scar above his left Eyebrow, of about an Inch and an Half long, one End goes down thro' his Eyebrow, a small Scar or two across it, two of his Nails on one Hand are ridg'd in the middle, and much thicker than common. He had on a dark colour'd Fustian Coat with slash Sleeves, a linnen Jacket and Breeches, chequer'd trowsers, grey or black worsted Stockings, Cow-mouth Shoes, a Linnen Cap, and good Hat. Whosoever takes up the said Apprentice, and secures him again, shall have Forty Shillings Reward, and reasonable Charges   paid by   WILLIAM BAKER.
N. B. *He is supposed to be gone to New-York.*
The Pennsylvania Gazette, August 28, 1746.

Philadelphia, August 28. 1746.
RUN away from Samuel Bettle of Birmingham, in the County of Chester, an Irish Servant Man, named Richard Fitz Simmons, he pretends to be a Baker by Trade, but hath since his coming is wrought at the Farmer's Trade; about 22 Years of Age, a bold impudent looking Fellow, and in his Conversation is very apt to say, *Myself did so and so*: Had on when he went away, a good Racoon Hat, a fine Shirt, Floretta Jacket, check Trowsers, good Shoes, no Coat nor Stockings, unless got since, his Hair cut off, and wears a Cap. Whoever takes up and secures the said Servant, so that his Master may have him again, shall have Forty Shillings Reward, and reasonable Charges,
paid by   SAMUEL BETTLE.
The Pennsylvania Gazette, August 28, 1746; September 4, 1746; September 11, 1746.

Philadelphia, September 4, 1746.
RUN away, on the 26th of August, from the Subscriber, at Warwick Furnace, in Chester County, an Irish Servant Lad, named Patrick Linch, about 20 Years of Age, of middle Stature, short black Hair, Down looking, round shoulder'd, and smooth faced: Had on, and took with him, when he went away, a coarse Snuff coloured Broadcloth Coat and Breeches, brown Cloth Jacket, with Metal Buttons, without Lining or Sleeves, Buckskin Breeches, Oznabrigs Shirt and Trowsers, old Beaver Hat, a Cap, and half worn Shoes; 'tis likely he may have changed his Cloaths; he writes a pretty good Hand, and is a Fellow of few Words, until he is in Liquor, and then very talkative.

good Hand, and is a Fellow of few Words, until he is in Liquor, and then very talkative.

Whoever takes up said Servant, and brings him to the Furnace aforesaid, or secures him in any Goal, and gives Notice thereof, shall have Fifty Shillings Reward, and all reasonable Charges,

          paid by   *George Taylor.*

N. B. 'Tis supposed he is conceal'd in Capt. Trent's Company.

The Pennsylvania Gazette, September 4, 1746; September 11, 1746.

RUN-away on the 16th Day of *August* from *Joseph Ridder* of the County of *Lancaster,* and Township of *Leacock,* a Servant Man named *Timothy Connor,* of a middle size, freckel'd Face, with a Scar on his Nose, aged 20 Years: Had on when he went away, a coarse felt Hat, white Lincey Jacket without Flaps or Lineing, a coarse Shirt, a white pair of Breeches with a patch between the Legs of Lincey, a pair of blueish worsted Stockings, and a pair of Women's Shoes with flat Heels. Whoever takes up and secures the said Servant, so that his Master may have him again, shall have Twenty Shillings reward and reasonable Charges

          paid by   JOSEPH RIDDER.

The Pennsylvania Journal, or, Weekly Advertiser, September 4, 1746; September 11, 1746; September 18, 1746; October 2, 1746, October 9, 1746; October 16, 1746; October 23, 1746; October 30, 1746; November 6, 1746; November 13, 1746; November 20, 1746; November 27, 1746; December 2, 1746; December 9, 1746; January 6, 1747.

                                    Philadelphia, Sept. 11. 1746.

RUN away the 30th of August, from Stephen Jenkins, of Abington Township, Philadelphia County, a native Irish Servant Man, named Bryan Murray, about 24 Years of Age, has much of the Brogue. Had on when he went away, an old Hat, with a Hole in the Brim, a blue Cloth Coat much torn, a Flannel Jacket lac'd in the Breast, Leather Breeches much worn, blue gray Stockings, and old Shoes, with Strings. Whoever takes up said Servant, and brings him said Jenkins, or to John Beard, at Neshaminy, in Bucks County, shall have Twenty Shillings Reward, and reasonable Charges,

          paid by   ROBERT BEARD.

N. B. He was seen in Capt. Trent's Company, the 5th Inst. and 'tis supposed he inlisted in said Company. All Masters of Vessels, and others, are forbid harbouring or concealing him, at their Peril.

The Pennsylvania Gazette, September 11, 1746; September 18, 1746.

Philadelphia, Sept. 11. 1746.
RUN away from George Aston, of Whiteland, in Chester County, on the 25th of August, an English Servant Man, named Daniel Mills, a Tanner by Trade, of middle Stature, a lively Fellow, sandy Complexion: Had on when he went away, an old white Coat, and a Camblet double-breasted Jacket, of a brown Colour; had with him a Pair of Leather Breeches, and coarse Tow Trowsers, two Shirts of Homespun Linnen almost new, Yarn Stockings of a gray Colour, Neats-Leather Shoes newly tapped; he also took a Horse belonging to his Master, of a sorrel Colour, his four Feet and Legs white very high up, bald Face, not much Mane or Tail, shod before, branded on the near Shoulder with Letters, not remember'd, saving a Figure of 2 above the other Brand. Whoever takes up the said Servant, or secures him, so that his Master may have him again, shall have Three Pounds Reward, with reasonable Charges
paid by   GEORGE ASTON.
The Pennsylvania Gazette, September 11, 1746; September 18, 1746.

Philadelphia, September 18. 1746.
RUN away, on the 11th Instant, from John Stinson, in Walnut-street, an Irish servant girl, named Mary Brown, about 19 or 20 years of age, a lusty, jolly, fresh complexion'd girl, with red hair. Had on when she went away, a green gown, a quilted paned petticoat or linnen and calicoe, check'd apron, with large cheeks, no shoes nor stockings; she was seen over Schuylkill, between the ferry and Darby. Whoever takes up and secures said servant girl, so that her Master may have her again, shall have *Thirty Shillings* reward, and reasonable charges,
paid by   JOHN STINSON.
The Pennsylvania Gazette, September 18, 1746; October 2, 1746; October 9, 1746; October 16, 1746.

Philadelphia, September 15, 1746.
RUN away yesterday, from Conrad Waltecker, butcher, of this city, an Irish servant man, named James Rey, about 18 years of age, round face, short black curl'd hair, pock mark'd, can talk Dutch, and when he talks seems to smile: Had on when he went away, a new twenty shilling hat, a new homespun shirt, a new light-coloured cloth coat, jacket, and breeches, of the same cloth of capt. Diemer's company of soldiers, with Swisser buttons, the coat has slash sleeves, and lin'd in the body and sleeves with ozenbrigs; coarse thread stockings, and new neats-leather shoes, with steel buckles. Whoever takes up and secures said servant, so that his master may have him again, if taken in this city, or within ten miles of it, shall have Forty shillings reward, but if further Three pounds, and reasonable charges,
paid by   CONRAD WALTECKER.

The Pennsylvania Gazette, September 18, 1746; Otober 2, 1746; October 9, 1746.

Philadelphia, Octob. 2. 1746.
RUN away from the Ship Griffin, John Chubbard, master, the following seamen and servants, viz. *Lawrence Gilcrist*, sailor, a lusty young fellow, fresh coloured, lately recovered from sickness, about twenty three years of age. *John Ferguson*, sailor, middle siz'd, brown complexion, thin, being lately sick, about twenty two years of age. *James Jordan*, sailor, pale coloured, middle siz'd slender, and sickly, looking about twenty years of age. *Richard Davis*, sailor, short and broad set, black complexion, just recovered from sickness, about eighteen years of age. *Thomas Cunningham*, a servant man, lusty, well set, pretty tall, brown complexion, given to swearing, about eighteen years of age. *John Dunbar*, servant, lusty, middle siz'd, fresh looking, about eighteen years of age, Whoever takes up the said sailors and servants, and brings them to Philadelphia, shall have Three Pounds for each, and reasonable charges
paid by   GEORGE OKILL.

The Pennsylvania Gazette, October 2, 1746; October 16, 1746; October 23, 1746.

Philadelphia, October 2. 1746.
RUN away, from George Dowllenger, of Strasburgh township, Lancaster County, on the 21st of September last, an Irish servant man, named William Harley, about 19 years of age, 5 foot 9 inches high, or thereabouts, slender made, thin face, much freckled, dark brown hair: Had on when he went away, a dark brown jacket, and a short jacket under it, flax shirt, and took another shirt with him, a good felt hat, old tow trowsers, dark coloured coarse stockings, good shoes, and steel buckles. Whoever takes up said servant, and secures him, so that his master may have him again, shall have Forty Shillings reward, and reasonable charges,
paid by   GEORGE DOWLLENGER.

The Pennsylvania Gazette, October 2, 1746; October 9, 1746; October 16, 1746.

Philadelphia, October 2. 1746.
RUN away from Matthias Meuris's paper mill, on Wissahickon creek, about 3 miles from Germantown, an apprentice, named David Collins, born at Stanford or Stratford, both lying on the road leading to Boston: Had on when he went away, an oznabrigs shirt, large check trowsers, much spotted with logwood dye, dark coloured jacket, without lining, double channel pumps, much wore, and trod down at the heels, white metal buckles, a blue and white cotton cap, an old hat; he is a tall, well-set fellow, about 5 foot 10 inches

high, down looking, and commonly wears his hat flapped down before; he took with him, besides what he wore, a double breasted jacket, of a whitish colour, much spotted with logwood dye. Whoever takes up said apprentice, and secures him, so that his master may have him again, shall have Twenty Shillings reward, if taken in this province, with reasonable Charges, and Thirty Shillings, if taken out of this province,
    from *Matthias Meuris.*
The Pennsylvania Gazette, October 2, 1746; October 9, 1746.

              Philadelphia, October 17. 1746.
RUN away, the 13th Instant, from the Snow Anne, Robert Macky, commander, then lying at Reedy island, 5 sailors, viz. Bartholomew Barrell, a tall, black fellow, and lodged in Pewter Platter Alley; Bartholomew Thomas, John Dean, Robert Anderson, and Archibald Mackelvy; they took with them said vessel's long boat, and 'tis supposed they are come to this city. Whoever secures said sailors, shall have Two Pistoles reward for each,
    from JOHN GILLEYLIN.
The Pennsylvania Gazette, October 23, 1746; November 20, 1746.

              Philadelphia, October 30. 1746.
YEsterday morning absented himself from his master, one Joseph Willard, about 19 years of age, has a down look, straddles as he walks, by trade a blacksmith: Had on when he went away, an old brown kersey or plain coat, with metal buttons, a green waistcoat if any, an ozenbrigs shirt, wide trowsers, yarn stockings, coarse blue cloth breeches, an old castor hat, woollen cap, and 'tis suppos'd he took a new check'd shirt with him; 'tis also imagined he has took a cannoe in order to get on board of some vessel, or to go up the river to get towards New-York. Whoever takes up the said apprentice, or secures him in some Goal, so that his master may have him again, shall have Forty Shillings reward, and reasonable charges,
    paid by WILLIAM PARKER.
N. B. All Persons are hereby forewarned not to entertain him at their peril.
 The Pennsylvania Gazette, October 30, 1746; November 6, 1746; November 13, 1746.

              Philadelphia, November 6. 1746.
RUn away from the subscriber, on the 3d instant, an Irish servant man, named George Terret, by trade a stocken-weaver, of middle stature, has a large wen on his right cheek, long strait brown hair, slow spoken, and thin visage: Had on when he went away, a dark brown homespun cloth coat, an old brown broad cloth jacket, a pair of old check'd trowsers, old grey worsted stockings,

with one shoe and one pump. Whoever takes up said servant, and brings him to his master, shall have Fifteen shillings, if taken in this city, and if taken above ten miles from hence, Thirty shillings, but if taken in any other province, Forty shillings reward, and reasonable charges,
    paid by JOHN NEEDHAM.
N. B. All masters of vessels and others, are forbid harbouring or concealing him at their peril.
 The Pennsylvania Gazette, November 6, 1746; November 13, 1746; November 20, 1746.

         Philadelphia, November 13. 1746.
RUN away on the 2d inst. from John Rowland, of Whiteland, in Chester county, a Welch servant lad, named Amos David, about 19 or 20 years of age, a lusty lad, with black hair, and smooth face: Had on when he went away, a blue coat, lined with blue, flat white metal buttons, a scarlet jacket, lined with red, leather breeches, or perhaps white cloth breeches, good fine shirt and hat, dark grey yarn stockings, a large flag handkerchief, and old shoes. He may have taken other clothes with him. Whoever takes up the said servant, so that his master may have him again, shall have Forty-shillings reward, and reasonable charges,
    paid by JOHN ROWLAND .
 The Pennsylvania Gazette, November 13, 1746; November 20, 1746; December 2, 1746.

         Philadelphia, November 20. 1746.
Absconded from his bail, in Bucks county, one William White, a little short fellow, very much pock-marked, between 40 and 50 years of age, pretends to be a tinker: He rid a likely black horse, with a blaze down his face, and a trimm'd mane, and some white feet. Whoever apprehends the said White, and brings him to David Wilson, in Southampton, Bucks county, or to Newtown goal, or the nearest goal where taken up, and give speedy notice thereof to the said Wilson, shall have Twenty Shillings,
    paid by *DAVID WILSON.*
 The Pennsylvania Gazette, November 20, 1746; November 27, 1746; December 2, 1746; December 9, 1746; December 16, 1746.

         Philadelpia, Nov. 20. 1746.
MADE his escape out of Newtown goal, in the county of Bucks, the 10th inst. in the afternoon, between the hours of two and three o'clock, John Warren, aged between 50 and 60 years, and is very hard of hearing; had on a blue duroy coat, with slash sleeves, oznabrigs trowsers and shirt, and very bad pair of shoes on; took with him some cloaths belonging to another

prisoner, and had irons on when he made his escape. Whoever secures him, so that he may be had again, shall have *Three Pounds* reward,
        paid by   Amos Strickland, Sheriff.
The Pennsylvania Gazette, November 20, 1746. See *The Pennsylvania Gazette*, July 3, 1746.

                                Philadelphia, November 27, 1746.
RUN away from Robert Meade, in January 1744-5, two Dutch servants, man and wife; the man's name Joannes Harmonius Fretzel, a smart lively fellow, with a scar under his lower jaw, as it were from an evil. 'Tis said they are settled in a place call'd the camp, back of New-York; where he has past some times for a doctor or physick, and some times for a preacher. Whoever brings the good couple to said Meade, shall have for Reward TEN PISTOLES.
The Pennsylvania Gazette, November 27, 1746; December 2, 1746; December 9, 1746. See *The American Weekly Mercury*, From May 16, to May 23, 1745.

                                Philadelphia, Dec. 8. 1746.
RUN away last night, from Samuel Evans, of Marple township, Chester county, a native Irish servant man, named Peter Conoly, about 20 years of age, speaks broguish, of a dark brown complexion, and short brown hair: Had on when he went away, an Irish cap, an old felt hat, a pair of new shoes, dark colour'd stockings, a pair of buckskin breeches, with yellow buttons, a good tow short, a long light colour'd jacket too large for him, with a short dark colour'd one under it, without sleeves. Whoever secures said servant, so that his master may have him again, shall have Forty shillings reward,
        paid by   SAMUEL EVANS.
The Pennsylvania Gazette, December 9, 1746; December 23, 1746; January 6, 1747.

                                Philadelphia, Decem. 16. 1746.
RAN away the 8th Instant from Gunpowder Iron-works, a servant man belonging to James Evins, in West Nottingham, Chester County, named Joseph Carr; about twenty years of age, near 6 foot high, pale complexion, brown eyes, and his hair cut off. Had on when he went away, a striped cotton cap, mostly white, a brown coloured coat, with round white metal buttons, black jacket, wanting the sleeves, two pair of breeches, one of them blue cloth, and the other red plush, blue yarn stockings, and sharp toed shoes. He had about twenty or thirty shillings of Maryland money about him, is given to drink, and has been a soldier, which he is apt to talk of. Whoever takes up said servant, so that his master may have him again, shall have Three Pounds reward, and reasonable charges,   paid by James Evins.
The Pennsylvania Gazette, December 16, 1746.

Philadelphia, December 16, 1746.
RAN away the 11th Instant from the subscriber, living in Charlestown, Chester County, a native Irish servant man named William Reardon; between twenty and thirty years of age, a short thick well set fellow, with black hair, lisps very much, was born near Cork, and has been out a privateering. He served some time prisoner in Chester goal. Had on when he went away, a brown drugget coat, lined with yellow shalloon, whitish cloth-coloured waistcoat, and a red one, lined with the same, and good shoes and stockings. he is supposed to be in company with one Mary Sullivan, a short thick woman, and notorious thief. Whoever takes up the said servant, so that his master may have him again, shall have two pistoles reward, and reasonable charges,   paid by   William Reynolds.
N. B. masters of vessels, and others, are hereby cautioned not to entertain him at their peril.

The Pennsylvania Gazette, December 16, 1746; December 23, 1746; December 30, 1746. See *The Pennsylvania Gazette*, December 10, 1745, *The Pennsylvania Gazette*, June 4, 1747, and *The Pennsylvania Gazette*, July 30, 1747.

Philadelphia, December 23. 1746.
RUN away the 8th instant, from Matthias Kerlin, tavernkeeper, in Concord, Chester county, an English servant woman, named Rachel Pickerin, about 30 years of age, thick set, pretty fat, pale complexion, dark colour'd hair, somewhat pock fretten: Had on when she went away, a worsted orange coloured gown, several strip'd worsted petticoats, peak toed mens shoes; she had a fat man-child with her, about 6 months old, and wore a whitish callicoe gown, a red and white strip'd linsey frock, another frock strip'd blue and yellow; she was carried up from New-Castle county to Philadelphia in a boat, she has been heard to enquire for one Timothy Conner, who she says is her husband, but he is only her bastard's suppos'd father; he serv'd his time with one William Peters, fuller, living near said Concord. Whoever takes up said servant, and brings her to her master, or secures her, so that he may have her again, shall have Forty Shillings reward, and reasonable charges,
paid by   MATTHIAS KERLIN.
The Pennsylvania Gazette, December 23, 1746; December 30, 1746; January 20, 1747.

1747

Philadelphia, Dec. 31. 1746.
RUN away the 30th inst. from Joseph Jeanes, of the mannor of Moreland, Philadelphia county, a servant lad, named John Hughes, about 17 years of

age, has dark colour'd hair. Had on when he went away, a coarse shirt, new felt hat, two linsey jackets, one of them strip'd, and patch'd with other colours, and has pewter buttons, white linsey beeches, lightish yarn stockings, and new shoes; and took with him an old great coat without a cape. Whoever secures the said servant, so that his master may have him again, shall have Thirty-shillings reward,
              paid by   JOSEPH JEANES.
The Pennsylvania Gazette, January 6, 1747; January 13, 1747; January 20, 1747.

RUN away on the 12th of *December* last, from *John Willson* of *Coventry* Township in *Chester* County, a Native Irish Servant-Man, named *Derby Delaney*, speaks bad English, is about 23 Years of Age, near five foot ten Inches high, is a thick well-set Fellow, with short blackish Hair, is somewhat Negro-nos'd, thick Lips, heavey Browed, and is apt to Swear, had on when he went away an old felt Hatt, an ash colour'd Cloath Jacket with brass Buttons, a new Linnen Coat and the Buttons cover'd with Thread, a Flannel Jacket without Sleeves, a course Tow Shirt and Buck-skin Breeches with brass Buttons, old brown Stockings and new Shoes with picked Toes, tyed with Thongs: Whoever takes up and secures said Servant-Man, so as his Master may have him again, shall have forty Shillings Reward,
              paid by   JOHN WILLSON.
N. B. He was seen at the Widow *Mc. Neal's* Tavern, in the great Valley, on the 20th of *December* and is suppos'd to go towards *New-Port* or *Newcastle*.
The Pennsylvania Journal, or, Weekly Advertiser, January 6, 1747; January 20, 1747; January 27, 1747; February 3, 1747; February 10, 1747; February 24, 1747; March 3, 1747; March 10, 1747; March 17, 1747; March 24, 1747; April 2, 1747; April 9, 1747.

                             Philadelphia, January 20. 1746-7.
RUN away the 18th instant, from William Hudson, of this city, tanner, an Irish servant man, named Daniel Brady, about 20 years of age, sandy complexion, 5 feet 9 or 10 inches high. Had on a black Irish frize coat, a brown waistcoat, and another of a lighter colour without sleeves, a fine homespun shirt, leather breeches, and good shoes and stockings: Took with him besides, a pair of stockings and shoes, two brown homespun shirts, and a pair of linnen breeches. 'Tis probable he will endeavour to pass for a tanner, tho' he is not a workman. Whoever secures the said servant, so that he may be had again, or brings him to his Master, shall have Twenty-shillings reward,

if taken within 10 miles of this city, or Forty if farther, and reasonable charges, paid by   WILLIAM HUDSON.

The Pennsylvania Gazette, January 20, 1747; January 27, 1747; February 3, 1747.

Philadelphia, January 27. 1746-7.
RUN away the 17th inst. from Nehemiah Allen, of this City, an apprentice lad, named Joseph Crispin, a cooper by trade, about nineteen years of age, and five foot eight inches high: Had on when he went away, a narrow brimm'd beaver hat, a linnen cap, a mixt coloured homespun coat lin'd with the same, a light colour'd cloth waistcoat with brass buttons, a pair of buckskin breeches, a check shirt, and a pair of dark coloured yarn stockings. Whoever secures the said apprentice, so that his master may have him again, shall have Thirty-shillings reward, if taken within thirty miles of this city, and Three Pounds if taken further off, and reasonable charges,
            paid by   *Nehemiah Allen.*
N. B. 'Tis supposed he is gone towards Amwell, in New- Jersey; or to New-York, as he was seen pass thro' Trenton.

The Pennsylvania Gazette, January 27, 1747; February 3, 1747; February 10, 1747; February 17, 1747. See *The New-York Gazette, Revived in the Weekly Post-Boy*, February 9, 1747.

Philadelphia, February 3, 1746-7.
ON the 11th of last month was committed to the goal of this city, a person who called himself John Bland, on suspicion of his having stolen a Negro boy, a stallion, and a gelding, which he brought with him to this place. He is well set, about 24 years of age, fresh complexion, and light brown hair. The Negro is a likely lad, named Peter, about ten years old; by whose account it appears, that he was stolen by the prisoner from his master, one Giffin, who lives at a place called Pon Pon, in South Carolina.

The stallion mentioned above, is a sorrel, about 14 hands high, with a white mane and tail, branded on the near buttock **R W**. The gelding is a light roan, about 14 hands high, has a short tail, and looks as if lately cut with a knife; he is branded on the near shoulder **T B** in one, and on the near buttock, **D B**; they have both saddle spots, and are natural pacers.

The prisoner above-mentioned, since his commitment, has confest his true name to be Uttie Perkins; and that some time in May, 1743, he made his escape from the sheriff of Baltimore county, in Maryland. It also appears, by a letter found about him directed to one Louns, that he has broke prison in some part of South Carolina. And a person who has seen him here, and knows him well, informs, That he has, for a long time, been a noted horse stealer in

Virginia and South Carolina, and that a very great reward has been offered for apprehending him.   NICHOLAS SCULL, Sheriff.
> *The Pennsylvania Gazette*, February 3, 1747; February 17, 1747; *The Maryland Gazette*, February 17, 1747; February 24, 1747. Minor differences between the papers.

RUN away the 17th January, from Nehemiah Allen, of Philadelphia, an Apprentice Lad, named Joseph Crispin, a Cooper by Trade, about 19 Years of Age, and 5 Foot 8 Inches high: had on when he went away, a narrow brimm Bever Hat, a Linnen Cap, a mixt-colour'd homespun Coat lined with the same, a light-coloured cloth Wastcoat with brass Buttons, a pair of Buckskin Breeches, a check Shirt, and a pair of dark-colour'd yarn Stockings. Whoever secures the said Apprentice, so that his said Master may have him again, shall have Thirty Shillings *Reward if taken within* 30 Miles *of* Philadelphia, *and* Three Pounds *if farther off, and reasonable Charges,*
paid by   Nehemiah Allen.
N. B. *It is supposed he is gone towards* Amwell, *in* New-Jersey; *or to* New-York, *as he was seen pass through* Trenton.
> *The New-York Gazette, Revived in the Weekly Post-Boy*, February 9, 1747; February 16, 1747; February 23, 1747. See *The Pennsylvania Gazette*, February 3, 1747.

Philadelphia, February 24. 1746-7.
Run away the 19th instant, from John Stevenson, of Norrington township, Philadelphia county, a native Irish servant fellow, named Hugh Cavenaugh, about 20 years of age, full faced, down look'd, middle sized; well set, has brown hair, speaks a little on the brogue, and is very apt to lie: Had on when he went away, a whitish Kersey Jacket, with brass buttons, a brown one under it, a leather apron, leather breeches, grey yarn stockings, old shoes, old felt hat, and coarse shirt. Whoever secures said servant, so that his master may have him again, shall have Twenty Shillings reward, if taken within ten miles, or Fifty of further, and reasonable charges,
paid by   JOHN STEVENSON.
> *The Pennsylvania Gazette*, February 24, 1747; March 3, 1747; March 10, 1747; March 16, 1747.

Philadelphia, March 3. 1746-7.
RUN away the 22d day of January last, from Hugh M'Cleland, of the township of Salisbury, Lancaster county, an Irish servant boy, named Michael Galacher, about 14 years of age, speaks much on the brogue, of thin visage, fair complexion, and dark brown hair: Had on when he went away, an old castor hat, a brown coat, with carved metal buttons, and a jacket of the

same, old cloth breeches and blue yarn stockings, patched with white cloth on both heels, good shoes, tied with strings; and he is much pitted with the small-pox. Whoever takes up and secures the said servant, so that his master may have him again, shall have Thirty-shillings reward, and reasonable charges, paid by   Hugh M'Cleland.
The Pennsylvania Gazette, March 3, 1747; March 10, 1747; March 16, 1747.

Philadelphia, March 3. 1746-7.
RUN *away the* 23d *of last month, from William Hartley, of Charlestown, Chester County, an Irish Servant man, named Peter Fowler, about 25 years of age, a thick well set fellow, and has short black hair, and is very much given to drinking; he has been several years in this province, but by running away, and other misdemeanors, is still a servant: Had on when he went away, a brown linsey jacket, with pewter buttons, old cloth breeches, fine check trowsers, and good shoes and stockings, Whoever takes up and secures said servants, so that his master may have him again, shall have Five Pounds, Pennsylvania currency, reward, and reasonable charges,*
          from   William Hartley.
N. B. *If the above servant is taken out of the province, Six Pistoles reward.*
The Pennsylvania Gazette, March 3, 1747; March 10, 1747; March 16, 1747; March 24, 1747. See *The Pennsylvania Gazette,* February 24, 1743, *The Pennsylvania Gazette,* June 27, 1745, *The Pennsylvania Journal, or, Weekly Advertiser,* June 27, 1745, and *The Pennsylvania Gazette,* April 9, 1747.

Philadelphia, March 10. 1746-7.
RUN away, on the 26th of February last, from John Keppler, of Perkyoman, by Pawling's mill, Philadelphia county, an Irish servant lad, named James Barly; but it is supposed he will call himself Jacob Barly; he is about 17 years of age, of middle stature, pretty much mark'd with the small-pox, has short black hair, cut but last summer, and speaks pretty good English, and good Dutch: Had on when he went away, an old pair of shoes, check trowsers, brown coat, half worn, and afterwards bought new cloaths in Philadelphia, viz. a blue jacket, a silk handkerchief, a hat, and shoes and stockings: He took with him a roan gelding, about 13 or 14 hands high, shod before, not long trimm'd, paces and trots; he has also taken some money. Whoever takes up said servant, and secures him, so as his master may have him again, shall have Three Pounds reward, if taken within 50 miles of Philadelphia, if farther, for every 10 miles Five Shillings, and reasonable charges, paid by *JOHN KEPPLER.*
The Pennsylvania Gazette, March 10, 1747; March 16, 1747; March 24, 1747.

Philadelphia, March 10. 1746-7.
RUN away, the 17th of February last, from John Climson, of Salisbury township, Lancaster county, an Irish servant lad, named Edward Loller, about 17 years of age, of middle stature, well-set, fresh complexion, red hair, freckled in the face: Had on when he went away, an old drab coloured coat, old brown jacket, without sleeves, good leather breeches, tow shirt, old brown stockings, old shoes, and an old felt hat, and wore an iron collar. Whoever takes up and secures said servant, so that his master may have him again, shall have Twenty Shillings Reward, and reasonable charges,
   paid by JOHN CLIMSON.
The Pennsylvania Gazette, March 10, 1747; March 16, 1747; March 24, 1747. See *The Pennsylvania Journal, or, Weekly Advertiser*, March 10, 1747.

RUN away about the 17*th* of *February, from John Clemson*, of the Township of *Salisbury*, in *Lancaster* County, a Servant Lad named *Edward Coller*, aged about 17 Years, of fresh Complexion, red Hair, and freckled Face, had on when he went away, an Iron Collar, an old Drab-colour'd Coat, an old brown Jacket with no Sleeves, old brown Stockings, old Shoes, good Leather Breeches, a Tow Shirt, and an old Felt Hat. Whoever takes up said Servant and secures him so that his Master may have him again, shall have Twenty Shillings Reward, and reasonable Charges
   paid by JOHN CLEMSON.
The Pennsylvania Journal, or, Weekly Advertiser, March 10, 1747; March 24, 1747; April 9, 1747; April 24, 1747; April 30, 1747. See *The Pennsylvania Gazette*, March 10, 1747.

        Philadelphia, April 2. 1747.
RUN away on the 15th of March, from Jost Dubs, at Reading iron-works, an Irish servant man, named James Rees; he is a short lad, about 19 years of age, very much pitted in the face with the small-pox, has short black hair, and can talk Dutch. Had on when he went away, a fine hat, a light colour'd cloth coat and jacket, with brass buttons; new homespun shirt, with large buttons at the collar, made of the same as the shirt; light worsted stockings, a little old, and new pumps, with two odd buckles in them. Whoever takes up the said servant, and secures him in any goal, shall have Forty Shillings reward, and reasonable charges,
   paid by JOST DUBS.
The Pennsylvania Gazette, April 2, 1747; April 9, 1747.

Philadelphia, April 9. 1747.

RUN away the 23d of February last, from William Hartley, of Charlestown, Chester county, and province of Pennsylvania, an Irish servant man, named Peter Fowler, about 25 years of age, a thick well set fellow, has short black hair, and is very much given to drinking; he has been several years in this province, but by running away, and other misdemeanours, is still a servant: Had on when he went away, a brown linsey jacket with pewter buttons, old cloth breeches, fine check trowsers, and good shoes and stockings. Whoever takes up the said servant, and gives notice thereof to Mr. Benjamin Franklin printer in Philadelphia, so that his master may have him gain, shall have Ten Pounds Pennsylvania currency as a reward, and reasonable charges,

paid by   *William Hartley.*

N. B. All masters of vessels and others, are hereby cautioned not to entertain him at their peril.

The Pennsylvania Gazette, April 9, 1747; April 23, 1747; *The New-York Gazette, Revived in the Weekly Post-Boy,* April 13, 1747; April 27, 1747. Minor differences between the papers. See *The Pennsylvania Gazette,* February 24, 1743, *The Pennsylvania Gazette,* June 27, 1745, and *The Pennsylvania Gazette,* March 3, 1747.

Philadelphia, *April* 9. 1747.

RUN away from John Foulks, tanner, of the borough of Lancaster, on the 5th inst. an Irish servant man, named Archibald M'Kaghan: Had on a brown cloth coat, a plad jacket, a pair of leather breeches newly wash'd, a pair of black stocking, good shoes, a felt hat, and a brown wig. He is of a middle stature, dark complexion, bluff face, and very well set. Whoever takes up said servant, and secures him so that his master may have him again, shall have Forty shillings reward, and reasonable charges,

paid by   JOHN FOULKS.

N. B. He procur'd a pass from one Clark now in Lancaster goal, and 'tis suppos'd he will change his name to that of Clark.

The Pennsylvania Gazette, April 9, 1747; April 23, 1747.

Philadelphia, *April* 16. 1747.

RUN away on the 8th of this instant, from Alexander Crage, of New-London township, Chester county, an Irish man, named William Anderson, of a dark complexion, down look, black bushy hair; had on when he went away, a white flannel jacket, leather breeches, of sheep skin, white yarn stockings, old shoes, and an old felt hat, and is supposed to have an old grey twiled jacket under the flannel jacket, speaks very broad and slow. Whoever takes up the said servant, and secures him, so as his master may have him again;

shall have Forty Shillings reward, and reasonable charges,
        paid by   Alexander Crage.
The Pennsylvania Gazette, April 16, 1747; April 23, 1747; April 30, 1747.

Philadelphia, April 16. 1747.
RUN away on the 18th of last month, from Benjamin Fred, of New Garden township, Chester county, a servant man, named John Wilson, about 21 years of age, of middle stature, well set, full faced, short dark brown hair, cut off last summer. Took with him, a new light grey, or skie- blue coloured cloth coat without lining, has cross pockets, with large open cuffs to the sleeves, mohair buttons on it, and buttonholes wrought with blue worsted; another coat of twilled stuff, of a flesh colour, well lined, and is full narrow for him; two jackets, one of white fustian, the other an old cloth Jacket, of a brown colour; a pair of leather breeches with white metal buttons, one pair of grey yarn stockings, a worsted pair, and one pair of white thread; an old felt hat, old shoes, two new shirts, and an old fine one. Whoever takes up the said servant, so that his master may have him again, shall have Thirty shillings reward,   paid by   BENJAMIN FRED.
The Pennsylvania Gazette, April 16, 1747; April 23, 1747; April 30, 1747.

Philadelphia, April 24, 1747.
RUN-away on the 26th of *March* last from *Hugh Patten*, of *Hempfield* Township, *Lancaster* County, an Irish Servant Man named *Mortough Smith*, had on when he went away a good Felt Hat, short black Hair if not cut of, Orange Colour Jacket, with brass Buttons, a Linsey one under it, old cloath Breeches, and Trowsers, black Stockings, old Shoes, and of a Dark Complexion, and is a great Snuffer. Whoever takes up and secures the said Servant, so that his Master may have him again, shall have FIVE POUNDS reward, and reasonable Charges
        paid by   *HUGH PATTEN*
The Pennsylvania Journal, or, Weekly Advertiser, April 24, 1747; May 7, 1747; May 14, 1747.

Philadelphia, May. 7. 1747.
RUN away the fourth Inst. from Thomas Griffith, of Vincent township, Chester county, an Irish servant boy, named John Coffee, about 17 years of age, short and well set, red hair, freckled, and is pretty talkative. Had on when he went away, a striped linnen jacket, and an old pea one, black cloth breeches, two shirt, old yarn stockings, good shoes, and an old felt hat. Whoever takes up and secures said servant, so that his master may have him

again, shall have Thirty shillings reward, and reasonable charges,
paid by   *Thomas Griffith.*
N. B. All masters of vessels are forbid to take him on board at their peril.
The Pennsylvania Gazette, May 7, 1747; May 14, 1747; May 21, 1747.
See *The Pennsylvania Gazette,* July 30, 1747.

Philadelphia, May 7. 1747.
RUN away from his bail, on the 26th of April last, Thomas Bentley, but may have changed his name to that of Vincent. he's an Englishman, about 25 years of age, 5 foot 6 inches high, fair complexion, talks much, and is much addicted to company. Had on, a grey cloth jockey coat, and waistcoat of the same, leather breeches, a castor hat, and a linnen cap. Whoever takes up and secures said Bentley, so that he may be had again, shall have Three-pounds reward, and reasonable charges, paid by Benjamin Vanhorne,   in Northampton township, Bucks county.
The Pennsylvania Gazette, May 7, 1747; May 14, 1747; May 21, 1747.

Philadelphia, May 7. 1747.
RUN away, on the first inst. from Edward Wells, of this city, an English servant man, named John Jones, about 25 years of age, 5 feet 6 inches high, pretty well set, round shoulder'd, large nose, and pretty much pitted with the small-pox; he is a bold talkative fellow, and wears his own black short curled hair. Had on when he went away, a butcher's frock, trowsers and shirt, all new oznabrigs, new shoes, and a coarse felt hat. Whoever takes up said runaway, and secures him, so as his master may have him again, shall have if taken within ten miles of this city, Ten-shillings reward, and if twenty, Twenty shillings, and reasonable charges,
paid by   EDWARD WELLS .
The Pennsylvania Gazette, May 7, 1747; May 14, 1747; May 21, 1747.

Philadelphia May 21. 1747.
RUN away about three weeks ago, from the snow Bonetta-packet, Charles Lyon, master, a sailor, named William Cross, an Irishman, and has a good deal of the brogue on his tongue, about 35 years of age, about 5 foot and a half high, a well-set fellow, and much pockfretten: Had on when he went away, an old hat, a linnen cap, blue jacket, and a white flannel one under it, trowsers, good yarn stockings, and old shoes. Whoever takes up said Cross, and secures him, so as he may be had again, shall have Forty-shillings reward,
paid by   SAMUEL POWELL, junior.

N. B. He had a month's pay from the owners of said vessel, and is supposed to be lurking about town.
The Pennsylvania Gazette, May 21, 1747; May 28, 1747; June 4, 1747.

Philadelphia, May 21. 1747.
RUN away the 13th instant, from Chester, an Irish servant man, named Patrick M'Donnell, aged about 28 years, a short thick fellow, with short brown curl'd hair, hollow eyes, large eyebrows, sour countenance, goes close with his knees, and is very apt to get drunk, when he is very impudent and talkative. Had on when he went away, a bluish broad cloth jacket, ozenbrigs shirt, black plush breeches, much torn, with sheepskin lining, grey yarn stockings, round toed shoes, too large for his feet. he serv'd his time to John Clemson, of Pequa, on the edge of Chester county, and has been brought in again as a servant, for his fine and prison fees, being indicted for felony. He has been a privateering in the new George, from Philadelphia, and with Capt. Tingley, from New-York. Whoever secures him, so that he may be had again, shall have *Two Pistoles* reward, and reasonable charges
   paid by *John Hanly.*
All masters of vessels are requested not to take him on board.
The Pennsylvania Gazette, May 21, 1747; May 28, 1747; June 4, 1747.

Philadelphia, May 21. 1747.
RUn away, on the 17th instant from John Holland, of Whiteland township, Chester county, Pennsylvania, an English servant man, named William Thomas, about 20 years of age, low stature, squints much with his right eye: Had on when he went away, a felt hat, a light coloured coat, with white metal buttons, leather breeches, with brass buttons, grey yarn stockings, and round toed shoes, tied with strings. Whoever takes up and secures said servant, so that his master may have him again, shall have *Three Pounds* reward,
   paid by *JOHN HOLLAND.*
The Pennsylvania Gazette, May 21, 1747; May 28, 1747; June 4, 1747.

Philadelphia, May 21. 1747.
RUn away, on the 18th day of April last, from the subscriber, at Coventry forge, in Chester county, an Irish servant man, named Charles Barker, a thick, well-set, smooth faced fellow: Had on when he went away, a beaver hat, cotton cap, a good brown fustian jacket, and no coat, grey worsted stockings, and leather breeches, if he has not changed his apparel. Whoever takes up and secures the said servant, so that his master may have him again, shall

have *Five Pounds* reward, and reasonable charges,
paid by   SAMUEL MEREDITH.
The Pennsylvania Gazette, May 21, 1747; May 28, 1747; June 4, 1747.

Philadelphia, May 25. 1747.
FIVE PISTOLES REWARD.
RUN away last night, from John Veneman, of Chester, in Pennsylvania, a servant man, named Sion Wentworth, born in New-England, aged about 25 years, by trade a Blacksmith, about 5 feet 6 inches high, well set, dark complexion, down-cast look, slow of speech, walks wide with his knees, lately had the Small-pox. Had on when he went away, an old beaver hat, sharp cocked, and a small brim, white cap, dark brown broad-cloth coat and jacket, the Jacket double breasted, and more worn than the Coat, having most of the buttons worn off, and darned near the pocket, old leather breeches, blue yarn stockings, halk-worn [sic] calfskin shoes, with holes burnt in the upper leathers, a white homespun shirt, and a check one. Whoever secures him in any goal, or otherwise, so that his mater may have him again, shall have the above Reward, and reasonable Charges,
paid by   JOHN VENEMAN.
The Pennsylvania Gazette, May 28, 1747; June 4, 1747; June 11, 1747.

Philadelphia, May 28. 1747.
RUN away on the 24th instant, from the subscriber, near Warwick furnace, Chester county, an Irish servant man, named Bryan Dignan, about 20 years of age, a short well-set fellow, fresh complexion, with short brown hair, if not cut off: Had on when he went away, a felt hat, ozenbrigs shirt and trowsers, an orange colour'd jacket, without lining, with Brass Buttons, Leather Breeches, new pumps, and some money with him, and may have changed his cloaths. He formerly ran away from Edward Goff, and was taken up near the Forks of Delaware. Whoever brings him to the subscriber, or secures him in any goal, so that his master may have him again, shall have Forty Shillings reward, and reasonable charges,
paid by   *Randal Marshall.*
N. B. All masters of vessels are desired not to take him on board.
The Pennsylvania Gazette, May 28, 1747; June 4, 1747; June 11, 1747.

Philadelphia, May 28. 1747.
RUn away, on the 19th instant, from John Potts, Esq; of Colebrookdale township, Philadelphia county, an Irish servant man, named Francis

Henderson, aged about 24 years, a tall, thin faced fellow, much pitted with the small-pox, of sandy complexion, pretends to be a scholar, and apt to drink, if he can get it: Had on when he went away, a felt hat, cotton cap, a freeze or napt whitish jacket, and ozenbrigs shirts and trowsers, old shoes, and may have a pair of red plush breeches. Whoever takes up said servant, and secures him in some goal, or brings him to his said master, if taken within 45 miles, shall have *Thirty Shillings* reward, and if further Three Pounds,
    paid by JOHN POTTS.
The Pennsylvania Gazette, May 28, 1747; June 4, 1747; June 11, 1747; June 18, 1747.

           Philadelphia, June 4. 1747.
RUn away, on the 24th of last month, from Joseph Kelly, of Bristol township, Bucks county, an Irish servant man, named Richard Savage, about 25 years of age, of dark complexion, a well set fellow, and very active and brisk: Had on when he went away, a coarse linnen jacket and breeches, and an iron coloured waistcoat over the linnen one, check shirt, coarse stockings, old shoes, new soaled, coarse hat, old black wig, and a striped cap; he was seen going by the widow Amos's, and has on leather breeches, and white stockings, which 'tis supposed he got from some body for some of his clothes; he is a cunning, artful fellow, and can do something at the cooper and butcher's trade. Whoever takes up and secures said servant, so that his master may have him again, shall have *Forty Shillings* reward, and reasonable charges, paid by said
    Kelley, or Charles Edgar, in Philadelphia.
N. B. 'Tis supposed he will change all his clothes.
  The Pennsylvania Gazette, June 4, 1747; June 11, 1747; June 18, 1747. See *The Pennsylvania Journal, or, Weekly Advertiser*, June 4, 1747, and *The Pennsylvania Journal, or, Weekly Advertiser*, October 1, 1747.

           Philadelphia, June 4. 1747.
      TEN POUNDS Reward.
RUN away on Sunday night last, from the subscribers, living in Chester county, two native Irish servant men, one named William Reardon, the property of William Moore; is a short, thick, well set fellow, between 20 and 30 years of age, talks pretty fast, and lisps much, has black hair, was born near Cork, is well acquainted with every part of Pennsylvania, and understands all sorts of country work, of which he is apt to bragg, and has been a privateering. He formerly served Mr. Hugh Evans, of Merion, Philadelphia county; but since that has for his roguery lain a considerable Time in Chester goal; has taken no clothes with him but what are very

indifferent, except two pair of shoes, and two shirts, marked on the bosom W.

The other named *Derby Clark*, the property of James Star, by trade a weaver, about 5 feet 9 inches high, dark complexion, Had on when he went away, a dark blue broadcloth coat, with blue mohair buttons, a new homespun ash coloured jacket, with broad white flat metal buttons, white jacket, without sleeves, two shirts, a pair of brown cloth breeches, two pair of trowsers, old shoes, felt hat, and a pair of brown yarn stockings, and is about 28 years of age. Whoever apprehends the said servants, and delivers them to their respective masters, shall have *Five Pounds* reward for each, and reasonable charges, paid by   WILLIAM MOORE, and JAMES STAR.

The Pennsylvania Gazette, June 4, 1747; June 11, 1747; June 18, 1747.

See *The Pennsylvania Gazette*, December 10, 1745, *The Pennsylvania Gazette*, December 16, 1746, and *The Pennsylvania Gazette*, June 4, 1747, for Reardon.

Philadelphia, June 4. 1747.
RUN away on the 24 of May, from *Joseph Kelly*, of *Bristol* Township, and County of *Bucks*, an Irish Servant Man, named *Richard Savage*, aged about 25 Years, a dark Complexion, a well-set Fellow, very brisk and active, Had on when he went away, a coarse linnen Jacket and Breeches; an Iron-coloured Waistcoat over the linnen one, a check'd Shirt, coarse Stockings and Hatt, an old black Wig, and a striped Cap, old Shoes new soled; he was seeming coming by the Widow *Amos's* and had leather Breeches and white Sockings, suppos'd to have changed with some one, he is a cunning artful Fellow, he can do a small Matter at the Cooper's and Butcher's Trade. Whoever takes up and secures said Servant, so that his Master may have him again, shall have Forty Shillings Reward, and reasonable Charges paid by said
   Kelly, or *Charles Edgar*, in *Philadelphia*.
N. B. It is supposed he will change his Cloaths.

The Pennsylvania Journal, or, Weekly Advertiser, June 4, 1747; June 11, 1747; June 18, 1747; June 25, 1747; July 2, 1747; July 9, 1747; July 16, 1747; July 23, 1747; July 30, 1747; August 6, 1747. See *The Pennsylvania Gazette*, June 4, 1747, and *The Pennsylvania Journal, or, Weekly Advertiser*, October 1, 1747.

Philadelphia, June 11. 1747.
Run away, the 4th instant, from Samuel Evans, of Marple township, Chester county, a native Irish servant man, named Peter Connoly, about 29 years of age, middle stature, brown complexion, brown short hair, has a blemish in the right eye, by the poak of a cow's horn. Had on, a half worn felt hat, light coloured jacket, too short, with metal buttons, and a pair of trowsers, his shoes too large for him and one of them has a cut in the upper leather, near

the toe. Whoever secures said servant, so that he may be had again, shall have Twenty Shillings reward, and reasonable charges,
   paid by *Samuel Evans.*
The Pennsylvania Gazette, June 11, 1747; June 18, 1747; July 2, 1747.

              Philadelphia, June 11. 1747.
RUn away, on the 19th of last month, from Oley Forge, in Philadelphia county, an Irish servant man, named William Palmer, of low stature, down looked, brown complexion, thin visaged, wears his own hair, is about 18 years of age, speaks but poor English, and has an impediment in his speech: Had on when he went away, a half worn light coloured jacket, and ozenbrigs shirt, striped linnen trowsers, new shoes, and old castor hat. Whoever takes up and secures the said servant, so that his master may have him again, shall have *Two Pistoles* reward,
   paid by *John Lesher and Company.*
The Pennsylvania Gazette, June 11, 1747; June 18, 1747; July 2, 1747.

              Philadelphia, June 18. 1747.
Run away from the subscriber, of Strawsborough township, Lancaster county, an English servant man, named John White, about 40 years of age, fresh complexion, middle stature, has dark brown hair, and is apt to change his name: Had on when he went away, a brown homespun jacket, tow trowsers, grey yarn stockings, and pumps; he took with him a pair of buckskin breeches, two hats, one of them new, value twenty shillings, the other an old felt hat, a red silk handkerchief, and a coarse shirt. Whoever takes up and secures said servant, so as his master may have him again, shall have *Thirty Shillings* reward, and reasonable charges,
   paid by *Philip Ward.*
The Pennsylvania Gazette, June 18, 1747; June 25, 1747; July 2, 1747; July 16, 1747.

              Philadelphia, June 18. 1747.
Run away, the 14th instant, from Thomas Fletcher, of Abington township, Philadelphia county, two Irish servant men; one named Patrick Macguire, middle stature, thin visage, whitish complexion: Had on a homespun lead coloured jacket, with pewter buttons, two pair of tow petticoat trowsers, check shirts, old shoes, square toed, yarn stockings, and a large brimmed felt hat; he is a bold, talkative fellow, and perhaps will call himself a forgeman.
 The other named Patrick Matthews, a short, well-set fellow, down looked, reddish complexion, and somewhat pockfretten: Had on a new homespun lead coloured jacket, with mohair buttons, check shirts, two pair

of tow trowsers, new shoes, worsted stockings, and broad brimmed hat; they both wear caps, their hair cut off, but one of them has a wig; and have been but about two months in the country. Whoever takes up said servants, and secures them, so as they may be had again, shall have *Forty Shillings* reward for each, and reasonable charges,
    paid by Thomas Fletcher.
The Pennsylvania Gazette, June 18, 1747; June 25, 1747.

              Philadelphia, June 18, 1747.
RUN away on Saturday last from *George Bradley* of this City an *Irish* Servant Man named *Charles Smith*, aged about 25 Years, a lusty stout Fellow, fresh Complexion, short dark Hair, had on when he went away, a blew cloath Coat, full trim'd, a cloth Jacket, much peic'd, Leather Breeches and oznabrigs Trowsers, good Stockings, and a felt Hat. His Legs is remarkable thick and large, and affects to walk very stately, and has the Brogue on his Tongue. Whoever takes up the said Servant and secures him so that his Master may have him again, shall have *Forty Shillings* Reward and all reasonable Charges
    paid by GEORGE BRADLEY.
The Pennsylvania Journal, or, Weekly Advertiser, June 18, 1747; June 25, 1747; July 2, 1747; July 9, 1747; July 16, 1747; July 23, 1747.

              Philadelphia, June 18. 1747.
RUN away on Sunday Night last, from *Alexander Alexander*, and *James Rynells*, of this City, two Irish Servant Men: The one belonging to *Alexander Alexander*, named *Daniel M'Bride*, aged about 25 Years, has the Brogue on his Tongue, about 5 Foot 6 Inches high, well-set, pretty fresh Complexion, by Trade a Blacksmith, and has two of his Fingers shot off his Right Hand. Had on when he went away, a dark brown cloth Coat, blueish Jacket, oznabrig Trowsers, yarn Stockings, good Shoes, a dark colour'd Wig, and a felt Hat.

  The other belonging to *James Rynells*, named *Bryant Boyles*, has the Brogue on his Tongue, aged about 25 Years, is a well-set Fellow, and has black Hair. Had on when he went away, an old felt Hat, a new oznabrig Jacket, Breeches, Trowsers and Shirt, new yarn Stockings, and old Shoes.

  Whoever takes up and secures said Servants, so that their Masters may have them again, shall have *Twenty Shillings* Reward for each, if taken within ten Miles of *Philadelphia*, and *Forty Shillings* if further off,
    paid by Alexander Alexander, James Rynells.
N. B. 'Tis suppos'd they have taken with them, a dark bay Horse, and a black Mare.

The Pennsylvania Journal, or, Weekly Advertiser, June 18, 1747; June 25, 1747; July 2, 1747.

Philadelphia, June 25. 1747.
RUn away from Moses Macilvaine, of Lancaster county, the 16th instant, an Irish servant, named Catherine O'Harra, well-set, fair hair, speaks bad English, and is apt to swear; she has been about ten months in the county, and had on, and took with her, a plad gown, and an old striped blue and white one, a yellow petticoat, worsted stockings, silk handkerchief, high heel'd shoes, a hoop, a little black silk bonnet for a child, and several other things not here mentioned. Whoever takes up said servant, and secures her in any goal, so that she may be had again, shall have Forty Shillings reward, and reasonable charges,
        paid by   Moses Macilvaine.
The Pennsylvania Gazette, June 25, 1747, July 2, 1747; July 9, 1747; July 16, 1747; July 23, 1747.

RUN away on the 17th Instant past, from *Patrick Marrow*, of *Radnor* in *Chester* County, an Irish Servant, named Dennis M'Coy, of middle Stature, black Hair; having on a light colour Jacket, Breeches, and Stockings, good Shoes and a felt Hat, hath taken with him several Shirts and a Wallet, his age about Twenty. Whoever takes up and secures the said Servant, so that his Master may have him again, shall have THREE POUNDS Reward, and reasonable Charges,
        paid by   PATRICK MARROW.
The Pennsylvania Journal, or, Weekly Advertiser, July 2, 1747; July 9, 1747; July 16, 1747; July 23, 1747; July 30, 1747; August 6, 1747; August 13, 1747; August 20, 1747; August 27, 1747; September 3, 1747. See *The New-York Gazette, Revived in the Weekly Post-Boy*, July 27, 1747.

Philadelphia, July 9. 1747.
RUN away the 5th of this instant, from John Yoder, of Oley township, Philadelphia county, two Irish servant men; the one named Daniel Donahew, about 40 years of age, of middling size, long thin visage, much pock mark'd, has a large scar on his left cheek, and another on his neck, black hair, if not cut off, by trade a miller. Had on when he went away, a felt hat, homespun shirt, a light brown linsey jacket, with brass buttons, two trowsers, yarn stockings, and half worn shoes. The other named Thomas Lynch, about 20 years of age, well set, much freckled in his face, black hair, if not cut off. Had on when he went away, a chestnut colour'd linsey jacket, a fine hat, an ozenbrigs shirt, tow trowsers, and new shoes. They took some other cloaths

with them. and perhaps may change those describ'd above. Whoever takes up and brings the said servants to their master, or secures them in any goal, so that he may have them again, shall have THREE PISTOLES reward for each, and reasonable charges,
     paid by JOHN YODER.
The Pennsylvania Gazette, July 9, 1747; July 16, 1747; July 23, 1747.

       TEN POUNDS Reward.
            Philadelphia, July 9. 1747.
RUN away the 5th Inst. from Samuel Howell, of this city, hatter, two Irish servant men, one named Edward Cain, about 35 years of age, 5 feet 10 inches high, thin visage, short black hair, down look, stoops in his shoulders, very subject to get drunk, speaks very good English. Took with him a good cloth great coat, with horse hair buttons, too little for him, and 'tis suppos'd will wear it as a close body'd coat; old blue damask jacket, three good check shirts, a pair of check trowsers, and a new pair of shoes. He or the other took a new thirty shilling hat, and may offer it to sale. The other named David Castillow, about 22 years of age, 5 feet 8 inches high, pretty well set, and full faced. Has the brogue on his tongue. Took with him an Irish cloth surtout coat, an old pair of sheepskin breeches, two good check shirts, and one white one, an Irish grey wig, and a good pair of shoes. They are both hatters by trade.
  Whoever takes up and secures said servants, so that their master may have them again, shall have FIVE POUNDS reward for each, and reasonable charges, paid by Samuel Howell.
  The Pennsylvania Gazette, July 9, 1747; July 16, 1747; July 23, 1747.

            Philadelphia, July 16. 1747.
RUN away from James Pryor, of Kenet, in Chester county, an Irish servant man, named John Denison, of a short thick stature, black complexion, and a red face; took with him, a brown half-worn coat, with slash sleeves and cross pockets, flat white metal buttons, and not made for himself; an old grey jacket, two old shirts, one tow and one flax, a tow pair of trowsers, two wool hats, one old and the other new, a pair of brogues, a check linnen cap, and a pair of leather breeches, seamed up the thighs. Whoever takes up said servant, and secures him in any goal, or elsewhere, and gives notice to his master, shall have Three Pounds reward, if taken within 20 miles of his master's, if further, Five Pounds, and all reasonable charges,
     paid by me JAMES PRYOR.
  The Pennsylvania Gazette, July 16, 1747; July 23, 1747; July 30, 1747.
  See *The Pennsylvania Journal, or, Weekly Advertiser,* July 16, 1747.

Philadelphia, July 16. 1747.

WHereas a vile impostor who gave himself the name of Foster Pierce, did, on Tuesday, 7th Instant, come to the subscriber, and inform'd him of his father's Death, whereby a considerable fortune was descended to him: In confirmation of which, he produced a Letter, as from the subscriber's uncle John Fortescue, acquainting the subscriber, that his said uncle was one of the executors of his late father's testament, and desiring him upon receipt, to return home; and also produced bills drawn on the bank of London, for Seven Thousand Pounds, signed with the name of the subscriber's step-mother; which bills were so drawn upon condition that the subscriber releas'd certain town lands in Ireland: All which he the said impostor, further confirmed, by giving a particular account of the funeral, place, situation of the subscriber's family burial-place, with several family affairs, too tedious to mention. But forasmuch as the subscriber hath since (by a letter secretly convey'd to his house, last Sunday night, by a person unknown) discovered the premises to be imposture, deceit and knavery, and that the letters were forged, and the story of the subscriber's father's death villainously contriv'd by the said Foster Pierce, in order to get ten or twelve pounds, as said last mentioned informs, from the subscriber; as likewise that the said villain had withdrawn himself, for fear of a discovery, last Friday. All which wicked hellish, forgery and contrivance, hath been of very great loss and damage to the subscriber, by occasioning him to break up school, and to dispose of a considerable part of his house furniture, so that the subscriber is now in a manner out of all business. Therefore, the intent of this is to give warning to all persons to be careful of, and guarded against this devilish impostor; who is a person of about five feet eight inches high, well set, full faced, hath a blemish in one of his eyes, had brownish clothes, a black wig, talks good English, and eloquently. There subscriber is almost persuaded that the said impostor hath lived in his father's family, or with some neighbouring gentleman, and that he hath for some wicked action been obliged to come to America.
    CHARLES WALKER FORTESCUE.
The Pennsylvania Gazette, July 16, 1747; July 23, 1747; August 6, 1747.

Philadelphia, July 16. 1747.

ON the 14th day of this inst. July, made their escape out of Newtown Jail, in Bucks county, Malachi Walton, that formerly kept an Inn in Bristol; he had on when he went away, an old hat half worn, linnen caps, an old flower'd coat, leather breeches, check shirt, worsted stockings, calfskin shoes; he is a middle siz'd man, of a brown complexion. And one Paul Messenger, a wheelwright by trade; had on when he went away, an old fine hat, oznabrigs shirt, a light coloured coat half-worn, oznabrigs trowsers; he is a Dutch man, and had his hair cut off. And also one Henry Thornton, a servant man,

belonging to Amos Strickland; he had on when he went away, a felt hat, brownish hair, oznabrigs shirt, a light coloured coat, with brownish lining, a long pair of petticoat trowsers, made of tow, old shoes, with brass buckles in them. Whoever takes them up, and secures them, so that they may be had again, shall have Forty shillings reward for each,
    paid by me AMOS STRICKLAND, Sheriff.
 The Pennsylvania Gazette, July 16, 1747; July 23, 1747; July 30, 1747. See *The Pennsylvania Gazette*, August 13, 1747, and *The Pennsylvania Gazette*, October 29, 1747, for Walton and Messenger.

          Philadelphia, July 16. 1747.
RUN-away on the 6th instant, from James Pryor, of *kennet*, in chester county, an irish servant man, named *John Denison*, of a short thick stature, black complexion, and a red face; took with him, a brown halfworn coat, with slash sleeves and cross pockets, flat white mettle buttons, and not made for him, an old grey jacket, two old shirts, one tow and the other flax, a tow pair of trowsers, two wool hats, one old the other new, a pair of brogues, and a check linen cap: he had also a pair of leather breeches seemed up the thighs. Whoever takes up and secures said servant, so that his master may have him again, shall have THREE POUNDS reward if taken within twenty miles, if further FIVE POUNDS and reasonable charges,
    paid by *JAMES PRYOR.*
 The Pennsylvania Journal, or, Weekly Advertiser, July 16, 1747; July 23, 1747; July 30, 1747; August 6, 1747; August 13, 1747; August 20, 1747; August 27, 1747; September 3, 1747. See *The Pennsylvania Gazette*, July 16, 1747.

          Philadelphia, July 23. 1747.
RUN away the 19th inst. at night, from Thomas Anderson, of Upper Merion, Philadelphia county, an Irish servant man, named Bartell Durham, about 23 or 24 years of age, five feet six inches high, much pock-pitted, and black complexion: Had on and took with him, a cloth scarlet jacket without sleeves, and a dark coloured frize one, check trowsers, grey worsted stockings, pretty good shoes, too large for him, a good beaver hat, an old brown wig, and a snuff colour'd broad-cloth coat. Whoever takes up and secures said servant, so as his master may have him again, shall have Forty-shillings reward, and reasonable charges,
    paid by THOMAS ANDERSON.
 The Pennsylvania Gazette, July 23, 1747; July 30, 1747; August 6, 1747.

Philadelphia, July 23. 1747.
RUN away on the 18th inst. from Lawrence Potter, of the Northern-liberties of this city, an Irish servant lad, named Thomas Erwin, about 20 years of age, pretty tall, well set, no beard, red complexion, red hair, but has a pale face by reason of sickness, and has a scar on one of his cheeks: Had on when he went away, a check shirt, oznabrigs trowsers, twenty shilling hat, linnen cap, and a new pair of shoes. Whoever takes up and secures said servant, so that his master may have him again, shall have Forty-shillings reward, and reasonable charges,
   paid by LAWRENCE POTTER.
N. B. The said runaway is both a brickmaker and a Miller.
 The Pennsylvania Gazette, July 23, 1747; July 30, 1747; August 6, 1747.

RUN away on the 17th of June past, from Patrick Marrow, of Radnor in Chester County, Pennsylvania, an Irish Servant Man, named Dennis M'Coy, of middle Stature, black Hair; having on a light colour'd Jacket, Breeches and Stockings, good Shoes, and a Felt Hat; hath taken with him several Shirts and a Wallet; his age about Twenty. Whoever takes up and secures the said Servant so that his Master may have him again, shall have Three Pounds Reward, and reasonable Charges,
   paid by P. Marrow.
 The New-York Gazette, Revived in the Weekly Post-Boy, July 27, 1747; August 10, 1747; August 17, 1747. See *The Pennsylvania Journal, or, Weekly Advertiser,* July 2, 1747.

         Philadelphia, July 30. 1747.
RUN away from the ship Domville, Robert Young commander, now lying at Mr. Goodman's wharff, on Saturday evening the 25th inst. James Hannah, born in the north of Ireland, is about 5 feet 8 inches high, or something better, of a sandy complexion, speaks slow, and has a mole on one cheek, wears generally a black velvet cap, a brown cloth coat, a brown wig, or white cap, a striped cotton waistcoat, with flat silver buttons, black flowered shag breeches, and generally white thread stockings, sometimes wears a ruffled shirt, with a silk handkerchief about his neck. Whoever apprehends the said James Hannah, and gives notice to the commander aforesaid, shall have Forty Shillings reward, and all expenses born,
   by me ROBERT YOUNG, Commander.
 The Pennsylvania Gazette, July 30, 1747; August 6, 1747; August 13, 1747.

Philadelphia, July 30. 1747.
RUN away the 24th Instant, from Thomas Griffith, of Vincent township, Chester county, an Irish servant boy named John Coffel, about seventeen years of age, middle stature, reddish hair, and freckled in the face. Had on when he went away a white cloth coat, with mohair buttons, a striped linnen jacket, black cloth breeches, home-spun shirt, felt hat, old shoes and stockings. Whoever takes up and secures said servant, so that his master may have him again, shall have Forty Shillings reward, and reasonable charges paid by   THOMAS GRIFFITH.

The Pennsylvania Gazette, July 30, 1747; August 6, 1747; August 13, 1747. See *The Pennsylvania Gazette,* May 7, 1747.

Philadelphia, July 30. 1747.
FIVE POUNDS REWARD.
RUN away on the 7th of June last, from William Moore, of Moorehall, in the county of Chester, an Irish servant-man named William Reardon; a short, thick, well-set fellow, between twenty and thirty years of age, talks pretty fast, lisps much, has black hair, but keeps it cut, was born near Cork, is well acquainted with every part of Pennsylvania, understands all sorts of country work, of which he is apt to brag; he has been a privateering. He formerly served Mr. Hugh Evans of Merion, in Philadelphia county, but since that has for his roguery been a considerable time in Chester goal. The clothes he is supposed to have stolen and taken with him are not certainly known. His own shirts are marked at the bosom W. There is gone in company with him a native Irish woman, with a child of about five months old. The woman is a most notorious thief. They have with them a false pass. Whoever apprehends the said run-away, and delivers him in Chester goal, shall receive FIVE POUNDS Reward, and reasonable charges from
WILLIAM MOORE.
N. B. The person that apprehends the above runaway, is desired to secure the pass (which I am informed he has directions from the writer to destroy immediately upon his being taken) and they shall be reward upon delivering it to W. Moore.

The Pennsylvania Gazette, July 30, 1747; August 6, 1747; August 13, 1747. See *The Pennsylvania Gazette,* December 10, 1745, *The Pennsylvania Gazette,* December 16, 1746, and *The Pennsylvania Gazette,* June 4, 1747.

Philadelphia, August 6. 1747.
RUN away on the 1st of this inst. from the subscriber in Oxford township, Philadelphia county, an Irish servant man, named James Dugan, about five feet ten inches high, well set, round visage, and pock-broken of a small sort,

thick bushy hair, and speaks indifferent good English: Had on when he went away, a black coat and jacket, light coloured cloth breeches, check shirt, light coloured yarn stockings, new felt hat, round tow'd shoes, with indifferent large white metal carv'd buckles. Whoever takes up and secures the said servant, so as his master may have him again, shall have *Twenty Shillings* reward, if taken within six miles of Philadelphia, and if further *Fifty Shillings*, and reasonable charges,
        paid by   Daniel Stuard.
N. B. His coat and jacket are lined with red shalloon.
    The Pennsylvania Gazette, August 6, 1747; August 13, 1747; August 20, 1747; August 27, 1747. See *The Pennsylvania Gazette*, September 10, 1747.

                                    Philadelphia, August 6. 1747.
RUn away, on Sunday night last, from Samuel Hurford, of this city, a servant boy, named *George Parks*, aged about 17, a short, thick set lad, and had his hair cut off: Had on wide trowsers, snuff coloured jacket, good shoes, large brass buckles in them, a homespun shirt, and a brownish bobb wig.

    Also an apprentice lad belonging to Thomas Pristly, joiner, in this city, named *James Yeats*, an English lad, came from Eling, in Hampshire, about 18 years of age, thick and chunky, stoops as he walks, very thick legs, white hair, cut off, and down look: Had on a garlix shirt, or an old check one, a kersey jacket, or a drugget coat, about half worn, the jacket of a drab colour, the coat of an olive colour, a castor hat, this county made, about half worn. He was an apprentice to Giles Lawrence, joiner, who lately lived at Bristol, Bucks county.

    Likewise from Peter Lawrence, shoemaker, in this city, an apprentice lad, named *William Sherrett*, a slim fellow, and has a down look: Had on and took with him, an old beaver hat, ozenbrigs shirt and trowsers, plush breeches, new stockings and shoes, a brown holland jacket, lined with white linnen, is ript in the side, and has buttons of the same, and a reddish chocolate coloured short jacket; he also took with him a new piece of linnen, and three pair of new shoes.

    And from Isaac Dawson, hatter, an apprentice lad, named *Henry Tuckness*, a thin spare lad, about 5 foot 6 inches high, of a fair complexion, his hair cut off, except a little on the back of his head, and wore a white cap: He took with him a light brown silk camblet jacket, an old castor hat, a pair of homespun tow trowsers, and old shoes.

    Whoever takes up said lads, or either of them, and secures them in any goal, shall have *Forty Shillings* reward for each, paid by
    Samuel Hurford, Thomas Pristly, Peter Lawrence, and *Isaac Dawson.*
    The Pennsylvania Gazette, August 6, 1747.

Philadelphia, August 6. 1747.
RUN away from the Ship Domville, Robert Young commander, now lying at Mr. Goodman's Wharff, on the 5th Instant, in the Evening, Patrick O-Hara, an Apprentice to the Ship; he is about 5 feet 9 inches high, pretty gross, and is much mark'd with the small pox, has a blush in his cheeks, and is of a dark complexion; generally wears a strip'd worsted cap, or a wig, and has a little black lock of Hair in the back of his neck, which generally curls, wears a strip'd flannel waiscoat, a grey frize jacket, has a very odd gait, and his knees seem to have a bent to one another; he speaks after the Scotch accent, and was born in the north of Ireland. Whoever apprehends and secures the said Patrick O-Hara, so that he may be had, and gives Notice to Messrs Allen and Turner, or the Commander aforesaid, shall receive *Fifty Shillings* reward, and all expences, from me   ROBERT YOUNG.
The Pennsylvania Gazette, August 6, 1747; August 13, 1747; August 20, 1747; August 27, 1747.

Philadelphia, August 13. 1747.
RUN away on the 8th of this instant, from the subscriber, living in Londonderry township, Chester county, an Irish servant man, named William Martin, 22 years of age, speaks good English, is a tall likely fellow, has black hair, but cut off; had on a reddish brown cloth jacket, with carv'd brass buttons, lined with old cloth of near the same colour, leather breeches, grey worsted stockings, good shoes, and large brass buckles, a fine shirt, and took with him a coarse shirt, trowsers, and a good felt hat. He is a miller and cooper, can write, and may have written himself a pass. Whoever takes up and secures said servant, so that he may be had again, shall have, if taken within twenty miles of the subscriber's house, Twenty Shillings, and if further, Three Pounds reward, and reasonable charges,
            paid by   JOB RUSTON.
The Pennsylvania Gazette, August 13, 1747. See *The Pennsylvania Gazette*, August 27, 1747.

Philadelphia, August 13. 1747.
RUN away on the 29th of July last, from the subscriber, an Irish servant man, named John M'Nemare, aged 25 years, 5 feet 4 inches high, swarthy complexion, thin visage, much pock-mark'd: Had on when he went away, a brown jacket, without lining, only about the neck it was lin'd with red cloth; also a striped ticken jacket, of a dull colour, and breeches of the same, check shirt, clumsy shoes, blue grey yarn stockings, and felt hat; he has his hair cut off pretty short, and speaks broken English. It is supposed he has stolen some other clothing. Whoever takes up and secures the said servant, so that his master may have him again, or brings him, to Prince's Iron-works, shall have Three Pounds reward, and reasonable charges,

paid by   PETER DOWNEY.
The Pennsylvania Gazette, August 13, 1747; August 20, 1747; August 27, 1747.

Philadelphia, August 13. 1747.
TWENTY POUNDS REWARD.
MAde their escape on the 14th day of July last, out of Newtown jail, in Bucks county, Malachi Walton, a smooth tongu'd man, and formerly kept an Inn in Bristol: had on when he went away, an old hat half-worn, linnen caps, an old flower'd coat, leather breeches, check shirt, worsted stockings, calfskin shoes; he is a middle siz'd man, of a brown complexion. And one Paul Messenger, a wheelwright by trade; had on when he went away, an old fine hat, oznabrigs shirt, a light coloured coat half-worn, oznabrigs trowsers; he is a Dutchman, and had his hair cut off. Whoever takes them up, and secures them, so that they may be had again, shall have TEN POUNDS reward for each, and reasonable charges,
paid by   AMOS STRICKLAND, Sheriff.
The Pennsylvania Gazette, August 13, 1747; August 20, 1747; August 27, 1747. See *The Pennsylvania Gazette,* July 16, 1747, and *The Pennsylvania Gazette,* October 29, 1747.

FIVE POUNDS Reward.
Philadelphia, August 20. 1747.
Run away from Reading Furnace, the 9th of this instant August, a lusty, stout, native Irish man, about 6 foot high, well proportioned, about 30 years of age, has much of the brogue, slow of speech, and low voice, and is a comely man: Had on when he went away a good felt hat, light coloured coat, made of English plains, of a surtout fashion, buttons of a lighter colour than the cloth, and large cape, a double breasted jacket, of an olive colour, and breeches of the same, check trowsers over them, and a fine white shirt: He took with him a sorrel natural trotting horse, white faced, marked **OR**, with an **A** over them on the near shoulder. Whoever takes up said servant, Manus Kerregan, and will bring him to his master, Richard Hughs, of West Caln, Chester county, or to Samuel Flower, at Reading Furnace, or confines him in any goal, so that his master may have him again, shall have Five Pounds reward, and reasonable charges,   paid by   *Richard Hughes.*
The Pennsylvania Gazette, August 20, 1747; August 27, 1747; September 3, 1747.

Philadelphia, August 20. 1747.
Run away, on the 9th of this instant August, from John Jerret, of Horsham township, Philadelphia county, a Dutch servant lad, about twenty years of

age, named Loranz Howsar, has brownish curl'd hair, small limbs, is full faced, has large eyes, and speaks better English than Dutch: Had on when he went away, a linnen jacket and breeches, yarn stockings, old pumps, and felt hat, almost new. Whoever takes up said servant, and secures him, so that his master may have him again, shall have Forty Shillings reward, and reasonable charges, paid by *John Jerret.*

The Pennsylvania Gazette, August 20, 1747; August 27, 1747; September 3, 1747.

Philadelphia, August 27. 1747.
Run away from Capt. Thomas Tyrer, a servant boy, about eighteen years of age: Had on when he went away, a pair of white wide trowsers, a coarse dark grey jacket, and a new hat: He is blind of one eye, much pock-pitted, and speaks very bad English. Whoever brings the said servant to his master, at Mr. George Okill's, merchant in Front-street, shall receive Three Pounds reward, and reasonable charges,
from *Thomas Tyrer.*
N. B. All masters of vessels, and others, are forbid to carry off or harbour said servant, he having taken with him some things of value.

The Pennsylvania Gazette, August 27, 1747; September 3, 1747; September 10, 1747.

Philadelphia, August 27. 1747.
Run away, last Week, from the subscriber, living in Londonderry township, Chester county, an Irish servant man, named William Martin, 21 years of age, speaks good English, is a tall, slim fellow, has black hair, but cut off; had no clothes, except a coarse shirt and trowsers, but may have stolen others; he is a miller and cooper, can write, and may have written himself a pass. Whoever takes up and secures said servant, so that he may be had again, shall have, if taken within 20 miles of the subscriber's house, Twenty Shillings, and if further, Three Pounds reward, and reasonable charges,
paid by   JOB RUSTON.
The Pennsylvania Gazette, August 27, 1747. See *The Pennsylvania Gazette*, August 13, 1747.

Philadelphia, August 27. 1747.
RUn away, the 21st of this instant August, from on board the snow City of Cork, Daniel Jappie commander, an Irish servant man, named Alexander Macmahan, about 25 years of age, has a sullen, downcast look, his right-hand very remarkably larger than the other, which he generally carries either in his bosom or pocket, to conceal the blemish: Had on when he went away, a blue jacket, grey wig, half worn shoes and stockings, and canvas trowsers. Whoever takes up and secures said servant, so that the subscribers may have

him again, shall, if taken in town, receive *Twenty Shillings* reward, if in the country, Thirty Shillings, and reasonable charges,

    from *Conyngham* and *Gardner.*

The Pennsylvania Gazette, August 27, 1747; September 3, 1747; September 17, 1747; October 1, 1747.

            Philadelphia, Sept. 3. 1747.

RUN away on the 30th of August last, from Robert Boyle, tanner, of Fallowfield township, Chester county, two servant men, one named Laughlin Tracy, about 6 foot high, 22 years of age, lately came from Ireland. Had on, a brown short jacket, a waiscoat of strip'd flannel, black breeches, with blue old stockings, tow trowsers, coloured with tann, and some other clothes, a coarse hat, his hair cut of, and sometimes wears a wig; he has a large mark from his breast to his navel, as if it had been burnt. The other named Michael Vaughan, aged 30 years, about 5 feet high, pock-mark'd, curled black hair, wanting a tooth before, swarthy complexion, and bad countenance. Had on, a large strait brown coat, not made for him, tow trowsers coloured with tann, a pair of shoes sit in both the upper-leathers, several shirts, some coarse and some fine, he is given very much to Liquor. Whoever takes up and secures said servants, so that their master may have them again, shall have Three Pistoles reward, and reasonable charges,

    paid by *Robert Boyle.*

N. B. All masters of vessels and others, are warned not to entertain them at their peril.

The Pennsylvania Gazette, September 3, 1747; September 10, 1747; September 17, 1747. See *The Pennsylvania Gazette,* July 7, 1748.

FOURTEEN POUNDS REWARD.

            Philadelphia, Sept. 3. 1747.

Run away on the 29th of August last, at night, from George Fudge, bricklayer, in Dock-street, Philadelphia, an Irish servant man, named Patrick Fitz Patrick, about 6 feet high, pock-mark'd, his right knee bends in, aged about 22 years. Had on, an old beaver hat, a white cap, or an old wig, a blue coat with metal buttons, an old searsucker jacket, two speckled shirts, and one white ditto, brown holland breeches, old oznabrigs trowsers, blue worsted stockings, thick strong shoes, with brass buckles. And from Simon Shirlock, ship-wright, on Society-hill, an Irish servant man (a ship-mate of the above one) named Paul Mahon, a sawyer by trade, about 24 years of age, middle stature, well set, brown complexion, black short hair, his forehead shav'd. Had on, a snuff-coloured Spanish broad cloth coat, with silver twist buttons almost the colour of the coat, a white dimity jacket, with white flat buttons, oznabrigs shirt, and speckled ditto, buckskin breeches, blue worsted

stockings, old shoes, one of them ript at the heel, and brass buckles, a brown wig, and large castor hat; he was in the Pretender's army, and is a talkative fellow. Whoever takes up and secures said servants, if taken within forty miles of this city, Five Pounds reward for each, and if farther, Seven pounds a piece, and reasonable charges,
                paid by   GEORGE FUDGE, and SIMON SHIRLOCK
   The Pennsylvania Gazette, September 3, 1747; September 10, 1747; September 17, 1747.

                              Philadelphia, Sept 10. 1747.
RUN away on the 1st of August last, from the subscriber, in Oxford township, Philadelphia county, an Irish servant man, named James Dugan, about 28 Years of Age, 5 feet ten inches high, well set, round visage, and pock-broken of a small sort, thick bushy hair, and speaks indifferent good English: had on when he went away, a black coat and jacket, light coloured cloth breeches, check shirt, light coloured yarn stockings, new felt hat, round toed shoes, with indifferent large white metal carv'd buckles. Whoever takes up and secures said servant, so that his master may have him again, shall have Five Pounds reward, and reasonable charges,
                paid by   *Daniel Steward.*
N. B. His coat and jacket is lin'd with red shalloon.
   The Pennsylvania Gazette, September 10, 1747; September 17, 1747; September 24, 1747. See *The Pennsylvania Gazette*, August 6, 1747.

                              Philadelphia, Sept. 10. 1747.
RUN away on Sunday night last, from Thomas Paxton, of Conestogoe mannor, and Benjamin Ashleman, of Conestogoe township, two native Irish servant men; one named Edward Cuisick, about 20 years of age, 5 foot 6 inches high, a slim fellow, a little freckled, and talks good English: had on, an old brown serge coat, broken in several places, coarse trowsers, grey yarn stockings, old shoes, felt hat, and a reddish wig. He is a pretty good scholar, and probably may pass for a schoolmaster, he has got several books with him, and it is supposed he will write a pass for himself and the other runaway. The other named Thomas Doyle, about 24 years of age, of middle stature, well set, a little pock-fretten, and has a down look: had on when he went away, an old ash coloured camblet coat and jacket, lined with red silk, coarse trowsers, stockings, new shoes, old beaver hat, and his hair shaved off. Whoever takes up said servants, and secures them in Lancaster goal, so as their masters may have them again, shall have Three Pounds reward for each, and reasonable charges, paid by   *Thomas Paxton,* and *Benjamin Ashleman.*
   The Pennsylvania Gazette, September 10, 1747; September 17, 1747; September 24, 1747.

Philadelphia, October 1. 1747.
RUN away on the 15th of last month, from Robert Miller, of Pensborough township, Lancaster county, the two following servants; one a man, named Reynold M' Donald, about 26 years of age, 6 foot High, small-pockmarked, fresh complexion; had on, a felt hat, his hair cut off, white kersey jacket with white metal buttons, ozenbrigs trowsers, and old shoes. The other a woman, named Catharine M' Namee, black hair, aged about 34 years: had on a striped linsey woolsey gown, a black linsey woolsey bed gown, has but one petticoat, and bare-footed. They have both the brogue on their tongues, and 'tis probable they may pass for man and wife. Whoever takes up and secures said servants, so that their master may have them again, shall have Three Pounds reward for the fellow, and Two-pounds for the woman, and all reasonable charges, paid by   ROBERT MILLER.

The Pennsylvania Gazette, October 1, 1747; October 8, 1747; October 15, 1747.

Philadelphia, September 24, 1747.
RUN-away from JOSEPH KELLY of Bucks County, a Servant Man named Daniel Murphey, a slender thin Fellow, blind of one Eye, and redish Hair; had on a linnen Jacket and Breeches, check Shirt, dark grey Coat with metal Buttons, a felt Hat, and has a great Brouge. Whoever takes up said Servant and secures him so that his Master may have him again, shall have THREE POUNDS Reward and reasonable Charges
         paid by   Joseph Kelly or Charles Edgar in Philadelphia.

N. B. Richard Savage who run away from the above mentioned Kelly, and was advertised in May last, has not yet been taken up, and it is supposed they are both gone up to Donegal or Maryland.

Whoever takes up the said Savage shall also have Three Pounds Reward.

The Pennsylvania Journal, or, Weekly Advertiser, October 1, 1747; October 8, 1747; October 22, 1747; October 30, 1747; November 5, 1747; November 12, 1747; November 19, 1747. See *The Pennsylvania Gazette*, June 4, 1747, and *The Pennsylvania Journal, or, Weekly Advertiser*, June 4, 1747, for Savage.

Philadelphia, October 1, 1747.
WHEREAS Hugh Thompson, *alias* John Thompson, came to the House of the Subscriber in Gray's Alley, between Second and Front-streets, and there lodged and dieted for a Month and upwards, being in appearance afflicted with the Fever and Ague, thought it a piece of Humanity to take him in, but the said Thompson, who is a thin Man, fair hair'd and of a sandy Complexion, left his said Lodging the 23d of last Month, and took with him two Shirts, one ruffled the other plain, mark'd on the Lap AL, and one white flannel

Jacket the Foreparts striped with green and white, and one pair of thread Stockings half worn, and half worn blue camblet Coat with red Linings, short waisted, and a blue changeable duroy Coat and Breeches, a felt Hat half worn, and a black Wig, he is about 6 Feet high, pale and freckled: Whoever secures the said Person so as the Subscriber may have him, shall have Forty Shillings,, if taken within 5 Miles of this City, and if 40 Miles or farther Five Pounds, He is supposed to be gone towards Salem, with a pair of worn oznabrig Trowsers; he sometimes pretends to be a Seaman and is acquainted with Plantation-Work, say he has a brother a Weaver in Salem, who lives next door to Mr. S[ ]ns a Taylor.   JOHN CLARK.

The Pennsylvania Journal, or, Weekly Advertiser, October 1, 1747; October 8, 1747.

Philadelphia, October 8. 1747.
Absented, or run away, from the ship Freer, John Peters commander, Edward Swinny, an Irishman, a middle sized person: Had on (when he received Five Pounds advance money) a white flannel jacket, black wig, and trowsers, and lodged at Patrick Roberts's, in Arch-street. Whoever secures and brings him to said master, or Thomas Lloyd, shall have Forty Shillings reward. N. B. All masters of vessels, or others, are hereby forbid to entertain him at their peril, he having engaged to proceed the voyage.

The Pennsylvania Gazette, October 8, 1747; October 22, 1747.

Philadelphia, October 15. 1747.
Run away, on the twelfth of this instant October, from William Moses, jun. of this city, blacksmith, an Irish servant man, named John Hughes, about 20 years of age, 5 feet 5 inches high, has a down look, is very talkative, and much addicted to drinking: Had on when he went away, a white double-breasted surtout coat, with white metal buttons, a blue and white striped jacket, buckskin breeches, flourished at the knees, grey yarn stockings, pretty good shoes, a cotton cap, and old hat. Whoever takes up said servant, and brings him to his master, shall have Fifty Shillings reward, and reasonable charges,   paid by   WILLIAM MOSES, jun.

The Pennsylvania Gazette, October 15, 1747; October 22, 1747; October 29, 1747.

Philadelphia, October 15. 1747.
Run away, on the 6th of this instant October, from the subscriber, of Townamenson, Philadelphia county, a servant man, named John Wamsley, about 23 years of age, of low stature, grey eyes, near sighted: Had on when he went away, a light brown linsey woolsey coat and jacket, also a brown and blue tammy waiscoat, check trowsers, red plush breeches, half worn, purple

blue yarn stockings, neats leather shoes, large brass buckles, besides other cloathing he took away with him, and he is supposed to have taken the road towards Newcastle. Whoever takes up said servant, and brings him to his master, or secures him, so that he may have him again, shall be handsomely rewarded by me   DANIEL WILLIAMS.
The Pennsylvania Gazette, October 15, 1747; October 22, 1747; October 29, 1747. See *The Pennsylvania Gazette*, November 1, 1750.

Philadelphia, October 15. 1747.
THIS is to give notice, that Israel Henton, stole out of the house, of John Miller, of Plymouth township, Philadelphia county, with whom he lodged, on the 13th instant at night, the following things, a great coat, and close-bodied coat, of a snuff colour, with large brass buttons a fine shirt, a twenty shilling hat, a pair of worsted breeches, & a pair of shoes: Said Henton, is of middle stature, pale faced, and when laughing shews his teeth and gums very much: Had on when he went away, a whitish colour coat, buckskin breeches lined, a slash pocket. Whoever takes up said Henton, and secures him, so as he may be had again, shall have forty shillings reward, and reasonable charges   paid by   John Miller.
He is a Newenglandman, and speaks Scotch well.
The Pennsylvania Gazette, October 15, 1747; October 22, 1747; October 29, 1747.

Philadelphia, October 15, 1747.
RUN away on the 11th Instant from the Ship Lydia, William Tiffin Master, a Servant-Man, named Thomas Howson, aged about 21 Years, of short Stature, thick-set, round faced, a little pock-fretten, and short black Hair: Had on when he went away a black leather Cap, a blue pea Jacket and a serege Waistcoat, a pair of blue Drawers and Trowsers, grey worsted Stockings, good Shoes, and a spotted silk Handkerchief about his Neck, Whoever takes up and secures said Servant so that his Master may have him again, shall have THREE POUNDS Reward,
   paid by   WILLIAM TIFFIN.
The Pennsylvania Journal, or, Weekly Advertiser, October 15, 1747; October 22, 1747.

Philadelphia, October 22. 1747.
RUn away on the 19th inst. from Hugh Lindsay, house-carpenter, an Irish apprentice lad, named Samuel Pearson, about 19 years of age, very lusty, fresh coloured, smooth face: Had on when he went away, a new castor hat, a whitish wig, blue cloth coat, two jackets, one a light blue stuff, the other with the forepart black flowered silk damask, two shirts, one fine linnen, the other

oznabrigs, blue cloth breeches, yarn stockings. Whoever takes up and secures said apprentice, so that his master may have him again, shall have Twenty-shillings reward, and reasonable charges,

        paid by   Hugh Lindsay.

N. B. He speaks very quick and hoarse. All masters of vessels are warned not carry him off at their peril.

The Pennsylvania Gazette, October 22, 1747.

                              Philadelphia, Octob. 29. 1747.
              TWENTY POUNDS REWARD.

MAde their escape on the 14th day of July last, out of Newtown Jail, in Bucks county, Malachi Walton, a smooth tongu'd man, and formerly kept an Inn in Bristol; had on when he went away, kept an Inn in Bristol; had on when he went away, an old hat half worn, linnen caps, an old flower'd coat, leather breeches, check shirt, worsted stockings, calfskin shoes; he is a middle siz'd man, of a brown complexion. And one Paul Messenger, a wheelwright by trade; had on when he went away, an old fine hat, oznabrigs shirt; he is a Dutchman, and had his hair cut off. Whoever takes them up, and secures them, so that they may be had, shall have TEN POUNDS reward for each, and reasonable charges,

        paid by   AMOS STRICKLAND, Sheriff.

The Pennsylvania Gazette, October 29, 1747; November 5, 1747; August 12, 1747. See *The Pennsylvania Gazette*, July 16, 1747, and *The Pennsylvania Gazette*, August 13, 1747.

                            Philadelphia, November 12. 1747.

Run away, the third of August last, from Alexander Craig, of New London township, and county of Chester, an Irish servant man, named William Anderson, about 22 years of age, of a dark complexion, down look, speaks broad, and slow: Had on when he went away, a coarse homespun shirt and trowsers, an old brown coat, flannel jacket, old shoes, and old felt hat; has short black hair, and had an iron collar about his neck. Whoever takes up said servant, and secures him, so as his master may have him again, shall have *Twenty Shillings* reward, and reasonable charges,

        paid by   ALEXANDER CRAIG .

The Pennsylvania Gazette, November 12, 1747; November 19, 1747; November 26, 1747; December 3, 1747.

                            Philadelphia, November 12. 1747.

RUn away on the 4th instant, from Frances Scholey, of Springfield, an Irish servant man, named John Furio, about 30 years of age, short and well-set,

dark complexion, yellow strait hair, talks very bad English, and has much of the brogue. Had on when he went away, a brownish coloured coat, half worn dark coloured Jacket, linnen breeches, worsted grey stockings, footed above the ancle of a darker colour than the rest, half worn neats leather shoes, single soaled, with buckles in them, fine white shirt, and pretty good felt hat. Whoever takes up said servant, and secures him, so that his Mistress may have him again, shall have *Three Pounds* reward, and reasonable charges,
   paid by FRANCES SCHOLEY
The Pennsylvania Gazette, November 12, 1747; November 19, 1747; November 26, 1747; December 12, 1747.

Philadelphia, November 19, 1747.
RUN away, on Friday last, from the shallop Speedwell, William Phillips, master, an Irish servant man, named John Patterson, a blacksmith by trade, about 22 years of age, a thick, well-set fellow, of a fair complexion, his upper lip remarkably thick, and speaks broad: Had on an old frize coat, and a red great coat over it, old check shirt, leather breeches, half-worn, old shoes and stockings, and old felt hat. Whoever takes up said servant, and brings him to Captain John Phillips, in Water-street, Philadelphia, shall have Twenty Shillings reward, and reasonable charges, besides what the law allows,
   from JOHN PHILLIPS.
N. B. All masters of Vessels, and others, are forbid to harbour him at their peril.
The Pennsylvania Gazette, November 19, 1747; November 26, 1747; December 3, 1747.

Philadelphia, November 26. 1747.
RUN away the 22d instant, from James Greenfield of Newlin township, Chester county, an Irish servant man named Robert Clinton, a weaver by trade. He is of a middle stature, with black curled hair, swarthy complexion, and about twenty years of age: Had on when he went away, a new felt hat, a dark brown coat, greet jacket, flaxen shirt, and fine stock, tow trowsers, black stockings, footed with brown worsted, old patched shoes, with large brass buckles. He was enticed away by one Sylvester Eagon an Irishman, by trade a weaver, and speaks very brogueish, but no servant. Whoever secure said servant, and sends word to his master, so as he may have him again, shall have Five Pounds reward, and reasonable charges,
   paid by *James Greenfield.*
The Pennsylvania Gazette, November 26, 1747; December 3, 1747; December 12, 1747.

Philadelphia, November 26. 1747.
RUN away on Saturday last, from the snow Dragon, William Andrew master, two sailors, both Irishmen, one named Lawrence Doyle, about 26 years of age, 5 foot 6 inches high, well set, fair complexion, speaks good English, and is a very talkative likely fellow: Had on when he went away, a blue jacket, and a pair of trowsers. The other named James Cangling, about 26 years of age, five foot and a half high, pretty well set, and is a well looking fellow: Had on when he went away, a blue grey jacket, and a plad jacket under it, trowsers, and a black wig. Whoever takes up said sailors, and brings them to William and David Macilvaine, in Front-street, Philadelphia, shall have Forty shillings reward for each, and reasonable charges,
paid by   WILLIAM and DAVID MACILVAINE.
The Pennsylvania Gazette, November 26, 1747; December 3, 1747; December 12, 1747; December 15, 1747; December 22, 1747; December 29, 1747; January 5, 1748.

Philadelphia, December 3. 1747.
RUn away from William Hasleton, of this city, an apprentice lad, named Charles Badmin, about 17 years of age, short, and round shoulder'd, round face, but pale, he speaks English, French, Spanish and Dutch, writes a good hand, and may have forged a pass: Had on an old blue jacket, striped flannel waistcoat, and ozenbrigs trowsers.

Likewise a Negroe man, about 23 years of age, named Cicero, a black, short fellow, round shoulder'd, has a scar on his under lip, is a blockmaker by trade, and had sundry clothes, among which a new fustian coat, and a blue broadcloth one; he took also with him 3 *Pistoles*, and a *Twelve Shilling* bill.

Whoever takes up said runaways, and secures them, so as their master may have them again, shall have 20 shillings reward for the white boy, and 30 shillings for the Negroe, and reasonable charges,
paid by   *William Hasleton.*
N. B. *All masters of vessels and others, are forbid to carry them off, or harbour them, at their peril.*
The Pennsylvania Gazette, December 3, 1747; December 12, 1747; December 15, 1747; December 22, 1747.

Philadelphia, December 10. 1747.
RUn away, the 28th of November last, from John Spencer, of this city, shipwright, a lusty Dutch servant woman, named Elizabeth Cowren, about 25 years of age, full breasted, fair complexion, full faced, has a large mole on the right-side of her chin, speaks good English, lisps a little, and talks loud

and coarse: Had on when she went away an English made cap, with a double cambrick border, a red flag silk handkerchief, an ozenbrigs shift, a brown shaloon bed gown, and brown linsey woolsey petticoat, blue stockings, and new shoes. Whoever secures said servant, so that her master may have her again, shall have 3 pounds reward, and reasonable charges,
    paid by JOHN SPENCER.
N. B. All persons are forbid at their peril to harbour or conceal said servant woman.
 The Pennsylvania Gazette, December 12, 1747; December 15, 1747; December 22, 1747; December 29, 1747.

            Philadelphia, December 10. 1747.
Run away from the sloop William and Agnes, Alexander Martin master, belonging to Barbados, a Dublin Boy, named James Underhill, of a fair complexion, with long yellow hair: Had on when he went away, a blue jacket, and a pair of trowsers. Whoever takes up said boy, and secures him, so as he may be had again, shall have 40 shillings reward, and reasonable charges, paid by John Harrison, merchant in Philadelphia, or by said master. All masters of vessels, and others, are forbid to carry him off at their peril.
T *The Pennsylvania Gazette*, December 12, 1747; December 15, 1747.

1748

            Philadelphia, February 2. 1747.
RUN away, on the 30th of January, from John Miller, of Lampeter township, Lancaster county, an Irish servant man, named Dennis Ryan, aged about 18; of middle stature, fair complexion, with strait fair Hair. Had on when he went off, a whitish colour'd coat, lin'd with blue, brown linsey jacket, blue stockings, Dutch-made shoes, and had cloth and leather breeches. He took with him a large bay horse, with a blaze on his forehead, a switch tail, and round shod, with a good saddle, and new bridle. Whoever secures said Ryan and Horse, so as they may be had again, shall have Three Pounds reward, and reasonable charges, from JOHN MILLER.
 The Pennsylvania Gazette, February 2, 1748; February 9, 1748; February 16, 1748; February 23, 1748; March 8, 1748.

            Philadelphia, Feb. 9. 1747-8.
RUN away from Elizabeth Weekes, of this city, shopkeeper, on the 6th of this inst. a Dutch servant girl, named Elizabeth Stormer, of about 15 years of age, middling tall, light brown hair, and muddy complexion, heavy down

look, has a small mole or wart on her upper lip, speaks broken English, and has been about three months in the country. Had on when she went away, a dark jacket, flannel petticoat, burnt before, linsey ditto, new Dutch shoes, with nails in the heels, 2 pair of worsted stockings, one pair yellow, and the other white, one pair thread ditto, blue and white linnen handkerchief, Dutch black cap, with goose border, two coarse linnen shifts; she took with her, a new dark coloured stuff gown, with a small red stripe, and bordered with yellow; English caps, several linnen hankerchiefs, an oznabrigs apron, one blue ditto, a new white linsey petticoat, bound at the bottom with black, but not plaited at the top, with several other things, so that it is likely she may alter her dress. Whoever secures said servant, so that her mistress may have her again, shall have Three Pounds reward, and reasonable charges,
    paid by ELIZABETH WEEKES.
N. B. All persons are forbid, at their peril to harbour, conceal, or carry her off.
 The Pennsylvania Gazette, February 9, 1748.

             Philadelphia, March 15. 1747-8.
Run away, on the 24th of February last, from the subscriber, in Coventry, Chester county, an Irish servant man, named Thomas Head, a lusty, downlookin fellow, speaks good English and Irish, is about 22 years of age: Had on when he run away, a good felt hat, worsted cap, a large flag handkerchief, a brown coat, without buttons, and long side pockets, a grey ragged jacket under it, also a grey jacket, with brass buttons, and wooden buttons. with sleeves, a cinnamon coloured linsey jacket, and a white flannel jacket, without sleeves, greasy leather breeches, with brass buttons, tow shirt, brown stockings, and single soaled shoes, with good brass buckles in them, one of the tongues broke. Whoever takes up and secures said servant, and secures him in any goal, or brings him to his master, shall have Five Pounds reward, and reasonable charges,
    paid by CHARLES REILLES.
 The Pennsylvania Gazette, March 15, 1748; March 22, 1748; April 5, 1748.

             Philadelphia, March 15. 1747-8.
RUN away from the subscriber on Sunday, the 5th instant, a servant man, named Anthony Rietz, a Dutchman, about 19 or 20 years of age, of a dark brown complexion, has very black eyes and hair, is a well set fellow, about five feet high, and talks pretty good English. He took with him his indentures, and has a year and a half to serve; it is supposed he changed his clothes. Whoever apprehends said runaway, and secures him in any goal, so as his

master may have him again, shall have Forty Shillings reward, and reasonable charges, paid by `HENRY KLEIN.
The Pennsylvania Gazette, March 15, 1748; March 22, 1748; April 5, 1748.

               Philadelphia, March 29.1748.
RUN away from the subscriber, on the 15th instant, a servant woman named Ann Fortey, had on when she went away, a grey linsey wolsey gown, and carried with her a striped cotton and callico gown, a holland quilted, a brown, and a striped flannel pettycoat, a black hat, and red cloak; she took with her a strawberry roan mare, that paces well, and branded on the off buttock **R**, with a red side-saddle; she had several shifts, caps, stockings, aprons, and other things of value; she is supposed to go away with one Samuel Collear, a blacksmith; he had on a dark cloth coat, and dark bearskin riding-coat, and rode a black horse branded on the near buttock **NO**. Whoever takes up the said woman, and secures her, so that she may be had again, shall have Five Pounds reward, or if brought home to the subscriber in Baltimore county, or to captain Robert North's, shall have Ten pounds, Maryland currency,
    paid by *John Fortey.*
N. B. The woman is short and thick, with a scar on her arm.
The Pennsylvania Gazette, March 29, 1748; April 5, 1748; April 16, 1748; April 21, 1748.

              Philadelphia, March 29, 1748.
WHEREAS William Callahon, who lately work'd with Richard Singleton, Shoemaker, of this City, having absented himself from his Work on the 21st Instant, and has taken Tools with him, a new worsted Cap, two Wigs one a light Colour the other grey, a new castor Hat, a large flag Handkerchief, a genteel light colour'd homespun stuff Coat with slash Sleeves and mohair Buttons, and Breeches of the same, two white corded dimity Waistcoats without lining, two pair of blue-grey worsted Stockings, one lighter than the other, a pair of mill'd Stockings, a pair of new Pumps and a pair of old ones, and plain copper Buckles: He has also taken with him a fine white Shirt ruffled at the Bosom and slits with a red Stamp on the Tail, two check Shirts, one oznabrigs, an old blue Jacket, a striped flanel Jacket, an old pair of leather Breeches, and a pair of homespun Trowsers; he is well-set, about 40 Years of age, middle siz'd, fresh coloured, high cheek boned, blue Eyes, has been in the late Expedition, and is very talkative. Whoever takes up and secures said Callahon shall have THREE POUNDS Reward
    paid by RICHARD SINGLETON.
The Pennsylvania Journal, or, Weekly Advertiser, March 29, 1748; April 5, 1748; April 14, 1748; April 21, 1748.

Philadelphia, April 5. 1748.
THREE POUNDS Reward.
RUn away, the 26th of last month, from Robert Grace, at Coventry Forge, an Irish servant man, named Hugh Gallaspy, of middle stature, thick set, black curled hair, much pitted with the small-pox, a scar on one cheek, a down-look, and speaks with the Scotch tone: Had on a light coloured cloth great coat, torn, a strawberry rone colour'd kersey coat and breeches, ozenbrigs shirt, mill'd yarn stockings, and shoes. Whoever secures said servant in any goal in this province and gives notice thereof to said Grace, or brings said servant to said Grace, shall have Three Pounds reward,
    paid by ROBERT GRACE.
The Pennsylvania Gazette, April 5, 1748; April 16, 1748; April 21, 1748.

Philadelphia, April 4. 1748.
RUN away last night, from John Dobbin, of this city, blacksmith, an Irish servant man, named Garret Condon, about 28 years of age, 5 foot ten inches high, and has short black hair: had on a half worn beaver hat, an old blue broad cloth coat, lined with red shalloon, a grey homespun jacket, a coarse white shirt, old breeches, old stockings, and half worn shoes. Whoever takes up and secures said servant, so that his master may have him again, shall have Twenty shillings reward if taken in town, and Forty shillings if ten miles from town, and reasonable charges,
    paid by *John Dobbin.*
N. B. He has been in the county six or seven years, but by his running away, and other misdemeaners, bro't himself to serve for a longer time; he is well acquainted with all the neighbouring colonies.
The Pennsylvania Gazette, April 5, 1748.

Philadelphia, April 14. 1748.
RUn away from the Ship Rachel, of London, Isham Randolph commander, 5 seaman, viz. Thomas Robson who is a well-set man, about 5 Foot 6 inches high, brown complexion, and had on when he went away, a blue duffle waistcoat, canvas trowsers, a cap or wig, and a hat.) *Joseph Smith* (a slim, spare man, about 5 foot 7 inches high, brown complexion, and had on a blue serge waistcoat, canvas trowsers, a hat, and brown wig.) *John Jeffris,* (a little, thin man, about 5 foot 5 inches high, brown complexion, and had on a blue serge waistcoat, trowsers, wears his own black hair, and a hat.) *Henry Jones* (a tall, well-set man, about 5 foot 8 inches high, swarthy complexion, and had on a blue waistcoat, canvas trowsers, a brown bob wig, and a hat) And *James Boyle,* a tall slender lad, about 5 foot nine inches high, and had on a

green duffle waistcoat, a blue kersey jacket, canvas trowsers, a wig and hat. Whoever secures said men, or either of them, so that they may be brought back to their Ship, shall have *Forty Shillings* reward for each, and reasonable charges, paid by   ISHAM RANDOLPH.
The Pennsylvania Gazette, April 16, 1748; April 21, 1748; April 28, 1748.

Philadelphia, April 21. 1748.
RUn away from the subscriber, on the 13th of this instant, a servant woman, named Grace M'Swain; she is an Irishwoman, about 25 years of age, speaks very broad, of small stature, is round shoulder'd, and has brown hair: Had on when she went away, a deep blue gown, cuffed with red, and something torn about the cuffs, wore a check cotton handkerchief, brown and white petticoat, coarse tow linnen apron, coarse cap, no shoes nor stockings. Whoever takes up said servant woman, and brings her to the subscriber, her master, living in Bohemia Mannor, shall have *Forty Shillings* reward, and reasonable charges,
        paid by me   MANASETH LOGUE.
The Pennsylvania Gazette, April 21, 1748; April 28, 1748; May 5, 1748.

Philadelphia, April 21. 1748.
RUn away, on the 18th of this instant, from Jonathan Willis, of Radnor, Chester county, an Irish servant man, named James Bigley, about 18 years of age, slim and tall, of a fresh complexion, blind of an eye, the middle finger of his right hand broke, and is very crooked, speaks bad English, and wears his own hair: Had on a new felt hat, eat in the brim by the rats, two jackets, one a light coloured coarse kersey, the other an old flannel one, coarse tow trowsers, neither shoes nor stockings. Whoever takes up said servant, shall have *Three Pounds* reward, and reasonable charges,
        paid by   JONATHAN WILLIS.
N. B. All masters of vessels, and others, are forbid to carry him off, or harbour him, at their peril.
The Pennsylvania Gazette, April 21, 1748; April 28, 1748; May 5, 1748; May 12, 1748.

Philadelphia, April 28. 1748.
RUn away from his bail, about a month ago, an Irishman, named Hugh Braslam, a blacksmith by trade, but commonly works at country-work, about 25 years of age, a short, well-set fellow, has a down look, and talks pretty good English: Had on an old brown camblet coat and jacket, check shirt, check trowsers, and linnen drawers under them, felt hat, and worsted cap, worsted stockings, and good shoes. Whoever takes up said Braslam, and

brings him to Peter Widdifield, at Poole's Bridge, Philadelphia, shall have Five Pounds reward, and reasonable charges,
    paid by PETER WIDDIFIELD.
 The Pennsylvania Gazette, April 28, 1748; May 5, 1748; May 12, 1748.

            Philadelphia, May 5. 1748.
      FIVE POUNDS Reward.
STolen away, last Night, from William Clayton's pasture, in Upper Chichester, a natural pacing bay horse, three years old this spring, with one white foot behind, branded on the near shoulder something like a T with a C through the middle of it, and a cross at the end of it, not very plain; he is supposed to be taken by one Benjamin Gould, a short, thick fellow, and wore a bluish grey coat, with white metal buttons, a striped flannel jacket, tow trowsers, a black wig or cap, but may have changed his clothes, having stolen several other Things of Value; such as a dark great-coat, with mohair buttons, three check shirts, and a silver headed cane, Thomas Clayton engraved round the head. Whoever secures said horse, and the thief, so as he may be brought to justice, shall have *Five Pounds* reward,
    paid by THOMAS CLAYTON.
 The Pennsylvania Gazette, May 5, 1748; May 12, 1748; May 19, 1748.

            Philadelphia, May 12. 1748.
RUn away last night, from Nathaniel Grubb, of Willistown, Chester county, an English servant man, named John Ridgway, about 35 years of age, down-look, has black curled hair, talks pretty broad, is of middle size, and slender, and knows the country exceedingly well: had on when he went away, a good castor hat, homespun light coloured cloth coat, leather breeches, grey yarn stockings, good shoes, a fine white shirt, and took with him some check shirts, a piece of broad cloth for a jacket, and several other things. He also took with him a likely deep sorel stallion, about 8 years old, paces well, is well-set, and has little or no white about him. Whoever takes up and secures said Man and horse, so as the owner may have them again, shall have Six Pounds reward for the man and horse, if taken together; but if separate, Five Pounds for the Man, and Twenty shillings for the horse, and reasonable charges, paid by *Nathaniel Grubb.*
 The Pennsylvania Gazette, May 12, 1748; May 19, 1748. See *The Pennsylvania Gazette*, May 26, 1748.

            Philadelphia, May 9. 1748.
RUn away last night, from Nathaniel Grubb, of Willistown, Chester county, an English servant man, named John Ridgway, about 35 years of age, down-

look, has black curled hair, talks pretty broad, is of middle size, and slender, and knows the country exceeding well: had on when he went away, a good castor hat, homespun light-coloured cloth coat, leather breeches, grey yarn stockings, good shoes, a fine white shirt, a blue great coat, and a pair of boots, and took with him some check shirts, a piece of broad cloth for a jacket, and several other things. He also took with him a likely deep sorrel stallion, who was found in the Great Valley, near Schuylkill. Whoever takes up and secures said servant, so as he may be had again, shall have Five Pounds reward and reasonable charges, paid by   *Nathaniel Grubb.*

The Pennsylvania Gazette, May 26, 1748; June 2, 1748; June 9, 1748; June 16, 1748. See *The Pennsylvania Gazette,* May 12, 1748.

Philadelphia, June 16. 1748.
RUN away from Edmund Woolley,   house-carpenter, an aprentice, named John Jones, 5 feet 4 or five inches high, walks upright, of a fresh complexion, and about twenty years of age, being marked on the root of his left thumb 1*1 he is English born, tho' he speaks very good Dutch and Welch: Had on when he went away, a yellow serge waistcoat, striped trowsers, a check shirt, white thread stockings, a half worn beaver hat, a silk cap, speck'd red and white, a muslin neckcloth, a pair of calve skin shoes, with steel buckles. He also took away with him a half trimm'd broadcloth coat, of a dark walnut colour, lin'd with blue shalloon, open cuff'd, a light coloured flowered worsted damask waistcoat, with a pair of light coloured cloth, and a pair of blue camblet breeches, two white shirts, three white caps, one muslin neckcloth, one pair of cotton, and one pair of thread stockings, a pair of new calveskin shoes, and a pair of silver knee buckles. He is supposed to be gone to Manhawtany or else to his father in law's, Jenkin Williams, who lives on the other side of Susquehannah, where lives Thomas Jones, brother to said John Jones, who was in Philadelphia about a week ago, and is supposed to have let him have money to go off with. Whoever takes up and secures said lad, so as his master may have him again, shall receive Three Pounds reward, exclusive of all reasonable charges, that is to say, if taken on the other side of Susquehannah Three Pounds, if at Chester Thirty Shillings, if at Newcastle Forty Shillings, if in Philadelphia, or on board any vessel, Twenty Shillings, to be paid by   Edmund Woolley.

N. B. If the above John Jones thinks fit to return to his said master, and save himself of the charges herein mentioned, he may in safety; it is supposed he has an indenture with him, by which he was bound to John Scull, or the Northern Liberties of Philadelphia, of whom he bought his time out since that bound himself to the subscriber.

The Pennsylvania Gazette, June 16, 1748.

Philadelphia, June 30. 1748.

RUN away on the 15th instant, from James Smith, of Donnegal, Lancaster county, a servant man, country born, named Thomas Bentley, but probably may change his name, of low stature, well set, fresh complexion, thin visage, and much addicted to swearing, talks much, and likes to keep much company: Had on when he went away, a blue grey surtout coat, and jacket of the same, and a linsey woolsey jacket under it, homespun Trowsers and shirt, blue and white thread stockings, shoes, with large brass buckles in them. Whoever takes up said servant, and secures him so as his master may have him again, shall have Four Pounds reward, and reasonable charges,
   paid by JAMES SMITH.
The Pennsylvania Gazette, June 30, 1748; July 7, 1748.

Philadelphia, June 30. 1748.

RUN away on the 29th inst. from Alexander Watson, of this city, an Irish servant man, named Carberry Cloath, aged about 27 years, of middle stature, and speaks good English: Had on when he went away, a grey jacket with brass buttons, a short pair of Trowsers, an old check shirt, and old shoes; he is marked with the smallpox, and stoops in the shoulders. Whoever takes up and secures said servant, so that his master may have him again, shall have Twenty shillings reward, and reasonable charges,
   paid by ALEXANDER WATSON.
The Pennsylvania Gazette, June 30, 1748; July 14, 1748.

Philadelphia, June 30, 1748.

RUN away on the 26th Instant, from John Dabbin, of this City, Blacksmith, an Irish Servant Man, named Garret Condon, about 5 feet 10 inches high: Had on when he went away, a white dimitty Jacket, new white Shirt, half worn beaver Hat, a black Wig or white Cap, new check Trowsers, worsted Stockings, and half worn Shoes Whoever takes up and secures said Servant so as his Master may have him again, shall have FIVE POUNDS Reward, and reasonable Charges,
   paid by JOHN DABBIN.

N. B. He had been in Country seven Years, but by his running away and other Misdeameanours, has brought him in for lone Time, he is well acquainted with all the neighbouring Colonies.

The Pennsylvania Journal, or, Weekly Advertiser, June 30, 1748; July 7, 1748; July 14, 1748; July 21, 1748; August 4, 1748; August 11, 1748.

Philadelphia, July 7. 1748.

Run away from the subscriber, on the 12th of last month, a servant man, named Hugh Montgomery, about 20 years of age, is round shoulder'd, has

short curled hair: Had on a good felt hat, an olive green jacket, a fine shirt, a pair of petticoat trowsers, coarse linnen; he is pitted with the small-pox, the pitts small. Whoever takes up said servant, and secures him, so as he may be had again, shall have *Five Pounds* reward, and reasonable charges,
   paid by JOHN KELL, or WALTER DENNY.
The Pennsylvania Gazette, July 7, 1748; July 14, 1748; July 21, 1748.

              Philadelphia, July 7. 1748.
RUn away, on Monday last, from Robert Boyle, of Fallowfield Township, Chester County, an Irish servant man, named Laughlin Tracey, 6 foot high, 21 years of age, thick nosed, with a down looking countenance, and speak pretty good English: Had on when he went away, a whitish coloured coat, with black lining, rather too long for him, a new olive coloured jacket, wanting the sleeves, with cloth buttons, a worsted cap, coarse tow trowsers, and a felt hat; he has a scar from his right breast to his navel with burning, has taken with him a gun, and a large powder horn, almost full of powder, and several other things. Whoever takes up or secures said servant, so as his master may have him again, shall have Forty-shillings reward, and reasonable charges,
   paid by ROBERT BOYLE.
The Pennsylvania Gazette, July 7, 1748; July 14, 1748; July 21, 1748.
See *The Pennsylvania Gazette*, September 3, 1747.

              Philadelphia, July 7. 1748.
RUn away from Charles Williams, of Bucks county, near Tohikan , an apprentice lad, named Francis Hamilton, about 19 years of age, near 6 foot high, is slim, has brown hair, no beard, has long fingers, and is lame of his left thigh by a strain. Had on when he went away, an old felt hat, a blue serge jacket, homespun linnen shirt and trowsers, thread stockings, and good shoes. He carried with him a pair of striped linnen trowsers, an old brown linsey jacket, and a new sickle. Whoever takes up and secures said apprentice, so that his master may have him again, shall have *Thirty Shillings* reward, and reasonable charges,
   paid by me CHARLES WILLIAMS.
The Pennsylvania Gazette, July 7, 1748; July 21, 1748; July 28, 1748.

              Philadelphia, July 7. 1748.
RUN away, on the third Instant from John Baldwin, of Neshaminy Ferry, in the province of Pennsylvania, an Irish servant man, named William Boat, about 20 years of age, a shoemaker by trade, a pretty lusty, well set fellow,

and his head lately shaved: Had on when he went away, a new felt hat, and linnen cap, old fine shirt, linnen jacket, two trowsers, worsted stockings, and new shoes, single soled. Whoever takes up said servant, and secures him, so as his master may have him again, shall have Forty shillings reward, and reasonable charges,
    paid by JOHN BALDWIN.
 The Pennsylvania Gazette, July 7, 1748; July 14, 1748; July 21, 1748; July 28, 1748.

                Philadelphia, *July* 21. 1748.
RUN away from Henry Mitchell, of Bristol township, on the thirteenth inst. at night, an Irish servant man, named John Burn, about 20 years of age, short and well-set, walks pretty upright, and has a little of the brogue on his Tongue: Had on and took with him, two coats, one a copper coloured duroy, the other a dark coloured coarse coat, a light coloured camblet waistcoat, without Sleeves, short wide trowsers, leather breeches, thread and yarn stockings, and shoes and pumps. Whoever takes up and secures said servant, so as his master may have him again, shall have Three Pounds reward, and reasonable charges,
    paid by HENRY MITCHELL.
 The Pennsylvania Gazette, July 21, 1748; July 28, 1748; August 4, 1748. See *The Pennsylvania Gazette*, January 31, 1749.

                Philadelphia, July 21, 1748.
RUN away from the Sloop *Daniel*, lying at Bickley's Wharff, and supposed to be Idleing about Town, *Abel Inman*, tall and lusty Rhode-Island born. *Robert Shurgold*, short and slender, sandy Complexion. *Edward Davis*, pretty lusty, born in Wales, about 50 Years of Age. *Alexander Jackson*, a small Scotch Lad: *William Johnson* middle size, born in Cumberland. Whoever secures any of them so that they may be had again, shall be well Rewarded,
      by THOMAS CROSTHWAITE.
 The Pennsylvania Journal, or, Weekly Advertiser, July 21, 1748; August 4, 1748; August 11, 1748.

                Philadelphia, July 21, 1748.
RUN away on the 15th Instant, from the Ship *Macclesfield*, then at Anchor near Billingsport; *Henry Forster* a Sailor, and took with him a new Moses with one Oar, said *Forster* is about 5 feet 6 Inches high, round Faced some what mark'd with the small Pox, had on a blue Jacket with oznabrigs Trowsers. Whoever takes up and secures him in any Goal, shall have THREE POUNDS Reward, and Twenty Shillings for taken up the Moses and delivering her in Philadelphia.

CUZZINS and SMYTER.
The Pennsylvania Journal, or, Weekly Advertiser, July 21, 1748; August 4, 1748; August 11, 1748.

Philadelphia, July 28. 1748.
RUN away last night from the subscriber, a servant lad, named Timothy Scannell, born in Ireland, of a thick short stature, full face, wears his own short black hair, very talkative, and speaks very fast; he wears a frock and trowsers, a pea jacket, and has other cloths with him; he is by trade a ropemaker. Whoever secures him, so as his master may have him again, shall have Twenty-shillings reward,
   paid by WILLIAM SPAFFORD.
The Pennsylvania Gazette, July 28, 1748.

Philadelphia, August 4, 1748.
Run away from Joseph Gaven, of this city, shoemaker, on the 24th of last month, an Irish servant man, named Teddy O Lanshahin, but may change his name, a shoemaker by trade, about 21 years of age, has a red spot on his right-eye, by a stroke he received on it, is long faced, has long black hair, is well-set, talks little, and has a down look: Had on when he went away, a brown duroy coat, full trimmed, and lined with the same, breeches of the same stuff and colour, a white corded jacket, white shirt, blue and white speckled worsted stockings, and peek-toed pumps; has with him a speckled worsted cap, and 'tis supposed will cut off his hair. Whoever takes up said runaway, and secures him, so as his master may have him again, shall have, if taken within 20 miles of town, 30 shillings reward, and if further 3 pounds, and reasonable charges,
   paid by JOSEPH GAVEN.
The Pennsylvania Gazette, August 4, 1748; August 18, 1748; August 25, 1748.

Philadelphia, August 4. 1748.
RUn away, on the 29th of last month, from Rebecca Leech, of Cheltenham township, Philadelphia county, an Irish servant lad, named Bernard Macclue, about 16 years of age, about 5 feet high: Had on a fine shirt, marked in the bosom IP, a beaver hat, half worn, a light blue suit of duroy, white thread stockings, neats leather shoes, half worn, with copper buckles; he has lost his foreteeth, speaks much on the brogue, is a great liar, passes for a tanner or shoemaker, walks with his legs very wide apart, wears a cap, and has short black hair. He took with him a new coarse homespun shirt, but very white, a pair of light blue worsted stockings, two pair of tow petticoat trowsers, a pair of calf-skin shoes, half worn, a brown homespun great coat, and a pair of elk-

skin breeches. Whoever takes up and secures said servant lad, so that his mistress may have him again, if taken in this government, shall have *Three Pounds* reward, and if in any other, *Five Pounds*, and reasonable charges,
    paid by REBECCA LEECH.
The Pennsylvania Gazette, August 4, 1748.

              Philadelphia, August 4. 1748.
RUN away, last night from Richard Richison, of Whiteland township, in the Great Valley, Chester county, a servant man, named Samuel Kennedy, aged about 23, born in the north of Ireland, and talks something of the Scotch, but lived several years in France, and can talk their language, and a little Dutch, was a soldier in the French service; he is about 5 feet 8 inches high, well set, full faced, swarthy complexion, and sour look'd, wore his own hair, but supposed has cut it off; he took with him two coats, the one a soldier's red coat, the other a brown one, with broad metal buttons, no lining, a brown linnen jacket, leather breeches, with brass buttons, brown yarn stockings, a coarse felt hat, and three new shirts, one of them a homespun one, and one of the others of a french make, with narrow wrist-bands, and collar, and several rows of back stitching; he also took with him a large brown horse, with a snip and a blaze, shod before, and a buckskin seated saddle, blue cloth housing, edged with red leather, but supposed he will part with some of them for want of money. Whoever secures the said servant and horse, so that the owner may have them again, shall have Four Pounds for both, if taken together, or Three Pounds for the man, and Twenty Shillings for the horse, if apart, and reasonable charges,
    paid by Richard Richison.
The Pennsylvania Gazette, August 4, 1748; August 18, 1748; August 25, 1748. See *The Pennsylvania Gazette*, November 24, 1748.

              Philadelphia, August 4. 1748.
Run away on the 26th Instant, from Robert Erwin, of this city, an English servant man, named William Brown, of middle stature, round shoulder'd: had on when he went away, a new hat, white cap, check shirt, red jacket, tow trowsers, and old pumps. Whoever takes up said servant, and secures him, so as his master may have him again, shall have Three Pounds reward, and reasonable charges,
    paid by ROBERT ERWIN.
The Pennsylvania Gazette, August 4, 1748; August 11, 1748.

              Philadelphia, August 5. 1748.
This day made his escape out of the prison of this city, one William Rise, five feet eight inches high, born in England, about 26 years of age, marked on one

of his hands, between the thumb and wrist, with W*R, and has short black hair: Had on when he went away, a light coloured shaloon jacket, speckled shirt, old patched trowsers, no stockings, and old pumps. Whoever takes up said Rise, and brings him to the prison, shall receive *Twenty Shillings* as a reward, if taken in the city, and if five miles distance, or further, *Forty Shillings*, and reasonable charges,
    paid by JOSEPH SCULL.
The Pennsylvania Gazette, August 11, 1748; August 18, 1748; August 25, 1748.

           Philadelphia, August 18. 1748.
Run away from his bail, Josiah Wilkinson, of Bucks county, on the 12th instant, one Benjamin Beal, this country born, a lusty well set man, about 23 Years of age, fresh coloured, sandy hair, but may wear a cap, a small beard, with a smooth face: had on a bluish coloured worsted coat, pretty much patched, also a leaden coloured jockey coat, with metal flat buttons, white shirt and trowsers; took with him from his said bail, a young grey horse, about 13 hands and a half high, branded on the near shoulder I E, with a Russet saddle and bridle, with blue housing, also a drugget coat, of a lightish brown, with mohair buttons, almost new. Whoever takes up the said runaway and horse, and secures him in any goal and sends word to his said bail, so that he may have them again, shall have Three Pounds reward and, reasonable charges paid by *Josiah Wilkinson.*
The Pennsylvania Gazette, August 18, 1748; August 25, 1748; September 1, 1748; September 8, 1748.

          Philadelphia, August 25. 1748.
Run away, on the 23d inst. at night, from Benjamin Engle, of Germantown, an Irish servant man, named James Hagan, short and well set, and pretty talkative, is full fac'd, black eye-brows, and his head is full of scars: Had on a good new castor hat, brown coat, much worn, with mohair buttons, white jacket and breeches, and good leather breeches, with brass buttons, worsted stockings, and good pumps, has two shirts, one white homespun, and the other of finer linnen. Whoever takes up and secures said servant, if taken within 10 miles of his Master's, shall have Forty Shillings; but if further Three Pounds, and reasonable charges,
    paid by BENJAMIN ENGLE.
The Pennsylvania Gazette, August 25, 1748; September 1, 1748; September 8, 1748.

          Philadelphia, August 25. 1748.
RUn away, the 3d of last month, from Alexander Scott, of Hempstead township, Lancaster county, an Irish servant women, named Catherine

Deyerman, by her husband Ginnena, she is short and thick, full fac'd, freckled, and pale complexion'd: Had on when she went away, an olive colour'd linsey gown, flannel quilted petticoat, striped black and white, linnen handkerchief, coarse shift and apron, short blue cloth mantle, no shoes nor stockings. Whoever takes up said servant in the aforesaid county, and secures her, so that her master may have her again, shall have Thirty Shillings reward, and if taken out of the county Forty Shillings, and reasonable charges,
          paid by   ALEXANDER SCOTT.

The Pennsylvania Gazette, August 25, 1748; September 1, 1748; September 8, 1748.

Philadelphia. September 1, 1748.
RUn away, the 27th of last month, from Nehemiah Allen, an apprentice lad, named Thomas Claborne, about 18 years of age, of short stature, round fac'd, and swarthy complexion: Had on when he went away, an old beaver hat, a linnen cap, short blue jacket, with brass buttons, ozenbrigs short and trowsers, shoes that have been soal'd, but not stockings. Whoever takes up and secures said apprentice, so that his master may have him again, shall have Thirty Shillings reward, and reasonable charges,
          paid by   NEHEMIAH ALLEN.

The Pennsylvania Gazette, September 1, 1748; September 8, 1748; September 15, 1748.

Philadelphia, September 8. 1748.
RUn a way, from Joseph Oldman, an Irish servant man, named Thomas Middleton, by trade a nailor, and part of a black-smith, a thick set, coarse favour'd fellow, much marked with the small pox: Had on when he went away, a grey forrest cloth coat, with mettle buttons, a kersey cloth colour'd vest, with brass buttons, old hat, new ozenbrigs shirt and trowsers, grey worsted stockings, pumps, large brass buckles, he may have chang'd his name to Thomas Gorgin, whoever takes up or secures the said servant, so that his master may have him again, shall have Thirty Shillings reward and reasonable charges,
          paid by   JOSEPH OLDMAN.

The Pennsylvania Gazette, September 8, 1748; September 15, 1748; September 22, 1748.

Philadelphia, September 29. 1748.
RUn away from the subscriber of Donegal, the 14 of this instant September, a Servant man, named Francis Nealis about 18 years of age, a little stoop shoulder'd, his head hangs forward, speaks with a coarse voice, had on when he went away an old hat, his hair about two months grown, a coarse linsey woolsey jacket of a brown colour, a coarse new shirt, old leather breeches

with brass buttons, a pair of worsted stockings of sky blue colour, old shoes, and steel buckles. Whoever secures said servant, so as his master may have him again, shall have *Twenty Shillings* reward, and reasonable charges
    paid by JAMES ALLISON.
The Pennsylvania Gazette, September 29, 1748; October 13, 1748; October 20, 1748. See *The Pennsylvania Gazette*, October 27, 1748.

             Philadelphia, October 6. 1748.
Run away, on the 29th of last month, from Joseph M'Farlan, of Tenicum township, Bucks county, a native Irish servant man, named Bryan O Murry, about five foot six inches high, dark complexion: Had on when he went away a good felt hat, very short black hair, white shirt, brown linsey jacket, leather breeches, white yarn stockings, and old shoes. Whoever takes up said servant, and secures him, so that his master may have him again, shall have Forty Shillings reward, and reasonable charges,
    paid by Joseph M'Farlan.
The Pennsylvania Gazette, October 6, 1748; October 13, 1748; October 20, 1748.

             Philadelphia, October 6. 1748.
RUn away, on Tuesday last, from William Scott, of Province island (formerly East Jersey) an Irish servant girl, named Mary Burk, about 18 years of age, is short, very fat, has large breasts, is full faced, and down-look'd: Had on blue and green ragged patch'd gown, and quilted petticoat, no shoes nor stockings. Whoever takes up said girl, and secures her, so as she may be had again, shall have Forty Shillings reward, and reasonable charges,
    paid by *William Scott.*
The Pennsylvania Gazette, October 6, 1748; October 13, 1748; October 27, 1748.

             Philadelphia, October 20, 1748.
RUn away from the Morning-star privateer of New-York, an Irish servant man, named Hugh Kelly, belonging to Samuel Hodge, of New-York. Periwig-maker; he is of low stature, has a long sharp nose, black beard, is long visaged, and much addicted to drinking. He left the Privateer at Bermuda, came in a vessel to this place, but is supposed to be gone towards Virginia, or lurking about Christine. Whoever takes up and secures said servant, so as he may be had again, shall have Three Pounds reward, paid by William Cannon, taylor, in Front-street, Philadelphia,
    or said Samuel Hodge, in New-York.
The Pennsylvania Gazette, October 20, 1748; October 27, 1748; November 10, 1748.

Philadelphia, October 27. 1748.

RUn away, the 14th of this instant, from the subscriber, in Donnegal, a servant man, named, Francis Nellis, about eighteen years of age, stoop shouldered, his head leans forward, of a pale complexion, out mouth, goes strait at the knees: Had on when he went away, an old hat, a linsey woolsey jacket, of a brown colour, a coarse shirt, leather breeches, with a pair of trowsers over them, a pair of sky blue stockings, old shoes, and steel buckles; took with him a black mare, natural pacer, with a small star, and two white feet behind, a large hunting saddle, with a small pad under the housing, an old snafle bridle. Whoever secures the said servant and mare, so as his said master may have them again, shall have *Forty Shillings* reward,

    paid by me *James Allison.*

The Pennsylvania Gazette, October 27, 1748; November 10, 1748. See *The Pennsylvania Gazette*, September 29, 1748.

Philadelphia, November 3. 1748.

RUn away, the 25th of last month, from Thomas Fitzwater, blacksmith, living in Whitpain, Philadelphia county, an Irish servant man, named James Knox, a blacksmith by trade; he is about 5 feet 6 inches high, well-set, much freckled, and a great boaster of his pitching the bar, throwing the stone, and the like: Had on when he went away, a light colour'd jacket, double breasted, 'tis thought, leather breeches, sailor's trowsers, grey yarn stockings, and a half-worn fifteen shilling hat. Whoever takes up and secures said servant, so as his master may have him again, shall have Forty Shillings reward, and reasonable charges,

    paid by me THOMAS FITZWATER.

The Pennsylvania Gazette, November 3, 1748; November 10, 1748; November 24, 1748.

Philadelphia, November 3. 1748.

Run away, on the 30th of last month, from Edmund Conoly, of Kennet township, Chester county, an Irish servant man, named James Thompson, by trade a weaver, lusty and well-set, long face, and has a long nose, very thick legs, long brown hair, and a sandy beard: Had on when he went away, an old felt hat, old brown coat and jacket, old leather breeches, old brown worsted stockings, and calf-skin shoes, with steel buckles in them. Whoever takes up and secures said servant, so that his master may have him again, shall have Forty Shillings reward, and reasonable charges,

    paid by EDMUND CONOLY .

The Pennsylvania Gazette, November 3, 1748; November 10, 1748; November 24, 1748.

Philadelphia, November 3. 1748.

RUn away from Obadiah Bonsall, of Birmingham township, Chester county, an Irish servant man, named John Costeloe, a shoemaker by trade, about 23 years of age, of middle size, is slim, has large eyes, and pretty much of the brogue on his tongue: Had on when he went away, a light coloured coat, with brass buttons, a black callimancoe jacket, without sleeves, greesy buckskin breeches, light colour'd yarn stockings, old pumps, and large new felt hat. Whoever takes up said servant, and secures him, so as he may be had again, shall have Three Pounds reward, and reasonable charges,
   paid by   OBADIAH BONSALL.
The Pennsylvania Gazette, November 3, 1748; November 10, 1748; November 24, 1748.

Philadelphia, November 3. 1748.

RUn away, on Sunday last, from John Michener, of the Manor of Moreland, Philadelphia county, an Irish servant man, named John Ryley, about 20 years of age, of middle size, well-set, speaks pretty good English, has a down-look, and wears his own brown hair: Had on when he went away, an orange cloth jacket, without lining, flat pewter buttons, and a coarse linnen jacket over it, linsey breeches, and linnen drawers, blue yarn, and coarse thread stockings, neat-leather shoes, with steel buckles in them, homespun linnen shirt, pretty good felt hat, and a new check linnen handkerchief, with a seam across it. Whoever takes up said servant, and secures him, so as his master may have him again, if within ten miles of Philadelphia, shall have Forty Shillings reward, and if further Three Pounds, and reasonable charges,
   paid by   JOHN MICHENER.
N. B. All masters of vessels are forbid to carry him off at their peril.
The Pennsylvania Gazette, November 3, 1748; November 10, 1748; November 17, 1748.

Philadelphia, November 3. 1748.

Run away, on Sunday night, the 23d of last month, from his master, Thomas Potts, senior, at Colebrookdale, in the County of Philadelphia, an indented servant man, named Cornelius Bower, aged about 30 years, fair hair, somewhat curled, freckled complexion, fresh colour'd, small peeked nose, a lusty square shoulder'd fellow, walks very upright, about five foot ten inches high, has been several years out a privateering from New-York, and some parts of the West-Indies, and values himself much upon that account, and very forward to boast of his exploits that way: had on when he went off, an old half worn small brimm'd castor hat, usually wore it cock'd up sharp behind, and down before, a garlix shirt, brown cloth turn'd jacket, metal buttons, red plush breeches, with short petticoat trowsers, blue yarn stockings, and pretty good shoes, may have an old shirt with him, and a small

matter of other things unknown. Whoever secures said servant in any goal in this province, and sends word to his said master, shall have *Forty Shillings* reward, and if in any other province, *Three Pounds*, and reasonable charges,
   from THOMAS POTTS, Senior.
N. B. All masters of vessels are forbid to carry him off at their peril.
 The Pennsylvania Gazette, November 3, 1748; November 10, 1748; November 17, 1748.

             Philadelphia, November 3. 1748.
RUn away, on Monday last, from Samuel Evans, of Ridley, in Chester county, an Irish servant lad, named James Boucher, about 18 years of age, full faced, of middle size, brown complexion, short brown hair, and has a pass of his own writing: Had on when he went away, a half-worn orange colour'd cloth jacket, with metal buttons, and a yellow colour'd linsey coat, lines with striped linsey, half-worn felt hat, new shoes, with large brass buckles, new light grey stockings, buckskin breeches, with brass buttons, and buckles at the knees. Whoever takes up said servant, and secures him, so that his master may have him again, shall have *Forty Shillings* reward, and reasonable charges,
   paid by SAMUEL EVANS.
 The Pennsylvania Gazette, November 3, 1748; November 10, 1748; November 17, 1748.

            Philadelphia, November 17. 1748.
RUn away, on Sunday last, from John M'Call, of Warminster township, Bucks County, an Irish servant man, named John Purfield, about 35 years of age, five feet eight inches high, speaks pretty good English, has red hair, smooth face, large mouth and nose: Had on when he went away, a half-worn blue coat and vest, brown cloth breeches, and leather ones under them, a felt hat, and grey wig, and has with him a new blue red and white worsted cap, light grey worsted stockings, old pumps, and large pewter buckles in them. Whoever takes up and secures said servant, if within thirty miles of Philadelphia, shall have *Thirty Shillings* reward, and reasonable charges,
   paid by JOHN M'CALL.
N. B. He has with him a forged pass, and is a taylor by trade.
 The Pennsylvania Gazette, November 17, 1748.

             Philadelphia, November 24. 1748.
RUN away, on the 30th of October last, from James David, of Charles town, in Chester county, an Irish servant woman, named Hannah Swainy, short and thick, with grey eyes, and lightish hair: had on, a plat hat, light coloured camblet cloak, striped linnen gown, blue camblet petticoat, and a yellow

quilted one, homespun linnen shift and apron, calfskin shoes, and steel buckles, and took with her some other clothes. Whoever takes up and secures said servant, so that her master may have her again, shall have Fifty shillings reward, and reasonable charges,

          paid by   JAMES DAVID.

N. B. The said servant has been in the country seven or eight years, and served her former time with David Haistins, at Ochterara.

The Pennsylvania Gazette, November 24, 1748; December 8, 1748; December 13, 1748; December 20, 1748.

                          Philadelphia, November 24. 1748.

RUN away the 4th of August last, from Richard Richison, of Whiteland, in Chester county, a servant man, named Samuel Kennedy, aged about 23 years, born in the North of Ireland, but liv'd many years in the king of France's service, and can talk French, and some Dutch; he is about 5 feet 8 inches high, well set, full face, bold look, swarthy complexion, and wore his own hair: He took with him two coats, one a soldier's red coat, the other a brown coat, with broad metal buttons, without lining, a brown linnen jacket, leather breeches, with brass buttons, yarn stockings, boots, felt hat, and three new shirts, one French-make, with several rows of backstitching on the collar and wristband. 'Tis suppos'd be took with him a dark bay horse, about 15 hands high, with a blaze and a star, shod before, trimm'd mane, a natural pacer, and goes with a sweep and rough when strained, aged about 14, with a long switch tail, and branded on the near shoulder **I D**, the letters dim; has a buckskin seated saddle, with blue cloth housings. 'Tis thought he is gone towards the French settlements. Whoever secures the said servant and horse, so that the owners may have them again, shall have Five Pounds for the man, and Three Pounds for the horse, if taken either together or apart, and reasonable charges,

          paid by   RICHARD RICHISON.

The Pennsylvania Gazette, November 24, 1748; December 8, 1748; December 20, 1748. See *The Pennsylvania Gazette,* August 4, 1748.

                          Philadelphia, November 24. 1748.

Run away, on the 16th instant, at night, from John Stokes, near hay-cock, in bucks county, a servant man, named James Ray, about twenty-one years of age, a thick, short, well-set fellow, has curl'd bushy hair, is pitted with the small-pox, has grey eyes, and a long nose: had on when he went away, an old beaver hat, without linning, two linsey-woolsey jackets, one of which is striped, with leather buttons, and patched on the shoulder; the other a new one, made up without milling, with a large brass button at top and bottom, and smaller pewter and brass buttons between them, and has dark linning,

homespun shirt, fill'd in with tow, old leather breeches, pretty dirty, and seam'd round the button holes at the knees, new yarn stockings, has with him a pair of shoes, besides what he wore, one pair soal'd and patched. the other half-worn, and both pairs hob-nail'd. Whoever takes up and secures said servant so that his master may have him again, shall have *Forty Shillings* reward, and reasonable charges,
    paid by JOHN STOKES.
 The Pennsylvania Gazette, November 24, 1748; December 8, 1748; December 13, 1748. See *The Pennsylvania Gazette*, October 17, 1745, and *The Pennsylvania Gazette*, July 10, 1746.

             Philadelphia, December 1. 1748.
RUN away, from his bail on Saturday the 19th of November last, one John Murphy, late of Whiteland, in Chester county: He had several suits of apparel along with him, so that it is uncertain which of them he may have on, he wore his own hair of a sandy colour, he is a little freckled and pockmarked, he is a lame man, occasioned by a hurt, is very much addicted to drink, he rode a dark bay horse that has but one eye, a natural pacer, the boot that he wore on his lame leg, is split on the outside almost to the foot, and laced up with a thong, it is supposed he is gone towards New England. Whoever secures said runaway in any goal, so that his security may have him again, shall have Three Pounds reward, Pennsylvania currency, and reasonable charges,
   paid by Joseph Bourgoin, John M'Dearmon, or Mathias Lamey.
 The Pennsylvania Gazette, December 1, 1748; December 8, 1748; December 13, 1748.

             Philadelphia, December 8. 1748.
RUn away, on the 28th of last month, from James Eldridge, of West Caln, Chester county, an Irish servant lad, named John Steward, about sixteen years of age, slim, and pretty tall of his age, is pockmark'd, and has short black hair: Had on when he went away, a dark homespun jacket, leather breeches, light yarn stockings, footed with blue to above his shoes, and new homespun shirt. Whoever takes up and secures said servant, so that his master may have him again, shall have *Thirty Shillings* reward, and reasonable charges,
    paid by JAMES ELDRIDGE.
 The Pennsylvania Gazette, December 8, 1748; December 13, 1748; December 20, 1748; December 27, 1748.

                 December 13. 1748.
RUn away, on Sunday last, from John Femel, of this city, baker, a Dutch servant man, his christian name Michael, about 25 years of age, about 4 foot 9 inches high, no beard, pale complexion: had on a brown coat, blue coarse

jacket, two pair of speckled trowsers, brown stockings, and half-worn pumps. Whoever takes up and secures said servant, so as his master may have him again, shall have *Three Pounds* reward, and reasonable charges,
        paid by   JOHN FEMEL.
The Pennsylvania Gazette, December 13, 1748; December 20, 1748; December 27, 1749; January 3, 1749; January 10, 1749.

                              Philadelphia, December 13. 1748.
RUn away, last Tuesday night, from Jacob Asleman, in Conestogoe, a Dutch servant lad, middle stature, a fat, chunky fellow, and of a fresh complexion: Had on when he went away, a blue linsey woolsey jacket, white trowsers, new felt hat, and red silk handkerchief about his neck. Whoever take up and secures said servant in any goal, so as his master may have him again, shall have *Forty Shillings* reward, and reasonable charges,
        paid by   JACOB ASLEMAN.
N. B. All masters of vessels, and others, are desired not to entertain said servant at their peril.
The Pennsylvania Gazette, December 13, 1748; December 20, 1748; December 27, 1749; January 3, 1749.

                              Philadelphia, December 20. 1748.
Run away from his bail, in the month of April last, William Allison, born in the north of Ireland, aged about 28 years, a well set man, has red hair, and much marked with the small-pox; he formerly lived at Conestogoe, and followed raising hemp; 'tis supposed he keeps either about Philadelphia, or in the Jerseys. Whoever secures the said Allison, in any goal of this, or any neighbouring province, and gives notice to the printers hereof, or to the subscriber, living in the Borough of Lancaster, shall have *Four Pistoles*,
        paid by   GEORGE SMITH.
The Pennsylvania Gazette, December 20, 1748; December 27, 1748; January 3, 1749; January 10, 1749.

1749

                              Philadelphia, January 3. 1748-9.
RUn away, from the subscriber, of Lampiter township, county of Lancaster, the ninth day of last month, a dutch servant man, named John Weyant, about 20 years of age: Had on when he went away, a dark colour'd coat, a blue jacket, and a short stript ditto, a pair of leather breeches, and a pair of tow trowsers, a reddish pair of stockings, a wool hat; is full fac'd, and has thick lips, black short straight hair. Whoever secures said servant, so that his master

may have him again, shall have *Fifty Shillings* reward, and reasonable charges, paid by HENRY DAMOOD.
The Pennsylvania Gazette, January 3, 1749; January 10, 1749; January 17, 1749; January 31, 1749.

Philadelphia, January 10. 1748-49.
RUn away, on the 29th of December last, from John Vernor, of Leacock township, Lancaster county, an Irish servant lad, named Bryan, or Barnabe M'Glew, about 18 years of age, speaks good English, is about 5 feet 4 inches high, fresh colour'd, short curl'd black hair, wants his fore-teeth, has a fresh cut in his forehead, and one on his nose; had on when he went away, a duroy light blue coat, jacket and breeches; also a brown cloth coat, with horse-hair buttons, and is supposed to have a light coloured great coat with him; has a large felt hat, with several coarse and fine shirts: He took with him a light bay horse, with a large star in his face, about ten years old, of good courage, and paces a little, also a saddle and bridle. Whoever takes up said servant and horse, and secures them, so that their master may have them again, shall have Five Pounds reward for both, or Four Pounds for the servant, and reasonable charges, paid by JOHN VERNOR.
The Pennsylvania Gazette, January 10, 1749; January 17, 1749; January 24, 1749; January 31, 1749. See *The New-York Gazette, Revived in the Weekly Post-Boy,* March 20, 1749.

Philadelphia, January 17. 1748-9.
RUn away, the 13th instant, from Jacob Lewis, of the city of Philadelphia, carpenter, an apprentice lad, named Abraham Wood, a tall well-set fellow, about nineteen years of age: Had on when he went away, a bearskin coat, with slash sleeves, and a verst of the same, leather breeches, grey worsted stockings, a pair of pumps, with large brass buckles, and generally wears a cap. He is supposed to be gone in company with a sort of molattoe, named George Shirley, servant to Samuel Rowland, of Lewes-town. Whoever takes up said apprentice, and secures him, so as his master may have him again, shall have, if taken in town, *Twenty Shillings* reward, and if any distance from town, *Three Pounds,* and reasonable charges,
paid by JACOB LEWIS.
N. B. Said Lewis will likewise give Forty Shillings reward, and reasonable charges, for the above George Shirley.
The Pennsylvania Gazette, January 17, 1749; January 24, 1749; January 31, 1749.

Philadelphia, January 24. 1748-9.
RUn away, on the 15th instant, at night from Isaac Lemon, of Lampiter township, Lancaster county, an Irishman, named James Muirhead, lately a

servant; he took from said Lemon, a new brown stuff coat, about Forty Shillings value, a Thirty Shilling beaver hat; he was seen going over Schuylkill Ferry, towards Philadelphia. Whoever takes up said Muirhead, and secures him in any goal, so as said Lemon may have his things again, and the person brought to justice, shall have Three Pounds reward,
    paid by ISAAC LEMON.
 The Pennsylvania Gazette, January 24, 1749; January 31, 1749; February 7, 1749.

             Philadelphia, January 24. 1748-9.
*R*Un *away from James Galbreath, Esq; of Lancaster county, on the 20th of December last, a Welsh servant man, named John Davis, and will be known by his tongue to be a Welshman, about 25 years of age, a well-set fellow, dark complexion, black curl'd hair, black eye-brows, and fresh colour'd: Had on when he went away, a bluish grey strait coat, lined with linsey, much of the same colour, a dark brown jacket, slash sleeves, lined with linsey of a dark colour, and a small flannel jacket, old leather breeches, the coat, jacket and breeches, are mounted with brass buttons; he had also with him a pair of white demity home-made breeches, two shirts, the one coarser than the other, a pair of new white wool stockings, and a dark pair, a pair of new white wool stockings, and a dark pair, a pair of half wore shoes, with brass buckles, a felt hat, half wore; he is much given to drinking, and is very quarrelsome, and swears much, when drunk, and it is thought he will change his name. Whoever takes up said servant, and secures him, so as his master may have him again, shall have Three Pounds reward, and reasonable charges,* paid by JAMES GALBREATH.
 The Pennsylvania Gazette, January 24, 1749; January 31, 1749; February 7, 1749; February 14, 1749.

             Philadelphia, January 31. 1748-9.
RUN away, on the 23d of this instant January, at night, from Henry Mitchell, of Bristol township, Bucks county, an Irish servant man, named John Bourne, but probably will go by the name of James Johnston, is about twenty years of age, short, and well-set, has a rough voice, and speaks pretty good English: Had on when he went away, an old kersey jacket, and a bluish colour'd one under it, without sleeves, old leather breeches, double soal'd good shoes, a good hat, and tow shirt. Whoever takes up and secures said servant, so as his master may have him again, shall have Forty Shillings reward, and reasonable charges,
    paid by HENRY MITCHELL.
N. B. It is supposed he is gone in company with a Dutchman, a freeman, named Henry Anks, and intends for Conestogoe.

The Pennsylvania Gazette, January 31, 1749; February 7, 1749; February 14, 1749. See *The Pennsylvania Gazette,* July 21, 1748.

                          Philadelphia, *January* 31. 1748-9.
RUn away, last night, from Benjamin Kendall, an English servant man, named Richard Holland, by trade a shoemaker, about 23 years of age; near 5 feet 4 inches high, his left thigh and leg much smaller than the right, which occasions his walking very lame, pretty much mark'd with the small pox: Had on when he went away, a brown broad cloth coat, lined with scarlet, shalloon, yellow metal buttons, a half worn castor hat, one white, and one check shirt, a coarse broad-cloth jacket, and new buckskin breeches, worsted stockings, new pumps, silver shoe and knee buckles; took with him a large brown horse, with a star in his forehead, his hind feet white, his mane hangs on both sides, shod before, and paces well; also a good new saddle, with blue broad-cloth housings, and an old curb bridle. Whoever takes up said servant and horse, and secures them, so that the owner may have them again, shall have *Three Pounds,* if taken within 40 miles of Philadelphia, and *Five Pounds,* if farther off, and reasonable charges,
        paid by   BENJAMIN KENDALL.
N. B. It is supposed he is gone towards New-York.
   The Pennsylvania Gazette, January 31, 1749; February 7, 1749; February 14, 1749; February 21, 1749.

                          Philadelphia, January 31. 1748-9.
RUN away from the subscriber, on the 23d of this instant January, a servant man, named John Grace, alias John Jones, about 5 feet 9 inches high, black complexion, round shoulders, much fretted with the small-pox, and very hairy: Had on when he went away, a light coloured cloth jockey coat, light plush breeches, lined with doe-skin, his shoes too big for him, is well acquainted with the iron-work business, and was born in Maryland. Whoever takes up the said servant, or secures him in any goal, so as his master may have him again, shall have Forty Shillings reward, and reasonable charges, paid by   JOHN PENNILL, in Chester.
   The Pennsylvania Gazette, January 31, 1749; February 7, 1749; February 14, 1749; February 21, 1749.

                          Philadelphia, February 28. 1748-9.
RUN away from Thomas Green, a lusty apprentice lad, named James Pummell, hath two years to serve the 22d of next March; he was born and bred by French creek; if any person hath him at work there, that hath a mind

to buy him, the above Green will sell him; or if any body will bring him to his master, shall have Twenty-shillings reward, and reasonable charges,
        paid by said   Thomas Green.
The Pennsylvania Gazette, February 28, 1749; March 7, 1749; March 14, 1749.

                      Philadelphia, March 28. 1749.
ABsented himself on the 17th instant from his mistress, Margaret Pocklenton, an English apprentice lad, named Renard Fosset, a calker by trade, has about three years and nine months to serve, is master of his business, about five foot high, well set, of fair complexion, light short hair, and lightish eye-brows, grey eyes: had on when he went away a lead coloured cloath pee jacket, with brass buttons, one old blue ditto, with leather buttons, one red and white flower'd ditto, with fringe around the pocket flaps, coarse shirts, with one fine ditto, two hats, both half worn, new buckskin breeches, with brass buttons, scarlet cloth ditto, half worn, calf-skin shoes, large white metal carved shoe buckles, two pair of light grey yarn stockings. He took with him all his masters tools. Whoever takes up and secures said apprentice, so that his mistress may have him again, shall have Six Pounds reward, and reasonable charges,
        paid by   MARGARET POCKLENTON.
N. B. All masters of vessels are desired not to carry him off upon their peril.
The Pennsylvania Gazette, March 28, 1749; April 5, 1749; April 13, 1749.

                      Philadelphia, March 28. 1749.
RUn away from his master, Joseph Gray, at the sign of the Conestogoe waggon, a servant man, named John Bell, was born at Albany, of Dutch and Swedish parents, is of small size, about 33 years of age, has very little hair, and is bald on the crown of his head: Had on when he went away, an old beaver hat, white shirt, old lead colour'd broadcloth coat, turn'd, old olive colour'd fustian jacket, old coarse blue plush breeches, grey worsted stockings, and old shoes. He says his mother lives at New-York. Whoever brings said servant to Joseph Gray, or secures him, so as his master may have him again, shall have Three Pounds reward, and reasonable charges,
        paid by   JOSEPH GRAY.
The Pennsylvania Gazette, March 28, 1749; April 5, 1749; April 13, 1749. third ad does not have the location and date at the top.

RUN away from the Subscriber hereof, living in the Province of Pennsylvania, *County of* Lancaster, *and Township of* Leacock, *an* Irish *Servant Lad, about* 18 *or* 19 *Years of Age, speaks good English, about* 5 *Foot*

4 *or* 5 *Inches high, fresh complexion'd, short black Hair curl'd, wants his fore Teeth, a fresh Scar on his Forehead and Nose: Had on when he went away, a Duroy light blue Coat, Jacket and Breeches; also a brown Cloth Coat trim'd with Horse-Hair Buttons, and a light colour'd great Coat trim'd with Mohair Buttons, a large Felt Hat, several coarse and fine Linnen Shirts, took a light colour'd bay Horse with him, with Saddle and Bridle: The Horse is about 9 or 10 Years old, and paces a turnay Rate, and hath a Star on his Forehead; a square well made Horse. Whoever takes up said Servant and Horse, and secured them, so that the Owner may have them again, shall have Five Pounds Reward for both, or Four for the Servant, and reasonable Charges paid, by me*   JOHN VERNOR.

The New-York Gazette, Revived in the Weekly Post-Boy, March 20, 1749; March 27, 1749. See *The Pennsylvania Gazette*, January 10, 1749.

Philadelphia, March 31. 1749.
RUn away, on Monday last, from Brian Wilkinson, of this city, ship carver, an Irish servant man, named William Mooney , a little fellow, about twenty years of age, much mark'd with the small-pox, by trade a carver: Had on when he went away, a castor hat, almost new, cotton cap, new light grey coat, with slash sleeves, flat metal buttons, striped ticken stockings, old shoes. Whoever takes up the said servant, and secures him, so that his master may have him again, if taken within ten miles of Philadelphia, shall have Fifteen Shillings reward, if further, Three Pounds, and reasonable charges,
paid by   BRIAN WILKINSON.
The Pennsylvania Gazette, April 5, 1749; April 13, 1749.

Philadelphia, April 6, 1749.
Run-away Yesterday, from Maurice *and* Edmund Nihell, *Brewers, an Irish Servant Man named* Owen Smith, *about 35 Years of Age, six Feet high, with thick black Eye-brows, his Eyes much sunk in his Head, very coarse in all Features, round shoulder'd, small Legs in Respect of his Body, large clumsey Feet, cramp'd in his Toes, by which he walks goutify'd, speaks tolerable English, is much adicted to swear, has a deep cut on the third Finger of his left Hand, cough's much as consumptive: Had on a dark grey Frieze Jacket with flat Pewter Buttons, lined with white Flannel, a pair of light colour'd Cloth Breeches somewhat too short for him, a pair of dark gray Yarn Stockings, a very bad old Hat trim'd all round; principally remarkable for his coarse Features and goutified Walking. Whosoever secures said Servant and brings him to his Master, if taken within 30 Miles of this City, shall have* Three Pistoles *Reward, if* 40 *Miles or upwards, shall have* Five Pistoles. *Whoever secures said Servant in any County Goal, so that his Master may*

have Intelligence of him, shall have Two Pistoles *Reward, paid by the said* Maurice *and* Edmund Nihell, *or the Printer hereof in* New-York.
The New-York Gazette, Revived in the Weekly Post-Boy, April 10, 1749; April 17, 1749; April 24, 1749. See *The New-York Gazette, Revived in the Weekly Post-Boy,* July 10, 1749.

Philadelphia, March 30, 1749.
RUn away on the 28th Instant, from *George Dewksbury,* Pilot, of this City, an Apprentice, named *Thomas Brown,* a middle siz'd Lad of a dark Complexion, wears his own black curl'd Hair: Had on when he went away, a slate colour'd Jacket, check Shirt, check Handkerchief, old red Breeches, a pair of short Trowsers, light colour'd Stockings, and half worn Pumps, with pewter Buckles, has an impediment in his Speech, and is given to Drink. Whoever takes up and secures said Apprentice, so that his Master may have him again, shall have *Thirty Shillings* reward, and reasonable Charges,
   paid by GEORGE DEWKSBURY.
The Pennsylvania Journal, or, Weekly Advertiser, April 13, 1749, April 20, 1749.

Philadelphia, April 20. 1749.
RUN away from James Graham, living in West-Nantmell township, and county of Chester, a servant man, named Jacob Johnston, born in old England, and has travelled in most parts of this country; he has been in Scotland and Ireland, and been a privateering, 'tis suppos'd he will pass for a sailor, aged twenty-four years, smooth-faced, a long beard, full ey'd, with a down look, a large nose, and big mouth, with a cut across his two first fingers on his right-hand; he has also a large pocket book, full of papers and notes, with sixty pounds in gold, silver and paper: Took with him when he went away, a beaver hat, daubed with tar on the crown, two grey wigs, and an old worsted cap, a tow shirt, a worsted homespun double-breasted jacket, of a light brown, lined with brown linnen: Had on, an old olive green broad cloth coat, made fashionable, a pair of old tow trowsers, and a pair of country shoes, with pewter buckles. Whoever takes up and secures said servant, so that his master may have him again, if the money be found with him, shall have Fifteen Pounds reward, if no money is found with him, Seven Pounds,
   paid by JAMES GRAHAM.
N. B. he is about six foot high.
The Pennsylvania Gazette, April 20, 1749; April 27, 1749; May 4, 1749.

  Buckingham, in Bucks county, April 17. 1749.
RUn away from John Hirst, on Sunday, the sixteenth day of April instant, an English servant man, named William Blows, aged about twenty eight years:

Had on when he went away an ash-coloured coat, blue calimancoe jacket, pretty much worn, a pair of sheep skin breeches, unfashionable made, brown yarn stockings, old shoes, with steel buckles in them, a tow and linnen shirt, an old white linnen handkerchief, with an old hat; he is a little man, curled black hair, with small legs, and very talkative; he took with him a new strong leather pocket book, with an old indenture that he had of a former servitude. Whoever secures said servant in any goal, so that his master may have him again, shall have Five Pounds reward, and reasonable charges,
   paid by JOHN HIRST.
N. B. He took also with him an old brown kersey jacket, with white metal buttons, without lining.
 The Pennsylvania Gazette, April 20, 1749; April 27, 1749; May 4, 1749; May 18, 1748; June 1, 1749; June 15, 1748; June 22, 1749. See *The Pennsylvania Gazette*, September 28, 1749.

           Philadelphia, April 11. 1749.
RUN away, on the 11th inst. from John Brown, of Pequa, in Lancaster county, an Irish servant man, named John Welch, about twenty-one years of age, of a swarthy complexion, nigh 6 foot high, with short black hair: Had on when he went away, a felt hat, an old blue linsey coat, a coarse homespun shirt, and new leather breeches, coloured by working at the shoemaking trade, half-worn stockings, of white and blue yarn twisted together, and old shoes; likewise he took with him a new brown homespun coat, lined with shalloon, an old sky-blue serge jacket, lined with green, a new fine hat, and two new fine shirts, a pair of thread stockings, two silk handkerchiefs, one of them a red flag, the other red and white check; he also took shoemaker's tools and leather, and it is supposed he will make up the leather, he being a shoemaker by trade; he has somewhat of the brogue on his tongue. Whoever takes up and secures said servant, so that his master may have him again, shall have Three Pounds reward, and reasonable charges,
   paid by JOHN BROWN.
The Pennsylvania Gazette, April 20, 1749; April 27, 1748; May 4, 1749.

           Philadelphia, April 27. 1749.
RUN away in the morning of the 21st inst. from Thomas Pryor, in Solbury township, Bucks county, a servant man, named John Morgan, about 18 years of age, has a very thin visage, was born in Ireland, but talks English tolerably well: Had on when he went away, a worsted cap, a new Felt hat, linsey woolsey coat and jacket, lined with red shalloon, and a linnen jacket under them; tow trowsers, and half-worn shoes. Whoever takes up and secures said

servant in any goal, and gives notice to the subscriber, shall have Forty shillings reward, and reasonable charges,
paid by THOMAS PRYOR.
The Pennsylvania Gazette, April 27, 1749; May 4, 1749; May 11, 1749.

Run away, on Tuesday night last, from George Fling, of the Northern Liberties of this city, a hired man, named Thomas Dene, born in Ireland, a silversmith by trade, about 30 years of age, is very short, much pitted with the small-pox, and is a very artful fellow: Had on when he went away, a blue fearnothing greatcoat, a sort of sailor's jacket, speckled trowsers, two new speckled shirts, and a coarse homespun one, a good hat, old thread stockings, and old pieced shoes, with large silver buckles in them, mark'd LF. Whoever takes up said runaway, and secures him, shall have Two Pistoles reward, paid by GEORGE FLING, or JOHN CLARE, at the Golden-fleece,
in Second-street, Philadelphia.
The Pennsylvania Gazette, May 4, 1749; May 11, 1749; May 18, 1749.

Philadelphia, May 18. 1749.
RUn away, on the 14th instant, from Samuel Read, of this city, baker, an Irish servant man, named Hugh Williams, about 19 years of age: Had on when he went away, a very mealy hat, worsted cap, his head newly shaved, ozenbrigs jacket and trowsers, and good shoes. He took with him two pair of buckles, one carved silver, the other brass. Whoever takes up and secures said servant, so as his master may have him again, shall have Forty Shillings reward, if taken within ten miles of this city, and Five Pounds if further,
paid by SAMUEL READ.
N. B. It is supposed he is lurking about this city.
The Pennsylvania Gazette, May 18, 1749; June 1, 1749; June 8, 1749.

Philadelphia, May 25. 1749.
RUN away on the 15th day of this instant, from Dennis Cunrads, of Lower Merion, Philadelphia county, an Irish servant girl, named Mary O Donnel, of low stature, round visage, has lost the forefinger of her right-hand, has the brogue on her tongue, and is 22 years of age. Had on when she went away, a blue flannel petticoat, a linsey bed gown, white apron and cap, cotton handkerchief, blue yarn stockings, good shoes, and has taken with her a pair of new shammy gloves, and some other clothing, as 'tis supposed. Whoever takes up the said servant, and brings her to her master, or secures her, so as

she may be had again, shall have Twenty Shillings reward, and reasonable charges, paid by   DENNIS CUNRADS.

The Pennsylvania Gazette, May 25, 1749; June 1, 1749; June 8, 1749; June 22, 1749.

Philadelphia, May 25. 1749.
RUN away on the 17th inst. from Jonathan Ingham, of Solbury, Bucks county, a servant man, named Stephen Greenleaf, middle stature, brown complexion, about 23 years of age, and has short black hair: Had on, a red worsted cap, an old castor narrow brimmed hat, a blue jacket, an old cloth coloured jacket without skirts, an old check shirt, old wide canvas trowsers, daub'd with tar, old white stockings, old shoes, without heels, one brass buckle, and one pewter one; he pretends to be a sailor. Whoever takes up and secures said servant, so that his master may have him again, shall have Thirty shillings reward, and reasonable charges,
           paid by   JONATHAN INGHAM.

The Pennsylvania Gazette, May 25, 1749; June 1, 1749; June 15, 1749; June 22, 1749.

Philadelphia, May 25. 1749.
RUN away from his special bail, living in North-wales, Philadelphia county, one Robert Moore, of middle stature, a house-carpenter by trade, mostly has his hair cut off, and wears a white cap: Had on when he went away, a blue grey cloth coat, Jacket and breeches. Whoever takes up and secures said Moore in any goal, so that his bail may have him again, shall have Forty shillings reward, and reasonable charges,
           paid by   JOSEPH HUBBS.

The Pennsylvania Gazette, May 25, 1749; June 1, 1749; June 8, 1749; June 22, 1749.

Philadelphia, May 25. 1749.
WHereas the house of Jeremiah Piersal, of West Nantmel, Chester county, was robb'd on the 19th inst of a small trunk, with a considerable sum of money, and writings of value; the said robbery is suppos'd to have been committed by one Patrick Higgins, who us a short well set man, of sandy complexion, and wears a beaver hat, and a worsted cap, a light coloured cloth jockey coat, with cross pockets, a white linnen jacket, and check trowsers. Whoever takes up the said man, and brings him to Dennis Wellen, at the Three-tuns, in Nantmell township, or James Way, tavernkeeper, in the township of Caln, or secures him so a she may be brought to justice, shall have Five Pounds reward, and reasonable charges,
           paid by   JEREMIAH PIERSAL.

N. B. 'Tis supposed he may be between 25 and 30 years of age, and hath two blue letters on one of his hands.
The Pennsylvania Gazette, May 25, 1749; June 1, 1749; June 8, 1749.

RUn away, from John Leadlie, of Wright's town, Bucks county, on the 28th of last month, an Irish servant woman, named Margaret Brown, about thirty six years of age, much given to smoking tobacco, has large rowling eyes, with much white in them, and is very talkative: Had on a brown linsey gown, a black and white striped linsey petticoat, blue and white linsey apron, a pretty good cap, a new red flag handkerchief, with a small piece cut out of one of the corners, no shoes nor stockings. Whoever takes up and secures said servant woman, so as her master may have her again, if taken within ten miles of her master's, shall have *Twenty Shillings* reward, and if twenty miles, or in any other province, *Three Pounds*, and reasonable charges,
        paid by   JOHN LEADLIE .
The Pennsylvania Gazette, May 25, 1749; June 1, 1749; June 8, 1749; June 22, 1749. See *The Pennsylvania Gazette*, January 21, 1746.

Run away from the subscriber, of Leacock township, Lancaster county, the 29th of last month, a servant man, named John Lowe, a lusty fellow, about five foot six Inches high, red faced, heavy browed, and about 23 years of age. He took with him four jackets, one a fine whitish broadcloth, well worn, few buttons, and without sleeves, a new black ratteen jacket, made out of an old coat, a striped linnen one, and an old black one, check'd trowsers, new shoes, a large calf-skin apron, and a new hat; he is much addicted to drinking, and will be apt to swap his clothes for others, in order to git off. Whoever secures said servant, so as his master may have him again, shall have Three Pounds reward, and reasonable charges,
        paid by   Robert Stewart, or Peter Worrel, Esq.
Another fellow went away with the aforesaid servant, named Hugh M'Laughlin, a native Irishman, well set, pock marked, swarthy complexion, and had on two brown jackets, buckskin breeches, linnen trowsers, an old hat, and is about 5 feet 3 inches high. It is supposed they are gone toward the Many-sinks.
The Pennsylvania Gazette, June 8, 1749; June 22, 1749; June 29, 1749.

RUn away, on the 5th instant, from William Pennell, of Middletown, Chester county, a servant man, New-England born, named James Steell, about 22 years of age, middle stature, sandy complexion, and lively countenance: Had on when he went away, a new castor hat, with pretty large brims, a red worsted cap, and a cotton one, white and blue, has two check shirts, and a white coarse one, an old broadcloth double-breasted jacket, with slash sleeves, and large metal buttons, and a blue and white flannel under jacket, with large stripes, two pairs wide short trowsers, grey yarn stockings, with strong shoes, and strings in them. Whoever takes up and secures said servant, so that his master may have him again, shall have *Three Pounds* reward, and reasonable charges,

    paid by WILLIAM PENNELL.

N. B. He was seen at George Gray's Ferry, and 'tis supposed he intends to go towards New York.

The Pennsylvania Gazette, June 8, 1749; June 22, 1749; June 29, 1749.

              Philadelphia, June 6. 1749.

RUn away, last night, from George Polley, of this city, shoemaker, an Irish servant man, named Robert Carroll, about two or three and twenty years of age, about five feet, eight inches high, well-set, pock pitted a little, has a lively look, and has a good deal of the brogue on his tongue: Had an old broadcloth coat, with old brass buttons, a new felt hat, check shirt, old cloth breeches, blue ribbed stockings, and good shoes.

  Whoever takes up and secures said servant, so as his master may have him again, if taken in town, shall have Twenty shillings reward, and if twenty miles from town, Five Pounds reward, and reasonable charges,

    paid by me GEORGE POLLEY.

N. B. It is supposed he will pass for a sailor, wherefore all masters of vessels are forbid to carry him off at their peril.

The Pennsylvania Gazette, June 8, 1749; June 15, 1749; June 22, 1749.

RUn away, on Tuesday last, from Swan Boon, of Darby township, Chester county, a servant man, named James Wickrey, this country born, about 28 years of age, of a sandy complexion, pock-pitted, short hair, if not cut off, thin visage: He took with him three jackets, one of bearskin, double breasted, with leather buttons, an old green ratteen ditto, with leather buttons, one thick ditto of blanketing, stamped on the outside, but white in the inside, two old check shirts, one patched with white linnen, petticoat trowsers, half-worn, buckskin breeches,r almost new, yarn stockings, without the feet, two pairs strong half-worn shoes, and one pair of new calf-skin pumps, two hats, one an old felt one, the other a rackoon one, almost new. He stole and took with him his master's part of the indentures for three years servitude; they were written, and a former indenture printed, for 96 working days, without any loss of time. He went off in an old chestnut canoe, mended at one, if not both ends, and is supposed to be gone over the river Delaware, or on board some

vessel as a sailor, having been formerly a privateering. Whoever takes up and secures said servant, so as his master may have him again, shall have forty shillings reward, and reasonable charges,
   paid by SWAN BOON.
N. B. All masters of vessels are forbid to harbour him at their peril.
The Pennsylvania Gazette, June 8, 1749; June 22, 1749; June 29, 1749.

RUn away from Patrick Heany, of little Conewago, Lancaster county, the 14th day of last month, a servant man, named James Mackellick, by trade a weaver, born in Ireland, about 29 years old, of short stature, freckled face and hands, sandy colour'd hair, and red beard, large nose, somewhat awry, pretty much pockfretten, speaks good English, and can talk Irish; took with him a good felt hat, a blue home-made cloath coat, half worn, a drab colour'd jacket; also a good broad cloath blue coat, with a red lining, and white metal buttons, in the form of silver twist, new linnen breeches, two pair of tow cloth trowsers, one tow shirt, two fine shirts, one pair of grey worsted hoes, one pair of brown yarn hoes, good shoes, no buckles, hath a considerable sum of money, and several Roman books with him. Whoever secures the said servant, so that his master may have him again, shall have Three Pistoles reward, and reasonable charges,
   paid by me PATRICK HEANY.
The Pennsylvania Gazette, June 8, 1749; June 22, 1749; June 29, 1749.

          Philadelphia, June 15. 1749.
RUN away, the 3d inst. from the subscriber's house, at Germantown, a Scotch servant man, named James Robinson, lately brought over by Capt. Stupart: He is a well made fellow, and walks well, seem'd to about 37 or 38 years old, has jet black hair, which curls a little; he has hardly any of the Scotch accent, he carried nothing with him, but a coarse blue jacket, narrow striped ticken breeches, a check shirt, a new felt hat, and shoes and stockings. Whoever takes up and secures the said servant, so that his master may have him again, shall have Three Pounds reward,
   paid by SAMUEL M'CALL sen.
The Pennsylvania Gazette, June 15, 1749; June 22, 1749; June 29, 1749.

          Philadelphia, June 15, 1749.
RUN away on the 9th Inst. from WILLIAM VAUGHAN, of Chichester, Shipwright, an *Irish* Servant Man, named *Thomas Head,* alias *Tom Johnson,* of middle Stature, full faced, short brown Hair, down look, aged about 27 Years: Had on and took with him when he went away, a striped linen Jacket

and Breeches, thread Stockings, half worn Pumps an old felt Hat, oznabrigs Shirt and Trowsers, a white home-spun Shirt, and an old brown Jacket. Whosoever takes up said Servant and secures his so as he may be had again, shall have *Thirty Shillings* Reward, and reasonable Charges,
    paid by WILLIAM VAUGHAN.
 The Pennsylvania Journal, or, Weekly Advertiser, June 15, 1749; June 22, 1749; June 29, 1749; June 13, 1749; June 20, 1749; June 27, 1749; August 3, 1749.

            Philadelphia, June 29. 1749.
RUn away, on the 25th instant, from Samuel Read, of this city baker, an Irish servant lad, named William Tucker, about 17 years of age, low stature, pale complexion, and looks very sickly: Had on a good hat, but too little for him, this country made cotton cap, lines with speckled linnen, check shirt, ozenbrigs jacket, with white metal buttons, ozenbrigs trowsers, blue yarn stockings, old shoes, with odd buckles in them. Also a Negroe man, named Wiltshire, about 35 years of age, a short thick fellow, has a scar in his forehead: Had on a good felt hat, ozenbrigs shirt and trowsers, took with him two pair of shoes, one new, the other old. Whoever takes up and secures said servant, so that his master may have him again, shall have Three Pounds reward; and for the Negroe *Twenty Shillings* reward, and reasonable charges,
    paid by SAMUEL READ.
N. B. All masters of vessels are forbid to carry them off at their peril.
 The Pennsylvania Gazette, June 29, 1749; July 6, 1749.

RUn away, the 25th of last month, from the subscriber, in East- Nottingham, Chester county, an Irish servant girl, named Frances Duffy, aged about 18 years, of a pale complexion: Had on when she went away, an old linsey bed gown, and blue stuff petticoat. Whoever takes up said servant, and secures her, so that her master may have her again, shall have Two Pounds reward, and reasonable charges,
    paid by JOHN GLENN, junior.
N. B. It is supposed she is gone towards Philadelphia.
 The Pennsylvania Gazette, July 6, 1749; July 13, 1749; July 20, 1749.

RUn away, from the subscriber hereof, living in Lancaster county, and Colerain township, a servant man, named William Wilkison, a little well set fellow, about 20 years of age, fair faced, and fair hair: Had on, when he went away, a brownish coat, mounted with buttons of the same, homespun trowsers, shirt of the same, and another finer, half worn wool hat, has grey stockings, and half worn shoes; he speaks good English, and is a pretty good

scholar; it is supposed he has taken a wallet with him. Whoever takes up the said servant, and secures him, so that his said master may have him again, shall have *Three Pounds* reward, and reasonable charges,
    paid by me JOHN BARCLAY.
The Pennsylvania Gazette, July 6, 1749; July 13, 1749; July 20, 1749.

           Philadelphia, July 6. 1749.
RUn away, on the 28th of last month, from Benjamin Weatherby, of Marple township, Chester county, a native Irish servant man, named John M'Neal, alias Oneal, about 24 years of age, pale complexion; thin visage, has the brogue on his tongue, has a lump on the nuckle of one of his forefingers: Had on a half worn raccoon hat, searsucker cap, two shirts, one check, the other white, three jackets, one a blue double-breasted, with brass buttons, that has an impression of a man's head on them, one linnen double-breasted, one striped flannel one, two pair of old trowsers, blue ribb'd stockings, old shoes ty'd with strings. Also took with him a lightish coloured great-coat almost new, a light sorrel horse, with a broad bald face, whitish mane and tail, white feet, paces middling well, an old hunting saddle and bridle, with a long lash, he served some time in Talbot, in Maryland. Whoever takes up and secures said servant, so as his master may have him again, shall have *Forty Shillings* reward and reasonable charges,
    paid by BENJAMIN WEATHERBY.
The Pennsylvania Gazette, July 6, 1749; July 13, 1749; July 20, 1749.

RUN away on the 27th of last month, from John Patrick, of East-Nantmell, in Chester county, an Irish servant man, named John Standly, but 'tis supposed he will change his name to John Wright, speaks good English, he is about 5 feet seven inches high, well set, has a small lump on one of his wrists, which makes it stiff, he is of a sandy complexion, pock-mark'd and freckled: Had on when he went away, an old brown homespun cloth coat, torn under the arms, tow shirt and trowsers, old shoes, no stockings, and wears a cap; he serv'd his former time with one Martin, near the town of Chester; he is well acquainted in some parts of the Jerseys. Whoever takes up and secures said servant, so as his master may have him again, shall have Three Pounds reward, and reasonable charges,
    paid by JOHN PATRICK.
The Pennsylvania Gazette, July 6, 1749; July 13, 1749; July 20, 1749.

RUn away from Alexander Cruikshanks, an Irish servant man, named Valentine Strong, a young fellow, about 20 years of age, well-set, black

complexion, and has a down-look: had on when he went away, an old grey german serge coat, a flannel jacket, with the stripes round his body, old leather breeches, large felt hat, old wig, grey yarn stockings, and new shoes. Whoever takes up and secures said servant in any goal, so as his master may have him again, shall have *Forty Shillings* reward, and reasonable charges,
    paid by ALEXANDER CRUIKSHANKS.
The Pennsylvania Gazette, July 6, 1749.

RUN away the 24th of June last, from Maurice *and* Edmund Nihell, *Brewers in* Philadelphia, *an* Irish *Servant Man named* Owen Smith, *about 35 Years of Age, six Feet high, with thick black Eye Brows, his Eyes much sunk in his Head, very coarse in all Features, round shoulder'd, small Legs in Respect of his Body, large clumsey Feet, cramp'd in his Toes, by which he walks goutify'd, speaks tolerable English, is much addicted to swear, has a deep Cut on the third Finger of his left Hand, has an old Sore on his left Shin, near the Anckle, coughs much as consumptive: is accustomed to wink with one Eye: Took with him a dark grey Frize Jacket with flat Pewter Buttons, lined with white Flannel, an Ozenbrigs Jacket, two pair of Trowsers, a new Shirt of the same, blue Camblet Breeches, a pair of white rib'd Stockings, a pair of Pumps, A Beaver Hat better than half wore, a grey Wig, and two Linnen Caps; says he is a Miller, principally remarkable for his coarse Features and goutified Walking. Whoever secures said Servant and brings him to his Master, if taken within 30 Miles of this City, shall have* Three Pistoles *Reward, if 40 Miles or upwards, shall have* Five Pistoles. *Whoever secures said Servant in any County Goal, so that his Master may have Intelligence of him, shall have* Two Pistoles *Reward,*
    paid by the said MAURICE *and* EDMUND NIHELL.
N. B. *He went in Company with* Daniel Mulhall, *the Servant under mentioned.*
RUN away at the same Time, from on board the Snow Jenny & Sally, Brice M'Clelland Master, from Dublin, now lying at Philadelphia, an Irish Servant Man, named Daniel Mulhall, by Trade a Blacksmith, about 21 Years of Age, 5 Foot 7 Inches high, well set, full smooth fac'd, black short curled Hair, talks good English, has a Mark on his Breast as from a Burn. Had on when he went away, a blue Cloth Coat and Jacket with small metal Buttons, a Pair of Sailor's Trousers, a good Beaver Hat, new Shoes, a blue and white striped Shirt, and a Flag Handkerchief. He has been at Sea, and may pass for a Sailor, of which he has much the Looks, and went away in Company with one Owen Smith, as above described. Whoever secures the said Servant in any Goal, and gives Intelligence to the Subscriber, or to the Printer hereof, so that he may be had again, shall have Two Pistoles Reward,
    paid by JAMES WALLACE.

One of their Companions has reported, that they design'd to go to Long Island.

The New-York Gazette, Revived in the Weekly Post-Boy, July 10, 1749; July 17, 1749; July 24, 1749. See *The New-York Gazette, Revived in the Weekly Post-Boy*, April 10, 1749.

Philadelphia, July 13. 1749.
STolen the night before last, out of the stable of Rees Francis, of Whiteland, Chester county, a bright bay stallion, with black mane and tail, shod before, natural pacer, the near hind foot white, a black spot as large as an English crown on the far buttock, about 14 hands high; the person supposed to have stolen him goes by the name of Joseph Wilson, a slender fellow, of a fair complexion, had scars round his neck under his chin, can speak Welsh, pretends to be a taylor; had on a dark brown coat and jacket, lined with blue, a castor hat, and black wig, a linnen cap with a border, a fine shirt, black leather breeches, with brass buttons, grey wilted worsted stockings, calfskin shoes, with large brass buckles that were not fellows; he took a buckskin seated saddle, with blue cloth housings, and a bridle. Whoever takes up and secures said horse and thief, so as he may be brought to justice, shall have Ten Pounds reward; and in case the thief escapes, shall have Five Pounds reward for the horse, if delivered to John Hunt, in Black-horse alley, Philadelphia, or to John Hambricht, at the White-horse,
on the Conestogoe road.

The Pennsylvania Gazette, July 13, 1749; July 27, 1749; August 3, 1749.

RUn away from Thomas Lewis, of Pikeland township, Chester county, an Irish servant man, named John Bronon, about 23 years of age, has a down look, and his hair cut off; Had on when he went away, an old felt hat, homespun shirt, a darkish grey coarse jacket, lined, check trowsers, new strong neats leather shoes, with large brass buckles; he is a labouring man, but may pretend to be a tanner, as he has been some time at that business. Whoever takes up said servant, and secures him in any goal in this province, so as his master may have him again, shall have *Forty Shillings* reward, and reasonable charges; but if taken in any other province, *Three Pounds* reward, and reasonable charges, paid by Thomas Lewis, or John Garrick,
or Joseph Holloway, both in Chestnut-street.

The Pennsylvania Gazette, July 27, 1749; August 3, 1749; August 10, 1749.

RUn away from John Rowan, near Marcus Hook, the 30th of July last, a servant man, named Daniel M'Brid, by trade a weaver: Had on when he went away, a pair of ozenbrigs trowsers, a green waistcoat, with lapells, a blue grey coat, the rest of his clothes unknown to his master. Whoever secures said servant in any goal, shall have *Thirty Shillings* reward, and all charges,
        paid by   JOHN ROWAN.

The Pennsylvania Gazette, August 17, 1749; August 24, 1749; August 31, 1749.

Run away from the subscriber, of Lebanon township, Lancaster county, a servant man, named George Doude, a short thick well set fellow, about twenty years old, or upwards: Had on when he went away, a linnen jacket, check trowsers, and old shirt, about eight hundred, no shoes, cap, nor hat. Whoever takes up the said servant, and secures him, so that his said master may have him, again, shall have Three Pounds, reward, and reasonable charges, paid by me,   RALPH WHITSITT.

The Pennsylvania Gazette, August 17, 1749; August 24, 1749; August 31, 1749.

Philadelphia, August 24. 1749.
RUn away on the 21st instant from Walter Comly, of the mannor of Moreland, in Philadelphia county, an English servant man, named Joseph Weaver, about 24 years of age, middle stature, palish complexion, a blemish in one eye, pock-mark'd, short brown hair, and has on his arm a coat of arms with Jerusalem, and his own name, done, as 'tis suppos'd, with gunpowder: Had on when he went away, a coarse felt hat, double breasted light kersey jacket and breeches, with mohair buttons, woollen stockings, old shoes, and a pair of silver buckles, mark'd W.C. he took with him an old tarry jacket, and two pair of tow trowsers. Whoever takes up and secures said servant, so as his master may have him again, shall have Forty Shillings reward, and reasonable charges, paid by   WALTER COMLY.

The Pennsylvania Gazette, August 24, 1749; August 31, 1749; September 7, 1749. See *The Pennsylvania Gazette*, March 19, 1751, and *The Pennsylvania Gazette*, April 16, 1752.

Philadelphia, August 24. 1749.
RUN away on the 20th of this inst. from Alexander Parker, of this city, an English servant man, named Coles Hardwich, about 23 years of age, middle stature, well set, down look, somewhat pock-mark'd, yellowish complexion: Had on when he went away, a good felt hat, grey wig, white shirt, linnen coat,

jacket and breeches, grey worsted stockings, darned in the legs with silk, new double-soal'd sharp toed shoes; took with him, a thick short blue jacket, without lining, and an ozenbrigs shirt, and an old check one. Whoever takes up and secures said servant, so as his master may have him again, shall have Three Pounds reward, and reasonable charges,
   paid by ALEXANDER PARKER.
N. B. He went off with a slender fellow, named Thomas ——, who had a blue jacket, and old leather breeches, wore his own hair, and serv'd his time with William Morris, at Trenton.
 The Pennsylvania Gazette, August 24, 1749; August 31, 1749; September 7, 1749. See *The New-York Gazette, Revived in the Weekly Post-Boy*, August 28, 1749.

           Philadelphia, August 24. 1749.
RUN away from Isaac Coran, an English servant man, named Thomas Francis, about 22 years of age, about 5 foot 5 inches high, and by trade a skinner: Had on when he went away, a linnen coat, without sleeves, a homespun linnen shirt, oznabrigs trowsers, and new shoes, had no hair, and wears a linnen cap: He stole and took with him, a blue cloth coat, full trimmed, and lined with red, a striped Bengal jacket and breeches, quite new, a pair of new sheep-skin breeches, with brass buttons, a pair of grey worsted stockings, and a beaver hat, about half-worn, and two white dirty shirts. Whoever secures the said servant, with the clothes, in any goal, so that he may be had again, shall have Forty shillings reward, and reasonable charges,
   paid by ISAAC CORAN.
 The Pennsylvania Gazette, August 24, 1749; August 31, 1749; September 7, 1749.

           Philadelphia, August 24. 1749.
ON the 19th inst. in the morning, made his escape from Joseph Scull, of this city, a servant lad, named Aaron Allen, this country born, about 17 years of age, he has a down look, and a sickly countenance: Had on when he went away, a blue sailor's jacket, much too big for him, a coarse homespun shirt, old tarry trowsers, old shoes, and no stockings, old hat, and has black short hair.
 Whoever takes up said servant, and brings him to the prison, in this city, shall have Twenty shillings reward, and reasonable charges,
   paid by JOSEPH SCULL.
 The Pennsylvania Gazette, August 24, 1749; August 31, 1749.

Philadelphia, August 24. 1749.

RUN away on the 20th Instant from *William Murdock* of this City, Taylor, an Irish Servant Man named *Richard O Donnel*, about 25 Years of Age, about 5 foot 4 inches high, of a pale Complexion, long Nose, tender Ey'd, has a mark under his right Eye, looks always half Drunk, and is a great Snuff-taker: Had on when he went away, a black Coat much worn, a pair of dark cloth Breeches, and speckled worsted Stockings, a black Wig, a white Shirt, one check Ditto; and is supposed to be gone with a Sailor towards New-York, or else by Water towards the Capes.

Whoever takes up and secures said Servant, so that his Master may have him again, shall have THREE POUNDS Reward, and reasonable Charges,
   paid by WILLIAM MURDOCK.

The Pennsylvania Journal, or, Weekly Advertiser, August 24, 1749; August 31, 1749.

Philadelphia, August 24. 1749.

RUN away on the 18th Instant from Ann Weldon, of this City, an Irish Servant Man, named *Ephraim Boggs*, about 5 foot 6 inches high, much mark'd with the Small-Pox, a tallow-Chandler by Trade, about 21 Years of Age: Had on when he went away, a good Hat, wollen Cap, flag Handkerchief, a good brown broad-cloth Coat, a light colour'd Jacket, and a pair of new buckskin Breeches; took also with him, a black Jacket, and a pair of brown Stockings. Whoever takes up and secures said Servant, so that he may be had again, shall have *Forty Shillings* Reward, and reasonable Charges,
   paid by ANN WELDON.

N. B. All Masters of Vessels are desired not to Harbour or Conceil him, at their Peril.

The Pennsylvania Journal, or, Weekly Advertiser, August 24, 1749; August 31, 1749; September 7, 1749; September 14, 1749; September 21, 1749; September 28, 1749; October 5, 1749; October 12, 1749; October 19, 1749; October 26, 1749; November 2, 1749.

RUN-away on the 20th of this Instant August, *from* Alexander Parker, *of the City of* Philadelphia, *an English servant man, named* Coles Hardwich, *about 23 Years of Age, middle Stature, well set, down Look, somewhat Pock mark'd, yellowish Complexion: Had on when he went away, a good Felt Hat, grey Wig, white Shirt, Linnen Coat, Jacket and Breeches, grey worsted Stockings, darned in the Legs with Silk, new double soald sharp toed Shoes; took with him a thick short blue Jacket, without Lining, an Oznabrig Shirt, and an old Check one. Whoever takes up and secures said Servant, so as his Master may have him again, shall have* Three Pounds *Reward, and reasonable Charges,*
   paid by ALEXANDER PARKER.

N. B. *He went off with a slender Fellow, named* Thomas Pearse, *who had a blue Jacket, and old leather Breeches, wore his own Hair, and serv'd his Time with* William Morris, *at Trenton. If they are both taken in Company, shall receive* Five Pounds Reward.

The New-York Gazette, Revived in the Weekly Post-Boy, August 28, 1749; September 4, 1749; September 11, 1749. See *The Pennsylvania Gazette,* August 24, 1749.

Philadelphia, August 30. 1749.
RUN away Yesterday Morning from *John Howard,* of this City Joyner, two Servant Men, one named *John Kent,* an *Englishman,* about 42 years of Age, has a down look red rough Face, about 5 Foot 9 Inches high: Had on when he went away, a Snuff colour'd broad-cloth Coat, with metal Buttons, a bushey brown Wig, and old beaver Hat, with other Cloaths unknown. The other an *Irish* Lad about 19 Years of Age, about 5 Feet 7 Inches high, pitted with the Small-Pox, had a lump on his Cheek, occasioned by a Boyle, named *George Davall,* has short Hair; it is supposed he hath a speckled Shirt, and Trowsers, a striped Jacket and breeches, an old beaver Hat, pretty large, both Joyners by Trade, and given to Drink. Whoever takes up and secures said Servants, so as their Master may have them again, shall have *FIVE POUNDS* Reward, and reasonable Charges

paid, by John Howard.
The Pennsylvania Journal, or, Weekly Advertiser, August 31, 1749.

RUN away, on the 10th inst. from Michael Hutchinson, of Makefield township, Bucks county, an Irish servant, named Abraham Magee, by trade a taylor, a slim middle siz'd fellow, and has no hair: Had on when he went away, an ash colour'd drugget coat, with round cuffs, lin'd with striped stuff, a linnen jacket, half-worn beaver hat, a fine shirt, and a coarse one, and took with him two pair of shoes, half-worn, with brass buckles, two pair of stockings, one pair yarn, the other pair blue grey worsted, and wears a cap. He went away with one Bartle Maquire, an Irish man, a short thick, well-set fellow, mark'd with the small-pox; and had on when he went away, a double breasted brown jacket, a pair of tow trowsers, and two check shirts. Whoever takes up the said Abraham Magee, and secures him, so as his master may have him again, shall have Three Pounds reward, and reasonable charges, if taken within thirty miles of home, and if further Four Pounds,

paid by   MICHAEL HUTCHINSON.
The Pennsylvania Gazette, September 14, 1749; September 21, 1749; October 5, 1749.

STOLEN from the subscriber, living in London-grove township, Chester county, the first of this inst. a dark bay horse, about fourteen hands high, with a star and a snip, one of his hind-feet white, and paces and trotts. The supposed thief is a middling set fellow, dark complexion, down-looking, has black [h]y hair, wants one of his fore-teeth, and speaks very much on the brogue: Had on a blue broadcloth coat, brown callimancoe jacket, blue breeches, blue stockings, fine shoes, and fine hat, and goes by the name of John Owen. Whoever takes up said horse and thief, shall have Forty Shillings reward, of the horse, without the thief, Twenty Shillings, and reasonable charges,   paid by   SARAH WALLACE.
N. B. The horse has neither brand nor ear-marks.
The Pennsylvania Gazette, September 14, 1749.

RUn away, the 17th instant, from John Hutchinson, of Bristol, in Bucks county, Pennsylvania, joiner, an apprentice lad, named William Heaton, a lusty healthy fellow, about 5 feet 9 inches high, is this country born, between 19 and 20 years of age, and has about 18 months to serve; he can neither read nor write, is of a bold countenance, and one of his ancles bends inwards, from a cut thereon: He had on, and with him, when he went away, a light blue duroy coat, jacket and breeches, new, a snuff colour'd drugget jacket, a pair of trowsers, one pair thread stockings, a pair coarse blue stockings, and two pair light blue worsted stockings. He has also found means to get his indentures, which he has probably with him. Whoever takes up the said apprentice, and secures him, so that his master may have him again, shall have Five Pounds reward, and reasonable charges,
          paid by   JOHN HUTCHINSON.
The Pennsylvania Gazette, September 21, 1749; September 28, 1749; October 5, 1749.

NOTE: The next two ads run together for three weeks.

                       Buckingham, in Bucks county, April 17. 1749
RUn away from John Hirst, on Saturday, the Sixteenth day of April instant, an English servant man, named William Blows, aged about 28 years; Had on when he went away, an ash-colour'd coat, blue calimancoe jacket, pretty much worn, a pair of sheep-skin breeches, unfashionable made, brown yarn stockings, old shoes with steel buckles in them, a tow and linnen shirt, an old white linnen handkerchief, with an old hat; he is a little man, can neither read nor write, has curled black hair, small legs, and is very talkative; he took with him a new strong leather pocket book, with an old indenture that he had of a former servitude. Whoever secures said servant in any goal, so that his master

may have him again, shall have Five Pounds reward, and reasonable charges, paid by   JOHN HIRST
N. B. He took also with him an old brown kersey jacket, with white metal buttons without lining.
The Pennsylvania Gazette, September 28, 1749; October 5, 1749; October 12, 1749. See *The Pennsylvania Gazette*, April 20, 1749.

Philadelphia, September 28. 1749.
RUN away from John Hirst, of Buckingham, in the county of Bucks, on the 19th of this inst. September, an English servant man, named Aaron Leidinburg, about 31 years of age, is a very good scholar, and will pass for a school-master; he is of a very black complexion, a broad built man, and about 5 foot 9 inches high: Had on, and took with him, when he went away, a good beaver hat, with three cocks in it, a light flaxen colour'd wig, two caps, one linnen, the other double worsted, a blur grey coat, with mohair buttons, and reddish lining, a short striped linsey jacket, blur and white, and a fine shirt, ruffled at the breast; his breeches the same with his coat, two pair of blue grey stockings, one ridge, and the other worsted, with good shoes, and copper buckles. Whoever takes up and secures the said servant, so that his master may have him again, shall have Forty Shillings reward and reasonable charges,   paid by   JOHN HIRST.
The Pennsylvania Gazette, September 28, 1749; October 5, 1749; October 12, 1749.

RUn away from the subscriber, on the 24th of last month, an Irish servant man, named George Sweeney, of middle stature, fresh coloured, aged about 20 years: Had on, a blue camblet jacket, a pair of cloth breeches, without lining, a pair of white cotton stockings, and a pair of new peeked toed shoes, a great coat, with black hair buttons, and a brown jacket; he has taken with him a large silver spoon. Whoever takes up the said runaway, and puts him in any goal, or delivers him to me, shall have Forty Shillings reward, paid by   JOHN WILCOCKS.
The Pennsylvania Gazette, October 5, 1749; October 19, 1749; October 26, 1749.

Run away, on Saturday last, the 7th of this inst. from the subscriber, two High German servants, a man and a woman: The man had on when he went away, a red waistcoat, a white jacket, black breeches, white stockings, old shoes, and old hat, with a metal button on one side; has short pale coloured hair, is a slim man, of middle stature, about 22 years of age. The woman is thick and

well set, has pale coloured hair, clothed in a black Palantine dress. Their names, Christopher and Regina Hausse, in Dutch, Stofel and Lany Hausse. Whoever takes up the said servants, and secures them, so that their master may have them again, shall have Five Pounds reward, and all reasonable charges, paid by me JAMES COMINGS, living in Northampton township, Bucks county.
 The Pennsylvania Gazette, October 12, 1749; October 19, 1749; October 26, 1749.

RUn away from Robert Simonton, of Lancaster county, an Irish servant man, named John Donesan, about 24 *years of age, red faced, short black hair, a lusty big fellow, speaks bad English: Had on a new felt hat, Irish worsted cap, brown jacket, double breasted, not lined, a small collar, lined with red, a small white freeze jacket, coarse shirt, old trowsers, bagging breeches, old shoes, with brass carved buckles; he has also with him a pair of good buckskin breeches, new wash'd, two pair stockings, one pair blue and white, the other grey, and a pair of good boots. Whoever takes up and secures said servant, so as his master may have him again, shall have Three Pounds reward, and reasonable charges*
   paid by   ROBERT SIMONTON.
 The Pennsylvania Gazette, October 19, 1749; October 26, 1749; November 9, 1749. See *The Pennsylvania Gazette*, November 16, 1749.

RUN away from the Sloop Speedwell *of Philadelphia, Nathan Solly Master, Thomas Nichols, of a small Stature, long thin visag'd, very swarthy, a long Nose, something pitted with the small Pox, and wore a light colour'd old Wig. George* ——, *something larger than the other, full fac'd and smooth, except some Pimples occasioned by drinking, and wore a Worsted Cap: It is supposed they have stolen a new Rateen Coat of a light brown, with two large white Buttons, a pair of black Breeches, a Gingham Jacket, two white and two Check Shirts, two pair of Worsted Stockings, an old Castor Hat with a Hole in the Crown, and Fifteen or Twenty Pounds in Cash: Had on when they went away, blue Jackets, Check Shirts, white tary Trowsers, old Shoes and Stockings, old Hats and very dirty. Whoever takes up and secures said Fellows, so that Capt. Solly may have then again, shall have Thirty Shillings Reward for each, and reasonable Charges,*
   paid by   NATHAN SOLLY.
 The New-York Gazette Revived in the Weekly Post-Boy, October 23, 1749.

Philadelphia, October 26, 1749.
RUN away, on the 16th instant, from John Hallowell, of Philadelphia, shoemaker, a servant lad, named John Iden, about 19 years of age, down look: Had on when he went away, a half worn castor hat, with a large brim, and no loops, mixt coloured drugget coat, strip'd linsey waistcoat, brown Bengall breeches, white shirt, old worsted stockings, and wooden heel'd shoes, with broad toes. Whoever takes up and secures said servant, so that his master may have him again, shall have Twenty Shillings reward, and reasonable charges,
        paid by   JOHN HALLOWELL.
N. B. He speaks thick, and is very apt to feign himself religious where he is not known.
   The Pennsylvania Gazette, October 26, 1749; November 2, 1749; November 16, 1749.

RUN away on the 6th inst. from James Wilson, of West-caln, in Chester county, a native Irish fellow, named Darby Henry, sometimes calls himself Jeremiah Henry, about 26 years of age, a well-set fellow, about 5 foot nine inches high, a very surly fellow when in liquor; had on when he went away, a slip on coat, ash coloured, with yellow metal buttons, and a blue jacket, wanting sleeves, and a check shirt, the jacket and coat home-made cloth, both having yellow buttons, and breeches of a light blue, with buttons of the same, took with him a blue jacket, double breasted, with clear flat buttons, he took with him a gun of a Dutch fashion, he is a down-looking fellow, with short black hair, had with him a black wig, sometimes wore a cap, had old stockings, and old shoes half soaled, has scars on his forehead. Whoever secures said servant, so that his master may have him again, shall have Three Pounds reward, and reasonable charges,
        paid by   JAMES WILSON.
N. B. he had on coarse petticoat trowsers.
   The Pennsylvania Gazette, November 9, 1749; November 16, 1749; November 23, 1749. See *The Pennsylvania Gazette*, August 30, 1750.

RUn away, on the first day of this instant November, from Edward Hill, of Dunks's Ferry, a Low Dutch servant man, named in his indenture Frederick Vandyke, but goes by several names, and sometimes says he is a sailor, sawyer, or carpenter, is a little man, of a swarthy complexion, has short black hair, and black eyes: Had on an old felt hat, check shirt, green jacket, with a brown worsted homespun jacket over it, much too big for him, a pair of brown camblet breeches, also too big for him, with old trowsers over them, and a pair of neat's leather shoes. He took with him a black Spanniel dog, his

hair curl'd all over, and a white stripe down his face. Whoever secures said servant and dog, so as the owner may have them again, shall have Forty Shillings reward for both, or Twenty Shillings for either,
    paid by EDWARD HILL.
N. B. All masters of vessels are forbid to carry off said servant at their peril.
 The Pennsylvania Gazette, November 9, 1749; November 16, 1749; November 23, 1749.

           Philadelphia, November 9, 1749.
RAN away from *Joseph Farmer* of White-Marsh, in the County of Philadelphia, an Irish Servant Man, named Thomas Moran, about 40 Years of age, has a red Face, is a lusty Fellow, speaks bad English, has a Sore on his Right Leg which caused it to be larger than the other, and Ring-worm or Sore over his Right Eye: Had on when he went away, a brown Coat with slash Sleeves, light-colour'd linsey woolsey Jacket patch'd on the Button-holes with brown cloth, a green Jacket without Sleeves, old brown cloth Breeches, new blackish Stockings, and new Shoes. Whoever takes up and secures the said Servant so that his Master may have him again, shall have Forty Shillings Reward and reasonable Charges,
    paid by JOSEPH FARMER.
 The Pennsylvania Journal, or, Weekly Advertiser, November 9, 1749; November 16, 1749.

           Philadelphia, Nov. 16. 1749.
RUN away from Daniel Hathorn, of this city, taylor, on Sunday last, an Irish apprentice lad, named Samuel Adams, about 17 years of age, of middle size, slender, and of a pale complexion, and speaks much with the Scots accent. Had on a dark olive coloured camblet coat, with long pockets in the sides, green breeches, blue ribbed yarn stockings, pretty good felt hat, good shoes, with brass buckles in them, and a good check shirt. Whoever takes up and secures said apprentice, so as he may be had again, shall have Thirty shillings reward, and reasonable charges,
    paid by DANIEL HATHORN.
N. B. As said lad has been some time at sea, all masters of vessels are forbid to carry him off at their peril.
 The Pennsylvania Gazette, November 16, 1749; November 23, 1749; November 30, 1749.

RUN away from John Wily, of Maiden creek, on the 8th inst. at night, an Irish servant lad, named Richard Watson, about 18 years of age, middle stature, short visage, black complexion, short hair, speaks on the brogue: Had on when he went away, a new felt hat, white shirt, blue cloth jacket, with stripes of white linnen down the seams, a brown cloth jacket, too big for him, a pair of old torn breeches, with leather buttons on the knees, a pair of brown stockings, old shoes, with linnen strings in them, and mended with a leather thong, and a new check handkerchief. Whoever takes up and secures said servant, so that his master may have him again, shall have Forty Shillings reward, and reasonable charges,

    paid by me JOHN WILY.

The Pennsylvania Gazette, November 16, 1749; November 23, 1749; November 30, 1749.

Broke out of the Bucks county goal, the 11th inst. at night, one Michael Redding, an Irishman (for felony) about 5 feet 6 inches high; had on when he went away, a grey lincey woolsey coat, a whitish woollen jacket, leather breeches, blue yarn stockings, a linnen cap, is about 40 years of age. Also one Henry Ancts, a Dutchman, about 5 feet 10 inches high; had on when he went away, a dark brown coat, with silk lining, and jacket of the same, leather breeches, a beaver hat, wears his own hair, is a lusty well-set fellow, had with him a pair of check trowsers, green shag breeches, a pair of large brass buckles, old shoes, and brown stockings. And also an Irish servant man, named John Doneson, about 24 years of age, red fac'd, short black hair, a worsted cap, a seaman's dark brown jacket, leather breeches, blue yarn stockings, shoes cut from the legs of boots, a middle sized man, speaks bad English. Whoever takes up and secures either of said persons, so as they may be had again, shall for the said Henry Ancts have Five Pounds reward, for Michael Redding Three Pounds, and for the said John Doneson, Forty Shillings, and reasonable charges,

    paid by WILLIAM ANDERSON, deputy sheriff.

The Pennsylvania Gazette, November 16, 1749; November 23, 1749; November 30, 1749. See *The Pennsylvania Gazette*, October 19, 1749, for Doneson/Donesan.

RUN away from Michael Brand, in Hanover township, commonly call'd Falkner swamp, in the county of Philadelphia, on the first day of November inst. a Dutch servant man, came this Fall into the province, named George Shriner, about 22 years of age, or younger, of low stature, smooth face, sandy hair, lately cut off: had on when he went away, a blue cloth coat, lin'd with red, and a blue jacket, lin'd with blue, linnen breeches, and thread stockings, and an old felt hat, and new shoes. Whoever takes up the said servant, and brings him to the said Michael Brand, or secures him so that his master may have him again, shall have Four Pounds reward,

    paid by MICHAEL BRAND.

The Pennsylvania Gazette, November 16, 1749; November 23, 1749; November 30, 1749.

Philadelphia, November 23. 1749.
RUn away from George Enterkin, of East Bradford, Chester county, on first Day, the 19th instant, an Irish servant man, named Bartholomew Maguire, but commonly goes by the name of Bartly; he has served one servitude in the country already, and knows many parts of it, has been a privateering, is a talkative fellow, and has a little of the brogue on his tongue; he is a short chunky man, a little pock-mark'd, and has brownish colour'd bushy hair: Had on when he went away, a brown double breasted jacket, with slash sleeves, and a green and yellow worsted jacket under it, without sleeves, a pair of thick buckskin breeches, and blue woollen stockings, newly footed with grey yarn, strong neat's leather shoes, with buckles in them; had with him two new ozenbrigs shirts, and probably other things. Whoever takes up and secures said servant man, so that his master may have him again, shall have Five Pounds reward, and reasonable charges,
   paid by GEORGE ENTERKIN.
N. B. All masters of vessels, and others, are forbid to carry him off at their peril.

The Pennsylvania Gazette, November 23, 1749; November 30, 1749; December 5, 1749.

Philadelphia, November 24. 1749.
Run away, last night, from William Williams, in Bucks county, New-Britain township, a servant man, named James Hayes, about twenty years of age, of middle stature, sandy complexion: Had on a new cotton cap, large felt hat, commonly cock'd up, a tammy coat, full trimm'd before, with some of the buttons off above and below, with a brown camblet lining, a pale tammy jacket, lined with Bristol stuff, old leather breeches, with a flap before, or Dutch fashion, oznabrigs shirt, blue stockings, calfskin pumps, with block-tin buckles; he has also with him, a cloth, serge, and flannel jacket, without sleeves; he stole from his master twenty dollars in silver, and a considerable quantity of paper money, the value not known. Whoever takes up said servant, and brings him to his master, or secures him in any goal, so that he may be had again, shall have Three Pounds current money of Pennsylvania, and reasonable charges,
   paid by WILLIAM WILLIAMS.
N. B. He is an Irishman, but speaks pretty good English.

The Pennsylvania Gazette, November 30, 1749; December 5, 1749; December 12, 1749.

Philadelphia, November 30. 1749.
Run away from the subscriber of Conestogoe, Lancaster county, on the 15th of October last, an Irish servant man, named John Dunnoghon, about 24 years of age, a lusty fellow, fat, and red faced, has short dark hair, a thin beard, swarthy skin, a big belly, and speaks bad English. Had on when he went away, a new felt hat, an Irish worsted cap, a brown jacket, made sailor fashion, not lined, double-breasted, a collar, lined with red; under it a little white jacket, short grey stockings, old shoes, and brass buckles; he carried with him a pair of buckskin breeches, a little worn, but newly wash'd, a fine hat, a little worn, with a new loop, a pair of boots almost new, and a pair of blue and white stockings. Whoever secures the said servant, so that his master may have him again, shall have Five Pounds Reward, and reasonable charges,
      paid by   ROBERT SIMINTON.
The Pennsylvania Gazette, November 30, 1749; December 5, 1749; December 12, 1749. See *The Pennsylvania Gazette,* December 19, 1749, *The Pennsylvania Gazette,* March 13, 1750, and *The Pennsylvania Gazette,* May 31, 1750.

Philadelphia, Nov. 30. 1749.
RUn away on the 7th of this inst. from James Moore, of East Caln township, in Chester county, an Irish servant man, named John Roche, about 5 foot 6 inches high: Had on when he went away, a short yellowish wig, a brown homespun coat and jacket, and a striped ditto, brown cloth breeches, yarn stockings, and old shoes, with square steel buckles, an old wool hat, cut about the brim; took with him when he went away about Five Pounds in cash, and sundry accounts, to a considerable value. Whoever takes up and secures the said servant, so that his said master may have him again, shall have *Forty Shillings* reward, and reasonable charges,
      paid by   JAMES MOORE.
N. B. He speaks broken English.
The Pennsylvania Gazette, November 30, 1749; December 5, 1749; December 12, 1749.

Philadelphia, December 5. 1749.
RUn away on the 26th of last month, from Luke Morris of this city, Ropemaker, an Irish servant man, named Patrick Kirk, about 21 years of age, of middle stature, has a hitch or uncommon way of walking, as if his hip or knees had been hurt: He carried with him several shirts, a pair of leather breeches, and kersey jacket, both with brass buttons, a green napt jacket, new lined with blue, a green under waistcoat, and an old brownish colour'd great coat, with the nap wore off, with sundry other clothes; his clothes are a little tarr'd; and may pass for a sailor, by the name of Richard Sweet. Whoever

takes up said servant, and secures him, so that he may be had again, shall have Five Pounds reward, and reasonable charges,
        paid by   LUKE MORRIS.
The Pennsylvania Gazette, December 5, 1749; December 12, 1749; December 19, 1749. See *The New-York Gazette, Revived in the Weekly Post-Boy*, December 11, 1749.

RUN-away on the 26th of last Month, from Luke Morris, *of* Philadelphia, Rope-Maker, *an Irish Servant Man, named* Patrick Kirk, *about* 21 *Years of Age, of middle Stature, has a Hitch or uncommon Way of walking, as if his Hip or Knees had been hurt: He carried with him several Shirts, a pair of Leather Breeches, and Kersey Jacket, both with Brass Buttons, a green napt Jacket, new lined with blue, a green under Waistcoat, and an old brownish colour'd Great Coat, with the Nap wore off, with sundry other Clothes; his Clothes are a little tarr'd; and may pass for a Sailor, by the Name of* Richard Sweet. *Whoever takes up said Servant, and secures him, so that he may be had again, shall have Five Pounds Reward, and reasonable Charges,*
        paid by   LUKE MORRIS.
The New-York Gazette, Revived in the Weekly Post-Boy, December 11, 1749; December 18, 1749; December 25, 1749. See *The Pennsylvania Gazette*, December 5, 1749.

RUn away the 3d inst. from Samuel Swift, of Bustletown, an Irish servant man, named Roger Flanagen, is of a sandy complexion, has short hair, and is used to tumbling and antic tricks: Had on when he went away, a homespun cloth coat and jacket, buckskin breeches, with brass buttons, black wool stockings, new shoes, with strings in them, and an old hat. Whoever takes up and secures said servant, so as his master may have him again, shall have Five Pounds reward, and reasonable charges,
        paid by   SAMUEL SWIFT.
N. B. He will probably pass for a chimney-sweeper.
The Pennsylvania Gazette, December 12, 1749; December 19, 1749; December 26, 1749; January 2, 1750; January 9, 1750; January 16, 1750; January 30, 1750; February 6, 1750.

NOtice is hereby given, that there is now in the goal of this city a man, supposed to be John Dunnoghon, a runaway servant of Robert Siminton's, of Conestogoe, Lancaster county, tho' he goes by the name of William Davis; wherefore said Siminton is desired to come or send to know whether he is his servant or not; and if he is, to pay charges, and take him away. He talks a little French, but is an Irishman.

    N. B. Any other person that has had a servant run away from him lately, is also desired to come and see the above person, in case he should not prove to be Robert Siminton's. MARTIN REARDON.

The Pennsylvania Gazette, December 19, 1749; December 26, 1749. See *The Pennsylvania Gazette*, November 30, 1749, *The Pennsylvania Gazette*, March 13, 1750, and *The Pennsylvania Gazette*, May 31, 1750.

INDEX

Abbott, Robert, 20
Adams, James, 213
Adams, Samuel, 442
Adder, Scilis, 300
Adogan, Dennis, 187
Agnew, James, 234
Aharns, Andrew, 232
Ainsworth, William, 152
Aldeburgh, Richard, 20
Alexander, Alexander, 378
Alexander, Robert, 19
Allcorn, James, 132
Allen, Aaron, 435
Allen, Mr., 386
Allen, Nehemiah, 366, 367, 410
Allen, Patrick, 269
Allen, Richard, 8
Allison, James, 411, 412
Allison, Joseph, 285
Allison, William, 417
Alpden, Matthias, 173
Amos, Ann, 147
Amos, Mrs., 376
Amyet, John, 19
Ancts, Henry, 443
Anderson, Enoch, 230
Anderson, James, 127
Anderson, Richard, 108, 109
Anderson, Robert, 254, 310, 361
Anderson, Thomas, 306, 382
Anderson, William, 82, 370, 394, 443
Andrew, William, 396
Andrews, Mr., 103
Anks, Henry, 419
Annely, Edward, 172
Annis, John, 25
Armirage, James, 13
Armit, Joseph, 235
Armit, Stephen, 116
Armitage, Benjamin, 62, 164, 284

Arnold, Melchizedeck, 65
Arrold, Thomas, 63
Ashbrook, John, 272
Ashfield, Richard, 69
Ashleman, Benjamin, 390
Ashton, Richard, 139, 140, 211
Ashton, Thomas, 37
Asleman, Jacob, 417
Aston, George, 137, 359
Attwood, Capt., 231, 233
Attwood, William, 162, 232, 233
Atwood, Capt., 220
Austin, Samuel, 180
Awbrey, John, 264
Ayres, Absalom, 4
Backer, Mr., 52
Bacley, Thomas, 120
Badmin, Charles, 396
Bagg, Thomas, 171, 172
Bailey, Joel, 325
Baily, Richard, 154
Baird, Ann, 283
Baird, Patrick, 29
Baker, Isaac, 291
Baker, Joseph, 309
Baker, Joshua, 184, 191, 291
Baker, William, 299, 357
Baldwin, James, 242
Baldwin, John, 73, 76, 405
Baldwin, William, 21
Ball, John, 33, 50, 94
Ball, Roger, 147
Bannet, William, 37
Bantoff, William, 42, 44
Barber, Edward, 260
Barber, Elizabeth, 170
Barclay, John, 431
Bard, John, 259
Bard, Peter, 339, 340
Bare, Blasius, 246
Barecrost, Ambrose, 14
Bareford, William, 51

Barker, Charles, 373
Barker, John, 268
Barly, James/Jacob, 368
Barnes, William, 160
Barone, Isaac, 72
Barrell, Bartholomew, 361
Barret, Richard, 178
Barry, Michael, 280
Barry, Richard, 41
Bartam, Joseph, 70
Bartholomew, Joseph, 295
Bartleson, Bartle, 272
Baseener, Andreas, 126
Basker, John, 338
Basnet, Capt., 330
Bate, Thomas, 319
Bavenson, Richard, 14
Bayley, John, 57
Bayly, John, 90
Baynton, Peter, 92
Beakes, Stephen, 309
Beaks, Joseph, 323
Beaks, Samuel/Samuell, 12, 18
Beal, Benjamin, 409
Bealey, John, 17
Beard, Robert, 358
Beaumont, William, 14
Beddall, John, 292
Beddes, Richard, 214
Bell, Henry, 26
Bell, James, 131
Bell, John, 67, 421
Bell, Tom, 289
Bell, William, 125
Beman, George, 96
Benn, James, 104
Benn, John, 200
Bennerman, James, 135
Bennet, James, 168
Bennet, John, 21
Bennet, Thomas, 249
Bennet, William, 31
Bennett, James, 266

Bentley, John, 61
Bentley, Thomas, 372, 404
Bently, Thomas/Tho., 130
Berry, Michael, 221
Bethel, Samuel, 154
Betterton, Benajmin, 271
Bettle, Samuel, 357
Bevan, Evan, 159
Biddle, James, 100
Biddle, William, 90, 102
Biederey, John Barnhard, 301
Bigley, James, 401
Bile, William, 71
Biles, Thomas, 97
Billet, William, 30
Bingly, Thomas, 15
Bird, William, 305, 318
Bissell, William, 29
Blair, Thomas, 204
Blair, William, 220, 234, 236
Blake, Charles, 79
Blakely, Henry, 267
Blakey, Charles, 85
Blanchet, John, 43
Bland, John, 366
Blare, Thomas, 199
Bleakley, John, 247, 279, 280
Bleakly, Henry, 276, 281
Blowden, John, 64, 89, 118, 124, 125, 152, 237
Blows, William, 423, 438
Boat, William, 405
Boddiscurte, John, 185
Bogert, Nicholas, 122
Boggs, Ephraim, 436
Boham, Sarah, 168
Bonar, William, 302
Bond, James, 190, 191, 302
Bond, John, 207
Bond, Joseph, 260
Bond, Samuel, 42
Bonell, John Dod, 343
Bonham, Samuell, 17

Bonsal, Obadiah, 113
Bonsall, Obadiah, 413
Boon, Swan, 428
Booth, Thomas, 161
Bordman, George, 94
Bostock, George, 22
Bostuck, Martha, 207
Boucher, James, 414
Boude, Thomas, 53
Bouman, Jacob, 294
Bourgoin, Joseph, 416
Bourne, John, 419
Bowels, George, 43
Bowen, Henry, 206
Bowen, Richard, 55, 74, 76
Bower, Cornelius, 413
Bowls, Samuel, 55
Boyd, Ann, 262
Boyd, James, 111, 131
Boyd, John, 166
Boyd, Patrick, 5, 7
Boyle, James, 400
Boyle, Robert, 293, 389, 405
Boyle, Thomas, 390
Boyles, Bryant, 378
Brackenbury, John, 39, 46
Bradford, Andrew, 1, 9, 22, 36,
   40, 51, 52, 64, 69, 80, 135,
   141, 208
Bradford, William, 1, 36, 52, 136
Bradley, Darby, 245
Bradley, George, 378
Bradley, John, 22
Brady, Daniel, 365
Brady, Richard, 192
Braiser, Jane, 80
Brame, John, 302
Brand, Michael, 443
Brandon, John, 315
Brandriff, Timothy, 56
Branson, William, 1, 51, 71, 188,
   240, 304, 310
Braslam, Hugh, 401

Brazil, Michael, 57
Brendly, James, 79
Brennan, Timothy, 299
Breuster, Margaret, 311
Brewer, Henry, 72
Brian, Daniel, 98
Briggs, Edmund, 310
Briggs, William, 310
Bright, Anthony, 215
Brimer, Lawrance, 231
Bringhurst, John, 141
Broderick, Daniel, 289
Brogden, Edward, 342, 344
Bromadge, Capt., 165, 183
Bromage, Samuel, 61
Bromley, John, 38
Bronon, John, 433
Brookman, Sarah, 284
Brooks, Edward, 5, 7, 68, 224
Brooks, John, 350
Brothers, Daniel, 289
Brown, Charles, 17
Brown, David, 148
Brown, Edward, 154
Brown, George, 283
Brown, Hugh, 46
Brown, John, 101, 156, 275, 424
Brown, Margaret, 339, 427
Brown, Mary, 359
Brown, Peter, 230, 320
Brown, Philip, 207
Brown, Thomas, 262, 423
Brown, William, 80, 120, 121,
   408
Browne, Peter, 330
Brustall, Richard, 25
Bryan, James, 321
Bryan, John, 181
Bryan, Joseph, 338, 340
Bryan, Michael, 257
Bryant, John, 42, 278
Bryant, Joseph, 356
Buchanan, Robert, 141

Budd, John, 86
Bull, John, 31
Bunting, Samuel, 3, 85
Burgain, Patrick, 108, 109
Burgan, Patrick, 106
Burge, William, 96
Burk, John, 63
Burk, Mary, 411
Burk, Patrick, 170
Burleigh, Joseph, 149
Burn, Ann, 332
Burn, Hugh, 196
Burn, John, 406
Burn, Matthew, 241
Burn, Roger, 54
Burne, Dennis, 267
Burrass, Mathew, 262
Burrass, Mrs., 262
Burroughs, Elizabeth, 170
Burrows, Arthur, 262, 263
Burrows, William, 229
Bush, David, 209, 211
Butcher, Samuel, 325
Butler, James, 165, 183
Butler, Sarah, 314
Butler, Thomas, 338
Butt, Samuel, 189
Bye, Hezekiah, 337
Cain, Edward, 380
Cain, William, 99
Calaghan, Cornelius, 312
Calahan, Charles, 102
Caldwel/Caldwell, Andrew, 219
Callahon, William, 399
Callehan, Charles, 90
Callender, Ephraim, 188
Cambell, Charles, 207
Cammock, Samuel, 128
Campbel, Tho., 126
Canadey, Thomas, 285
Canby, Benjamin, 260
Cangling, James, 396
Cannon, William, 411

Cannor, Cornelius, 260
Canon, Joseph, 236
Carawan, John, 196
Cardiff, John, 302
Carey, Roger, 54
Carhalt, John, 341
Cario, Michael, 313
Carlisle, Abraham, 307, 308
Carman, Joseph, 286
Carman, Macaja, 286
Carmichael, William, 327
Carne, James, 248
Carnell, John, 345
Carpenter, Henry, 268
Carpenter, Nicodemus, 107
Carr, James, 24
Carr, Joseph, 363
Carrel, John, 322
Carrel, Mary, 322
Carrigan, Patrick, 97
Carrol, John, 162
Carroll, James, 343
Carroll, Robert, 428
Carson, Mr., 242, 283
Cartar, George, 30
Carter, Henry, 85
Carvel, Thomas, 219
Cary, John, 143
Casdorp, Jacob, 212, 213
Casey, James, 257
Cassell, Arnold, 26
Cassell, John, 25
Castillow, David, 380
Castle, Elizabeth, 316
Castle, Nicholas, 185, 186
Caughlan, Samuel, 158
Caughland, Elinor, 222
Cavannah, Garret, 191
Cavenaugh, Hugh, 367
Cavenaugh, James, 137
Cavenaugh, Thomas, 315, 317
Cavenough, Eleanor, 299
Cell, Luke, 72

Center, William, 228
Chads, Capt., 189, 197
Chalfin, Robert, 134
Chalkley, Thomas, 238
Chalmers, James, 62
Chamberlain/Chamberlin Richard, 20, 21
Chambers, Jonathan, 213
Chancellor, William, 7, 28
Chaplen, Mrs. Samuel, 26
Chaplen, Samuel, 26
Chapman, Abraham, 80
Chapman, John, 14
Chapman, Richard, 248
Charadon, Clament, 47
Chard, Martin, 163
Cheribly, Cornelius, 260
Childs, William, 326
Chit, Thomas, 60
Christie, Robert, 255
Chubbard, John, 360
Claborne, Thomas, 410
Clare, John, 345, 425
Clare, Peter, 34
Clare, William, 223
Clark, Derby, 376
Clark, Henry, 186
Clark, John, 71, 392
Clark, Joseph, 304, 321
Clark, Mr., 370
Clark, Robert, 25
Clark, Valentine, 144
Clarke, Valentine, 117
Clarke, William, 268
Clarkson, Mathew, 165
Classon, Nicholas, 52
Claxton, James, 356
Claypoole, James, 149
Clayton, Edward, 101
Clayton, Richard, 61
Clayton, Thomas, 402
Clayton, William, 334, 402
Clement, Jeremiah, 76

Clemmons, Hugh, 347
Clemson, John, 373
Clemson, Thomas, 354
Clerk, Valentine, 157
Clever, Derick, 305
Clevet, John, 241
Cliff, John, 19
Climson/Clemson, John, 369
Clinton, Robert, 395
Cloath, Carberry, 404
Clows, John, 114
Clymer, Christopher, 338, 340
Clymer, Mr., 104
Clymer, Richard, 121
Coasher, Josiah, 137
Coates, Moses, 260
Coats, John, 29
Coats, William, 1
Coats/Courts, Mrs. William, 26
Coats/Courts, William, 26
Cochran, Mary, 322
Cock, Gregory, 45
Cockran, Thomas, 289
Codgall, John, 349
Codgdill, John, 336, 337
Coes, Anthony, 273
Coffee, John, 371
Coffel, John, 384
Cogdill, John, 293
Coger, Josiah, 148
Coging, Nicholas, 301
Cole, Stephen, 188
Cole, William, 107, 354
Collemore, William, 307, 308
Collet, John, 229
Collet, Robert, 34
Collick, Peter Mack, 56
Collin, John, 44
Collings, Edward, 206
Collings, Joseph, 10
Collins, David, 360
Colson, Edward, 288
Colston, William, 133

Coltis, James, 214
Comeley, Henry, 74, 76
Comely, John, 90
Comings, James, 440
Comins, Thomas, 193
Comly, Walter, 434
Condon, David, 286
Condon, Garrat, 279
Condon, Garret, 400, 404
Condon, James, 95
Connal, John, 172
Conner, Timothy, 254, 364
Conner/Connor, Roger/Rodger, 296, 297, 298
Connoly, Peter, 376
Connoly, Simon, 349
Connor, Patrick, 102
Connor, Timothy, 358
Conoly, Edmund, 412
Conoly, Peter, 363
Conrad, Peter, 329
Conron, Edward, 57
Conyngham, Mr., 389
Cook, John, 331
Cook, John George, 317
Cook, Samuel, 316, 343
Cooke, Edward, 14
Cooke, William, 17
Cookson, Daniel, 202
Coombes, Thomas, 16
Cooper, Daniel, 320
Cooper, Jonathan, 70
Cooper, William, 37
Copson, John, 15
Coran, Isaac, 435
Corbet, John, 10
Corbie, William, 281
Corby, William, 290
Corin, Isaac, 98
Cornish, Andrew, 58
Cornish, James, 185, 186
Correy, George, 341, 345
Correy, John, 345

Coryell, Manuel, 260
Costeloe, John, 413
Cottinger, John, 314
Cowley, John, 3
Cownden, James, 63
Cowpland, Caleb, 181
Cowpland, Joshua, 82
Cowren, Elizabeth, 396
Crab, Thomas, 78
Craddock, William, 296
Crage, Alexander, 370
Craig, Alexander, 394
Crane, Charles, 282
Cratho, John, 25
Crawley, Henry, 195
Creighton, John, 177
Cremeing, Daniel, 162
Cresswel, John, 66
Crispin, Joseph, 366, 367
Crispin, Thomas, 122
Croasdale, Thomas, 204, 258, 271, 275
Croker, John, 103, 163
Crosbe, Faril, 180
Crosbery, William, 153
Crosby, John, 36
Crosdale, Thomas, 238, 284, 289
Crosleys/Crosly, Charles/Charls, 54
Cross, William, 372
Crosset, Thomas, 46
Crosthwait, William, 222
Crosthwaite, Thomas, 406
Crosthwaite, William, 215, 219, 237
Crosthwaite/Crossthwaite, William, 181
Crotty, William, 318
Crouders, James, 40
Crowley, Dennis, 325
Cruikshank, Alexander, 350
Cruikshanks, Alexander, 431
Crukshank, Alexander, 149, 229

Cuff, Peter, 107, 108, 119
Cuisick, Edward, 390
Culford, Patrick, 226
Cumly, Joseph, 150
Cummings, Thomas, 227
Cummins, Joseph, 73
Cundun, James, 58
Cunningham, Mr., 334
Cunningham, Patrick, 306
Cunningham, Redmond, 262
Cunningham, Thomas, 360
Cunrad, Anthony, 197
Cunrads, Dennis, 425
Cunrod, John, 241
Curren, George, 66, 93
Curry, James, 77, 79
Curtis, John, 330
Cuthbert, John, 309
Cuugh, Wiliam, 189
Cuzzins, Mr., 406
Cyphers, Elizabeth, 42
Dabbin, John, 244, 245, 281, 290, 404
Dailey, Dennis, 305
Daley, Dennis, 318
Dalloway, Joseph, 83
Damood, Henry, 418
Dampsey, Margaret, 243
Damsel, Henry, 92, 94
Daniels, Richard, 323
Danis, David, 14
Darby, Francis, 88, 91
Davall, George, 437
Daveis, James, 205
David, Amos, 362
David, James, 414
David, John, 341, 342
Davies, David, 66
Davies, Ellis, 252
Davies, William, 100
Davies/Davis, David, 93, 175
Davis, Benjamin, 240, 266, 287, 353
Davis, Daniel, 132
Davis, Edward, 406
Davis, George, 267
Davis, James, 306, 307, 308, 327
Davis, James, 351
Davis, John, 1, 320, 419
Davis, Joseph, 223
Davis, Lawrence, 337
Davis, Llewlling, 257
Davis, Mary, 94
Davis, Richard, 360
Davis, Robert, 123
Davis, Samuel, 196
Davis, Thomas, 32, 65, 91, 104
Davis, William, 45, 138, 446
Davison, William, 350
Davy, Mr., 242, 283
Dawfitt, Philip, 31
Dawson, Isaac, 385
Dean, John, 361
Dean, Thomas, 313
Deaver, Antil, 287
Debler, Lodowick, 218
Deglish, Robert, 60
Delaney, Derby, 365
Delaplane, Mr., 314
Dene, Thomas, 425
Denhall, Benjamin, 2
Denison, John, 380, 382
Denison, Timothy, 231, 233
Dennis, John, 232, 234, 310
Dennison, Patrick, 279
Denny, Walter, 173, 405
Denormandie, John Abraham, 259
Dent, Lawrence, 235
Dent, William, 226
DePeyster, Gerardus, 166
Devoe, Peter, 205
Dewees, William, 65
Dewksbury, George, 423
Dexter, Henry, 60
Dexter, John, 25, 80

Deyerman, Catherine/Ginnena, 409
Dicker, Samuel, 18
Dickie, William, 111
Dickinson, John, 25
Dicks, Peter, 3
Dickson, James, 282
Dickson, Margaret, 282
Diemer, Capt., 359
Dignan, Bryan, 374
Ditchett, William, 204
Dix, Nathan, 88
Dixson, Robert, 235
Dobbin, John, 400
Dod, Anne, 68
Dodson, John, 72
Doharthy, Mary, 226
Dollaha, William, 316
Doller/Dollar/Dollard, Patrick, 296, 297, 298
Domingo, John, 259
Donahe, Michael, 86
Donahew, Daniel, 379
Donelan, John, 230
Donesan/Doneson, John, 440, 443
Donnever/Donnevan, Cornelius/Cobernelius, 264, 265
Dorborow, Joseph, 170
Dorrell, William, 120, 121
Dorrington, William, 123
Double, John, 30
Doude, George, 434
Dougherty, James, 317
Douglas, John, 330
Dowen, Philip, 200
Dowllenger, George, 360
Downey, Peter, 387
Downing, Anstis, 71
Downing, John, 87
Downing, Thomas, 235
Doyle, John, 141

Doyle, Lawrence, 396
Draper, Stephen, 215
Driver, Robert, 224
Dryskyl, William, 129
Dubs, Jost, 369
Dudy, Patrick, 311
Duffy, Frances, 430
Dugan, James, 384, 390
Dulany, Matthew, 10
Dummond, Duncan, 53, 54
Dun, Philip, 195
Dunbar, John, 360
Dunevan, Charles, 304
Dunn, Daniel, 228
Dunning, Thomas, 139, 140
Dunnoghon, John, 445, 446
Durborow, Daniel, 15
Durey, Edward, 269
Durham, Bartell, 382
Durham, Bartholomew, 332
Dussell, Thomas, 74
Dwalt, Mathew, 122
Dyck, Thomas, 260
Dyke, Thomas, 312
Eades, Michael, 82
Eagen, John, 191
Eagon, Sylvester, 395
Earle, John, 12
Eastbourn, Samuel, 66
Eastburn, John, 212
Eavenson, Nathaniel, 217
Ebberman, Jacob, 267
Edgar, Charles, 326, 375, 376
Edgell, Simon, 78, 207
Edwards, Evan, 35
Edwards, Henry, 106
Edwards, John, 67, 100, 131
Edwards, Richard, 343
Edwards, Thomas, 161, 304, 321
Edwards, William, 163
Effreth, Jeremiah, 32
Eisman, Hans Wulf, 126
Eldridge, James, 416

Eldridge, Obediah, 110, 129
Elford, John, 42
Elfreth, Jeremiah, 65
Elfreth, John, 65, 149
Elliot, Peter, 256
Ellis, Evan, 204
Ellis, Robert, 25, 40
Ellis, William, 288
Eme, William, 18
Emerson, Mr., 251
Emlen, George, 120, 121, 352
Emlin/Emlen, George, 307, 308
Emmit, Abraham, 240
Engelbert, Anthony, 225
England, Joseph, 77
Engle, Benjamin, 409
Engle, Frederick, 37
Enoch, Henry, 35
Enocks, Henry, 32
Ensworth, James, 33
Enterkin, George, 444
Erwin, Robert, 408
Erwin, Thomas, 383
Esington, James, 133, 134
Evan, William, 256
Evans, David, 160
Evans, Edward, 232, 234
Evans, Hugh, 375, 384
Evans, John, 38
Evans, Morgan, 285
Evans, Owen, 174
Evans, Samuel, 363, 376, 414
Evins, James, 363
Eyre, Ambross, 208
Fagan, Henry, 322, 339
Fairbrother, Thomas, 353
Faires, Samuel, 223
Fairman, Benjamen/Benjamin, 47
Fare, Thomas, 1
Fareis, John, 291
Farguhar, Adam, 286
Farinton, George, 45

Farmar, Edward, 299
Farmar, Joseph, 356
Farmer, Edward, 3, 265
Farmer, Joseph, 442
Farmer, Justice, 82
Farmer, Richard, 231
Farra, Samuel, 158
Farrall, Roger, 333
Farrel, Edmond, 34, 36
Farrel, Edmund, 110, 119
Farrell, Martin, 150
Faulkner, Alexander, 10
Femel, John, 416
Fenton, John, 2
Fenuel, Nicholas, 321
Ferguson, John, 360
Ferguson, Samuel, 59
Fetterly, Johannes, 69
Field, Richard, 129
Fields, Samuel, 343
Finch, William, 296
Finly, William, 314
Fishar, Jonathan, 249
Fishbourn, William, 165, 183, 194
Fisher, Jonathan, 81, 84
Fitzgerald, James, 84, 98
Fitzgerrald, John, 252
Fitzpatrick, Richard, 389
Fitzsimmons, Richard, 357
Fitzwater, Thomas, 412
Flanagan, Hugh, 156
Flanagen, Roger, 446
Fleming, George, 126
Fleming, John, 309
Flemming, Arthur, 262, 263
Flemming, John, 10
Flening, Arthur, 74
Fletcher, Thomas, 161, 377
Flexney, Daniel, 148
Fling, Cornelius, 209
Fling, George, 425
Fling, Rebecca, 294

Flower, Joseph, 84, 172
Flower, Samuel, 304, 311, 387
Flud, John, 109
Ford, John, 78
Ford, Nathaniel, 70
Forde, Thomas, 114
Forest, William, 149
Forlindey, Jendey, 93
Forrest, Thomas, 81
Forrester, John, 111
Forster, Henry, 406
Fortescue, Charles Walker, 381
Fortescue, John, 381
Fortey, Ann, 399
Fortey, John, 399
Fortune, William, 39
Fosset, Renard, 421
Foster, Arthur, 347
Foster, Joseph, 86
Foster, William, 300
Foulks, John, 370
Fowler, John, 266
Fowler, Peter, 283, 368, 370
Fowler/Powler, Peter, 324
Fox, Daniel, 294
Foy, Edward, 39
Frame, Alexander, 48
Francis, Rees, 433
Francis, Thomas, 435
Francklin, John, 21
Franklin, Benj., 203
Franklin, Benjamin, 370
Fred, Benjamin, 371
Fred, Nicholas, 156
French, Jonathan, 114
French, Thomas, 92, 107
Fretzel, Gertrude, 320
Fretzel, Joannes Harmonius, 363
Fretzel, John Harmon, 319
Frivall, Harmon, 314
Frivall, Mrs., 314
Frost, John, 75
Fruin, John, 102

Fry, John, 317
Fudge, George, 389
Fulham, Peter, 296
Fulks, Elizabeth, 150
Fulks, John, 150
Furio, John, 394
Furlong, Peter, 20
Galacher, Michael, 367
Galbreath, James, 419
Galbreth, John, 101
Gallachar, Thomas, 300
Gallaspy, Hugh, 400
Gambarto, Peter, 157
Gamble, Richard, 313
Gammon, Philip, 39
Ganthony, James, 338, 340
Gardiner, William, 286
Gardner, James, 331
Gardner, Mr., 334, 389
Gardner, Peter, 196
Garlach, John Ierich, 19
Garland, Edward, 67
Garland, William, 199, 204
Garrad, Anthony, 146
Garrat, Samuel, Jr., 124
Garrick, John, 433
Garrigues, Francis, 272
Garvi, Malachi, 117
Garwood, William, 140
Gatchel, Justice, 138
Gathen, Mary, 236
Gaven, Joseph, 407
Gay, Nathaniel, 224
Gesson, William, 343
Gibbens, David, 45, 47
Gibbs, John, 84
Gibson, George, 282, 297
Gilbert, John, 255
Gilbert, Joseph, 316, 343
Gilcrist, Lawrence, 360
Gill, Richard, 347
Gilleylin, 361
Gilliam, William, 69

Gilling, John, 94
Glandon, Michael, 121
Glasford, Henry, 350
Glenn, John, Jr., 430
Goard, Solomon, 51
Goddin, William, 301
Godfrey, Thomas, 170
Godsel, John, 302
Goff, Edward, 374
Gooch, John, 142
Gooch, Joseph, 142
Goodenough, John, 247
Goodfellow, William, 356
Goodman, Mr., 383, 386
Goodman, William, 319
Goodson, Andrew, 307, 308
Goodwin, Joseph, 324
Goodwin, Thomas, 306
Gordon, Patrick, 105
Gorgin, Thomas, 410
Gorrel, James, 251
Gould, Benjamin, 402
Gould, William, 280
Grace, John, 420
Grace, Robert, 400
Grady, Barnaby, 335
Graham, James, 423
Granger, John, 63
Grant, Thomas, 171
Grassholt, Christian, 126
Gray, George, 428
Gray, John, 61
Gray, Joseph, 126, 322, 354, 421
Gray, Robert, 242
Gray, Thomas, 190
Gray, William, 301
Graydon, Mr., 251
Greagin, Edward, 88
Green, John, 255
Green, Thomas, 94, 348, 420
Green, William, 90, 134, 216
Greenfield, James, 395
Greenleaf, Stephen, 426
Greenstreet, Benjamin, 123
Greenwich, Giles, 94
Greevy, John, 317
Grefith, David, 202
Gregory, Richard, 300
Grevill, Aylmer, 329
Griffin, Robert, 78
Griffin, William, 189
Griffis, Michael, 125
Griffith, David, 282, 297, 320
Griffith, Thomas, 371, 384
Griffiths, John, 213
Griffiths, Thomas, 259
Griffitts, John, 84
Griffitts, Philip, 211
Grigg, Thomas, 83
Grimes, Joseph, 132
Gross, Charles, 138
Grove/Grover, Joseph, 271, 272
Grub, Nathanael, 163
Grubb, Henry, 39
Grubb, Nathaniel, 41, 178, 402
Grubb, Peter, 281
Gryer, John, 142
Gubby, John, 206
Guest, Edward, 64
Gumly, Nathan, 13
Guttery, Ann, 351, 352
Guy, John, 294
Hackett, John, 332
Hadley, Thomas, 239
Hadly, Simon, 143
Hagan, Daniel, 219
Hagan, James, 409
Hagget, John, 154
Haines, John, 266
Haistins, David, 415
Hale, Samuel, 135, 136
Hall, Archiba, 35
Hall, Archibald, 347
Hall, John, 35, 156, 294
Hall, William, 243
Hallowell, John, 441

Hambleton, Edward, 114, 179
Hambleton, Robert, 149
Hambricht, John, 433
Hamilton, Edward, 175, 178
Hamilton, Francis, 405
Hamilton, John, 157, 181, 294
Hamilton, Robert, 263
Hamilton, William, 189, 315
Hamlin, Michael, 13
Hanaway, Thomas, 313
Hancock, Robert, 92
Handlin, Valentine, 236
Haney, Thomas, 170
Hanly, John, 342, 344, 373
Hannah, James, 383
Hannum, John, 148
Hannum, Robert, 129
Hanraty, Thomas, 356
Harbert, William, 57, 250
Harding, Edward, 302
Harding, John, 95
Hardman, Thomas, 2
Hardwich, Coles, 434, 436
Hargrave, Charles, 117
Hargrave, Joseph, 148
Harlen, Joseph, 292
Harlen, Ruth, 292
Harley, William, 360
Harmson, Henry, 20
Harpe, Peter, 116
Harper, John, 326
Harper, Mrs., 262
Harris, George, 239
Harris, John, 258, 341, 342
Harris, Richard, 12
Harris, Robert, 17, 340
Harris, Thomas, 82
Harris, William/Wm., 127
Harris/Harriss, Robert, 338
Harrison, John, 397
Harrison, Joseph, 112
Harrison, William, 177
Harry, John, 271

Hart, Charles, 284
Hart, John, 84, 203
Hart, Thomas, 83, 100
Hartley, Henry, 156
Hartley, Thomas, 228
Hartley, William, 173, 283, 324, 368, 370
Harvey, Benjamin, 253, 325
Harvey, Job, 160, 169, 196, 221, 257
Hasey, William, 123
Hasleton, William, 396
Hassert, Arent, 166
Hastings, Samuel, 193, 208, 220, 221
Hathorn, Daniel, 442
Hatton, Peter, 112
Hausse, Christopher/Stofel, 440
Hausse, Regina/Lany, 440
Hawley, Joseph, 4
Haxley, David, 209
Hay, John, 221
Hay, William, 221
Hayes, James, 444
Hayes, John, 27
Hayes, Joseph, 111
Hayes/Hays, William, 16
Haygen, John, 291
Haynes, George, 127
Hays, William, 38
Hayward, Thomas, 16
Hazely/Hazeey, John, 338, 340
Head, Thomas, 398, 429
Heany, Patrick, 429
Hearcoat, David, 259
Heath, John, 355
Heaton, William, 438
Hedford, John, 75
Hemphill, Edward, 134
Henderson, Francis, 375
Henderson, James, 251
Henderson, Samuel, 168
Hendricks, Mr., 40

Hendry, John, 151, 152
Henry, Darby, 441
Henry, Jeremiah, 441
Henton, Israel, 393
Herbert, William, 145
Hern, Daniel, 264
Herne, Launcelot, 55
Herne, Lawrence, 69
Herring, Benjamen, 25
Hethcot, John, 168
Hether, Richard, 56
Heurtin, William, 144
Hewes, Moses, 68
Hibberd, John, 238
Hickey, Francis, 338, 340
Hickey, Lancaster, 199
Hickinbottom, Alexander, 277
Hicks, Benjamin, 239, 240
Hicky/Hickay, John, 248, 249
Higgins, John, 109
Higgins, Patrick, 426
Higgins, Timothy, 27
Hill, Anthony, 277
Hill, Edward, 441
Hill, George, 349
Hill, John, 51
Hill, Samuel, 258, 280
Hill, Thomas, 165
Hillegas, Michael, 192
Hilliard, Benjamin, 20
Hillyard, Benjamin, 12
Hilton, Andrew, 42, 87
Hirst, John, 423, 438, 439
Hister, Daniel, 330
Hockley, Henry, 229
Hodge, Samuel, 411
Hodges, James, 231
Hodges, Joseph, 56
Hogg, George, 235
Holcolm, John, 226
Holiday, Robert, 179
Holland, John, 373
Holland, Richard, 420

Holland, William, 346
Hollingsworth, Stephen, 72
Hollington, Hannah, 330
Holloway, Joseph, 433
Holmes, James, 229
Holt, John, 217
Holt, Samuel, 42
Holt, Thomas, 116, 242
Homer, John, 104, 295
Hood, John, 87
Hooper, John, 182
Hooper, Samuel, 149
Hoopes, John, 185
Hoopes, Stephen, 216
Hopkins, David, 123
Hopkins, John, 53, 126, 149
Hore, Capt., 91
Horley, Daniel, 278
Horne, Edward, 58, 146
Horrom, Moses, 343
Horsley, Joseph, 87
Hoskins, Ruth, 45
House, George, 46, 151, 152
House, John, 192
Howard, Edmond, 212
Howard, Edward, 213
Howard, John, 437
Howard, Thomas, 306
Howell, David, 286
Howell, John, 331, 339, 340
Howell, Nicholas, 6
Howell, Samuel, 380
Howlet, John, 169
Howsar, Loranz, 388
Howson, Thomas, 393
Hoyet, John, 303
Hubbs, Joseph, 426
Huddleston, Henry, 207
Huddy, Christopher, 246, 247
Hudson, William, 47, 365
Hudson, William, Jr., 110
Huff, Samuel, 4
Huffey, Rebecca, 294

Hugh, Jenkin, 256
Hughes, Bryan, 193
Hughes, John, 289, 296, 364, 392
Hughes, Matthew, 78
Hughes, Richard, 154, 244
Hughes, William, 89
Hughes/Hughs, Richard, 387
Hughs, John, 325
Hughs, Richard, 18
Hughs, Samuel, 73, 168
Huling, Michael, 193
Hulings, Marcus, 318
Humphrey, John, 44
Humphreys, John, 315
Humphries, Peter, 102
Humphry, John, 43
Hunt, James, 256
Hunt, John, 433
Hunt, Roger, 284
Hunt, William, 12, 15, 17
Hunter, Alexander, 200
Hunter, Mr., 37
Hurfoot, Samuel, 117
Hurford, Samuel, 385
Husbands, Thomas, 338, 340
Hutchins, Zachariah, 32, 60
Hutchins, Zechariah, 13
Hutchinson, John, 60, 102, 438
Hutchinson, Michael, 437
Hutton, John, 33
Hyat, John, 2, 51
Hyatt, John, 128, 144, 231, 275
Hyde, Cesar, 65
Hynes, John, 34, 36
Iddings, Wm., 61
Iden, John, 441
Impy, John, 183
Indians, 1; Ham, 90; Maria, 29; Peter, 29; Robin, Jeremiah, 231; Robin, Nehemiah, 231; Tamerlane, Thomas, 79; Tamerlin, Thomas, 85; Tobey, 1

Indians, Tomlinson, Thomas, 37; unnamed, 251
Ingham, Jonathan, 260, 426
Ingledew, Blakeston, 171, 172
Inglis, John, 135
Ingram, John, 156
Ingray/McGray, Nicholas, 244, 245
Inman, Abel, 406
Jackson, Alexander, 406
Jackson, John, 36, 306, 314, 343
Jackson, Joseph, 44, 111, 279
Jackson, Mr., 171
Jackson, Stephen, 43, 44
Jacobs, James, 348
James, John, 185
James, Joseph, 194, 324, 325
James, Thomas, 345
Jappie, Daniel, 388
Jeanes, Joseph, 364
Jefferis, Elizabeth, 354
Jeffris, John, 400
Jenkin, David, 283
Jenkins, Captain, 242
Jenkins, Nathaniel, 143
Jenkins, Stephen, 358
Jenkinson, John, 78
Jennings, John, 39
Jennings, Thomas, 318
Jerrard, Richard, 269
Jerret, John, 387
Jodon, Francis, 260
Johnson, John, 47, 215, 218, 222
Johnson, Miner, 260
Johnson, Samuel, 98
Johnson, Thomas, 130
Johnson, Tom, 429
Johnson, William, 406
Johnston, Dr., 10
Johnston, Jacob, 423
Johnston, James, 419
Johnston/Johnson, Obadiah, 169
Jones, Daniel, 202

Jones, David, 302
Jones, Edmund, 16
Jones, George, 172
Jones, George Rice, 168, 220
Jones, Henry, 400
Jones, John, 22, 41, 48, 50, 84, 109, 182, 197, 241, 285, 306, 307, 308, 372, 403, 420
Jones, Joseph, 9, 10
Jones, Mary, 196
Jones, Morgen/Morgan, 307, 308
Jones, Mr., 266
Jones, Oliver, 253
Jones, Reece, 123
Jones, Rees, 18
Jones, Samuel, 48
Jones, Thomas, 3, 6, 8, 403
Jordan, James, 360
Josep, Abraham, 255
Kahar, John, 204
Kairlin, Matthias, 303
Kann, Conrad, 50
Kann, Marina, 50
Kanton, Francis, 326
Kastner, George, 305
Katts, Lodowick, 302
Kavanaugh, James, 153
Kees, Andrew, 16
Kees, John, 120
Kehind, William, 101
Keifer, George, 246
Keimer, James, 304
Keith, William, 20, 21, 26, 29
Kell, John, 405
Kelley, Peter, 74
Kelly, Cornelius, 88
Kelly, Daniel, 158, 159
Kelly, Dennis, 202
Kelly, George, 315, 317
Kelly, Hugh, 411
Kelly, Joseph, 375, 376
Kemp, William, 258
Kendall, Benjamin, 420

Kenedy, Patrick, 53
Kennedy, Bryan, 241
Kennedy, David, 269, 270
Kennedy, Samuel, 408, 415
Kenny, Lazarus, 194
Kensey, John, 333
Kent, John, 437
Keppler, John, 368
Kerk, Samuel, 4
Kerlin, Matthias, 364
Keron, Lawrence, 142
Kerregan, Manus, 387
Kerril, Morris, 193, 194
Kerrill, Morris, 165
Kerslake, Abraham, 215
Kettsendorff, William, 201
Kigler, Christopher/Hans, 234
Kindley, Peter, 200
King, George, 49
King, John, 114
King, John Landman, 114
Kirk, Jacob, 227
Kirk, James, 195
Kirk, Patrick, 445, 446
Kirk, Roger, 235
Kirkbride, Joseph, 85
Klein, Henry, 399
Knight, Joseph, 33, 34
Knowles, John, 46
Knox, James, 412
Kuhl/Kühl, Marcus, 150; 301
Kures, Peter, 19
Lamb, Thomas, 67
Lamborn, Robert, 255
Lamenon, Patrick, 60
Lamey, Mathias, 416
Lamey, Matthias, 332
Lamy, Mathias, 298
Lancilus, Thomas, 192
Land, Joseph, 139
Landsdown, Thomas, 110
Lang, Alexander, 333, 335
Langhorne, Judge, 103

Larrance, Thomas, 164
Laverdy, Alexander, 289
Lawden, Richard, 54
Lawless, Michael, 287
Lawrence, Joshua, 31
Lawrence, Peter, 385
Layworthy, William, 29
Lea, Anthony, 134, 138
Lea, Roger, 23
Leacock, John, 114, 133, 134, 139, 180
Leadlie, John, 339, 427
Lee, Anthony, 133, 322
Lee, John, 11
Leech, Jacob, 263
Leech, Rebecca, 407
Leech, Tobias, 9
Lees, Ralph, 129
Leicester, Thomas, 7
Leidinburg, Aaron, 439
Leik, John, 295
Lemon, Isaac, 418
Leonard, John, 163
Lesher, John, 377
Lester, William, 90
Letcher, James, 51
Lewis, Enos, 327
Lewis, Jacob, 418
Lewis, James, 97
Lewis, Jenkin, 283
Lewis, Lewis, 197
Lewis, Nathan, 192, 201
Lewis, Robert, 311
Lewis, Samuel, 2
Lewis, Susannah, 250
Lewis, Thomas, 433
Leycet, John, 346
Lican, Hance, 122
Licet, John, 303
Lightfoot, Jacob, 138
Lightle, Nathaniel, 278
Linch, Patrick, 357
Lindley, Thomas, 83, 106

Lindsay, Hugh, 393
Lindsay, John, 259
Lindsay, William, 187
Linsey, David, 252
Linsey, Michael, 309
Lion, George, 241
Lipscomb, John, 212
Littleford, David, 171
Lloyd, Ebenezer, 270
Lloyd, Edward, 202
Lloyd, John, 83, 236
Lloyd, Judge, 49
Lloyd, Thomas, 247, 263, 392
Lloyd, William, 203
Lob, Joseph, 77
Lock, John, 133
Logan, J., 7
Logan, James, 5
Logue, Manaseth, 401
Loller/Coller, Edward, 369
Londergan, Larke, 251
Looney, Edward, 257
Loonin, James, 132
Loudon, Richard, 53
Louns, Mr., 366
Low, Robert, 119
Lowdon, Esther, 83
Lowdon, Richard, 199
Lowe, John, 427
Lownes, Mary, 316
Loyd, Richard, 319, 328
Loyd, Thomas, 174
Lycon, Peter, 115
Lyn, Joseph, 74, 141
Lynch, Thomas, 379
Lynch, William, 253
Lynn, Joseph, 185, 190, 191
Lyon, Charles, 372
Mabbot, Richard, 61
Macall, Philip, 179
Macarslon, William, 327
Macarty, Dennis, 252
Maccahee, John, 1

Macclue, Bernard, 407
MacClure, Nathan, 173
MacColester, Alexander, 39
MacCollister, Allexander, 46
MacConnel, Alexander, 77
MacDaniel, Agnes, 71
MacDaniel, James, 119
MacDoniel, John, 161
MacDonnell, Nicholas, 83
MacGinnis, James, 80
Macguire, Patrick, 377
MacHafee, John, 198
Macilvaine, David, 396
Macilvaine, Moses, 379
Macilvaine, William, 396
Mack, William, 99, 130
Mackay, James, 97
Mackay, Mr., 141
Mackelanen, Janes, 68
Mackellick, James, 429
Mackelvy, Archibald, 361
Mackenny, Westlock, 338, 340
Mackenzie, Duncan, 84
Mackey, James, 153
Mackey, John, 296
Mackintosh, Joseph, 1
Mackmaman, John, 62
MacKnapp, Thomas, 157
Macky, Robert, 244, 361
Macmahan, Alexander, 388
Macmullen, John, 327
MacNayle, John, 41
Macnemar, Francis, 5
Macward, Grace, 4
Macward, Miles, 5, 7
Magee, Abraham, 437
Maguire, Bartholomew/Bartly, 444
Maguire, Bartle, 437
Maguire, James, 193
Maguire, Thomas, 99
Mahany, John, 220
Mahegan, Daniel, 232

Mahon, Paul, 389
Mahone, Alexander, 202
Major, Edward, 179
Makee, John, 1
Makseron, Patrick, 290
Mallary, Ebenezer, 10
Malone, James, 196
Maloughlan, Thomas, 266
Man, John, 48
Mansfield, James, 243
Manthorpe, Samuel, 34
Marceloe, Isaac, 144
Margison, John, 295
Mark, Wm., 130
Markland, Charles, 71
Marks, Joseph, 326
Marle, Thomas, 7
Marpole, David, 24
Marpole, George, 301
Marrow, Patrick, 379, 383
Marshal, Thomas, 217
Marshall, John, 23
Marshall, Randal, 374
Marshall, Thomas, 14, 210
Martin, Alexander, 397
Martin, Daniel, 11
Martin, Lancelot, 198
Martin, Mr., 78, 431
Martin, William, 350, 386, 388
Masterson, Hugh, 26
Mathewson, William, 268
Matlock/Matlack, Timothy, 307, 308
Matson, Peter, 312
Matthews, John, 146
Matthews, Patrick, 377
Maugridge, William, 233, 249, 250
Maule, Thomas, 346
Maxwell, James, 356
May, Thomas, 281
Mayberey, Thomas, 114
Maybery, Thomas, 179

Mayburry, Thomas, 175, 178
Maybury, Thomas, 312
McAlhany, Samael, 274
McAtee, Thomas, 269, 270
McBrid, Daniel, 434
McBride, Daniel, 378
McBride, Nathaniel, 143
McCall, George, 19
McCall, John, 414
McCall, Samuel, 429
McCall, William, 325
McCallon, Thomas, 140
McCarty, Richard, 236
McClauskey, William, 153
McClelan, Hugh, 311
McCleland, Hugh, 367
McClelland, Brice, 432
McClenny, Margaret, 186
McColbem, John, 303
McCollister, Margaret, 266
McComb, John, 173
McComb, John, Jr., 1
McConnal, Francis, 241
McConoll, James, 265
McCormick, John, 353
McCoun, Thomas, 155
McCown/McCoun, Jane, 351, 352
McCoy, Dennis, 379, 383
McCoy, Neal, 55
McCra, James, 166
McCrackan, William, 279
McCullock, Robert, 135
McDaniel, John, 179
McDaniel, Randal, 191
McDearmon, John, 416
McDermot, Terrence, 192
McDonald, Arthur, 260
McDonald, Reynold, 391
McDonnell, Patrick, 373
McDowel, Dugel/Dennis, 235
McDowell, John, 183
McFarlan, Joseph, 411

McFerson/McFarson, John, 105
McGee, Thomas, 156
McGill, Thomas, 223
McGinnis, Francis, 116
McGlachon, Charles, 241
McGlew, Bryan/Barnabe, 418
Mcguire, John, 284
Mcguire, Mary, 284
McGuire, Michael, 109
McGuire, Patrick, 247, 266
McGuire, William, 115, 116
McKaghan, Archibald, 370
McKennan, Charles, 217
McKenny, Charles, 210
McKenny, Peter, 286
McKinsey, Mundo, 295
McKinzey/Mackenzy, John, 107, 108
McKoy, John, 159
McLaughlin, Hugh, 427
McLoughlan, Farrel, 229
McMachin, John, 267
McMackin, John, 276, 281
McMahon, Hugh, 343
McManus, Brian, 162
McMollin, Thomas, 317
McNahme, Sarah, 93
McNamee, Catharine, 391
McNeal, John, 431
McNeal, Mrs., 365
McNemare, John, 386
McOnagel, Charles, 285
McQuatty, David, 166, 167, 176
McQueen, John, 335
McQuire, Thomas, 264
McSwain, Grace, 401
McSwine, Thomas, 223
Mead, Samuel, 160, 169
Meade, Robert, 314, 320, 363
Medcalf, Jacob, 123
Megloughlin, Neal, 196
Men, unnamed, 38, 84, 93, 111,

Men, unnamed, 251, 258, 265, 388, 416, 417, 421, 435, 440
Mercer, Daniel, 337
Meredith, Reese, 228
Meredith, Samuel, 374
Meredith, William, 18
Merratty, James, 158, 159
Messenger, Paul, 381, 387, 394
Meuris, Mattias, 360
Michener, John, 293, 413
Mick, Rudolph, 329
Middleton, Richard, 9, 61
Middleton, Thomas, 410
Mifflin, Benjamin, 268
Milburn, Leonard, 141
Miller, Grissel, 155
Miller, John, 393, 397
Miller, Robert, 47, 248, 391
Miller, William, 103, 200
Millholland, Arthur, 213
Millnors, John, 67
Millord, William, 330
Mills, Daniel, 359
Mills, Hezekiah, 158
Mills, John, 181
Mills, Thomas, 104
Millwater, Joseph, 132
Minneman, William, 1
Miranda, Mr., 10
Mitchel, James, 65, 86, 91
Mitchel, John, 145
Mitchell, Henry, 406, 419
Mitchell, James, 170
Mohegan, Daniel, 233
Montgomery, Archibald, 326
Montgomery, Hugh, 404
Moode, William, 145, 343, 349
Mooney, William, 422
Moor, Charles, 223, 345
Moor, Roger, 276, 277, 291
Moor, Thomas, 19
Moor/Moore, John, 248, 249
Moore, James, 445

Moore, John, 26, 91
Moore, Robert, 426
Moore, Walter, 236
Moore, William, 37, 184, 375, 384
Moorhouse, Peter, 99
Moran, Thomas, 442
Morgan, Alexander, 201
Morgan, Darby, 255
Morgan, Edward, 226
Morgan, Evan, 75, 94, 171
Morgan, Francis, 331
Morgan, George, 172
Morgan, James, 66
Morgan, John, 174, 424
Morgan, Morgan, 241
Morgan, Thomas, 346
Morgan, William, 161, 216, 322, 339
Morrey, Elizabeth, 316
Morris, Isaac, 233
Morris, James, 27
Morris, Luke, 445, 446
Morris, Samuel, 336, 337, 349
Morris, William, 291, 435, 437
Morrison, John, 60
Morrow, Charles, 280
Morrow, John, 280
Morton, John, 214
Mosely, Charles, 209
Moses, William, Jr., 392
Moyes, James, 140
Mugglew[ay], Charles, 41
Muirhead, James, 418
Mulhall, Daniel, 432
Mulholland, Arthur, 41
Mullan, Thomas, 247
Mullin, John, 334
Mullins, Harper, 233
Mulloan, Matthew, 275
Mundle, James, 311
Murdock, William, 436
Murfy, James, 292

Murley, Cornelius, 269
Murphey, Lawrence, 76
Murphy, Arthur, 328
Murphy, Henry, 162
Murphy, John, 272, 273, 330, 416
Murphy, Richard, 69
Murphy, Robert, 310
Murray, Bryan, 358
Murray, John, 199
Murray, Robert, 345
Murrey, John, 115
Murry, Thomas, 70
Myers, Philip, 329
Naglee, John, 69
Nailor, Robert, 203
Naylor, John, 28, 278, 290
Naylor, Richard, 333, 336
Naylor, Robert, 71, 82
Neal, Dennis, 113
Nealis, Francis, 410
Nealson, Alexander, 110
Needham, John, 362
Neglee, Jacob, 253
Negroes, Cicero, 396; Cunfy, Jo, 132; Harry, 199; Jo, 96; Limos, 51; Peter, 366; Quam, 12, 18; Shirley, George, 418; Tom, 256; unnamed, 201, 287; Wiltshire, 430
Nellis, Francis, 412
Nelson, Alexander, 119
Nelson, Henry, 96
Nelson, John, 325
Newberry, William, 8
Newell, Joseph, 33
Newlin, Jane, 111
Newlin, John, 218
Newman, George, 57
Newton, Thomas, 259
Nichols, Rhomas, 440
Nichols, William, 92, 94, 189
Nicholson, John, 136

Nihell, Edmund, 422, 432
Nihell, Maurice, 422, 432
Noble, Anthony, 185
Noble, Joseph, 6
Noble, Roger, 248
Noble, William, 5, 269
Noblit, William, 303
Norrel, James, 152
Norris, Isaac, 100
Norris, John, 77, 79
Norry, Robert, 244
North, Robert, 399
Northove, Richard, 231
Northover, Richard, 233, 275
Norton, James, 122
Norwood, Henry, 213
Nowlan, John, 306
Nut, Samuel, 71
Nutt, Mr., 226, 229
Nutt, Robert, 262
Nutt, Samuel, 51, 166, 167, 176, 177
Nutty, John, 168
O'Donnel, Mary, 425
O'Durish, Patrick, 354
O'Hara, Patrick, 386
O'Harra, Catherine, 379
O'Lanshahin, Teddy, 407
O'Murry, Bryan, 411
O'Brian, John, 151
Odonally, James, 220
O'Donnel, Richard, 436
O'Donolly, Owen, 82
Ogden, David, 228
Ogleby, James, 271
Ohare, Michael, 350
Okill, George, 295, 350, 360, 388
Oldham, Robert, 138
Oldman, Joseph, 410
Oldman, Thomas, 124
Oliver, Christopher, 218, 245
Oliver, John, 253

O'Neal, Charles, 104
O'Neal, Fernando, 184
Oneal, John, 431
Onion, Stephen, 215
Onions, Thomas, 190
Orin, Joseph, 337
Orr, John, 86, 91
Orton, John, 8
Osborne, Samuel, 218
Osbourn, Alexander, 264
Osburn, Samuel, 245
Ottinger, Christopher, 267
Oughtopay, Daniel, 10
Oungess, Thomas, 242
Over, Thomas, 11
Overthrow, William, 195
Overton, Thomas, 287
Owen, Edward, 206
Owen, James, 23, 24
Owen, John, 90, 99, 349, 438
Owen, Obediah, 95
Owen, Owen, 38, 136, 139, 182, 184, 242
Pain, Edward, 135, 136
Paine, John, 10
Palmer, Daniel, 65
Palmer, John, 9, 10
Palmer, William, 377
Palmore, George, 62
Paris, Mr., 77
Paris, Mrs., 79
Park, John, 184
Park, Jonathan, 95
Park, Nicholas, 41
Parker, Alexander, 434, 436
Parker, George, 87
Parker, John, 71, 82, 94
Parker, Nicholas, 72
Parker, Samuel, 217
Parker, Thomas, 171
Parker, William, 120, 361
Parks, George, 385
Parks, William, 51, 52

Parr, Samuel, 145, 268
Parry, John, 115, 189, 207
Paschall, Benjamin, 177
Paschall, Thomas, 23, 24
Pasmore, John, 54
Patrick, Hugh, 344
Patrick, John, 431
Patridge, John, 145
Patten, Hugh, 371
Patterson, Gray, 296
Patterson, James, 1
Patterson, John, 395
Patterson, Mr., 34
Patterson, Samuel, 252
Patterson, William, 183
Paxton, Thomas, 390
Payne, James, 347
Pearce, Ann, 87
Pearce, Thomas, 437
Pearne, Richard, 179
Pearson, Abel, 6
Pearson, Corlius, 104
Pearson, Francis, 280
Pearson, Henry, 41
Pearson, Samuel, 393
Peasley, Jonathan, 239
Peckford, Richard, 49
Peecock, John, 3
Peele, Anthony, 104
Peers, Edmund, 155
Pelican, Robert, 162
Pemberton, Israel, 3, 85
Pennell, William, 427
Pennill, John, 420
Penquite, John, 352
Perey, Elisha, 27
Perkenson, Ralph, 209
Perkins, Uttie, 366
Perkins, William, 152
Perkinson, Robert, 154
Perry, Frederick, 225
Peters, John, 310, 392
Peters, William, 142, 254

Philips, Abel, 74, 76
Philips, John, 353
Phillips, William, 395
Pickerin, Rachel, 364
Pickford, Richard, 53
Pierce, Foster, 381
Pierce, Henry, 111
Pierce, Thomas, 284
Piersal, Jeremiah, 426
Pile, Ralph, 27
Pipe, John, 343
Plumly, John, 9, 10
Plumsted, William, 343
Plunkett, Eleanor, 299
Pocklenton, Margaret, 421
Poet, Benjamin, 213
Pollatto, John Baptist, 23
Polley, George, 428
Pollock, Thomas, 113
Poluck, Johannes, 165
Pombark, Leonard, 275
Pooles, Nathaniel, 123
Portell, James, 88
Porter, Mary, 347, 351, 352
Postgate, Christopher, 140
Postlethwait, Mr., 103
Potter, Lawrence, 383
Potter, William, 21
Potts, David, 91, 187
Potts, John, 374
Potts, Jonathan, 243, 275
Potts, Thomas, 132, 187, 413
Powel, Evan, 9
Powel, John, 153
Powel, Thomas, 201
Powell, John, 122
Powell, Samuel, Jr., 372
Power, Peter, 160
Prat, Abraham, 106
Prat, Richard, 44
Preston, Abel, 123
Preston, Belchior, 250
Price, Evan, 145

Price, Rees, 350
Price, Richard, 310
Price, Thomas, 1
Prichard, Daniel, 58
Prichard, Henry, 88
Prichard, Rice, 66
Prichard, Samuel, 341, 342
Pricket, John, 220
Pricket, William, 16
Pride, Abraham, 11
Pristly, Thomas, 385
Pritchard, Rees, 142, 197
Pritchard, Reese, 187
Pritchett, Hannah, 78
Probert, Thomas, 119
Prouse, James, 28
Prowse, Joseph, 65
Pryer, Thomas, 41
Pryor, James, 380, 382
Pryor, Thomas, 424
Pugh, Henry, 56
Pugh, John, 271
Pugh, Joseph, 320, 351, 352
Pullen, William, 197, 198
Pummell, James, 420
Punch, David, 205, 229
Purcell, Edward, 344
Purfield, John, 414
Purnel, James, 55, 74, 76
Pywell, William, 102
Que, William, 225
Queen, James, 125
Quin, Michael, 267
Quin, Neil, 188
Radford, Andrew, 1
Raffardy, Henry, 295
Ragan, William, 292
Ramsey, William, 350
Randolph, Isham, 400
Rannels, Edward, 305
Ranstead, Caleb, 98
Ransted, Caleb, 59
Raulisson, Paul, 141

Raulisson, Sarah, 141
Rawle, Francis, 41
Rawle, Martha, 41
Rawle, William, 41
Rawlinson, Mary, 58
Ray, James, 331, 353, 415
Rea, James, 334
Read, Charles, 40, 65, 95, 105
Read, John, 286
Read, Samuel, 425, 430
Reading, Matthew, 226
Reardon, Martin, 447
Reardon, William, 334, 364, 375, 384
Redding, Michael, 443
Reddy, John, 103
Redman, Adam, 305
Reed, Peter, 96
Rees, David, 248, 249
Rees, Isaac, 205, 229
Rees, James, 369
Rees, Thomas, 214
Reeves, David, 17
Reeves, John, 317
Reichard, Michael, 253
Reid, James, 223
Reilles, Charles, 398
Ren, Roger, 227
Reney, Robert, 145
Rennalds, Lawrence, 144
Renolds, John, 6
Renton, Henry, 39
Rey, James, 359
Reyner, Joseph, 115, 116
Reynes, Daniel, 31
Reynolds, Francis, 282, 310
Reynolds, Humphrey, 115
Reynolds, John, 157, 267
Reynolds, Lawrence, 26, 34, 157
Reynolds, Patrick, 192
Reynolds, William, 364
Reynolds/Rynolds, Lawrence, 30
Rhodes, Benjamin, 35

Rice, Henry, 72
Richards, Edward, 196
Richards, Joseph, 93
Richards, Thomas, 60
Richards, William, 261
Richardson, Capt., 234
Richardson, Francis, 144
Richardson, Joseph, 113, 120, 121
Richardson, Samuel, 62
Richardson, Thomas, 102
Richey, John, 214
Richey, Samuel, 143, 327
Richison, Richard, 408, 415
Richman, William, 129
Ridder, Joseph, 358
Ridgway, John, 328, 402
Ridinan, Thomas, 33
Ridsley, James, 144
Rietz, Anthony, 398
Rigbie, Nathan, 300
Rigby, George, 61
Righby, John, 326
Right, John, 151
Rigley, James, 128
Rigley, John, 107
Rikard, Michael, 261
Riley, James, 37
Riley, John, 106
Riley, Timothy, 309
Ring, Nathaniel, 196
Rion, Morgan, 185
Riscarrick, George, 28
Rise, William, 408
Rives, David, 15
Roach, Catherine, 223
Roach, Edmond, 311
Roach, Nicholas, 82
Roads, Peter, 12
Robert, Owen, 30
Roberts, Ann, 151
Roberts, Hugh, 61, 62
Roberts, John, 151

Roberts, Patrick, 392
Roberts, Robert, 206
Roberts, Thomas, 2, 63, 147
Robertson, James, 266
Robeson, Jonathan, 258
Robeson, Malchum, 351
Robeson, Peter, 333
Robin, Jeremiah, 231
Robin, Nehemiah, 231
Robinson, Andrew, 131
Robinson, James, 17, 429
Robinson, John, 101, 195
Robinson, Jonathan, 177
Robinson, S., 116
Robinson, Thomas, 72, 234
Robison, George, 130
Robison, John, 242
Robson, Thomas, 400
Roche, John, 445
Rochell, George, 128
Rochet, Emanuel, 78
Rode, John Mitchel, 217
Roe, James, 135, 139
Roe, John, 83, 106
Roe, Stephen, 97
Roe, William, 161, 179
Rogers, George, 30
Rogers, John, 51
Rogers, Joseph, 331, 353
Rogers, Nicholas, 83
Rogers, Thomas, 242, 246, 247
Rogers, William, 31
Rogger, Joseph, 334
Rogharty, John, 344
Rolfe, Thomas, 14
Ronane, William, 148
Roney, John, 309
Roof, Coonrade, 187
Roof, Michael, 187
Ross, James, 192
Rothwel, Henry, 8
Rouke/Rourke, Hugh, 271, 272
Roult, James, 175

Rowan, John, 434
Rowland, John, 362
Rowland, Samuel, 418
Rowlands, William, 147
Ruddock, Joseph, 20
Rudulph, Hanse, 224
Rue, Joseph, 357
Rugstone, Elizabeth, 170
Rush, Joseph, 301
Rush, Thomas, 112
Rush, William, 279
Russan, David, 119
Russel, Thomas, 111
Ruston, Job, 386, 388
Ruttenhousen, William, 64
Rutter, John, 8, 56
Rutter, Mrs., 222
Rutter, Thomas, 8
Ryan, Daniel, 332
Ryan, Dennis, 397
Ryan, John, 227
Ryan, William, 230
Ryley, Bryan, 340
Ryley, John, 413
Rynells, James, 378
Ryon, James, 112
Ryon, Peter, 187
Ryon, Thomas, 52
Salkeld, John, 134
Salkeld, Wm., 230
Sampson, Edward, 273
Sandiford, Charles, 80
Sandiford, Ralph, 114
Sandimont, Joseph, 111
Saples, Bartholomew, 287
Saunders, Peter, 180
Savage, Henry, 157
Savage, Richard, 375, 376, 391
Savage, Samuel, 214
Scandelan, John, 111
Scannell, Timothy, 407
Scarth, Timothy, 191
Scholey, Frances, 394

Schowthrip, Thomas, 28
Scot, George, 78
Scot, William, 233
Scott, Alexander, 409
Scott, William, 411
Scull, John, 403
Scull, Joseph, 250, 338, 353, 409, 435
Scull, Nicholas, 69, 177, 367
Scuten, Jacob, 109
Seamore, Thomas, 43
Searle, John, 199
Sedimon, John, 218
Sellers, Samuel, 287
Sembler, Sarah, 164
Sempell, John, 276, 281
Setgriffon, William, 62
Sewers, John, 37
Shad, George, 63
Shae, Francis, 312
Shanay, John, 124
Sharp, Thomas, 61
Sharples, James, 206
Shaughnesay, Thomas, 7
Shauney, Thomas, 7
Shaver, Peter, 258, 304
Sheed, George, 17, 23, 97, 261, 273
Sheed, Mr., 24
Sheerer, David, 354
Shelley, Abraham, 279, 328
Shelly, Abraham, 299
Shelton, Richard, 17
Shephard, Robert, 33, 34
Sheppard, Aemy, 43
Sherburn, John, 38, 55
Sherradon, Patrick, 181
Sherrett, William, 385
Shewell, Robert, 103
Shewell, Walter, 225
Shewen, Tobias, 155
Shields, James, 149, 274
Shields, John, 274

Shipley, Thomas, 323
Shippen, Edward, 130, 183, 211, 212, 232, 240
Shippen, Mr., 127, 128
Shirlock, Simon, 389
Shoar, Reuben, 224
Shoemaker, George, 92
Shoemaker, Thomas, 120
Shoogle, Timothy, 260
Shriner, George, 443
Shurgold, Robert, 406
Sill, James, 251
Siminton, Robert, 445, 446
Simmons, James, 212
Simonton, Robert, 440
Singin, John, 306
Singleton, Richard, 399
Sitch, John, 47
Skelton, Richard, 3
Skit, Elizabeth, 58
Slack, John, 223
Sloane, Alex., 62
Slough/Slouch, Jacob, 275
Smart, James, 32, 35
Smith, Armstrong, 84, 147
Smith, Charles, 281, 378
Smith, Christopher, 59
Smith, George, 40, 73, 76, 417
Smith, Henry, 130, 182, 239, 240, 288
Smith, James, 11, 297, 404
Smith, John, 278, 287, 290, 310, 349
Smith, Joseph, 334, 400
Smith, Mortough, 371
Smith, Owen, 422, 432
Smith, Robert, 190
Smith, Samuel, 31
Smith, Thomas, 84, 278
Smith, Timothy, 67, 96, 171
Smith, William, 19, 53, 54, 77, 79, 118, 124, 125, 153, 164, 258

Smout, Edward, 45, 47
Smyter, Mr., 406
Snaggs, Rich., 50
Snags, Richard, 61
Snevely, John, 159
Snooke, Thomas, 172
Sober, Thomas, 84
Sobers, Thomas, 20
Solly, Nathan, 440
Somers, Timothy, 174
Soward, Lawrence, 323
Spafford, William, 407
Spaggs, William, 210
Spencer, John, 396
Spicer, Thomas, 201
Spring, John, 38
Spurstew, John, 207
Stackhouse, Thomas, 63
Stading, Francis, 98
Standly, John, 431
Stanley, Richard, 93
Stapleford, Thomas, 139
Star, James, 376
Steadman, David, 147
Stedman, Capt., 211
Stedman, John, 209
Steel, Alexander, 234
Steel, James, 155
Steel, John, 2
Steell, James, 427
Steuart, William, 343
Stevenson, John, 367
Steward, Daniel, 390
Steward, James, 48, 50
Steward, John, 416
Stewart, Robert, 427
Stillman, Augustin, 323
Stinson, John, 359
Stokes, John, 415
Stone, Christian, 157
Stone, Joseph, 153
Stormer, Elizabeth, 397
Strawbridge, Ann, 284

Stretch, Samuel, 117
Strickland, Amos, 363, 382, 387, 394
Strong, Valentine, 431
Stroud, George, 188
Stuard, Daniel, 385
Stuart, William, 348
Stupart, Capt., 429
Sturgus, Joseph, 59
Suckly, Joseph, 35
Sugar, Thomas, 221
Sulavan, John, 216
Sullevand, James, 19
Sullivan, Andrew, 257
Sullivan, Mary, 317, 364
Sunderland, Edward, 92
Sunley, Richard, 80
Sutherland, James, 295
Sutton, John, 12
Swaim, James, 6
Swain, James, 11
Swainy, Hannah, 414
Swane, Edward, 238
Sweeney, George, 439
Sweet, Richard, 445, 446
Sweney, Cornelius, 285
Swift, Samuel, 446
Swindall, Jonathan, 23
Swinny, Edward, 392
Sykes, James, 65
Symmonds, James/Cyrcus, 250
Taft, John, 85
Talbot, Joseph, 200
Talbott, Joseph, 198
Talifero, John, 72
Tally, William, 181
Tamerlane, Thomas, 79
Tamerlin, Thomas, 85
Tamplan, Samuel, 292
Tanner, George, 261, 273
Tate, Anthony, 326, 328, 348
Tatnal, Jonathan, 103
Tatnall, Thomas, 92, 107

Tayler/Taylor, Philip, 6
Taylor, George, 358
Taylor, Isaac, 348
Taylor, John, 16, 287
Taylor, Joseph, 199
Taylor, Joseph, Jr., 56
Taylor, Mr., 75
Taylor, Philip, 14
Tearney, Patrick, 97
Templeton, Hugh, 275
Templeton, James, 333, 335
Teringer, Henry, 329
Ternan, Thady/Timothy, 59
Terret, George, 361
Tesdall, George, 67
Thernbury, Thomas, 63
Thomas, Aaron, 121
Thomas, Bartholomew, 361
Thomas, Evan, 68, 132, 223
Thomas, John, 24, 217
Thomas, Philip, 174
Thomas, Richard, 99
Thomas, Robert, 160
Thomas, Samuel, 173
Thomas, Thomas, 316
Thomas, William, 287, 298, 332, 373
Thompson, Cornelius, 95
Thompson, Edward, 27
Thompson, James, 412
Thompson, John, 42, 44, 326
Thompson, John/Hugh, 391
Thompson, Thomas, 32
Thomson, Joseph, 162
Thomson, Joshua, 237
Thomson, Thomas, 263
Thornton, Henry, 381
Thwaits, James, 34
Tickum, Richard, 35
Tidman, Tho., 33
Tiffin, William, 197, 393
Timothy, Alexander, 232
Tingley, Capt., 373

Todder, George, 343
Tomlinsom, Thomas, 37
Tommins, Patrick, 179
Tompson, Hannah, 257
Toms, Robert, 158
Tomson, Jacob, 90
Tomson, Neal, 21
Toole, Terrence, 220
Toppin, Christopher, 70
Tough, Arthur, 126
Tough, Capt., 164
Town, Benjamin, 300
Townley/Townly, George, 228, 233, 249, 250
Townshend, Joseph, 16
Tracey, Laughlin, 405
Tracy, Laughlin, 389
Travett/Travatt, John Christian, 209, 211
Trego, James, 341, 342
Trener, Patrick, 156
Trent, Capt., 358
Trimble, Francis, 246
Trone, Michael, 320
Tub, William, 210
Tucker, William, 430
Tuckness, Henry, 385
Tunbroll, Robert, 12
Turcy, Henry, 39
Turner, Francis, 25
Turner, George, 267
Turner, John, 323
Turner, Mr., 386
Turner, Robert, 265
Twig, John, 303
Tyler, John, 79
Tyrer, Thomas, 388
Ullrich, Caspar, 273
Umphrey, Mary, 322
Underhaven, Abraham, 353
Underhill, James, 397
Vachen, Michael, 293
Vandyke, Frederick, 441

Vanhorn, Bernard, Jr., 315
Vanhorn, John, 315
Vanhorne, Benjamin, 372
Vanhorne, Isaac, 318
Varnall, William, 81
Varnell, William, 81
Varner, John, 252
Varnill, William, 6, 14
Vaughan, Michael, 389
Vaughan, Thomas, 274
Vaughan, William, 429
Vaughen, Valentine, 22
Veneman, John, 374
Vepon, William, 322
Vernon, Catherine, 299
Vernon, Moses, 187
Vernor, John, 418, 422
Vidal, Stephen, 243
Vippin, William, 68
Waldron, Edward, 253
Walker, Daniel, 113
Walker, George, 340
Walker, Isaac, 73
Walker, Mrs., 78
Walker, Thomas, 209
Walker, William, 276, 277, 290, 292
Wall, John, 168
Wall, Joseph, 288
Wallace, James, 432
Wallace, John, 73, 87
Wallace, Sarah, 438
Walley, Shadrach, 4
Waln, Joseph, 304
Waln, Richard, Jr., 268
Waltecker, Conrad, 359
Walton, Malachi, 381, 387, 394
Wamburg, Frederick, 246
Wamsley, John, 392
Ward, Barnet, 352
Ward, Philip, 377
Warde, Thomas, 352
Warner, Christian, 302

Warren, John, 85, 351, 362
Wathell, Thomas, 11
Watkins, Henry, 201
Watkins, Thomas, 49
Watson, Alexander, 404
Watson, Nathan, 19
Watson, Richard, 442
Watson, William, 163, 174
Watt, Joseph, 121
Way, James, 426
Waye, Robert, 177
Wead, Connerd, 305
Wear, Hugh, 97
Weatherby, Benjamin, 431
Weaver, Joseph, 434
Webb, Joseph, 212
Webb, William, 13
Weekes, Elizabeth, 397
Welch, Henry, 238
Welch, James, 198, 200
Welch, John, 424
Weldon, Ann, 436
Weldon, William, 31
Wellen, Dennis, 426
Wells, Abraham, 103
Wells, Arthur, 64, 89, 124, 125, 153
Wells, Edward, 372
Wells, Susannah, 235
Welsby, George, 71
Welsh, Nathaniel, 181
Welsh, Samuel, 234, 306
Wenn, Thomas, 237
Wentworth, Sion, 374
West, Charles, 42
Weston, Edward, 22
Westron, John, 28
Weyant, John, 417
Weyman, Richard, 5
Wharton, Joseph, 209
Wheldon, John, 11, 57
Wheldon/Wleldon, John, 6
Wheler, Samuel, 202

Whellen, John, 324
Whitacer, Charles, 195
White, Charles, 242
White, Edward, 57
White, Garrett, 84
White, John, 120, 197, 198, 328, 345, 377
White, Moses, Jr., 94
White, Mr., 75
White, Thomas, 180
White, William, 362
Whitehead, Edward, 252
Whitehill, James, 292
Whitelock, Isaac, 333
Whithill, James, 290
Whitsitt, Ralph, 434
Whitten, Richard, 58
Wickrey, James, 428
Wicks, John, 84
Widdifield, Peter, 402
Wier, Hugh, 127
Wikerson, Anthony, 53
Wilcocks, John, 439
Wilcox, Thomas, 52
Wildeer, Thomas, 220, 221
Wildeere, Thomas, 193
Wiley, David, 263
Wilkins, Alice, 294
Wilkinson, Anthony, 49, 136
Wilkinson, Brian, 422
Wilkinson, Josiah, 409
Wilkison, William, 430
Willard, Joseph, 354, 361
Willcox, Hugh, 4
Willcox, Thomas, 196
Willdear, Thomas, 208
Williams, Charles, 405
Williams, Daniel, 77, 393
Williams, Ennion, 31
Williams, Francis, 333, 335
Williams, Hugh, 425
Williams, Jenkin, 403

Williams, John, 3, 9, 91, 127, 128, 160, 210, 237, 238
Williams, Joseph, 244
Williams, Lewelin, 319
Williams, Lewis, 254
Williams, Samuel, 233
Williams, Thomas, 183, 210
Williams, William, 9, 48, 216, 244, 322, 444
Williamson, John, 227
Williamson, Robert, 230
Williamson, Timothy, 35
Willing, Charles, 278
Willing, Mr., 127, 128
Willis, Jonathan, 401
Willis, Robert, 84
Wills, Robert, 5
Wills, Thomas, 200
Willson, Ebenezer, 270
Willson, Edward, 34
Willson, Elizabeth, 42
Willson, John, 13, 34, 365
Willy, Peter, 240
Wilson, David, 362
Wilson, Edward, 304
Wilson, James, 88, 441
Wilson, John, 10, 371
Wilson, Joseph, 165, 433
Wilson, Lewis, 278
Wilson, Mary, 59
Wilson, Thomas, 51
Wilson, William, 295
Wiltshire, Thomas, 137
Wily, John, 442
Winter, Robert, 122, 225
Wister, John, 253
Witt, Caril, 329
Wittaher, Thomas, 51
Woldridge, Michael, 347
Wolff, Henry, 294
Wolfrys, Edeth, 219
Women, unnamed, 1, 29, 90, 106, 139; 146, 165, 317, 384

Wood, Abraham, 72, 418
Wood, David, 345
Wood, James, 38, 234
Wood, John, 23, 100
Wood, Samuel, 125, 127, 128
Wood, Sarah, 58
Woods, Glowd, 227
Woods, Manasses/Menasses, 224
Woods, Mark, 83
Woodward, Edward, 245, 304
Woodward, Henry, 185
Woodward, John, 239
Woolley, Edmund, 403
Woore, Joseph, 84, 180
Wormley, Henry, 284
Worral, John, 39
Worrel, Peter, 427
Worrial, Peter, 264
Worthington, James, 347
Worthington, Samuel, 55, 62, 74, 76, 117
Wragg, Mary, 95
Wright, Jacob, 108, 109

Wright, John, 431
Wright, Joseph, 273
Wright, Mr., 215
Wright, Patrick, 106
Wright, Richard, 107
Wright, William, 146, 223
Wyatt, Edward, 213
Wynne, Thomas, 155
Yarnal, Philip, 113
Yarnal, Samuel, 190
Yarnall, Nathan, 302
Yates, James, Jr., 104
Yawes, Henry, 145
Yeardley, Thomas, 171, 306
Yeats, James, 385
Yerbury, William Farmer, 59
Yoder, John, 379
York/Yorke, Thomas, 264, 265
Young, David, 350
Young, Henry, 164
Young, James, 348
Young, Robert, 383, 386
Zenger, John Peter, 136, 317

www.ingramcontent.com/pod-product-compliance
Lightning Source LLC
Chambersburg PA
CBHW071221290426
44108CB00013B/1251